HANDBOOK OF
Cognitive-Behavior Group Therapy
with Children and Adolescents

HANDBOOK OF
Cognitive-Behavior Group Therapy with Children and Adolescents

Specific Settings and Presenting Problems

Edited by

Ray W. Christner • Jessica L. Stewart • Arthur Freeman

Routledge
Taylor & Francis Group

New York   London

Routledge
Taylor & Francis Group
270 Madison Avenue
New York, NY 10016

Routledge
Taylor & Francis Group
2 Park Square
Milton Park, Abingdon
Oxon OX14 4RN

© 2007 by Taylor & Francis Group, LLC
Routledge is an imprint of Taylor & Francis Group, an Informa business

Printed in the United States of America on acid-free paper
10 9 8 7 6 5 4 3 2 1

International Standard Book Number-10: 0-415-95254-9 (Hardcover)
International Standard Book Number-13: 978-0-415-95254-5 (Hardcover)

Library of Congress Cataloging-in-Publication Data

Handbook of cognitive-behavior group therapy with children and adolescents : specific settings and presenting problems / [edited by] Ray W. Christner, Jessica L. Stewart, Arthur Freeman.
    p. ; cm.
  Includes bibliographical references.
  ISBN 0-415-95254-9 (hb : alk. paper)
  1. Cognitive therapy for children--Handbooks, manuals, etc. 2. Cognitive therapy for teenagers--Handbooks, manuals, etc. 3. Family psychotherapy--Handbooks, manuals, etc. I. Christner, Ray W., 1972- II. Stewart, Jessica L. III. Freeman, Arthur, 1942-
  [DNLM: 1. Cognitive Therapy--methods. 2. Adolescent. 3. Child. 4. Psychotherapy, Group--methods. WS 350.6 H23645 2007]

RJ505.C63H3644 2007
618.92'89142--dc22
                                          2006028456

Visit the Taylor & Francis Web site at
http://www.taylorandfrancis.com

and the Routledge Web site at
http://www.routledge-ny.com

My wife, Andrea, and my girls, Alyssa and Sydney, provide me the inspiration and love that guide and make my life so meaningful and rewarding. They are the motivation for everything I do. And to my parents, Ray and Theresa, and to my grandmother, Pauline, to whom I dedicate this book, thank you for believing in me and encouraging my scholarship. Finally, to the children and families who continually inspire me and let me be a part of their life...thank you.

—Ray W. Christner

In dedication to my mother, Sally Stewart, for my sincere and unending appreciation of her sacrifices, generosity, and guidance...without which I, thankfully, can only imagine a life less directed and rewarding. And for the children, families, and adults who have allowed me the honor of sharing in their intimacy and vulnerabilities, and to benefit professionally and personally from their strengths and resilience.

—Jessica L. Stewart

I dedicate this book to my family, who are my supports, and to my colleagues and friends at the Philadelphia College of Osteopathic Medicine, who over the years contributed and collaborated on many new and exciting projects.

—Arthur Freeman

Contents

About the Editors

Ray W. Christner, PsyD, NCSP, is an assistant professor and director of the Educational Specialist Certification Program at Philadelphia College of Osteopathic Medicine (PCOM). Dr. Christner is licensed as a psychologist in Pennsylvania, and he also holds certification as a school psychologist by the Pennsylvania Department of Education and the National School Psychology Certification Board. In addition to his work at PCOM, he maintains a private practice for children, families, and adults, and he conducts consultation work with various schools. Dr. Christner is coeditor of *Cognitive-Behavioral Interventions for Educational Settings: A Handbook for Practice* (with Rosemary B. Mennuti and Arthur Freeman).

Jessica L. Stewart, PsyD, earned her doctorate in clinical psychology from Philadelphia College of Osteopathic Medicine (PCOM). She is a licensed clinical psychologist in Rhode Island, Massachusetts and Pennsylvania, and a licensed school psychologist in Massachusetts. She currently works as a school psychologist for Old Rochester Regional School District in Mattapoisett, Massachusetts, and works in private practice in Rhode Island.

Arthur Freeman, EdD, ABPP, ACT, is a professor in the Department of Psychology at Philadelphia College of Osteopathic Medicine (PCOM). He is past president of the Association for the Advancement of Behavior Therapy (now the Association for Behavioral and Cognitive Therapies), and he is a fellow of the Academy of Cognitive Therapy and the American Board of Professional Psychology. He has published over 45 books and has lectured in 25 countries.

Contributors

Lamia P. Barakat, PhD, is an associate professor of psychology at Drexel University, specializing in pediatric psychology. Her research is focused on applying risk and resilience models to develop interventions to improve adaptation of children with chronic illness and their families.

Andrea Bloomgarden, PhD, maintains private psychology practice in Pennsylvania. Dr. Bloomgarden specializes in the treatment of eating disorders.

Caroline Boxmeyer, PhD, is a research scientist in the Department of Psychology at The University of Alabama. She currently trains elementary school counselors and mental health professionals to implement the Coping Power prevention program to foster healthy coping skills and prevent substance use, violence, and delinquency in school-age children. Dr. Boxmeyer received her doctoral degree in clinical psychology from the University of California at San Diego and specializes in early intervention and prevention of disruptive behavior problems.

Lauren Braswell, PhD, is a licensed clinical psychologist who teaches courses in counseling and psychotherapy, psychopathology, and general psychology at the University of St. Thomas in St. Paul, Minnesota. In the past she has worked in both hospital and outpatient clinic settings and conducted treatment research involving children with ADHD and their families. Dr. Braswell is a frequent presenter for parent support groups and teacher workshops on meeting the needs of students with ADHD and on the use of service-learning activities in the teaching of psychology.

Lydia Brill, MS, is a doctoral student at the Philadelphia College of Osteopathic Medicine where she is completing her PsyD in school psychology. She also currently works as a school psychologist in Pennsylvania.

Emily R. Chernicoff, PsyD, maintains a private practice in Bala Cynwyd, Pennsylvania. She is the executive director of Spring Garden Psychological Associates and teaches group and family therapy in the Department of Psychology at the Philadelphia College of Osteopathic Medicine.

April Conti, MS, is a doctoral student in the PsyD School Psychology program at the Philadelphia College of Osteopathic Medicine. She also currently works as a school psychologist in New Jersey.

Diana Coulson-Brown, MS, is currently a student at the Philadelphia College of Osteopathic Medicine in the PsyD program in clinical psychology. She has eight years experience in the helping professions. Her current interests include resilience, systems, and traumatic stress.

Annie M. Deming, MA, is a doctoral candidate in clinical psychology at the University of Alabama. She received her BA in psychology from the University of Montana and her MA in psychology at the University of Alabama.

Richard J. Erdlen, Jr., PhD, earned his school psychology certification and completed his doctoral training in school psychology at Temple University. He completed a post-doctoral fellowship in rehabilitation psychology at the duPont Children's Hospital in Wilmington, Delaware. Dr. Erdlen supervises school psychology services at the Lincoln Intermediate Unit, a regional educational agency that provides school psychology services to 19 school districts in a three-county area.

Christina Esposito, PsyD, is a clinical assistant professor at the Philadelphia College of Osteopathic Medicine. She has extensive experience providing service to the PCOM Community Health Care Centers.

Shaheen R. Fazelbhoy, PsyD, currently practices as a certified school psychologist in the School District of Philadelphia. She is also certified as a Montessori educator. She recently completed her PsyD in school psychology at the Philadelphia College of Osteopathic Medicine.

Ellen Flannery-Schroeder, PhD, ABPP, is a member of the faculty at the University of Rhode Island. Her research interests include the nature of anxiety and depressive disorders in children and adults; efficacy of cognitive-behavioral treatment and prevention programs for children at risk for anxiety; parent training; and the role of family factors in the onset, maintenance, and treatment of anxiety disorders.

Robert D. Friedberg, PhD, is an associate professor and postdoctoral fellowship director in the Department of Psychiatry at the Penn State Milton Hershey Medical Center, Penn State College of Medicine. Dr. Friedberg has written extensively, and he is author of *Clinical Practice of Cognitive Therapy with Children and Adolescents: The Nuts and Bolts* (with Jessica M. McClure).

Marika Ginsburg-Block, PhD, is an assistant professor in the School of Education at the University of Delaware. Her research investigations focus on school-based prevention and intervention programs for vulnerable urban youth, with an emphasis on the efficacy of peer- and parent-mediated strategies.

Elizabeth R. Gonzalez, BS, is a graduate student in Drexel University's PhD program in clinical psychology. Her research interests include quality of life and resilience factors for pediatric populations. Specifically, she is interested in the beneficial effects of pediatric summer camps on chronic illness populations.

Elizabeth A. Gosch, PhD, ABPP, is the director of the master's program in counseling and clinical health psychology at the Philadelphia College of Osteopathic Medicine. Much of her work has focused on the treatment of anxiety and depression in youth. She has conducted NIMH-funded psychotherapy outcome research at the University of Pennsylvania's Center for Psychotherapy Research, the Department of Child and Adolescent Psychiatry at the Children's Hospital of Philadelphia, and the Child and Adolescent Anxiety Disorders Clinic at Temple University.

David C. Hill, PhD, is an associate professor of psychology at Millersville University of Pennsylvania where he has taught since 1986 after completing his PhD at the University of Arizona. He also maintains a private consulting practice as a PA licensed psychologist since 1988.

Daniel H. Ingram, PsyD, has worked with special needs children for 33 years. He has concentrated in the assessment and treatment of children with autism spectrum disorder. Dr. Ingram has been involved in the development of a functional behavior checklist to assess and diagnose autism spectrum disorder.

Mark J. Johnson, PsyD, is a clinical psychologist at the Milton Hershey School in Hershey, Pennsylvania. Dr. Johnson is a graduate of the Clinical Psychology program at Baylor University in Waco, Texas. He completed his internship and post-doctoral training at Children's Hospital of Oklahoma where he specialized in pediatric psychology, child maltreatment, and children with sexual behavior problems.

Annita B. Jones, PsyD, has worked with the ageless victims of trauma for over 30 years. She has presented internationally on the treatment of self-injury used as a way of coping with urgency of overwhelming stimulation. She is in private practice in Allentown, Pennsylvania, and she is working on a book regarding the clinical treatment of SIB.

Linda K. Knauss, PhD, ABPP, is an associate professor and director of internship training at the Institute for Graduate Clinical Psychology at Widener University. Her professional interests include training and supervising psychologists; ethics and professional issues; and child, adolescent, and family therapy.

Andrew Livanis, MS, is currently a faculty member at Long Island University – Brooklyn Campus within the School of Education. Prior to this position, he worked as a school psychologist for 10 years where he helped to establish and initially coordinate a program for students diagnosed with Asperger's disorder in a mainstream school setting. He received his master's degree in school psychology from St. John's University, and is currently completing his PhD in educational psychology from the City University of New York Graduate Center.

John E. Lochman, PhD, ABPP, received his PhD in clinical psychology from the University of Connecticut in 1976, and he is presently professor and Doddridge Saxon chairholder in clinical psychology at the University of Alabama, and adjunct professor of psychiatry and behavioral sciences at Duke University Medical Center. Dr. Lochman is the editor of the *Journal of Abnormal Child Psychology*, and serves on the editorial board for the *Journal of Clinical Child and Adolescent Psychology, Developmental Psychology, Behavior Therapy,* and the *Journal of School Psychology.* Dr. Lochman has written over 190 journal articles, book chapters and books, primarily addressing social-cognitive, peer and family factors associated with children's antisocial behavior, and the effects of cognitive-behavioral interventions designed to reduce children's conduct problems. He has received grant funding from the National Institute of Drug Abuse, the National Institute of Mental Health, the Centers for Disease Control and Prevention, and the Center for Substance Abuse Prevention to pursue these research aims.

Rosemary B. Mennuti, EdD, NCSP, is a professor and director of School Psychology programs in the Department of Psychology at the Philadelphia College of Osteopathic Medicine. She is coeditor of the recently published book, *Cognitive Behavioral Interventions in Educational Settings: A Handbook for Practice* (with Arthur Freeman and Ray W. Christner).

Carol L. Oster, PsyD, is a clinical psychologist and associate professor of clinical psychology at the Illinois School of Professional Psychology at Argosy University, Chicago. She maintains a private practice in cognitive-behavioral psychology, working primarily with children and adolescents, in Deerfield, Illinois.

Nicole Powell, PhD, MPH, received her doctoral degree in clinical psychology from the University of Alabama in 2000 and currently holds the position of research scientist in the Department of Psychology at the University of Alabama. Her interests include the implementation and evaluation of manualized interventions for disruptive children and their parents.

Marcy R. Rickrode, EdS, received her educational specialist certificate in school psychology from the Indiana University of Pennsylvania in 2005 and is currently a school psychologist with the Lincoln Intermediate Unit No. 12. She serves students in grades 4 through 8 within the Conewago Valley School District, New Oxford, Pennsylvania.

Barbara A. Schaefer, PhD, is an associate professor of education serving as director of training for Pennsylvania State University's School Psychology program. Her primary research interests are in applied psychometrics, empirically supported interventions, and educational and behavioral assessment.

Laura M. Sharp, PsyD, is a graduate from the PsyD program in clinical psychology at the Philadelphia College of Osteopathic Medicine. She is currently working for Lincoln Intermediate Unit No. 12 in New Oxford, Pennsylvania. She has worked in the public school system for several years providing counseling and interventions to youth.

Christine B. Sieberg is a doctoral student in the Clinical Psychology program at the University of Rhode Island. She provides cognitive-behavioral treatment to children with anxiety disorders in the Child Anxiety program at the Psychological Consultation Center, University of Rhode Island.

Kimberly Simmerman, MS, currently practices as a certified school psychologist in New Jersey. She is also a doctoral student in the PsyD School Psychology program at the Philadelphia College of Osteopathic Medicine.

Diane L. Smallwood, PsyD, NCSP, is an associate professor and director of clinical training in School Psychology at the Philadelphia College of Osteopathic Medicine. She joined the PCOM faculty after working in public schools for over 25 years. For the past 20 years, Dr. Smallwood has been involved in leadership activities at both the state and national levels. She is also a former president of the National Association of School Psychologists.

Esther R. Solomon, MSEd, MA, is the school psychologist and coordinator of a program for students diagnosed with AS in a mainstream school setting. Her background is in both clinical and school psychology. Her current research interests include a variety of issues in ADHD and Asperger's disorder. She is currently completing her PhD in educational psychology from the City University of New York Graduate Center.

Mark H. Stone, EdD, PsyD, ABPP, is a core professor at the Adler School of Professional Psychology in Chicago. He is a licensed clinical psychologist and maintains a private practice in addition to business consulting. His publications span two areas—clinical psychology and statistics.

Christopher Summers, PsyD, LCSW, currently works as a clinician for Fox Valley Women & Children's Health Partners in Aurora, Illinois. His experience with residential treatment began when he was employed as a therapist for KidsPeace National Centers in Orefield, Pennsylvania, and later completed his pre-doctoral internship at Lydia Home Association in Chicago, Illinois, through the Chicago Area Christian Training Consortium.

Ann Vernon, PhD, LMHC, is professor and coordinator of counseling at the University of Northern Iowa in Cedar Falls. She has written extensively on applications of REBT to children and adolescents, and she presents workshops on this topic around the world. In addition to teaching, writing, and presenting workshops, Dr. Vernon has a private practice.

McKenzie L. Walker, MS, graduated with her BS and MS in clinical psychology from Millersville University. She is a graduate student at the Philadelphia College of Osteopathic Medicine in the clinical PsyD program. She is the president-elect for the Student Special Interest Group of ABCT and the state advocacy coordinator for Pennsylvania's Psychological Association of Graduate Students.

Beverley Slome Weinberger, MS, is a graduate student at Drexel University's PhD program in clinical psychology. Her research interests include cultural differences in coping among children and adolescents with chronic illnesses and their families, as well as sleep and its relationship to children's health.

Andrea B. Weller, MA, is completing her doctoral degree in clinical psychology at the Philadelphia College of Osteopathic Medicine. She currently works as an outpatient therapist at Northwestern Human Services, Harrisburg, and as an adjunct instructor for Harrisburg Area Community College and Drexel University (Behavioral and Addictions Counseling Sciences program).

Alicia Young, PhD, is currently completing her post-doctoral residency at Psychological Health Affiliates in Manheim, Pennsylvania. She earned her PhD in clinical psychology at Fuller Theological Seminary in Pasadena, California, in September 2005. Her doctoral dissertation focused on factors that promote resiliency and thriving among youth who had been exposed to family violence. Dr. Young specializes in working with families who have experienced family violence, and verbal, physical, and sexual abuse.

Laura Young, BA, is a doctoral candidate in clinical psychology at the University of Alabama. She received her BA in psychology from the University of Notre Dame. Her areas of interest include the social cognitions of aggressive children, parenting practices, and intervention/prevention programs for aggression.

Part One

GROUP THERAPY ESSENTIALS

Chapter One

An Introduction to Cognitive-Behavior Group Therapy with Youth

Jessica L. Stewart, Ray W. Christner, & Arthur Freeman

Cognitive-behavior therapy (CBT) with youth clients has received considerable attention and support over the past several years for a variety of presenting problems experienced by youth, including depression, anxiety, anger and aggression, eating disorders, and such (Ollendick & King, 2004). With the growing interest in CBT among practitioners, a number of experts in the field have compiled thorough and useful resources for implementing CBT with child and adolescent clients (see Kendall, 2000; Reinecke, Dattilio, & Freeman, 2003). Not only has CBT been applied to a variety of presenting problems experienced by youth, but also there is growing implementation of CBT interventions in a variety of settings in which youth interact. Recently, Mennuti, Freeman, and Christner (2006) offered a resource specifically for addressing child and adolescent issues a school setting.

The focus for a number of the CBT resources for youth clients, however, is mostly on individual psychotherapy or intervention; yet, many professionals in the field are being faced with greater time constraints and increasing numbers of referrals. For this reason, therapists are looking for alternative and time efficient ways to work with youth. Freeman, Pretzer, Fleming, and Simon (2004) suggest that cognitive-behavior group therapy (CBGT) can be a natural alternative, or in some cases, a supplement to individual treatment. To date, there is a growing evidence-base for CBGT, as it has shown positive outcomes with youth for a variety of issues, including anger and aggression (Feindler & Ecton, 1986; Larson & Lochman, 2002), depression (Clarke, Rohde, Lewinsohn, Hops, & Seeley, 1999), and anxiety (Albano & Barlow, 1996; Flannery-Schroeder & Kendall, 2000; Ginsburg, Silverman, & Kurtines, 1995). Others have contributed excellent practical resources (Dryden & Neenan, 2002; Rose, 1998). Given the opportunities that CBGT offers for clinicians in a number of settings, it is only fitting that a comprehensive resource be available.

Our goal when deciding to develop this handbook was to fill the void for a comprehensive resource that presents not only the theoretical constructs of CBT and group therapy, but also to capture the innovative practices of CBGT with various presenting problems and in specific settings. As such, we hope this volume offers a complete guide designed to provide professionals working with youth a focused and structured model of group intervention, guided by cognitive-behavior theory, principles, and strategies. Whether experienced in CBT or new to the model, each chapter provides a basic review of the components of CBT relevant to the treatment being discussed and direction on how to apply them effectively in group therapy with youth. However, we encourage readers to also consult the already existing guides that present many of the essential tenets of using CBT with children and adolescents (see Friedberg & McClure, 2002; Reinecke, et al., 2003).

BRIEF HISTORY OF THE GROUP MODALITY

The modern form of group psychotherapy was pioneered by Joseph H. Pratt in the 20th century in the United States (Dreikurs & Corsini, 1954). On July 1, 1905, Pratt used group education to treat groups of patients with tuberculosis. The original intent of this approach was to expedite educating his patients on their condition of pulmonary tuberculosis. He quickly realized, however, the psychological benefits this approach demonstrated with his patients and proceeded to generalize this approach to other medical populations. Pratt later went on to work with psychiatric patients where he began to focus more on the emotional responses to their illnesses and the impact the illness had on the patients' psychological condition. This occurred in the group setting and eventually became one of the staples to Pratt's work in therapy (Pratt, 1945; Blatner, 1988). Although Pratt was most likely unaware at that time, he had created a methodical approach to the use of groups as a treatment modality.

Between 1908 and 1911, not long after Pratt began utilizing group methods, Jacob Moreno implemented the idea of creative drama with children in Vienna. This was among the first group methods implemented that did not focus on the concepts of individual therapy (Dreikurs & Corsini, 1954). Creative drama has become a valuable vehicle for teaching social skills, self expression, and ways of learning to groups of children. Compiling his insights from this process, in 1912 Moreno began the first known self-help group. He gathered together a group of prostitutes in Vienna to discuss their concerns, health issues, and life problems. During this group process, Moreno expected that each woman would become the therapeutic agent for the other women by sharing stories and experiences to which each woman could relate. These groups brought about a sense of community, of self-awareness, and an enhanced ability to solve problems. Moreno later applied the process of group psychotherapy to working with inmates in the prison system, focusing on the interaction between group members with less emphasis on education. In presenting this work at the American Psychiatric Association conference in Philadelphia in 1932, Moreno used the terms "group therapy" and "group psycho-therapy" for the first time.

Group Therapy with Children

Alfred Adler was most likely the first psychiatrist to use the group method in an orderly and prescribed way in his child guidance clinics (Dreikurs & Corsini, 1954). In 1921,

Adler and Rudolph Dreikurs engaged in the first family oriented group work which consisted of counseling and case planning for children and their families. Adler's early work, consistent with his social philosophy, consisted of service within the poorer sections of Vienna, focusing on children in schools. He believed that "people are understood best in relation to their social environment" (Sweeney, 1999, p. 427), and therefore established child and family education centers where Adlerians worked with children, their parents in child-rearing groups, and marriage discussion groups. This work carried over to the United States when Dreikurs established these services in Chicago.

In 1934, Slavson initiated a shift from group therapy with adults to group therapy with children. At his child guidance clinic, he worked with groups of children to provide them with a myriad of tools for creativity. As a psychoanalyst, his group work consisted of goals similar to individual therapy that included the resolution of unconscious conflict that was blocking the function and productivity of the children in home and school settings. Slavson had two foci in his work. The first was on the group treatment of children who were judged as disturbed. A second focus was to work with parents of troubled children in what he termed child-focused group treatment of adults. In 1943, Slavson introduced the idea of activity group therapy (AGT) for children in *The Introduction to Group Therapy* (1943), and addressed the importance of understanding child development because of the constant change and growth. He believed that it was important to address the differences among age and developmental trends in childhood in play therapy, particularly when using play therapy in a group setting. He believed that children will have the greatest benefit from participating in a group with peers who have skills which fall within their own realm of understanding and by being challenged in a way that will allow a child to be successful. Other early group work with children includes Lauretta Bender's use of play therapy groups for emotionally disturbed children at Bellevue hospital (Bender, 1937, Blatner, 1988).

"Certain problems, especially involving social skills, empathy, and interaction problems are best dealt with in a group setting. Groups are also used to facilitate discussion, to provide support, to normalize disorders, and to motivate otherwise disinterested children" (Kronenberger & Meyer, 2001, p. 34). By putting children together in a group they can see that their behaviors, feelings, thoughts, and families, are not strange or "weird." It also allows children to see the impact of their behavior on other children. Whether or not this will add to their insight, help them change what they do, or effect a change on their out-of-group behavior is unclear. Yet, it is the contention of an ever-growing body of literature, and the authors and editors of this volume, that such a process is a viable and effective option for improving the service delivery of psychological services to children and adolescents.

BENEFITS AND CAUTIONS OF COGNITIVE-BEHAVIOR GROUP THERAPY

Group treatments can have a number of distinct advantages for clinicians, as well as clients. However, clinicians must use their judgment in determining the appropriateness of group intervention for particular clients, as it is not always the treatment of choice. We offer several thoughts for clinicians to consider when deciding to provide CBGT services. Some of these highlight the inherent benefits, while others draw attention to particular cautions.

Convenience

A primary benefit of the group modality is simply the capability to reach a large number of children and adolescents at one time. For some professionals, this has become a primary modality as a matter of necessity, based on healthcare limitations and restrictions on resources, rather than a desire to work with groups of clients. Yet for other clinicians, group interventions afford them the ability to deliver therapy to multiple clients within a limited timeframe, thus maximizing efficiency while not compromising effectiveness. While this is convenient from time, space, staffing, and financial standpoints, groups also (and more importantly) allow clinicians to begin seeing clients sooner to prevent the increase in difficulties or the decline in coping that may arise during a long wait period (Freeman et al., 2004). This issue of convenience can also have some disadvantages, as well. For instance, although clinicians may be able to see individuals in group sooner, it also means that there will be less time devoted to each individual client.

Ongoing Assessment

Many child and adolescent patients who present for therapy do so because of difficulties interacting with others. This may manifest for some through social anxiety, while for others may relate to being disrupting or disturbing, as is the case with children with anger problems or difficulty with behavioral inhibition. In individual therapy, it is difficult to see patients demonstrate skills with others and more challenging to facilitate the generalization of skills outside of the therapeutic setting. Goldstein and Goldstein (1998) suggest that interventions must occur in a setting in close proximity to where the problem occurs. In this case, a group format offers an ideal way for clinicians to directly observe participants' emotional and behavioral reactions and interactions with peers. This affords valuable information regarding members' repertoire of interpersonal responses and skills (e.g., decision making, coping, problem solving, communication), as well as their abilities to implement them successfully. Clinicians can use this information to refine their ongoing conceptualization of the client, as well as to monitor his or her progress. For children or adolescents with social problems, monitoring can occur with specific skills (e.g., listening to others when they are talking, making eye contact) by establishing a baseline during the initial one or two group sessions and then collecting data on the skills through observations. This information can be tracked and compared to baseline data over the course of the group treatment.

Psychoeducation

Groups also provide an increased emphasis on psychoeducation, which facilitates *skills acquisition.* This is a primary premise to providing psychotherapy to children and adolescents—that is, educating them about specific skills they can apply to their daily life in order to deal with their presenting problem. It is implausible to expect children and adolescents to apply skills that they have not yet mastered, or in some case have not yet learned. Thus, group interventions often begin by simple teaching of the skills necessary to remediate deficits or just to refine their existing skills for effectiveness.

In addition to building skills, it is important when conducting CBGT to orient the children or adolescents to the CBT model (described in further detail below)—teaching them to recognize that a relationship exists between situations, beliefs, emotions, and behaviors. Subsequently, sessions will involve exercises used to modify their thoughts and acquire skills. We suggest that when socializing children and adolescents to the cognitive-behavioral connections, it is best to begin by using generic situations, different from their own, albeit situations they understand. For instance, with younger children we use stick figure drawings of common situations, such as a child holding a present, playing with a dog or cat, or swinging on a swing, with an empty thought bubble to demonstrate how changing thoughts may change feelings and behaviors. Friedberg and McClure (2002) explain a similar procedure in their book, *Clinical Practice of Cognitive Therapy with Children and Adolescents: The Nuts and Bolts.* For adolescents, while the pictures can be used, we often use a diagram demonstrating the interaction and select common scenes for the adolescents to discuss (e.g., talking on the phone, shopping at the mall, playing a sport). Figure 1.1 is an illustration of the diagram used.

Another area in which psychoeducation is useful is to expose the clients to facts and basic information regarding their diagnosis, symptoms, or experiences that have led to inclusion in group therapy. Many group programs include the presentation of written materials or working folders or notebooks at the start of group for the development of skills in an orderly sequence.

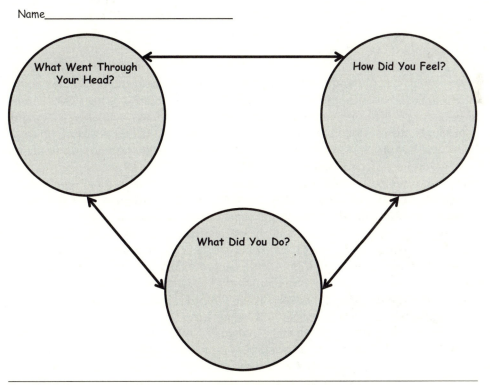

Figure 1.1 Thought-Feeling-Behavior Connection. (© 2004 R. W. Christner. This form can be copied for clinical use. All other situations, please contact the author.)

Social Comparison and Support

According to Festinger's (1954) social comparison theory, change is internally motivated and occurs more readily when relevant others are available for social comparison, particularly in the presence of an ambiguous situation. The situations that typically produce the emotional and behavioral disturbances for young people are oftentimes new and ambiguous to them, as they are largely unaware of their mental processes (Reneicke, et al., 2003). Observing and hearing others who are similar to them, in terms of presenting problems or circumstances, affords group members reference points to offer information and increase motivation to adapt to their challenges and difficulties, as well as to help normalize what makes members feel "different" or alone. Yalom (2005) offered that "normalizing behavior" promotes a sense of universality that is one of the most helpful features of group therapy. It is common, especially in working with adolescents, for patients to discount the therapist's ability to understand what they are "going through." However, the group setting makes it less feasible for members to dismiss the observations of others who share similar problems.

In general, this is a significant benefit to group interventions, though for some youth, there can be a negative impact. We recall a 10-year-old boy in group who became very discouraged because he did not see himself as making similar gains as his groupmates, though his progress was commendable on an individual level. For him, this reinforced his thought, "I'm a failure." To overcome this, we recommend setting specific goals for each child and having a target that they should meet for themselves. This requires celebrating the moments that each client achieves the steps leading to his or her goal.

Natural Laboratory

As noted earlier, group therapy settings offer a unique opportunity for clients to interact and practice skills in a safe setting. In essence, the group therapy setting serves as a natural laboratory in which members can "test out" their beliefs, as well as newly acquired strategies and interventions they have learned during the *skill acquisition* phase. This *skill implementation* aspect of group therapy offers an environment for group members to have the opportunity to experiment with new behaviors. This can occur naturally during group interactions or through role-play and practice activities used to prepare them before trying the new skills out in the "real world." While members may practice any number of skills, the group setting is especially beneficial for experimenting with effective coping strategies (e.g., relaxation, feeling identification and tracking, goal setting, problem solving) and interpersonal skills (e.g., appropriate self-disclosure, effective communication and listening skills, developing empathy, conflict management). As participants often model the behaviors of other group members or the therapists, group facilitators must be mindful, however, of the potential for ineffective or dysfunctional thoughts and behaviors to be repeated and strengthened, or acquired by other members. Group therapy requires that therapists have strong management skills to avoid being sidetracked and to be cognizant of negative patterns occurring within the group. One individual can negatively affect the experience for the entire group (Freeman et al., 2004).

Engagement and Motivation

Many children and adolescents presenting for group therapy may have no prior experience with psychological intervention nor desire any. They may not be familiar with the process or their role in effecting change, and, therefore, may be more passive than active if left without guidance on this matter. The group therapy environment encourages members to be active participants in their treatment, as this expectation is modeled by the facilitator and other members. Members are encouraged to participate actively in defining goals, exposing thought patterns and irrational beliefs, practicing skills in group exercises, offering feedback and support to others, and developing homework to continue practicing new skills outside of session (Freeman & Stewart, in press).

BASIC TENETS OF COGNITIVE-BEHAVIOR GROUP THERAPY

Discussing all aspects of the CBT model and its basic components is beyond the scope of this chapter. There are many outstanding texts available that are resources on CBT in general (see J. Beck, 1995; Freeman et al., 2004), as well as on CBT specific to child and adolescent treatment (see Friedberg & McClure, 2002; Reinecke et al., 2003). Readers are referred to those volumes for a more detailed review of CBT. However, before using the resources provided within this handbook, we feel it is important to offer a brief review of the basic goals, structure, and components of CBT, specifically as they relate to group therapy with children and adolescents.

Brief Overview of CBT

The aim of CBT in general is to identify and restructure irrational or distorted beliefs and schema related to the self, others, and the world that produce emotional distress and maladaptive behaviors (Beck, Rush, Shaw, & Emery, 1979; J. Beck, 1995). This same fundamental goal is maintained for each participant when CBT is provided in a group format, though the group modality offers the additional benefits of support, peer modeling, a sense of commonality, and an environment in which to practice the variety of skills acquired. Through CBT and CBGT, each individual is encouraged to be active in the collaborative process of therapy, even when working with young people. However, the therapy process is typically guided by the clinician, which, as noted above, is essential in group therapy to avoid disruption.

CBT is often described in a linear manner, in which situations, thoughts, feelings, and behaviors are connected. For instance, a youngster who is afraid to give a speech in the front of the classroom (situation) begins to think he is going to embarrass himself or throw-up in front of the class (thought), and subsequently, he becomes nervous and afraid (feelings) and refuses to get in front of the class and walks out of the room (behavior). For most situations with children and adolescents, this clear and direct connection is not as simplistic. Instead, these factors likely influence and, at times, exacerbate each other (e.g., the feelings of anxiety make his stomach upset, which in turn, reinforces his thoughts he will throw-up). Thus, clinicians must be aware of the multiple, interacting factors affecting children and adolescents (Murphy & Christner, 2006). Readers are encouraged to reference the case conceptualization framework developed by Murphy and Christner specifically designed for therapeutic work with youth clients.

In general, the CBT model postulates that the way a child responds to situations depends on the ways in which he or she interprets those experiences (Friedberg & McClure, 2002), and that these interpretations and responses can have an effect on each other. Distorted thinking will, naturally, result in irrational and unnecessary emotional reactions and exaggerated behavioral responses. These are usually the symptoms that result in referral for psychological intervention and, in this case, inclusion in group psychotherapy. CBT aims to use the therapeutic situation to identify distorted thinking and responding to modify both. The identification of distorted perceptions and beliefs may be direct or indirect, depending on the age and cognitive flexibility of group members (discussed in more detail below). Modification of beliefs can be through various cognitive techniques and means, or through behavioral experiments that result in "evidence" that counters or corrects distorted thinking. Similarly, ineffective emotional and behavioral responding can be modified through behavioral techniques and interventions that aim to build more effective coping and skills. The inherent benefits of the group setting highlighted above facilitate the goals of identifying and restructuring distorted perceptions and beliefs and facilitating the development of more effective skills, making CBGT a natural extension of individual CBT.

There are two primary elements in CBT or CBGT—(1) cognition and (2) behaviors. The CBT literature uses numerous terms to describe the various levels of cognition (e.g., core beliefs, schema, intermediate beliefs, irrational beliefs, automatic thoughts). To simplify these terms for use in working with young people, we suggest using two levels—schema and automatic thoughts. *Schemas* are an individual's basic beliefs or assumptions through which he or she perceives and interprets various events (Freeman et al., 2004; Friedberg & McClure, 2002; Young, 1999). They are shaped by our life's experiences and are often reinforced throughout our development. They are, essentially, the lenses through which people view themselves, others, the world, events, and interactions. Schema are not easy to identify in younger children, and in many cases, their schema are just developing. However, it is much easier to identify *automatic thoughts*, which are the immediate, superficial level of cognition (Beck, 1995; Freeman, et al., 2004).

Automatic thoughts are situation specific and occur spontaneously without cognitive effort (Freeman, et al., 2004; Friedberg & McClure, 2002). These thoughts typically produce immediate emotional or behavioral responses to a particular situation, are usually easy to identify, and provide a basis for the patterns in thinking that identify schemas to target for change. When a child's or adolescent's thinking affects his or her behavior, there are two possible cognitive explanations—*cognitive deficiencies* and *cognitive distortions* (Kendall & MacDonald, 1993). *Cognitive deficiencies* refer to a deficit in a child's or adolescent's cognitive-processing ability (Kendall & MacDonald, 1993). For instance, consider the child who responds impulsively without thinking in social situations, which results in peer conflicts. The second cognitive factor is *cognitive distortions*, which generally refers to errors or inaccuracies in thinking (Freeman, et al., 2004). These errors lead to the child misperceiving or misinterpreting a situation that subsequently alters his or her feelings and behaviors. For example, an adolescent girl is waiting outside of school and her best friend walks past her without saying hello. The girl thinks, "Jenny must be mad at me; she didn't say anything to me," without considering other more reasonable options, such as, "Jenny must not have seen me waiting for her." Not all cognitive distortions are negative, though individuals tend to alter incoming information to fit their schema.

Several experts in the field have identified a number of cognitive distortions or errors in thinking common to several disorders (J. Beck, 1995; Burns, 1999; Freeman, et al., 2004). These distortions serve to invalidate or modify information that poses a threat to a person's existing schematic framework so that the incoming information is, instead, compatible with what the person already believes (even if that framework is irrational or maladaptive). In Table 1.1, we offer a sample of common cognitive distortions we have seen in our work with children and adolescents in both individual and group settings. Not only may the cognitive distortions of youth clients influence their feelings and behaviors in general, but they may also effect the youth's group participation (e.g., "If I say the wrong thing, the group will make fun of me," "The other kids are going to think my problems are silly.").

The second element to CBT and CBGT is the focus on <u>behaviors</u>. This also can be br<u>oken down int</u>o two areas—*skills deficits* and *skills application difficulty*. Those children with skills deficits are viewed as not having particular skills, and through

Table 1.1   Common Cognitive Distortions of Children and Adolescents

1. *Dichotomous thinking*—The child views situation in only two categories rather than on a continuum. The world is either black or white with no shades of gray. For example, "I'm either loved or I am hated."

2. *Overgeneralization*—The child sees a current event as being characteristic of life in general, instead of one situation among many. For example, "Because she didn't invite me to the party, I'll never be invited to anyone else's either."

3. *Mind reading*—The child believes he or she knows what others are thinking about him or her without any evidence. For example, "I just know that my mother is disappointed in me."

4. *Emotional reasoning*—The child assumes that his or her feelings or emotional reactions reflect the true situation. For example, "I feel like no one likes me, so no one likes me."

5. *Disqualifying the positive*—The child discounts positive experiences that conflict with his or her negative views. For example, "Doing well on those quizzes was just because the teacher helped me and I got lucky."

6. *Catastrophizing*—The child predicts that future situations will be negative and treats them as intolerable catastrophes. For example, "I'm going to strike out and no one will want me on their team."

7. *Personalization*—The child assumes that he or she is the cause of negative circumstances. For example, "Michelle wouldn't talk to me in the hall today. I must have done something to make her so mad at me."

8. *Should statements*—The child uses should or must to describe how he or she or others are to behave or act. For example, "I must always say yes when my friends ask for my help, because I shouldn't be selfish."

9. *Comparing*—The child compares his or her performance to others. Oftentimes, the comparison is made to higher performing or older children. For example, "I can't read as well as my older sister. She must be smarter than me."

10. *Selective abstraction*—The child focuses attention to one detail (usually negative), and ignores other relevant aspects. For example, "My teacher gave me an unsatisfactory on the last assignment, so this means I must be one of his worst students!"

11. *Labeling*—The child attaches a global label to describe him or herself rather than looking at behaviors and actions. For example, "I'm a loser" rather than "Boy, I had a bad game last night."

skills acquisition exercises will learn new ways to approach situations. The simplest example is what we see in typical social skills groups. *Skills application difficulties*, on the other hand, are seen in children who have acquired the skill and can use it effectively in certain situations (e.g., the child who can use diaphragmatic breathing well in the session), yet they do not apply it to general situations. For children at this level, *skill implementation* exercises are essential for them to make progress.

CONSIDERATIONS FOR THE PROVISIONS OF CBGT WITH YOUTH

In applying CBGT with children and adolescents, professionals must consider several important components to the structure and process of service delivery. Each chapter reviews unique considerations fundamental to the specific setting or presenting problem discussed, though there are a number of common factors within CBGT that cross all settings and problem areas. Each of the considerations discussed are important to the flow and process of therapy, as well as to the general conceptualization of the group.

Therapeutic Relationship

Perhaps the most important tool a child and adolescent therapist can rely on is his or her working relationship with the youth. Those not familiar with cognitive-behavioral approaches often assume CBT or CBGT ignore the "therapeutic relationship," yet this is not accurate. In fact, Beck and his associates (1979) have stressed the importance of active interaction between client and therapist, and the therapeutic alliance or working relationship is a key element to effective CBT and CBGT. A number of experts have asserted that a positive, authentic connection between client and therapist can produce an opportunity for the client to make notable change and to enhance overall outcome (Corey, Corey, Callanan, & Russell, 1992; Mennuti, Christner, & Freeman, 2006).

In his influential work, Bordin (1979) identified the "working alliance" as the most important tool in effecting therapeutic change. He outlined three important components to its effectiveness, including (1) an agreement on goals, (2) an agreement on assigned tasks, and (3) the development of a personal bond. In order for intervention to be successful, clinicians need to attend to these components and monitor them throughout therapy—as one must not assume that just because a positive relationship has developed that it will be maintained. In the group context, the development of bonds relates not only to the relationship between the therapist and each child, but also between each of the group members as well. These dynamics will play an important role in the comfort level of each participant to engage in the process of therapy to the extent that change will be possible and lasting, and that will facilitate group cohesiveness and shared responsibility.

Cohesiveness and Shared Responsibility

Effective CBGT with children and adolescents promotes collaboration between members through goal setting, the establishment of rules for group, agenda setting, feedback and sharing of ideas, role-playing, and practice exercises. These ongoing opportunities for members to work together for the betterment of each other promotes a cohesiveness, which facilitates each member taking an active role and a personal investment in his or her own success and that of the group and other participants. This investment ideally leads each member to share in the responsibility for the group's maintenance, progression, and successful completion. Facilitators should monitor the degree to which members are actively collaborating and portraying an interest in working together, offering feedback to others, and working to meet group goals, so that challenges to group cohesiveness may be detected and addressed early and directly. Some members may be less willing than others to assume responsibility for their own progress, let alone the growth of the group as a whole. Facilitators must be cognizant of the motivation of these members to actively participate in the change process, which should be evident if the conceptualization of each group member's presentation and the group dynamics as a whole is adjusted for accuracy throughout the group process.

Types of CBGT Groups

One factor that can have a major impact on cohesion and sharing is the type of CBT group. Freeman and colleagues (2004) describe closed and open groups. Closed groups often have a set number of sessions and timeframe, and once they begin, no new members are added to the group. In this case, there is a greater chance for group unity, and the therapist has the opportunity to sequentially process through topics. With open-ended groups, conversely, new members may be added on an ongoing basis. While this may impact group cohesion, it does offer group members an opportunity to practice new skills, and in some cases, teach the new members what they have learned. Open groups are more likely seen in short-term settings, such as on inpatient units or in hospitals.

Another option for group format is a *rotating group*. In rotating groups, therapists design the group based on an 8 to 10 week cycle, and each session serves as a module of treatment. No matter when a new member enters, he or she remains in the group until they complete the full course of sessions. This format is ideal in some settings. For instance, we have used this approach in schools, as an alternative to suspension. Students would be assigned to the group for certain disruptive behaviors (e.g., anger outbursts) and they would be required to attend the full eight week program, which consisted of eight lessons, including relaxation training, understanding and modifying thoughts, social problem solving, self-monitoring, self-instruction, stress management, communication skills, and planning for the future. No matter where the student began the group, they continued until completing all modules.

Setting an Agenda

No matter which group type or format you use, consistent with individual CBT, CBGT relies on the use of session agendas. Freeman and colleagues (2004) note that some alterations will be necessary. The agenda helps structure the group format, though clinicians must be flexible to allow content and process to emerge. It is important to have a basic idea of the agenda for each session, though the session should be established and

Table 1.2   Examples of CBGT Agendas at Different Stages of Therapy

First Session	Middle Sessions	Last Session
Introducing the therapist	Greeting	Greeting
Setting agenda	Setting agenda	Setting agenda
Clarifying group rules	Eliciting feedback from previous session	Eliciting feedback from previous session
Getting to know you activity	Reviewing between session work	Reviewing between session work
Socializing to CBGT	Conducting activities	Developing a maintenance plan
Providing a summary	Obtaining examples from group	Identifying group members' plan for success
Developing between session work	Providing a summary	Providing a summary
Eliciting feedback	Developing between session work	Eliciting feedback
Adjourning	Eliciting feedback	Adjourning
	Adjourning	

implemented in a collaborative manner. Some of the common elements include checking in since the last session, reviewing between session work, discussing specific issues planned for the session, obtaining feedback from the members, setting new between session work, and adjourning. White (2000) suggests an alternative approach of having group members determine the agenda. While setting the agenda collaboratively is recommended, White's alternative approach could be counterproductive with youth clients. Instead, we suggest that therapists using CBGT with children and adolescents should have a relatively standard agenda, but allow the opportunity for the group to discuss and negotiate tasks. In Table 1.2 we offer a suggested agenda format for various stages of group. This is a guideline that therapists can use in planning their sessions.

Goals and Treatment Plans

The CBGT model is solution-focused and time-limited, and also relies on the development of specific goals to direct the implementation of interventions. This remains an important component in all treatment, but perhaps even more so when the modality is group therapy. Goals for group treatment may vary, and for some groups the goals may be established before the children or adolescents arrive. This is especially true for groups that have a specific purpose in mind (e.g., CBGT to reduce social anxiety). However, we believe it important to also maintain some focus on obtaining goals for each individual group member, as it will give them a sense of ownership. In addition, individual goals provide a benchmark for youth clients to try to achieve on an individual basis rather than competing against each other. We often use a metaphor for establishing goals, called *Raise the Bar* (Christner, 2006). We talk to the group members about high bar jumpers, and how they must clear one height before moving on to the next. CBGT is the same in that we look at what "height" you have cleared so far, and then set the next height for you to achieve. While in some cases, individual member goals are identified in the initial interview, in other cases this will be done in a group setting. At these times, it is important to include each member in the establishment of goals, as collaborative goal setting facilitates not only the working relationship but also provides the motivation for members to be personally invested.

Assessment and Group Inclusion

A thorough assessment of group members is crucial to the development and conduction of any group therapy. This assessment may vary based on the setting or presenting problem, and thus, readers are encouraged to review specific chapters in this handbook. Clinicians must consider multiple factors that may influence group composition and make-up (e.g., developmental level, individual experiences, ethnicity and cultural factors), as well as presenting symptoms and their severity, desired goals for treatment, and readiness to engage in the therapeutic process. Assessment should include standardized objective measures, observations (when possible), and a comprehensive interview with potential group members, their families, teachers, etc. The information gathered guides the clinician in formulating a thorough and accurate conceptualization of the presentation, needs, skill deficits, competencies, and strengths of each member through the CBGT framework. Once an individual is determined to be appropriate for group, additional baseline data not included in the initial assessment must be considered for progress monitoring. For instance, the *Beck Depression Inventory—Youth, Second Edition* (BDI-Y; Beck, Beck, & Jolly, 2005) is an excellent tool for assessing and monitoring relevant symptoms in youth with depression.

Interventions

The selection of specific interventions and techniques will depend on the group's focus, setting, and goals, as well as on the individual factors of members (e.g., age, developmental level, availability of supportive resources). Interventions may be more cognitively-based for some, while more behaviorally based for others. We suggest that child and adolescent clinicians determine the mixture of cognitive and behavioral interventions based on the client's age (e.g., younger clients use a higher ratio of behavioral to cognitive interventions) and symptom severity (e.g., more severe behaviors may initially require a greater proportion of behavioral to cognitive strategies to stabilize symptoms). In all cases, we believe that treatment should involve a combination of both. There are a number of resources available on CBT interventions in general (Freeman, et al., 2004), as well as specifically with children and adolescents (Friedberg, Friedberg, & Friedberg, 2001; Friedberg & McClure, 2002; Vernon, 2002). While it is beyond the scope this chapter to offer a full description of all interventions, we list some general strategies we have found useful within our group sessions in Table 1.3. The previous resources mentioned also offer some fun and unique ways of presenting and implementing these interventions to children.

Homework

The inclusion of between-session practice (typically referred to as "homework" in CBT) is a primary component of the CBGT model, given that the emphasis is on skill building, making newly learned skills automatic, generalizing skills across settings, and altering the ways in which group members perceive events within their environments. Essentially, homework attempts to "put in action" the skills discussed and learned in group. Home-

Table 1.3   Specific Interventions for Use in CBGT with Youth

Behavioral

Systematic Desensitization
Exposure
Relaxation Techniques (Progressive Muscle Relaxation, deep breathing)
Social Skills Training
Social Problem Solving
Activity Scheduling
Communication Skills

Cognitive

Self-Monitoring
Self-Instructional Training
Dysfunctional Thought Record
Problem-Solving Skills Training
Thought Stopping
Socratic Dialogue

work is often first practiced within a group session, then planned for practice between sessions, and finally reviewed in the following session. Members work together to learn and practice skills and then support and provide feedback to one another on the success or failure of completion of homework. Homework in CBGT has particular value, as it offers members the chance to learn from one another's experiences.

An important consideration for facilitators, beyond the assignment of meaningful homework, is how to handle the situation when group members fail to follow-through with between-session work. This consideration is one that cannot be underscored enough, as it contributes to the perceptions and beliefs that members have about themselves, others, and the process of therapy. If a particular member is having compliance difficulty, the facilitator must seek to accurately understand his or her difficulty, rather than automatically attributing noncompliance to behavioral difficulties or resistance. Some group members may have difficulty with follow-through because of a lack of support or resources outside of group (e.g., a reliable adult to help facilitate the assigned activities, lack of opportunities to generalize the skills). Others may be experiencing self-doubt, feelings of incompetence, or confusion about the assignment that must be understood as part of the conceptualization of the automatic thoughts and schemas of the individual members at work within the group.

Reasons for missed homework must be accurately and directly ascertained and addressed by facilitators within the group, to prevent the members from perceiving that homework is not important. Also, understanding the reason for noncompliance can be an assessment tool to help determine factors that may hinder or impede an individual client's change. In addition, it can lead the group to help the one member by sharing ideas to overcome particular obstacles. When a therapist does not address issues of completion of between-session work, it may lead to members feeling that the therapist "doesn't care." For example, consider a socially rejected child who is not completing assignments but the therapist does not directly address the issue. The child may perceive, "She really doesn't care that I am a member of the group" or "She doesn't even notice me." These perceptions result from and, worse, reinforce his beliefs that he is worthless, dispensable, and lacks value in the eyes of others.

Social Loafing

Whether related to compliance with homework or in-session exercises, the social psychology concept of social loafing is important to consider within the group modality. Essentially, facilitators must be cognizant of the possibility that when involved in a group, each member may potentially experience the perception that he or she does not need to engage in an activity because other members will and that will be enough to guide the exercise. This concept of social loafing exists given that, by nature of a group, members' individual identity is lessened to the extent that they contribute to the identity of the group as a whole. Therefore, the sense of individual responsibility or contribution is lessened also, as the emphasis typically shifts to the production of the group as a whole. It is important for facilitators to actively address members' perceptions of their accountability to individual growth and goal-attainment, and to the simultaneous contribution of the success of other members. By being cognizant of drawing attention to individual contributions and gains, facilitators help to minimize the likelihood that members will engage in social loafing.

One way we have found to encourage participation from all members is to use the members' real life experiences for group problem-solving, but to do so in a manner that gives all members a chance—even those who may not be that outgoing. We use a technique called *This is My Life* (Christner, 2006) in which all group members are given a 3 × 5 card as they come into the group session and are asked to briefly write down one recent personal situation related to the topic being discussed (e.g., "Write down a situation that made you angry this week."). All of the cards are then placed into a paper bag, randomly selected, and read out loud to the group without identifying the group member. As a group, they begin talking about thoughts, feelings, and behaviors (both positive and negative) related to the chosen situation and work to come up with a positive thought-feeling-behavior connection. This is a form of group problem-solving. Then, the person who wrote the situation identifies him or herself and describes what he or she did in the situation and then evaluates how he or she thinks the group's suggestions would help him or her next time.

Readiness to Change

The idea of readiness to change is not a new concept to psychotherapy, as it has been supported in the literature for a number of years (Prochaska & DiClemente, 1982; Prochaska, DiClemente, & Norcross, 1992), and has been applied to a number of psychological, psychosocial, and medical issues (see Prochaska, Redding, Harlow, Rossi, & Velicer, 1994). Freeman and Dolan (2001) provided a revision to the original model, including the following 10 stages: (1) Noncontemplation, (2) Anticontemplation, (3) Precontemplation, (4) Contemplation, (5) Action Planning, (6) Action, (7) Prelapse, (8) Lapse, (9) Relapse, and (10) Maintenance. See Freeman and Dolan (2001) for a thorough review of each stage.

Despite literature focusing on these stages, there remains minimal data on the use of this very important model with children and adolescents. The group context presents an additional dynamic, as the stage of change of each member potentially influences the stages of others (both in positive and negative directions). In a positive way, for example, a member who is just thinking about the need to change but has yet to take action may move more quickly toward the action planning and action phases by observing the successes of other group members. However, we have had cases where the opposite has occurred and members' reluctance to attempt change strategies occurs because of a negative report of another member. It is necessary for the group therapist to be aware of this possible dynamic and use session time to problem-solve less than positive experiences and to encourage further attempts.

Challenging Group Members

When we think of challenging group members, the term *resistant* often comes to mind. Malekoff (2004) noted that *resistance* can be manifested in a number of ways, including denial of the problem, superficial compliance, testing the limits, silence, blaming others, and so forth. However, while on the surface these resistant behaviors appear planned and deliberate, in many cases, these behaviors stem from sources outside of awareness (Yalom, 2005). Although *resistance* is a commonly used word, we feel it is pejorative and blaming of the client. Thus, we prefer to use the term *challenging*. In our experiences, disruptive and challenging behaviors in group may be the result of a number of cognitive errors or distortions.

Take for instance, the group member who needs to be "the center of attention." This is the child who responds to every question, but does so in a manner that is disruptive and often superficial (e.g., "If I look like I know this stuff, I won't get put on the spot."). Sometimes, however, there is another need being met for this child (e.g.,"I need to be noticed, or people will forget about me."). Another common presentation within child and adolescent groups is the *silent challenger*. This is the child who attends every group, but rarely responds, and if he or she does, it is usually, "I don't know." Many of these children have concern regarding social perception in the group (e.g., "I don't want to embarrass myself."). However, in our work, we have seen a number of children and adolescents whose silence was because they did not believe the intervention would work for them. We recall one adolescent in a depression group who, while discussing his silence individually, reported having thoughts of, "I've screwed up so bad, nothing will make it better." By addressing the underlying cognition, we were able to work with him to alter his perception serving as a barrier to his participation and treatment. Finally, there is the *active challenger*. This is the participant who is more actively noncompliant and often disruptive. Again, there are many thoughts that may be contributing to the behavior. We have had some clients who have expressed thoughts like, "If I change I will be vulnerable," or "If I try in group, I'm admitting I have a problem." These are just a few basic examples and we encourage therapists to explore the cognitive factors that may be at the root of challenging behaviors.

In addition, while the individual is often looked at when a client's behavior is challenging, we suggest that therapists also look at other potential factors that may impede change. These can include family factors, systems or setting factors, peer factors, and provider factors (e.g., teachers, nurses, physicians), to name a few. Each of these, as well as other potential influences, should be considered when a client presents as challenging in group. We have found that through keeping an open mind and exploring various factors, we can often identify the reason for the challenge and work with the child or adolescents individually to overcome the difficulty.

Therapist Cognitions

Finally, when conceptualizing the needs, participation, and progress of each group member, facilitators must consider the influence of their own cognitions on the functioning of group members. Just as the schemas, automatic thoughts, and resulting emotional and behavioral responses of members influence one another, so do these factors of the group facilitator. As clinicians, we often take for granted that we are just as likely to possess our own less-than-entirely-accurate perceptions that may negatively impact our responses. When conducting group therapy, it is especially important to be mindful of our beliefs related to our competencies and abilities and the intentions, motivations, behaviors, and abilities of others (namely, our group members). The group setting creates a very different situation with an additional set of challenges than individual therapy and may activate underlying schema that would otherwise be less of an issue in a one-to-one situation. For example, beliefs related to incompetence are more salient in the group setting, as the idea of making a mistake or not being skilled enough, for example, is far more threatening given an audience of six to eight children as opposed to one. Facilitators may also possess beliefs related to their ability to work with a cofacilitator, which is often a benefit or even, at times, a necessity in certain group programs. Another example may relate to our beliefs about the intentions or motivations of youth in our group, in that we may maintain the assumption that adolescents would be resistant to engaging in role-play exercises and, therefore, be less likely to assign these practice situations. Maintaining an awareness of the impact that our own cognitions, attitudes, and behaviors may have on the dynamics of the group or the participation or progress of individual members is crucial to the effectiveness of group therapy.

SUMMARY

CBGT offers a systematic, theoretically driven model that allows for appropriate conceptualization of information related to each participant and to the group as a whole, anticipation of obstacles, and determination of structured intervention approaches. Throughout this chapter we have mentioned the importance of an accurate, adjustable conceptualization of each member's presentation and of the group as a whole. The individual chapters to follow will highlight this conceptualization according to specific presenting problems. What we have emphasized is that the needs and goals for each member should be viewed through the CBGT framework so that thoughts, emotions, and behaviors at work in the presentation of each child and within the dynamics of the group as a whole can be understood by facilitators in a way that guides the group program and selection and application of specific interventions and strategies. This includes the facilitator's own cognitions and behaviors influencing group dynamics and the success of members. As the CBGT model emphasizes the interaction between thoughts, feelings, and behaviors, within the group setting this potentially includes dozens of reactions influencing each other at any given time.

It is our hope that throughout this handbook, readers will recognize that, while the application of CBGT with children and adolescents presents some challenges different than those of individual therapy, it also presents many benefits especially relevant for work with children and adolescents. These challenges are more than manageable within the framework of the CBGT model so long as facilitators maintain an awareness of these potential obstacles, adhere to the guiding principles of CBGT, work to maintain an accurate conceptualization of the various factors influencing the group dynamics, and direct the group toward the accomplishment of defined goals for individual members and the group as a whole.

ACKNOWLEDGMENTS

We would like to thank Diana Coulson-Brown and Mckenzie L. Walker for their contribution and assistance with obtaining background and historical research for this chapter.

REFERENCES

Albano, A. M., & Barlow, D. H. (1996). Breaking the vicious cycle: Cognitive-behavioral group treatment for socially anxious youth. In E. D. Hibbs & P. S. Jensen (Eds.), *Psychosocial treatments for child and adolescent disorders: Empirically based strategies for clinical practice* (pp. 43–62). Washington, DC: American Psychological Association.

Beck, A. T., Rush, A. J., Shaw, B. F., & Emery, G. (1979). *Cognitive therapy for depression.* New York: Guilford.

Beck, J. S. (1995). *Cognitive therapy: Basics and beyond.* New York: Guilford.

Beck, J. S., Beck A. T., & Jolly, J. (2005). *Manual for the Beck Youth Inventories of Emotional and Social Adjustment* (2nd ed.). San Antonio, TX: The Psychological Corporation.

Bender, L. (1937). Group activities on a children's ward as a method of psychotherapy. *American Journal of Psychiatry, 93,* 151–173.

Blatner, Adam (1988). *Foundations of psychodrama: History, theory, and practice* (3rd ed.). New York: Springer.

Bordin, E. (1979). The generalizability of the psychoanalytic concept of the working alliance. *Psychotherapy: Theory, Research and Practice, 16,* 252–260.

Burns, D. D. (1999). *Feeling good: The new mood therapy* (Rev. ed.). New York: Avon.

Christner, R. W. (2006). *Fundamentals of psychotherapy with children and adolescents: Overlooked variable and effective strategies.* Invited workshop presented at Midwestern Intermediate Unit, Grove City, PA.

Clarke, G. N., Rohde, P., Lewinsohn, P. M., Hops, H., & Seeley, J. R. (1999). Cognitive-behavioral treatment of adolescent depression: Efficacy of acute group treatment and booster sessions. *Journal of the American Academy of Child and Adolescent Psychiatry, 38,* 272–279.

Corey, G., Corey, M. S., Callanan, P. J. & Russell, J. M. (1992). *Group techniques,* 2nd ed. Pacific Grove, CA: Brooks/Cole.

Dreikurs, R., & Corsini, R. (1954). Twenty years of group psychotherapy: Purposes, methods, and mechanisms. *American Journal of Psychiatry, 110*(8), 567–575.

Dryden, W., & Neenan, M. (2002). *Rational emotive behaviour group therapy.* London: Whurr Publishers.

Feindler, E.L., & Ecton, R.B. (1986). *Adolescent anger control: Cognitive behavioral techniques.* Boston, MA: Allyn & Bacon.

Festinger, L. (1954). A theory of social comparison processes. *Human Relations, 7,* 117–140.

Freeman, A., & Dolan, M. (2001). Revisiting Prochaska and DiClemente's stages of change theory: An expansion and specification to aid in treatment planning and outcome evaluation. *Cognitive and Behavioral Practice, 8,* 224–234.

Freeman, A., & Stewart, J. L. (in press). Group cognitive-behavior therapy (CBT) for personality disorders. In P. Bieling, M. Antony & R. McCabe (Eds.), *Cognitive behavioral groups: Skills and process.* New York: Guilford.

Freeman, A., Pretzer, J., Fleming, B., & Simon, K. M. (2004). *Clinical applications of cognitive therapy.* New York: Plenum.

Friedberg, R. D., & McClure, J. M. (2002). *Clinical practice of cognitive therapy with children and adolescents: The nuts and bolts.* New York: Guilford.

Friedberg, R. D., Friedberg, B. A., & Friedberg, R. J. (2001). *Therapeutic exercises for children: Guided self-discovery using cognitive-behavioral techniques.* Sarasota, FL: Professional Resource Press.

Ginsburg, G. S., Silverman, W. K., & Kurtines, W. K. (1995). Family involvement in treating children with phobia and anxiety disorders: A look ahead. *Clinical Psychology Review, 15,* 457–473.

Goldstein, S., & Goldstein, M. (1998). *Managing attention deficit hyperactivity disorder in children: A guide for practitioners* (2nd ed.). New York: Wiley.

Kendall, P. C. (Ed.) (2000). *Child and adolescent therapy: Cognitive-behavioral procedures.* New York: Guilford.

Kendall, P. C., & MacDonald, J. P. (1993). Cognition in the psychopathology of youth and implications for treatment. In K. S. Dobson & P. C. Kendall (Eds.), *Psychopathology and cognition* (pp. 387–430). San Diego: Academic Press.

Kronenberger, W. G., & Meyer, R. G. (2001). *The child clinician's handbook* (2nd ed.). Boston: Allyn & Bacon.

Larson, J., & Lochman, J. E. (2002). *Helping schoolchildren cope with anger: A cognitive behavioral intervention.* New York: Guilford.

Malekoff, A. (2004). *Group work with adolescents: Principle and practices* (2nd ed.). New York: Guilford.

Mennuti, R. B., Christner, R. W., & Freeman, A. (2006). An introduction to a school-based cognitive-behavioral framework. In R. B. Mennuti, A. Freeman, & R. W. Christner (Eds.), *Cognitive-behavioral interventions in educational settings: A handbook for practice* (pp. 3–19). New York: Routledge.

Mennuti, R. B., Freeman, A., & Christner, R. W. (Eds.). (2006). *Cognitive-behavioral interventions in educational settings: A handbook for practice.* New York: Routledge.

Murphy, V. B., & Christner, R. W. (2006). A cognitive-behavioral case conceptualization approach for working with children and adolescents. In R. B. Mennuti, A. Freeman, & R. W. Christner (Eds.), *Cognitive-behavioral interventions in educational settings: A handbook for practice* (pp. 37–62). New York: Routledge.

Ollendick, T. H., & King, N. J. (2004). Empirically supported treatments for children and adolescents: Advances toward evidence-based practice. In P. M. Barrett & T. H. Ollendick (Eds.), *Handbook of interventions that work with children and adolescents: Prevention and treatment* (pp. 3–25). New York: Wiley.

Pratt, J. H. (1945). Group method in the treatment of psychosomatic disorders. *Sociometry, 8,* 323–331.

Prochaska, J. O., & DiClemente, C. C. (1982). Transtheoretical therapy: Toward a more integrative model of change. *Psychotherapy: Theory, Research and Practice,* 276–288.

Prochaska, J. O., DiClemente, C.C., & Norcross, J. C. (1992). In search of how people change: Applications to addictive behaviors. *American Psychologist, 47,* 1102–1114.

Prochaska, J. O., Redding, C. A., Harlow, L. L., Rossi, J. S., & Velicer, W. F. (1994). The transtheoretical modal and HIV prevention: A review. *Health Education Quarterly, 21,* 471–486.

Reinecke, M. A., Dattilio, F. M., & Freeman, A. (Ed.). (2003). *Cognitive therapy with children and adolescents: A casebook for clinical practice* (2nd ed.). New York: Guilford.

Rose, S. D. (1998). *Group therapy with troubled youth: A cognitive-behavioral interactive approach.* Thousands Oaks, CA: Sage.

Slavson, S. R. (1943). *Introduction to group therapy,* New York: Commonwealth Fund.

Sweeney, T. J. (1999). *Adlerian counseling: A practitioner's approach.* (4th ed.). New York: Taylor & Francis.

Vernon, A. (2002). *What works when with children and adolescents: A handbook of individual counseling techniques.* Champaign, IL: Research Press.

White, J. R. (2000). Depression. In J. R. White & A. S. Freeman (Eds.), *Cognitive-behavioral group therapy: For specific problems and populations* (pp. 29–62). Washington, DC: American Psychological Association.

Yalom, I. (2005). *The theory and practice of group psychotherapy* (5th ed.). Cambridge, MA: Basic Books.

Young, J. E. (1999). *Cognitive therapy for personality disorders: A schema-focused approach* (3rd ed.). New York: Professional Resource Press.

Chapter Two

CBT Group Treatment with Children and Adolescents: What Makes for Effective Group Therapy?

Mark H. Stone

Effective group treatment with children and adolescents rests upon three essential considerations: the clients that compose the group, the therapists responsible for conducting the group, and the setting in which the group occurs. Careful attention to each factor is important in order to assure the most beneficial treatment possible, as each element enhances or inhibits the others. This chapter will discuss the impact of these three major considerations on the process of group therapy with children and adolescents, and in particular discuss the specific issues related to each factor that must be considered from the initiation and design of group treatment through maintenance and eventual termination. As this handbook outlines the application of the cognitive-behavioral group therapy (CBGT) model to group therapy with children and adolescents, the influence of these client, therapist, and setting variables will be discussed within this theoretical framework.

Youth client variables to consider include age, gender, education level, developmental level, race, culture, ethnicity, socioeconomic status, personal attributes, psychosocial strengths and weaknesses, the presenting problems, and levels of cooperation and motivation. For group therapy to be effective, these issues must be taken into account (Cohen & Rice, 1985). Variables related to the therapist(s) conducting group therapy with children and adolescents relate to skill level, personal attributes, and approach to the role assumed, as group success initially rests upon the role of the therapists. Several references address this matter in detail (Bates, Johnson, & Blaker, 1982; Durkin, 1964; Weiner, 1983). Leaders must model behavior for the group members and facilitate the cognitive-behavioral treatment approach. Leaders must also recognize that growth and change are the result of their modeling and the progressive interactions of group members as they gain insight and skills and, therefore, leaders must monitor these processes and guide in the direction of conceptualization as needed. Finally, the setting in which the group operates may facilitate or impede group progress. The importance of the setting cannot be minimized because it bears a close relationship to group outcome. The setting must support the role of group treatment by commitment to the treatment goals and process. This includes practical considerations to accommodate the group, but especially the commitment of the organization and leaders to the role of CBGT.

Effective group psychotherapy requires that each of these three elements be considered in more detail. The specific issues outlined below are meant to guide the reader by providing further explanation of the importance of addressing these three broad factors in the provision of CBGT with children and adolescents. Topics are not necessarily presented as specific to only one of those factors, as some issues relate to both client and therapist variables, for example (i.e., ethnic diversity considerations). The dynamics of group treatment with children and adolescents comprise similar manifestations to group work with adults. While consideration of age and development are important to bear in mind when working with children and adolescents, the generic operation of effective group psychotherapy rests upon broad and general principles. References for further reading are given within these sections. Some of the classic references in group psychotherapy are also provided because they have chapters that discuss various issues of group treatment important to working with children and adolescents (Alonso & Swiller, 1993; Corey, 2000; Dies & MacKenzie, 1983; Gazda, Ginter, & Horne, 2001; Kaplan & Sadock, 1993; Vanderkolk, 1985; Yalom, 1994). This chapter concludes with a checklist for effective practice to summarize all the issues discussed.

CONSIDERATION OF POTENTIAL GROUP MEMBERS

A careful assessment of the behavior of each participant will facilitate the group process. This is especially important given the range and variability in social and emotional development for children and adolescents. Maladaptive behaviors may suddenly erupt in group to the surprise of leaders unless this assessment is made (Stock, Whitman, & Lieberman, 1958). An individual interview prior to inclusion in group is useful in order to make an initial assessment and diagnosis of each individual to determine their appropriateness for participating in group therapy and individual goals, strengths, and weaknesses that may impact the overall group (Piper & Perrault, 1989). In general, almost all persons can profit from group treatment; however, there can be an individual whose behavior and goals do not coincide with the mutual benefit of others, or whose social skills are very limited (Stock et al., 1958). Those individuals with severe psychopathology or antisocial tendencies can present problems to the development of group cohesion, and therefore, therapists should remember that group therapy is not possible with every individual (Stone, 1993). While rare, these persons ought not to be included in the typical group, and/or the leaders must be aware of the potential difficulty that any child with a severe emotional disturbance may present in a group that is not comprised specifically of similar peers. Careful initial assessment usually keeps this problem from arising unexpectedly, and allows for a better fit of individual needs and goals for all members when the degree of pathology, skill levels, maturation, and social skills are considered.

It is useful to establish limits or conditions during this individual session, and especially to be explicit with the child or adolescent regarding the process, rules, procedures, and expectations. Children will generally accept these conditions without much ado, but adolescents may sometime resist any constraint on what they consider their freedom. Each member of the group should be assessed as to their readiness for successful group participation and potential for contributing to the group process. Where time is limited for this task, even a short individual session pays off greatly in beginning a successful group. The leaders can appraise the status of the individual, and tentatively determine which behaviors seem most important to address with each member. An individual session with each participant allows the leaders to enter the first session without becoming subject to any unknown factors that could have disastrous consequences, and which could have been foreseen, as well as afford each group member with enough information to make transition into a (perhaps) unknown situation more successful from the onset.

ESTABLISHING SPECIFIC, OBTAINABLE, AND MEASURABLE GOALS

Effective treatment requires that specific goals be determined. Furthermore, these goals must be clearly expressed, and they must be measurable. These tasks, when carefully addressed, are the hallmarks of successful group treatment. The leaders and participants will be gratified when they can see progress and ascertain movement. Everyone understands the function of a ruler for measuring length. The ubiquitous ruler is a simple analogy to assist the leaders and participants, especially young people, to develop and affirm mutually determined goals that can be measured as progress is monitored.

Begin with the obvious, but necessary first goal, which is attendance. This is an important goal, but also illustrative of a clear and simple goal. Attendance is indispensable to group facilitation and progress. It is vital for the group that members be regular and committed to group attendance. Keeping attendance records is a simple task, but useful to illustrate the clear and measurable goal of commitment to the group.

Successive goals can be developed by the group and the leaders. Many ideas might be suggested. The group can begin its first work by determining which of these ideas are most useful to serve as the group goals. Do not underestimate the capacity for children and adolescents to address and help monitor this task. They can be successful in developing goals that are clear and specific. Leaders can add more expertise for how they will be explicitly stated and measured. Who in the group is to be responsible for implementing and recording these goals must be designated. Some measures can be monitored by group members so as to facilitate commitment to the group. Other measures may be the responsibility of the leaders, developed by and solely for the leader's use only. Nevertheless, mutually determined goals are exceedingly useful for the group to develop collectively, and these become the group members' responsibility for maintaining and sharing with other members of the group. Developing measurable goals is a very useful initial group task and one in which most participants can make an immediate contribution, which assists in the development of the collaborative relationship that is central and necessary for effective cognitive-behavior therapy (CBT). Goal-setting tends not to be a threatening task to most individuals, and it is one that participants immediately recognize as relevant and useful.

ASSESSING INTERACTIVE PATTERNS AMONG GROUP MEMBERS

The essence of group treatment is mutual interaction. This can take the form of affirming support, providing information, and raising questions. There are a host of negative behaviors that can be observed also (Bion & Rickman, 1943). The group is a micro-cosmic example of interactive living. It is an experimental setting by which participants can gain insight into the behavior of others and that of their own selves. The leaders have the task of appraising the level of insight observed in each participant who interacts with the other group members. The leaders also have the task of conveying these insights to the group, and to an individual member when appropriate. Members may bluntly or more skillfully convey their insight. Leaders have to take into account the skill levels evident in different individuals in order to utilize their input effectively. Each member has considerable influence upon the other members, so leaders must sometimes temper a group member's remarks. Effective groups are those in which useful input by any participant is skillfully utilized by the leaders to the benefit of all. Leaders influence, first and most important, by their modeling of appropriate group behavior. Participants learn from this modeling how to improve their skill levels. Specific tasks, exercises, and leader input will further add to these developing skills, and this is especially true with children and adolescents who are familiar with learning environments that utilize exercises and concrete examples to gain skill and knowledge.

DIVERSITY: TAKING INTO ACCOUNT GENDER, RACE, ETHNICITY, AND CULTURE

Groups tend to be diverse, but they often do not reflect the full range of diversity. Diversity is often a function of the setting and the auspices under which the group occurs. By diversity it is not simply meant of racial, ethnic, cultural, or social background, but also in terms of diversity of experience, history, or perspective. The appreciation of individual differences can be effectively enhanced when the participants represent the many aspects of diversity. This is an ideal, but sometimes groups are only what they come to be according to the setting. Even then, diversity can be addressed, but not as richly as by utilizing participants who are reflective of greater diversity than can occur in a group merely by talking about the issues of diversity (Lazerson & Zilbach, 1993).

It is effective to have diverse co-therapists. Often this can be accomplished most easily in terms of gender, by having both a male and female group leader. The unique tasks of co-therapy are discussed in more detail later, but it is important to mention in reference to diversity that it is useful when the co-therapists can represent different aspects of diversity. Every individual member's comments or questions represent one or more aspects of diversity. Effective groups are those that profit from drawing upon the resources available through these diverse viewpoints. Group leaders should not simply acknowledge the viewpoints expressed, but plumb the underlying bases and circumstances that give rise to these expressions of opinion and differences. An essential role for leaders is to skillfully probe a response for the underlying issues, and not simply rely upon the expression itself as sufficient (Whitaker, 1985). In general, the more diversity represented in the group, the richer and more effective the group process will be. Sometimes this can be arranged through pre-selection, and at other times, this is not an option given setting or population limitations so groups must operate as initiated. Sometimes, however, a group that is too heterogeneous may distract members from developing cohesiveness and similarity in purpose or goals.

Group process becomes a powerful tool for addressing what lies beneath expressions of intolerance in any aspect. Expressions of intolerance should not be dismissed, but explored in order that those who express these thoughts and those who hear them learn the proper forms for expression and listening. The group cannot adopt a single moral viewpoint, but two essential attributes are especially important to effective group interaction: (1) the paramount importance of reason guiding actions, and (2) proper respect for every member. Leaders must take the initiative, and lead in the adoption of these two essential behaviors. The discussions of the group, however, must not be allowed to invade the fields of politics, sociology, law, and the like, but to focus upon the interactive elements within the confines of group interaction. The role of the group is not to lament the current ills of society, their future, or the causes, but to address interaction by group members whose goals support the affirmation of everyone. Though this may be less of an issue, per se, for group therapy with children and adolescents, this notion of focus and purpose to discussion is relevant in that youth may also be prone to diversion to social chatter or discussions of dissatisfaction with teachers or staff (i.e., in school or inpatient settings). Leaders have to be alert to this tendency for comments to move off-center to the goals of the group. This tendency should be identified when it occurs so that participants learn what facilitates group progress and what defeats it. Group goals should not be sacrificed to pursue hidden or private agenda (Rosenbaum & Berger, 1963).

Leaders who are unfamiliar with or inexperienced working with the diversity represented in their groups can utilize other persons as possible resources to the group for insight and information. Leaders should also seek supervision from other persons with insight into the diversity represented in their groups if this is the case. Useful resources include Salvendy (1999) and Weinberg (2003).

SETTING THE GROUP AGENDA AND ESTABLISHING NORMS

As is the case in individual CBT, the agenda is a useful tool to aid in outlining the process of group sessions and in maintaining focus and best use of limited time for all group members. There are certain agenda issues that must be clearly established by about the end of the first or second sessions. This process can be enhanced through the use of the individual screening that was advocated earlier. The leaders have the obligation to set certain rules for the behavior of participants in the group. These should be few in number, but explained as the essential ones for group success. Attendance is vital and the conditions for absence should be clearly explained. Verbal participation is best facilitated and not demanded. It is not useful to require overt participation. Children and adolescents vary in their level of verbal skills, group experience, and anxiety among other personal qualities that may inhibit participation, none the less of which may be the social pressures that are inevitable given this developmental level. Many participants learn from careful listening and reflection. Those who talk the most are not always insightful. Support and careful solicitation of responses will generally work with almost every person, although some persons will require more time and encouragement than others (Gans, 1996). Moderating the group in this respect depends greatly upon the skill of the leaders in orchestrating the participants as working members of a group.

Some groups establish specific rules against meeting or communicating beyond scheduled times. This is a useful rule although participants may not understand it at first. The most useful approach is to show how external meetings defeat the group process by the formation of pacts that may or may not be known to the other group members. Fundamental group interaction occurs within the group, and when these are usurped by pacts, the group process is endangered. Members usually subscribe better to a rational explanation of how this behavior adversely affects the group as a whole, than to offer a consequence for these external meetings. This may also be difficult to prevent or monitor in some settings whereby the children and adolescents may attend school together, share a room if in an inpatient or medical settings, be neighbors in a community mental health group, or the like. By directly addressing the potential negative consequences of external communication related to internal group happenings, many youth may be able to maintain that boundary on their own successfully even if interacting socially outside of group.

ETHICAL CONSIDERATIONS

Core Ethics for Leaders and Members

There must be mutual respect for everyone in the group. Those not present as well as the external diversity represented in society at large deserve respect. Reason and rational means must always be employed to engender an effective group so as to reconcile differing views. The ethical treatment of all persons is a fundamental aspect of the group process. Lakin (1986) and Mullan (1988) deal specifically with such ethical issues in group psychotherapy.

Ethical Issues for Group Members

There is no end to a list of ethical issues that might occur. To lead an effective group the emphasis must be upon establishing the fundamental ethical guidelines for group process. Most group members voluntarily choose to subscribe to the group norms as the only means for effective interaction. During the individual assessment session, it can be stated that any member's concerns and problems can and should be raised in the group, or possibly by requesting a meeting with the leaders to first discuss the matter. Early establishment of these conditions usually prevents many problems from occurring that would otherwise impede the progress of the group.

LEADER STYLES AND TASKS

Good leadership is indispensable to effective groups (Kotter, 1994). Preference is for co-facilitators. The tasks of leadership are far too complex to be assumed adequately handled by one person working alone. Sometimes groups must be operated with only one leader, but this should not be considered optimum for effective group interaction to occur. A rousing group of children or teens will challenge even two leaders, and two facilitators allows for greater objectivity, observation, and better conceptualization of the process and interactions within the group.

    Co-leadership, however, can present special problems. How two leaders behave toward each other in the presence of the group is evident for all to see and hear (Rice, 1995). Because modeling is so important, it is paramount that the leaders work together so as to present a facilitating role for group members to emulate. Working together effectively requires a pre-session meeting and a post-session review for leaders. Slighting these meetings will not facilitate cooperative leadership, and may eventually slow group progress.

Sometimes there is a clear hierarchy in the two leaders because of their titles and roles. One leader may be more experienced, the senior by training, or administratively assigned this role. Even in these situations, cooperation is essential. Pre-session meetings to anticipate the issues and goals of the upcoming session and to evaluate the status of the group are very important. Post-session meetings to process and evaluate each session are likewise essential. These meetings need not be long in time, but they should never be neglected or minimized. When cooperation in the group declines or fails to progress, it is usually because good communication between the co-therapists has been neglected.

Co-Leadership

Co-leading a group requires more than just having two leaders present in the group. This is especially true in the provision of CBGT, given the importance of both members having familiarity with the underlying tenets of this model. Co-leaders can often make better observations, stimulate interaction, encourage participation, and keep the group focused. Modeling by both leaders is important. The group members will be looking to the leaders, as well as observing them overtly and clandestinely to see how they behave. This is especially true for children and adolescents in group treatment, who are often adept at observing and learning from the interactions of parents and other influential adults.

If one leader is clearly senior with respect to experience and training, then the hierarchy is established even though this does not imply domination or one-sidedness in operating the group. However, it does indicate which of the two likely bears ultimate responsibility. In most circumstances, it is important for the two leaders to know one another as well as possible. This should include both their personality attributes and clinical skills. This working relationship requires something more than just a superficial acquaintanceship. The leaders should determine the roles of each in the group, and especially, how to handle the dividing and triangulating behavior that manipulating children and adolescents may frequently engage in with adults.

Leaders should share a common orientation to group treatment. Leaders must also have knowledge of the common impediments that may occur between leaders so as to establish a clear method for how to handle these problems when they arise. Above all, they must commit to the treatment modality goals undergirding cognitive-behavioral treatment. The pre-session meetings and post-session reviews will maintain good communication between leaders and usually forestall any potential problems (Nobler, 1983). Above all leaders must have the willingness and forthrightness to raise issues and resolve them. One matter in particular that is usually problematic occurs when the words, actions, or behavior of one leader raise an issue with the other. Good sense requires them to work out such matters between them at a later time and in a private conference. They might choose to inform the group of what happened in order to utilize that experience for the benefit of all. However, this should not be attempted until the matter between them is thoroughly resolved and comfortable to both. Co-leadership provides the group members with an abundance of skill and insight, but it also contains problematic issues that must be prepared for by close communication between the two leaders (Beck, Dugo, Eng, & Lewis, 1986).

Leaders should use the time immediately after each session to record notes of interaction and progress. Do not wait until later. Using just five minutes immediately after a session is worth many more minutes of time spent trying to recollect events much later, or worse yet, forgetting important matters altogether. Leaders who share this time together make this process invaluable and contribute to a more accurate recollection and perspective of the interaction in the group and process for each of the individual members.

SUPERVISION: CLINICAL AND ADMINISTRATIVE

Everyone needs supervision although not everyone believes they do. Wise leaders know they can profit from the insight and guidance that a capable supervisor can provide and, more importantly, so can the children and adolescents they service. The role of a supervisor is varied. Sometimes, it is to offer another viewpoint, to confirm an interpretation, or to suggest alternative strategies. Sometimes specific guidance and skills can be enhanced by supervision with an expert in CBT. At other times, simple assurance that one is on the right track conceptually and in implementing appropriate strategies is often all that is required. Supervision, however, requires advanced planning, and the details should be worked out ahead of time so as to avoid an emergency. A simple contract is useful and helps keep everyone on track.

Sometimes, administrative oversight requires contact with agency heads. Wise managers will not request confidential information, but they ought to be forewarned of any serious difficulties, and no administrator wants to be caught blind-sighted. Many group leaders need assistance in coping with the unique needs of children and adolescents. Good supervision by persons experienced in working with children and adolescents is necessary for effective group growth with the youth population to result.

GROUP STRATEGIES AND INTERVENTIONS

Cognitive-Behavioral Group Strategies

The essence of effective group treatment rests upon employing specific strategies. CBT has shown itself to be an effective approach in clinical treatment, and no less so in group therapy (White & Freeman, 2000). Many, if not most, of the CBT strategies employed for individual treatment have their analog or similarity in group work. Most strategies can be adopted with allowance for the consideration that leaders are addressing the group even when focusing upon an individual.

CBT directly addresses the manner in which individuals think, act, and behave. Unless they have productive ways of behaving, most children and adolescents get into trouble. Children and adolescents especially need to cultivate appropriate ways of thinking and behaving. A few of them may already have this insight, while others may have adopted maladaptive strategies. CBT group therapy offers a useful approach to fostering productive behavior.

CBT addresses the basic assumptions and core beliefs that are central to the perception and interpretation of life's experiences. These core beliefs serve as the rules for living as formed by the child early in life in combination with their upbringing. These core beliefs (schema) serve to guide and dominate one's mode of behaving. They give structure and meaning to life as viewed from the subjective perspective of the individual. Schema serve as a blueprint encompassing the belief system of the person. Such an understanding may become so ingrained that they operate as automatic thoughts, which function without conscious monitoring. In this sense, they become dogma and dictate a subjective understanding of how to behave according to these inner rules.

When children and adolescents have learned a mode of behaving that is self-serving, but not truly effective, they do not know what to do about changing. Hence, they lack support to learn and try alternative ways. CBT offers very specific skills that are easily learned by most children and adolescents. CBT focuses first upon what thoughts are initiated, and how those thoughts maintain behavior. CBT group therapy seeks to make the group a working laboratory by which to understand what causes people to be dissatisfied and unsuccessful and how to better themselves. It does so in a setting that confronts, but does so supportively, and in a context of helping children and adolescents understand their behavior and initiate change.

Change can be threatening, which is usually why most people persist in their learned behaviors. The group format facilitates the normalizing of issues members are struggling with, and supplies an instant network of relevant peers from whom to gain support, examples, models, and practice. Leaders introduce CBT concepts and strategies to assist in developing alternative solutions (Brandler & Roman, 1991). Many presenting problems are complex. Leaders will assist group members by breaking large problems into separate, manageable tasks that are prioritized for action. The group will serve as a supportive laboratory for action steps in addressing these initial changes. Group members will collectively learn these skills, and each member will apply these new skills to problems of their own and work them out in the supportive environment of the group.

The process of rational problem-solving and skill-building is the focus of CBT interventions. This structured approach is applied to problems presented by group members. Developing a systematic approach to problem-solving and skill-building is the essence of treatment. This approach is frequently oriented to social skills training because children and adolescents often lack insight into their social behavior, cannot correctly interpret communication from others, and therefore, behave with little success. Leaders assist cognitive restructuring so that participants learn how to understand the misguided self-talk and misguided logic directing their maladaptive behavior. Multiple observations of this process in action are a decided advantage of working in a group. This is why the group process can be so effective. Members learn about their own faulty styles of thinking and acting, but they also have the opportunity to observe this over and over again as other members work on their problems.

The utilization of homework by advocating bibliotherapy, and utilizing audio and video tapes can reinforce new learning. Such techniques must be enhanced by ample preparation and follow-up or else this homework will be neglected in a manner similar to school assignments. Make these activities interesting, and don't call them *homework*.

Devise useful, but clear and simple tasks, and refer to them using terms such as "experiments" or "between session practice" (Mennuti, Freeman, & Christner, 2006). For example, "Observe how you respond to your friends versus how you respond to your parents. Determine what is different, what is the same, and report back to the group."

Strategies from Other Theoretical Approaches

There are many other theoretical approaches for group therapy. Some approaches blend nicely with CBT, while many other approaches are too disparate to match well with this model. The best and most effective approach is not to introduce disjuncture by a hodge-podge mixture of modalities, but to supplement and utilize, if needed, those models that might be employed without disorienting everyone in the group or detracting from the style and method of CBT. Two modalities are given for illustration of approaches that augment CBT, including Gestalt group psychotherapy and Adlerian group psychotherapy.

Group therapy understood from a Gestalt perspective can offer insight to children and adolescents. With this modality, the behavior of group members is thought to reflect how they deal with the world. Issues and needs move to the forefront or back according to the demands of the situation and the personality of the person. Gestalt therapy fosters expression of thoughts and feelings. These thoughts and feelings can be "acted-out" in gestalt group treatment using informal drama exercises that allow the participants to express themselves, but more importantly, to eventually understand the meaning of their behavior. Expression and observation combine to foster a better understanding of the operating motives in their behavior. Participants learn that these behaviors are created and constructed. They can be controlled. Alternatively, better models of behaving can also be constructed that serve the person more usefully. Understanding the levels of revealed behavior can be insightful when identified and illustrated productively by the leaders. There are many exercises that can be utilized from Gestalt group therapy that are exciting and useful for children and adolescents. Blatner (1996) and Kipper (1986) are useful resources for ideas that can be incorporated in CBT group sessions.

Adler used a group approach to the treatment of children in Vienna as far back as the 1920s. Adlerian group psychotherapy dovetails closely to CBT, in fact, much of CBT has its roots in Adler's Individual Psychology (Corsini & Rosenberg, 1955; Dreikurs, 1957). Adlerian group therapy may, in fact, be the earliest systematic use of groups in treatment. The essence of Adlerian group treatment is the identification of one's Life Style and how that Life Style influences thoughts and behavior. One's Life Style expresses the "marching orders" that guide a person's thoughts and actions. Life Style analysis identifies what CBT explains as *schema*. In Adlerian treatment the focus is upon recognizing the 'guiding line' of orientation that dictates behavior. One comes to rationalize thoughts and behavior so completely that any challenge to their foundation can appear as a revelation. Adlerian treatment is designed to make this revelation manifest rather than allow it to remain latent and unrecognized. Life Style analysis addresses the latent operating motives of the person so as to make them recognized and understood. Life Style analysis can be revealing to each person. Understanding birth order and its influence upon self-understanding is also enlightening to children and adolescents because they experience these issues daily in dealing with siblings. Children and adolescents learn that one's interpretation of birth order can produce a perspective on self and others that needs to be recognized and understood. It may need to be changed. Addressing the family atmosphere and the faulty premises underlying many so-called family values is also important. These values may embody virtuous goals, but more frequently they represent hidden agenda about perceiving others behavior and the surrounding world. Often these interpretations are faulty and only serve to mislead the person. These perceptions are misinterpretations and most noticeable in social interactions where children and adolescents present with little insight and maturity.

GROUP DEVELOPMENT: PROCESS AND STAGES

Therapy usually progresses in stages and group therapy especially so. This is because many persons participate in the process, and that makes stage analysis more evident. Group development is generally considered to progress in an orderly fashion through successive stages; however, no rigid parameters should be expected and stage theories have themselves been critiqued for being too rigid. Even so, it is useful to model stage progression as a guide for treatment only so long as it is not treated too rigidly. While much of this theory and research has been done with adults, the general implications are no less important in working with children and adolescents. Research by Beck, Dugo, Eng, and Lewis (1986) identified several stages. Other theorists and different models can be found in Beck and Lewis (2000).

The initial stage, usually occupying the first few sessions, is generally exploratory as the group members look to the leaders for direction and affirmation. This is the time for the leaders to clarify the rules and goals of the group. Trust and openness need to be established and this takes time. Defensiveness, resistance, and reticence need to be worked through. How the leaders handle these issues will determine how quickly this stage progresses. Group members may explore roles, but they will initially express their standard operating mode for dealing with others. The developing task in this stage is to move the focus of the group from the leaders to the collective membership of the group (Lewis & Beck, 1983). This progresses by developing trust and respect, and when the members feel mutual support from one another.

As this stage evolves, more exploration is evident by members. This is important because the group should now be at a place where new behaviors can be initiated and explored. The group should become a safe haven for such exploration. This atmosphere allows the development of new alternatives in thinking, feeling, and acting. Group members will vary in how much exploration they engage in, but when these initiations are greeted by support and interest, their tentativeness can move to new levels of awareness and self-improvement. During this period, indications of closeness and trust should become more evident. Leaders should observe that the members occupy more of center stage than occurred in the initial sessions. A more cohesive and work-oriented stage becomes evident when a deeper level of communication is evident in the group.

A time-oriented commitment makes everyone aware of the end of the group's meetings. This can be difficult for some due to the high level of commitment made to group members and the support received. Termination can appear ominous (Kauff, 1977). This is the time for the leaders to affirm the growth and progress of the group. Reporting by leaders on previous assessments of progress may assist the group to see how much was gained by working together. This matter is discussed further under evaluation. Identifying progress and offering strategies for the future are important tasks for the leaders so that group members do not feel abandoned. An unpublished research study recently completed by Stone, Lewis, and Beck (2005) has identified three stages that evolve as groups work through their issues. The data documents and supports the evolving stage model discussed.

Group Dynamics and Interactive Patterns

Careful observation and attention to group dynamics is essential. Group dynamics tap the forces and processes that evolve in the life of a group (Bion & Rickman, 1943; Greenberg & Pinsof, 1986). Group leaders essentially initiate and drive these forces in the initial stage. The power of group processes occurs when members adopt and utilize them, transforming the process from one or two initiates to everyone. Group leaders remain part of this process, but group members will adopt more and more useful influence as the group progresses. While leaders initiate the process, it is the members who will drive the process forward in successive sessions.

The dynamics of the group may begin in usefully advantageous ways, but groups can regress and blunder as they work their way along. It is the role of the leaders to offer insight into the course of the group endeavors with respect to these dynamics (Lewis, 1984, 1985). These insights on dynamics are important because they supply the group members with knowledge about how their work is progressing and what these dynamics mean for progress to occur. In this way, group members learn more productive ways to function, and they can abandon old or ineffective ones.

The dynamics and interaction of group members encompass verbal and nonverbal behaviors. Physical manifestations and bodily positions and gestures are important to understand. The leaders will want to identify manifestations of these behaviors and offer illustrative interpretation so that the group members can learn from these illustrations.

Role behavior is important for leaders to understand to facilitate effective group therapy, and there are several models for describing the interactive process of individuals in group treatment. Among these models, Beck et al. (1983, 1986) identify four emergent leadership roles, including, Task, Emotional, Scapegoat, and Defiant, and a nonleader remaining member role. These are hypothesized to be role-consistent during the life of the group. These roles are, however, informal, emerging roles and are not the fixed, formal roles that might be assumed to exist. Research has suggested validity to this model and the roles assumed to operate (Brusa, Stone, Beck, Dugo, & Peters, 1994). Helping children and adolescents understand past roles and how they can change and modify their behavior into new roles offers a powerful incentive to members when they come to understand that they can change and have the tools to do so.

TYPICAL AND UNIQUE PROBLEMS

There are a variety of problematic situations that can arise in group treatment. Initial screening can help identify most of them, but many behaviors do not make their appearance until the dynamics of the group bring them forth. Chapter 5 in Yalom's classic text (1994) identifies the major ones. The most difficult individuals are those whose personality and character challenge the general goodwill of most group members (Gans & Alonso, 1998). While this might not be fully expected in most young children and adolescents, it can appear as full-blown pathology (Silverstein, 1997). This phenomenon often occurs because process in group treatment may uncover or bring to the surface problematic situations such as abuse, neglect, and such. Interestingly, many of the psychoanalytically oriented texts and articles often deal insightfully with how leaders can recognize and deal with problematic situations when they arise (Rosenbaum & Berger, 1963).

EVALUATING THE EFFECTS OF GROUPS

The key to evaluating the effects of cognitive-behavioral group therapy is to work from clearly established and measurable goals (Dies & MacKenzie, 1983; MacKenzie & Livesley, 1986; Stone, Lewis, & Beck, 1994). The importance of making these goals clear and measurable was discussed in an earlier section. Clear, measurable goals allow specific determination of what has or has not occurred. Evaluation need not be esoteric or overly sophisticated. Simple counts will suffice for producing data. However, these counts must be based upon a standard method for determining them. To use attendance as an example, we record absent/present with a 0/1 count. We place these counts in a two-way matrix similar to a checkerboard so that the rows are persons and the columns are the meeting dates. The sums of each row give the attendance by person and the sums of each column give attendance by date. Tabulation and reporting is simple and straightforward for the counts and their conversion to percentages.

Each goal to be measured must be clear so there is no ambiguity about what is counted. It can be objective such as attendance or follow some similar strategy. Consider the following four criteria for group participation: (1) alert and listening attentively, (2) accepting of other members comments, (3) making supportive statements to other members, and (4) productive personal work. These can be rated 1/0 for each session, or 1, 2, 3 for gradations of success. Ask each member to rate themselves on the 3rd, 6th, 9th, and 12th sessions on each criterion. This simple scale can be modified in any way for use by children or adolescents. Some instruction and practice would be needed to orient and train members to use the scale. On the specified days, each member would rate themselves. The ratings are tallied by person and session date on a matrix similarly to the way attendance was recorded and summarized. As the group gains insight and skill, we would expect the ratings to improve as the sessions progressed. Members would also become more accurate in recording their ratings with greater insight and understanding as time progressed. This should be taken into account in reviewing the data. Similar goals could likewise be determined and measured. Corcoran and Fischer (2000) offer a large selection of informal measures that can be employed directly or adapted to serve local requirements. Sociometric-oriented procedures are very useful in evaluating group process and progress. For whatever methods are selected, the group should be evaluated using simple tools that can easily be incorporated into the sessions without consuming large amounts of time. Keeping the measures short and simple will encourage their use. They can provide both members and leaders with useful information about what has occurred. Evaluation is important for effective group psychotherapy to occur.

A checklist for effective group practice with children and adolescents that follows a CBT approach is provided as a summary in Figure 2.1. Use the checklist as a guideline

	Planned/ Awareness	In Progress	Complete/ Operating
Individual assessments prior to group sessions	1	2	3
Clear and measurable goals for treatment	1	2	3
Constant observation of interaction among participants	1	2	3
Diversity sensitivity	1	2	3
Ethical issues for leaders and group members	1	2	3
Co-leader facilitating by pre- and post-session meetings	1	2	3
Supervision	1	2	3
Implementing CBT strategies and interventions	1	2	3
Supplementing with other interventions	1	2	3
Observing group development/stages	1	2	3
Attending to group/individual dynamics	1	2	3
Preparing for problems to occur	1	2	3
Evaluating the effects of group treatment	1	2	3

Figure 2.1   A Checklist for Effective Group Therapy.

to establishing more effective group therapy, as well as to ascertain both the current and optimum status for improving upon the effectiveness of group treatment. A copy of the research report can be obtained from carolmlewis@sbcglobal.net or markhstone2@sbcglobal.net.

REFERENCES

Alonso, A., & Swiller, H. (1993). *Group therapy in clinical practice.* Washington, DC: American Psychiatric Press.

Bates, M., Johnson, C., & Blaker, K. (1982). *Group leadership: A manual for group counseling leaders* (2nd ed.). Denver: Love.

Beck, A. Dugo, J., Eng, A., Lewis, C., & Peters, L. (1983). The participation of leaders in the structural development of therapy groups. In R. Dies & R. MacKenzie (Eds.), *Advances in group psychotherapy: Integrating research and practice* (pp. 137–158). New York: International Universities Press.

Beck, A., Dugo, J., Eng, A., & Lewis, C. (1986). The search for phases in group development: Designing process analysis measures of group interaction. In L. Greenberg & W. Pinsof (Eds.), *The psychotherapeutic process: A research handbook* (pp. 615–705). New York: Guilford.

Beck, A., & Lewis, C. (2000). *The process of group psychotherapy*. Washington: American Psychological Association.

Bion, W., & Rickman, J. (1943). Intra-group tensions in therapy: Their study as the task of the group. *Lancet, 245*, 678–681.

Blatner, A. (1996). *Acting-in: Practical applications of psychodramatic methods*, 3rd ed. New York: Springer.

Brandler, S., & Roman, C. (1991). *Group work: Skills and strategies for effective intervention*. Binghamton, NY: Haworth Press.

Brusa, J., Stone, M., Beck, A., Dugo, J., & Peters, L. (1994). A sociometric test to identify emergent leader and member roles. *International Journal of Group Psychotherapy, 44*(1) 79–100.

Cohen, S., & Rice, C. (1985). Maximizing the therapeutic effectiveness of small psychotherapy groups. *Group, 9*, 3–9.

Corcoran, K & Fischer, J. (2000). *Measures for clinical practice*. New York: Free Press.

Corey, G. (2000). *Theory and practice of group counseling* (5th ed.). Belmont, CA: Brooks/Cole.

Corsini, R., & Rosenberg, B. (1955). Mechanisms of group psychotherapy. *Journal of Abnormal and Social Psychology, 15*, 406–411.

Dies, R., & MacKenzie, K. (1983). *Advances in group psychotherapy: Integrating research and practice*. New York: International Universities Press.

Dreikurs, R. (1957). Group psychotherapy from the point of view of Adlerian psychology. *International Journal of Group Psychotherapy, 7*(4), 363–375.

Durkin, H. (1964). *The group in depth: Styles methods techniques*. New York: International Universities Press.

Gans, J. (1996). The leader's use of indirect communication in group therapy. *International Journal of Group Psychotherapy, 46*, 209–228.

Gans, J., & Alonso, A. (1998). Difficult patients: Their construction in group psychotherapy. *International Journal of Group Psychotherapy, 48*, 311–326.

Gazda, G., Ginter, E., & Horne, A. (2001). *Group counseling and group psychotherapy*. Boston: Allyn & Bacon.

Greenberg, L., & Pinsof, W. (Eds.). (1986). *The psychotherapeutic process: A research handbook*. New York: Guilford.

Kaplan, H., & Sadock, B. (1993). *Comprehensive group psychotherapy* (3rd ed.). Baltimore: Williams and Wilkins.

Kauff, P. (1977). The termination phase: Its relationship to the separation-individual phase of development. *International Journal of Group Psychotherapy, 27*(17), 3–18.

Kipper, D. (1986). *Psychotherapy through clinical role playing*. New York: Brunner/Mazel.

Kotter, J. (1994). *Advanced group leadership*. Pacific Grove, CA: Brooks/Cole.

Lakin, M. (1986). Ethical challenges of group and dyadic psychotherapies: a comparative approach. *Professional Psychology, Research and Practice, 17*, 454–461.

Lazerson, J., & Zilbach, J. (1993). Gender issues in group psychotherapy. In H. Kaplan & B. Sadock (Eds.), *Comprehensive Group Psychotherapy* (3rd ed., pp. 682–693). Baltimore: Williams and White

Lewis, C. (1984). The impact of tasks of group development on the psychotherapeutic treatment of depression in groups. *International Journal of Mental Health, 13*(3–4), 105–118.

Lewis, C. (1985). Symbolization of experience in the process of group development. *Group, 9*(2), 29–34.

Lewis, C., & Beck, A. (1983). Experiencing level in the process of group development. *Group, 7*(2), 18–26.

MacKenzie, K., & Livesley, W. (1986). Outcome and process measures in brief group psychotherapy. *Psychiatric Annals, 16*(12), 715–720.

Mennuti, R. B., Freeman, A., & Christner, R. W. (Eds.) (2005). *Cognitive-behavioral interventions in educational settings: A handbook for practice*. New York: Routledge.

Mullan, H. (1988). The ethical foundations of group psychotherapy. *International Journal of Group Psychotherapy, 37*, 403–416.

Nobler, H. (1983). When group doesn't work: an examination of the types and causes of individual group and leader failure. *Group 10*(2), 103-110.

Piper, W., & Perrault, E. (1989). Pretherapy preparation of group members. *International Journal of Group Psychotherapy, 39*, 17–34.

Rice, C. (1995). The dynamics of the co-therapy relationship: The junior-junior team. *Group, 19* (2), 87–99.

Rosenbaum, M., & Berger, M. (Eds.). (1963). *Group psycho-therapy and group function: Selected readings*. New York: Basic Books.

Salvendy, J. (1999). Ethno-cultural considerations in group psychotherapy. *International Journal of Group Psychotherapy, 49*(4), 429–464.

Silverstein, J. (1997). Acting out in group therapy; Avoiding authority struggles. *International Journal of Group Psychotherapy, 47*, 31–45.

Stock, D., Whitman, R., & Lieberman, M. (1958). The deviant member in therapy groups. *Human Relations 11*, 341–372.

Stone, M. (1993). *Abnormalities of personality*. New York: Norton.

Stone, M., Lewis, C., & Beck, A. (1994). The structure of Yalom's curative factors scale. *International Journal of Group Psychotherapy, 44*(2), 239–245.

Vanderkolk, C. (1985). *Introduction to group counseling and psychotherapy*. Columbus: Charles R. Merrill.

Weinberg, H. (2003). The culture of the group and groups from different cultures. *Group Analysis, 36*(2), 253–268.

Weiner, M. (1983). The role of the leader in group psychotherapy. In Kaplan & Sadock (Eds.), *Comprehensive Group Psychotherapy* (pp. 54–63). Baltimore: Williams and Wilkins.

Whitaker, D. (1985). *Using groups to help people*. London: Routledge & Kegan Paul.

White, J., & Freeman, A. (2000). *Cognitive-behavioral group therapy*. Washington, DC: American Psychological Association.

Yalom, I. (1994). *The theory and practice of group psychotherapy* (4th ed.). New York: Basic Books.

Chapter Three

Developmental Considerations for Group Therapy with Youth

David C. Hill & Diana Coulson-Brown

Group interventions with children and adolescents have the potential to mobilize the power of prosocial peer influences, positive peer and adult role models, and the persuasive power of a social interaction and informal contracting process in the service of impressive therapeutic change among child and adolescent clients. At the same time, the inherent frustrations and setbacks that often characterize any therapeutic work with youth are frequently present in the context of group work as well. The power of peer influence can be positive or negative depending on the complex set of factors that interact within the therapeutic process in a child or adolescent group. This chapter addresses a number of important developmental considerations that are necessary in designing and implementing interventions for children and adolescents utilizing cognitive-behavioral techniques within a group modality. We present the major implications of theory and research in child-adolescent development and developmental psychopathology for Group Cognitive-Behavior Therapy (G-CBT) with youth by outlining considerations, implications, and recommendations related to current knowledge of the following specific factors: (a) current compelling epidemiological issues affecting children and adolescents; (b) biological, genetic, and neurological influences; (c) psychological, cognitive, and affective (emotional) developmental considerations; and (d) social, contextual, and cultural factors.

CURRENT ISSUES AND EPIDEMIOLOGY OF VARIOUS DISORDERS

This section provides an overview of the most important mental health problems, physical health problems, and sociocultural-contextual challenges (i.e., media influences, family dissolution/divorce, peer culture) confronting contemporary children and adolescents as they engage in the process of development. We also consider some of the implications of these problems and trends for psychotherapeutic group work with youth.

Recent Epidemiological Evidence

The *Diagnostic and Statistical Manual of Mental Disorders-IV-Text-Revision* (*DSM-IV-TR*; American Psychiatric Association, 2000) provides prevalence estimates for the various categories of mental disorders, including those that clinicians frequently diagnose and treat in children and adolescents. Although the diagnostic criteria for most disorders are the same regardless of age of the client being diagnosed, for certain disorders the *DSM-IV-TR* provides some developmental guidelines (e.g., the note that a depressed mood related to a Major Depressive Episode "in children and adolescents, can be irritable mood," or that one may "consider failure to make expected weight gains" when establishing the specific criterion related to weight loss or weight gain for children; American Psychiatric Association, 2000, p. 356). *DSM-IV-TR* also provides a separate section for disorders usually first diagnosed in infancy, childhood, or adolescence, but clearly specifies that clinicians may diagnose these disorders later in life providing that, in the opinion of the diagnosing clinician, the person's pattern of thoughts, feelings, and behavior met the diagnostic criteria within the specified developmental time period. Another example involves the diagnostic criteria for the Personality Disorders. The criteria for Antisocial Personality Disorder require that the person is at least 18 years of age and has a history of Conduct Disorder symptoms prior to age 15. For all of the other Personality Disorders, *DSM-IV-TR* does not expressly prohibit diagnosis under age 18, but does caution that diagnosing a Personality Disorder in people under age 18 requires that the "features must have been present for at least 1 year" (American Psychiatric Association, 2000, p. 687) and Personality Disorder features that appear under age 18 "will often not persist unchanged into adult life" (American Psychiatric Association, 2000, p. 687). The key point here is that *DSM-IV-TR* addresses developmental differences and concerns, but leaves a great deal of room for clinical judgment on the part of diagnosing clinicians.

Epidemiology of mental disorders affecting children, adolescents and adults.   In a recent epidemiological study, Kessler and colleagues (Kessler et al., 2005) surveyed almost 10,000 adults. They found that approximately 25% of those surveyed met diagnostic criteria for at least one *DSM-IV* diagnosis at the time of the study (point prevalence). In addition, 46% of the respondents had met criteria for a *DSM-IV* diagnosis at some point during their lifetimes (lifetime prevalence). Of particular salience for this exploration of mental health factors affecting group work with adolescents is the fact that three-fourths of the respondents reported that they had developed symptoms of one or more disorders prior to the age of 24 and fully one-half of them had symptoms before age 14! These data have compelling implications for therapeutic work with youth, in that they emphasize the need for the earliest possible identification, evaluation, intervention, and treatment because these symptoms begin to develop so early—often before 14 years of age—and can result in impairment in social, educational, occupational, and other important areas of functioning (as is a diagnostic indicator for a large majority of the diagnostic categories in *DSM-IV-TR*; American Psychiatric Association, 2000).

Other Important Recent Issues

Obesity epidemic among children and adolescents.   Media reports have highlighted the emerging epidemic involving the related conditions of overweight, obesity, Type

II diabetes, and metabolic syndrome not only among adults but among children and adolescents. Lifestyle choices, parental modeling of eating and self-care behaviors, media and advertising influences, peer influences, and biological-genetic predispositions all contribute to these interconnected problems. One recent analysis (NHANES, 2001) found that the prevalence of being overweight between 6 and 11 years of age increased 325% between 1974 and 1999 and that being overweight at 12 years of age means a 75% chance of being overweight as adults. The psychological consequences of this epidemic are many, ranging from depression to anorexia to binge-eating. The medical consequences including hypertension, diabetes, metabolic syndrome, hypercholesterol, cardiovascular disease, and stroke are widely publicized. Psychotherapeutic work with children must consider carefully this epidemic and the physiological, emotional, social, and behavioral effects being overweight may exert on children and adolescents as they relate to the development of youth and their participation in group therapy situations.

Epidemic of alcohol, drug, and tobacco addiction among children and adolescents. Extensive surveys of 50,000 adolescents (Johnston, O'Malley, & Bachman, 2004) revealed that drug and alcohol use among adolescents continues to be a significant problem despite some slight downward trends in the past 5 years. These surveys identify the United States as having "the highest rate of adolescent drug use of any industrialized nation" (Santrock, 2006, p. 375). The surveys most likely underestimate the extent of drug and alcohol use in the United States because they do not include school drop-outs who have higher alcohol and drug use patterns (Santrock, 2006, p. 375). Alcohol, drugs, and tobacco provide adolescents with an escape from tension, frustration, and boredom. Substances are also taken for social reasons allowing the adolescents to "fit in" with their peer group or as a means of escape from pressures bestowed by the peer group or other persons. This means of temporary escape carries with it a lasting price tag. The adolescent may become dependent on these substances, become disorganized socially and personally as well as predispose the adolescent to serious and sometimes fatal diseases (Gullotta, Adams, & Montemayor, 1995). Wodarski and Hoffman (1984) found that when adolescents discuss alcohol-related issues with peers in a school-based program, they reported less alcohol abuse at a 1-year follow-up than did peers who were not involved in these peer discussions. All group and individual psychotherapy with children and adolescents must recognize the widespread use of drugs and alcohol among both youth and their parents and guardians. Issues related to substance use by clients, parents, or both generally sabotage any attempts at cognitive restructuring, insight-building, self-exploration, and motivation enhancement, thus drastically weakening the prognosis of the psychotherapeutic process.

Epidemic of sexually-transmitted diseases (STDs), AIDS, and pregnancies among adolescents. The National Center for Health Statistics (NCHS) reported that the number of live births to 15–19 year olds in 2003 was 414,580, resulting in a birth rate for 15–19 year olds of 41.6 live births per 1,000 population (National Center for Health Statistics 2004). This number represents approximately a 21% decrease in the birth rate for adolescent girls 15–19 years of age since 1991. This is an encouraging trend, but "the United States continues to have one of the highest adolescent pregnancy and childbearing rates in the industrialized world today" (Santrock, 2006, p. 372). In addition, fully 25% of sexually active teens develop at least one Sexually-Transmitted Infection (STIs; Centers for Disease Control and Prevention, 2004). Among these, Human Immunodeficiency Virus/Acquired Immune Deficiency Syndrome (HIV/AIDS) continues to proliferate among the young. According to Santrock (2006), the incidence rate (i.e., number of new cases each year) involves 4,000 13–19-year-olds in the U. S. Despite the improved treatments for AIDS, it remains a very serious often fatal disease.

High-profile dramatic incidents involving mass murder of peers, school personnel, and family members by children and adolescent. The three leading causes of death among adolescents are accidents (mostly automobile accidents), homicide, and suicide, respectively (Gould, 2001). These data are notoriously difficult to interpret because an unknown proportion of single-car automobile accidents resulting in death are in actuality suicides but the victims did not leave any evidence. Therefore, these deaths are recorded as "accidents," not suicides. Included in the statistics about homicide rates among young people is an increase in publicized mass-killings involving students bringing weapons to school to murder other students and adults. Incidents beginning in 1979 with a female student killing her principal, through the most recent home-to-school shooting spree of a 16-year-old Minnesota boy in March of 2005, have drawn attention to the issues impacting young people that would lead to this level of emotional distress and violence (e.g., the influence of violence in multimedia, bullying and social rejection/isolation, the availability of firearms, the level of positive and effective adult guidance and modeling).

All three of these causes of death are potentially preventable with early identification, intervention, education, and, in some cases, therapy. While all such occurrences are not preventable, it seems quite apparent that alienation, lack of social support, extreme difficulty managing emotions, high levels of impulsivity, and very impaired decision-making and problem-solving skills contributed to these deaths. Intervention can certainly make a difference in at least some of these kinds of cases. Group contexts for delivering educational and therapeutic information are particularly well-suited to these kinds of efforts because of the strong influence of peer modeling and affirmation that can help to remediate some of the peer and social issues that may otherwise contribute to such high levels of desperation in some distressed young people.

High prevalence rates of family chaos, physical and sexual abuse/assault, spousal-partner violence, and Posttraumatic Stress Disorder (PTSD) and other disorders as a consequence. In contemporary America, the prevalence of family chaos, physical, and sexual abuse/assault, spousal/partner violence, and PTSD and trauma-related mental disorders is very high. Judith Herman (1992), John Briere (2002), Christine Courtois (1988; 1999), Murray Strauss and his colleagues (1997, 2001), and other authorities have focused attention on the long-term and multidimensional effects of chronic repeated experiences of trauma. Herman (1992) contributed the term "Complex PTSD" to describe these consequences.

Briere (2002) emphasized the multiple possible trajectories that may emerge in cases of complex psychological trauma, especially the kind of trauma that occurs when children are still in preverbal (or mostly preverbal) stages of development. Briere's integrative model rests fundamentally on cognitive-behavioral principles but recruits concepts from trauma theory, attachment theory, and psychodynamic approaches (self-psychology and object-relations theory) to elucidate the long-term consequences of abuse by "omission" and "commission" (Briere's terminology). Developmentally, children rarely have either the language skills or the long-term memory encoding-storage-retrieval skills that are necessary to process these events verbally. Nonetheless, the emotional memories and effects are compellingly salient and powerful in steering developmental (including pathological) outcomes. Courtois (1988; 1999) has studied the effects of sexual trauma including Dissociative Disorders, Posttraumatic Stress Disorder, and others. For example, Strauss (2001) and Strauss, Sugarman, and Giles-Sims (1997) have clearly established that physical discipline even if it is short of "physical abuse" produces antisocial behavior as well as measurable deficits in cognitive functioning.

Children who have experienced maltreatment evidence a greater prevalence of psychiatric symptoms and diagnoses when compared to peers who have not experienced maltreatment. Disorders that have been found to have a relationship with maltreatment run the gamut of anxiety disorders, eating disorders, affective disorders (Browne & Finkelhor, 1986b), Attention-Deficit/Hyperactivity Disorder, Posttraumatic Stress Disorder (Sternberg et al., 1993), and Antisocial Personality Disorder (Luntz & Widom, 1994). Dodge (2000) concluded as follows: "The experience of physical abuse during the first 5 years of life is one of the most consistent distal risk factors for later conduct problems, crime, and antisocial personality disorder" (p. 451).

The effects of child sexual abuse on the child include anger, aggression and hostility, fear and anxiety, depression, and sexually inappropriate behavior (Browne & Finkelhor, 1986a). Long-term effects of sexual abuse noted by Browne and Finkelhor (1986a; 1986b) include poor self-esteem, depression, self-destructive behavior, substance abuse, feelings of isolation and stigma, difficulty in trusting others, anxiety, a tendency toward revictimization, and sexual maladjustment. Children who have experienced sexual abuse are at greater risk of developing a number of disorders including Posttraumatic Stress Disorder (McLeer, Callaghan, Henry, & Wallen, 1994) and dissociative symptoms (Nash, Hulsey, Sexton, Harralson, & Lambert, 1993).

Compelling questions, controversies, and dilemmas.   These contemporary phenomena suggest the importance of many issues for practitioners who provide psychosocial, educational, and psychotherapeutic services to youth. Consideration must be given to: choices and decisions regarding health behaviors; lifestyle choices; emotional self-regulation; cognitive self-monitoring abilities; social skills; and decision-making strategies and skills. These are important issues to address regularly with children and adolescents across multiple contexts including at home, in the classroom, in extracurricular activities, in vocational, career, and educational counseling, and in individual and group psychotherapy. This text covers many of these issues within the context of various specific chapters involving particular settings and problems.

Key Definitions and Conceptual Questions

It is important that we provide definitions for the terms we are employing throughout this chapter. In this section, we provide answers to the following question: How do we define the terms *children, adolescents,* and *youth?*

Children.   Infants and toddlers are technically also children, but toddlerhood typically ends between 24 and 36 months of age. In this chapter, in discussing cognitive-behavioral group interventions with "children," we will assume that the term *children* refers to prepubertal children who are at least 4–5 years of age. Many children enter gonadarche (pubescence) by 10 or 11 years of age, but some do not do so until 13–14 years of age. Therefore, the endpoint for our definition of children must necessarily be somewhat flexible, ranging from 10 to 14 years of age. Cognitive-behavioral approaches do exist for preschool children, for example, the Interpersonal Cognitive Problem-Solving program developed by Shure and Spivak (1979). Most extant CBT interventions are designed for school-age children who are at least enrolled in kindergarten (i.e., 5–6 years of age). We examine the cognitive developmental skills necessary for a child to engage in group therapy in a later section of this chapter.

Adolescents.   Following the above logic, we define *adolescents* as people who have begun the puberty process (gonadarche). Therefore, the age range for the beginning of adolescence is the same as the age range for the endpoint of childhood (i.e., 10 to 14 years of age). The endpoint for the adolescent stage is also somewhat difficult to define with chronological precision. For some purposes, legal adult rights and responsibilities begin at 18. Major examples include the right to enlist in the armed forces without parental permission and the reality that the legal system considers crimes committed at age 18 to be the province of the adult criminal system, not the juvenile system. However, in other respects one is not an adult until a later age. For example, one may not purchase or consume alcoholic beverages until one is 21 years of age in the United States, and typically automobile rental companies will not rent a car to a person under 25 years of age. The age at which banks, credit unions, and loan companies will grant a mortgage or loan varies from state to state and from company to company, but generally, the age requirement is older than 18.

In terms of societal "rites of passage," and in sharp contrast to other nonindustrialized cultures, American society does not have a clear ritual or ceremony at which we unequivocally state, "You are now a fully enfranchised and independent adult in all ways." Receiving a driver's license (usually 16 years of age), graduating from high school (around 18–19 years of age), beginning college, graduating from college, and other typical societal achievements are all problematic in one way or another as a definition of *adulthood.* For our purposes, we define adolescents as people who have begun the puberty process and are not older than approximately 21 years of age. This is admittedly arbitrary, but practically speaking it works fairly well as a flexible definition that recognizes that some people may be nearly completely autonomous and independent at age 18 or 19 while others may be still quite dependent on their families of origin until their middle twenties.

Youth.   The term *youth* is an inclusive one that denotes both children and adolescents as we have defined them above, that is from entry into elementary school until end of adolescence (approximately 21 years). This use of the term *youth* is generally consistent with authors who have utilized the term in the literature such as Erik Erikson (1968) and Kenneth Kenniston (1970).

Commonalities among all youth.   In using the term *youth* in this inclusive way, the implication is that there is some set of shared characteristics and experiences that all youth have in common. What are these commonalities among all youth? Shared characteristics and experiences include the following: (a) Throughout the developmental time period we are using, i.e. elementary school through approximately 21 years of age, society generally expects that people are still dependent to some extent for financial resources, health care, shelter, and educational support on their parents or other legal guardians. (b) Most people do not subjectively consider people under 21 to be full-fledged "grown-ups" or adults. (c) Most people under 21 perceive themselves still developmentally not quite full adults.

Key differences between children and adolescents.   Having examined some commonalities across this broad developmental range, we must recognize great differences between children in the early elementary grades, for example, and college freshmen and sophomores. What are the key differences between children and adolescents? There are differences in cognitive capacities, emotional (affective) experiences, and social skills and behavior. We will consider these specific differences within each of the major subsections of this chapter.

Differences within categories. There exist not only differences across separate developmental categories, but also within categories. This principle recognizes the tremendous diversity that characterizes children who may be the same chronological age. For example, one 11-year-old girl may have reached nearly all of her adult height potential and may have nearly completed the puberty process to the point that she might be capable of ovulating and potentially conceiving. Her classmate, another female the same chronological age, could still be in every respect a young girl who is about 4 1/2 feet tall and has not yet begun to manifest any discernible signs of pubescence and may not be physically capable of ovulation and conception until she is 15 or 16 years of age. They are both "within the normal range." The various major subsections that follow contain answers to the following question: What important differences in terms of physical development, cognition, emotional development, and social behavior exist within categories (i.e., "young children" vs. "latency age children" or "young adolescents" vs. "older adolescents")?

Effects of commonalities and differences on group therapy with youth. The following crucial question is an integral part of each of the major sections of this chapter: How might these commonalities and differences affect cognitive-behavioral group therapy (CBGT) with children and adolescents? Each section of this chapter will provide answers to this general question.

BIOLOGICAL, GENETIC, AND NEUROLOGICAL INFLUENCES

This section provides a general overview of issues and influences involving primary biological factors including the following: (a) hormonal factors, (b) genetic contributions, (c) neurohormones and neurotransmitters, (d) brain growth and brain structures, and (e) interactions among these factors. The focus of this section is to present considerations, implications, and recommendations for CBGT with youth derived from the current knowledge of the biological, genetic, and neurological influences on development and developmental psychopathology.

Evidence of Continued Brain Growth through Late Adolescence/Young Adulthood

Prefrontal cortex "growth spurts." The last part of the brain to mature is the prefrontal cortex (PFC), which is responsible for higher order cognitive functions, such as making decisions, setting priorities, and suppressing impulses (Rubia et al., 2000). The PFC exerts effects on executive function (inhibition, planning, time perception, internal ordering, working memory, self-monitoring, verbal self-regulation, motor control, regulation of emotion, motivation), is the brain region that inhibits impulsivity, and is continuing to develop during adolescence (Casey, Giedd, & Thomas, 2000). That being said, it is not surprising to encounter adolescents who make rash decisions, do not plan ahead, and are often late for curfew. According to recent research (LeDoux, 2002), the amygdala, part of the limbic system (the "emotional brain"), matures more quickly than the PFC does. There is evidence that this produces differences between adolescents and adults in terms of the brain areas that process emotion. A study that used functional magnetic resonance imaging (fMRI) showed that the brain activity in 10- to 18-year olds when they viewed faces with fearful expression was centered in the amygdala, not the PFC while the opposite pattern occurred in 20- to 40-year-olds (Baird, Gruber, Cohen, Renshaw, & Yureglun-Todd, 1999).

Changes in neurotransmitter (NT) activity. Walker (2002) found that dopamine activity increases during puberty while serotonin activity decreases. Serotonin has an influence on mood regulation and many other functions. Dopamine affects mood regulation and impulse control and is also a prominent part of the "pleasure circuit" (reward pathways) in the brain. These changes may relate to many dimensions of adaptive functioning and vulnerability (risk and resilience), ranging from increased susceptibility to mood disorders to the typical age of onset for psychotic disorders such as Schizophrenia (18 to 25 years for males, 25 to mid-30s for females; *DSM-IV-TR*; American Psychiatric Association, 2000). Experimental research has demonstrated that mildly stressful experiences produce real changes in neurotransmitter levels in the brain. For example, Suomi (1997, 2000) reported that rhesus monkeys that were peer-raised (separated from mothers and other adults) had consistently lower levels of serotonin metabolites in their cerebrospinal fluid. These monkeys had more problems with aggression. Brain chemistry, therefore, can reflect environmental and experiential factors. Levels of brain neurotransmitters are not carved in "genetic stone" as some simplistic models of "chemical imbalances" might suggest.

Ongoing brain development and the continual interaction between genes and the environment. Neuroscientific research has established that brain structure continues to develop throughout the lifespan. The brain eliminates connections (synapses) that it no longer needs (pruning), creates new branches and connections where needed (dendritic spreading), builds new synapses with new learning, and under some conditions may produce new neurons—a possibility only recently established in the research. The brain is therefore exquisitely sensitive to environmental input, making children's and adolescents' brains vulnerable throughout the developmental years.

In recent years, biological, genetic, and behavior-genetic research has demonstrated the complex nature of the process of gene-environment interaction, including that experiences produce actual changes in brain cells and synapses (Rosenzweig, 1969) by "switching on" or "switching off" genes, producing changes in levels of neurotransmitters, increased synaptic growth, extended dendritic spreading, and frequent pruning of unused or unnecessary pathways. Abuse and neglect, for example, produce direct effects on brain development by interacting with the genes that regulate the neurodevelopmental processes. Perry (2002) summarized the body of research as follows: "Abuse studies from the author's laboratory, studies of children in orphanages who lacked emotional contact, and a large number of animal deprivation and enrichment studies point to the need for children and young nonhuman mammals to have both stable emotional attachments with and touch from primary adult caregivers, and spontaneous interactions with peers. If these connections are lacking, brain development both of caring behavior and cognitive capacities is damaged in a lasting fashion" (Perry, 2002, p. 79).

Hormonal Effects on Cognition, Affect Regulation, and Behavior

Adrenarche.   Adrenarche, the hormonal awakening of the adrenal glands, marks the earliest discernible evidence of the onset of puberty. This component of puberty begins between the ages of 6 and 9. During this period, blood levels of the adrenal androgens (male hormones) rise (Grumbach & Styne, 1992), and continue to increase throughout gonadarche (the later hormonal awakening of the ovaries and testes that follows adrenarche by 2–3 years) The initial hormone increases in adrenal androgens occur prior to noticeable physical changes such as breast or pubic hair development. At the same time that these adrenal androgens begin to rise, hormones from the hypothalamic-pituitary-gonadal axis (estrogens and testosterone) are dormant.

Gonadarche.   The second phase of puberty, gonadarche, is what most often is referred to as "puberty." Gonadarche begins at roughly 8 to 9 years of age for African American girls, at age 9 to 10 years in White girls (Herman-Giddens et al., 1997), and at age 10 to 11 years in boys (Grumbach & Styne, 1992). It is the stage during which sexual maturity, reproductive maturity (testes and ovaries), and secondary sex characteristics (pubic hair and breast growth) are realized. The peak of the "puberty" stage is menarche for girls and spermarche for boys.

The reality of this transformation from child to adult is that the actual pubertal stage does not have as strong a relationship to emotions and behavior as do the hormone levels during this developmental transition. The changes in sex steroids (testosterone and estrogens) and adrenal androgens at this time, coupled with physical changes, play a part in the increased prevalence of depression and physical aggression in adolescents.

Testosterone.   Theorists and researchers have implicated testosterone as a causal influence on provoked aggressive behavior in ninth grade boys, appearing to lower their frustration tolerance (Olweus, Mattson, Schalling, & Low, 1988). In this same study, higher levels of testosterone appeared to cause the boys to be impatient and irritable, thereby increasing their readiness to engage in unprovoked aggressive behavior. Conversely, Susman and colleagues (1987; 2003) reported a "negative relationship between testosterone and behavior problems... in healthy young boys" (2003, p. 302). At least two studies found no relationship between testosterone levels and girls' aggressive behaviors (Susman et al., 1987; Brooks-Gunn & Warren, 1989). In summary, the findings regarding testosterone and behavior are somewhat inconsistent depending on methods of measurement, gender, and other factors.

Estrogen.   Higher concentrations of estradiol (one of the estrogens) in 9- to 14-year-old girls correlated with dominance while girls were interacting with their interacting parents (Inoff-Germain et al., 1988). However, existing research has established no consistent relationship between estradiol and aggressive or delinquent behavior (Susman et al., 1987). In a study with girls who had delayed puberty, an administered dose of estrogen caused an increased self-report of aggression against peers and adults in girls given low and middle doses of estrogen but not in girls given the high doses (Finkelstein et al., 1997). Girls exhibited withdrawal behaviors with increased estrogen doses (Susman, et al., 1998) and reported increases in depression with increased estrogen (Angold, Costello, Erkanli, & Worthman, 1999).

Early vs. Late Maturation and Appraisal of Risk

Most of the original research literature suggested that for boys, it is advantageous to mature early rather than late (Simmons Blyth, Van Cleave, & Bush, 1987). For girls, early maturation leads to a number of significant problems (Graber, 2003). Early maturing girls are more likely to drink or smoke cigarettes. They are more likely to become depressed, develop an eating disorder, and have older friends. The maturation of their bodies may elicit interest from males that can lead to earlier dating as well as sexual experiences at a young age (Wiesner & Ittel, 2002). Social factors account for two to four times more of the variance than do hormonal factors in terms of adolescent girls' levels of depression and anger (Brooks-Gunn & Warren, 1989). Stattin and Magnusson (1990) found that early-maturing girls may have lower educational attainment and lower occupational status in adulthood.

Health Factors

Medical conditions affecting development.   In a previous section, we examined several health-related behaviors including obesity and substance use disorders. The increasing prevalence of these conditions has been a cause for great concern among medical and mental health professionals. This has been particularly salient because of the close relationship between obesity and cigarette addiction, on the one hand, and cardiovascular disease, stroke, and cancer, on the other, all leading causes of death in adulthood. Two additional health-related conditions that are often comorbid with certain mental disorders and deserve special attention are polycystic ovary syndrome (PCOS) and hypothyroidism, both very prevalent conditions in the population and both of which can have their origins during adrenarche and gonadarche.

   Polycystic ovary syndrome (PCOS).   PCOS is a syndrome caused by abnormally high androgen (male hormones) levels in a human female. Symptoms include menstrual irregularity, hirsuitism (hair on the face, navel, and other areas where males typically have hair growth), difficulty conceiving (infertility), acne (especially along the jaw), mood swings (irritability, aggressiveness, depression, etc.), and ovarian cysts. Testing for reproductive hormone levels can definitively establish the diagnosis. There is often a history of medical professionals' having prescribed oral contraceptives in order to regulate the menstrual cycle. PCOS is very prevalent in contemporary American females with estimated prevalence rates of 5 to 10% of women of childbearing age (Susman et al., 2003). PCOS often occurs in females who have early adrenarche and gonadarche. PCOS may also play a role in insulin resistance, a risk factor for later metabolic syndrome and Type II diabetes. The mood symptoms of PCOS can closely resemble a Major Depressive Episode or a Hypomanic Episode, and often a diagnosis of Major Depressive Disorder or Bipolar II Disorder occurs as a result. This can lead to a prescription of drugs for mood stabilization. Drugs in this class will worsen the symptoms of PCOS and will frequently contribute to rapid weight gain without producing significant change in mood status. We recommend that all adolescent females who have some of the symptoms outlined above should have a thorough medical physical including testing for androgen (especially testosterone) levels before assigning any mood disorder diagnoses.

Hypothyroidism.   Hypothyroidism is one of the most prevalent metabolic conditions and the fact that Synthroid is one of the most frequently prescribed medications provides further substantiation of this fact. The *Merck Manual of Medical Information* (Merck & Co, Inc., 1997) emphasizes the following: "In sharp contrast to hyperthyroidism, the symptoms of hypothyroidism are subtle and gradual and may be mistaken for depression" (p. 709). Therefore, as is repeatedly and thoroughly emphasized by the *DSM-IV-TR*, it is imperative that mental health treatment providers make certain that clients, including adolescent clients, have a thorough physical, complete with testing for thyroxin levels, before assigning any mood disorder diagnosis as certain antidepressants would be contraindicated in clients whose mood symptoms are actually produced by hypothyroidism. Unfortunately, diagnosing professionals often overlook this important caveat.

Diet and exercise.   In a previous section, we presented information on the current epidemics involving overweight, obesity, and Type II diabetes, including the increasingly early age of onset for these phenomena among American youth. Psychologists, psychiatrists, and other professionals who are delivering mental health services to youth must devote time and attention to diet and exercise in their consultations with children, adolescents, and their parents. This is important because poor diet and sedentary lifestyle (lack of exercise) often result in the development of chronic conditions that, in turn, develop into potentially life-threatening health conditions such as cardiovascular disease and stroke. Group work with youth will often include these issues more implicitly than explicitly, but group members will often raise these topics in one way or another. We must be prepared to address them forthrightly.

Substance use and comorbidity with other mental disorders.   We presented the epidemic of substance use disorders among children and adolescents in a previous section. However, in reviewing factors impacting child and adolescent development it is important to make two points. The *DSM-IV-TR,* when discussing various substance abuse and dependency diagnoses, consistently notes that prevalence rates tend to be higher in people under 25 years of age and that there is often significant comorbidity among the various Substance Use Disorders (SUDs) as well as among SUDs and other primary mental disorders such as Mood Disorders, Anxiety Disorders, Attention-Deficit/Hyperactivity Disorder, Conduct Disorder, and Personality Disorders. Most SUDs have relatively early onset and many adolescents and children will have some complications related to substances in their lives, either in terms of personal consequences or family involvement. Treatment professionals must be very mindful of these possibilities when conducting therapeutic interventions, given the pervasive effects of substances on thinking, feeling, and behavior, models of psychotherapy such as CBT that seek to mobilize thinking processes to manage behavior and feelings will inherently encounter major roadblocks with clients who are surreptitiously using substances or suffering from SUDs in family members.

Complex interactions among factors.   The problems that youth bring with them to the group psychotherapy context are rarely unidimensional and neatly circumscribed. Instead, there invariably exist complex interactions involving dimensions of risk, factors favoring resilience, positive and negative peer and family influences, and biological-genetic predispositions. This complexity suggests the value of a diathesis-stress model, in which development of symptoms of one or more mental disorders is a product of the interaction of genetic predispositions with multiple possible environmental and experiential factors. In a group therapy context, professionals need to recognize that youth are in the process of growth and change. They have the opportunity to bring the resilience-enhancing dimensions of the group therapy subculture to bear on reducing personal emotional distress as well as making more self-protective behavioral choices. Group facilitators need to view child group therapy participants as capable of change, recovery, and growth, even when serious diagnoses are already present. Children and adolescent mental status is not "carved in diagnostic stone."

PSYCHOLOGICAL, COGNITIVE, AND AFFECTIVE (EMOTIONAL) INFLUENCES

This major section cannot provide an exhaustive presentation of the rich body of re-search in child and adolescent development in the realms of psychological, cognitive, and affective development. Each of these dimensions can consume at least an entire volume by itself. In addition, all of these factors interact with domains of social and personality development, both remarkably extensive in themselves. Therefore, we have of necessity selected key examples of theories and research with particular relevance for understanding the interaction of psychological, cognitive, and affective factors in the group context. The purpose of this section is to present considerations, implications, and recommendations for CBGT with youth that derive from the current knowledge of the psychological, cognitive, and affective (emotional) influences on development and developmental psychopathology.

Cognitive Developmental Considerations

Feldman (2002) reviewed the current status of our knowledge regarding cognitive devel-opment in childhood and emphasized the interacting but originally separate influences of Piaget's (1970) model of cognitive development, Vygotsky's (1962) sociocultural-cogni-tive constructivist model, Chomsky (1957), and others. Eccles, Wigfield, & Byrnes (2003) presented a review of cognitive development in adolescence, emphasizing structural change (knowledge and capacity) and functional change (deductive reasoning, decision making, gender differences). A key aspect of Eccles and colleagues' review that holds major implications for working with children and adolescents in a psychotherapeutic context involves the related concepts of decision making and risk taking. While there is some evidence consistent with Piaget's concept of formal operational thought that ado-lescents can engage in more cognitively sophisticated decision making in experimental situations, there is some question about whether or not adolescents actually use their decision making abilities to make self-protective decisions and avoid high-risk behavior. These authors concluded: "Regrettably, these studies reveal the opposite of what one would expect if decision-making skills improve during adolescence; instead these studies show that older adolescents are more likely than younger adolescents or preadolescents to engage in these (high risk) behaviors" (Eccles et al., p. 328). The implications of this conclusion are clear: When we work with adolescents, we must be aware that although their manifest capacity to verbally handle complex decision making in a controlled context such as group psychotherapy may be very impressive, they may do quite the opposite in the actual "real-world" situations when confronted with high-risk choices. This example highlights that not all areas of development (cognitive, affective, behavioral) progress at the same rate and may result in discrepancies impacting functioning within and outside of the group therapy context.

Freud: Ego integrity, ego defenses, and the reality principle. A frequent misconception regarding Freud's psychoanalytic model of personality functioning and psychological development is that it relies entirely on unconscious emotional processes and basic biologically driven drives. There is also a very prominent role for conscious processes and cognitive functioning including thinking, self-awareness, decision making, problem-solving, scientific reasoning, intellectual creativity, beliefs, attitudes, values, and other cognitive processes. Freud located these functions in the ego (i.e., "the I" or "self") and clearly articulated that the ego functions according to the "reality principle" as opposed to the id which responds to the "pleasure principle." Insight, the first step in the change process in psychoanalytically oriented models, is a product of the ego, the cognitive aspect of the self. Therefore, in assisting child and adolescent clients in examining evidence, "disputing irrational beliefs," exposing "automatic thoughts," examining "underlying assumptions," and discovering "core beliefs," cognitive-behavioral therapists are relying on ego functions in psychoanalytic terminology.

In classic psychoanalytical developmental terms, ego functioning begins with the "birth of the ego" in the anal period beginning at roughly 12–18 months and concluding around 30–36 months of age. In the phallic stage, ages 3–6 years, the ego develops important new sophisticated ego defense mechanisms including identification—the capacity to experience a degree of gratification vicariously by observing older powerful identification figures, especially their same-sex parents. In this process of resolving the Oedipal conflict (males) or Elektra conflict (females), the superego (conscience and ego ideal) is formed. The child then has the cognitive and emotional equipment to deal with more advanced demands of external reality including building skills for life functioning during the "latency stage" (ages 6–puberty). Most of the life skills (academic, athletic, self-care, etc.) involve heavy use of the ego's reality-oriented capacities. Most group counseling and psychotherapy would begin during this latency stage because of the advanced emotional and cognitive skills. This may make them relatively task-oriented and compliant participants in group psychotherapy until pubescence, a process that can start as early as 8 years of age in contemporary America.

However, according to Freud, the massive changes of adolescence will produce major new challenges as the sexual and hormonal changes no longer permit the ego to rely on the more primitive defense mechanisms formed during the first three stages of life (repression, splitting, introjection, denial, minimization, magical thinking, and projection). Adolescence demands a much more sophisticated defensive structure from the ego. Both Sigmund and Anna Freud emphasized that new defenses must develop. If this process fails massively, then the result can be "ego decompensation," the psychoanalytical conceptualization of psychoses such as Schizophrenia; essentially, the ego's capacity for "reality testing" has disintegrated. Clinicians who work with youth with serious mental health disorders such as major mood disorders with psychotic features, psychotic disorders, serious personality and/or conduct disorders involving self-destructive or other-destructive behavior (including suicidality, homicidality, or serious aggression), or severe potentially life-threatening Substance Use Disorders (including food-related disorders such as Anorexia Nervosa) will need to be very aware of the psychotic components of these disorders—in other words, serious impairment in ego functioning. Impairment in ego functioning will seriously challenge the capacity of people with these mental disorders to respond to cognitive and behavioral interventions. Nevertheless, there is ample evidence that CBT and other psychosocial interventions are effective even with clients with psychotic symptomatology (e.g., Frank et al., 2005; Rector & Beck, 2001) whether or not they are taking medications.

New defense mechanisms should be developing in adolescents to cope with the new challenges of emerging sexuality in the genital stage. These include sublimation, displacement, asceticism, intellectualization, humor, and reaction formation. These mechanisms comprise the more "sophisticated" defensive strategies. All can be patho-logical in extreme manifestations, but within limits constitute what most psychologists would characterize as mature psychological functioning, at least from a psychody-namic perspective. Many troubled adolescents will have the more primitive defenses of childhood rigidly in place and may have few or none of the more sophisticated ones. In terms of group work with adolescents, a major implication of this possibility is that clinicians can constitute groups with heterogeneous membership including people with more advanced defensive structures and use the power of the peer influence process to encourage more socially adaptive defensive functioning on the part of the less socially competent group members.

Adler's concepts of subjective perception, social affiliation, and "private logic," and purposeful behavior.   Dinkmeyer and Dinkmeyer (1991) and Monte (1999) pro-vided overviews of Adler's contributions. Adler proposed that the ideas and beliefs according to which a person operates are called private logic. In addition, he believed that humans' most fundamental motivation is to affiliate with others and derive a sense of social belonging and to make a contribution to the well-being of the group. Adler used the German term *Gemeinschaftsgefuhl* (community feeling or social interest) to express this need to belong and affiliate. Adler also emphasized that human behavior, thoughts, and feelings are all goal-driven (teleological or purposeful). Adler's theory is an approach that focuses on our thinking, feeling, and behavior within our social groups and is ideally suited for understanding children and adolescents in their peer and family contexts. It also emphasizes that cognitive development involves the influence of social drives and experiences.

Piagetian and Neo-Piagetian approaches to cognition.   According to Piagetian theory, formal operational thinking occurs in adolescence and adolescents begin to create make-believe situations and demonstrate an increased tendency to think about thought, a process known as *metacognition* (Flavell, Miller, & Miller, 2002). Adolescents are able to begin thinking like scientists and engage in hypothetical-deductive reasoning problem solving.

Elkind's (1976) concept of "adolescent egocentrism" entails two types of social thinking—imaginary audience and personal fable. Imaginary audience connotes the adolescents' belief that others are watching them and evaluating them, while the per-sonal fable refers to the adolescents' belief that the self is unique, invulnerable, and omnipotent. Adolescents believe that no one will ever understand what they are going through and tend to believe that they are of great interest to other people in the room. Egocentrism differs from the more common language terms "egotism" or "egotistical." The latter denotes something more Freudian in derivation, namely that the person is grandiose and narcissistic in a distinctly nonempathetic way. Egocentrism, in contrast, is primarily a social-cognitive characteristic focusing primarily on the way adolescents cognitively construe their social experience of themselves in relationship to others. These cognitive developmental considerations are especially important to bear in mind when working within a group therapy modality, as they represent possible factors at work within each group member and within the dynamics between members.

Vygotsky's concepts of "Zone of Proximal Development," "situated learning," embeddedness, contextual learning, and cultural influences: "A sociocultural-cognitive-constructivist approach." Feldman (2003) emphasized the integrative nature of Vygotsky's (1978) theory: "Although still arguably a cognitive developmentalist, Vygotsky's framework could be equally plausibly thought of as social, cultural, historical, or educational as easily as it could be called cognitive (Feldman, 2003, p. 198).

Attachment Theory and Bowlby's concept of "Internal Working Models" and social competence of securely attached children/adolescents. Attachment Theory (AT; Bowlby, 1940; 1969) provides an integrative approach that combines a genetically mediated predisposition to form close relationships in the service of personal and species survival with the psychological processes of thinking and feeling that support survival. Bowlby's concept of *internal working models* is particularly applicable to CBGT approaches because internal working models involve one's internalized expectations of worthiness in terms of love, care, protection, and nurturance. These internal working models derive from experiences in close relationships. Disruptions in these relationships produce distortions in one's capacity for self-regulation and social relatedness. Sroufe, Duggal, Weinfield, and Carlson (2000) utilized longitudinal methodology to establish a clear link between infant attachment security and later "self-esteem, social competence, prosocial behavior, ego resiliency, and overall adjustment" (2000, p. 82). We return to these concepts in the next section on affective and personality development, but mentioned them here as they relate to cognitive development in that these theories explain the formation of beliefs and mental representations that develop in children and adolescents related to themselves and their relationships with others.

Social cognition and decision-making involving ambiguous social stimuli. Dodge and colleagues (1995; 2000) have demonstrated that the cognitions involved in the encoding and processing of social stimuli, particularly ambiguous social stimuli, can exert a strong influence on whether or not children or adolescents select aggressive or nonaggressive responses. We discuss this again in the section on social cognition.

Affective and Personality Development

G. Stanley Hall's concept of "storm and stress." Early in the 20th century, G. Stanley Hall used the German expression "Sturm und Drang" ("storm and stress") to describe the turmoil that he believed was a central manifestation of normal adolescence. This attitude reflected the influence of Freud's model. The notion of tumultuous adolescence has been a very popular one throughout the past century. However, broad-based cross-cultural surveys suggest that adolescence is tumultuous for only a minority of adolescents and their parents (Offer, Ostrov, Howard, & Atkinson, 1988) and that the point prevalence of psychopathology among adolescents ranges from 20 to 25% (Casper, Belanoff, & Offer, 1996; Offer, Ostrov, Howard, & Atkinson, 1992). Therefore, while the most typical profile for adolescence is relatively smooth functioning and emotional stability, there is an important minority who experience considerable turmoil. The major implication for clinicians here is that the adolescents who participate in group psychotherapy and counseling most likely represent this latter "storm and stress" pattern.

Psychodynamically-oriented models.   We previously discussed the application of Freud's and Erikson's approaches in terms of cognitive development. Freud emphasized that in latency (middle childhood) there is a reduction in the pressure of the intense energy of the id and its demands for gratification. This provides an opportunity for developing ego strength as described earlier. The strengthening of the ego provides a foundation for coping with the challenges of puberty and the emergence of adult sexuality, and contributes to the development of tendencies toward emotional and behavioral functioning that comprise personality. Erikson emphasized the crisis of industry vs. inferiority during middle childhood. We return to Erikson's theoretical contributions below in the section on contemporary models of personality development.

Social belonging and subjective perception.   In the earlier section on cognitive development, we described the usefulness of Adler's pioneering contribution to cognitive approaches (subjective perception, private logic, social belonging, purposeful behavior). These concepts also relate directly to affective and personality development and to implications for group therapy. In particular, Adler's idea that emotions and affective expression have social meaning and goal-directedness is important in terms of understanding children's and adolescents' ability to benefit from group interaction. They want to belong and contribute to the group. The task of the facilitator is to mobilize and channel this inherent desire and to help group participants examine their own socially productive behavior as well as their maladaptive behavior.

Cognitive-developmental contributions to social cognition.   We previously noted Piaget's and Elkind's contributions to our understanding of child and adolescent cognitive development. In particular, Elkind has applied Piagetian concepts of cognitive development to children's and adolescents' social interactions and behavior. The concepts of adolescent egocentrism that we presented earlier have importance in terms of affective and personality development as well. Repeated experiences in which adolescent egocentrism including the "personal fable" and the "imaginary audience" manifests itself develop into a behavior pattern that becomes part of the personality. In CBGT, the facilitator will hopefully assist children and adolescents in consciously examining their own appraisal of the risks associated with their behavior and the evidence that supports certain behavioral choices and discourages others. This process can also help reduce the intense self-consciousness that manifests itself in the "imaginary audience."

Contemporary models of personality development.   Trust, self-identity, and the ability to be independent are crucial factors for personality development. Much of what we know of personality development derives from research using younger children or adults. Erikson (1968) labeled the first year of life the trust-vs.-mistrust stage of development. Erikson purported that infants learn that they can trust others if their caregivers attend to them in a consistent and warm manner. This stage does not terminate once the child leaves the first year of life. Instead this phenomenon of trust-versus-mistrust arises with each new developmental stage. Thus, when working with adolescents, the therapist may encounter mistrust from children who appeared to have a warm and structured first few years of life.

Children find and construct their own selves (Rochat, 2001), and Erikson (1968) believed that the stage of autonomy vs. shame/doubt (approximately 18–36 months) plays an important backdrop for the development of independence and identity during adolescence. When toddlers develop autonomy from their caregivers, they experience the courage to be independent and to choose which paths to take into the future.

It is in adolescence that personality styles begin to shape the person's life. One taxonomy, well known as the Big Five, and often given the mnemonic OCEAN, is a comprehensive model of personality factors. Costa and McRae (1980) developed the "Big Five" model in their Baltimore Longitudinal Study. The five factors included in this model are Openness/Intellect (curious about the world, imaginative), Conscientiousness (well organized and plans ahead), Extroversion (assertive and outgoing), Agreeableness (likable, kind, giving), and Neuroticism (anxious and self-pitying) (Caspi, 1998; Goldberg, 1993). When mothers of 12- to 13-year-old Caucasian and African American boys rated their children on this set of five factors, an additional two dimensions of personality emerged for adolescents: irritability (feelings are easily hurt, complains a lot), and positive activity (physically active and energetic; John, Caspi, Robins, Moffitt, & Stouthamer-Loeber, 1994). John and colleagues (1994) also demonstrated statistically significant relationships between these five personality factors and adolescents' emotional well-being. Boys who demonstrated externalizing problems were less agreeable, less conscientious, and more extroverted than their peers who did not demonstrate externalizing problems. Boys who demonstrated internalizing disorders were high on neuroticism and low on conscientiousness. Boys who scored low on conscientiousness and low on openness demonstrated poor school performance.

Kagan, Reznick, and Gibbons (1989) describe the temperament construct of behavioral inhibition as "a temperamentally based disposition of children to react consistently to unfamiliar events, both social and nonsocial, with initial restraint," (p. 301). Kagan (2002) classified children using a temperament category called "inhibition to the unfamiliar" based on the premise of their being either shy and timid, or sociable and extroverted. Children with high behavioral inhibition react to novel situations cautiously, perhaps withdrawing or behaving in a fearful way. Kagan (1992) noted that children react with behavioral inhibition beginning around 7 to 9 months of age and remain in this temperamental category through early childhood. This is important to keep in mind when working with youth as their temperament at a younger age may affect how people have come to view them as well as how they may view themselves (represented in schema at work within the group, as well, and possibly the targets of restructuring).

Buss and Plomin's (1984) temperament theory identifies another possible elucidation for understanding social behavior. The original model of Buss and Plomin (1975) characterized four temperaments: Emotionality, Activity, Sociability, and Impulsivity. Impulsivity is not included in Buss and Plomin's (1984) modern EAS model on temperament. Buss and Plomin projected the emotionality characteristic to include mostly negative affect, activity to be a high or low energy disposition, and sociability to be the degree to which shyness or extroversion prevails in a person.

MODELS THAT INTEGRATE COGNITIVE, AFFECTIVE, AND BEHAVIORAL INFLUENCES

Social Cognition

Integrative models involving socialization and cognition. In earlier sections on cognitive development, we introduced Elkind's (1976) concepts of adolescent egocentrism (imaginary audience and personal fable), Dodge and colleagues' (1995; 2000) model of social information processing of ambiguous social stimuli, Adler's concepts (Dinkmeyer & Dinkmeyer, 1991; Monte, 1999) of subjective perception and private logic, Bowlby's (1940; 1969) and Sroufe and colleagues' (2000) attachment theory (AT) and principle of internal working models, and Vygotsky's (1962; 1978) sociocultural-constructivist concepts of zone of proximal development and situated learning. All of these concepts are integrative because they focus on the ways that cognitive development affects social behavior and, conversely, the mechanisms by which social experiences affect cognitive development. Cognition and social behavior have a dynamic, ongoing, reciprocal relationship to each other; it is a systemic or interactive pattern.

Dodge's model. Social cognition has central relevance for CBT approaches, especially when applied in the group context as in CBGT. because the group provides an in vivo "laboratory" for improving social cognitive skills. Dodge's research establishes that individuals who act out aggressively are much more likely to cognitively appraise ambiguous social cues as provocative or threatening. Group facilitators can build goals and objectives that help participants improve their thinking about various alternative explanations regarding social interactions as well as alternative behavioral choices following appraisal of ambiguous social cues.

Attachment Theory. In similar fashion, the AT concept of internal working models addresses internalized cognitive appraisals and expectations—however, specifically related to one's worthiness of love, protection, care, and nurturing. These internalized cognitive-affective expectations derived from the repeated reciprocal interactions in the early years. When these patterns involve neglect, abuse, and violence, children's and adolescents' internal working models are very likely to involve notions such as the following, most of which are unrecognized or unconscious: (a) "I am not worth being protected." (b) "I don't deserve to be loved or cared for." (c) "I can't expect people to reach out to me or nurture me." (d) "I can't do anything right." (e) "My efforts do not get people's love and attention." (f) "I never know when I might be criticized or abused."

In the language of CBT, these internal working models form the basis for core beliefs about self, world, and future. Children apply these internal working models to their academic and vocational behavior, their social choices and peer associations, their intimate relationships, and their self-care and self-protective choices (or lack thereof). In essence, they tend to care for themselves and protect themselves in the same way that their caregivers and close family members cared for and protected them. When there were deficiencies in these relationship experiences, children's internal working models are likely to be impaired and deficient. Group facilitators can help "repair" some of these deficiencies by providing a safe and trusting context in which children and adolescents can explore and discover some of their internal beliefs and expectations and replace them with more socially adaptive and personally protective ones. The therapeutic relationship or alliance provides the foundation for this exploratory process.

SOCIAL, CONTEXTUAL, AND CULTURAL INFLUENCES

The goal of this section is to present considerations, implications, and recommendations for CBGT with youth derived from the current knowledge of the social, contextual, and cultural influences on development and developmental psychopathology. This section briefly revisits Vygotsky's model, further applies Dodge's research on social cognition, examines peer influences in more detail, explores parent and family systems influences, and analyzes cultural and media influences as they pertain to group work with youth.

A Sociocultural Cognitive-Constructivist Approach: Vygotsky

Vygotsky's theory, mentioned briefly above, seems remarkably well-suited to the contemporary needs of children and adolescents. The group context contains the essential ingredients for the application of Vygotsky's concepts of "Zone of Proximal Development" (ZPD), "situated learning," embeddedness, contextual learning, and cultural-mediated learning. In the CBGT applications, the general goal regardless of specific treatment setting or particular types of psychopathology is to help clients learn ways of thinking differently about their feelings and behaviors in order for their feelings and behaviors to be more consistent with better adaptation and less subjective distress. In the group setting, each participant is potentially at once a mentor and a mentee. Vygotsky's concept of the ZPD suggests that a child or adolescent group participant might demonstrate the most adaptive and least disruptive behavior when a mentor who could be a group member or facilitator/therapist helps this mentee stretch beyond her/his typical level of social functioning, cognitive exploration, and/or emotional self-awareness. Other group members might switch roles from mentee to mentor frequently depending upon the issue that surfaces at the time. Building on each others' strengths is a key Vygotskian notion. This learning potential is "embedded" within the group process and the group itself constructs a kind of subculture that can potentially support new learning and new levels of adaptive behavior. While there always remains the risk that group members might facilitate each others' learning in maladaptive directions, it is the unique role of the therapist/facilitator to help with the "sociocultural construction" of group norms and standards that reinforce the positive direction.

Peer Influence

From school to sporting activities to weekend sleepovers, youth spend an ever-increasing amount of time with their peers. Friendships can be a valuable commodity for healthy psychological development. A classic study using Rhesus monkeys established just how important peers are for youth development. Suomi, Harlow, and Domek (1970) found that monkeys became depressed and less socially advanced when they were separated from the peers with which they were raised. The classic Bulldogs Bank (Freud & Dann, 1951) study evidenced that children show resilience when bonded together.

Influences of Parents and the Family System

Family breakup is a major modern issue. The number of adolescents growing up in single-parent families or in stepfamilies is remarkable. According to the National Center for Health Statistics, approximately 1,000,000 children experience a divorce each year. An estimated 23% of youth are living in single-parent homes (Santrock, 2006). Most studies have concluded that children in nondivorced families show better adjustment compared to their peers in divorced families (Amato & Keith, 1991). Children in non-divorced families are less likely to have academic difficulty and internal and external problems (Conger & Chao, 1996). Conger and Chao also reported that children in these intact families tend to be more socially responsible and do not become sexually active as young as their peers from divorced homes. Amato and Keith argue that these effects are becoming smaller as divorce is becoming more widespread in the United States. Hetherington and Stanley-Hagan (2002) found that the adjustment of the youth prior to the divorce, the gender of the youth, and their temperament all affect the eventual outcomes following the experience of divorce.

Cultural and Media Influences

The media is one influence in the shaping of eating disorders and adolescents' dissatis-faction with their body image. Thompson and Heinberg (1999) demonstrated that inter-nalization of societal pressures such as what body shape is attractive has a moderating effect on the media's impact on body dissatisfaction and eating disorders of females. Adolescents become increasingly more aware of their bodies during the transition from childhood to adulthood. For females, this transition requires greater fat deposits on the body. Oftentimes the societal ideal is not possible and does not reflect the image of a physically healthy body.

In stark contradiction to the striving for the ideal "thin" body image is the increased focus on fast meals such as "drive-thru's" and microwavable frozen dinners. These meals are high in saturated fat and frequently provide only "empty calories." These meals cause an increase in body fat when consumed over an extended period of time not only by their high fat and high caloric content, but also by the lack of vitamins, minerals, and protein necessary for adolescents to remain active and healthy. Adolescent activity may also have an impact on the epidemic of overweight and obese children. Motor-scooters, all-terrain vehicles, automobiles, computers, cellular phones, television, and videogames all contribute to an inactive lifestyle and for many teens this will lead to increased body weight and poorer self-image.

CONCLUSIONS AND RECOMMENDATIONS

The following conclusions essentially take the form of recommendations to practitioners of group psychotherapy, specifically CBGT. CBGT facilitators can draw on these recom-mendations in designing their group interventions. The recommendations assume a generic format so that the details of implementation are the province of individuals who design CBGT interventions in specific settings for particular sets of problems.

Diversity across Developmental Stages

We recommend continued attention to the wide variation that we encounter in terms of cognitive, affective, and behavioral capacities in delivering group services to children as young as 5–6 years of age or adolescents as old as 18–23 years of age. We have presented a great deal of information to help group facilitators understand this diversity.

Age-Specific Cognitive Changes, Competencies, and Limitations

Group facilitators need to tailor their interventions to address the information-processing capacity (memory, language, metacognition), conceptual sophistication, and limitations of the children and adolescents comprising their groups. Therefore, for children under 11 years of age, psychological qualities and dynamics need to be reduced to very concrete behavioral terms and not delivered in abstract ways. Abstract thought begins with pubescence at approximately 11–13 years of age with even wider variation possible.

Affective and Personality Changes, Competencies, and Limitations

CBGT attempts to use cognitive self-exploration, examining evidence, disputing irrational beliefs, and two-sided problem-solving and decision-making skills to help children and adolescents with affective self-regulation and emotional self-monitoring. Group facilitators need to recognize that the lexicon of emotions develops slowly and that prepubescent children may lack rich vocabularies in terms of feeling words. Many children may exhibit signs of alexithymia, a condition in which they have a true deficiency in ability to label feelings and appropriately identify these feelings in themselves or others. Patience is required to tailor our vocabularies to the appropriate developmental level of our youthful clients.

Social and Systemic Changes, Competencies, and Limitations

Group facilitators need to be aware of the ways that social support (or lack thereof) and the social systems that surround children and adolescents change as development proceeds through the elementary years into middle school and high school. Their social worlds broaden very rapidly and their freedom and mobility increase in exciting but simultaneously potentially hazardous ways. Access to automobiles, for example, provides the foundation for the leading cause of death in adolescents—accidents. Helping children and adolescents choose self-protective and self-enhancing social and systemic involvement while avoiding high-risk choices is always an important goal in group work. This goal may be explicit or implicit, but it will always be there.

Value of Cognition and Limitations of Cognition

In this chapter, we have emphasized the development of a wide range of cognitive skills including logical thought, alternative thinking, and consequential thinking. These skills develop to varying extents among children as they move from elementary age into adolescents. By definition, many of the clients in CBT groups will have more delays or impairment in terms of the cognitive developmental capacities. Group facilitators find themselves in a position to help children and adolescents to strengthen these skills and apply them more effectively to their decision-making and problem-solving in "real world" situations.

Strengthen Risk-Appraisal Skills

Additional cognitive skills that develop in these years are risk-appraisal skills, especially as children reach Piaget's formal operational stage at around 11 or 12 years of age. Consistent with this stage is presumably the capacity to think about the various possible solutions to a problem, to assess the risks and benefits associated with each one, and then make the appropriate choice. This theoretical formulation often breaks down when children and adolescents actually encounter temptations in the "real world." The group context provides helping professionals with opportunities to strengthen these skills.

Strengthen Decision-Making and Problem-Solving Skills

The recommendations above regarding logical thought, alternative thinking, consequential thinking, and risk-appraisal skills also apply directly to decision-making and problem-solving skills. Group facilitators and group members can provide the conversation and self-exploration activities that can reinforce thoughtful problem solving and decision making while minimizing the frequency of impulsive and ill-considered choices.

Cultural and Cross-Cultural Considerations

Group facilitators must be ever mindful of the fact that behavior and beliefs considered pathological in one culture may be entirely normal and typical in another. *DSM-IV-TR* has now included many "culture-bound syndromes" in its appendices. Practitioners need to familiarize themselves with those beliefs and practices that are typical for the children and adolescents with whom they work in groups, and remember the utility of Vygotsky's Sociocultural Cognitive Constructivist Model and concepts such as the ZPD, mentoring, peer influence in the group setting, and the embeddedness of learning within cultural contexts.

CONCLUDING SUMMARY

This chapter has explored the many dimensions of child and adolescent development in the contemporary sociocultural context and has presented the implications of these developmental and contextual dimensions for group cognitive-behavior therapy with youth. A major emphasis throughout involves the excellent opportunities that CBGT provides for both group facilitators and group members to influence group members in terms of their cognitive processing of problematic behavioral choices and painful emotional experiences.

REFERENCES

Amato, P. R., & Keith, B. (1991). Parental divorce and the well-being of children: A meta-analysis. *Psychological Bulletin, 110*, 26–46.

American Psychiatric Association. (2000). *The diagnostic and statistical manual of mental disorders* (4th ed., text rev.). Washington, DC: Author.

Angold, A., Costello, E. J., Erkanli, A., & Worthman, C. (1999). Pubertal changes in hormone levels and depression in girls. *Psychological Medicine, 29*, 1043–1053.

Baird, A. A., Gruber, S. A., Cohen, B. M., Renshaw, R. J., & Yureglun-Todd, D. A. (1999). MRI of the amygdala in children and adolescents. *American Academy of Child and Adolescent Psychiatry, 38*, 195–199.

Bowlby, J. (1940). The influence of early environment in the development of neurosis and neurotic character. *International Journal of Psycho-Analysis, 21*, 1–25.

Bowlby, J. (1969). *Attachment and loss* (Vol. 1). London: Hogarth Press.

Briere, J. (2002). Treating adult survivors of severe childhood abuse and neglect: Further development of an integrative model. In J. E. B. Myers, L. Berliner, J. Briere, C. T. Hendrix, T. Reid, & C. Jenny (Eds.), *The APSAC handbook on child maltreatment* (2nd ed., pp. 1–26). Newbury Park, CA: Sage.

Brooks-Gunn, J., & Warren, M. P. (1989). The psychological significance of secondary sexual characteristics in 9- to 11-year-old girls. *Child Development, 59*, 161–169.

Browne, A., & Finkelhor, D. (1986a). Impact of child sexual abuse: A review of the research. *Psychological Bulletin, 99*, 66–77.

Browne, A., & Finkelhor, D. (1986b). Initial and long-term effects: A review of the research. In D. Finkelhor (Ed.), *A sourcebook on child sexual abuse* (pp. 143–179). Beverly Hills, CA: Sage.

Buss, A.H., & Plomin, R. (1975). *A temperament theory of personality development.* New York: Wiley.

Buss, A.H., & Plomin, R. (1984). *Temperament: Early developing personality traits.* Hillsdale, NJ: Erlbaum.

Casey, B., Giedd, J., & Thomas, K. (2000). Structural and brain development and its relation to cognitive development. *Biological Psychology, 54*, 241–257.

Casper, R. C., Belanoff, J., & Offer, D. (1996). Gender differences, but no racial group differences, in self-reported psychiatric symptoms in adolescents. *Journal of the American Academy of Child and Adolescent Psychiatry, 35*, 500–508.

Caspi, A. (1998). Personality development across the life course. In W. Damon (Ed.), *Handbook of child psychology* (Vol. 3, pp. 311–388). New York: Wiley.

Centers for Disease Control and Prevention. (2004). *Sexually Transmitted Diseases.* Atlanta: Author.

Chomsky, N. (1957). *Syntactic structures.* The Hague, The Netherlands: Mouton.

Conger, R. D., & Chao, W. (1996). Adolescent depressed mood. In R. L. Simons (Ed.), *Understanding differences between divorced and intact families: Stress, interaction, and child outcome* (pp. 157–175). Thousand Oaks, CA: Sage.

Costa, P. T., & McRae, R. R. (1980). Influence of extraversion and neuroticism on subjective well-being: Happy and unhappy people. *Journal of Personality and Social Psychology, 38*, 668–678.

Courtois, C. (1988). *Healing the incest wound: Adult survivors in therapy.* New York: W. W. Norton.

Courtois, C. (1999). *Recollections of sexual abuse: Treatment principles and guidelines.* New York: W. W. Norton.

Dinkmeyer, Jr., D. & Dinkmeyer, Sr., D. (1991). Adlerian family therapy. In A. M. Horne & J. L. Passmore (Eds.), *Family counseling and therapy* (2nd ed., pp. 383–401). Itasca, IL: F. E. Peacock.

Dodge, K. A. (2000). Conduct disorder. In A. J. Sameroff, M. Lewis, & S. M. Miller (Eds.), *Handbook of developmental psychopathology* (2nd ed., pp. 447–463). New York: Kluwer/Plenum.

Dodge, K. A.., Pettit, G. S., Bates, J. E., & Valente, E. (1995). Social information processing patterns partially mediate the effects of early physical abuse on later conduct problems. *Journal of Abnormal Psychology, 104*, 632–643.

Eccles, J., Wigfield, A., & Byrnes, J. (2003). Cognitive development in adolescence. In I. B. Weiner (Ed.), *Handbook of Psychology* (Vol. VI, pp. 325–350). New York: Wiley.

Elkind, D. (1976). *Child development and education: A Piagetian perspective.* New York: Oxford University Press.

Erikson, E. H. (1968). *Identity: Youth and crisis.* New York: W. W. Norton.

Feldman, D. H. (2002, June). *Piaget's stages revisited (and somewhat revised).* Presented at the Annual Meeting of the Jean Piaget Society, Philadelphia, PA.

Feldman, D. H. (2003). Cognitive development in childhood. In I. B. Weiner (Ser. Ed.) & R. M. Lerner, M. A. Easterbrooks, & J. Mistry (Vol. Eds.), *Handbook of psychology: Vol. 6. Developmental psychology* (pp. 198–210). Hoboken, NJ: Wiley.

Finkelstein, J. W., Susman, E. J., Chinchilli, V. M., Kunselman, S. J., D'Arcangelo, M. R., Schwab, J., Demers, L. M., Liben, L. S., Lookingbill, G., & Kulin, H. E. (1997). Estrogen and testosterone increases self-reported aggressive behaviors in hypogonadal adolescents. *Journal of Clinical Endocrinology and Metabolism, 82*, 2433–2438.

Flavell, J. H., Miller, P. H. & Miller, S. (2002). *Cognitive development* (4th ed.). Upper Saddle River, NJ: Prentice Hall.

Frank, E., Kupfer, D. J., Thase, M. E., Mallinger, A. G., Swartz, H. A., Fagiolini, A. M., et al. (2005). Two-Year outcomes for interpersonal and social rhythm therapy in individuals with Bipolar I Disorder. *Archives of General Psychiatry, 62*, 996–1004.

Freud, A., & Dann, S. (1951). Instinctual anxiety during puberty. In A. Freud (Ed.) *The ego and its mechanisms of defense.* New York: International Universities Press.

Goldberg, L. R. (1993). The structure of phenotypic personality traits. *American Psychologist, 48,* 26–34.

Gould, M. (2001). *Science for all: Just growing pains? The mental health of our children.* Washington, DC: National Institute of Mental Health.

Graber, J. A. (2003). *Early puberty and drug use.* Unpublished data, Department of Psychology, University of Florida, Gainsville.

Grumbach, M. M., & Styne, D. M. (1992). Puberty: Ontogeny, neuroendocrinology, physiology, and disorders. In J. D. Wilson & P. W. Foster (Eds.), *Williams textbook of endocrinology* (pp. 1139–1231). Philadelphia: Saunders.

Gullotta, T. P., Adams, G. R. & Montemayor, R. (Eds.). (1995). *Substance misused in adolescence.* Newbury Park, CA: Sage.

Herman, J. L. (1992). Complex PTSD: A syndrome in survivors of prolonged and repeated trauma. *Journal of Traumatic Stress, 5*(3), 377–391.

Herman-Giddens, M. E., Slora, E. J., Wasserman, R. C. Bourdony, C. J., Bhapkar, M. V., Koch, G. G., & Hasemeier, C. (1997). Secondary sexual characteristics and menses in young girls seen in office practice: A study from the Pediatric Research in Office Settings Network. *Pediatric, 99*, 505–512.

John, O. P., Caspi, A., Robins, R. W., Moffitt, T. E., & Stouthamer-Loeber, M. (1994). The "little five": Exploring the nomological network of the five-factor model of personality in adolescent boys. *Child Development, 65*, 160–178.

Johnston, L. D., O'Malley, P. M., & Bachman, J. G. (2004). *Monitoring the future with national results on adolescent drug use: Overview of key findings, 2003.* Bethesda, MD: National Institute of Drug Abuse.

Kagan, J. (1992. Yesterday's promises, tomorrow's promises. *Developmental Psychology, 28*, 990–997.

Kagan, J. (2002). Behavioral inhibition as a temperamental category. In R. J. Davidson, K. R. Sherer, & H. H. Goldsmith (Eds.), *Handbook of affective sciences* (pp. 320–331). New York: Oxford University Press.

Kagan, J., Reznick, J. S., & Gibbons, J. (1989). Inhibited and uninhibited types of children. *Child Development, 60*, 838–845.

Kenniston, K. (1970). Youth: A "new" stage of life. *American Scholar, 39*, 631–654.

Kessler, R. C., Berglund, P., Demler, O., Jin, R., Merikangas, K. R., & Walters, E. E. (2005). Lifetime prevalence and age-of-onset distributions of DSM-IV disorders in the national comorbidity survey replication. *Archives of General Psychiatry, 62*, 593–602.

LeDoux, J. E. (2002). *The synaptic self.* New York: Viking.

Luntz, B., & Widom, C. (1994). Antisocial personality disorder in abused and neglected children grown up. *American Journal of Psychiatry, 151*, 670–674.

McLeer, S. V., Callaghan, M., Henry, D., & Wallen, J. (1994). Psychiatric disorders in sexually abused children. *Journal of the American Academic of Child and Adolescent Psychiatry, 33*, 313–319.

Merck & Co., Inc. (1997). *The Merck manual of medical information.* Whitehouse Station, NJ: Author.

Monte, C. F. (1999). *Beneath the mask: An introduction to theories of personality* (6th ed.). New York: Harcourt Brace.

Nash, M. R., Hulsey, T. L., Sexton, M. C., Harralson, T. L. & Lambert, W. (1993). Long-term sequelae of childhood sexual abuse: Perceived family environment, psychopathology, and dissociation. *Journal of Consulting and Clinical Psychology, 61*, 276–283.

National Center for Health Statistics (2004). *Births.* Atlanta: Center for Disease Control and Prevention.

NHANES (2001, March). *National Health and Nutrition Examination Surveys.* Washington, DC: U.S. Department of Health and Human Services.

Offer, D., Ostrov, E., Howard, K. I., & Atkinson, R. (1992). A study of quietly disturbed and normal adolescents in ten countries, In A. Z. Schwartzberg & A. H. Esman (Eds.), *International Annals of Adolescent Psychiatry* (pp. 285–297). Chicago: University of Chicago.

Offer, D., Ostrov, E., Howard, K. I., & Atkinson, R. (1988). *The teenage world: Adolescents' self-image in ten countries.* New York: Plenum.

Olweus, D., Mattson, A., Schalling, D., & Low, H. (1988). Circulating testosterone levels and aggression in adolescent males: a causal analysis. *Psychosomatic Medicine, 50,* 261–272.

Perry, B. D. (2002). Childhood experience and the expression of genetic potential: What childhood neglect tells us about nature and nurture. *Brain and Mind, 3,* 79–100.

Piaget, J. (1970). Piaget's theory. In P. Mussen (Ed.), *Carmiachael's manual of child psychology* (pp. 703–732). New York: Wiley.

Rector, N. A., & Beck, A. T. (2001). Cognitive behavioral therapy for schizophrenia: An empirical review. *Journal of Nervous & Mental Disease, 189*(5), 278–287.

Rochat, P. (200i). Origins of self concept. In G. Bremner & A. Fogel (Eds.), *Blackwell handbook of infant development* (p. 191-212). Malden, MA: Blackwell.

Rosenzweig, M. R. (1969). Effects of heredity and environment on brain chemistry, brain anatomy, and learning ability in the rat. In M. Monosevitz, G. Lindzey, & D. D. Thiessen (Eds.), *Behavioral genetics.* New York: Appleton-Century-Crofts.

Rubia, K., Overmyer, S., Taylor, E., Brammer, M., Williams, S., Simmons, A., et al. (2000). Functional frontalization with age: Mapping neurodevelopmental trajectories with fMRI. *Neuroscience & Behavioral Reviews, 24,* 13–19.

Santrock, J. W. (2006). *Life-Span Development* (10th ed.). Boston: McGraw-Hill.

Shure, M. & Spivak, G. (1979). Interpersonal cognitive problem-solving and primary prevention: Programming for preschool and kindergarten children. *Journal of Clinical Psychology, 8,* 89–94.

Simmons, R., Blyth, A., Van Cleave, E., & Bush, D. (1987). Entry into early adolescence: The impact of school structure, puberty, and early dating on self-esteem. *American Sociological Review, 44,* 948–967.

Sroufe, L. A., Duggal, S., Weinfield, N., & Carlson, E. (2000). *Relationships, development, and psychopathology.* In A. J. Sameroff, M. Lewis, & S. M. Miller (Eds.), *Handbook of developmental psychopathology* (2nd ed., pp. 75–91). New York: Kluwer/Plenum.

Stattin, H., & Magnusson, D. (1990). *Pubertal maturation in female development.* Hillsdale, NJ: Erlbaum.

Sternberg, K., Lamb, M., Greenbaum, C., Cicchetti, D., Dawud, S., Cortes, R., et al. (1993). Effects of domestic violence on children's behavior problems and depression. *Developmental Psychology, 29,* 44–52.

Strauss, M. A. (2001). *Beating the devil out of them* (2nd ed.). New Brunswick, NJ: Transaction Publications.

Strauss, M. A., Sugarman, D. B., & Giles-Sims, J. (1997). Spanking by parents and subsequent anti-social behavior in children. *Archives of Pediatrics and Adolescent Medicine, 151,* 761–767.

Suomi, S. J. (1997). Early determinants of behaviour: Evidence from primate studies. *British Medical Bulletin, 53,* 170–184.

Suomi, S. J. (2000). A behavioral perspective on developmental psychopathology: Excessive aggression and serotonergic dysfunction in monkeys. In A. J. Sameroff, M. Lewis, & S. M. Miller (Eds.), *Handbook of developmental psychopathology* (2nd ed., pp. 237–256). New York: Kluwer/Plenum.

Suomi, S. J., Harlow, H. F., & Domek, C. J. (1970). Effects of repetitive infant-infant separations of young monkeys. *Journal of Abnormal Psychology, 76,* 161–172.

Susman, E. J., Dorn, L. D., & Schiefelbein, V. L. (2003). Puberty, sexuality, and health. In I. B. Weiner (Series Ed.) & R. M. Lerner, M. A. Easterbrooks, & J. Mistry (Vol. Eds.), *Handbook of psychology: Volume 6. Developmental psychology* (pp. 295–324). Hoboken, NJ: Wiley.

Susman, E. J. Finkelstein, J. W. Chinchilli, V. M., Schwab, J., Liben, L. S., D'Arcanagelo, M. R., Meinkle, J. M. D. L., Lookingbill, G., & Kulin, H. E. (1998). The effect of sex hormone replacement therapy on behavior problems and mood in adolescents with delayed puberty. *Journal of Pediatrics, 133,* 521–525.

Susman, E. J., Inoff-Germain, Nottelmann, E. D., Cutler, G. B., Loriaux, D. L., & Chrousos, G. P. (1987). Hormones, emotional dispositions, and aggressive attributes in early adolescents. *Child Development, 58,* 1114–1134.

Thompson, J. K., & Heinberg, L. J. (1999). The media's influence on body image disturbance and eating disorders: We've reviled them now can we rehabilitate them? *Journal of Social Issues, 55*(2), 339–353.

Vygotsky, L. (1962). *Thoughts and language.* Cambridge, MA: MIT Press.

Vygotsky, L. (1978). *Mind in society.* Cambridge, MA: MIT Press.

Walker, E. F. (2002). Adolescent neurodevelopment and psychopathology. *Current Directions in Psychological Science, 11,* 24–28.

Wiesner, M., & Ittel, A. (2002). Relations of pubertal timing and depressing symptoms to substance use in early adolescence. *Journal of Early Adolescence, 22,* 5–23.

Wodarski, J. S., & Hoffman, S. D. (1984). Alcohol education for adolescents. *Social Work in Education, 6,* 69–92.

Chapter Four

Legal and Ethical Issues in Providing Group Therapy to Minors

Linda K. Knauss

Two important factors combine that highlight the importance of ethical issues in group therapy with children and adolescents. The first is the fact that groups are a powerful force, and the second is the fact that children and adolescents are especially influenced by peer pressure (Terres & Larrabee, 1985). In addition, group treatment strategies have been rapidly expanding to apply to a variety of populations and disorders including grief, depression, physical and sexual abuse, substance abuse, and eating disorders. In many settings, group interventions are the primary treatment modality (Glass, 1998).

This chapter will highlight a sample of ethical and legal concerns that often arise when conducting group therapy with minors. These issues include (1) ethical decision making, (2) competence, (3) recruitment of group members, (4) screening and selection, (5) consent to treatment, (6) informed consent, (7) confidentiality, (8) child abuse, and (9) record keeping.

ETHICAL DECISION MAKING

Ethical dilemmas usually arise in an interpersonal context. This makes ethical decision making in practice much more difficult than on an exam. There are many considerations that compete for the group therapist's attention and inclination. Thus, it is essential to understand the personal and interpersonal nature of ethics. Most therapists do not plan to engage in unethical behavior. Violations most often occur because of poor judgment, insensitivity to ethical standards, or as a means to justify one's actions.

There are many available ethical codes and guidelines to help therapists resolve ethical dilemmas. Some of these codes have been developed by professional organizations such as the Ethical Principles of Psychologists and Code of Conduct (American Psychological Association, 2002), the Code of Ethics and Standards of Practice (American Counseling Association, 1995), and the NASW Code of Ethics (National Association of Social Workers, 1999). Additional codes have been developed by organizations devoted to the advancement of group therapy such as the American Group Psychotherapy

Association (2002) and Ethical Guidelines for Group Counselors of the Association for Specialists in Group Work (1989).

Regardless of the specificity of existing ethical guidelines, there will always be situations that go beyond the written code or pit one ethical standard against another (Brabender, 2002). Typically, most ethical dilemmas are ambiguous which gives clinicians discretion in determining an ethical course of action. The course that is chosen is influenced by the therapist's training, moral standards, and prevailing values of the community (Yanagida, 1998). Thus, it is essential for therapists to be familiar with a model of ethical decision making to further aid in making appropriate choices.

Many ethical decision-making models exist (Abeles, 1980; Eberlein, 1987; Haas & Malouf, 2002; Koocher & Keith-Spiegel, 1998; Kitchener, 1984; Rest, 1982; Tymchuk, 1986). The model that will be presented here is both systematic enough to include all of the relevant information and flexible enough to apply to a variety of situations. This model, developed by Knapp and VandeCreek (2003), is comprised of five steps that are common across most of the models.

1. *Identification of the problem.* This includes obtaining information from the parties involved and from relevant sources. It also includes consulting existing guidelines or ethics codes such as those mentioned earlier in this chapter. This process may lead to contradictions, or there may be no relevant standard. However, it is important to take this step so one does not disregard existing policy.
2. *Development of alternatives.* This includes considering whether there is a reason to deviate from an existing standard, perhaps because the standard is vague or in a particular case, it may lead to more harm than benefit by adhering to the standard. It is also necessary to evaluate the rights, responsibilities, and welfare of all affected parties. When generating alternatives, all possible actions should be included. A decision that was initially unacceptable may later be the most feasible.
3. *Evaluation of alternatives.* At this time, it is important to list the risks and benefits of making each decision as well as evaluating the probability that those risks and benefits will actually occur. Often there is no evidence to help make this decision. The alternative that results in the optimum resolution for the greatest number of interested parties should be chosen.
4. *Implementation of the best option.* It is not enough to be aware of what needs to be done. Being ethical requires action and taking responsibility for the consequences of those actions. These decisions should also be documented both for the protection of the practitioner and for future use.
5. *Evaluation of the results.* One way to evaluate the decision is to ask if it was satisfactory to the needs and preferences of the affected parties. It can also be helpful to ask: Would you recommend that everyone do this? In thinking about how to advise another person to act in a similar situation, it provides an opportunity to reflect on a particular choice.

The shortcoming of any cognitive model of ethical decision-making is that it does not require therapists to consider emotional or situational factors affecting their decision. Also, it is necessary to have time to reflect on the ethical problem (Knapp & VandeCreek, 2003). In order to improve ethical decision-making in crisis situations, it is helpful to anticipate the type of problems that might occur, and develop an action plan for high probability situations.

COMPETENCE

Competence to provide group therapy to minors encompasses several areas, competence as a therapist, competence as a group therapist, and competence to work with children. In addition, group therapists must be competent to work with racially and culturally diverse clients and may need to be competent to work with specialty populations such as eating disorders or substance abuse.

Competence as a Therapist

Competence may refer to the use of a technique (assessment, hypnosis), skills in working with particular problem areas (group therapy), a particular population (children), or emotional stability (emotional competence). To become proficient in a certain area of practice, psychologists or other therapists submit their work to external feedback. This occurs when students attend graduate programs and receive feedback from faculty and clinical supervisors. It is more difficult for individuals in practice to demonstrate competence in new areas or with new techniques (Knapp & VandeCreek, 2003).

It is not considered sufficient to read a book or attend a workshop in order to gain competence in a new domain of practice. This is because neither of those activities guarantees that therapists have acquired the knowledge and skills necessary to provide intervention in the new domain. Often competent performance in an area of practice requires skills that take practice rather than just factual knowledge (Knapp & VandeCreek, 2003). Working with children and leading therapy groups are both areas that require skills, practice, and feedback to perfect.

Competence as a Group Therapist

Group therapists come from very diverse backgrounds. Preparation for leading groups ranges from no formal training to graduate level training with supervised experience. Some group leaders have been in groups as members while others have not. Sometimes leaders are individuals who have been diagnosed with the disorder being treated. This is especially true in the area of substance abuse. The assumption is that having experienced the problem is an essential leader qualification. In contrast, some professionals may possess an advanced degree and a license to practice but they have no training or supervised experience in leading groups (Glass, 1998).

According to Brabender (2002), "organized training in group therapy has not been prevalent in graduated training programs in the mental health professions" (p. 250). In comparison to training in individual therapy, group therapy is given minimal treatment in most programs. However, many mental health professionals are called upon to lead groups in their jobs. Some are clinical groups such as groups for children with diabetes and others are administrative groups such as treatment teams. Most agencies or organizations do not provide training opportunities in this valuable skill to make up for weaknesses in graduate training (Brabender, 2002).

Thus, individuals are responsible to spend their own resources of time and money to ensure competence. Many professional organizations such as the American Psychological Association and the American Group Psychotherapy Association provide training experiences in group therapy (Brabender, 2002). As was mentioned previously, didactic training alone is not enough. Brabender (2003) notes, "To achieve competence the group therapist will require competent supervision" (p. 251). Cotherapy provides the most ideal opportunity for supervision because the supervisor has access to all of the interventions made by the supervisee as well as nonverbal cues such as posture and head nodding. When co-therapy is not possible, process notes, audio tapes, and videotapes provide various amounts of information (Brabender, 2002).

Specific guidelines for the training of group therapists have been developed by professional organizations such as the American Group Psychotherapy Association (AGPA) and the Association for Specialists in Group Work (ASGW). Both organizations specify a combination of knowledge, skills, and experience competencies to prepare therapists to lead groups adequately (Glass, 1998). However, the requirements of the two organizations differ with respect to minimum expectations for group participation and supervision. Since guidelines provided by professional organizations can only provide models for consideration, individuals who conduct group therapy need to be aware of their own strengths and weaknesses in the areas of knowledge, skills, and experience and seek means to strengthen any deficiencies.

Competence to Work with Children

Numerous ethical and legal issues confront group therapists that are unique to working with children and adolescents. Often, groups are designed for children of divorced parents, physically ill parents, children who have been abused, or children with developmental delays. While in most situations in which therapists work with children their work is not monitored, some situations may place them under professional scrutiny with regard to the courts (Koocher & Keith-Spiegel, 1990). A group therapist could be asked to testify in a child custody case or a case involving child abuse. Similar to the situation with group therapy, there are no written guidelines in the area of child or family work with respect to establishing a basic threshold of competence. It is possible to complete a doctoral degree in psychology as well as advanced training in social work, psychiatry, and other mental health fields without ever assessing or treating a child.

Due to the lack of training standards or guidelines for working with minors, Koocher and Keith-Spiegel (1990) have made the following suggestions. Therapists who are planning to pursue assessment or intervention with children or adolescents should have completed formal course work in developmental psychology or human development, including educational components on physical, social, and personality development as well as psychopathology of childhood and adolescence. In addition, practitioners should have completed formal supervised experience such as a practicum or internship in a setting where they have the opportunity to work with children. This is an ideal way to combine training in group work with training in working with minors because many educational and agency settings offer group therapy or specialized groups for children and adolescents.

It is especially important for anyone working with minors to be aware on a continuing basis of the statutes or regulations in the state or agency that apply to minors (such as child abuse reporting laws). Therapists must also maintain an awareness of and sensitivity to the effects of their own emotional needs and reactions when working with children and adolescents. Sexual abuse of child and adolescent clients or providing illegal substances in an effort to build rapport and be liked by clients are not rare or isolated events (Bajt & Pope, 1989; Koocher & Keith-Spiegel, 1990). For this reason, it is also important to be alert for indications of possible sexual abuse by prior therapists when working with children and adolescents. If a child client does behave in a manner that suggests that abuse may have occurred in a prior professional relationship, the current therapist must explore the situation and make a report of abuse if warranted.

Although it may not always be possible to avoid all dual role situations, it is very important to consider the potential effect of such relationships when working with children and adolescents. Dual role relationships may also grow out of relationship with people other than the identified client. These types of relationship often go unnoticed until a crisis occurs. These suggestions by Koocher and Keith-Spiegel (1990) are especially valuable because they focus attention on the most common ethical dilemmas that are faced by therapists working with children and adolescents.

Specialty Populations

Often therapy groups and especially groups for children and adolescents are developed for a specific purpose. For example, there are groups for children who have been sexually abused, groups for clients with eating disorders or substance abuse, groups for children with cancer, diabetes, or terminal illnesses and groups for children who have lost a parent. It is necessary to have adequate training in the etiology, typical needs, common symptom patterns, and interpersonal capabilities of these clients in order to develop an effective group design (Glass, 1998). It is not possible to address the needs of such diverse client populations through a generic group design. To practice competently, the group therapist must be familiar with the client population he or she will be serving. This can be accomplished through reading, observations, co-leading a group, consultation, or supervision (Glass, 1998).

In many employment settings there is a great deal of pressure to provide services to new or emerging clinical populations. Glass (1998) notes, "Administrators and supervisors often assume that the professionals they hire ought to be capable of carrying out every professional task the agency may require. To decline such an assignment may put the professional in the position of appearing either uncooperative or incompetent" (p. 102). However, professionals in this situation should indicate their willingness to do group work with the specified client population but only after appropriate experience.

Diversity

Society is becoming increasingly multiethnic. In order to work effectively with ethnic and culturally diverse clients, it is necessary for therapists to understand not only racial, ethnic and gender issues, but also to develop an increased awareness of their own personal values and attitudes. According to Corey and Corey (1992), "Effective delivery of group counseling services must take into account the impact of the client's culture" (p. 299). They go onto say that culture influences the client's behavior and the group therapist's behavior whether or not one is aware of this process. The APA Ethical Principles of Psychologists and Code of Conduct (2006) address diversity in standard 2.01b:

Where scientific or professional knowledge in the discipline of psychology establishes that an understanding of factors associated with age, gender, gender identity, race, ethnicity, culture, national origin, religion, sexual orientation, disability, language, or socioeconomic status is essential for effective implementation of their services or research psychologists have or obtain the training, experience, consultation, or supervision necessary to ensure the competence of their services, or they make appropriate referrals, except as provided in Standard 2.02, Providing Services in Emergencies.

In spite of the best intentions to create effective, cross-cultural ethical guidelines, it is difficult to do this effectively. One reason for this is that in the process of defining what constitutes correct, appropriate, and ethical behavior in any ethics code, reflects the values and norms of the dominant culture (Glass, 1998).

Cultural differences can be magnified in group therapy. For example, not all cultures value insight. Thus in an insight-oriented therapy group, a client's lack of success may be related to cultural factors (Brabender, 2002). Leong (1992) cites other examples of ethnocentrism that can be detrimental in group therapy. These include the belief that emotional openness is better than emotional inhibition, and the belief that independence and self-sufficiency are signs of maturity in contrast to interdependence and group loyalty. Other behaviors such as expecting verbalizations of thoughts and feelings, confrontations and conflicts, and asking questions to probe feelings can be uncomfortable for members of various cultural groups (Hurdle, 1991). However, it is equally important not to stereotype minority clients using broad generalizations such as, "Asian clients are always quiet." An additional challenge for the group therapist working with culturally diverse children and adolescents is the tendency of children to identify and exaggerate differences in negative ways. Thus, it is important to discuss issues of diversity in the group and hopefully begin the process of intercultural acceptance and understanding (Glass, 1998). Group leaders also need to be aware of their own personal feelings and model appropriate behaviors of respect and acceptance.

In general, group therapy can be easily adapted to a multicultural population. There is nothing inherent in group approaches that make them inappropriate to any culture. Thus, group therapy does not require major alterations of general principles of group process to work with clients of a non-majority culture. Group therapists should find culturally inviting ways to include members of diverse populations in their therapy groups. Until training in diversity becomes an integral part of all professional education, it is an aspirational goal for group therapy practitioners to examine their attitudes, assumptions and values to become as effective as possible in working with clients from multicultural backgrounds (Glass, 1998).

Additional Considerations

Self-care is an important component of competence for mental health professionals. This is magnified for group therapists who work simultaneously with multiple clients as well as for therapists working with children and adolescents. There is growing literature on the stressors facing health care professionals according to Knapp and VandeCreek (2003). In addition, individuals and institutions should attempt to help reduce distress, prevent impairment, and assist in making the workplace as pleasant and desirable as possible. In recent years, there has been a focus on general self-care, meaning anticipating and learning to handle stressors and to focus on positive self-care. The focus on positive self-care is especially important for mental health professionals where emotional competence is directly related to the quality of their work (Knapp & VanderCreek, 2003).

The APA Ethical Principles of Psychologists and Code of Conduct have two standards related to impairment (2.06 a&b). These standards state that impairment is grounds for disciplinary actions, and psychologists who are impaired have a responsibility to stop practicing or seek supervision to ensure the quality of their work. At times therapists may find it helpful, or necessary to participate in their own personal therapy. For group therapists, involvement in a therapy group may be especially helpful (Brabender, 2002). In addition, many state and provincial psychological associations have created colleague assistance programs designed to help psychologists who are having difficulties (Barnett & Hillard, 2001). Stress or other personal or situational factors may cause a noticeable decline in effectiveness that does not cause one to become impaired or incompetent. However, a reduced ability to empathize with clients or to handle countertransference feelings may result in a decline in positive patient outcomes (Knapp & VandeCreek, 2003).

Life-long learning is another important aspect of competence. The research base of group therapy and techniques for working with children and adolescents is continually expanding, as are empirically supported treatments. Other knowledge becomes obsolete over time. Both formal and informal continuing education is needed to keep pace with the latest developments in the field. Many licensing boards require continuing education as a condition of licensure renewal. However, this represents a minimal requirement. Life-long learning is fundamental to ensure that teaching, research, and clinical practices have an ongoing positive effect on clients (Fisher, 2003).

RECRUITMENT

Recruitment is the first stage in the process of group therapy. Groups for children and adolescents may be held in schools, community agencies, or be run by private practitioners. Recruitment begins by advertising the group or soliciting referrals from parents, teachers, or other therapists. In a school setting, the school counselor could put a notice on the bulletin board, send a memo to teachers asking for referrals, or put a notice in handbooks and newsletters that go to parents, inviting them to nominate their child for a particular group (Ritchie & Huss, 2000). In community agencies, therapists could notify other therapists in their agency or related agencies of their intention to begin a group on a particular topic. They can also form groups from their own caseloads by starting a group with several children and adolescents with similar concerns. Therapists in a community agency or private practice can work with school counselors for referrals. They also advertise groups through direct mail, radio, newspapers, and the Internet (Ritchie & Huss, 2000).

Often well-intentioned school counselors solicit members for groups on wide ranges of topics such as children of divorce, children of alcoholics, (COA), and attention deficit/hyperactivity disorder (ADHD) by asking teachers to identify potential members. Unfortunately, this can create ethical problems. Receiving a referral from a concerned or observant teacher is not unethical, but labeling students who exhibit problem behaviors with a diagnosis of ADHD or even COA or "at risk" can be problematic.

The primary ethical issue in the recruitment of minors for participation in a group experience is privacy. This refers to both the therapeutic relationship as well as being identified as a client. This right to privacy also extends to people before the therapeutic relationship begins such as those who are interested in becoming a group member, or people who have been recommended to be a group member. Thus, group therapists in schools or community agencies need to be careful that their recruitment process does not label potential group members and violate their rights and the rights of their parents to privacy (Ritchie & Huss, 2000).

Based on the literature and ethical guidelines, Ritchie and Huss (2000) suggest the following guidelines for recruitment and advertising for minors for group therapy. First, do not give the group a name that might label children or imply a diagnosis. Next, it is best not to have a pre-group meeting in school at an announced time and place, especially if children of alcoholics or divorced parents are being recruited. This would compromise the privacy of anyone seen in that area. It would be preferable to have students make an appointment with the therapist at their own discretion to discuss their interest in the group. Finally, if the group therapist gives teachers a checklist of observable behaviors, it is best not to identify those behaviors as characteristic of a particular label. This is also true of checklists included in newsletters or other communications to parents for recruitment. In most cases, the lists of behaviors are very similar regardless of the issue of which they are supposed to be symptomatic (children of divorce, COA, at risk, and so on). Although recruitment for group members often takes place in schools, and minors can be referred or express interest in participation, they cannot become group members without the consent of their parent or legal guardian and a thorough informed consent process.

SCREENING AND SELECTION

A critical element of success for any therapy group is the appropriateness of the group experience for the specific child or adolescent. The ASGW (1998) Best Practice Guidelines state that group therapists select group members whose needs and goals are compatible with the goals of the group, who will not impede the group process, and whose well-being will not be jeopardized by the group experience. Although there are several possible options for pre-group screening, individual interviews with potential members are the most effective. The primary purpose of pre-group screening is to determine the appropriateness of the potential member for the group. However, a pre-group interview also allows the group leader to discuss the purpose and procedures of the group as well as identify the needs, expectations, and commitment of the potential group member (Couch, 1995).

Group interviews, which require less time than individual interviews, also allow the group leader to observe communication and interaction skills of potential members (Ritchie & Huss, 2000). The group interview can take the form of an activity such as having each child interview another child and introduce that child to the group. This provides an opportunity for children to talk about themselves, listen to others, and sit quietly while listening. One drawback to this method is that children may not be as forthcoming about their concerns in a group interview as they would be individually

(Ritchie & Huss, 2000). Although consent of a parent or legal guardian may not be necessary in certain situations at the prescreening level of group therapy, it is advisable to have parental (legal guardian) consent whenever one is working with a minor.

In selecting children and adolescents to participate in group therapy, the group leader must judge the suitability of potential members, not only with regard to the selection criteria, but also based on the probability that the child will cooperate in the group setting. Ritchie and Huss (2000) suggest that "Group leaders should be aware of specific client characteristics that would warrant exclusion from the group" (p. 152). Selection criteria are usually obvious in groups that are established for a specific purpose such as children of divorced parents.

Several client characteristics have been identified as desirable for group membership. These include interest in the group, the capacity for empathy, and age appropriate social skills. These characteristics can be evaluated during pre-screening. It is also important for children and adolescents to be available at the time the group is scheduled. Contraindications for outpatient or school based group therapy include children or adolescents who present a danger to themselves or others, who are overly aggressive, or those who are overly sensitive to criticism (Toseland & Siporin, 1986). However, groups for children and adolescents in residential facilities or inpatient settings are often composed of individuals with difficult behaviors and complex treatment needs. In general, the goal of the screening and selection process is to include children and adolescents who will benefit from the group therapy experience, who will not be harmed by the experience, and whose participation will not be harmful to others.

CONSENT TO TREATMENT

The concepts of consent to treatment and informed consent are different, but they have many overlapping elements. The law and society presume that children are not able to make major life decision on their own, and the rules that exist to deny children the right to make decisions independently, generally serve to protect them (Koocher & Keith-Spiegel, 1990). When a decision is to be made on behalf of minors, it is usually made by a parent or legal guardian. This is the person who consents to treatment for the child. It is assumed that the adult is acting in the child's best interest, although situations do arise that question this assumption. Courts traditionally respect the sanctity of the family unit and seldom become involved unless there is abuse, severe neglect or other dramatic reasons. Thus decisions that may not be in the child's best interest, especially with regard to mental health treatment, often do not rise to the level of intervention (Koocher & Keith-Spiegel, 1990).

It is also important to differentiate between the concepts of consent, permission, and assent. Consent implies the ability to understand the facts and consequences relative to a decision, and be able to make that decision voluntarily. The idea of informed consent indicates that all of the data needed to reach a thoughtful decision have been both considered and understood. In many jurisdictions, a person must meet a legal age requirement, usually age 18, in order for their decision to be considered legal, or binding. Thus, it is imperative for mental health professionals working with children or adolescents to know the legal age of consent in their locale. In addition, there can be many subtle nuances in laws regarding age of consent. For example, some states may have different ages for consent to inpatient or outpatient treatment. Or there could be different circumstances related to consent to treatment versus release of information. Many state professional organizations can be helpful in providing this information and in offering continuing education in this area.

Consent is sometimes defined as a decision that one can only make for oneself. Thus, parents or legal guardians are those from whom *permission* must be sought as both a legal and ethical requirement before providing mental health services to minors (Koocher & Keith-Spiegel, 1990). Assent, is used to mean that although minors may not be able to give consent as a result of their age and accompanying developmental level, they are still able to have and express a preference. However, exercising this power usually can only be done in the negative, by refusing to participate such as in individual or group therapy. It is also disrespectful to solicit the assent of a child, if refusal would not be honored (Corrao & Melton, 1988). Assent involves the minor in the decision-making process, although the child's level of participation is limited.

In general, adults are considered competent and minors are considered incompetent in almost all legal contexts. Unfortunately, the law has seldom been guided by psychological principles. Because minors are considered incompetent, even if they are determined to be competent for a particular purpose, such as to stand trial as an adult, they are still considered incompetent in other decision-making situations, such as consenting to their own medical treatment. The status as an "emancipated minor" can be given at a court hearing. This status, which is seldom based on the cognitive or reasoning ability of the minor, gives them some rights of the majority, such as the right to consent to medical care, but not all rights, such as voting or consuming alcohol (Koocher & Keith-Spiegel, 1990).

Conflicts of interest can arise among various parties including the child, parents, and mental health professionals. However, it is the ethical responsibility of the professional to obey the law and protect the best interests of the client while delivering competent services (Koocher & Keith-Spiegel, 1990). This can be a difficult task. Children are usually brought to therapy by adults who have a definite agenda in mind (my child is disruptive, uncooperative, or lazy). Although the adult's agenda may be consistent with the child's, it would be an error to just assume this to be true. In assessing minors for appropriateness to participate in group therapy, group leaders need to recognize that different family members may have different goals for the same child. Any treatment plan that is developed should take into consideration the best interests of all parties. Accomplishing this goal may require assertiveness and strong mediation skills.

When providing mental health services to minors, therapists always have two clients, the minor and his or her parent(s) or legal guardian. Services should not be provided to any minor without the knowledge and consent of the parents or guardian unless it is an emergency or the child is old enough to give consent on his or her own. It is the duty of every mental health professional "to know and understand the legal obligations and responsibilities that apply when children are clients" (Koocher & Keith-Spiegel, 1990, p. 17). This is especially true with regard to the age at which a person can consent to treatment.

INFORMED CONSENT

Informed consent for group therapy with minors takes place between the parents, child or adolescent, and the therapist. It is important for the minor to hear all of the information that is part of the informed consent process and to give his or her assent. The purpose of informed consent is to provide an adequate basis for making a decision about whether or not to give permission for the child to join a particular group and to enable minors to decide on their level of participation once they are in the group (Brabender, 2002). Informed consent generally includes the qualifications of the leader; the purpose and goals of the group; expectations of members; methods and procedures to be used; potential risks and benefits of participation; confidentiality and its limits; times, location, and duration of the group; fees for participation; and the ability to withdraw from the group at any time (ASGW, 1998; Corey & Corey; 1992, Gladding, 1999). The information needs to be presented in language that is understandable, including in the client's native language if that is different from the language used by the group leader. Group leaders also need to be able to explain their reasons for recommending group therapy as the treatment of choice (Glass, 1998), and comparing and contrasting group therapy with other possible treatment options (Brabender, 2002).

Informed consent can be either written or verbal. If informed consent is given verbally, this should be documented in the client's record. Sometimes, verbal informed consent is used when there is not enough time to get written consent. If this is the case, written informed consent should follow at a later time. Written informed consent provides evidence that the person has consented, however a signature is not proof that the person truly understood the conditions of treatment. Thus, the therapist needs to make every effort to assure that the client understands the information in the informed consent document (Brabender, 2002). This can be accomplished by asking the client questions about what they understand or by asking them to explain in their own words the informed consent information. This is also a good time to address any questions or misconceptions about the group process.

Group membership may not be voluntary on the part of a minor when consent is given by a parent or guardian. However, the group member is always empowered to make choices about his or her behavior during the group, including how much and what information to share (Brabender, 2002). This is one reason for including minors in the informed consent process. They need to know whether their behavior will be the basis for any decision-making process such as custody decisions or probation. The minor also needs to know the limits of confidentiality, both to his or her parents, as well as any other parties such as teachers, school administrators, or probation officers.

A very important part of the informed consent process involves a discussion of the risks and benefits of participation in the particular therapy group. The therapist does not necessarily need to share every possible risk. Some risks, although possible, are extremely unlikely, while others are much more common. Thus, the therapist needs to consider the probability that a potential risk may occur in deciding whether to discuss it as part of informed consent. Therapists who are overly inclusive run the risk of discouraging clients who would benefit from group therapy. According to Glass (1998), "Some group leaders prefer to focus on the positive benefits of group participation and are reluctant to detail possible, but unlikely risks" (p. 112). Research data on the probability of various risks in group treatment is extremely limited (Brabender, 2002). However, the most common risk seems to be violations of confidentiality by other group members. This will be discussed in detail in the next section. Other possible risks include receiving negative feedback, physical aggression, and lack of progress toward treatment goals.

Even if the group's process can be accurately explained to minors and their parents, this cognitive level of understanding is still very different from the actual experience of group participation. Even with the best intentions of providing thorough informed consent, exact information about what will happen in the group and how other group members will behave can not be accurately predicted (Glass, 1998). It is not possible to prepare anyone for all of the possibilities that may occur during group treatment. However, in spite of these limitations, group leaders are ethically bound to do the best job possible of informing clients as fully as possible. Although not every possible consequence can be anticipated, prospective members (and their families in the case of minors) deserve a realistic and comprehensive overview of the nature of group therapy and the expectations for the specific group being considered.

CONFIDENTIALITY

Two of the most common questions asked by children and adolescents about group therapy are, "What can I say in the group?" and "Can I really trust the other group members with my problems?" (Ohlsen, 1974). These questions indicate that confidentiality is central to effective group therapy. Group participants, especially children and adolescents, are not going to reveal themselves in a meaningful way unless they feel sure that they can trust both the group leader and the other group members to respect what they say (Corey, Corey, Callanan, & Russell, 1992). One of the most important tasks of a group leader is to clearly define confidentiality as well as to help group members recognize how important and at times difficult it can be to maintain confidentiality.

The best time to discuss confidentiality as well as the limits to confidentiality is during the informed consent process. As in all therapy situations, there are legally mandated limits to confidentiality. These exceptions to confidentiality include threats of physical harm to oneself or others (including the duty to warn identifiable victims), mandated reporting of child abuse, and responding to a court order. Thus, therapists should never imply that everything that is shared in the context of therapy is confidential. This is especially true in group therapy where the therapist-client relationship is not the only variable.

In group therapy with minors, there are certain unique dimensions of confidentiality. One dimension has to do with information that is shared with parents or legal guardians in contrast to information that is shared with other parties. Although the dimension of therapist-client confidentiality is shared with other forms of therapy, client-to-client confidentiality is unique to group therapy.

From a legal perspective, children do not have the same rights as adults. In most circumstances, parents or legal guardians make all decisions regarding confidentiality for children under 18 years of age. This includes signing for release of information, accessing school or hospital records, and learning the content of therapy sessions. Koocher and Keith-Spiegel (1990) observe, "In the strictest legal sense, children are not generally entitled to have secrets from their parents unless the parents permit it" (p. 81). Thus, it is very important for group therapists to discuss the limits of confidentiality with both parents and their children before beginning treatment.

Autonomy and privacy are concerns of great importance to adolescents. In establishing a trusting, therapeutic relationship, treating children and adolescents with honesty, respect, serious consideration, and involvement in goal setting is more important than the promise of absolute confidentiality (Koocher, 1976). Minors need to know the nature and extent of information to be shared with others as well as the reasons for sharing it.

Although it is not legally or ethically required to get the permission of a child client before disclosing confidential information, it is clinically wise to do so. If it is not likely that the child will give his or her permission, it is good clinical practice to tell the child what information you will be disclosing and to whom, rather than doing this without the child's knowledge. This connotes a level of respect for the child's cognitive, social, and emotional level of functioning (Koocher & Keith-Spiegel, 1990).

Thus, it is best to discuss the "ground rules" of confidentiality in advance with parents and children together. Information that is ordinarily confidential from other parties is usually not confidential from parents or guardians of children under the age of 18. However, it is important for group leaders to know the laws of the jurisdiction in which they are practicing. For example, in some states the right to confidentiality may extend to children as young as age 14 years.

When conducting groups with children and adolescents, therapists may be confronted with issues of illegal substance use, sexual activity, pregnancy, or tobacco use. Again, it is important to know the laws regarding age limits of confidentiality in the area in which one is practicing. For example, in some locations, minors of any age may seek treatment for substance abuse in a facility licensed for this purpose, and this treatment is confidential including confidentiality from parents and legal guardians.

Generally, when working with children and adolescents, treatment may not be successful if children are concerned that everything they say will be shared with their parent or guardian. Therapists can develop "agreements of confidentiality" with parents where parents agree to restrict their access to the information obtained by the therapist from or about the child. This is a voluntary agreement between the therapist, parent, and minor that limits the amount of information the therapist will tell the parents without the consent of the child. The purpose of such agreements is to encourage the child to disclose more in therapy. Of course, information regarding danger to self, others, and mandated reporting of child abuse are always disclosed to parents. Parents can limit the information they want to know to danger to self, others, and child abuse, or they can include sexual activity, substance use or any other category in which they are interested. However, the minor would know in advance what information will be shared with parents and can make their disclosures accordingly.

Group leaders may adhere to strict standards of confidentiality themselves, but confidentiality in a therapy group cannot be guaranteed. Information that is discussed in a group format is shared by many people, so the leader alone cannot insure confidentiality. According to Brabender (2002), "Where as the therapist's inappropriate disclosures about a group member can lead to stiff legal and professional sanctions, with some rare exceptions such consequences do not exist for group members" (p. 260). The burden of responsibility rests with the group leader to establish a confidentiality rule by which group members agree to protect the identities of the other group members and agree not to share material discussed in the group context with individuals outside of the group. Unfortunately, therapists have very little power to enforce this rule. Therefore, group leaders need to educate members in the importance of maintaining confidentiality (Glass, 1998). Children and adolescents may need to be reminded frequently of the importance and necessity of confidentiality. It is helpful to include examples of how violations of confidentiality can be hurtful both to individual group members and to the effectiveness of the group.

Confidentiality is especially difficult when groups are conducted in institutions, agencies, or schools where members know each other, and have frequent contact with each other outside of the group. In these settings, the idea that group members not have contact with one another except during group is not practical.

Although no group therapist can promise group confidentiality, five steps have been identified by Brabender (2002) that can be taken to increase the probability that members will protect each other's confidentiality. This must become part of the group process. The first step is to obtain a commitment from the minor before entering the group to observe confidentiality. Before the child makes that promise, the therapist should explain that the child must not talk about what he or she hears in group with anyone outside of the group, even a close friend. It is also important to specify that confidentiality should be maintained even after the group has ended.

The second step is to let all group members know the consequences of violations of confidentiality. The consequences need to be stringent enough to discourage breaches of confidentiality yet flexible enough to account for the various ways in which violations occur. Some group leaders terminate group membership for a violation of confidentiality, but this is not effective with children and adolescents who are often not highly motivated to participate in the group.

The third step is to provide regular reminders to the group of the need for confidentiality. This is especially important when working with children and adolescents. It cannot be assumed that because confidentiality has been discussed once in group that it will be thoroughly understood or remembered (Terres & Larrabee, 1985). An important discussion to have in group is how members should act when they meet each other outside of group (when this is not a frequent or regular occurrence). There is a natural tendency to greet people that one knows, however when it is another group member, this may not be in his or her best interest. If the person is with colleagues or friends, it may create an awkward situation or a compromise of that person's confidentiality if someone asks how you know each other. In contrast, a group member may be concerned that ignoring another group member outside of group may be considered impolite or cause the other person to feel slighted or rejected. This situation is easier to rectify by subsequently discussing it in group. It can usually be explained as an effort to respect the person's confidentiality and prevent an awkward moment. Experienced group leaders are aware of the probability of out-of-group encounters although group members may not anticipate them. Therefore, group leaders should provide the opportunity for the group to discuss unexpected encounters before they occur, and develop guidelines for handling them (Brabender, 2002).

The fourth step is to be sure to discuss thoroughly within the group any violations of confidentiality that do occur. Violations of confidentiality can interfere with the functioning of the group, even if the violation has not caused any harm outside of the group (Brabender, 2002). Group members may feel betrayed and become less likely to participate in the group process. By discussing the issue in an open and honest manner, group members can gain empathy for both sides of the situation and hopefully progress to an even higher level of functioning while becoming more sensitized to the issue in the future.

Finally, it is important to stress that group leaders should model ethical behavior, especially with regard to confidentiality. Group therapists may be more aware of the types of issues that can compromise confidentiality, but nonetheless, ethical dilemmas do arise. One example of this situation may occur when group leaders are asked for information about a group member by a third party. Although receiving the necessary release of information from a parent or guardian may be time consuming and cumbersome, it is an ethical obligation.

There are several additional considerations regarding confidentiality. Audio or video recording of group sessions may be useful for training or supervision purposes. Prior consent of group members and their parents or guardians is required as well as an understanding of how this material is to be used. Written consent is recommended in this situation. Also, consent is needed if someone such as a student or intern will be observing the group or using information from the group for research, training, or supervisory purposes (Glass, 1998). When third parties such as teachers, probation officers, or referral sources need to know about a minor's progress or participation in group therapy, this either needs to be agreed to as part of the informed consent process, or a release of information form needs to be completed. Clients or their legal guardians can always have information about their progress in therapy shared with outside parties through the release of information process. This may be necessary for insurance reimbursement or coordination of care if the minor is also being seen in individual therapy or by a psychiatrist. Thus, every effort is made to protect the confidentiality of information that is shared in group therapy, except when disclosure is legally mandated or requested by the client.

MANDATED REPORTING OF CHILD ABUSE

Group therapists who work with minors are likely to encounter a situation of suspected child abuse in their careers. The decision to report suspected abuse is always difficult, and is sometimes referred to as an ethical dilemma. The reasons that therapists find it difficult to report abuse fall into three general categories, violations of confidentiality, the consequences of reporting, and diluting the professional role (Kalichman, 1993). Mandated reporting of child abuse is an exception to confidentiality. Therefore, it needs to be thoroughly discussed as part of the informed consent process. Many therapists fear that by telling clients, especially children and adolescents that they are mandated reporters, the minors will not talk about abuse if it is occurring. This may be true in certain situations, so it is best that clients know the consequences of their behavior and can choose accordingly. However, many minor clients do reveal abuse in therapy with the knowledge that the therapist is a mandated reporter. This is an appropriate method to obtain protection and assistance.

One reason that therapists are reluctant to report abuse is that they believe reporting suspected abuse will have a negative effect on therapy. Specifically, they fear that the client will terminate treatment and may also be reluctant to seek treatment in the future. However, failure to report suspected abuse is illegal and it puts vulnerable children at risk. There is no guarantee that keeping a minor or even his or her family in treatment will prevent further abuse (Koocher & Keith-Spiegel, 1990). However, reporting does not have to result in the termination of the therapeutic relationship. In a study by Harper & Irvin (1985), it was found that when cases were reported in the context of ongoing therapy, clients were unlikely to terminate treatment. Watson and Levine (1989) found that reports of suspected abuse tend to occur early in the course of treatment. In this study, a careful review of the cases showed that most cases of mandated reporting did not have negative effects on the therapeutic relationship.

Even when it is clear that a report needs to be made, the therapist has a number of clinical options regarding how the report is made. There are ways to reduce the negative effects of a child abuse report. When the therapist learns of abuse, remind the client (and his or her parents) that it must be reported. This follows from the discussion of mandated reporting during informed consent. From a clinical perspective, it is best if the client makes the report. This can be done from the therapist's office, or the client can make the report on his or her own. However, if the report is not made in the presence of the therapist, after being informed that the report was made, the therapist should check with the agency where the report was given to be sure the suspected abuse was reported. Even if the client makes the report, the therapist is still responsible for abuse getting reported. If the report was not made, it can be made at this time. If the client does not want to make the report, the therapist should make the report with the client present. In this way, the client (and his or her parents who should also be present) knows exactly what was said. This is very important to the therapeutic relationship. If the client and legal guardian are not present when the report is made, it is helpful if they are informed that a report will be made. Although it is both legal and ethical to make a report of suspected child abuse without the client being present or informed, this is the least preferable choice from a therapeutic perspective. Nonetheless, there may be times, based on the specifics of a particular case, when this is the best option.

Concerns about the adverse effects on therapy are not the only reason therapists are reluctant to report suspected abuse. Another significant factor is concern about a lack of enough evidence to report abuse (Kalichman, 1993). Some therapists struggle with the decision of whether or not abuse has occurred, especially when working with young children. Other professionals who suspect abuse may feel that having a reasonable suspicion, which is the standard set by most child abuse reporting laws, is not enough to make a report. According to Kalichman (1993), "Human service professionals also find themselves in a precarious situation of seeking further information to justify reporting in response to vague statues, despite the fact that the law does not require them to do so, and that such actions may compromise their roles as helping professionals" (p. 42). Thus with respect to mandated child abuse reporting laws, therapists need to understand the threshold for making a formal report. The use of professional discretion as a rationale for not reporting is not ethically acceptable (Koocher & Keith-Spiegel, 1990). There is little evidence to support the perception that reporting abuse has detrimental effects on the quality and efficacy of professional services.

When facing an ethical dilemma, it is often helpful to consult a colleague. This is also useful when considering making a report of suspected child abuse. Discussing the circumstances of the specific case with a colleague brings an additional perspective to the situation. Kalichman and Brosig (1993) found that many practicing psychologists discuss cases of suspected child abuse with colleagues. In addition, therapists who discuss cases with colleagues more consistently make reports of child abuse (Kalichman, 1993). In contrast to the position that reporting suspected child abuse is an ethical dilemma, when therapists discuss the limits of confidentiality, and report all cases of suspected abuse, they have met both their legal and ethical obligations. Consistently reporting suspected abuse also eliminates the temptation to seek additional information to validate the occurrence of abuse beyond the legal standard of suspicion. Thus, mandatory reporting laws limit the use of clinical judgment when child abuse is suspected. As with many other legal issues discussed here, mandated reporting laws vary from state to state. Group therapists need to be familiar with the laws governing the jurisdiction in which they practice.

RECORD KEEPING

The central dilemma with regard to record keeping in group psychotherapy is whether to keep records separately for each individual group member, or to keep one record for the group as a whole (Knauss, 2006). If records are kept for the group as a whole, which may correspond more closely to the way the therapist experiences and thinks about the group session, it creates a problem of confidentiality with regard to access to records by group members, release of the record to third parties, and subpoenas of the entire record if a court proceeding involves one of the group members. However, if records are kept for each individual group member, it may be difficult to capture the context of a group member's comments, and how he or she related to the other group members. The challenge is to maintain the confidentiality of group members while still being able to follow the flow of the session. This makes record keeping more complex for group therapists than for individual therapists.

Many authors (Brabender, Fallon, & Smolar, 2004; Leupker, 2003; Slovenko, 1998) recommend writing individual notes about each group member, after each meeting, to be kept in the individual's file. No reference to other group members in a manner that would identify them should be included in any individual chart. This includes specific characteristics of background and behavior as well as the person's name. Many factors determine the content of session notes. The following are commonly included: Date of Service; Diagnostic Impression; Treatment Goals; and Progress toward achieving those goals. Group therapists may also include the theoretical orientation of the group, the relationship between the group member's behavior and his or her presenting problems, and any significant feedback the member received from others in the group (Brabender et al., 2004).

Group therapists cannot predict who might want to read their records. It may be the client, his or her parents, a teacher, or an attorney. Progress notes may also be read in court. It is for these reasons as well that it is preferable to keep individual files for participants in group therapy rather than creating an integrated record of the whole group. Although an integrated group progress note can better capture the focus and themes of the group sessions, it would be difficult to include an adequate amount of detail about each individual in such a note.

In addition to the issue of the content of session notes, each group therapy participant needs to have an individual client record file with identifying information such as name, address, telephone number, birth date, legal guardian, school, billing and financial information, relevant history, medical history, presenting problem, testing or school reports, and records of any consultations about the client. Other factors that may influence the content of a group member's record are requirements of third-party payers such as insurance and managed care companies, as well as requirements of schools or probation officers when relevant (Brabender et al., 2004).

In order to ensure confidentiality, convenient access to records, and proper release of information, group therapists need to maintain separate documentation in individual charts on each group member. Although it is easier and more convenient to write a single comprehensive note about the entire group session, it is worth the extra time after each group meeting to write individual notes to protect each group member's confidentiality. It takes skill and practice to write individual notes that capture important group-level issues.

ADDITIONAL CONSIDERATIONS

Peer pressure can have a negative effect on group members, especially in groups for children and adolescents. Group leaders have an ethical obligation to respond to undue peer pressure toward any group member (Corey, Corey, Callanan, & Russell, 1992). It is always a judgment call to achieve a balance between appropriate pressure and unethical coercion. The relevant ASGW (1989) guideline states, "Group counselors protect member rights against physical threats, intimidation, coercion, and undue peer pressure in so far as is reasonably possible" (p. 122). One technique for dealing with peer pressure in group therapy is to make it the topic of group discussion. This acknowledges the feelings of the group members who are exerting the pressure and hopefully reframes those feelings in a more productive direction. It is also the role of the leader to remind the group of the need to respect the wishes of an unwilling member (Corey, Corey, Callanan, & Russell, 1992).

Group members also must have the freedom not to participate in activities or discussions. This information should be part of the informed consent process, and frequent reminders during group may be helpful. In addition, group leaders need to demonstrate that it is acceptable for members to choose not to participate at times. This is especially true for minors because many times they have been referred by parents or teachers and are especially reluctant to participate. Similarly, when group members are discussing a particular issue, they can decide to stop at any point. The leaders may explore their reason for stopping, and let them know that if they want to continue the discussion at a later time, to let the leader know.

In contrast to peer pressure, group leaders can also abuse their power. This can take the form of excessive focus on one member, pressuring a minor to reveal certain information, or making group members feel defensive. When these techniques are used, clients tend to withdraw and stop participating. Thus, it has the opposite of the intended effect. Other group members also may model abuse toward a client by the group leader. This causes a serious disruption in the functioning of the group and destroys any atmosphere of trust. Instead of giving thoughtful answers to questions, a client who feels attacked will try to find the "right" answer to get the questions to stop. Although confrontation can be an effective therapeutic technique, it needs to be done carefully and with concern for the client being confronted (Corey, Corey, Callanan, & Russell, 1992).

Giving group members the freedom to leave the group is a difficult decision when working with minors, especially since in some circumstances it is not the minor's choice to be a member of the group. Regardless of how the group leader wishes to handle this issue, it should be discussed as part of informed consent so that group members are aware of what is expected of them. If group members have the option to leave the group, and wish to do so, they also have a responsibility to inform the group members and leader of their intention to leave as well as their reasons for wanting to leave. It can be therapeutic for the person who plans to leave to tell the group what they considered negative in the experience. Also, if the child or adolescent is leaving because of feedback they have received, this discussion provides the opportunity to clarify any misunderstanding that may have taken place. Other group members may feel that the child is leaving because of something they said or did. Corey and colleagues (1992) point out that "By having the person who is leaving present reasons to the group as a whole, (it gives) the other members an opportunity to verify any concerns they may have about their responsibility for that person's decision" (p. 27). In most groups, members are expected to attend all sessions and inform the leader if they plan to miss a session or withdraw. When members choose to leave the group, it does have a significant effect on the whole group, especially if they do so without discussing their reasons. If a child who is still in need of mental health services chooses to leave group therapy, it is good practice to provide his or her parents with a referral for additional treatment.

SUMMARY AND CONCLUSIONS

There are many legal and ethical issues that confront group therapists working with minors. It is the responsibility of the group leader to both act ethically, and create an ethical climate in the group (Glass, 1998). Although there are ethical guidelines and codes to aid group therapists in making good decisions, they do not provide answers for all ethical dilemmas. Thus, in addition to knowing the ethics code of the group leader's profession and the laws of his or her specific jurisdiction, it is helpful to have an ethical decision-making framework to use in resolving ethical dilemmas (Brabender, 2002). This chapter presented the model developed by Knapp and VandeCreek (2003) that is made up of five steps that are common across most ethical decision-making models.

The area of competence was discussed from several perspectives; such as competence as a therapist, competence as a group therapist, competence to work with children, competence with specialty populations and competence to work with a diverse clientele. The importance of life-long learning in maintaining competence throughout one's career was also stressed.

Recruitment, screening, and selection of minors for participation in group therapy were also addressed. Some of the issues discussed included the negative effects of labeling children and adolescents in the recruitment process, how to best involve teachers and parents, and how to identify children who will benefit from group treatment.

The next area focused on consent to treatment of minors. In most jurisdictions when a decision is to be made on behalf of a person who has not yet reached the age of 18, it is usually made by a parent or legal guardian. Even though group therapy clients below the age of 18 can not legally consent to treatment, it is important to obtain their assent, or willingness to participate in the group.

Informed consent is a very important part of the group therapy process. Informed consent provides the basis for parents to make the decision about whether or not their child should participate in group treatment. The elements of adequate informed consent were discussed, including the risks and benefits of group participation.

Confidentiality is central to all mental health treatment. Group therapy with minors presents many challenges in the area of confidentiality. For example, the amount of information to be shared with parents needs to be negotiated, and agreed on in advance. Also, in group therapy, the leader can control therapist-client confidentiality, but not client-to-client confidentiality. Children and adolescents need frequent reminders of the importance and necessity of confidentiality. Five steps were discussed that can be taken by group leaders to increase the probability that group members will respect each other's confidentiality.

Mandated reporting of child abuse was included because group therapists working with minors are likely to encounter a situation that requires reporting. Knowing the reasons that therapists are reluctant to make a report is as important as knowing when and how to report suspected child abuse. Options were provided to reduce the negative effects on treatment of making a child abuse report.

Records of group therapy sessions can be written either about the entire group or about each individual member. The pros and cons of each format were discussed and recommendations were made to maintain the confidentiality of group members.

Finally, the issues of peer pressure in group therapy, the freedom not to participate in group activities or discussions, and the freedom to leave the group were presented. These topics are especially important when working with children and adolescents who are easily influenced by the behavior of others.

Ethical dilemmas arise when they are least expected and most inconvenient. It is beneficial to discuss ethical issues with colleagues and to provide necessary training to graduate students and interns. Consultation in complex situations provides an additional perspective (Glass, 1998). "The group therapist can deliver effective treatment only by acting ethically and within the limits of the law" (Brabender et al., 2004, p. 202).

REFERENCES

Abeles, N. (1980). Teaching ethical principles by means of value confrontation. *Psychotherapy: Research and Practice, 17*, 384–391.

American Counseling Association. (1995). *The code of ethics and standards of practice.* Alexandria, VA: Author.

American Group Psychotherapy Association and National Registry of Certified Group Psychotherapists. (2002). *Guidelines for ethics.* New York: Author.

American Psychological Association (2000). Ethical standards and code of conduct. *American Psychologist, 57*, 1060–1073.

Association for Specialists in Group Work. (1989). *Ethical guidelines for group counselors.* Washington, DC: American Association for Counseling and Development.

Bajt, T. R., & Pope, K. S. (1989). Therapist-patient sexual intimacy involving children and adolescents. *American Psychologist, 44*, 455.

Barnett, J. E., & Hillard, D. (2001). Psychologist distress and impairment: The availability, nature and use of colleague assistance programs for psychologists. *Professional Psychology: Research and Practice, 32*, 205–210.

Brabender, V. (2002). *Introduction to group therapy.* New York: Wiley.

Brabender, V.A., Fallon, A. E., & Smolar, A. I. (2004). *Essentials of group therapy.* Hoboken, NJ: Wiley.

Corrao, J., & Melton, G. B. (1988). Legal issues in school-based behavior therapy. In J. C. Witt, S. N. Elliot, & F. M. Gresham (Eds.), *Handbook of behavior therapy in education* (pp. 377–399). New York: Plenum.

Corey, M. S., & Corey, G. (1992). *Groups: Process and practice* (4th ed.). Pacific Grove, CA: Brooks/Cole.

Corey, M. S., Corey, G., Callanan, P., & Russell, J. M. (1992). *Group techniques* (2nd ed.). Pacific Grove, CA: Brooks/Cole.

Couch, R. D. (1995). Four steps for conducting a pregroup screening interview. *Journal for Specialists in Group Work, 20*, 18–25.

Eberlein, L. (1987). Introducing ethics to beginning psychologists: A problem-solving approach. *Professional Psychology: Research and Practice, 18*, 353–-359.

Fisher, C. B. (2003). *Decoding the ethics code: A practical guide for psychologists*. London: Sage Publications.

Gladding, S. T. (1999). *Groundwork: A counseling specialty* (3rd ed.). Upper Saddle River, NJ: Prentice Hall.

Glass, T. A. (1998). Ethical issues in group therapy. In R. M. Anderson, T. L. Needels, & H. V. Hall (Eds.), *Avoiding ethical misconduct in psychology specialty areas* (pp. 95–126). Springfield, IL: Charles C. Thomas.

Haas, L. J., & Malouf, J. L. (2002). *Keeping up the good work: A practitioner's guide to mental health ethics* (3rd ed.). Sarasota, FL: Professional Resource Press.

Harper, G., & Irvin, E. (1985). Alliance formation with parents: Limit setting and the effect of mandated reporting. *American Journal of Orthopsychiatry, 55,* 550–560.

Hurdle, D. E. (1991). The ethnic group experience. In K. L. Chau (Ed.). *Ethnicity and biculturalism: Emerging perspectives of social group work* (pp. 59–69). New York: Haworth Press.

Kalichman, S. C. (1993). *Mandated reporting of suspected child abuse: Ethics, law, and policy*. Washington, DC: American Psychological Association.

Kalichman, S. C., & Brosig, C. L. (1993). Practicing psychologists' interpretations of and compliance with child abuse reporting laws. *Law and Human Behavior, 17,* 83–93.

Kitchener, K. S. (1984). Intuition, critical evaluation and ethical principles: The foundation for ethical decisions in counseling psychology. *Counseling Psychologist, 12*(3), 43–55.

Knapp, S., & VandeCreek, L. (2003). *A guide to the 2002 revision of the American Psychological Association's ethics code*. Sarasota, FL: Professional Resource Press.

Knauss, L. K. (2006). Ethical issues in record keeping in group psychotherapy. *International Journal of Group Psychotherapy, 56*(4), 415–430.

Koocher, G. (Ed.) (1976). *Children's rights and the mental health profession*. New York: Wiley-Interscience.

Koocher, G. P., & Keith-Spiegel, P. C. (1990). *Children, ethics, and the law: Professional issues and cases*. Lincoln: University of Nebraska Press.

Koocher, G. P., & Keith-Spiegel, P. (1998). *Ethics in psychology: Professional standards and cases* (2nd ed.). New York: Oxford University Press.

Leong, F. T. L. (1992). Guidelines for minimizing premature termination among Asian American clients in group counseling. *Journal for Specialists in Group Work, 17*(4), 218–228.

Leupker, E. T. (2003). *Record keeping in psychotherapy and counseling*. New York: Brunner- Routledge.

National Association of Social Workers. (1999). *NASW code of ethics*. Washington, DC: Author.

Rest, J. R. (1982). A psychologist looks at the teaching of ethics. *Hastings Center Report*, pp. 29–36.

Ohlsen, M. M. (1974). *Guidance services in the modern schools*. New York: Harcourt Brace Jovanovich.

Ritchie, M. H., & Huss, S. N. (2000). Recruitment and screening of minors for group counseling. *Journal for Specialists in Group Work, 25*(2), 146–156.

Slovenko, R. (1998). *Psychotherapy and confidentiality: Testimonial privileged communication, breach of confidentiality, and reporting duties*. Springfield, IL: Charles C. Thomas.

Terres, C. K., & Larrabee, M. J. (1985). Ethical issues and group work with children. *Elementary School Guidance and Counseling, 19*(3), 190–197.

Toseland, R. W., & Siporin, M. (1986). When to recommend group treatment: A review of the clinical and the research literature. *International Journal of Group Psychotherapy, 36,* 171–201.

Tymchuk, A. J. (1986). Guidelines for ethical decision making. *Canadian Psychology, 27,* 36–43

Watson, H., & Levine, M. (1989). Psychotherapy and mandated reporting of child abuse. *American Journal of Orthopsychiatry, 59,* 246–256.

Yanagida, E. H. (1998). Ethical dilemmas in the clinical practice of child psychology. In R. M. Anderson, T. L. Needels, & H. V. Hall (Eds.), *Avoiding ethical misconduct in psychology specialty areas* (pp. 47–77). Springfield, IL: Charles C. Thomas.

Part Two

SPECIFIC SETTINGS

Chapter Five

Applying Cognitive-Behavior Therapy Groups in School Settings

Diane L. Smallwood, Ray W. Christner, & Lydia Brill

According to statistics from the U.S. Department of Education (National Center for Education Statistics, 2005), almost 50 million children and adolescents attend public elementary and secondary schools in the United States, with an average daily attendance of over 44 million students. Even without considering the additional numbers enrolled in private educational programs, it is clear that schools are an ideal access point for provision of a broad range of services for the school-age population.

It is estimated that at least 10% of children and adolescents in the United States meet criteria for emotional disorders that have significant impact on their daily functioning (National Institute of Mental Health, 2004). These disorders can disrupt learning, not only for individual students but in some cases for their classmates as well. Thus, schools cannot ignore the mental health needs of such a substantial proportion of the student population. Moreover, as noted by Ehly and Garcia-Vazquez (1998), students often experience difficulties within the context of their peer group, making school-based group interventions an important aspect of school mental health programs.

Although the primary mission of schools is education, early attention to mental health factors can prevent more serious disorders that may result in school failure or dropout. In fact, some researchers have noted that mental health concerns and stressors are a major barrier to learning (Adelman & Taylor, 1998; 2000). The final report of the President's *New Freedom Commission on Mental Health* (2003) provides additional support for addressing children's mental health in school settings, concluding that "strong school mental health programs can attend to the health and behavioral concerns of students, reduce unnecessary pain and suffering, and help ensure academic achievement" (p. 58).

In this chapter, we offer a multilevel framework for school-based group interventions using cognitive-behavioral techniques. The chapter initially addresses the unique characteristics of school environments with regard to factors that facilitate and hinder effective use of group interventions. In addition, a discussion of multiple levels of intervention is followed by a brief review of research demonstrating the effective use of school-based cognitive-behavior therapy (CBT) groups to support children's healthy emotional development and to address specific mental health needs. Finally, we provide suggestions regarding the assessment and identification of individuals who would likely benefit from school-based group CBT interventions.

UNIQUE CHARACTERISTICS OF SCHOOLS

The concept of providing mental health services in schools continues to be a topic of debate. While some argue that such services are difficult to "fit" into the culture of schools, others have advocated for these services. Specifically, several have noted the parallel between CBT and other educational services, which increases its acceptability among educators in general (Christner & Allen, 2003; Christner, Stewart-Allen, & Mennuti, 2004; Mennuti & Christner, 2005; Mennuti, Christner, & Freeman, 2006). CBT's present-oriented, solution-focused approach offers a flexible model that can fit into an existing school-based problem-solving approach, as well as provide a continuum of interventions at differing levels of specificity, complexity, and intensity. Although this chapter focuses specifically on group interventions, Mennuti, Freeman, and Christner (2006) provide a text that reviews CBT interventions in school settings addressing a continuum from prevention to early identification to direct individual service.

Although CBT is a natural fit in many ways within school settings, there also exist a number of challenges to offering group interventions within the culture of an educational setting. One of the greatest challenges incumbent in school settings is obtaining "buy in" from the many players of the educational team that interact with students. Schools are under increased pressure from national legislation (e.g., No Child Left Behind) to improve outcomes for students. For many educators, this equates to *academic* success, and the focus for a number of schools is placed on moving through the curriculum and raising test scores. Because of these constraints on student time and pressure on teachers to ensure academic success, clinicians providing mental health services must be mindful of their approach. Our experience has found that being flexible in scheduling group interventions is essential. Flexible scheduling can occur in a number of ways, though we found that using a rotating group format provided the best results. This consists of rotating the time of the group each week, so that students do not miss the same class time each week (e.g., session one 8:00 a.m–9:00 a.m., session two 9:00 a.m.–10:00 a.m., session three 10:00 a.m.–11:00 a.m., etc.).

Interventions typically provided within school settings are conducted and/or monitored through a team process (e.g., prereferral teams, multidisciplinary teams, etc.). Yet, a common mistake among mental health service providers in school is that they attempt to conduct interventions in isolation. Although content of what occurs in a group session should remain confidential between members and facilitators, clinicians can involve other school team members in various aspects, such as initial assessment and referral and progress monitoring. In addition, it is important for mental health providers to educate teachers, administrators, parents, and others involved with students how emotional and behavioral difficulties can affect learning. One way to do this is to provide resources to school staff and parents regarding various issues facing children. We have also found that teaching school staff about the approaches and their benefits has a great impact on their understanding of mental health intervention. For instance, one of us (RWC) has conducted relaxation workshops with school staff to educate them about the intervention and then also discussed how it could be used in the classroom.

Finally, providing counseling services in school creates a collaborative, working relationship between student and clinician. While this relationship is beneficial for therapeutic purposes and, in many cases, key to successful group intervention, it also can create some conflict within a school setting. In the school environment, clinicians are more likely to have casual interactions with students outside of group (e.g., passing in the hallways) than would be experienced in other settings. These informal interactions in many ways are positive, as they may help facilitate the collaborative relationship with the student. However, clinicians must be cautious of boundary issues and confidentiality in these cases. Not only should confidentiality be discussed regarding student and clinician interactions, but also those interactions between students. It is imperative for those providing CBT group intervention in educational settings to discuss these issues with group members from the start (e.g., What do we do when we pass in the hallways? What are some ways we can be sure to protect confidentiality?).

SCHOOL-BASED CBT GROUPS AT MULTIPLE LEVELS OF INTERVENTION

In educational settings, professionals can address mental health factors most appropriately and effectively within a multilevel framework of prevention and intervention. At the *primary prevention*, or universal, level, programs and services are targeted to the entire school population with the goal of establishing social and emotional competence in all members of the community. Examples at this universal level would include a comprehensive school curriculum using strategies and activities that foster resilience and positive skills for coping effectively with life demands. At the *secondary prevention* level, services are designed for a target group of individuals identified as being "at risk" for maladaptive reactions to daily stresses and extraordinary life events. The goal at this selective level is to intervene early in order to activate social supports and to develop enhanced coping strategies to minimize difficulties in functioning. The most intensive level of intervention is that of *tertiary prevention*, which provides assistance for those individuals who are showing fully developed symptoms of behavioral or emotional disorders. At this targeted level, intensive clinical services are needed, which typically calls for collaboration between school and community resources.

These individual levels of intervention are not exclusive of one another, and instead, should be viewed as a system that builds upon each component (see Figure 5.1). With effective services offered at the universal and early intervention levels, school-based referrals at the intensive or tertiary level should be fewer. By coordinating programs and services at all three of these levels, schools can address the goals of: (a) maximizing social, emotional, and academic competence for the entire school community; (b) intervening early with individuals who are at-risk for developing personal or educational problems or who are just beginning to encounter social, behavioral, emotional, or learning difficulties; and (c) minimizing the impact of established emotional or educational disorders. For the remainder of this section, we discuss the applications of CBT group interventions at these multiple levels within the educational system.

Universal Intervention (Primary Prevention)

Universal (primary) prevention programs in school settings typically aim to prevent the onset of learning or behavioral disorders (Rapp-Paglicci, Dulmus, & Wodarski, 2004). Although a number of programs are targeted to prevent specific problem behaviors, such

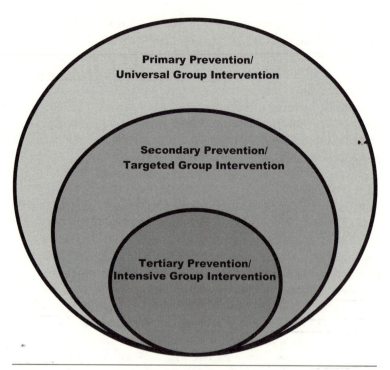

Figure 5.1   Multi-levels of Group Intervention.

as substance use (LeCroy & Mann, 2004), school dropout (Doll & Hess, 2004), suicide (McCarter, Sowers, & Dulmus, 2004), or teenage pregnancy (Armistead, Kotchick, & Forehand, 2004), a recent trend has been the establishment of more global prevention efforts that are intended to promote resilience and emotional and physical wellness among the general school population.

Resilience refers to the capacity to thrive despite the presence of risk factors or exposure to stressful conditions (Dulmus & Rapp-Paglicci, 2004). Several protective factors are commonly identified as contributing to resilience, including social competence, positive peer relationships, and the presence of one or more caring adults in the child's life. As the empirical research on resilience has grown, more attention has been given to implementing school-wide and district-wide programs that target social competence. Such programs usually are designed to teach all students the fundamental skills needed for effective social behavior, including (1) self-awareness, (2) social awareness, (3) self-management, (4) relationship skills, and (5) responsible decision-making (CASEL, 2003).

Cognitive-behavioral perspectives are evident in many programs that promote social competence. For example, programs that utilize a basic social problem-solving format (e.g., *I Can Problem Solve*, Shure, 2001; PATHS, Kusche & Greenberg, 1994) focus on teaching students to develop and apply a set of cognitive problem-solving skills that include alternative solution thinking, consequential thinking, and means-end thinking (Weissberg & Gesten, 1982). Such programs usually include an emphasis on recognizing emotional states in oneself and others, self-regulation, empathy, and decision making.

School classrooms provide naturally occurring groups for applying cognitive-behavioral interventions. At the universal level of prevention/intervention, classroom groups offer a "built-in" vehicle for delivering programs designed to enhance students' performance with regard to both academic and social/emotional skills.

Early Intervention (Secondary Prevention) for Students At-Risk

At the level of early intervention, students identified as being in a particular high-risk group or who are beginning to show early warning signs of difficulty in personal adjustment might participate in small group interventions designed to increase problem-solving and coping strategies. Cognitive-behavioral strategies for anger management and impulse control are often utilized for this purpose.

It is important to identify students within this at-risk category, so that additional supports can be organized and implemented. Although some students will be included in the high-risk group by virtue of their preexisting vulnerabilities to stress or difficult life circumstances, others may have newly emerging symptoms that need to be recognized early and addressed as soon as it is feasible. In most cases, students in need of services at this early intervention level will be identified through an instructional support program or other building-based problem-solving team process.

Intensive Intervention (Tertiary Prevention) for Students with Psychological Symptoms

It is a well-known fact that most of our school mental health resources are devoted to a limited number of students who have significant behavioral and emotional needs. Schools that have implemented comprehensive programs of positive behavioral supports at the universal and selective levels have found that the number of students with severe symptoms can be reduced, yet there will continue to be a small group of individuals who require more extensive and intensive psychological supports for a variety of reasons. Collaboration between school personnel and community agencies is needed to ensure that these students receive needed treatment services in addition to whatever is available at school, on either an outpatient or an inpatient basis.

Although intensive therapy groups are more often provided in community or outpatient settings, therapeutic CBT group interventions could be included as part of a comprehensive school counseling program. This would be appropriate particularly within school programs designed to meet the needs of students with significant emotional or behavioral disorders. It is important to recognize that some students may require individual treatment in addition to or in lieu of group interventions.

Responding to Crisis Situations on Multiple Levels

Crisis events often create special challenges for mental health professionals working in schools. Although many crisis situations are limited in scope, affecting small numbers of individuals, there often are situations that impact an entire school community. Intervening at the group level in such situations is an efficient and necessary approach, and classrooms offer an ideal environment for school-based group crisis intervention (Brock, 2002).

With respect to crisis intervention services, universal activities to address the needs of all students might include classroom sessions for talking about the traumatic event, providing opportunities to defuse emotional reactions, and to begin to activate positive coping strategies (that presumably have been strengthened through other primary prevention programs). The emphasis at this level would be to reestablish a sense of safety and security, and to resume normal school operations as soon as possible after the crisis. Most students will respond to these efforts to promote wellness through the use of normal coping strategies, and will not require additional follow-up services from mental health professionals.

Cognitive-behavioral principles provide an appropriate framework for conceptualizing reactions to trauma and for intervening with individuals and groups following a crisis event. Discussions based on beliefs about the nature and causes of the crisis, as well as schemas for coping with unexpected and tragic events, can assist trauma victims and survivors throughout the healing process. In addition, when the effects of trauma are not readily resolved, CBT techniques have proven to be highly effective in addressing symptoms of posttraumatic stress disorder in children and adolescents (Cohen, Berliner, & March, 2000). Specific to school situations, Smallwood, Williams, and McDonald (2006) offered a review of cognitive-behavioral interventions for crisis response in school settings.

REVIEW OF THE RESEARCH ON CBT GROUPS IN SCHOOL SETTINGS

School-based mental health services have moved in new directions in recent years, including consultation and other mental health services. These new directions also include the development of "tailor-made" programs for students at risk for school failure or who have been affected by crises, such as suicide or other traumatic events (Hoagwood & Erwin, 1997). In addition, national and state level policy changes are now placing more pressure on schools to ensure positive educational outcomes for all students. To that end, a thorough review of the evidence of the effectiveness of specific school-based mental health services is critical in informing policy changes (Hoagwood & Erwin, 1997).

Positive group interventions that have a solid evidence base offer the most promising strategies aimed at addressing behavioral problems with young people (Amendola & Scozzie, 2004). In general, one of the major benefits of group therapy is that it offers a more realistic environment for individuals to learn about and change their behavior than therapy that is done on an individual basis in a clinical setting (Lacey, 2004). Also, group therapy situations present interactions that, for many people, may provoke experiences of anxiety, anger, and other problems. As a result, group work is much more likely than individual therapy to provide the kinds of variables that trigger and reinforce these behaviors, and allow for direct observations that more accurately represent members' functioning than self-explanation that is often inaccurate. In fact, people's misperceptions of their anxiety, anger, and other emotional states often lead to a range of self-critical attitudes that may foster a depressed mood that often accompanies severe anxiety and other mental health disorders. However, therapeutic group situations allow members to more accurately observe their own and others' behavior, which can lead to a more realistic understanding of exactly what variables trigger the anxiety, depression, or anger (Lacey, 2004), instead of members' making global attributions about themselves.

Creating and facilitating groups can be a challenging process given the numerous considerations from development through assessment of appropriate members and the actual conduction of therapy. One challenge that a group leader faces is the ability to present the types of thinking patterns causing group members distress in a manner that does not blame or reject the individual members. In order to be a skilled group leader, one must possess the ability to detect an entire range of problem thinking, analyze patterns and functions of behavior, and appear human and approachable in the process (Lacey, 2004). Because of these demanding responsibilities, Lacey recommends that groups should be facilitated by more than one leader and that these facilitators should work closely together and form and maintain a collaborative relationship at all times.

There are a number of problem areas that present in school. Some of the most common areas addressed by group intervention in schools include anger and aggression, anxiety, and depression. A number of excellent programs exist to address these topics, and many of them have been evaluated for use within school settings. Some of the programs were designed for clinical setting, though they can be easily adapted for use in schools. Below we offer a brief review of each area and discuss several group interventions for clinicians to consider.

School-Based Group CBT with Anger and Aggression

Research shows that aggressive behavior in children is a predictive factor of later delinquency, substance use, school dropout, early parenthood, and depression (Amendola & Scozzie, 2004). In addition, if a child's aggressive behavior is left untreated, it can have damaging effects on their overall success in school, work, social situations, and overall quality of life. Therefore, it is essential to choose violence-prevention programs that are comprehensive, evidence-based, and serve to build positive skills and strengths in the young people of today's society (Amendola & Scozzie, 2004). Moreover, effective early intervention is needed when working with angry children because research shows that when children become aggressive at a young age, the tendency toward violent behavior seems to remain fairly stable (Fraser, 1996).

In a school setting, a disproportionate amount of a teacher's time and attention can be consumed by the inappropriate conduct of a single student. In addition, these behaviors also create difficulties for principals and other administrators whose responsibility it is to maintain classroom discipline. Overall, disruptive behavior interferes with class conduct, student learning, and models inappropriate behavior that may then be imitated by other students (Larkin & Thyer, 1999). Frequently referred by parents and teaches to therapists and other professionals for help are those children who are often regarded as disruptive, noncompliant, aggressive, out-of-control, and oppositional (Larkin & Thyer, 1999). Because disruptive behaviors have such an effect on students, teachers, and administrators, research addressing the needs of adolescents with anger difficulties is mounting.

Feindler and Goldstein are two researchers who have focused on developing cognitive-behavioral skill-building approaches for assisting a wide range of emotionally troubled adolescents in a variety of settings. These settings include outpatient, public school, and institutional settings to control anger. Included in their treatment efforts have been individual, group, and psychoeducational modalities (Kellner & Bry, 1999).

Feindler and Ecton (1986) reported that anger management training typically includes three skills. First, training should provide information regarding the cognitive and behavioral aspects of anger. Second, training should teach cognitive and behavioral techniques to manage anger. Third, effective training should facilitate the application of newly acquired skills. Specific skills typically emphasized include relaxation, assertiveness, anticipation, self-instruction, role-play or rehearsal and problem solving.

Larkin and Thyer (1999) have noted that many school-based interventions have been designed to improve self-esteem. This is because a number of studies identify low self-esteem as one of the leading causes of behavior problems on the part of school-age children (Burnett, 1994; Hwang, 1995; Lochman & Lampton, 1986; Wiggins & Wiggins, 1992). These researchers have, thus, conducted a study in order to evaluate the effectiveness of cognitive-behavioral group counseling aimed at improving the self-esteem, self-control, and classroom behavior of disruptive children at school. Group therapy focused on problem-solving strategies, self-instruction, modeling, role-play, alternative thinking, social skills training, and covert imagery. Although some adjustments and modifications were made, the group followed the protocol of O'Rouke and Worzbyt (1996) closely. In this study, students were assigned to either an Immediate Treatment (IT) group or a Delayed Treatment (DT) group. Results indicate that the Immediate Treatment groups' self-esteem, perceived self-control, and teacher and teacher aide grades of classroom deportment significantly improved while children assigned to the Delayed Treatment did not substantially change (Larkin & Thyer, 1999).

The "Keeping Cool" anger management program was developed by Dwivedi and Gupta (2000). The program used a cognitive-behavioral approach in order to improve the responses of students in anger-provoking situations. This approach promoted an understanding of anger as a process, increased awareness of personal triggers, and expanded the inventory of coping responses in trying situations. This program is based on the framework developed by Feindler and Ecton (1986). The group consisted of 10-weekly 40-minute sessions that focused on education, triggers, relaxation techniques, assertiveness skills, thought-stopping and thought-directing, and problem solving. In addition, students used a log to document threatening encounters they experienced between sessions. These experiences were then role-played and used as a basis to apply the new skills they acquired in the group. Dwivedi and Gupta (2000) found that the group interventions demonstrated short-term positive effects beyond the predominant behaviorist approach most often used in schools.

Specific Anger Management Groups Used in Schools. A number of anger management programs are available for use, with many of them having an adequate evidence base. In chapter 18 of this text, Lochman, Powell, Boxmeyer, Deming, and Young offer a review of aggression, with a specific focus on the *Coping Power Program*. Given their extensive review, we do not discuss it here and readers are encouraged to consult that chapter for further specifics. We do provide a review of several other programs that can be used at varying intervention levels in school (e.g., universal, targeted, intensive).

The Second Step: A Violence Prevention Curriculum. Committee for Children (1997) is a school-based curriculum that targets students in preschool through junior high. The program focuses on social skills and on altering attitudes and behaviors that lead to violence through empathy, impulse control, and anger management. This program has been shown to decrease physical aggression and increase pro-social behavior. In addition, this program provides children with the skills they need to create safe environments and to become successful adults later in life, and is an example of universal intervention aimed at improving the overall functioning and success of students. One major advantage of this program is that lessons are easy to teach and require minimal teacher preparation time. Moreover, while children learn how to recognize and understand feelings, make positive and effective choices, and keep anger from accumulating into violence, teachers recognize how to deal with disruptions and behavior issues (Amendola & Scozzie, 2004).

Responding in Peaceful and Positive Ways.   RIPP (Meyer, Farrell, Northup, Kung, & Plybon, 2000) is a school-based violence prevention program that is used with students in middle and junior high school. This program combines classroom curriculum of social/cognitive problem-solving with real life skill building opportunities. The key concepts of this program include the importance of significant friends or adult mentors, relationships between self-image and gang-related behaviors, and the effects of environmental influence on personal health. Students who take part in this program learn about physical and mental development during adolescence. In addition, they learn to analyze the consequences of personal choices on health and well-being. Most importantly, students learn that they have nonviolent options when conflicts arise (Amendola & Scozzie, 2004).

Research shows (Amendola & Scozzie, 2004; Farrell, Meyer, Sullivan, & Kung, 2003) that students who participated in RIPP were significantly less likely to have discipline code violations for carrying weapons, were less likely to have in-school suspensions, had lower reported rates of fight-related injuries, and were more likely to participate in their school's peer mediation program. In addition, during a 6-month follow-up, RIPP students reported lower rates of peer pressure to use drugs and an increase in pro-social responses to hypothetical problem situations.

Aggression Replacement Training.   ART (Goldstein, Glick, & Gibbs, 1998) is one of the most widely recognized cognitive-behavioral interventions being used in schools and treatment programs. ART was developed by Arnold Goldstein, the former director of Syracuse University's Center for Research on Aggression. ART is recognized as a promising program by the U.S. Department of Education's Expert Panel on Safe, Disciplined, and Drug Free Schools, and has been designated as a model program by the U.S. Department of Justice, The American Correctional Association, and The United Kingdom's Home Office. This program teaches social skills building/skillstreaming, anger control training, and moral reasoning (Amendola & Scozzie, 2004).

School-Based Group CBT Treatment with Anxiety

According to statistics, anxiety problems occur in 10–20% of school-age children. In addition, more general anxiety disorders that have a major impact on children's functioning such as overanxious disorder, separation anxiety, and social phobias are found in approximately 5–10% of children (Barrett, 1998). Moreover, according to Bernstein and Borchardt (1991, as cited in Cartwright-Hatton, Roberts, Chitsabesan, Fothergill, & Harrington, 2004). Anxiety disorders are the most common psychiatric disorders of childhood. If left untreated, anxiety is a serious condition that can have negative effects on academic and interpersonal functioning.

In addition, anxiety experienced during childhood and adolescence is often unremitting into adulthood and is associated with other serious conditions such as depression and substance misuse. Unfortunately, Generalized Anxiety Disorder (GAD) often follows a chronic, fluctuating course associated with a significant burden on health service resources. Furthermore, GAD is estimated to cause a similar magnitude of psychosocial disability to that of chronic somatic disease and depression (Durham, Fisher, Dow, Sharp, Powers, Swan, & Morton, 2004).

According to Beck and colleagues (Beck, Rush, Shaw & Emery, 1979) the cognitive model of anxiety is based on the premise that emotional reactions to stressful events are produced and stimulated by an interpretation of the situation as threatening in some way. In addition, the perceptions or cognitions stimulated by an event not only stimulate emotion, but also influence behavioral responses. Research conducted by Cartwright-Halton et al. (2004) indicated that CBT was an effective intervention for anxiety disorders of childhood and adolescence, when compared to a no-treatment control. Although reviews of literature on CBT used with adults are now able to examine CBT in the context of specific anxiety disorders, this is not yet possible within the literature on children and adolescents. In addition, while evidence indicates that CBT is a promising intervention for childhood and adolescent anxiety, it is likely that different children will respond to different types of CBT. One thing that is clear is that more quality research is needed in the area of treating anxiety disorders in young people.

According to Silverman (2003), there has been strong and consistent evidence from randomized clinical trials over the past decade that indicates that CBT can play an important role in reducing social phobia, separation anxiety, and generalized anxiety (GAD) in children and adolescents. In fact, Silverman (2003) concluded that that it is critical to include primary therapeutic procedures, such as exposure exercises, in any treatment plan for children who present with anxiety disorders. In addition, strategies such as contingency contracting and self-control procedures may be used to help increase the likelihood that children will engage in successful exposures (Silverman & Kurtines, 1996).

According to reviews of the efficacy of psychotherapy for GAD, CBT that focuses on either excessive worry or physiological arousal offers the most advantages (Borkovec & Ruscio, 2001; Fisher & Durham, 1999). Treatment strategies that precisely target the vulnerabilities and psychological processes that keep GAD going are likely to be more effective. A number of promising candidates for future clinical trials include worry exposure, worry behavior prevention, cognitive therapy focused on metacognition therapy for interpersonal difficulties, mindfulness training, and a therapeutic focus on intolerance of uncertainty (Durham et al., 2004). Furthermore, research shows that CBT has been found to be an effective treatment for anxiety disorders such as OCD and PTSD. Although psychiatric medications are typically the first line of treatment, cognitive and behavioral interventions can complement and possibly replace pharmacotherapy for relief of symptoms of OCD and PTSD. In fact, according to research, individuals treated with CBT experience a significantly greater reduction in symptoms and are more likely to achieve remission compared to control groups (Basco et al., 2000).

Generally speaking, when individuals learn to reduce anxiety associated with stressful events, begin to override anxiety symptoms with a relaxation response, practice logical thinking, and develop alternative coping responses to replace avoidance and other nonproductive attempts at coping, anxiety symptoms are reduced by uncoupling the association between the stimulus events and the anxiety response (Basco et al., 2000). By reducing avoidance behaviors and controlling anxiety, CBT increases the likelihood that an individual suffering from anxiety can resume normal functioning and live a life that is not limited or controlled by fear (Basco et al., 2000).

Barrett conducted a randomized clinical trial investigating the effectiveness of cognitive-behavioral and family management training procedures presented in a group format for childhood anxiety disorders. This study consisted of two treatment conditions that were a child-only CBT group treatment and a CBT plus family management training group. First, the child-only CBT group was a 12-week program that was run by two therapists and used the Coping Koala Group Workbook (Barrett, 1995). Each session was 2 hours long and covered topics such as recognizing anxious feelings and somatic reactions to anxiety, cognitive restructuring in anxiety provoking situations, coping self-talk, exposure to feared stimuli, peer modeling, and administering self- and peer reinforcement. This program also used in vivo exposure to feared situations by systematic desensitization (Barrett, 1998). Second, the CBT plus family management training group used the Group Family Anxiety Management Workbook (Barrett, 1995) which was used in parallel with the Coping Koala Workbook. During this group, two therapists met with six families in groups for 2-hour sessions on a weekly basis. The focus of these groups was on responding to conflict, daily discussions, problem solving, and anxiety management. Results of this study indicated that both active treatment conditions produced significant change compared to the waitlist control condition. As a result, this study demonstrated the effectiveness of using group CBT procedures with anxious children. In fact, group interventions for childhood anxiety proved as effective as individual interventions (Barret et al., 1996). Moreover, the inclusion of a structured group intervention for families improved the outcomes in the cognitive behavioral treatment of anxious children (Barret, 1998).

Specific CBT treatment groups used with anxiety. As mentioned earlier, the literature regarding the use of CBT with children and adolescents with anxiety is very limited. Chapter 11 of this text (Flannery-Schroeder, Sieberg, & Gosch) offers the most current research on anxiety disorders and treatments for anxiety. In addition to what they offer, we provide a review of two programs frequently used with adults, but through modification can be implemented with children and adolescents in schools, as well.

Stress Inoculation Training (SIT; Meichenbaum, 1977) was developed as an attempt to integrate the research on the role of cognitive and affective factors in coping with that of cognitive behavior modification. Foa and colleagues. (1999) have used SIT to treat fear and anxiety experienced by rape victims through an 8- to14-session program, which consists of three phases including (1) education, (2) skill building, and (3) application.

Emphasis is placed on progressive muscle relaxation, coping skills, diaphragmatic breathing, thought stopping, covert rehearsal, guided self-dialogue, and role playing.

Jones and Menzies (1998) originally developed *Danger Ideation Reduction Therapy* (DIRT) for OCD, though it can be used to treat symptoms of PTSD, as well. This strategy includes interventions focused on fear of contamination, such as filmed interviews, expert testimony, and corrective information regarding germs, cognitive restructuring, microbiological experiments, and a probability of catastrophe assessment task.

Group CBT Treatment with Depression

According to Dopheide (2006), cognitive behavioral therapy (CBT) has been proven to be efficacious in the treatment of depression in children and adolescents. Depression is a common and persistent illness in youth that affects 0.3% of preschoolers, 2% of elementary school-age children, and 5 to 10% of adolescents. It is important to note, that while the rates of pre-pubertal depression are similar for boys and girls, these rates double in females after puberty. Two influences thought to contribute to this dramatic increase in adolescent female depression are hormonal and environmental influences. Regardless of gender, however, rates of depression radically increase as children enter into adolescence. In fact, by age 18 years, it is estimated that at least 10 to 20% of adolescents have experienced at least one major depressive episode (Dopheide, 2006).

Depression affects the developmental process and is associated with difficulties in concentration and motivation, which may lead to poor academic performance, impaired social functioning, poor self-esteem, and a higher rate of suicide. The characteristics of depression vary depending on the age of the depressed individual, as some children who are depressed are irritable, have temper tantrums, and exhibit problem behaviors such as shouting and lack of interest in playing with friends, and the like. Older children (9 to 12 years of age) may display behaviors such as talking about running away from home and exhibiting boredom, low self-esteem, guilt, or hopelessness. Moreover, at this age they may begin developing a fear of death. Adolescents with depression display more sleep and appetite disturbances, and they may be more prone to reckless behavior, delusions, suicidal ideation and acts, and impairment of overall functioning.

First-line treatment options for depression in youth include CBT, interpersonal psychotherapy, antidepressants, psychosocial intervention, or a combination of non-drug and pharmacologic options (Dopheide, 2006). However, many of these have not yet demonstrated effectiveness in preschoolers or children younger than 8 years of age. One reason for this is that younger children may not yet have the verbal and cognitive processing skills needed to benefit from CBT (Reinecke, Dattilio, & Freeman, 2003).

For children over the age of 8 years with nonpsychotic major depression, CBT has been found to be superior to interpersonal psychotherapy and other nonspecific psychotherapeutic interventions in some studies (Dopheide, 2006). Those CBT interventions that are effective combine general skill building (e.g., problem-solving) with the process of identifying and counteracting cognitive distortions. Several researchers have discussed the effectiveness of CBT techniques delivered in a school setting for children with depression (Clarke, Rohde, Lewinsohn, Hops, & Seeley, 1999; Reynolds & Coates, 1986).

Specific depression groups used in schools. The *Adolescent Coping with Depression Course* (CWD-A; Clarke, Lewinsohn, & Hops, 1990) has been shown to decrease depressive symptoms significantly. CWD-A is used with adolescents from 14 to 18 years of age, and it consists of 2-hour sessions, 2 times a week for 8 weeks. The program is a very structured group intervention that makes use of a treatment manual with scripts, student workbooks, and a brief workbook for parents. Sessions include direct instruction, modeling, individual assignments, and homework. During this group, there is a focus on developing skills to better cope with or prevent future episodes of depression (Donoghue, Wheeler, Prout, Wilson, & Reinecke, 2006). The major techniques taught include social learning, reducing tension, changing one's thinking, disputing irrational thinking, social skills, stating feelings, problem-solving, and goal-setting.

Stark and Kendall (1996) developed the *Action Program,* which is a cognitive-behavioral group intervention designed for use with children and adolescents. This program consists of 30 1-hour sessions and involves developing a therapeutic relationship, helping youth understand emotional experiences, as well as teaching the relationship of thoughts, feelings, and behaviors. Additionally, skill building activities are conducted to enhance coping and focus on the development of relaxation skills, social skills, and problem-solving skills. The sessions of the *Action Program* are not scripted, though a student workbook is used to facilitate treatment. During group meetings, therapists can work individually with specific students (Donoghue, Wheeler, Prout, Wilson, & Reinecke, 2006).

IDENTIFICATION AND REFERRAL OF STUDENTS FOR SCHOOL-BASED CBT GROUPS

General referrals for students for therapeutic services in school are different from what clinicians experience in other settings with children. Whereas referrals are typically individually made by professionals, physicians, parents, and such, and then assessment is conducted as part of the initiation of services, within school settings student referrals for psychological services often involve aspects of their involvement within the educational system (observations and data from administrators, consideration of grades and disciplinary and attendance records, etc.). Through the use of a systematic problem-solving model (Iverson, 2002), educational professionals can provide an efficient and effective service delivery system at multiple levels of school-based intervention, including the referral process, which can assist schools in addressing state and national requirements to facilitate safe and supportive environments that foster educational success.

The problem-solving process uses a multidisciplinary team of professionals to identify and track at-risk students and develop and evaluate intervention plans that improve the school performance and behavior of all students in general (Tilly, 2002). A problem-solving model begins with attention to problem definition, using multiple sources of data to measure performance. The second stage of problem-solving is an analysis of the problem, with a focus on identifying variables that contribute to the problem and using this information to develop an intervention plan. Implementation of the intervention plan represents the third stage of the problem-solving process, including attention to treatment integrity and progress monitoring. The final step of the problem solving process involves evaluation of the responsiveness of the student or group of students to the intervention plan (often referred to as "response to intervention," or RTI). It should be noted that, although these stages of the problem-solving process are described here in a linear fashion, in reality this is a fluid and circular process. The process moves through defining a problem, analyzing available data, implementing and evaluating an intervention plan, and then using all of this information either to validate the original problem definition or to rework the process from the beginning.

Through the use of a building-based problem-solving team, school personnel can identify and address individual and programmatic needs for the entire student population. At the universal level, the problem-solving team can use information such as discipline referrals, attendance rates, and academic assessments to identify issues that may require system-wide interventions through changes to curriculum or staff training. As noted previously, classroom groups provide a ready-made setting for CBT interventions designed to increase coping skills or social/emotional competence of all students.

Through the problem-solving process, the school-based team can set benchmarks for student behavior and academic performance, and review individual performance in accordance with these benchmarks. Small group CBT interventions can be targeted for students identified with specific intra- or interpersonal problems, such as anxiety or anger management. In the course of comparing students' performance with benchmarks, it is critical that attention be given to making comparisons not only between individual performance and benchmarks, but also between individual performance and peer group norms. When performance of individuals deviates significantly from both established benchmarks and peer group norms, those students should be consider for an appropriate referral for some type of intervention services. When peer group norms deviate substantially from benchmarks, however, the appropriate unit of intervention would be the entire class or school (i.e., intervention at the universal level).

The progress monitoring and plan evaluation (RTI) stages of the problem-solving process are critical with regard to identifying students who are benefiting from universal or targeted interventions. Analysis of data related to outcomes of group interventions can be used as the basis for referrals of students as needed for more intensive group interventions or individual treatment. There are many tools that could be used to assess students mental health needs and to monitor progress of group treatment. Murphy and Christner (2006) offer a review of some basic assessment tools for mental health in school settings.

CONCLUSION

Providing mental health interventions in general, and specifically CBT group interventions, within educational settings has considerable promise. Schools are an ideal setting to conduct these interventions, not only because of the convenience of accessibility to students, but also because of the social aspects that create a "laboratory" for students to practice newly learned skills. The current culture of schools has embraced the systemic problem-solving approach, which allows for interventions at various levels including prevention, early intervention, and intensive treatment. CBT group interventions can play a significant role at each of these levels. We offered a brief review of several evidence-based group interventions for anger, anxiety, and depression. However, we recommend that readers review individual chapters to address these specific problems within this text, and other current resources regarding the implementation of school-based CBT interventions (see Mennuti, Freeman, & Christner, 2006).

RECOMMENDED READINGS

Hoagwood, K., & Erwin, H. (1997). Effectiveness of school-based mental health services for children: A 10-year research review. *Journal of Child and Family Studies, 6*(4), 435–451.

Mennuti, R., & Christner, R. W. (2005). School-based cognitive-behavioral therapy (CBT). In A. Freeman (Ed.), *International Encyclopedia of Cognitive Behavior Therapy*. New York: Springer/Kluwer.

Mennuti, R. B., Freeman, A., & Christner, R. W. (Eds.) (2006). *Cognitive-behavioral interventions in educational settings: A handbook for practice.* New York: Routledge.

REFERENCES

Adelman, H. S., & Taylor, L. (1998). Reframing mental health in schools and expanding school reform. *Educational Psychologist, 33,* 135–152.

Adelman, H. S., & Taylor, L. (2000). Looking at school health and school reform policy through the lenses of addressing barriers to learning. *Children services: Social policy, research, and practice, 3,* 117–132.

Amendola, A., & Scozzie, S. (2004). Promising strategies for reducing violence. *Reclaiming Children and Youth, 13*(1), 51–53.

Armistead, L., Kotchick, B., & Forehand, R. (2004). Teen pregnancy, sexually transmitted diseases, and HIV/AIDS. In L. A. Rapp-Paglicci, C. N. Dulmus, & J. S. Wodarski (Eds.), *Handbook of preventative interventions for children and adolescents* (pp. 227–254). New York: Wiley.

Barrett, P. (1998). Evaluation of cognitive-behavioral group treatments for childhood anxiety disorders. *Journal of Clinical Child Psychology, 27*(4), 459–468.

Barrett, P. M. (1995). *Group coping koala workbook.* Unpublished manuscript, School of Applied Psychology, Griffith University, Austraila.

Barrett, P.M. (1998). Evaluation of cognitive-behavioral group treatments for childhood anxiety disorders. *Journal of Clinical Child Psychology, 27*(4), 459–68.

Basco, M., Glickman, M., Weatherford, P., & Ryser, N. (2000). Cognitive-behavioral therapy for anxiety disorders: Why and how it works. *Bulletin of the Menninger Clinic, 64*(3), 19.

Beck, A. T., Rush, A. J., Shaw, B. F., & Emery, G. (1979). *Cognitive therapy for depression.* New York: Guilford.

Borkovec, T.D., & Ruscio, A.M. (2001). Psychotherapy for generalized anxiety disorder. *Journal of Clinical Psychiatry, 62,* 37–42.

Brock, S. E. (2002b). Group crisis intervention. In S. E. Brock, P. J. Lazarus, & S. R. Jimerson (Eds.), *Best practices in school crisis prevention and intervention* (pp. 385–399). Bethesda, MD: National Association of School Psychologists.

Burnett, P.C. (1994). Self-concept and self-esteem in elementary school children. *Psychology in the Schools, 31,* 164–171.

Cartwright-Hatton, S., Roberts, C., Chitsabesan, P., Fothergill, C., & Harrington, R. (2004). Systematic review of the efficacy of cognitive behavior therapies for childhood and adolescent anxiety disorders. *British Journal of Clinical Psychology, 43,* 421–436.

CASEL. (2003). Creating connections for student success: Annual Report. Chicago: Author.

Christner, R. W., & Allen, J. S. (2003, Spring). Introduction to cognitive-behavioral therapy (CBT) in the schools. *Insight, 23*(3), 12–14.

Christner, R. W., Stewart-Allen, J., & Mennuti, R. B. (2004, August). School-based cognitive-behavior therapy (CBT). *Pennsylvania Psychologist Quarterly, 64*(8), 22–23.

Clarke, G. N., Lewinsohn, P. M., & Hops, H. (1990). *Instructor's manual for the adolescent coping with depression course.* Eugene, OR: Castalia Press.

Clarke, G. N., Rohde, P., Lewinsohn, P. M., Hops, H., & Seeley, J. R. (1999). Cognitive-behavioral treatment of adolescent depression: Efficacy of acute group treatment and booster sessions. *Journal of the American Academy of Child and Adolescent Psychiatry, 38,* 272–279.

Committee for Children (1997). *The second step: A violence prevention curriculum.* Seattle, WA: Author.

Cohen, J. A., Berliner, L., & March, J. S. (2000). Treatment of children and adolescents. In E. B. Foa, T. M. Keane, & M. J. Friedman (Eds.), *Effective treatments for PTSD: Practice guidelines from the International Society for Traumatic Stress Studies* (pp. 106–138). New York: Guilford.

Doll, B., & Hess, R. (2004). School dropout. In L. A. Rapp-Paglicci, C. N. Dulmus, & J. S. Wodarski, *Handbook of preventative interventions for children and adolescents* (pp. 359–380). New York: Wiley.

Donoghue, R., Wheeler, A., Prout, M., Wilson, H., & Reinecke, M. (2006). Understanding depression in children and adolescents: Cognitive-behavioral interventions. In R. B. Mennuti, A. Freeman, & R. W. Christner (Eds.), *Cognitive-Behavioral Interventions in Educational Settings: A Handbook for Practice.* New York: Routledge.

Dopheide, J. (2006). Recognizing and treating depression in children and adolescents. *American Journal of Health-System Pharmacology, 63,* 233–243.

Durham, R., Fisher, P., Dow, M., Sharp, D., Power, K., Swan, J., & Morton, R. (2004). Cognitive behavior therapy for good and poor prognosis generalized anxiety disorder: A clinical effectiveness Study F. *Clinical Psychology and Psychotherapy, 11,* 145–157.

Dwivedi, K., & Gupta, A. (2000). "Keeping cool:" Anger management through group work. *Support for Learning, 15*(2), 76–81.

Dulmus, C., & Rapp-Paglicci, L. (2004). Prevention and resilience. In L. A. Rapp-Paglicci, C. N. Dulmus, & J. S. Wodarski (Eds.), *Handbook of preventative interventions for children and adolescents* (pp. 3–11). New York: Wiley.

Ehly, S. W., & García-Vázquez, E. (1998). Groups in the school context. In K. C. Stoiber & T. R. Kratochwill (Eds), *Handbook of group intervention for children and families* (pp. 9–28). Boston: Allyn & Bacon.

Feindler, E. L., & Ecton, R. B. (1986). *Adolescent anger control: Cognitive behavioral techniques.* Boston, MA: Allyn & Bacon.

Farrell, A., Meyer, A., Sullivan, T. & Kung, E. (2003). Evaluation of the responding in peaceful and positive ways (RIPP) seventh grade violence prevention curriculum. *Journal of Child and Family Studies, 12*(1), 101–120.

Fisher, P. L., & Durham, R. C. (1999). Recovery rates in generalized anxiety disorder following psychological therapy: An analysis of clinically significant change in STAI-T across outcome studies since 1990. *Psychological Medicine, 29*, 1425–1434.

Foa, E. B., Dancu, C. V., Hembree, E. A., Jaycox, L. H., Meadows, E. A., & Street, G. P. (1999). A comparison of exposure therapy, stress inoculation training, and their combination for reducing posttraumatic stress disorder in female assault victims. *Journal of Consulting and Clinical Psychology, 67*, 194–200.

Fraser, M. W. (1996). Aggressive behavior in childhood and early adolescence: An ecological-developmental perspective on youth violence. *Social Work, 41*, 347–361.

Friedman, R. M., Katz-Levy, J. W., Manderscheid, R. W., & Sondheimer, D. D. (1996). *Prevalence of serious emotional disturbance in children and adolescents* (No. DHHS Pub. No. 96-3098). Washington DC: US Government Printing Office.

Goldstein, A. P., Glick, B, & Gibbs, J. C. (1998). *Aggression replacement training: A comprehensive intervention for aggressive youth.* Champaign, IL: Research Press.

Hoagwood, K., & Erwin, H. (1997). Effectiveness of school-based mental health services for children: A 10-year research review. *Journal of Child and Family Studies, 6*(4), 435–451.

Hwang, Y. E. (1995). Student apathy, lack of self-responsibility and false self-esteem failing American schools. *Education, 115*, 484–490.

Iverson, A. M. (2002). Best practices in problem-solving team structure and process. In A. Thomas & J. Grimes (Eds.), *Best practices in school psychology IV* (pp. 21–36). Bethesda, MD: National Association of School Psychologists.

Jones, M. K., & Menzies, R. G. (1998). Danger ideation reduction therapy (DIRT) for obsessive-compulsive washers: A controlled trial. *Behaviour Research and Therapy, 36*, 959–970.

Kellner, M., & Bry, B. 1999. The effects of anger management groups in a day school for emotionally disturbed adolescents. *Adolescence, 34*(136), 645–652.

Kusche, C. A., & Greenberg, M. T. (1994). *The PATHS (Promoting Alternative Thinking Strategies) curriculum.* Seattle, WA: Developmental Research and Programs.

Lacey, T. 2004. Group therapy and CBT. *Counseling & Psychotherapy Journal, 15*(2), 34–35.

Larkin, R., & Thyer, B. (1999). Evaluating cognitive-behavioral group counseling to improve elementary school students' self-esteem, self-control, and classroom behavior. *Behavioral Interventions, 14*, 147–161.

LeCroy, C. W., & Mann, J. (2004). Preventing substance abuse among youth: Universal, selected, and targeted interventions. In L. A. Rapp-Paglicci, C. N. Dulmus, & J. S. Wodarski (Eds.), *Handbook of preventative interventions for children and adolescents.* New York: Wiley.

Lochman, J. E., & Lampton, L.B. (1986). Situation social problem-solving skills and self-esteem of aggressive and nonaggressive boys. *Journal of Abnormal Child Psychology, 14*, 605–617.

McCarter, A. K., Sowers, K. M, & Dulmus, C. N. (2004). Adolescent suicide prevention. In L. A. Rapp-Paglicci, C. N. Dulmus, & J. S. Wodarski (Eds.), *Handbook of preventative interventions for children and adolescents.* New York: Wiley.

Meichenbaum, D. (1977). *Cognitive behavioral modification: An integrative approach.* New York: Plenum Press.

Mennuti, R., & Christner, R. W. (2005). School-based cognitive-behavioral therapy (CBT). In A. Freeman (Ed.), *International Encyclopedia of Cognitive Behavior Therapy* (pp. 343–347). New York: Springer/Kluwer.

Mennuti, R. B., Freeman, A., & Christner, R. W. (Eds.) (2006). *Cognitive-behavioral interventions in educational settings: A handbook for practice.* New York: Routledge.

Meyer, A. L., Farrell, A. D., Northup, W., Kung, E., & Plybon, L. (2000). *Promoting non-violence in middle schools: Responding in peaceful and positive ways, a volume in the series of prevention in library practice.* New York: Plenum.

Meichenbaum, D. (1977). *Cognitive behavioral modification: An integrative approach.* New York: Plenum.

Murphy, V. B., & Christner, R. W. (2006). A cognitive-behavioral case conceptualization approach for working with children and adolescents. In R. B. Mennuti, A. Freeman, & R. W. Christner (Eds.), *Cognitive behavioral interventions in educational settings: A handbook for practice.* New York: Routledge Publishing.

National Center for Education Statistics (2005). *Digest of education statistics, 2004.* Publication # NCES 2006005. Retrieved May 16, 2006, from http://nces.ed.gov/programs/digest/d04/

National Institute of Mental Health (2004). *Treatment of children with mental disorders* [NIH Publication No. 04-4702]. Bethesda, MD: National Institute of Mental Health, National Institutes of Health, US Department of Health and Human Services.

O'Rourke, K., & Worzbyt, J. C. (1996). *Support groups for children.* Washington, DC: Accelerated Development.

President's New Freedom Commission on Mental Health (2003). *Final report to the President: Full version.* Washington, DC: Author.

Rapp-Paglicci, L. A., Dulmus, C. N., & Wodarski, J. S. (Eds.) (2004). *Handbook of preventative interventions for children and adolescents.* New York: Wiley.

Reinecke, M. A., Dattilio, F. M., & Freeman, A. (Ed.). (2003). *Cognitive therapy with children and adolescents: A casebook for clinical practice* (2nd ed.). New York: Guilford.

Reynolds, W. M., & Coates, K. I. (1986). A comparison of cognitive-behavioral therapy and relaxation training for the treatment of depression in adolescents. *Journal of Consulting and Clinical Psycholology, 54,* 653–660.

Silverman, W. (2003). Using CBT in the treatment of social phobia, separation anxiety and GAD. *Psychiatric Times.* Retrieved May 16, 2006, from http://www.kpchr.org/public/acwd/acwd.html

Silverman W. K., & Kurtines W. M. (1996). *Anxiety and phobic disorders: A pragmatic approach.* New York: Plenum.

Shure, M. B. (2001). *I can problem solve (ICPS): An interpersonal cognitive problem-solving program.* Champaign, IL: Research Press.

Smallwood, D., Williams, B., & McDonald, D. (2006). Cognitive-behavioral approaches to school crisis response. In R. B. Mennuti, A. Freeman, & R. W. Christner (Eds.), *Cognitive-behavioral interventions in educational settings: A handbook for practice* (pp. 407–427). New York: Routledge.

Stark, K. D., & Kendall, P. C. (1996). *Treating depressed children: Therapist manual for "Action."* Ardmore, PA: Workbook Publishing.

Tilly III, W. D. (2002). Best practices in school psychology as a problem-solving enterprise. In A. Thomas & J. Grimes (Eds.), *Best practices in school psychology IV* (pp. 21–36). Bethesda, MD: National Association of School Psychologists.

Weissberg, R. P., & Gesten, E. L. (1982). Considerations for developing effective school based social problem-solving (SPS) training programs. *School Psychology Review, 11*(1), 56–63.

Wiggins, J. D., & Wiggins, M. M. (1992). Elementary students' self-esteem and behavioral ratings related to counselor time-task emphases. *The School Counselor, 39,* 377–381.

Chapter Six

Application of Rational Emotive Behavior Therapy to Groups within Classrooms and Educational Settings

Ann Vernon

From its inception, rational emotive behavior therapy (REBT) has been educative in nature, its goal being to help people help themselves by teaching them positive mental health concepts. Early in the practice of REBT, Albert Ellis and his colleagues began applying the theory to children and found it to be a very effective approach (DiGiuseppe, 1999; Vernon, 1997; 2002). A long-time proponent of the application of REBT in educational settings, Ellis established the Living School, a small private grade school housed at the Institute for Advanced Study in Rational Psychotherapy (now called the Albert Ellis Institute). From 1971–1975, teachers presented REBT principles in the classroom to improve children's emotional well-being (DiGiuseppe, 1999; Vernon, 2006a).

Although the Living School has long since ceased to exist, there has been concerted effort over the years to translate REBT principles into structured lessons and curriculums (Knaus, 1974; Vernon, 1989a, b; 1998a, b, c; 2006a, b). In addition, Bernard (2001) developed a program to improve school achievement through classroom lessons that address topics such as procrastination, low-frustration tolerance, perfectionism, anxiety, and self-rating, all of which interfere with school performance.

There is also long-standing history of REBT and its applications to small group therapy. Ellis started his first REBT group in 1959, noting several advantages to a group approach. Perhaps most significant is the fact that many people enter therapy for interpersonal and relationship problems, so because the group is a social situation, Ellis maintained that many problems can be more easily assessed and treated than they can in individual therapy (Ellis, 1992; 1997). In addition, Ellis noted that clients have a better opportunity to discover others' irrational beliefs and help them dispute them, which gives them practice in identifying and disputing their own beliefs. A further caveat is that group members are more likely to follow through with homework assignments when they are accountable to an entire group. They can also help each other identify effective homework assignments (Ellis, 1997).

REBT groups have been used with a variety of client problems such as depression, interpersonal anxiety, self-esteem, bulimia, test anxiety, parenting, assertion, attention deficit hyperactivity disorder, and marital problems (Dryden, 2002). Dryden also noted that groups have been used in many different settings such as hospitals, the work place, schools, and universities to help clients apply rational principles to problems of every day living.

The purpose of this chapter is two-fold. First, to describe applications of REBT to children and adolescents in classroom groups through implementation of a rational emotive education (REE) curriculum. The core REE principles, implementation considerations, and specific REE lessons that illustrate the process will be addressed. Several other methods of reinforcing REBT principles in the classroom setting will also be described. Second, applications of core principles to various types of small groups (REBGT) in school or mental health settings with children and adolescents will also be discussed.

CLASSROOM APPLICATIONS

A Prevention Approach

Unlike other forms of therapy, an integral part of REBT is its emphasis on teaching and prevention. Knaus (1974) described it as a therapeutic approach "by which children can be taught sane mental health concepts and the skills to use these concepts" (p. 1). Inherent in this definition is the notion that there are identifiable concepts that should be presented to children. While it may seem as if this is stating the obvious, most therapeutic approaches do not emphasize skill acquisition in a deliberate manner; thus, the concept of teaching mental health skills to children and adolescents is a significant distinguishing feature of REBT.

Skill acquisition is critical given that children and adolescents are increasingly dealing with more complex challenges in this contemporary society. Young people often have very little if any control over things that affect their lives. For example, they do not have any say if their parents divorce, remarry, move, change jobs, or abuse them. They have no choice about whether their parents belittle them, ignore them, or ridicule them. Despite this lack of control, they still have to deal with the problems associated with these events. In addition, they also have to contend with normal developmental challenges: the physical, cognitive, and emotional upheaval associated with puberty; peer relationships and issues related to belonging and rejection; transitions; sexual identity; and achievement and mastery, to name but a few.

How children and adolescents deal with more serious situational challenges as well as normal developmental issues is compounded by the fact that school-age children are concrete thinkers. The shift from concrete to formal operational thinking begins at about age 11, but it is not attained until age 15 or 20 (Kaplan, 2000). As they move into formal operational thinking, adolescents begin to think more abstractly, develop the ability to hypothesize, and consider alternatives, according to Kaplan. However, they apply these skills erratically and are often unable to link events, feelings, and situations.

The level of cognitive development plays a central role in how children and adolescents interpret and respond to their life experiences (Vernon & Clemente, 2005).

For example, as concrete thinkers they will have more difficulty understanding why their parents are divorcing, but as formal operational thinkers, they are better able to understand complex relationships and consider multiple perspectives. However, until they have achieved formal operational thinking, children and adolescents are limited in their ability to make good judgments, to conceptualize situations accurately, and to understand ramifications of their own and others' behavior.

There is a strong interface between cognitive development and rational thinking. Vernon (2002) noted that concrete thinkers overgeneralize and "awfulize," lack the ability to put problems in perspective, and fail to distinguish between facts and assumptions. In addition, children and adolescents' sense of time is in the "here and now," which predisposes them to more impulsive behavior that can have consequences far beyond their ability to comprehend. Teaching them how to think more rationally in order to more effectively deal with problematic issues is imperative.

Wilde (1992) noted that REBT empowers children by "arming" them with knowledge and skills, emphasizing that this information can be utilized in present as well as future problematic situations. While these skills can be taught to children individually, in small groups, and through classroom approaches, the psycho-educational nature of rational emotive education (REE) is uniquely suited for classroom group approaches for several reasons. First, the principles can be easily transferred into lessons that teach children the core REBT concepts. Second, it is a comprehensive approach in that by identifying irrational beliefs that perpetuate problems, children gain a better understanding of how to change negative feelings and self-defeating behaviors. Third, the concepts can be adapted to different age levels, ethnicities, and intelligence levels. In addition, various learning styles are accommodated for by the wide variety of rational emotive methods that can be employed in delivering the lessons. Finally, it is a skills-oriented approach that equips children with cognitive, emotive, and behavioral strategies to apply to problems of daily living, both in the present and the future (Vernon, 2004a).

Given that almost 70% of children and adolescents who receive mental health services do so only at school, coupled with the fact that the number of students needing mental health services is increasing (Farmer, Burns, Phillips, Angold, & Costello, 2003), it is important to identify effective emotional education programs to implement in the school setting. According to Gonzalez and colleagues (2004), "Rational emotive behavior therapy has emerged as a popular form of therapy with many applications for mental and nonmental health professionals" (p. 222). The core REBT principles upon which rational emotive education are based will be subsequently described.

Core Principles

Rational-emotive education (REE) is based on the assumption that it is possible and highly desirable to teach children and adolescents how to help themselves deal more effectively with the situational and developmental challenges they will encounter throughout life. The core principles of REBT—that emotional problems result from irrational beliefs about the event rather than from the event itself, and that these irrational beliefs can be disputed, resulting in more moderate, healthy feelings and productive behaviors—form the basis of a REE program. In addition, an understanding of the A-B-C-D-E-F paradigm is an integral component of REE (Dryden & Neenan, 2002; Dryden, DiGiuseppe, &

Neenan, 2003). The internal or external activating event (A), which results in feelings and behaviors (C, consequences) that are generated by rational or irrational beliefs (B). If the beliefs are rational—that is, they are in the form of wishes and preferences, and they are logical, flexible, and consistent with reality, the feelings are moderate and appropriate and the behaviors are self-enhancing. In contrast, irrational beliefs result in more extreme negative emotions and self-defeating behaviors. Irrational beliefs which exist in the form of "shoulds" and dogmatic "musts" are rigid or extreme, illogical, inconsistent with reality, and detrimental (Dryden, 2003).

Helping individuals identify the four core irrational beliefs (demands, awfulizing, low frustration tolerance, and depreciation) is an integral part of the REBT process. According to Ellis (1994), demands form the core of unhealthy responses to the activating event. Dryden (2003) described a demand as "a rigid belief where the person dogmatically insists that certain conditions must or must not exist" (p. 12). As Dryden noted, demands may be directed towards oneself, others, or the conditions of the world. Awfulizing beliefs emanate from the demand that things should not be bad, and these beliefs tend to be extreme exaggerations. Awfulizing is characterized by thinking that it is the end of the world or that things are terrible. Low frustration tolerance is the notion that frustration should not exist and that it cannot be tolerated. Depreciation beliefs can relate to self, others, or life conditions and stem from the demand that people or life's conditions must conform to one's desires (Dryden, 2003).

If irrational beliefs exist, the next step in the paradigm is to dispute these beliefs (D). The major goal of disputation is to engage individuals in questioning the logic, productivity, and reality of the irrational beliefs (Dryden, DiGiuseppe, & Neenan, 2003). Empirical, logical, and pragmatic Socratic disputes, in combination with didactic disputations, are commonly used to help achieve the effective new philosophy (E) and the effective new feeling (F). With younger clients, however, disputing must be employed in more creative, developmentally appropriate ways (Vernon, 2002; Vernon, 2006a, b).

Rational-Emotive Education Lessons

REE lessons are typically experiential, with a significant amount of student involvement and group interaction, which increases the likelihood that children will be engaged in the activity. Understandings are deduced from the use of such methods as games, role-playing, art activities, simulations, bibliotherapy, experiential activities, guided discussions, music and writing activities, and worksheets. In addition, considerable time is spent debriefing the lesson so that children master the content through carefully guided discussions.

REE lessons are developed around the following basic REBT concepts: self-acceptance, feelings, beliefs, and disputing beliefs (Vernon, 2004a).

1. *Self-acceptance.* REBT practitioners prefer not to use the word self-esteem, since it implies a rating of self. Rather, they use the term self-acceptance, which implies that individuals strive to accept themselves with their strengths as well as their weaknesses. In developing this realistic self-concept, they also learn that there is no such thing as a perfect person; everyone is a fallible human being who will make mistakes. Accordingly, people who make mistakes, have weaknesses, or behave

badly are not bad people because in this theory self-worth is not equated with one's performance.

2. *Feelings.* A common misconception of rational emotive behavior therapy is that it does not deal with emotions. On the contrary, a critical component of REE lessons is learning the connection between thoughts, feelings, and behaviors. Developing a feeling vocabulary, learning to deal with emotional overreactions, assessing the intensity of feelings, and distinguishing between healthy and unhealthy ways to express feelings are also important. Understanding that feelings can change, that the same event can result in different feelings depending on how the event is perceived, and that it is natural to have feelings, are significant concepts.

3. *Beliefs.* A key component of REE is that there are two types of beliefs, rational and irrational. Rational beliefs are self-enhancing and result in moderate feelings that help people achieve their goals; they are realistic preferences that typically result in constructive behaviors (Dryden, 1999). Irrational beliefs result in negative feelings that can lead to self-defeating behaviors. These irrational beliefs manifest themselves in the form of a basic "must" that falls into three main categories: self-demandingness, other-demandingness, and world-demandingness (Ellis, 1994). Self-demandingness refers to the idea that one must always perform well and win others' approval; and if one does not, he or she is incompetent, unworthy, and deserves to suffer. Other-demandingness implies that people with whom one associates must always treat that person kindly, considerately, and fairly. If they do not, they are unworthy, bad, rotten, and deserve to be punished. World-demandingness means that the conditions in which one lives must be enjoyable, hassle free, safe, and favorable; and if they are not, it is awful and horrible and unbearable.

   It is also important that children understand the difference between facts and assumptions. As concrete thinkers, children and many adolescents readily misconstrue events by failing to distinguish between a fact (she didn't sit by me) and an assumption (she's mad at me and doesn't want to be my friend). As previously noted, because of their impulsive nature, it is all too common for young people to act on their assumptions and create more problems when others react to their overreaction.

4. *Disputing Beliefs.* The concept of disputing, a cornerstone of this theory, entails replacing irrational beliefs with rational beliefs in order to achieve a more sensible way of thinking, which in turn results in more moderate emotions and more self-enhancing behavior. The disputational process can take several forms: functional disputes, or questioning the practicality of the irrational beliefs (Ellis & MacClaren, 1998); the Socratic approach, in which questioning gives clients insight into the irrationality of their thinking (Dawson, 1991); the didactic approach, where the differences between rational and irrational beliefs are explained (Ellis & MacClaren, 1998); empirical disputes, which help people evaluate the factual aspects of their beliefs; logical disputes, which enable people to see how illogical it is to escalate desires into demands (Nelson-Jones, 2000), and use of exaggeration or humor.

These types of disputes can be taught directly to children in REE lessons or the concepts can be incorporated into lessons that indirectly teach children to apply the various types of disputations. As previously mentioned, because of their developmental level, children and many adolescents may not have the cognitive skills necessary to do these traditional types of disputations, so it is essential to be creative and develop age-appropriate strategies. For example, young children can be challenged to be "fact detectives," looking for facts as opposed to assumptions, which often result in irrational thinking. They can play games such as "Erase the Irrational" (Vernon, 2006a, pp. 247–248), where they use the analogy of erasing to identify effective disputes for identified irrational beliefs. Children as well as adolescents can engage in a reverse role play with one person being deliberately irrational and another attempting to dispute the other's beliefs. Adolescents respond well to an activity called "Let It Go" (Vernon, 2002, p. 93), where they identify irrational beliefs and write them on slips of paper. When they are able to identify disputes, they can put the slips in a balloon, blow it up, and "let it go," which is a symbolic way of helping them remember what can occur with disputation.

Designing Lessons

Lessons should also follow a specific procedure to assure that objectives are clearly introduced and reinforced throughout the sequence. The first step in this process is to identify the specific grade level. It is advisable to have separate lessons for each grade level if possible so that concepts can be sequentially developed and to ensure that there is no duplication of content. Next, identify one or two specific objectives per lesson. These objectives should be stated in measurable terms, such as "students will identify five irrational beliefs in the story" or "students will describe the difference between rational and irrational beliefs." These objectives must be appropriate for the designated grade level and be presented in a sequential hierarchy as previously noted.

Next, design a stimulus activity that reflects the content of the objectives and is engaging and developmentally/culturally appropriate. Stimulus activities should vary from lesson to lesson within a unit to maintain children's interest. For instance, if the first stimulus activity in a unit on beliefs for sixth graders is to participate in a game show format where players earn points for distinguishing between rational and irrational beliefs, the second stimulus activity could be a paper and pencil activity such as a worksheet where students match irrational beliefs with rational counterparts, and the third activity would engage students in creating rational limericks.

Although the stimulus activity is the heart of the lesson, it is very important to allow adequate time for debriefing in order for students to clarify what they learned and to share ideas. During the debriefing, a guided discussion occurs and consists of two types of questions: content and personalization/application. Content questions pertain to the content of the activity. Examples include: What were some examples of the rational and irrational beliefs you identified during the game show? What did you need to know about irrational and rational beliefs in order to complete the matching activity? How were you able to identify rational ideas to incorporate into your limericks? Personalization or application questions help students personalize the information and apply it to their own lives, such as: Do you usually think more rationally or irrationally? Which type of thinking works best for you? What can you do to help yourself think more rationally? The discussion allows students to learn more about specific skills, be introspective about particular concepts, and gain insights to help them learn more about themselves, their relationships, their behaviors, and their feelings.

Homework, a key component of REBT, can also be assigned as another way to reinforce concepts. Students could be asked to look for examples of rational thinking on

movies or television shows, explain the difference between rational and irrational thinking to parents, or write about a problem they are having and write a rational ending.

Implementation Considerations

The primary purpose of REE lessons is to teach students skills to facilitate their emotional, behavioral, and cognitive development. There is a heavy emphasis on prevention, and as Tollerud and Nejedlo (2004) stressed, the primary infusion of prevention
comes through curriculum offered in the classroom. There are several considerations in
implementing an emotional education curriculum in the classroom.

It is very important to present lessons that are appropriate to the developmental
level of the grade level with whom you are working. For example, it is appropriate to
use the terms *rational* and *irrational* with older adolescents, but with younger children,
the terms *sensible* and *insensible* would be easier for them to grasp. Likewise, younger
children will not understand the concept of disputing unless it is presented in a very
concrete manner, such as with the use of puppets in a dialogue, with one puppet being
insensible and the other being sensible. Similarly, whereas adolescents can more readily
understand how irrational beliefs result in negative feelings and unproductive behaviors, younger children need to have these concepts presented more specifically, such
as making a paper chain to visually illustrate how insensible thoughts create negative
feelings which result in poor behavioral choices.

Presenting the concepts in a sequential manner to assure greater mastery also needs
to be taken into consideration. It is best to introduce these concepts in units. If the first
unit is self-acceptance, all topics pertaining to that would be introduced, followed by
those relating to feelings, beliefs, and so forth. It is also advisable to have a sequential
progression of lessons within the specific units so that concepts can be introduced and
expanded on. For example, in a feelings unit the distinction between healthy and unhealthy feelings precedes the more difficult concept that feelings come from thoughts.
Likewise, when introducing beliefs, a first level would be to distinguish facts from beliefs
before moving on the notion of rational and irrational beliefs.

Several other considerations for implementing REE should be addressed. First, rules
should be established collaboratively with students and should be clearly identified so
that discussion can occur without interruptions. Second, because many of the activities encourage students to look at themselves and to share and learn from classmates,
it is imperative that an atmosphere of trust and group cohesion be established. If the
appropriate atmosphere exists, students often welcome the opportunity to share. It is
not unusual for some students to remain silent, but oftentimes just hearing the other
participants share and discuss is a valuable learning experience.

It is often necessary to utilize some simple get acquainted exercises to increase trust
and cohesiveness. For example, elementary aged children enjoy a simple game called
"People, Places, and Things" (Vernon, 2002, pp. 22–23). Children can be divided into
groups of four and each group is given a circle made out of tag board and divided into
3 areas labeled *people, places, things.* They take turns spinning an arrow (made out of
tag board and attached with a brass fastener so it spins). When it lands on one of the 3
areas, the child spinning responds with one of his or her favorites in that category. Allow
children to play for several minutes so that they all have several opportunities to share.
Introducing several strategies of this nature and varying the small group composition

eventually allows for children to interact with many different classmates, but it is less threatening to do so in small groups at the beginning. The ultimate goal is to increase the size of the groups so that a sense of community is developed with all students.

For older students, forming small groups and having them share three things from their purse or wallet that have personal meaning to them is an effective strategy, as is having them bring in musical selections or movie clips that reflect their values or beliefs. Again, encouraging sharing first in smaller groups ultimately builds trust throughout the class and makes it less threatening for students to share openly. A third consideration in implementing lessons is that during the discussion portion of the lesson, it is highly preferable to have students seated in a circle to facilitate discussion and exchange ideas. Fourth, it is important to make sure that during the discussion, the objectives are clearly reflected in the questions and that they are reinforced throughout the discussion.

For example, if one of the objectives was to identify rational coping self-statements to deal with self-downing, this should be the focus of the discussion rather than how to deal with negative feelings. Finally, it is important to maintain a balance between teaching or presenting the content and engaging in discussion. Utilizing a structure such as the one outlined in this chapter facilitates this and differentiates it from lessons that are less structured and rely more on random discussion as opposed to acquisition and application of specific concepts. Having clear objectives, developing the stimulus activity around these objectives, and identifying specific content and personalization/application questions that reflect the objectives helps the facilitator conduct a well-organized lesson that increases the likelihood that students will acquire the emotional education concepts.

A final note regarding length and frequency of emotional education lessons. Elementary students generally do best with 30-minute lessons, whereas adolescents benefit most if there is a 45-minute time block to allow for adequate discussion. Preferably, lessons can be introduced at least once a week, with reinforcement occurring in the form of the teachable moment, integration into the curriculum, and learning centers. These approaches will be subsequently discussed and followed by sample REE lessons.

Other Classroom Approaches

In addition to emotional education lessons presented to an entire classroom group, rational concepts can be introduced or reinforced in other ways. While these approaches do not present the ideas and teach the skills as specifically as in grade-level lessons, they are valuable in conjunction with an REE curriculum.

The teachable moment.   The basic assumption of this approach is that teachers will seize "teachable moments" to introduce and reinforce rational thinking concepts. There are numerous ways in which this can be done: with the entire class, individually, or with small groups of children.

As an example, suppose that a teacher returns a test and it is obvious that almost all the children are upset with their low scores. At this point, the teacher could introduce rational thinking in the classroom setting by asking children what the score says about them. Does it make them a better or worse person? Does this bad score mean that they will always do poorly on exams? Just because they did not do well on this test, does it necessarily mean they will not do well in the course? Is getting a bad score the worst possible thing that could ever happen to them? Raising disputations of this sort helps children avoid self-downing, awfulizing, and overgeneralizing. A next step could be to ask them what they could have done, if anything, to improve their score, which could result in appropriate goal setting for the next exam. Used preventively, a teacher or coach could spend a few minutes prior to a test, game, or performance and introduce discussion about what students are feeling and thinking about the upcoming event. Helping them identify and dispute irrational beliefs and develop rational coping self-statements and other methods to help them deal with the issue at hand can be very beneficial.

Similarly, this approach can be used with an individual. For example, Selina, a fourth-grader, frequently got upset when learning something new. She would throw down her pencil and tear up her paper and simply not finish the task. When the teacher approached her and asked her to explain what was wrong, Selina replied, "It's too hard—I'll never learn this." The teacher introduced some disputations. Had she ever tried to learn anything before and succeeded? Just because something was hard, did it mean she should give up? Although Selina responded appropriately to these questions, she remained frustrated, so the teacher drew two talking heads. On the first one, she listed Selina's irrational beliefs: "This is too hard—I'll never learn this." On the second one, she helped Selina identify rational self-talk, such as: "This is hard, but I just have to work harder to learn it; I don't like learning hard things, but I can stand it if I do a little at a time." The teacher instructed Selina to keep this visual inside her desk to use as a reminder when she felt frustrated and wanted to give up. As a homework assignment, she asked Selina to read *The Little Engine That Could* (Piper, 1986), a book that described how a little train chanted, "I think I can, I think I can" as he tried to make it up a mountain, and think about how this story applied to her situation.

The informal approach can also be used with small groups of students. For instance, as the teacher was walking through the hall, he noticed a group of young adolescents arguing with each other. As he approached the group, he heard all sorts of accusations being directed at one individual: "You're a horrible, selfish friend…you stole Katinka's boyfriend and we will never forgive you for it. We know you are the one who started all the rumors about us, and we are going to turn all the other girls against you so that no one in this class will ever speak to you again." The teacher wanted to diffuse the situation, so he pulled the group into an empty classroom and asked them to tell him more about the situation. As they talked, he began to challenge some of their assumptions. Where was the evidence that this girl had started all the rumors? Did they know for a fact that she "stole" another's boyfriend? Did they have so much power that they could turn *everyone* against her? Forever is a long, long time—do they really believe that they will *never* speak to her again, or is it possible that they will eventually get over being so upset? These disputations seemed to help de-escalate their emotions and put the problem in better perspective, and eventually they reached a point where they could communicate more effectively about how they felt and listen to the other side of the story.

In each of these situations, if the teacher had not intervened, the problems would have compounded themselves and interfered with the children's ability to concentrate in school. Furthermore, until the underlying beliefs are addressed, the problems would have perpetuated themselves. Nipping problems in the bud through this informal approach helps prevent this from occurring.

To use this approach, it is necessary to have a thorough understanding of the basic REBT principles and the disputation process. In addition, it is important to realize that while it might be easier to tell children how to feel or what to do to solve a problem, it is advisable that they be allowed to work things out for themselves, with proper guidance. Once they are able to dispute their irrational beliefs, they will have more moderate, healthy feelings and be in a better position to look at alternatives and to develop a plan to resolve the problem.

REE learning centers.   Oftentimes elementary and middle school teachers establish learning centers, where students work independently on activities to reinforce concepts presented in class or to introduce new ideas. REE activities can easily be incorporated into this type of format through worksheets, writing, or games. For example, Waters (1979) *Color Us Rational* stories lend themselves to a learning center activity. A copy of several of the stories can be placed at the center as models, along with paper and pencil. After reading one or more of the stories, students are instructed to write a rational story based on one of their own experiences.

Other good center activities involve having students write rational limericks or make rational bumper stickers or posters for their rooms, making up silly songs to help them deal with sad feelings, putting on rational puppet plays, or playing a game of hop scotch, where children have to identify rational self-talk to help them deal with anger or anxiety before jumping to the next space. The teacher is limited only by his or her creativity in designing center activities. They should be engaging and able to be completed independently.

Integration into the curriculum.   Yet another approach to REE emotional education is to integrate the concepts into an existing subject-matter curriculum. When teaching literature, teachers could select and discuss stories that present characters solving problems rationally or expressing feelings in a healthy manner. Topics for themes could be related to self-awareness such as making mistakes, identifying strengths and weaknesses, and the prices and payoffs for perfection. Vocabulary and spelling lessons could include feeling-word vocabularies and definitions.

Social studies lessons could focus on personal and societal values and on a rational understanding of the concept of fairness as it applies to societal groups or to law and order, for example. Students could examine the rational and irrational practices of politicians, the difference between facts and assumptions in political campaigns, or the concept of high-frustration tolerance as it applies to political leaders.

Integration into the curriculum is less direct than a structured lesson, but it is a viable way of reinforcing rational concepts and making them an integral part of the school structure. Although it may seem awkward and forced initially, once teachers become more familiar with the REE concepts, they will find that integration becomes more natural.

Sample Lessons

To illustrate the lesson plan format and the sequential progression of concepts within units, three lessons (elementary, middle school, and high school) are subsequently presented in Table 6.1 on the topic of beliefs. These activities are included in the *Thinking, Feeling, Behaving* emotional education curriculums (Vernon, 2006a, b).

Table 6.1 Sample Rational Emotive Education Lessons

Be A Fact Finder

Objective

To learn to differentiate between facts and assumptions

Materials

- Two sheets of poster paper, one labeled "Facts" and the other "Assumptions"
- Several objects, such as a large ball, a winter coat, a book, and a coloring book

Procedure

1. Introduce the lesson by taping the two sheets of poster paper on the board and offering a simple explanation of each term, such as: a fact is something that we know is true, and an assumption is something that we think is true but we don't have proof. Elicit examples from the children.
2. Next, hold up one of the objects and engage children in a discussion about the facts: for example, the ball is round, large, and red. As children state the facts, list them on the poster paper labeled "facts."
3. After they have identified several facts, ask what assumptions they have about this object when they look at it: for example, the ball can bounce high, the ball is slippery to hold, or the ball isn't heavy. Write these on the poster paper labeled "assumptions."
4. Continue this procedure with several other objects.
5. Next, explain that they can check out assumptions and that by doing that, they learn more facts. For example, the fact is that the book is thick and that there are a lot of pages. An assumption is that the book is good, but until they actually read the book, they won't know if it is good or not. Ask for other examples of how to check out facts.

Discussion

Content Questions

1. What is the difference between a fact and an assumption?
2. If you want to know whether an assumption is true, what can you do?
3. Do you think it is difficult or easy to identify facts? How do you do it?
4. Do you think it is difficult or easy to identify assumptions? How do you do it?
5. Do you think it is difficult or easy to tell the difference between a fact and an assumption? How can you tell the difference?

Personalization Questions

1. Do you think you are good at knowing the difference between a fact and an assumption? If so, how do you do it?
2. What is something you can do next time you want to check out an assumption to see whether or not it is a fact? Invite sharing of specific examples of things they want to check out.

O-S-A

Objective

To identify overgeneralizations and selective abstractions

Materials

- An *OSA* handout for each team of two students.

Procedure

1. Explain the concept of overgeneralization and selective abstraction: that they are forms of thinking that can create problems. Overgeneralizations are like exaggerated thinking, where a person assumes that things are always a certain way or never like that. For example, if you had one fight with a friend, an overgeneralization would be that you and your friend *always* fight and will *never* be friends again. Selective abstraction is when you focus on one small part of the whole picture, such as forgetting that up until yesterday, you had gotten perfect grades on all your science papers. Instead, you only focus on the fact that yesterday you missed two. With selective abstraction, you don't get the "big" picture.
2. Divide students into teams of two. Give each team a copy of the *OSA* handout and ask them to underline all of the overgeneralizations and circle all of the selective abstractions.
3. After several minutes, ask teams to share examples of the overgeneralizations and list them on the board. Do the same with the selective abstractions.
Clarify any questions about these concepts.
4. Once they have understood the concepts, put them in groups of four and have them make up a skit with examples of overgeneralizations and selective abstractions.
5. Invite each group to present the skit to the total group.

(Continued)

Table 6.1   Continued

Discussion

Content Questions

1. What is an overgeneralization?
2. What is a selective abstraction?
3. How difficult was it to distinguish between the two?
4. How did you identify examples for the skit?

Personalization Questions

1. Do you ever use overgeneralizations or selective abstractions? If so, are they helpful? If not, what is the effect?
2. What do you think you can do to avoid these types of thinking?
3. What did you learn from this lesson that might be helpful to you?

OSA Handout

Elena is in 6th grade. She doesn't like her teacher because she always picks on her. She says that other kids whisper and talk, but the teacher never yells at them. This really makes Elena mad. Elena is also upset with some of her friends. Today when she went into the lunchroom she saw several girls start to whisper. "They always whisper about me," thinks Elena, so she decides to sit at another table with the boys. But all during the lunch period, Elena can't stop thinking about the fact that she no longer has any friends.

After lunch Elena takes her spelling test and gets all the words right. She is happy about that, but as soon as she goes to science she forgets about how well she did in spelling because the teacher gave an unannounced quiz. Instead of getting all the answers right as she usually does, she missed three. The rest of the afternoon she couldn't think about anything else except how stupid she is.

After school Elena's mother drops her off at home to do her homework and takes Elena's sister shopping. Elena is really mad and accuses her mother of never taking her anywhere. Elena's mother reminds her that she took her shopping by herself just last week. Elena pouts as she does her homework and thinks about how unfair her parents are.

When her parents tell her that it is time for bed, Elena begs to stay up another hour to watch one of her favorite shows. She figures that they won't let her because they never let her do what she wants to do, but they tell her that she can watch the show. Elena is surprised, but happy. She asks again the next night and they tell her no, so once again she is upset because she never gets to do things she wants to do.

I'm a Believer

Objective

To distinguish between rational and irrational beliefs

Materials

- A copy of *I'm a Believer* sorting board and envelope of *I'm a Believer* belief strips for every 2 students
- Pencil for each student

Procedure

1. Introduce the lesson by asking students to define the word *belief* (Webster's definition is that a belief is an opinion or judgment or anything believed to be true).
2. Next, explain that some beliefs are *rational*—that is, they are reasonable,   consistent with reality, and help people achieve goals. Other beliefs are *irrational* because they represent overgeneralizations, exaggerations, and demands. They also are not very realistic or flexible and do not help people achieve goals.
3. Ask students to find a partner. Distribute the sorting boards and envelopes of beliefs to each pair and ask them to read each belief and put it in the rational or irrational belief column on the sorting board.

Discussion

Content Questions

1. How difficult was it to distinguish between the rational and irrational beliefs?
2. What are some of the negative outcomes from thinking irrationally? Invite discussion.

Personalization Questions

1. Do you think you tend to think more rationally or irrationally?
2. If you think irrationally, how has that affected your relationships, performance, and assessment of yourself?
3. What is something you learned from this lesson that you can apply in your life?

I'm a Believer Beliefs

Directions: Cut these beliefs into strips and place in an envelope; make enough sets for every 2 students.

Beliefs:

She's never there for me.

If I don't get all As, it doesn't mean I'm stupid.

I'd like to make first string orchestra.

I'll never speak to him again.

They are the most untrustworthy friends anyone could ever have.

I didn't get that job, but there are other possibilities.

My parents never let me do anything.

Everything I do is wrong.

I hope I do well on this test.

It's totally unfair that the coach picked him to be the captain of the team and not me.

I'm so far behind in my homework I'll never catch up.

I'd rather not have that part in the play, but I can do it if I have to.

I can't stand that teacher.

Nothing I ever do is good enough for them.

She's just doing that to annoy me.

I wish I could look as great as she does.

I wish my parents would let me have more freedom.

If she breaks up with me, my life will never be the same again.

I hope I do well on the job interview.

It is so hard to run the mile, but I just have to keep trying.

I'm a Believer—Sorting Board

Directions: Sort the beliefs in the envelope into the rational or irrational column

Rational

Irrational

Other Ideas for Stimulus Activities

As the above examples illustrated, there are numerous ideas to incorporate into age-appropriate stimulus activities, utilizing the lesson plan format. A few will be mentioned under several different categories, and the reader may refer to curriculums by Bernard (2001), Knaus (1974), and Vernon (1998a,b,c; 2002; 2006a,b) for additional suggestions and complete lessons.

Writing activities.   In a classroom or small group setting, writing can be used to help students develop perspective and learn rational concepts. Children can be invited to write rational limericks, such as the following:

> When I get so mad
> I sometimes act very bad
> And even though at first it seems strange
> I know that my thinking can change
> And then I stop acting like a cad.

They can also write rational endings to their problems. For example, a third-grader wrote about her parents' divorce, stating that at first it seemed like the end of the world. Now she knows that it could have been worse because her parents could have died and she would never see either one of them again.

Music activities.   Children of all ages love music. Younger children enjoy singing rational songs such as this one about overcoming procrastination to the tune of *Mary Had a Little Lamb* (Vernon, 2002, p. 185):

_____ (insert a child's name) had some chores to do, chores to do, chores to do
_____ had some chores to do that she just did not do.
So her mother chewed her out, chewed her out, chewed her out;
So her father chewed her out and said he'd give her two.
So _____ knew she had to work, had to work, had to work;
_____ knew she had to work or miss out on all the fun.
So _____ turned the TV off, TV off, TV off;
_____ put her book away and decided not to play.
Before _____ knew it, the chores were done, the chores were done
Before _____ knew it, the chores were done and she had some fun.

Adolescents, who often listen to depressing music when they are depressed, can be encouraged to rewrite songs to make them more rational.

Art activities. Art is not only very effective with nonverbal children, but it is also an excellent way to help children visualize various concepts. Creating rational bumper stickers or posters can be an effective way to help them remember to think rationally.

Another good strategy for helping adolescents understand consequences of their behavior is to ask them to make a paper chain (Vernon, 2006b, p. 35). On the first link, they identify a negative activating event. On the second link, they identify how they felt or thought, and on subsequent links, consequences of their thinking and behaving. They could also do another chain, identifying the same negative event but this time, identifying more rational thoughts and feelings and subsequent consequences. This visual is very helpful in illustrating the differences between thinking rationally versus irrationally.

Children dealing with anger issues can draw an anger alarm (Vernon, 2002), identifying advantages and disadvantages of hanging onto the anger and then writing down what "pushes" their anger buttons. After discussing what rational things they can tell themselves so that their anger alarm doesn't go off, they can write their responses around the alarm as a reminder to think rationally.

Another art activity to help students identify rational counterparts for irrational thoughts involves drawing around their hand. On each finger, they write their irrational thoughts, and in between the fingers, they write disputes to help them think more rationally.

Experiential activities. Actions often speak louder than words, and children and adolescents frequently remember what they have experienced more acutely than what they talked about. To help children deal with anxiety, have them make a list of what they are anxious or worried about. Then recruit several volunteers to play "Adios Anxiety" (Vernon, 2002, pp. 85–86), where they each use a hopscotch board made out of a plastic tablecloth or an old sheet. Before they can jump ahead, they need to read aloud one of the things they worry about and identify something they can tell themselves to be less worried. This procedure can be repeated with other students.

Another experiential activity relates to perfectionism. In a classroom setting, ask several volunteers to juggle tennis balls. Focus discussion on how perfectly they are doing it, whether it is possible to do everything perfectly, and what it says about people if they don't do things perfectly (Vernon, 2006a, p. 107).

Children and adolescents alike can learn more about the negative consequences associated with procrastination, as well as how they can change their self-talk to avoid this problem. First, students make a list of things they put off or procrastinate about.

Next, ask for several volunteers to illustrate the process. Ask the volunteers to lie down on the floor, face up. As the facilitator reads what each volunteer procrastinates about, he or she places a stack of newspapers on that individual. After all items for each person have been read, discuss how they feel with everything "piled up" and inform them that they can get rid of their piles if they can identify rational coping self-statements to help them stop procrastinating. Once they have done this and the newspapers have been removed, the procedure can be repeated with other volunteers or they can simply identify rational coping self-statements in relation to the list they had generated (Vernon, 2002, p. 183).

Games. A simple way to help younger children learn to differentiate between facts and assumptions is to give each pair of students a tic-tac-toe board. After they have designated themselves as X's or 0's, the facilitator reads a series of items such as: corn is a vegetable, Iowa is the best state in the United States, everyone likes to play tag, and there are many different types of dogs. As these are read, children take turns identifying each item as a fact or an assumption and putting a mark on the tic-tac-toe board. Before moving to the next item, the facilitator checks for verification that the response was correct, and if it was not, the child cannot make a mark (Vernon, 2006a, pp. 131–132).

Another game for younger children, designed to help them expand their feeling vocabularies and identify ways to deal with negative emotions, is to play "Feelings-Go-Round." The game is played like musical chairs. When the music stops, the person left standing draws a feeling word from a box, describes a time when he or she felt this way, and if it is a negative feeling, identifies a helpful way to deal with this negative emotion (Vernon, 2006a, p. 127).

RATIONAL EMOTIVE BEHAVIOR THERAPY: SMALL GROUP APPLICATIONS

According to DiGiuseppe (1999), Ellis has been a strong proponent of Rational Emotive Behavior Group Therapy (REBGT) and suggested that groups are most helpful for children with social difficulties because the exposure to others helps them develop social skills.

DiGiuseppe (1999) identified two REBGT group formats: an open-ended format in which group members take turns presenting problems they would like help with, and the homogeneous group, in which all members share a similar problem. In this type of group, the facilitator introduces exercises and discussion related to the problem and helps group members apply skills to their particular problem. Dryden and Neenan (2002) noted that these REBGT interventions are at least initially introduced by the facilitator, but after group members have learned how to use REBT, the facilitator takes a less active role unless a member is giving poor or inappropriate advice or when the group is off track in their efforts to intervene with each other. This may or may not be feasible with school-aged children, especially younger children, who would need the structure and a more directive facilitator style. However, high school students may be well equipped once they understand the REBT concepts to take on more responsibility for the group process.

Vernon (2004b) described two types of small groups: the problem-centered group and the preventive group. In the problem-centered group, which is similar to the open-ended format DiGiuseppe (1999) identified, members raise their current concerns and are taught to apply REBT principles for problem resolution by the group leader as well as by the group members, depending on their ability to do so. It is important to note that all members may be dealing with different problems and each member has the opportunity to receive the group's full attention to his or her individual concerns. As Bergin (2004) noted, this type of group may be more appropriate for intermediate, junior high, or high school students who are better able to articulate their problems, understand the concepts, and help others apply them. The format allows group members to learn from the problems they themselves present and also by observing how other members' problems are addressed. The group leader may use didactic methods to teach disputational skills, the ABC format, and problem-solving strategies as appropriate. Modeling rational thinking and helping group members apply rational principles to their every day problems is the primary goal. In a problem-centered group, members typically volunteer to participate, although teachers or parents may recommend that they attend. Counselors may also invite members to join a group as a follow-up to individual counseling.

A variation of the problem-centered group is to select a specific topic that all participants are grappling with, such as anger, procrastination, perfectionism, low-frustration tolerance, or conflict resolution. In addition, topics such as dealing with parental divorce or other types of loss, abuse, or transitions such as moving may be the focus. Group members may volunteer because they identify with the particular topic or they may be referred and requested to join. With this approach, the discussion is limited to the specific topic and the leader helps members apply REBT concepts to deal with current issues relative to the topic. Similar to the homogeneous group identified by DiGiuseppe (1999), group participants are encouraged to help each other, but the leader also assumes a more active role, at least initially and depending on the age and level of participation of the group members. The group setting provides the opportunity for members to learn more about their issues, explore and express feelings, and learn how their thoughts affect their feelings and behaviors.

Another type of group is the developmental, or preventive group. This group teaches children and adolescents how to apply REBT concepts to help them deal with the typical challenges involved in growing up. The approach is similar to the classroom group in that the focus is on prevention, but the small group is limited to 6-10 children, thus allowing for more interaction and personalization of concepts. Typically a theme is chosen for a 6-8 week module, with a different aspect of the topic targeted at each session. Topics may include relationships with parents, peers, or teachers; communication and assertion; school success; problem-solving and decision making; or self-acceptance. Or, the focus may be more specifically on teaching REBT concepts such as the ABC process, identifying and disputing irrational beliefs, and so forth. In the preventive group, the assumption is that participants do not have a particular problem, but that they are learning skills.

It is imperative that the specific content of the sessions be developmentally and culturally appropriate. This approach is generally more didactic, and a variety of techniques are used to introduce concepts: role playing, games, simulations, art and music activities, videos, or bibliotherapy, for example. The intent is to teach concepts and engage group members in discussions and activities that facilitate their understanding of rational principles that they can apply to present and future developmental concerns. Some of the topics may be similar to those presented in the general problem-solving groups, but there is not the assumption in forming these groups that students who volunteer or are asked to join have a significant problem; this approach is more appropriate for anyone and is more preventive than remedial.

Example of a Topic-Specific Problem-Centered Group Sequence

To illustrate the REBGT approach, a six-session group sequence will be outlined. The group is designed for high school students who are having difficulty in romantic relationships. Assume that the 6 students participating in the group volunteered because they are having relationship problems and that the group sessions are each 45 minutes in length.

Session 1.   Assuming that students do not know each other well, it is important to engage them in at least one get-acquainted exercise to help build trust. Following a go-around of introductions, participants will be asked to respond to the following on 4 quadrants of a large index card: (a) What is something others can't tell by looking at you? (b) What is one positive characteristic that you think is important in relationships? (c) What is one negative characteristic that you think is detrimental to relationships? (d) What would you like to learn as a result of this group? Individuals will be invited to share. After this sharing, it is advisable to involve the group in establishing some guidelines such as respecting others' opinions, maintaining confidentiality, and being honest about their issues.

In order to determine what types of relationship problems the group wishes to deal with, the first lesson involves group members in completing a short questionnaire which asks them to identify the following: (a) What is currently most troublesome about the relationship you are currently involved in? (b) On a scale of 1 (low) to 5 (high), how much does this problem affect you? (c) What are you telling yourself about this relationship? (d) What would you like to see as an outcome of this relationship?

Invite sharing, which will give the facilitator an idea about irrational thinking patterns and the relationship issues in general. Before adjourning, ask participants to come to the next session having identified (in writing) a specific negative activating event that occurred in the relationship during the week, how they felt about it, and what thoughts they had related to the specific event.

Session 2.   Begin the second session by reviewing the ground rules identified in the previous session and then inviting students to share their homework assignment. As they share, the facilitator helps members differentiate between rational and irrational beliefs and explains the A-B-C process, emphasizing that it is not the event itself, but what one thinks about the event that creates negative feelings. After adequate discussion and clarification, describe the four types of irrational beliefs: self-depreciation, demanding, low-frustration tolerance, and awfulizing/overgeneralizing and ask members to identify examples of these based on their current or past relationships. Conclude with a homework assignment which is to identify irrational beliefs in their relationship interactions throughout the next week.

Session 3.   At the beginning of this session, do a go-around, asking members to share examples of irrational beliefs from their homework assignment. Emphasize the B-C (beliefs, emotional/behavioral consequences) connection by pointing out how some members felt differently about a similar event because of what they were telling themselves. Because many relationship problems are based on assumption, play the "telephone" game, where one person shares a piece of information about his or her relationship, whispers it to the next person, and so on—with the person at the end stating out loud what he or she heard. Focus discussion on the negative consequences of rumors and basing behaviors on assumptions. To help them learn to identify specific cognitive distortions pertinent to relationships, give them a handout with examples:

> I can't stand it if we break up.
> If we break up, it will prove that I am worthless.
> I'll never find someone I care about as much as this person.
> Life will never be the same without this relationship.
> There must be something wrong with me or this wouldn't be happening.
> I can't think of anything worse than ending this relationship.
> I'll never get over this.

Invite participants to generate other examples and introduce the concept of disputing by helping them see that they could stand it, even if it will be difficult, and so forth. The homework assignment for the next session is to write out all of their irrational beliefs about this relationship and think of what they could say to themselves to challenge them.

Session 4.   Begin session 4 with an invitation to share the results of their homework assignment. Typically, this can take most of the session, with facilitator intervention about different types of disputes: where is the evidence? If this was your best friend going through this, would you tell this person he or she was worthless or that life isn't worth living? How many people do you know who have survived relationship breakups—and if they have, what makes you different? Demonstrating this through a role play with the facilitator modeling disputes based on an activating event presented by one of the group members may be helpful.

The homework assignment for the following week is to keep a self-help form where they identify in the first column the antecedents (A), the beliefs (B) in the second column, the emotional and behavioral consequences (C) in the third column, and possible disputes (D) in the next column.

Session 5.   Invite group members to share their self-help forms and encourage other group members to help each other distinguish between rational and irrational beliefs and to identify effective disputes. Next, break them into pairs and ask one person to role play the activating event and the partner to help them work through the A-B-C-D model. Debrief and then switch roles. After each person has had a turn to present a problem, process what occurred and address questions. As a homework assignment for the following session, ask participants to identify 4 things they learned about relationships as a result of the group and how these learnings have impacted the relationship.

Session 6.   In this final session, ask participants to share what they have learned and how this has impacted their relationships. Also encourage them to share irrational beliefs they are still struggling to dispute and as a group, generate alternative disputes. Review the A-B-C-D model and discuss how the disputational process results in an effective new philosophy (E) and more moderate, less troubling feelings (F). As a closing activity, have the group work together to make a rational poster as a reminder to think rationally about relationships (Copies can be made for all members).

Considerations in Forming Small Groups

Regardless of the type of group, the group leader must develop rapport, create a climate of trust and acceptance, and give positive reinforcement for rational behavior and for learning rational-emotive skills. DiGiuseppe (1999) advised that it is best to group children by presenting problems because having children with several different problems makes it difficult for them to focus on issues that may not pertain to them. He also advised grouping by age because differences in development (e.g., concrete versus formal operational thinkers) could create too many problems in selecting developmentally appropriate lessons or interventions.

As with any type of group, it is important to select participants carefully so as to create a balance between more verbal and less verbal students. Bergin (2004) recommended not putting best friends or worst enemies in the same group since this may interfere with the functioning of the group. Caution should also be exercised when putting students with severe discipline problems in the group since that can be very disruptive. Consulting with teachers is an important part of group selection.

Interviewing potential members prior to being enrolled is advisable (Bergin, 2004). This interview can ascertain their commitment to the group's purposes and their goals for wanting to join the group if they volunteered. In addition, it is an opportunity for the facilitator to determine how compatible individuals would be with other potential members and to address their questions.

CONCLUSION

Given the increasing need for mental health services for children, coupled with the fact that the majority of children and adolescents who receive these services do so in the school setting, it is suggested that educators and therapists take a serious look at how to best provide these services in an educational setting. Rational emotive therapy has been applied with children and adolescents for over 50 years, and Ellis has stressed the importance of a prevention curriculum designed to help young people help themselves by learning positive mental health concepts. Ironically, over 25 years ago, Pothier (1976) advocated for problem prevention, noting that we are in danger of wasting one of our major resources unless we initiate and support preventive mental health programs. He strongly suggested that these types of programs be implemented in the schools as a way of ensuring that all children are provided with a learning environment that promotes positive cognitive, social, and emotional growth. Pothier's concerns at that time are compounded in this contemporary society where more than ever before, young people need to develop emotional resiliency.

Evidence suggests that rational emotive education can be employed in a school setting with youth not only through a structured curriculum, but also through teachable moments, integration into the curriculum, through the learning center approach, and through small group counseling. REE lessons can easily be tailored to the developmental and cultural needs of specific populations through a wide variety of creative, engaging activities to help children and adolescents develop skills to enhance their development.

RECOMMENDED READINGS

Dryden, W., DiGiuseppe, R., & Neenan, M. (2003). *A primer on rational emotive therapy* (2nd ed.). Champaign, IL: Research Press.

Ellis, A.E. (1997). REBT and its application to group therapy. In J. Yankurs and W. Dryden (Eds.), *Special applications of REBT: A therapist's casebook* (pp. 131–161). New York: Springer.

Vernon, A. (2006). *Thinking, feeling, behaving: An emotional education curriculum for children* (Rev. ed.). Champaign, IL: Research Press.

REFERENCES

Bergin, J. J. (2004). Small group counseling. In A. Vernon (Ed.), *Counseling children and adolescents* (3rd ed., pp. 355–390). Denver, CO: Love Publishing.

Bernard, M. E. (2001). *Program achieve: A curriculum of lessons for teaching students how to achieve and develop social-emotional-behavioral well-being* (Vols. 1–6). Laguna Beach, CA: You Can Do It Education.

Dawson, R. W. (1991). REGIME: A counseling and educational model for using RET effectively. In M.E. Bernard (Ed.), *Using rational-emotive therapy effectively: A practitioner's guide* (pp. 112–132). New York: Plenum.

DiGiuseppe, R. (1999). Rational emotive behavior therapy. In H.T. Prout & D.T. Brown (Eds.), *Counseling and psychotherapy with children and adolescents: Theory and practice for school settings* (pp. 252–293). New York: Wiley.

Dryden, W. (1999). *Rational emotive behavioural counselling in action* (2nd ed.). London: Sage.

Dryden, W. (2002). *Fundamentals of rational emotive behaviour therapy: A training handbook*. London: Whurr.

Dryden, W. (Ed.). (2003). *Rational emotive behaviour therapy: Theoretical developments*. New York: Brunner-Routledge.

Dryden, W. & Neenan, M. (2002). *Rational emotive behaviour group therapy*. London: Whurrs.

Dryden, W., DiGiuseppe, R., & Neenan, M. (2003). *A primer on rational emotive therapy* (2nd ed.). Champaign, IL: Research Press.

Ellis, A. E. (1992). Group rational-emotive and cognitive-behavioral therapy. *International Journal of Group Psychotherapy, 42,* 63–80.

Ellis, A. (1994). *Reason and emotion in psychotherapy: A comprehensive method of treating human disturbances* (Rev.ed.). New York: Carol Publishing.

Ellis, A. E. (1997). REBT and its application to group therapy. In J. Yankurs & W. Dryden (Eds.), *Special applications of REBT: A therapist's casebook* (pp. 131–161). New York: Springer.

Ellis, A., & MacClaren, C. (1998). *Rational emotive behavior therapy: A therapist's guide*. Atascadero, CA: Impact Publishers.

Farmer, E. M. Z., Burns, B., Phillips. S. D., Angold, A., & Costello, J.E. (2003). Pathways into and through mental health services for children and adolescents. *Psychiatric Services, 54,* 60–66.

Gonzalez, J. E., Nelson, J. R., Gutkin, T. B., Saunders, A., Galloway, A., & Shwery, C. S. (2004). Rational emotive therapy with children and adolescents: A meta-analysis. *Journal of Emotional and Behavioral Disorders, 12,* 222–235.

Kaplan, P.S. (2000). *A child's odyssey: Child and adolescent development* (3rd ed.). Belmont, CA: Wadsworth.

Knaus, W. (1974). *Rational emotive education: A manual for elementary school teachers*. New York: Institute for Rational Living.

Nelson-Jones, R. (2000). *Six key approaches to counselling and therapy*. London: Continuum.

Piper, W.(1986). *The little engine that could*. New York: Platt and Munk.

Pothier, P.C. (1976). *Mental health counseling with children*. Boston, MA: Little, Brown.

Tollerud, T. R., & Nejedlo, R. J. (2004). Designing a developmental counseling curriculum. In A. Vernon (Ed.), *Counseling children and adolescents* (3rd ed., pp. 391–423). Denver, CO: Love Publishing.

Vernon, A. (1989a). *Thinking, feeling, behaving: An emotional education program for children*. Champaign, IL: Research Press.

Vernon, A. (1989b). *Thinking, feeling, behaving: An emotional education program for adolescents*. Champaign, IL: Research Press.

Vernon, A. (1997). Applications of REBT with children and adolescents. In J. Yankura & W. Dryden (Eds.). *Special applications of REBT: A therapist's casebook* (pp. 11–37). New York: Springer.

Vernon, A. (1998a). *The passport program: A journey through emotional, social, cognitive, and self-development, grades 1–5*. Champaign, IL: Research Press.

Vernon, A. (1998b). *The passport program: A journey through emotional, social, cognitive, and self-development, grades 6–8*. Champaign, IL: Research Press.

Vernon, A. (1998c). *The passport program: A journey through emotional, social, cognitive, and self-development, grades 9–12*. Champaign, IL: Research Press.

Vernon, A. (2002). *What works when with children and adolescents: A handbook of individual counseling techniques*. Champaign, IL: Research Press.

Vernon, A. (2004a). Rational emotive education. *Romanian Journal of Cognitive and Behavioral Psychotherapies, 4*, 23–37.

Vernon, A. (2004b). Applications of rational emotive behavior therapy with children and adolescents. In A. Vernon (Ed.), *Counseling children and adolescents* (3rd ed., pp. 163–187). Denver, CO: Love Publishing.

Vernon, A. (2006a). *Thinking, feeling, behaving: An emotional education curriculum for children* (Rev. ed.). Champaign, IL: Research Press.

Vernon, A. (2006b). *Thinking, feeling, behaving: An emotional education curriculum for adolescents* (Rev. ed.). Champaign, IL: Research Press.

Vernon, A., & Clemente, R. (2005). *Assessment and intervention with children and adolescents: Developmental and multicultural approaches*. Alexandria, VA: American Counseling Association.

Waters, V. (1979). *Color us rational*. New York: Institute for Rational Emotive Therapy.

Wilde, J. (1992). *Rational counseling with school-aged populations: A practical guide*. Muncie, IN: Accelerated Development.

Chapter Seven

Group Cognitive-Behavior Therapy in Outpatient Settings

Robert D. Friedberg

Clinical practice in outpatient settings represents the most common professional setting for cognitive-behavior group therapy (CBGT). Office visits are the most familiar entry points for young patients and their families. In fact, most outpatient mental health environments resemble the professional settings of other referral sources, such as pediatric clinics and schools, which help to facilitate a familiar transition. Given the diminishing financial resources and market pressures resulting in shortened residential and inpatient stays, outpatient settings are pivotal points on the mental health care continuum. Accordingly, conducting CBGT in outpatient settings is a very viable option.

This chapter presents a framework for considering and implementing CBGT in outpatient settings. The chapter's first section begins with a rationale for a group approach, lists several typical outpatient group programs, and briefly reviews the outcome literature supporting the approach. Measures for group member evaluation and selection such as the *Beck Depression Inventory, Second Edition* (BDI-II), *Children's Depression Inventory* (CDI), *Multidimensional Anxiety Scale for Children* (MASC), *Screen for Child Anxiety Related Emotional Disturbances* (SCARED), and *Conners Parent Rating Scales* (CPRS) are recommended. Further, a modular approach to group CBT, including introduction to treatment, self-monitoring, behavioral interventions, priming/problem-solving, self-instruction, rational analysis, and performance attainment is described. Helpful examples of specific interventions within each module are also given. Finally, cautions and considerations in group CBT are explicated.

RATIONALE AND ADVANTAGES OF GROUP CBT

Group therapy offers several advantages to the outpatient cognitive-behavior therapist. First, group therapy accommodates greater numbers of patients in fewer peak after school hours, which has been reported to improve access to care (Tynan, Schuman, & Lampert., 1999). Second, a cognitive-behavioral group offers a learning model characterized by psychoeducation, which makes it similar to school, and consequently, the group may be less stigmatizing for young people (Clarke, DeBar, & Lewinsohn, 2003). Further, group CBT represents a social learning laboratory, where therapists can work with patients to elicit and change thoughts and feelings (Friedberg & Crosby, 2001). Finally, CBGT includes powerful elements such as peer modeling, feedback, group problem-solving, and social comparison processes (Ginsburg, Silverman, & Kurtines, 1995; Lochman, Barry, & Pardini, 2003).

TYPES OF CBT GROUPS IN OUTPATIENT SETTINGS

CBGT is applicable to a plethora of problems typically encountered in outpatient settings. Externalizing disorders, such as oppositional defiant disorders, are suited to group treatment. Similarly, internalizing disorders, such as depression, anxiety, and eating disorders, can be effectively treated with group CBT. There is also promise for using CBGT skills training groups for children with Asperger's Disorder (see chapter 21 in this text).

Depending on the goals of treatment and the children's diagnoses, CBGT may elect a variety of group formats, including psychoeducational, skills training, and process-oriented groups. In purely psychoeducational groups, patients are typically given information about their disorder and possible coping strategies with limited opportunities to practice their acquired skills. Skills training groups directly coach patients in particular techniques such as relaxation, social skills, and problem-solving. Process groups emphasize the interpersonal dynamics occurring within the group. Most group programs combine psychoeducational, skill training, and process elements. There are a number of group protocols that have been developed and researched, several of which I describe below.

Social Effectiveness Therapy for Children (SET-C; Beidel & Turner, 1998) is a 12-week group program where children attend two sessions per week. Each child completes one group skills training session and one individual exposure session. The social skills components include greetings and interactions, initiating conversations, listening skills, joining, establishing and maintaining friendships, giving and receiving compliments, assertiveness with peers and adults, and telephone skills. SET-C also includes the use of non-anxious peers who act as models and helpers. The patients and peers are involved in 90-minute outings together, where patients practice skills, observe and learn from their models, and receive feedback.

Hinshaw (1996) described a group intervention for boys with Attention Deficit-Hyperactivity Disorder (ADHD). In this intervention, groups of four to five boys learn about ADHD, discuss medication, and rehearse social skills. Moreover, an anger management component is also a pivotal ingredient to the program. The anger management curriculum involves the child sharing the exact names, taunts, teases, and phrases that provoke him. Training continues with developing recognition of anger triggers and coping strategies. Next, children practice these coping strategies under gradually increasing provocative conditions.

The Chill Out Program for Adolescents (Feindler & Ecton, 1986; Feindler & Guttman, 1994) emphasizes anger management, which decreases impulsive responding and increases productive expression of anger. The program develops ways for tolerating emotional arousal, self-control strategies, problem-solving skills, reattribution, and communication skills. Five treatment foci for the 10-session program include (1) recognizing the interaction between cognitive, physiological, and behavioral components of angry arousal; (2) constructing a cost-benefit analysis examining the maladaptive and adaptive aspects of anger; (3) identifying the antecedents to their anger; (4) introducing the concept of choice and responsibility; and (5) learning methods to express anger appropriately.

The *Cognitive-Behavior Group Therapy-Adolescent* (CBGT-A; Albano, 2000) is a 16- session group protocol delivered by two therapists. Each session lasts 90 minutes and includes 4 to 6 adolescent group members. The initial four sessions occur in the first 2 weeks of treatment. Children meet weekly in sessions 5 through 11. The last sessions occur biweekly. The first eight sessions focus on psychoeducation and coping skills training, whereas sessions 9 through 16 emphasize exposure training. Homework assignments are part of each session, and parent involvement is encouraged through their attendance at sessions 1, 2, 8, and 15.

Positive Adolescent Choices Training (PACT; Hammond, 1991) is a behavioral-social skills training program that targets 12- to 15-year-old African American youngsters. The program is culturally responsive to racial, ethnic, and gender issues. Training includes communication training, negotiation, and problem-solving. More specifically, the adolescents learn to give positive and negative feedback, accept negative feedback, resist peer pressure, and negotiate conflicts. The program integrates direct instruction, videotape modeling, and role-plays. The role-plays and "mini" psychodramas are presented via videotaped vignettes featuring African American teen role models.

The *Coping with Depression-Adolescents* (CWDA; Clarke et al., 2003) is a 16-session skills training group for young people ages 13- to 18-years old. The group usually runs 8 weeks, including two sessions per week. This group program addresses depressive symptoms, such as anhedonia, guilt, hopelessness, social withdrawal, poor problem-solving, and impaired social skills. CWDA includes both behavioral activation and cognitive therapy. The specific skill modules, include cognitive restructuring, behavior therapy, problem-solving, communication, negotiation, relaxation training, and goal-setting.

Berman, Silverman, and Kurtines (2000) described their group intervention for youth traumatized by crime and violence. The program emphasizes three goals, including the reduction of PTSD symptoms, enhancement of adaptive coping resources, and increasing social support availability and utilization. Berman and colleagues integrated exposure-based activities, coping skills training, and mobilizing social support systems into this program. The exposure exercises are accomplished through youngsters writing about their experiences and reading them aloud in group, followed by group discussion about features of the trauma. The coping skills component teaches problem-solving and reattribution by employing the STOP acronym. Improving social support is done through modeling, role-playing, contingency contracting, and group feedback.

The *Child Anxiety Management Program* (CAMP) (Friedberg & Elamir, in preparation) at the Penn State Milton Hershey Medical Center is an eight week CBT group emphasizing psychoeducation and coping skills training for anxious children ages 8- to 12-years old. CAMP is a modular based program focusing on problem identification, self-monitoring, self-instruction, rational analysis, and performance attainment. The program includes tokens and prizes for participation, psychoeducational material, and homework assignments. A unique feature of the program is a weekly session feedback form completed by each child. Youngsters are referred to the group by parents, pediatricians, psychiatrists, and social workers. For many children, CAMP augments their individual treatment and/or medication management. For still others, CAMP is their only therapy experience. The approach is modified for younger children (5- to 7-years old, CAMP Jr.) and adolescents (Teen CAMP).

OUTCOME LITERATURE OF GROUP CBT

There is considerable promise for cognitive-behavior group therapy with children and adolescents. Specific literature has demonstrated support of group CBT for anxiety, depressive spectrum disorders, and disruptive behavioral disorders (Baer & Garland, 2005; Beidel, Turner, & Morris, 2000; Berman, Silverman, & Kurtines, 2000, Feindler, Marriott, & Iwata, 1984; Friedberg et al., 2003; Gillham, Reivich, Jaycox, & Seligman, 1995; Lochman et al., 2003; Muris, Meesters, & van Melick, 2003; Thienemann, Martin, Cregger, Thompson, & Dyer-Friedman, 2001; Silverman, Kurtines, Ginsburg, Weems, Lumpkin, & Carmichael, 1999; Tynan et al., 1999).

Anxiety Disorders

Muris and colleagues. (2003) found that CBT treatment was superior to emotional disclosure groups in reducing anxiety and depressive symptoms in 9- to 12-year-old children. *Social Effectiveness Therapy for Children* (SET-C), a cognitive behavioral approach for treatment of socially anxious youth, has demonstrated effectiveness in children ages 7 to 13 years of age. Specifically, Beidel and colleagues (2000) found that 67% of participants did not meet diagnostic criteria for social anxiety following treatment using SET-C. Most impressively, however, was that 85% of the children no longer met diagnostic criteria at a 6 month follow-up, which shows increased improvement over time. Silverman et al. (1999) conducted a randomized clinical trial evaluating group CBT with anxiety disordered children, which demonstrated improvement on all main outcome measures at the end of treatment, as well as at 3, 6, and 12 month follow ups. Similarly, Friedberg and others (2003) showed reductions in self-reported depressive and anxious symptoms in children who completed a cognitive-behavioral coping skills group.

Baer and Garland (2005) conducted a pilot study of community based group CBT for adolescents with social phobia. After receiving a course of group CBT, adolescents with social phobia showed symptom reductions on objective and subjective reports. Thienemann and colleagues (2001) evaluated manual driven group CBT for adolescents with Obsessive-Compulsive Disorder. Patients completed a 14-week course of CBT, based on March and Mulle's (1998) seminal manual. They found symptoms improved and adolescents reported high levels of satisfaction with treatment.

Depressive Disorders

Jaycox and colleagues (1994) found that children completing a brief, group cognitive-behavioral program that focused on preventing depressive symptoms experienced fewer depressive symptoms at both the end of treatment and at the 6 month follow-up. Evaluating the same program, Gillham and colleagues (1995) reported that only 7% of children in the program had moderate to severe depression one year after the program, as compared to 29% of the matched control counterparts. Further, only 12% of the treatment group were significantly depressed at an 18-months follow-up point, whereas 33% of the control group were depressed at this evaluation. The *Coping with Depression–Adolescent Version* (CWDA; Clarke et al., 2003) has been shown to be quite efficacious, as results have shown an improvement of depressive symptoms at post-intervention points. Specifically, 67% of the treatment groups showed decreased symptoms, while only 48% of their wait-listed counterparts showed a decrease in symptoms.

Disruptive Behavioral Disorders

Tynan and associates (1999) evaluated a group cognitive-behavioral training for children with ADHD. The group focused on following directions, taking turns, initiating conversation, recognizing emotions in others, and problem-solving. They found improvement in children's behaviors following 6.7 group therapy hours. Furthermore, there was high compliance and cooperation with a low attrition rate.

Feindler and colleagues' *Chillout* anger management program has been evaluated on groups of adolescents in inpatient and outpatient settings (Feindler, 1995; Feindler & Ecton, 1986; Feindler & Guttman, 1994; Feindler et al, 1984). Feindler and colleagues (1984) examined the effects of teaching self-control skills and anger management to disruptive junior high school students in an in-school program. They found that their intervention lead to decreases in fines and expulsions for disruptive and aggressive behavior. Additionally, students' problem-solving abilities improved.

Lochman and colleagues' group intervention entitled the *Anger Coping Program* has also enjoyed considerable support (Larson & Lochman, 2002; Lochman, Barry, & Pardini, 2003). Lochman, Nelson, and Sims (1981) found that 12 sessions of cognitive-behaviorally focused group interventions contributed to decreased aggressive behavior and teacher reported increases in on-task behavior for second and third grade African American children. Further investigation found that the *Anger Coping Program* led to decreased parent reported aggression, lower rates of time-sampled observations of disruptive classroom behavior, and higher self-esteem in elementary school boys (Lochman, Burch, Curry, & Lampron, 1985).

ASSESSMENT AND GROUP MEMBER IDENTIFICATION FOR OUTPATIENT SETTINGS

Specific Measures

A comprehensive clinical interview is recommended for assessment. More specifically, developmental, social, school, family, and physical history should be obtained. Substance abuse issues and cultural considerations need to be addressed, as well. Ideally, the best candidates are patients who do not present extreme behavior problems that will disrupt the group or claim excessive amounts of time to manage. Additionally, patients should have some minimal level of motivation to change, modest frustration tolerance, and an ability to appreciate, as well as profit, from peer feedback (Lochman et al., 2003)

Screening measures should be selected based on the treatment focus. For anxiety, narrow band measures such as the *Screen for Child Anxiety Related Emotional Disorders* (SCARED; Birmaher et al., 1997), the *Multidimensional Anxiety Scale for Children* (MASC; March, 1997), and the *Revised Child Manifest Anxiety Scale* (RCMAS; Reynolds & Richmond, 1986) are suggested. The SCARED is a 41-item measure of anxiety that yields a total anxiety score as well as separate factor scores for panic/somatic, generalized anxiety, separation anxiety, social anxiety, and school refusal. The MASC also produces a total score, as well as factor and subfactor scores. The MASC contains an inconsistency scale and an anxiety disorder index. MASC factor scores include physical symptoms, harm avoidance, social anxiety, and separation anxiety. Subfactor scores include tense/restlessness, somatic, autonomic, anxious coping, perfectionism, performance fears, and humiliation/rejection. Finally, the RCMAS produces a total score, three factors (Physiological, Worry, and Social), and a Lie Scale. These measures provide a molar assessment of distress and a more molecular evaluation of specific aspects of anxiety.

Narrow band measures such as the *Children's Depression Inventory* (CDI; Kovacs, 1992) and the *Beck Depression Inventory-Second Edition* (BDI-II; Beck, 1996) are recommended for groups focusing on depressive symptoms. The CDI is a 27-item inventory tapping pivotal depressive symptoms. It yields 5 factors (Anhedonia, Low Self-Esteem, Interpersonal Problems, Ineffectiveness, and Negative Mood). The CDI also has a short form that is useful for monitoring effects of treatment (CDI-S). The BDI-II is a 21-item inventory that taps physiological, cognitive, affective, and behavioral symptoms of depression. Both the CDI and BDI-II provide clinicians with clinically relevant psychometrically sound measures.

The *Conners Parent Rating Scales* (CPRS; Conners, 1990) is a 48-item scale measuring symptoms associated with AD/HD. The CPRS is highly focused on AD/HD symptoms and like other narrow band measures sacrifices breadth of coverage for in-depth assessment of specific symptoms (Kronenberger & Meyer, 1993). The 10-item Hyperactivity Index (HI) is recommended to assess treatment effects (Kronenberger & Meyer, 1993). The *Conners Teacher Report Scale* is similar to the CPRS and contains 39 items.

Member Characteristics

Lochman and colleagues (2003) suggested several general characteristics of good candidates for group intervention. Poor problem-solvers with low perceived hostility and an understanding that aggressive behavior is a problem are well-suited to group therapy. Moreover, Lochman and colleagues stated that children with internal attributions who are rejected by peers and are motivated to change are expected to profit from a group therapy experience. Friedberg and Crosby (2001) noted that children must possess sufficient self-control to benefit from group therapy. For instance, children who are so disruptive and dysregulated that they cannot stay seated or keep their hands and feet to themselves are not likely to gain from group experience. Additionally, symptom acuity is a determining issue, and a moderate level of acuity is ideal. A depressed child who suffers from paralyzing hopelessness and vegetative symptoms is initially better served with individual therapy, and then, when symptoms are relieved somewhat, therapists could consider group treatment.

COGNITIVE-BEHAVIORAL GROUP INTERVENTIONS

A modular or component approach to cognitive-behavior group therapy is recommended. Rudimentary modules of CBT, including introduction to treatment, behavioral interventions, problem-solving, self-instruction, rational analysis, and performance attainment, provide the basic intervention skeleton. Therapists then determine the number of sessions to allocate to each module depending on the patient and the goals of the group. Thus, interventions are organized under modular headings.

All the interventions should be employed while balancing structure, process, and content variables (Friedberg & Crosby, 2001). Structure refers to interventions, activities, and exercises group therapists employ, such as thought diaries, self-instructional practices, and behavioral methods. Content represents the material elicited from or emitted by the patient, such as thoughts and feelings by these methods. Process variables are the ways patients respond or complete the interventions, such as avoidance, opposition, non-compliance, irritation and engagement.

Group cognitive-behavior therapists should adhere to the fundamental notions of collaborative empiricism and guided discovery (A.T. Beck et al., 1979; J. S. Beck, 1995). By adhering to collaborative empiricism, group therapists actively involve patients as partners and make therapy observable. Group cognitive therapy is characterized by a guided discovery process propelled by empathy, Socratic dialogues, and behavioral experiments. Through collaborative empiricism and guided discovery, therapists act as coaches who help patients build their own data bases to cast doubt on their assumptions.

Group CBT typically integrates skill acquisition and application. Skills are acquired via psychoeducation, where therapists directly teach coping skills. Youngsters may be given reading material, sample worksheets, or see a skill demonstrated. Once the skill is acquired, the next phase requires application. In this more difficult phase of treatment, the skills become more portable and individualized. Children use the skills to cope with their own particular aversive circumstances, distressing emotions, and inaccurate appraisals, and replace problematic behavior with more functional alternatives. Application is enhanced through practice in the context of negative affective arousal. Simply, children should experiment with the acquired skills when they are feeling badly, both in session and through homework assignments

Introduction to Treatment/Self-Monitoring

The initial treatment module involves an introduction to treatment and self-monitoring. Early group sessions should expose youngsters to the nature and rationale of treatment. Young patients need to know the "rules of the therapy game." More specifically, therapists need to communicate that CBT focuses on physiological, emotional, cognitive, and behavioral symptoms. Further, they need to let youngsters know how the group processes will facilitate the acquisition and application of coping skills. Clarke and colleagues (2003) suggest therapists initially encourage patients to at least experiment with each skill once before they decide to accept or reject the tool.

Priming and Problem-Solving

Priming techniques ready the child's cognitive processes for direct interventions. They are designed to "loosen up" children's rigid cognitive processes. Additionally, they can stimulate group discussions and get children talking about non-threatening issues. *Are you an egg* is a problem-solving intervention modified from Vernon's (1989) creative workbook. In this exercise, the group therapist brings a raw egg and a bowl to group. She initially explains that the members will observe an experiment today. The therapist shows the egg to the group and generally asks one group member to examine the egg to verify its authenticity. The egg is then cracked on the side of the bowl and the results are shown to the group members. The therapist then asks the members to report their observations (e.g., What happened?). After the results are collected, the therapist then asks, "But did the egg choose to break?" The discussion continues with a dialogue on how they are similar and different from an egg. The exercise playfully illustrates the notion of choice in a non-threatening way.

Download This is an updated modification of a technique initially developed for inpatient children (Friedberg, Mason, & Fidaleo, 1992). The task presents groups members with $100.00 dollars of group money and a list of various musical artists. Their job is to spend exactly $100.00 downloading music from various artists. The artists are grouped in three different price categories ($20.00, $10.00, and $5.00), and the list includes some artists teenagers would typically prefer as well as many artists adolescents would not prefer.

The task is completed in three phases. In Phase I, children make their selections and share their choices aloud. The group therapist lists the choices by group member's names on a poster board or white board. After all the selections are shared and recorded, the group therapist instructs the patients to look at the lists on the board and asks them, "How many lists are identical or exactly the same?" There will be few if any identical lists. The next question is, "How many of you have the identical or exactly the same problem to solve?" Of course, they all did! The therapist then asks the synthesizing question, "What does it mean that you all had the same problem but came up with very different options?" The take away message from Phase I is that problems have many solutions.

Phase II builds on Phase I, as the therapist begins by asking each group member to identify which artists on their list they would spend their own money to buy. There will be some non-preferred choices on each child's list. Once all the children have identified the artists they would not buy on their own, the therapist asks, "What was it like to choose among things you did not like?" The point in Phase II is most times you have to choose among undesirable alternatives. This counters the common teenage belief that a choice has to occur among only desirable options.

Phase III involves the application phase. The therapist then invites the group members to experiment to generate a broad list of alternatives to their pressing problems. This list should include both ways they would prefer to solve the problem and solutions they would not like. Finally, they try to select productive alternatives from the preferred and non-preferred choices.

Building the Tool Kit is an excellent problem-solving and coping skills technique (Goldberg-Arnold & Fristad, 2003). Young patients create four categories of coping skills titled creative, social, physical, and rest and relaxation. Children then add strategies in each category. To make the activity more engaging, fun, and simple, the therapist could use colored adhesive labels with each category represented by a different colored adhesive label. The patient then only has to write the strategy on the label and then place it on an activity to record its use.

Behavioral Tasks

Behavioral skill training is another important module in group CBT. Social skills training, relaxation training, and pleasant activity scheduling are examples of behavioral interventions. Cartledge and Milburn's (1996) program contains many social skills training exercises that are culturally responsive, as well as ideal for outpatient groups. Completing a joint project is an excellent task that builds social skills and a sense of group "community." Each child is given an individual part of the group project to complete. The task requires the children to work together and offers *in vivo* practice opportunities for social skills (e.g., giving/receiving compliments/criticism, sharing, asking/getting help).

Relaxation training can also be done in groups. Developmentally appropriate procedures and scripts similar to the ones created by Kendall and colleagues (1992) are recommended for different ages and skill levels. Simple relaxation interventions are generally preferable to more complex ones. For example, Wexler (1991) created a *Ten Candles* exercise. Children imagine 10 lit candles in a row. Then, they blow out each candle with an effortful exhale. *Ten Candles* is useful because it combines imagery and controlled breathing, and it keeps the child engaged in the therapeutic task.

Self-Instruction

Self-instructional procedures change a child's inner dialogue. The focus of self-instruction is on replacing inaccurate appraisals with more accurate explanations and problem-solving strategies that guide adaptive coping. Therapeutic use of board games also lends itself nicely to outpatient CBT groups. Berg (1990a, 1990b, 1990c) has created several fun cognitive-behavioral games that are ideal for group work. Children take turns responding to various prototypical scenarios. The cards ask the child to identify and modify inaccurate thoughts. Therapists then can use the group process to help young people develop alternate self-instructions and problem-solving strategies. Further, once the common scenario is sufficiently processed, the therapist asks the children to apply the skill to their own lives (e.g., When have you felt like this? What popped into your head? What is something else you could have said to yourself?).

Changing Your Tune (Friedberg et al., 2001) is a general self-instructional technique useful for a variety of problems. The skill is taught via skill acquisition and application phases. In the acquisition phase, the analogy between troubling negative automatic thoughts and irksome song lyrics repeating in their mind is presented. Then, a simple self-instruction is taught. Next, prototypical situations, feelings, and negative automatic thoughts are presented. The child's task involves supplying an alternative response to common problematic situations. Once the children acquire the skill, they are given the applied assignment to complete a *Changing Your Tune* diary based on their individual experiences.

Goldberg-Arnold and Fristad (2003) described a very clever, yet simple self-instructional tool called *Naming the Enemy.* Children are given a sheet of paper, which they divide into two columns on both sides. One column on one half of one side of the paper is labeled, "Things I like about me." The child then turns the paper over and labels the other column on the opposite side, "My symptoms." The children are invited to list all of their symptoms (e.g., impulsivity, depression, not listening, irritability, etc.)

under the labeled symptoms. The children then turn the paper over and list their positive qualities (e.g., smart, good at sports, etc.). Next, they fold the symptom column over the strength column literally hiding the strength column. Children now have a concrete referent for the way symptoms camouflage strengths. The group then discusses the way symptoms can cover up positive characteristics.

Shout Out is a self-instructional technique based on the cognitive-behavioral protocol developed by March and Mulle (1998). The idea is to "boss back" the negative automatic thought and shout it out. The procedure makes use of the Beatles classic song *Get Back*. Shout out is a fun and active way to teach self-instruction. Singing/Shouting "Get Back" interrupts the chain of negative thoughts, empowers the child, and initiates the process. It is a way to "jump start" the self-instructional process. During the priming stage, the children listen to the lyrics and then sing along with the chorus, "Get Back, Get Back to where you once belonged." During the application phase, children identify their negative automatic thought and begin the self-instructional process by shouting/singing, "Get Back." After they shout out, the children construct their self instruction (e.g., "Being worried is also a feeling. It does not mean something bad will happen.").

Rational Analysis

Rational analysis techniques focus on modifying the illogical process of children's and adolescents' thoughts. Typically, constructing a Socratic dialogue that casts doubt on patients' assumptions is a pivotal task. A group format is well-suited to rational analysis because ideally the questioning and feedback comes from group members, as well as the therapist. Clarke and colleagues (2003, p. 125) remarked, " Even if teens like and trust the group therapist, they nonetheless may discount the therapist's feedback because she or he is an adult. Feedback from the other adolescent group members may be more palatable as it comes from a peer who understands my life." Indeed, when group members begin to question each other's conclusions Socratically, the group therapist is assured they have internalized the process of evaluating one's thoughts and started to apply their newly acquired skills.

Thought Digger is a rational analysis tool used with elementary school children in outpatient groups (Friedberg et al., 2001; Rambaldo et al., 2001). *Thought Digger* is presented in acquisition and application phases. In the acquisition phase, children are presented with 11 samples of Socratic questions, including: "What good things about myself am I ignoring?"; "Am I confusing maybe with forever?"; "Am I expecting too little from myself?"; and "Am I using my feelings as facts?" In the application phase, children record their problematic situations, feelings, and thoughts and circle thought digger questions that can help them rationally analyze their conclusions.

Goldstein and colleagues (1987) recommend a very innovative moral reasoning group intervention for aggressive youngsters. The program is based on Kohlberg's (1984) theory of moral development and includes several moral dilemmas. In their *Aggression Replacement Therapy* (ART), Goldstein and his colleagues provide adolescent group members moral dilemmas to resolve. The goal is to raise the youngster's levels of moral reasoning through group discussion, feedback, and rational analysis. While the Goldstein text includes prototypical vignettes, therapists need not be constrained by these stories. Using the game of *Scruples* is a nice alternative.

Performance Attainment and Experiential Activities

The *Circle of Criticism* (Feindler & Ecton, 1986; Feindler & Guttman, 1994) is an activity that encourages aggressive youngsters to demonstrate their coping skills. Patients are instructed to sit in a circle and make provocative slurs to each other (e.g., "You smell," "You are stupid," etc.) and the recipient responds with fogging, assertion, or any other anger control technique. Indeed, their exercise is an opportunity to practice the skills learned previously.

Say Cheese is a performance attainment exercise used in the CAMP program. Since socially anxious children are often uncomfortable posing for pictures and asking others to be in their pictures, children are instructed to ask each other to be in group pictures. The photographer selects the group and instructs them to make a silly pose. Children record their thoughts and feelings as the group members process any inaccurate appraisals and then problem solve difficulties.

Sharing the Persian Flaw is an experiential exercise inspired by the television series *Joan of Arcadia*. In one episode, Joan frets about making mistakes, being perfect, and trying to control everyone and everything around her. She learns that when Persian rugs are made, the rug-maker purposely creates a flaw in the rug as a defining feature and as a way to embrace humility. The Persian Flaw suggests that life must be lived and tolerated through its imperfections and unpredictability. This exercise is ideal for children plagued with perfectionism and an excessive need for control. A design is presented to the group members and they are instructed to complete the design and include a defining flaw. They can color outside the lines, rip, and crumble the paper, or even elect not to color it all. After they have finished the exercise, they must describe their flaw to the other group members. In sum, the exercise gives young people practice in making mistakes, going public with their mistake, evaluating people's reactions, and coping with possible negative reactions.

CHALLENGES TO OUTPATIENT GROUPS

Group cognitive-behavior therapists need to set rules and limits when groups begin. Friedberg and Crosby (2001, p. 78) noted, "Rules and limits allow the therapeutic process to unfold." While this process appears simple and straight-forward at first blush, clinical experience reveals it is a deceptively difficult practice. A few basic rules should be prepared by the therapist before the first group and then presented to the group members. It is generally best to collaboratively process and develop the rules. For instance, a prepared rule may be read aloud and then group members are invited to express their agreement or disagreement with the rule. In this way, the rules become an initial issue for group processing. After the prepared rules are discussed, children are encouraged to add their own rules. Of course, group therapists maintain "veto power" over the rules.

The rules should be recorded in written form, signed by the children, and each group member retains a copy. Poster boards displaying the rules may be hung on the walls and point charts reflecting children's compliance with the rules could be displayed (Lochman et al., 2003).   Once the rules are established, they must be enforced. When therapists fail to enforce limits and rules, they sabotage children's sense of safety. In fact, therapists are teaching patients they cannot be trusted or relied upon. When enforcing the rules, group cognitive-behavior therapists should remain faithful to the notions of guided discovery and collaborative empiricism. If the rules are initially transgressed, therapists should gently remind the offending member about the rules, process the reminder with the individual child (e.g., "What went through your mind when I reminded you about the rules?"), as well as elicit the thoughts and feelings from other members (e.g., "What popped into your mind when I reminded Joaquin about the rules?"). If transgressions continue, consequences need to be meted out (e.g., loss of points/tokens, time outs, or in severe cases removal from group).

Lack of rules and limits may reinforce deviancy training (Lochman et al., 2003). Lochman and his associates refer to deviancy training when group therapists unwittingly reinforce children's problematic thoughts and behaviors. This seems particularly likely when working with youngsters who have conduct, oppositional, and behavior problems. Moreover, this is precisely the reason group therapy with conduct disordered youngsters is contraindicated (Dishion, McCord, & Poulin, 1999). In these groups "gone wild," contagion effects predominate and young patients "catch" each other's dysfunctional attitudes, feelings, and actions. Lochman et al. advocate making clear expectations, using co-therapists, and dividing into subgroups as ways to inoculate the group from this contagion.

These problem strategies raise additional challenges involving the number of therapists in a group. Ideally, groups should be co-led. Fortunately, working in an academic or clinical training institution permits trainees to act as co-therapists. However, private practitioners and institutions without trainees may not enjoy the luxury of a co-therapist.

Regardless of whether the therapist has a "co-pilot" or "flies solo," clinical flexibility is a challenge. While homogeneous groups are the rule in Randomized Clinical Trials (RCT), they are commonly the exception in most practice settings. Addressing varying levels of psychopathology and cognitive emotional maturity is a pivotal task (Rambaldo et al., 2001). Therapists need to tailor techniques, exercises, and activities so that children with different problems can profit from the group experience. Further, the therapist must balance clinical tasks, such as delivering psychoeducation, Socratic processing, limit setting, and reinforcement.

Deciding between open and closed groups is another key issue. In closed groups, group membership remains constant throughout the course of group treatment. Thus, no new members are added once the group begins. In open groups, members continually enter and the group composition repeatedly changes. Time-limited versus open ended formats are frequently associated with decisions about closed and open groups. Time-limited groups impose a session limit (e.g., 8, 12, or 20 sessions), whereas in on-going groups, there is no set end point. Generally, time-limited groups lend themselves to closed enrollment, whereas an on-going group may more readily accommodate changing group composition.

The group structure and goals also impact decisions on open or closed enrollment. For instance, the group component of the Penn State University Milton Hershey Medical Center *Child Anxiety Management Program* (CAMP) includes eight sessions of group CBT. CAMP offers a sequential and structured approach in which each week builds upon the previous session. Since the curriculum is set, it is counterproductive to add patients in after the second week. However, a new group cycle begins every 8 weeks or so, and new groups are formed at that point.

Group size is another consideration. Size will depend on the number of therapists and costs. Larger groups with six or more children are likely best served with co-therapists. Therapists in outpatient settings may need to be mindful of the net revenue figures in order to set a minimum number of patients in a group.

Managing crises and intense emotional arousal in groups are additional challenges. Often, these considerations are shaped by group size, level of functioning, and number of available therapists. Therefore, groups need to be small enough for only one therapist to effectively manage and care for a member in crisis. If these groups are too large, then another therapist must be added. Therapists must take care there are not too many labile and vulnerable patients in one group. Not only will these patients' agendas overwhelm the group, but they will likely flood the therapist's resources. When individual issues predominate in a group context and consistently necessitate a therapist's "special attention," it is a recipe for disaster.

SUMMARY

CBT's landscape offers an expanding horizon. The range of applications appears quite wide and now includes work with bipolar depression, autism/aspergers disorders, and schizophrenic spectrum patients. CBT is transcending the traditional boundaries of individual therapy and is now being delivered in group and family formats. Indeed, group CBT in outpatient settings is an emerging and exciting clinical frontier.

While this chapter presented cognitive-behavioral approaches to group therapy in a common setting, proper application of group CBT may be an uncommonly productive intervention. Practitioners can reach more children in fewer clinic hours and equip them with empirically-tested skills. Young patients can profit from group support, peer feedback, and simply knowing they are not the only child who struggles with their particular emotional challenges. Continued theory building, clinical innovation, and empirical investigation will serve to bolster group cognitive-behavioral interventions. Collaboration between basic researchers, clinical scientists, and practitioners will propel group CBT toward even wider vistas.

RECOMMENDED READINGS

Beidel, D. B., & Turner, S. M. (1998). *Shy children, phobic adults.* Washington, DC: American Psychological Association.

Clarke, G. N., Lewinshon, P. M., & Hops, H. (2001). *Instructor's manual for the Adolescent Coping with Depression Course.* Retrievable from Kaiser Permanente Center for Health Research Web site www. kpchr. org/publicacwd.acwd.html.

Feindler, E. L., & Ecton, R. B. (1986). *Adolescent anger control.* Boston, MA: Allyn & Bacon.

Friedberg, R. D., & McClure, J. M. (2002). *Clinical practice of cognitive therapy with children and adolescents: The nuts and bolts.* New York: Guilford.

Larson, J., & Lochman, J.E. (2002). *Helping schoolchildren cope with anger: A cognitive behavioral intervention.* New York: Guilford.

March, J. S., & Mulle, K. M. (1998). *OCD in children and adolescents.* New York: Guilford.

REFERENCES

Albano, A. M. (2000). Treatment of social phobia in adolescents. Cognitive and Behavioral programs focused on intervention and prevention. *Journal of Cognitive Psychotherapy, 14,* 67–76.

Baer, S., & Garland, E. (2005). Pilot study of community-based cognitive behavioral group therapy for adolescents with social phobia. *Journal of the American Academy of Child and Adolescent Psychiatry, 44*, 258–264.

Beck, A. T. (1996). *Beck Depression Inventory-II.* San Antonio, TX: Psychological Corporation

Beidel, D. B., & Turner, S. T. (1998). *Shy children, phobic adults.* Washington, DC: American Psychological Association.

Beidel, D. C., Turner, S. M., & Morris, T. L. (2000). Behavioral treatment of childhood social phobia. *Journal of Consulting and Clinical Psychology, 68*, 1072–1080.

Berg, B. (1990a). *The anger control game.* Dayton, OH: Cognitive Counseling Resources

Berg, B. (1990b). *The anxiety management game.* Dayton, OH: Cognitive Counseling Resources.

Berg, B. (1990c). *The self-control game.* Dayton, OH: Cognitive Counseling Resources.

Berman, S. L., Silverman, W. K., & Kurtines, W. M. (2000). Youth exposure to crime and violence: Its effects and implications for interventions. *Journal of Cognitive Psychotherapy, 14*, 37–50.

Birmaher, B. Khetrapal, S., Brent, D., Cully, M., Balach, L., Kaufman, J., & Neer, S. M. (1997). The Screen for Child Anxiety-Related Emotional Disorders (SCARED): Scale construction and psychometric characteristics. *Journal of American Academy of Child and Adolescent, 38*, 1230–1236.

Cartledge, G.C., & Milburn, J.F. (Eds.), (1996). *Cultural diversity and social skills instruction: Understanding ethnic and gender differences.* Champaign, IL: Research Press.

Clarke, G. N., DeBar, L. L., & Lewinsohn, P. M. (2003). Cognitive-behavioral group treatment for adolescent depression. In A. Kazdin, & J. R. Weisz (Eds.), *Evidence-based psychotherapies for children and adolescents* (pp. 120–134). New York: Guilford.

Conners, K. C. (1990). *Conners Rating Scales.* Tonawanda, NY: Multi-Health Systems

Dishion, T. J., McCord, J., & Poulin, F. (1999). When interventions harm: Peer groups and problem behavior. *American Psychologist, 54*, 755–764.

Feindler, E. L., & Ecton, R. B. (1986). *Adolescent anger control: Cognitive behavioral techniques.* Boston, MA: Allyn & Bacon.

Feindler, E. L., & Guttman, J. (1994). Cognitive-behavioral anger control training. In C. W. LeCroy (Eds.), *Handbook of child and adolescent treatment manuals* (pp. 170–199). New York: Lexington, Books.

Feindler, E. L., Marriott, S. M., & Iwata, M. (1984). Group anger control training. *Cognitive Therapy and Research, 8,* 299–311.

Friedberg, R. D., & Crosby, L. E. (2001). *Therapeutic exercises for children: A professional guide.* Sarasota, FL: Professional Resource Press.

Friedberg, R. D., & Elamir, B. (In preparation). *Children's session by session perception of treatment in group cognitive behavioral therapy.*

Friedberg, R. D., Friedberg, B. A., & Friedberg, R .J. (2001). *Therapeutic exercises for children: Guided discovery through cognitive behavioral techniques.* Sarasota, FL: Professional Resource Press.

Friedberg, R. D., & McClure, J. M. (2002). *Clinical practice of cognitive therapy with children and adolescents: The nuts and bolts.* New York: Guilford.

Friedberg, R. D., Mason, C., & Fidaleo, R. A. (1992). *Switching channels; A cognitive-behavioral work journal for adolescents.* Sarasota, FL: Psychological Assessment Resources.

Friedberg, R. D., McClure, J. M., Wilding, L., Goldman, Long, M. P., Anderson, L, & DePolo, M. (2003). A cognitive-behavioral skills training group for children experiencing anxious and depressed symptoms: A clinical report with accompanying descriptive data. *Journal of Contemporary Psychotherapy, 33*, 157–175.

Fristad, M. A., Gavazzi, S. M., & Soldano, K. W. (1999). Naming the enemy: Learning to differentiate mood disorder symptoms from the self that experiences them. *Journal of Family Psychotherapy, 10*, 81–88.

Gillham, J. E., Reivich, K.J., Jaycox, L. H., & Seligman, M. E. P. (1995). Prevention of depressive symptoms in school children: Two year follow up. *Psychological Science, 6,* 343–351.

Ginsburg, G. S., Silverman, W. K., & Kurtines, W. S. (1995). Cognitive-behavioral group therapy. In A. R. Esien, C. A. Kearney, & C. E., Schaefer (Eds.), *Clinical handbook of anxiety disorders in children and adolescents* (pp. 521–549). Northvale, NJ: Jason Aronson.

Goldberg-Arnold, J. S., & Fristad, M. A. (2003). Psychotherapy for children with bipolar disorder. In B. Geller, & M. P. Delbell (Eds.), *Bipolar disorder in childhood and early adolescence* (pp. 272–294). New York: Guilford.

Goldstein, A. P. Glick, B., Reiner, S., Zimmerman, D., & Coultry, T. M. (1987). *Aggression replacement training.* Champaign, IL: Research Press.

Hammond, W. R. (1991). *Dealing with anger: Givin' it, takin' it, workin' it out.* Champaign, IL: Research Press.

Hinshaw S. P. (1996). Enhancing social competence: Integrating self-management strategies with behavioral procedures for child attention deficit hyperactivity disorder. In E. D. Hibbs, & P. S. Jensen, (Eds.), *Psy-*

chosocial treatments for child and adolescent disorders: Empirically-based strategies for clinical practice (pp. 285–309). Washington, DC: American Psychological Association.

Jaycox, L. H., Reivich, K. J., Gillham, J. E., & Seligman, M. E. P. (1994). Prevention of depressive symptoms in school children. *Behavioral Research and Therapy, 32*, 801–816.

Kovacs, M. (1992). *Children's depression inventory*. Tonawanda, NY: Multi-Health Systems.

Kohlberg, L. (1984). *Essays on moral development: Vol. II. The psychology of moral development*. San Francisco: Harper & Row.

Kronenenberger, W. G., & Meyer, R. G. (1996). *The child clinician's handbook*. Boston, MA: Allyn & Bacon.

Larson, J., & Lochman, J. E. (2002). *Helping schoolchildren cope with anger: A cognitive-behavioral intervention*. New York: Guilford

.Lochman, J. . Barry, T. D., & Pardini, D. (2003). Anger control training for aggressive youth. In A. E. Kazdin & J. R. Weisz (Eds.), *Evidence-based psychotherapies for children and adolescents* (pp. 263–281). New York: Guilford.

Lochman, J. E., Burch, P. P., Curry, J. F., & Lampron, L. B. (1984). Treatment and generalization effects of cognitive-behavioral and goal setting interventions with aggressive boys. *Journal of Consulting and Clinical Psychology, 61*, 1053–1058.

Lochman, J. E., Nelson, & Sims, J. P. (1981). A cognitive behavioral program for use with aggressive children. *Journal of Clinical Child Psychology, 13*, 146–148.

March, J. S. (1997). *MASC: Multidimensional anxiety scale for children technical manual*. Tonawanda, NY: Multi-Heatlh Systems

March, J. S., & Mulle, K. (1998). *Cognitive behavioral therapy for OCD*. New York: Guilford.

Muris, P., Meesters, C., & van Melick, M. (2002). Treatment of childhood anxiety disorders: A preliminary comparison between cognitive-behavioral group therapy and a psychological placebo intervention. *Journal of Behavior Therapy and Experimental Psychiatry, 33*, 143–158.

Rambaldo, L. R., Wilding, L. D., Goldman, M. L., McClure, J. M., & Friedberg, R. D. (2001). School-based interventions for anxious and depressed children. In L. Vandcreek, & T. L. Jackson (Eds.), *Innovations in clinical practice* (pp. 347–358). Sarasota, FL: Professional Resource Press.

Reynolds, C. R., & Richmond, B. O. (1985). *Revised Children's Manifest Anxiety Scale*. Los Angeles: Western Psychological Services.

Silverman, W. K., Kurtines, W. M., Ginsburg, G. S., Weems, Lumpkin, P., & Carmichael, D. (1999). Treating anxiety disorders in children with group CBT: A randomized clinical trial. *Journal of Consulting and Clinical Psychology, 67*, 995–1003.

Thieneman, M., Martin, J., Cregger, B., Thompson, H., & Dyer-Friedman, J (2001). Manual driven group cognitive behavioral therapy for adolescents with obsessive compulsive disorder: A pilot study. *Journal of the American Academy of Child and Adolescent Psychiatry, 40*, 1254–1260.

Tynan, W.D., Schuman, W., & Lampert, N. (1999). Concurrent parent and child therapy groups for externalizing disorder: From the laboratory to the world of managed care. *Cognitive and Behavioral Practice, 6*, 3–9.

Wexler, (1991). *The PRISM workbook: A program for innovative self-management*. New York: W. W. Norton.

Chapter Eight

Cognitive-Behavior Therapy Groups in Inpatient Settings

Mark H. Stone

This chapter focuses on the special conditions of inpatient settings for delivering group psychotherapy to children and adolescents. In order to focus solely upon these special considerations without overlapping other chapters, issues of general import and content are not typically discussed. Instead, those issues unique to an inpatient setting for the treatment of children and adolescents are given the most attention. Although I primarily focus on cognitive-behavior therapy (CBT) as the orientation of clinical treatment in this chapter, I provide some references from other orientations, as they address important aspects of treatment relating to client and therapist in this setting.

INTRODUCTION TO INPATIENT TREATMENT

Inpatient settings offer a unique approach to treatment, inasmuch as the care in such facilities usually covers 24 hours throughout the entire duration of residential placement and prescribed treatment. There are some programs that offer a partial-day or semi-residential program, but these programs are not discussed. Inpatient settings in this chapter will refer to environments typically considered within hospitals where admission is the result of acute emotional, cognitive, or behavioral distress that requires a high level of structure, stability, and safety to stabilize. What differentiates the inpatient setting (by this definition) from the residential settings (discussed within a separate chapter) is the severity of presentation of symptoms, the length of stay, and the goals of treatment—which are typically stabilization and step-down to a less intensive setting (including longer term residential settings). For a review of group considerations within longer term inpatient settings, readers are referred to the chapter within this text on residential group therapy.

Inpatient settings customarily address severe conditions, which make daily continuity of care a necessity. Two conditions make inpatient group psychotherapy noticeably different from that of outpatient or other nonresidential settings. First, group treatment is usually only part of the overall treatment milieu in inpatient settings, and it is only one segment of the total care and treatment of residential clients. It is not the single mode of treatment typical of outpatient treatment settings. Patients may receive both individual and group therapy, as well as other services to augment their care. Second, in inpatient settings, group sessions are typically conducted throughout the day and during the week. Patients in inpatient settings usually attend group sessions several times a week, and in some programs, multiple groups are scheduled every day. In many instances, there may be different groups that meet throughout the day, with each group addressing different treatment goals. For example, a client could attend one group focused upon her or his presenting problem, another group for a dual diagnosis condition, and another session dealing with residential issues. Additional groups may also address the family or even alcohol and drug abuse.

Both of these factors make the inpatient treatment process a complex one (Toseland & Siporin, 1986). Inpatient treatment settings usually require the group leaders to function as a part of an overall delivery-of-service team to patients rather than simply to function on a more independent level, as might occur when conducting groups in other settings (e.g., outpatient, etc.). Furthermore, inpatient treatment may be much more intensive than is typical of weekly sessions in an outpatient practice, as the severity of the presenting problems may warrant such intensity.

Immersion into the total milieu of inpatient treatment is an adjustment for patients in this setting. It requires adjustment to a regimen that may or may not be easily accepted and tolerated. Inpatient treatment may also require some adjustment for group leaders, even experienced outpatient leaders, who lack inpatient experience and are unfamiliar with operating in this setting. Because of conflict in scheduling, group members may or may not be present for all sessions. It is likely that they will not all share the same general symptoms as might be expected when conducting a scheduled outpatient group in which you can be more selective of your group members. This matter does depend, however, upon the setting, as admission pre-screenings can facilitate and help organize the process, which can place patients in groups that are fitting to meet their needs. However, it is doubtful that this is the set practice in all inpatient settings. A number of inpatient settings exist that serve a special function or population. When this is the case, the clients attend group sessions with a common presenting condition (e.g., depression, anxiety, substance abuse), and they usually attend these sessions in order to treat and resolve common problems (e.g., difficulty handling stress). Yet, in other inpatient settings, the clients may present with a wide array of conditions. Such groups may be composed of clients with a variety of conditions and presenting problems, and in these cases, the treatment approach will vary by client. The circumstances of how each inpatient setting operates will determine how this matter is addressed, but group leaders have to be much more flexible when working in these settings than might be imagined.

The typical inpatient placement usually follows a previously less restrictive setting for treatment, and it typically occurs only after other modes of treatment have been deemed less effective. Inpatient placement may also follow an extreme act, such as a suicide attempt, or result from a behavioral condition that requires immediate placement in a more restrictive environment, as when children and adolescents present with extreme manifestations of a conduct disorder. These conditions usually make the participants for group inpatient psychotherapy more severe in their disturbances, and often, more chronic in their condition than may be typically encountered in outpatient groups.

While voluntary admissions do occur, most inpatient placements of children and adolescents are involuntary. This makes for further complications in providing group psychotherapy. Group members frequently appear for their initial sessions with considerable anger, frustration, and resentment over what has occurred to bring about placement in an inpatient facility. Consequently, the role of the leaders in conducting inpatient sessions is much more complex than usually occurs in other settings. Unless the group members' issues and frustrations have been resolved or at least diffused, the initial group meetings may be the venue where these matters are first expressed. Leaders must be prepared for this behavior so as not to be surprised when these problematic issues occur in the form of anger, resentment, uncooperativeness, silence, and so forth. Therapists in an inpatient setting are encouraged to use the first session or at least a portion of it, to address these frustrations with the placement.

Inpatient groups are usually ongoing sessions, and often lack the outpatient parameters of a clearly determined beginning, middle, and end. Leaders who are new to inpatient groups are immediately introduced to what appears to be continuously revolving sessions produced by a variety of client circumstances that overall differ greatly from group therapy programs they might have conducted in other settings. Most leaders new to inpatient work experience their greatest frustration by the seemingly continuous flow of inpatient sessions and constant change in group members, as patients are discharged or admitted. Until leaders understand and acclimate to these phenomena, they may feel disoriented by the open-endedness of inpatient group sessions.

Leaders new to inpatient group psychotherapy will have to give very careful attention to all these issues. Seeking supervision and consultation from experienced leaders of inpatient groups are a benefit in making the adjustment to an inpatient setting.

REVIEW OF RESOURCES FOR GROUP INPATIENT TREATMENT

This section provides selected references for inpatient group psychotherapy to guide leaders to the literature dealing with specific problem areas. These references always pertain to group psychotherapy unless otherwise indicated. Yalom's comprehensive texts (2005) cover many of these areas and therapists should certainly consult these resources, as books are not specifically presented here and should be used independently as a reference. Rather than offering a traditional literature review on inpatient group therapy, I instead present annotated references arranged by presenting problems seen in this setting, as well as general information useful to inpatient therapists working with children and youth. Readers are directed to the individual chapters of this text for a more thorough review of these presenting problems, additional references, specific considerations for conducting problem-specific groups, and suggested interventions and techniques.

Inpatient Treatment

The works of Rice (1995) and Rice and Rutan (1987) are particularly useful for an orientation to inpatient group psychotherapy. They discuss the essential issues of conducting inpatient groups and offer suggestions on how to conduct sessions, and the issues that may arise.

Children and Adolescents

Corey (2000) offers very practical advice for conducting groups and presents specific sections dealing with groups for children and adolescents. Likewise, the works of Malekoff (1997), Rosenbaum (1972; 1996), Rosenbaum and Kraft (1972), and Shapiro, Peltz, and Bernadett-Shapiro (1998) provide excellent resources and specific information for conducting inpatient group treatment with children and adolescents.

Cognitive Behavioral Group Therapy

The White and Freeman (2000) book on group treatment using CBT is a valuable resource, which supplies leaders a general rationale of CBT together with many illustrative examples and vignettes. Although this text specifically addresses group psychotherapy, it is primarily addressing adult issues. Specific to CBT with children, though not necessarily group interventions, readers should consider various recent texts as resources (see Friedberg & McClure, 2002; Reinecke, Dattilio, & Freeman, 2003; Mennuti, Freeman, & Christner, 2005).

Difficult Clients

Numerous authors have addressed difficult clients. While many resources exist, readers should consider consulting Alonso (1992); Alonso and Rutan (1993); Fried (1954); Gans (1989); Gans and Alonso (1998); Ormont (1993); Roth, Kibel, and Stone (1990); Rosenthal (1996); Shields (2000); and Spotnitz (1976). Each of these supply a great deal of useful information on dealing with difficult clients, especially those who present with aggressive behavior, act-out in group settings, choose to be silent, and refuse to cooperate.

Eating Disorders

Brotman, Alonso, and Herzog (1985); Hall (1985); Harper-Giuffre and MacKenzie (1992); Laube (1990); and Reiss and Rutan (1992) offer excellent information on treating eating disorders. They provide specific treatment protocols and models for treating this condition specifically within an inpatient setting.

Trauma and Abuse

Beninati (1998); Grotsky, Camerer, and Grusznski (2000); Klein and Schermer (2000); Lesi and Hearn (1984); Peled and Davis (1995); van der Kolk (1993); and Webb and Leehan (1996) are valuable references in this area. These references give the reader very important information on dealing with trauma and abuse, including the treatment of battered women (Campbell, 1986; Gruszinski, Brink, & Edleson, 1988, Roberts, 1984) and their children (Peled & Davis, 1995; Schacht, Kerlinksy, & Carlson, 1990) in a group inpatient setting.

Shame

Shame is often ignored as a treatment variable. This usually occurs because patients do not directly manifest shame. It usually operates as a latent component of trauma and abuse, and especially so with cases of sexual abuse and incest. Silverstein (1993) specifically addresses the issues of secrecy and privacy that often prevail and how therapists can work with these matters in group treatment. Alonso and Rutan (1988), James (1992), and Scheff (1995) provide information on how issues of shame can be identified and appropriately addressed in groups. For comprehensive information on the dynamics of shame, readers should consult the classic work by Piers and Singer (1939), and more contemporary books by Kaufman (1989), Lewis (1992), and Nathanson (1987). The entire journal of the *American Behavioral Scientist* (vol. 38[8], 1995) is devoted to shame and its related emotions. All these references are very helpful for dealing with shame in group psychotherapy.

Medically Ill

Children and adolescents who present with chronic medical conditions may be overlooked for psychotherapy and mental health treatment. Leszcz (1998), Spira (1997), Stone (1996), and Ulman (1993) address these medical conditions together with suggestions for conducting group treatment for those who present with these complicated conditions.

Alcohol and Drug Abuse

Early abuse of alcohol and drugs by children and adolescents has made this a serious (and more often than not a chronic) condition even for young children. Voth (1963), in his historic volume, discussed issues regarding group psychotherapy for clients with alcohol problems, which still are of value today. Leaders of inpatient groups that deal with these conditions would be well advised to gain specific training in treating alcohol and drug abuse. This training would aid them in addressing substance abuse in conjunction with mental health conditions (Sciacca, 1991). Such training will also help them in conducting these groups with more specificity devoted to these special conditions and their influence on behavior. Leaders, when well versed in this area, will work more effectively with other treatment providers who may directly deal with substance abuse treatment. Alcohol and drug abuse are frequently components of other behavioral conditions, and usually produce a subsequent dual diagnosis. Failure to recognize this duality, or not work cooperatively in this area with other specialists, can raise difficulties and impede group treatment. Leaders of inpatient groups must specifically attend to the problem of alcohol and drug abuse because it compounds the behavioral problems of children and adolescents. Failure to recognize its impact frustrates treatment. The

Hazelden Foundation is one source that provides a wealth of information for the treatment of these conditions. These resources can be obtained at www.hazelden.org.

TYPES OF GROUPS CONDUCTED IN INPATIENT SETTING

The previous section provided literature according to the presenting conditions that are commonly treated within an inpatient environment for children and adolescents. This section discusses the variation in the conduction of inpatient groups that may operate in such settings. Group psychotherapists in inpatient settings must recognize the uniqueness of each patient, although the group membership may result from a common condition, similar presenting problem, or established setting.

Some settings foster expanding the group on certain occasions, when, for example, parents are invited to attend special sessions. Other establishments make these family-oriented meetings special events. Still other settings will schedule regular meetings for residents of inpatient programs, but will organize separate group meetings for a patient and his or her family. Some programs may offer what are called multiple family sessions, whereby all the families meet with all the group members. Conducting such mammoth sessions might seem daunting at first, but these sessions can have dramatic impact upon all who attend. Carl Whitaker (see Nichols & Schwartz, 2006) was a strong proponent for conducting large groups, including as *family* all the relatives, friends, and neighbors. Naturally, the leaders of such large groups need to be experienced and it is useful to have multiple leaders in such circumstances. All of these approaches are workable, but only if the structure of each approach is carefully delineated by the group leaders and the goals of the session are explained to each participant. These meetings can never be conducted impromptu; they must be carefully planned and orchestrated. The importance of a well-organized structure for any inpatient treatment program cannot be understated. Careful organization of the program to be conducted usually outweighs any differences in the strategy employed for its implementation.

The siblings of children and adolescents often suffer neglect because the identified siblings usually receive a great deal of negative attention for their behaviors and condition. It is important to address the other siblings' needs. I have run many groups for the siblings of children and adolescents in inpatient treatment. The universal concern of the children and adolescents in these groups is the expressed feeling that their siblings get all the attention due to their misbehavior or presenting problems, while they, the siblings, are often ignored. They report that parents expect them to take care of themselves in deference to the identified problem child or adolescent. Furthermore, these siblings indicate that parents expect them to always "behave," although the identified sibling is allowed free reign. Parents are frequently unaware of these perceptions of their nonidentified child, and offering group treatment for the siblings of inpatient youth can be an effective adjunct to addressing the issues of the entire family. Unfortunately, there is little published information on this matter. It is a problem area seen in inpatient treatment that is under-recognized and addressed, and thus, further inquiry and interventions must be pursued.

The exclusive focus upon a target client who is attending an inpatient program cannot produce the same therapeutic impact that can occur by addressing the entire family as part of the overall treatment milieu. Inpatient group psychotherapy must be part of an overall treatment approach for the entire family.

Gender and culture cannot be overlooked as consideration for groups within inpatient settings. However, these issues may be especially relevant for one group and less so for another, as the groups are often composed of admitted patients present at the time and are not always arranged in group a certain way. Whether the issues are gender (Garver & Glover, 1983), culture (de Mare, 1990), or general issues involving the group's organization (Glazer, 1969), leaders must be attentive to the impact of the overall membership upon individual group members and their behavior.

ASSESSMENT AND GROUP MEMBER IDENTIFICATION

Leaders of inpatient group therapy will usually not be part of the admission process. Their assessment of a potential group member will usually come from information taken from admission charts and by staff consultation. However, it is recommended that leaders also interview new members prior to their appearance in the group. This interview can enable the leaders to assess each of the member's unique traits, and especially their openness to therapy. Assessment allows leaders to be prepared to address any issues that might be unnecessarily disruptive to the group process when new persons join the sessions.

By using this screening process, leaders are not caught unaware by a member's issues when he or she joins the group. It also keeps the current momentum of the group productively employed when new members enter, and others leave. The coming and going of group members can become a useful adjunct to treatment by helping members address the issues of acceptance when new members arrive and learn to address closure when others leave. This potentially disruptive aspect can become a productive one when addressed correctly (e.g., via cognitive restructuring) in an ongoing group.

Assessment should include determining each client's behavioral repertoire. Leaders need to know what can be expected, and what clients are likely to do. It should include determining what may be difficult for them and what may be their strengths. It is especially important to know if the participants can anticipate the consequences of their actions. While forethought is important, some have to experience consequences before they can understand what they have done or what has occurred. They will need more help, that may be best provided, for example, via concrete behavioral interventions. It is also important to identify their key cognitions, both positive and negative. Are they open to new experiences or is it difficult for them to adjust? Can they recognize the supportive efforts of others? Are they generally cooperative? There are many more questions that might be asked, but leaders must certainly learn the extent to which each client can function within the group setting. Leaders must also evaluate the potential of each client for achieving growth in personal insight, behavior, and self-monitoring.

Such client assessments must usually be made much more quickly for inpatient settings than for outpatient or other settings, as the groups may have frequent changes in membership, and this often occurs on a day-to-day basis. Careful attention to initial client assessments will reap later rewards by providing a better understanding of the entering client and assuring the overall productive functioning for other members of the inpatient group.

Inpatient groups require ongoing assessments of each member. This information is often required for the inpatient chart to be completed following every session. In order to provide useful information, group leaders need to have clear goals for each client, as well as for the functioning of the entire group. Individual goals are developed from the initial assessments. These goals require some degree of measurement even if it is only based upon self-assessment and leader observations (Rice & Rutan, 1987).

Inpatient groups will likely have on-going criteria for evaluating group membership. Corcoran and Fischer (1987) provide two volumes of measures that can be used or easily adapted to provide a variety of instruments useful for evaluation in this setting.

GROUP INTERVENTIONS FOR INPATIENT SETTINGS

Because of the unique issues of inpatient settings, specific interventions must be targeted to the specialized treatment provided by the setting, but treatment must also address the unique conditions of each member of the group. For this reason, CBT stands out as an ideal treatment modality for inpatient groups. Leaders must operate within a group setting that will sustain constant changes in enrollment and varied duration for treatment. CBT offers the specific focus required for such varied conditions as may occur in an inpatient setting.

CBT has also been shown useful as a short-term mode of treatment. It is applicable to many conditions and especially suited for use by inpatient groups. The essential focus of CBT is upon the role of basic assumptions that underlay behavior (Beck, Rush, Shaw, & Emery, 1979). Such assumptions are the impetus for the thinking and acting of children and adolescents as they are for everyone. When these assumptions are practiced over years of development, they constitute schemas that provide meaning and structure for understanding the world. Unless children and adolescents have developed constructive schemas with appropriate ways of thinking and behaving, they will continue to follow the schema that has already produced their misbehaviors and emotional difficulties. Schemas are the blueprint for behavior (Beck & Weishaar, 1986). They can be identified through interviews and Socratic questions. Schema can also become apparent by observation of persons who incessantly repeat strategies already shown to be self-defeating. Self-defeating schemas in children and adolescents may arise from emotional deprivation, lack of positive models, and abuse, all of which produce limited self-understanding. Negative schemas disrupt effective cognitive processing.

Although all schemas can be identified and addressed, not all schemas are easily modified. However, group members can learn new ways of coping, observe others making efforts to improve, and learn to provide support to other group members who are gaining insight into themselves (McGinn & Sanderson, 2001). The straightforward approach of CBT makes it especially appealing to youth. CBT lacks the excessive overtones of pathology, and instead, it offers an alternative way of thinking and behaving. CBT appeals to children and adolescents because of its practical nature, as children and adolescents can be shown to use it in everyday circumstances.

Group leaders should begin session by fostering rapport and a sense of collaboration. Empathic understanding and careful listening create a climate of cooperation (Klein, 1985; MacKenzie, 1997). Modeling appropriate group behavior by leaders greatly assists other members to adapt to a productive atmosphere of cooperation.

Learning occurs throughout the group by means of observation and imitation. The group psychotherapy model greatly assists clients to understand their behavior by observing similar examples in other persons and evaluating the consequences. A stable group atmosphere allows members to exchange views and profit from supporting one another as they explore behavior in an environment free from oppression. In such circumstances, members feel more willing to try new roles and behaviors. This climate facilitates changes in thinking and behavior. When more than one leader is conducting the sessions, both must work cooperatively to provide modeling of cooperative behavior and to assist members in utilizing the advantages of member assistance in group psychotherapy (Roller & Nelson, 1991). Applying these exchanges and observations allows a member to explore new ways of operating, and the support of the group can enhance this process. This is the essence of group treatment (McKay & Paleg, 1992). Readers should consult the other chapters in this volume for further information on CBT applied to a variety of conditions and clients.

Children and adolescents greatly profit from participatory exercises (Morris & Cinnamon, 1974). Psychodrama and related experiential exercises are greatly enjoyed by many youth. While some individuals may be reluctant to volunteer, most group members readily respond to this approach, and eventually, the reluctant ones soon join in. Group leaders who need an orientation to this area, should consult the following references by Blatner (1996); Dyer and Uriend (1977); Jacobs, Masson, and Harvill (2002); Kellerman (1992); Kellerman and Hudgins (2000); Kipper (1986); Leveton (1992); and Moreno, Blomkvist, and Rutzel (2000). These references provide useful strategies with very practical exercises and activities useful for group sessions.

UNIQUE CHARACTERISTICS
OF INPATIENT SETTINGS

Group psychotherapy in an inpatient setting must be integrated with other modalities and services. Group leaders coming from other settings must learn to accommodate to multiple services, and usually to a much larger involvement with other treatment providers than may be encountered or typical of outpatient practice. Inpatient settings usually require that leaders give much more attention to coordination with other services. There are typically many more persons with whom to coordinate and communicate for inpatient work, far beyond the confines of conducting group psychotherapy. In an inpatient hospital setting, this would include physicians, psychiatrists, nurses, psychologists, social workers, and a host of other treatment and support personnel. Inpatient group psychotherapy requires accommodation to a multimodal treatment model.

Most inpatient settings will provide some form of individual treatment, family treatment, or supportive services. Participation in these multiple services also places a greater burden upon group leaders. It involves much more activity in the total milieu than merely conducting group psychotherapy. These multiple services also contain the strong possibility that some clients will attempt to divide and triangulate service providers. Careful attention to facilitating communication among all the providers is essential in order to keep this triangulating from occurring and for dealing with this phenomenon when it makes its appearance.

OVERCOMING OBSTACLES TO GROUP INPATIENT TREATMENT

The best way to overcome obstacles to group treatment in an inpatient setting is to be aware of these obstacles ahead of time, and before they can occur. To be forewarned is to be forearmed. In this chapter, I have presented the most prominent ones to keep in mind. It is important to address these matters appropriately without becoming disoriented by their seemingly sudden occurrence.

The most common obstacles that occur can be summarized into two categories: (1) those obstacles directly affecting the leaders and (2) those obstacles directly affecting the clients. Leader obstacles to success include the following:

1. Frequent group meetings with patients continuously entering and leaving group according to their changes in residence. Leaders must personally accommodate to this condition and use it productively.
2. Greater demands on coordination with other treatment providers. Considerable attention must be given to coordination and facilitation with other direct and ancillary treatment personnel and staff.
3. Greater severity in patient's condition and special considerations. Inpatient treatment assumes greater severity in presenting conditions and consequent longer expectations for change.
4. Need for flexibility in operating within an inpatient setting. Leaders must be accommodating to the demands of a complex organization.

   Client Obstacles are as follows:

1. Involuntary placement. This condition makes initial meetings potentially complex and fraught with latent issues.
2. Multiple treatment providers. Clients may become confused and divisive as a consequence.
3. Clients may or may not have group members with similar problems. This matter can be elevated beyond any usefulness by overattention to these differences, and by not giving attention to the commonality that prevails.

SUMMARY

This chapter has addressed inpatient group psychotherapy giving special attention to the role of leaders in operating these groups. Inpatient treatment typically serves severe and chronic conditions requiring a more restrictive environment following involuntary admission. Inpatient programs usually serve clients with special needs. The leaders of inpatient groups for children and adolescents must posses the capacity to work with difficult patients, to understand developmental aspects, and to participate in the total milieu of the patients. Conducting group psychotherapy within an institutional framework can be challenging as one deals with the special problems presented by clients whose needs require this focused attention.

There is great variety to the focus of the setting and the type of patients served. Some inpatient settings serve a specific function, while other settings deal with a broad array of client problems. References to these special needs as served by group psychotherapy have been given according to a number of categories. The requirements of group leaders operating within an inpatient setting are many and complex, especially while simultaneously dealing with the special problems and needs of inpatient group members. The problems and recommendations for the resolution of these issues have been given together with further readings.

Integrating group treatment with an individual, her or his family, and other modalities is both rewarding and challenging. Conducting these inpatient groups has both similarities and differences to operating groups in other settings, including other longer-term inpatient settings such as residential facilities. However, establishing goals and evaluating treatment for inpatient groups are similar tasks regardless of the setting. Readers should refer to the other chapters of this book for further information on specific *presenting problems*, and the chapter information on dealing with *other settings* and *issues*.

RECOMMENDED READINGS

A list of recommended readings was offered above, organized by presenting problem or condition, so the references are not repeated here. However, below is an outline for organizing one's reading around the focus of the chapter on inpatient treatment. Orientation to the inpatient treatment is paramount and suggested readings provide a basis for addressing this form of treatment as well as considerations for the ways in which conducting inpatient groups differ from conducting outpatient ones. CBT is recommended as the most useful mode of operating inpatient group psychotherapy. CBT offers the basis for treatment, and White and Freeman (2000) and Yalom (1994) should be consulted for additional information and further references.

Supplemental activities for conducting groups will be found in the references given at the end of the *Group Interventions for Inpatient Settings* section of this chapter. These references provide the foundation for learning useful activities for group work.

Specific attention to the variety of conditions treated by employing an inpatient model has been given by category in *Review of Resources for Inpatient Settings* section above.

Both chapters 1 and 2 of this volume offer further suggestions for conducting evaluations of the group's progress.

REFERENCES

Alonso, A. (1992). The shattered mirror: The treatment of a group of narcissistic patients. *Group, 16*, 210–219.

Alonso, A., & Rutan, J. (1993). Character change in group therapy. *International Journal of Group Psychotherapy, 43*, 439–451.

Alonso, A., & Rutan, J. (1988). The experience of shame and the restoration of self-respect in group therapy. *International Journal of Group Psychotherapy, 38*(1), 3–14.

Beck, A., Rush, A., Shaw, B., & Emery, G. (1979). *Cognitive therapy of personality disorders*. New York: Guilford.

Beck, A. & Weishaar, M. (1986). *Cognitive therapy*. Philadelphia: Center for Cognitive Therapy.

Beninati, J. (1998). Pilot project for male batterers. *Social Work with Groups, 12*(2), 63–74.

Blatner, A. (1996). *Acting-in: Practical applications of psychodramatic methods*. New York: Springer.

Brotman, A., Alonso, A., & Herzog, D. (1985). Group therapy for bulimia. *Group, 9*(1), 15–23.

Campbell, J. (1986). A survivor group for battered women. *Advances in Nursing Science, 8*, 13–20.

Corcoran, K., & Fischer, J. (1987). *Measures for clinical practice.* New York: The Free Press.

Corey, G. (2000). *Theory and practice of group counseling.* Belmont, CA: Brooks/Cole.

Dyer, W., & Uriend, J. (1977). *Counseling techniques that work.* Washington: American Counseling Association.

Fried, E. (1954). Benefits of combined therapy for the hostile withdrawn and the hostile dependent personality. *American Journal of Orthopsychiatry, 24,* 623–633.

Friedberg, R. D., & McClure, J. M. (2002). *Clinical practice of cognitive therapy with children and adolescents: The nuts and bolts.* New York: Guilford.

Gans, J. (1989). Effective management of hostility can benefit group therapy. *Psychiatric Times,* 12–13.

Gans, J., & Alonso, A. (1998). Difficult patients: Their construction in group therapy. *International Journal of Psychotherapy, 48*(3), 311-326.

Garver, C., & Glover, R. (1983). Gender issues in social group work. *Social Work with Groups, 6*(1), 5–18.

Glazer, H. (1969). Working through in group psychotherapy. *Journal of Group Psychotherapy, 19,* 292–306.

Grotsky, L., Camerer, C., & Damiano, L. (2000). *Group work with sexually abused children: A practitioners' guide.* Thousand Oaks: Sage.

Gruszinski, R. Brink, J., & Edleson, J. (1988). Support and education groups for children of battered women. *Child Welfare, 68,* 431–444.

Hall, A. (1985). Group psychotherapy for anorexia nervosa. In D. Garner, & P. Garfinkel (Eds.), *Handbook of psychotherapy for anorexia nervosa and bulimia* (pp. 117–131). New York: Guilford.

Harper-Giuffre, H., & MacKenzie, K. (Eds.). (1992). *Group psychotherapy for eating disorders.* Washington, DC: American Psychiatric Press.

James, S. (1992). Treatment of the shame involved in the experience of incest. In J. Rutan (Ed.), *Psychotherapy for the 1990's* (pp. 273–285). New York: Guilford.

Jacobs, E., Masson, R., & Harvill, R. (2002). *Group counseling: Strategies and skills.* New York: Wadsworth.

Kaufman, G. (1989). *The psychology of shame.* New York: Springer.

Kellermann, P. (1992). *Focus on psychodrama: The therapeutic aspects of psychodrama.* London: Kingsley.

Kellermann, P., & Hudgins, K. (2000). *Psychodrama and trauma: Acting out your pain.* London: Kingsley.

Kipper, D. (1986). *Psychotherapy through clinical role playing.* New York: Brunner/Mazel.

Klein, R. (1985). Some principles of short-term group therapy. *International Group Psychotherapy, 35,* 309–329.

Klein, R., & Schermer, V. (2000). *Group psychotherapy for psychological trauma.* New York: Guilford.

Laube, J. (1900). Why group therapy for bulimia? *International Journal of Group Psychotherapy, 40*(2), 169–187.

Lesi, J., & Hearn, K. (1984). Group treatment of children in shelters for battered women. In A. Roberts (Ed.), *Battered women and their families* (pp. 49–61). New York: Springer.

Leszcz, M. (1998). Group psychotherapy for the medically ill. *International Journal of Group Psychotherapy, 48*(2), 71–79.

Leveton, E. (1992). *A clinician's guide to psychodrama.* New York: Springer Publishing.

Lewis, M. (1992). *Shame.* New York: The Free Press.

MacKenzie, K. (1997). *Time-managed short-term group psychotherapy.* Washington, DC: American Psychiatric Press.

Malekoff, A. (1997). *Group work with adolescents: Principles and practice.* New York: Guilford.

de Mare, P. (1990). *Koinonia. From hate through dialogue to culture in the large group.* London: Free Association Press.

McGinn, L., & Sanderson, W. (2001). What allows cognitive behavioral therapy to be brief: Overview, efficacy, and crucial factors facilitating brief treatment. *Clinical Psychology: Science & Practice, 8*(1), 23–37.

McKay, M., & Paleg, K (1992). *Focal group psychotherapy.* Oakland, CA: New Harbinger.

Mennuti, R. B., Freeman, A., & Christner, R. W. (Eds.). (2005). *Cognitive-behavioral interventions in educational settings: A handbook for practice.* New York: Routledge.

Moreno, Z, Blomkvist, L., & Rutzel, T. (2000). *Psychodrama surplus reality and the art of healing.* London: Routledge.

Morris, K., & Cinnamon, K. (1974) *A handbook of verbal group exercises.* Springfield: Charles Thomas.

Nathanson, D. (1987). *The many faces of shame.* New York: Guilford.

Nichols, M., & Schwartz, R. (2006). *Family therapy.* New York: Allyn & Bacon.

Ormont, L. (1993). Resolving resistances to immediacy in the group setting. *International Journal of Group Psychotherapy, 43*(4), 399–418.

Peled, E., & Davis, D. (1995). *Groupwork with children of battered women.* London: Sage.

Piers, G., & Singer, M. (1939). *Shame and guilt.* Springfield, IL: Charles Thomas.

Reinecke, M. A., Dattilio, F. M., & Freeman, A. (2003). *Cognitive therapy with children and adolescents: A casebook for clinical practice*. New York: Guilford.

Reiss, H., & Rutan, J. (1992). Group therapy for eating disorders. *Group, 16*(2), 79–83.

Rice, C. (1995) The dynamics of the co-therapy relationship. *Group, 19*(2), 87–99.

Rice, C., & Rutan, J. (1987). *Inpatient group psychotherapy*. New York: MacMillan.

Roberts, A. (1984). *Battered women and their families*. New York: Springer.

Roller, W., & Nelson, V. (1991). *The art of co-therapy*. New York: Guilford.

Rosenbaum, M. (1996). *Handbook of short-term therapy groups*. New York: Jason Aronson.

Rosenbaum, M. (1972). Group psychotherapy with adolescents. In B. Wolman (Ed.), *Manual of Child Psychopathology* (pp. 294–311). New York: McGraw-Hill.

Rosenbaum, M., & Kraft, I. (1972). Group psychotherapy with children. In B. Wolman (Ed.), *Manual of Child Psychopathology* (pp. 110–127). New York: McGraw-Hill.

Rosenthal, L. (1996). *Resolving resistances in group psychotherapy*. New York: Jason Aronson.

Roth, B., Kibel, H., & Stone, W. (1990). *The difficult patient in group*. Madison, CT: International Universities Press.

Schacht, A., Kerlinsky, D., & Carlson, C. (1990). Group therapy with sexually abused boys. *International Journal of Group Psychotherapy, 40*, 401–417.

Scheff, T. (1995). Shame and related emotions. *American Behavioral Scientist, 38*(8), 1053–1150.

Sciacca, K. (1991). *An integrated treatment approach for severely mentally ill individuals with substance disorders*. New York: Jossey-Bass.

Shapiro, J., Peltz, L., & Bernadett-Shapiro, S. (1998). *Brief group treatment: Practical training for therapists and counselors*. Belmont, CA: Brooks/Cole.

Shields, W. (2000). Hope and the inclination to be troublesome. *International Journal of Group Psychotherapy, 50*, 33–48.

Silverstein, J. (1993). Secrets vs. privacy in group psychotherapy. *Group, 17*, 107–114.

Spira, J. (1997). *Group therapy for medically ill patients*. New York: Guilford.

Spotnitz, H. (1976). *Dealing with aggression in groups. Psychotherapy of Pre-oedipal conditions*. New York: Jason Aronson.

Stone, W. (1996). *Group therapy for people with chronic mental illness*. New York: Guilford.

Toseland, R., & Siporin, M. (1986). When to recommend group treatment: A review of the clinical and group literature. *International Journal of Group Psychotherapy, 36*, 171–201.

Ulman, K. (1993). Group psychotherapy with the medically ill. In H. Kaplan & B. Sadock (Eds.), *Comprehensive Group Psychotherapy* (3rd ed., pp. 459–470). Baltimore, MD: Williams & Wilkins.

van der Kolk, B. (1993). Group for patients with histories of catastrophic trauma. In A. Alonso, & H. Swiller (Eds.), *Group Therapy in Clinical Practice* (pp. 289–305). Washington, DC: American Psychiatric Press.

Voth, A. (1963). Group therapy with hospitalized alcoholics. *Quarterly Journal of Studies in Alcohol Abuse, 24*, 289–311.

Webb, L., & Leehan, J. (1996). *Group treatment for adult survivors of abuse*. Newbury Park, CA: Sage.

White, J., & Freeman, A, (Eds.). (2000). *Cognitive-behavioral group therapy for specific problems and populations*. Washington, DC: American Psychological Association.

Yalom, I. (2005). *The theory and practice of group psychotherapy* (5th ed.). New York: Basic Books.

Chapter Nine

Cognitive-Behavior Group Therapy in Residential Treatment

Christopher Summers

Residential programs are designed to provide 24-hour care for youth who are unable to be maintained in the community due to the severity of emotional and behavioral difficulties, or as a result of incarceration for criminal behaviors. Typically, these children are at risk for being a danger to themselves or others, and require a safe, fully-staffed setting to ensure the stabilization of dysfunction. Placement of children and adolescents in residential treatment occurs for a variety of reasons, ranging from severe psychopathology or extreme behavior problems (including legal involvement) to significant family dysfunction that interferes with healthy and successful academic, social, and community functioning. Many young people referred for residential treatment have a long history of family dysfunction that may include experiences of abuse, domestic violence, substance abuse in the home, or neglect, and often school failure and aggressive and self-destructive behaviors. Typical diagnoses include Major Depression, Borderline Personality Disorder, Psychotic Disorders, Conduct Disorder, Substance Abuse Disorders, Post-traumatic Stress Disorder, and other severe personality and psychological disorders. They often present with symptoms of oppositional/defiant behavior, anger outbursts, severe mood disturbance, anxiety, self-injurious behaviors, substance abuse, and poor social skills. It is widely accepted that placing children in the least restrictive placement possible is the goal; however, a child's referral for this level of care often results from the need for more intensive treatment than can be obtained through outpatient means.

While residential facilities may specialize in specific presenting problems (e.g., drug and alcohol intervention, eating disorder treatment, or juvenile detention), what they have in common is 24-hour supervised living that includes schooling and therapeutic intervention by professionals of all levels of training. Typical length of stay at a residential treatment facility can range from 1 month to 24 months (Underwood, Barretti, Storms, & Safonte-Strumolo, 2004) or longer. Staff-to-child ratios are typically similar to inpatient hospital programs, given safety and security needs both in terms of behavioral and emotional management. Most residential treatment facilities attempt to provide comprehensive treatment, including milieu therapy, individual therapy, group therapy, family therapy, psychiatric services, and education services. Milieu therapy includes providing corrective interactions and relationships with adults, training children and adolescents in daily living skills, and providing supervision. Many centers include contingency management programs, such as a token economy, that encourage prosocial and positive behaviors in order to obtain privileges. These components of the residential setting clearly represent the emphasis on skill-building, behavioral management and change, and improvement in interpersonal skills and relationships that are consistent with cognitive-behavioral therapy (CBT)—making it a natural environment in which to facilitate the inclusion of direct CBT services.

The focus of this chapter will be on the provision of group therapy services from a CBT framework within any residential facility. A brief description of the historical and current trends in residential treatment will be presented, with an emphasis on the role of group therapeutic intervention to address the increasingly difficult needs of residents within these environments. Specifically, CBT will be discussed as an effective approach to the provision of group psychological services with children and adolescents and as a fitting model and modality of service delivery within this setting given the demand for intensive therapeutic services. A cognitive-behavioral conceptualization of presenting problems for children with severe emotional and behavioral difficulties will be offered, and specific cognitive and behavioral techniques that would be especially beneficial given the nature of residential settings will be discussed. In addition, assessment of group members and considerations for implementation of group CBT in residential settings will be presented. Finally, some of the unique characteristics of the residential setting and obstacles faced in providing cognitive-behavioral group therapy in this environment will be offered. Given that the majority of presenting problems that warrant residential placement are covered in much more detail within the specific problem-topic chapters of this text, the bulk of this chapter will outline in general the incorporation of the CBT model into group treatment within residential treatment facilities (including detention centers, included within the term "residential" for the remainder of the chapter). Given the lack of literature on CBT group treatment in residential settings, the majority of this chapter will reflect my experience and the literature on group CBT in general with children and adolescents, emphasizing considerations relevant when incorporating this model into this unique setting.

CHANGES IN RESIDENTIAL TREATMENT

Changing Role of Patients

Dramatic changes in both children and adolescent populations treated in residential centers have been noted in the literature (Berridge & Brodie, 1998; Connor, Melloni, & Harrison, 1998). The populations of youth served in residential treatment centers are often children and adolescents who are unable to be maintained in the community. There is evidence that the acuity level of residential treatment centers has been increasing as limitations to inpatient hospital programs have led to referrals of increasing numbers of psychotic and severely personality-disordered youths to residential programs (Leichtman, Leichtman, Barber, & Neese, 2000). Other referrals to residential programs include young people being discharged from inpatient hospital programs and those who have failed in group home or foster care placements, as well as youths who have committed legal violations warranting consequences of removal from the community. It is clear that the level of psychopathology within residential treatment centers has increased over the past few decades (Berridge & Brodie, 1998; Connor, Melloni, & Harrison, 1998), with youth entering facilities with more challenging disorders and behaviors.

Changing Role of Therapy

The role of the therapist in residential facilities varies across programs and settings, but a general shift has occurred that typically includes more involvement of therapists in activities other than psychotherapy, including administrative tasks and milieu management. Psychotherapeutic emphasis in residential treatment for children and adolescents developed over the mid-twentieth century from a tradition of orphanages, training schools, and detention centers (Jemerin & Phillips, 1988). Historically, milieu therapy was the most common form of treatment and, if necessary, psychoanalysis initially took place off-site (Cohler, 2003). Eventually, therapy sessions more often took place in the residential setting as the living environment itself became more of a focus over time and the importance of having feedback from a therapist to structure the setting and its conditions led to more therapists being employed in residential facilities (Cohler, 2003). As the nature of residential treatment has shifted to shorter-term treatment with increased use of cognitive and behavioral techniques (Zimmerman, 1999), the role of the therapist began to expand in order to provide guidance for childcare workers, to facilitate group therapy, and to lead the treatment regimen of the child.

ROLE OF CBT IN RESIDENTIAL TREATMENT

Structured Nature of CBT

Over the last 20 years, many questions have arisen about the cost effectiveness of utilizing residential treatment. Historically, the effectiveness of residential treatment has not been examined closely, though it has consistently been one of the most expensive types of child welfare services (Barth, 2002; Bates, English, & Kouidou-Giles, 1997). Along with the increased examination of treatment costs and outcomes, the typical length of stay in a residential center has decreased. Despite mixed results on studies reviewing the effectiveness of residential treatment, almost one-fourth of U.S. funds spent on child mental health are utilized for residential settings (Burns, Hoagwood, & Maultsby, 1998). This large financial burden has brought about an emphasis on cost scrutinization and treatment outcomes. The trend in the provision of therapeutic services within residential settings, therefore, is to increase the effectiveness of services and decrease the time and course of treatment necessary for positive outcome. Cognitive-behavioral group treatment is an approach that maximizes staff efficiency, facilitates the establishment of objectives that can be easily measured, and requires a relatively shorter duration to achieve a greater level of stabilization and desired treatment results.

Flexibility and Applicability

Given the decreased length of stay at most residential centers, it is necessary to replace longer-term therapies with approaches that are more structured, direct, symptom-oriented, and skill-building. Hence, the applicability of approaches such as CBT has been strengthened. In addition, there is evidence demonstrating the use of cognitive-behavioral treatments to address a wide variety of presenting problems typically seen in children and adolescents within residential settings, including depression, anxiety, eating disorders, substance abuse, trauma histories, conduct disorders, and anger problems (e.g., Reinecke, Dattilio, & Freeman, 2003; Kendall, 2000). This level of flexibility inherent in cognitive-behavioral treatment approaches makes it a compatible match for the provision of therapeutic services within residential settings.

Adjunctive CBT Group Treatment vs. Comprehensive CBT Program

Cognitive-behavioral groups can be used as a supplemental group treatment or as a part of a comprehensive CBT program. In Witt-Browder's (2000) discussion of the partial hospital setting, she describes these two models for CBT in inpatient treatment as reported by Wright, Thase, Ludgate, & Beck (1993). Supplemental ("add-on") CBT groups have been utilized in inpatient (Freeman, Schrodt, Gilson, & Ludgate, 1993) and partial hospital programs (Loring & Fraboni, 1990). Witt-Browder (2000) proposed a model for a comprehensive CBT partial hospital program as has been implemented in inpatient programs (Wright et al., 1993). Similar to inpatient and partial hospital programs, CBT groups can be utilized in residential treatment as "add-on" groups, but may be more beneficial as part of a comprehensive CBT program. In the supplemental model, staff members' competing approaches may confuse clients (Wright et al., 1993) or treatment compliance may be weakened (Loring & Fraboni, 1990). While ideally the majority of residential staff will be trained and familiar with CBT concepts and treatment, staff members often have their own agendas and subscribe to other theoretical perspectives. If CBT treatment is offered as a supplemental group treatment and not part of a broader CBT treatment program, communication with line staff is even more crucial. In order to avoid client confusion and promote compliance, staff members should be trained in CBT and encouraged to assist in client's out-of-group work.

LACK OF LITERATURE ON EFFECTIVE GROUP TREATMENT IN RESIDENTIAL CARE

Despite the current trend focusing on treatment outcome research, there is very little literature on group CBT approaches with children and adolescents in residential centers. Stevens' (2004) review of this literature found few available studies and concluded that most had small sample sizes and provided limited follow-up data. One study of aggressive male adolescents in residential treatment found positive results of a CBT program, including improved problem-solving, conflict resolution, and increased self-esteem (Larson, Calamari, West, & Frevert, 1998). Another study found that a CBT program (along with increased structure in the residential setting) helped pre-adolescent boys with conduct problems to improve their decision-making and recognize the consequences for their actions (Wright, 1995). Other studies showed positive outcomes of CBT approaches when combined with consistent emotional support (Scholte & Van Der Ploeg, 2000), parent training programs (Matthys, 1997), and expressive therapies (Davis & Boster, 1993). Valliant's (1993) study of CBT treatment with 10 boys in a residential center yielded positive results in self-esteem and a reduction in verbal hostility, but 1-year follow-up results showed that 80% of the boys had committed crimes and been incarcerated. Overall, the limited literature suggests positive outcomes of CBT approaches in residential treatment. Stevens (2004) suggested that potential problems with generalizability and maintenance of treatment could be addressed with inclusion of peers (Duan & O'Brien, 1998) and parents (Scholte & Van Der Ploeg, 2000).

TYPES OF GROUPS CONDUCTED IN RESIDENTIAL CARE

Given the diversity of presenting problems of youth in residential programs, there are many problem areas that may be effectively addressed via CBT group treatments. Given the lack of research specific to the incorporation of these topic-specific treatments in residential centers, clinicians should rely on empirical approaches and monitor progress through the use of established symptom measures. A more extensive review of the format of these problem-specific CBT groups is provided in the respective chapters within this text. This section will outline a sample of typical problem groups and components of treatment easily incorporated within the residential setting. Some of the specific intervention components mentioned will be discussed in greater detail later in the chapter when presenting the unique characteristics of this setting that support the inclusion of CBT principles.

Depression

A large majority of the adolescents in residential treatment present with severe emotional disturbance, specifically with either primary or secondary depression. Children and adolescents in residential settings are often at a high risk for depression due to histories of abuse and neglect, as well as other trauma. Proper assessment is necessary because depression is often masked by outward behavioral problems or viewed as "normal" adolescent anger, irritability and hostility. Therefore, CBT groups should seek to address mood symptoms, regulation, and stabilization for youth residents. Cognitive-behavioral treatment programs for depression should include mood monitoring, social skills training, pleasant events scheduling, relaxation training, cognitive restructuring, communication skills training, conflict resolution, and maintenance training (Clarke, Lewinsohn, & Hops, 1990).

Anxiety Disorders and PTSD

Although children and adolescents in residential treatment may not present with a primary anxiety disorder, it is common for youth with depression and/or significant behavioral problems to be actually struggling with some form of anxiety (and often this anxiety relates to past trauma). A CBT group for anxiety typically involves a combination of components, including: psychoeducation, cognitive restructuring, self-reinforcement, modeling, exposure, relaxation training, role-play, and contingency management (Kane & Kendall, 1989). Many of the children placed in residential settings via the child welfare system have suffered abuse and neglect. Such experiences, as well as other trauma, lead to the need for effective trauma treatment in residential centers. For adolescents with Posttraumatic Stress Disorder, Erickson and Achilles (2004) summarize an approach by Cohen, Mannarino, Berliner, and Deblinger (2000) targeting trauma-related cognitive distortions, and including psychoeducation, relaxation therapy, thought stopping and replacement, and family involvement to provide support, address family dysfunction, and enhance maintenance of treatment effects.

Eating Disorders

Eating disorders are often treated in specialized hospital or residential programs that include a component of CBT. CBT approaches for eating disorders typically focus on operant techniques to increase weight gain, as well as cognitive restructuring, self-monitoring, and stimulus control (Fonagy, Target, Cottrell, Phillips, & Kurtz, 2002). Research has demonstrated efficacy of such approaches (Mitchell, Hoberman, Peterson, Mussell, & Pyle, 1996) with bulimia in conjunction with pharmacological treatment (Goldbloom et al., 1997) and with adolescents diagnosed with Anorexia Nervosa (Wilson & Fairburn, 1993). Despite mixed views about parental involvement with eating disorder treatment, parental support can often have a positive impact on treatment of adolescents with eating disorders and family therapy to change contributing patterns is generally appropriate.

Substance Abuse

In situations that require residential services with substance-abusing adolescents, a determination must be made whether mental health problems are of highest concern, whether mental health and substance abuse issues both require considerable attention (dual diagnosis program), or whether the treatment focus will primarily address alcohol or drug abuse problems (residential program specialized for substance abuse). It is clear that substance abuse problems often coexist with many of the problems that are treated in residential centers (Cocozza, 1997; Grosz et al., 1994) and comorbidity is associated with worse treatment outcomes than substance abuse by itself (Randall, Henggeler, Pickrel, & Brondino, 1999). Cognitive-behavioral treatment with adolescent substance abuse typically involves a heavy emphasis on skills training. It is especially important in treating substance abuse problems that clinicians guard against negative group processes that may counteract the positive effects of treatment. Typical components of treatment should include motivational enhancement, functional analysis, interpersonal skills (i.e., assertiveness, giving and receiving criticism, conflict resolution, etc.), managing negative emotions, and relapse prevention skills (e.g., identifying high risk situations, coping, refusal skills, and goal setting; Myers, Brown and Vik, 1998).

Anger, Aggression, and Conduct Problems

Despite coexisting with internalizing disorders, externalizing behaviors are often the problems that lead to placement in residential facilities (especially in the case of juvenile detention facilities). It has been estimated that more than half of the youth placed in residential programs have a history of aggressive behaviors (Grosz et al., 1994). Aggression and other behavior problems can have a severe negative impact on peer and family relationships, as well as academic performance. Anger management groups are common in residential treatment and include components of self-control training, problem-solving skills, social skills training, relaxation training, and role-play. Glick and Goldstein (1987) describe an approach that includes structured learning training (curriculum of 50 prosocial behaviors skills), anger control training (stress inoculation and anger control techniques), and moral education (fairness, justice, and empathy).

ASSESSMENT AND GROUP MEMBER IDENTIFICATION

Screening for Potential Group Members

As suggested earlier, the increasing acuity of children and adolescents typically presenting for residential treatment requires a careful approach to consideration for group involvement. On the other hand, the nature of the residential setting requires that residents typically participate in group treatment at least daily. This necessity for service delivery must be balanced with appropriateness of inclusion. Although there are cognitive or behavioral components that may be beneficial for the majority of children and adolescents in residential treatment, it is necessary to screen group members to assess level of pathology and readiness for involvement in group. When possible, pairing members with similar presentations into perhaps different sections of a particular topic-group should be considered (e.g., conducting two groups for eating disordered youth, one for those of a more severe presentation and a second for those already within the process of recovery). The screening process includes determination of members' cognitive and intellectual functioning, psychological functioning, ability to introspect, measures of symptoms, and level of motivation. While these considerations are not unique to groups conducted within the residential setting, what is unique to this setting is the heterogeneous population of residents, severity of pathology, and mandatory nature of group participation. It should be noted that while many residents in treatment facilities may not be appropriate for participation in CBT groups, many of the components can be effectively taught in individual treatment until they are more appropriate for group inclusion.

Cognitive and intellectual functioning. Given the degree of cognitive ability required for some tasks of cognitive-behavioral intervention, it is important to appraise potential group members' level of cognitive functioning. Many well-meaning clinicians have attempted to facilitate CBT groups without screening out lower functioning clients only to find that undue time is spent over-explaining concepts, "selling" the rationale for the group, and dealing with behavior problems from members that disengage from the group for lack of understanding. Meanwhile, those group members that are capable of actively participating in more cognitively oriented interventions are not receiving the focus of the facilitators. It is most important that clinicians consider whether potential group members have the ability to complete the cognitive tasks (i.e., monitoring symptoms, completing homework tasks, identifying and challenging thoughts, etc.). However, some of these tasks may be directly related to a client's ability to introspect, which may not be directly related to intelligence per se, but is central to many cognitive tasks. Determining a cutoff for intellectual functioning can be helpful, but should not be rigidly adhered. For example, an IQ of 90 or above has been suggested as a cutoff for some groups (Feindler & Ecton, 1986). This is not to say that CBT groups are totally incompatible with youth who have lower cognitive functioning levels, but instead that the focus of the task may be different. For instance, groups with lower cognitive abilities may be focused more on skills building (e.g., problem solving, life skills, social skills).

Psychological functioning.   A comprehensive assessment is important in identifying potential contraindications for CBT participation. Depending on the type of CBT group and problem areas addressed, a child's or adolescent's presentation of acute symptoms may necessitate that group CBT is not appropriate, such as delusional thinking, severe deficits in reality testing or other psychotic symptoms, severe suicidal ideation, and self-injurious behaviors. Once again, given the acuity level in most residential centers, it is most helpful to be flexible in considering such concerns rather than adopting strict rules regarding such matters (e.g., a group specifically targeting self-injurious behavior is obviously appropriate for active self-mutilators).

The two primary considerations are the impact of pathology on the potential group member's ability to participate and benefit from the group and how the group will be affected in its ability to work towards group goals given this member's symptom severity. In some situations, clinicians may decide that group CBT approaches should be utilized only once acute symptoms decrease to a manageable level (i.e., decreased severity of suicidal ideation, etc.) and have been addressed in individual treatment or other services. In others, it is likely necessary to allow clients with some level of suicidal ideation, for example, to participate in a CBT group for depression. Clinicians can assess symptom severity with a number of rating scales, such as the *Adolescent Psychopathology Scale* (Reynolds, 1998) or *Beck Depression Inventory* (Beck, Steer, & Brown, 1996), and through clinical interview and staff observation.

Symptom measures.   Throughout assessment and treatment, basic symptom measurement is needed to determine residents' need for a particular CBT group, their benefit of group participation, and the possibility of symptom worsening due to involvement in treatment. Measures are too numerous to list given the wide variety of presenting problems within a residential setting (see each problem chapter for specifics related to presenting topics). However, an example of symptoms and behaviors to monitor through objective and subjective means (such as staff observation and tracking) include mood symptoms, anxiety, hopelessness, dissociation, sleep and appetite disturbance, frustration tolerance, and peer interactions. For instance, anxiety-related symptoms may be objectively measured with the *Beck Anxiety Inventory* (Beck & Steer, 1993) and number of hours of sleep, as well as subjective staff and self-ratings of anxiety.

Motivation for tasks and homework.   As in any setting, a child or adolescent's level of motivation varies throughout placement in residential treatment. Many residents do not choose to be in treatment, and therefore, may have little motivation to make changes, especially initially. On the other hand, in my experience, I have often seen a "honeymoon" phase as part of the initial transition of youth to residential treatment.

During this time, children and adolescents may be more motivated for treatment and may not present behaviors and symptoms that were observed prior to intake. As the resident becomes more comfortable in the setting and with routines and expectations, they are likely to revert to previous ways of behaving, thinking, and feeling. As an adolescent nears discharge, they tend to have a higher level of motivation. There are times, however, when residents may also exhibit an increase of symptoms prior to discharge if there is resistance to returning to a less supportive environment or anxiety about their ability to succeed.

Each group member's level of motivation must be considered as part of the screening process due to the expectations of the group that include active session participation, peer interaction and support, and completion of homework tasks outside of group. Efforts should be made by the group facilitator to engage clients at the beginning of treatment. If clients are motivated and willing to engage in a CBT group and complete tasks soon after placement at a residential center, they are likely to benefit faster from skills they will learn and practice. Considering the stage of change of members provides insight into their cognitive schema related to their problems, needs, responsibility for making changes, resistance to intervention, etc. This understanding of the perceptions of group members affords the CBT group facilitator an awareness of possible distortions at work for intervention.

STAFF CONSIDERATIONS

In order to implement CBT groups, it is necessary to have competent group facilitators who are trained appropriately in cognitive-behavioral theory, principles, and techniques. In addition, it is necessary for residential staff (even those not facilitating groups) to be able to monitor and assist children and adolescents with their CBT homework and monitor expressed beliefs and possible distortions within the milieu.

Staff Training and Requirements

The basic requirements for cognitive-behavioral therapists include a working knowledge of CBT principles and methods. Naturally, the likelihood of success is improved for CBT groups in which facilitators have greater familiarity with CBT concepts. However, a facilitator's experience in conducting groups and his or her understanding of group development and processes in and of themselves can often be extremely valuable (Malekoff, 1997). Every clinician facilitates their "first" group at some point, but the value of observing and co-facilitating groups, as well as studying the literature on the role of the group leader and typical group development, should not be underestimated. Ideally, facilitators will have both experience in group therapy facilitation and in the application of the CBT framework and principles.

Group facilitators should be clinicians that possess a Master's degree in a mental health-related field. Due to staff unavailability, the fact remains that many properly trained group facilitators do not possess a Master's degree and are able to facilitate CBT groups adequately once they have gained experience and proper supervision. It is recommended in most situations that groups have two facilitators, and in many instances, it may be appropriate that the second facilitator not possess a Master's degree. As is a limitation within residential facilities, the majority of staff available to facilitate the large and various number of group treatments offered (in terms of problem topics and frequency of sessions per day) are primarily Bachelor-level counselors. Though their understanding of group process and skills once experience is gained may afford them the necessary skills to effectively facilitate groups, it is unlikely they have been properly trained in the CBT model and would require specific training and supervision by a skilled CBT clinician. Once this training has been established, childcare counselors may be quite successful at facilitating effective cognitive-behavioral groups, especially those focusing on skills building.

GROUP INTERVENTIONS IN RESIDENTIAL CARE

Once group members have been screened and selected for participation in a CBT group, the process of cognitive-behavioral group therapy begins with an orientation session that includes detailed group rules and expectations. The first phase of group treatment also includes psychoeducation regarding the CBT group process. Treatment planning is the next phase of treatment that will be dependent on the specific areas to be addressed (i.e., depression, PTSD, substance abuse, eating disorders, etc.) and includes setting goals, monitoring outcomes, and planning for discharge. The treatment phase is more specific to content and includes appropriate interventions, such as symptom and thought monitoring, problem-solving skill development, cognitive restructuring, social skills training, behavioral experiments, and relaxation skills training. Homework, follow-through, and progress monitoring are also central to the inclusion of group CBT within the residential setting.

Orientation to Cognitive Behavioral Treatment and Group Rules

The orientation to CBT treatment involves an explanation of the principles and goals of CBT and the rules for the group. Typically, this can be done in the first session of close-ended groups, but for open-ended groups may need to be done individually as part of an intake evaluation or otherwise periodically for a refresher for all members. Although the scope of this chapter does not allow for an in-depth explanation of CBT (see chapter 1), the foundation for the group should be laid, including a simplistic discussion of the relationship between thoughts, emotions, and behaviors. Facilitators should make efforts to sell the treatment and its proven effectiveness in order to motivate members to put forth the required effort. If members are apprehensive about the nature of CBT or the interventions incorporated, they should be encouraged to test the program principles through exercises and experiments within and outside of group to determine for themselves.

Group rules and expectations vary across settings, but should be agreed upon by group members. These rules typically include promoting confidential communication, providing equal group time among members, completing assigned homework, offering support to others, and staying positive. Confidentiality among group members is of great importance in residential treatment and should be communicated as crucial. In many cases, group members may spend much of their time within the same unit of the residential center or in school with other group members. It is likely that some of the residents may have difficulty trusting others in general because of past family problems, trauma or abuse history, and the fact that their placement reflects a lack of control over their very living conditions. When an adolescent has difficulty trusting other group members, they will be less likely to engage fully in the treatment process. These behavioral observations may provide insight to the facilitators regarding belief systems of the residents, and allow them to facilitate awareness in members of their own underlying automatic thoughts throughout work in group.

Psychoeducational Component

The psychoeducational component of cognitive-behavioral treatment is one of the most crucial aspects of treatment and involves a discussion of symptoms and presenting problems to educate members, but also the presentation and application of CBT concepts and skills. In an ideal situation, where cognitive-behavioral approaches are utilized as part of a comprehensive CBT program, psychoeducational groups may occur for all residents. Whether or not CBT principles are presented elsewhere, the psychoeducation component begins in the first session and continues throughout treatment. As the group progresses, psychoeducation topics may address a wide range of areas, including cognitive distortions that affect family problems, interpersonal relationships, coping, and self-esteem. The success of the group hinges on concepts being presented in a fashion that is understandable and practical. Members must clearly comprehend the materials in a way that they will be able to apply them to their day-to-day situations and interactions outside of group. When members are younger children or less cognitively developed, the direct instruction regarding cognitions and their restructuring may be less feasible, and be something that the skilled clinician aims to do by directing the group's discussion and interventions to promote indirect awareness and behavioral change.

Treatment Planning

In any setting, treatment planning is an essential part of a clinician's duties. However, in a residential center, it involves a great deal more. A typical residential treatment plan is designed to coordinate a myriad of interdisciplinary services that may include individual, group, and family therapy, psychiatry, nursing, recreational therapy, art therapy, etc. If possible, residents and their families should have input into the treatment plan. The following sections specifically address treatment planning in regards to cognitive-behavioral groups.

Focus of treatment.   As discussed previously, there are many potential focus areas for cognitive-behavioral groups, depending on the presenting issues of the residents. The treatment plan should clearly state the problem areas to be addressed in the group, and CBT facilitates this process as the model emphasizes specifying objectives of treatment and desired results for individuals (what improvement would "look like"). Given the long-term nature of residential treatment, it can be helpful to plan primary and secondary goals. Secondary goals may be addressed in additional groups, set for later in treatment, or in follow-up care after discharge.

Goal setting.   Goal setting is an important part of treatment planning in order to help residents (and their families, when possible) assume ownership of the treatment in the residential center. Goals should be individualized to each client and focused on specific problem areas addressed. Long-term goals should be broken down into several short-term goals in order to promote success. Group members should be encouraged to discuss and plan strategies for dealing with barriers to achieving goals. In addition, each problem area should be clearly defined in behavioral terms in order to measure outcomes (i.e., client will reduce score on CDI by 50%, etc.). Cognitive-behavioral interventions may then be designed to affect the desired outcomes for lasting change.

As mentioned previously, clients may prioritize primary goals to be addressed immediately and secondary goals for later in treatment. For instance, in situations with involvement of government social service agencies (i.e., the Department of Children and Family Services, DCFS), a client's family may be minimally involved at the outset of residential treatment and discharge planning may not be determined. Therefore, secondary goals, such as generalizing skills to the home environment and other goals of family therapy may be addressed later in treatment when transition plans are formulated, as well as after discharge.

Monitoring outcomes.   The effectiveness of treatment intervention will be monitored at designated times during treatment. A baseline screening should be done prior to starting treatment with follow-ups completed at regular intervals in order to determine the efficacy of the treatment and monitor growth and skill development. It may also be the case that as residents begin to improve coping, correct skill deficits, and change distorted belief systems that lead to more effective functioning, their goals for treatment will change. Monitoring this process closely will ensure that members do not become "stuck" within the same treatment plan despite those issues being modified (i.e., residents with abuse histories who continue to address certain components of their experiences even after they have already worked through restructuring beliefs about helplessness, guilt, etc. may actually experience greater difficulties if goals do not adjust accordingly to keep up with progress.). Specific measures for assessing progress on goals can be behavioral and emotional measures to assess functioning, as well as the measures used initially to assess symptom presentation for group readiness (those measures, depending on presenting problems, are suggested in individual subject chapters of this text.)

Planning for discharge.   Planning for discharge (and transitioning to the community) is an important part of treatment planning that begins when residents are first placed in centers. From the first day of programming, the ultimate goal is to help prepare the client for discharge. Each short-term goal should also lead toward the eventual long-term, discharge goals. It is often difficult to plan for discharge at the outset, however, as it may not be determined whether a resident will be returning home or to other less restrictive settings (i.e., group homes, foster care, independent living, etc.).

Cognitive Restructuring

The restructuring of distorted cognitions is one of the most central premises of a cognitive-behavioral approach. Children and adolescents in residential care typically present with a wide variety of negative and dysfunctional belief systems as a result of their experiences or disorders. The benefits of cognitive restructuring relate to children and adolescents learning to recognize their maladaptive schema and the resulting negative impact on emotional, behavioral, and social functioning, as well as become more realistic in their perceptions of themselves, others, and their circumstances.

Social Skill Development

Many youth in residential centers have a long history of interpersonal difficulties with peers and adults. There are many skill sets that can be taught in and of themselves, but also to improve residents' social skills, including communication skills, emotional awareness, assertiveness skills, and negotiation/problem-solving. When used effectively, they can be helpful in reducing aggression, increasing frustration tolerance, and improving relationships. These skills can be presented in the group and should also be practiced, role-played, and assigned for homework between sessions, as the residential setting affords group members with ample opportunities for practice and behavioral experimentation—as well as trained staff available to assist in facilitating growth-experiences and evaluating outcomes.

Pleasant Activities

Because of the isolation from family, friends, and the home community that results when children are placed in residential facilities, many residents may attend only to the negative aspects of constant supervision, continuous treatment, and feelings of failure or hopelessness for leading a "normal" life. The importance of increasing youths' enjoyable leisure activities should be emphasized as part of the group curriculum given it's potential for facilitating motivation, feelings of self-efficacy, a sense of normalcy, and hope. Lewinsohn and associates (1990), for example, emphasize the impact of reduced activity level in children and adolescent depression. Group members should be encouraged to identify activities that can be utilized for leisure or to be used as a distraction technique to provide them with the opportunity to feel something other than depressed, for example, and to encourage a natural task of youth—play and positive social interactions.

Relaxation Skills

Teaching children and adolescents to utilize relaxation skills can be helpful with many different presenting concerns. Relaxation training is most effective with those who struggle with mood instability and anxiety, controlling anger and aggressive impulses, issues of immediate gratification, and those who rely on unhealthy physiological methods of coping. Relaxation training helps residents cope more effectively with stress and tension that likely result from their other difficulties, or even from the placement itself. Group members are taught to achieve a state of relaxation through utilizing abdominal breathing, deep muscle relaxation, and imagery activities. Exercises are practiced in group and residents are expected to practice the skills between sessions so they become a natural option for the management of difficult emotional and physiological states.

Relaxation and imagery techniques also facilitate group members' ability to monitor automatic thoughts and develop greater cognitive control.

UNIQUE CHARACTERISTICS OF RESIDENTIAL CARE

Several characteristics of residential settings exist that are unique and affect the provision of group CBT treatment, including characteristics of the youth in residential settings, length of involvement in treatment, reduced level of family involvement, access to therapists within the milieu, and benefits of symptom, behavior, and homework management/monitoring by staff.

Characteristics of Adolescents in Residential Care

Children and adolescents that require placement in residential centers tend to present behavioral and emotional problems to a greater degree than their nonplaced peers. They tend to have more severe mental health and behavioral problems and a higher level of need for therapeutic services. Therefore, clinicians may need to modify the format of group accordingly or adjust the inclusion criteria for members based on the characteristics of residents available for group composition at a given time. In addition, group involvement is usually mandatory and residents attend several different groups as part of their treatment program. This may afford facilitators with more frequent opportunities to impart skill development and expose residents to therapeutic concepts.

Length of Stay in Residential Care

Although the typical length of stay in residential centers may be briefer than in the past, the extended length of stay in residential centers creates opportunities for longer participation in treatment groups and more comprehensive, in-depth addressing of problems and troubleshooting of skills learned. Residents are able to first practice their skills in a structured, secure environment, as well as practice them during family/home visits as discharge nears.

Therapist Role in the Milieu

Although arguably not as important as the continuity provided by childcare staff, the role of the therapist in the milieu can also help to reinforce the monitoring and use of CBT principles and skills. A significant advantage for residential therapists lies in their ability to observe, assist, and develop therapeutic relationships with children and adolescents in the residential center. In addition, the cognitive-behavioral therapist is able to incorporate CBT principles into other aspects of residents' treatment in addition to within group therapy, making the exposure to cognitive-behavioral principles more comprehensive. Knowing a resident's treatment needs, conceptualizing them from within the CBT framework, and adjusting environmental considerations allows for greater impact in facilitating change.

Benefits of Homework Management and Monitoring by Staff

This chapter has presented the importance of CBT homework tasks of monitoring symptoms and practicing skills. A benefit of the residential center is having trained childcare staff to assist in these tasks and facilitate the acquisition of concepts and skills, implement the treatment plan, and create a feedback loop for residents and group leaders. This can be especially helpful when adolescents struggle with completing their homework. For instance, younger and less mature adolescents tend to have difficulty with introspection at times and profit from consistent feedback and encouragement from staff members that spend much of the day with them and observe their behaviors.

Opportunities for Behavioral and Social Experiments

While participants in outpatient group therapy have the opportunity to engage in behavioral and social experiments outside of group with peers and family members, they may not have enough support to do so or the peers that may be available may not have similar difficulties, resulting in perhaps anxiety or resistance to draw attention to themselves or risk failure. The residential setting emphasizes therapeutic services and the need to address treatment problems continuously for all residents, including in the general living setting, during the school day, during meals, etc. Therefore, residents of treatment centers are surrounded by a treatment focus and similar peers available for social comparison, modeling, and practicing of newly learned skills.

Lack of Family Involvement

Involvement of families in residential treatment has been shown to produce greater outcomes (Landsman, Groza, Tyler, & Malone, 2001). For this reason, a big emphasis is placed on families of children and adolescents being involved in treatment. Parental involvement in treatment can be particularly helpful when parents get involved with monitoring and assisting residents with their CBT homework. For a variety of reasons, there is typically a low level of family involvement for youth in residential treatment. These reasons include large distances to the residential center, lack of transportation, and frustrations over problems that may have led to placement. In other situations, children and adolescents are placed in residential centers after parental rights have been terminated and/or no family resources are available. Some residents have been removed from the home of birth parents for reasons of abuse or neglect. All of these situations create barriers to family involvement. When possible, extended family members should be included in treatment to provide the additional support beneficial to treatment progress and a connection to outside support outside of the center for residents. At times, residents are discharged to foster homes when they are unable to return to their parents' homes. Involvement of foster families (once identified) in treatment should be encouraged, as well, and can provide opportunities for children and adolescents to practice and test their skills.

OVERCOMING OBSTACLES TO GROUP TREATMENT IN RESIDENTIAL CARE

There are several potential obstacles to positive outcome in providing effective cognitive-behavioral group treatment in residential facilities. Presented here are some of those obstacles to implementing and maintaining CBT groups in residential treatment, including competing theoretical approaches among staff members, lack of follow through by staff members on homework assignments, unwillingness of residents to put forth the effort required, and an undefined role of the therapist in the milieu. Considerations for resolving these barriers are also suggested.

Competing Theoretical Perspectives and Lack of Staff Support of CBT

As mentioned previously, a variety of treatment and childcare philosophies exist that contradict CBT approaches. For instance, there is a popular notion that young people need to vent their anger through physical means. Therefore, rather than addressing with CBT approaches, staff members may encourage clients to vent their anger physically (i.e., hitting a punching bag, etc.). Over 25 years ago, however, Geen and Quanty's (1977) review of the literature on catharsis did not support the notion that venting reduces hostility. Not only can such staff send mixed messages to residents participating in CBT groups, but they are also less likely to follow through in monitoring clients and assisting with their homework if they do not possess the same philosophical approach as group facilitators. It is necessary for clinicians to educate staff on the importance of consistency in approach, especially since childcare workers and staff are with residents 24 hours a day and have a greater influence on how treatment is actually implemented.

Effort Required for CBT

Another obstacle in providing CBT group treatment with children and adolescents involves their reluctance in completing homework and putting forth the "extra" effort involved in CBT treatment. As mentioned previously, there are many tasks required between group sessions. It is sometimes easier not to engage in practicing skills or monitoring of thoughts, emotions and behaviors—especially with the continuous emphasis on treatment day-in and day-out. Residents' motivation level tends to vary based on discharge plan, personal goals, and psychological functioning (i.e., adolescents nearing discharge may be more motivated to put forth extra effort in treatment, etc.).

Lack of Family Involvement

There is often a great deal of difficulty engaging the client's family in treatment. As discussed previously, residents are often unable to return home to their birth-parents.

When children and adolescents in RTF's are likely to be returning to their families, it is critical that family involvement begin at the time of placement. Even with the availability of family resources, it may be difficult for parents to travel consistently and regularly to the residential facility if distance is an issue, or as work schedules and other family commitments may limit (such as younger, more dependent children). As treatment progresses and residents near discharge, trial home visits are a necessary test of skills learned and generalizability to the home environment. The CBT skills learned in group therapy must be tested in the home environment and community and adjusted to ensure effective utilization after discharge. Parent Management Training (Kazdin, Siegel, & Bass, 1992) is designed to help parents improve their interactions with adolescents, promote prosocial behavior, and decrease deviant behavior. In combination with a CBT program for children with conduct problems, greater success was achieved in decreasing antisocial behavior, parental stress, and depression than either treatment alone (Kazdin, Siegel, & Bass, 1992).

SUMMARY

Residential treatment centers are an important and necessary part of the overall provision of mental health services to children and adolescents. Despite the high costs, there is a persistent need for placements in residential treatments that can provide services for young people that are unable to be maintained in the community. As the emphasis on outcome research, shorter lengths of stay, and cost scrutinization progresses, the need for short-term and outcome-based treatment approaches will become increasingly important. Cognitive-behavioral group therapy approaches have shown to be effective with youth in addressing many of the problems presented in residential treatment, and would be a natural framework for services in a setting that includes several inherent benefits for the provision of therapeutic services in general. Research into the effective inclusion of CBT group treatment is limited in the literature, and should be considered by mental health professionals contributing outcome research to the field of youth services.

RECOMMENDED READINGS

Erickson, S., & Achilles, G. (2004). Cognitive behavioral therapy with children and adolescents. In H. Steiner (Ed.), *Handbook of mental health interventions in children and adolescents* (pp. 525–556). San Francisco: Jossey-Bass.

Free, M. (1999). Cognitive therapy in groups: Guidelines and resources for practice. New York: Wiley.

Rosen, M. (1998). A cognitive therapy model for behaviorally disturbed adolescents at a residential treatment facility, *Education and Treatment of Children*, 21, 62–74.

REFERENCES

Barth, R. (2002). *Institutions vs. Foster Homes: The empirical base for the second century debate.* Chapel Hill, NC: School of Social Work, Jordan Institute for Families.

Bates, B., English, D., & Kouidou-Giles, S. (1997). Residential treatment and its alternatives: A review of the literature. *Child and Youth Care Forum*, 26, 7–52.

Beck, A., & Steer, R. (1993). *Beck Anxiety Inventory Manual.* San Antonio, TX: The Psychological Corporation.

Beck, A., Steer, R., & Brown, G. (1996). *Manual for the Beck Depression Inventory* (2nd ed.). San Antonio, TX: The Psychological Corporation.

Berridge, D., & Brodie, I. (1998). *Children's homes revisited.* London: Kingsley.

Burns, B., Hoagwood, K., & Maultsby, L. (1998). Improving outcomes for children and adolescents with serious emotional and behavioral disorders: Current and future directions. In M. Epstein, K. Kutash, & A. Duchnowski (Eds.), *Outcomes for children and youth with emotional and behavioral disorders and their families: Programs and evaluation best practices* (pp. 686–707). Austin, TX: Pro-Ed.

Clarke, G., Lewinsohn, P., & Hops, H. (1990). *Adolescent coping with depression course: Leader's manual for adolescent groups.* Eugene, OR: Castalia.

Cocozza, J. (1997). Identifying the needs of juveniles with co-occurring disorders. *Corrections Today*, June, 146–148.

Cohen, J., Mannarino, A., Berliner, L., & Deblinger, E. (2000). Trauma-focused cognitive behavioral therapy for children and adolescents: An empirical update. *Journal of Interpersonal Violence*, 15(11), 1202–1223.

Cohler, B. (2003). Foreword: Psychotherapy and the milieu: Issues posed for confidentiality and for the therapist's participation in the therapeutic environment. In P. Zimmerman, R. Epstein, M. Leichtman, & M.L. Leichtman (Eds.), *Psychotherapy in group care: Making life good enough* (pp. xiii–xix). Binghaptom, NY: Haworth Press.

Connor, D., Melloni, R., Jr., & Harrison, R. (1998). Overt categorical aggression in referred children and adolescents. *Journal of the American Academy of Child and Adolescent Psychiatry*, 37, 66–73.

Davis, D., & Boster, L. (1993). Cognitive-behavioural-expressive interventions with aggressive and resistant youth. *Residential Treatment for Children and Youth*, 10, 55–68.

Duan, D., & O'Brien, S. (1998). Peer-mediated social skills training and generalization in group homes. *Behavioral Interventions*, 17, 235–247.

Erickson, S., & Achilles, G. (2004). Cognitive behavioral therapy with children and adolescents. In H. Steiner (Ed.), *Handbook of mental health interventions in children and adolescents* (pp. 525–556). San Francisco, CA: Jossey-Bass.

Feindler, E., & Ecton, R. (1986). *Adolescent anger control: Cognitive-behavioral techniques.* New York: Pergamon.

Fonagy, P., Target, M., Cottrell, D., Phillips, J., & Kurtz, Z. (2002). *What works for whom? A critical review of treatments for children and adolescents.* New York: Guilford.

Freeman, A., Schrodt, G., Gilson, M., & Ludgate, J. (1993). Group cognitive therapy with inpatients. In J. Wright, M. Thase, A. Beck, & J. Ludgate (Eds.), *Cognitive therapy with inpatients* (pp. 121–153). New York: Guilford.

Geen, R., & Quanty, M. (1977). The catharsis of aggression: An evaluation of a hypothesis. In L. Berkowitz (Ed.), *Advances in experimental social psychology* (vol. 10; pp. 1–37). New York: Academic Press.

Glick, B. & Goldstein, A. (1987). Aggression replacement training. *Journal of Counseling and Development*, 65(7), 356–362.

Goldbloom, S., Halmi, K., Casper, R., Eckert, E., Davis, J. & Roper, M. (1997). A randomized controlled trial of fluoxetine and cognitive behavioral therapy for Bulimia Nervosa—Short term outcome. *Behaviour Research and Therapy*, 803–811.

Grosz, D., Lipschitz, D., Eldar, S., Finkelstein, G., Blackwood, N., Gerbino-Rosen, G., Faedda, G., & Plutchik, R. (1994). Correlates of violence risk in hospitalized adolescents. *Comprehensive Psychiatry*, 35, 296–300.

Jemerin, J. M., & Philips, I. (1988). Changes in inpatient child psychiatry: consequences and recommendations. Journal of the American Academy of Child and Adolescent Psychiatry, 27(4), 397–403.

Kane, M., & Kendall, P. (1989). Anxiety disorders in children: A multiple-baseline evaluation of a cognitive-behavioral treatment. *Behavior Therapy*, 20, 499–508.

Kazdin, A., Siegel, T., & Bass, D. (1992). Cognitive problem-solving skills training and parent management training in the treatment of antisocial behavior in children. *Journal of Consulting and Clinical Psychology*, 60, 733–747.

Kendall, P. (Ed.) (2000). *Child and adolescent therapy: Cognitive-behavioral procedures.* New York: Guilford.

Landsman, M., Groza, V., Tyler, M., & Malone, K. (2001). Outcomes of family-centered residential treatment. *Child Welfare*, 80, 351–379.

Larson, J., Calamari, J., West, J., & Frevert, T. (1998). Aggression management with disruptive adolescents in the residential setting: Integration of a cognitive-behavioral component. *Residential Treatment for Children & Youth*, 15(4), 1–9.

Leichtman, M., Leichtman, M. L., Barber, C., & Neese, D. T. (2000). Effectiveness of intensive short-term residential treatment with severely disturbed adolescents. *American Journal of Orthopsychiatry, 71*(2), 227–235.

Lewinsohn, P., Clarke, G., Hops, H., & Andrews, J. (1990). Cognitive behavioral treatment for depressed adolescents. *Behavior Therapy*, 385–401.

Loring, M., & Fraboni, E. (1990). The use of cognitive therapy in groups. *Journal of Partial Hospitalization*, *6*, 173–179.

Malekoff, A. (1997). *Group work with adolescents: Principles and practice*. New York: Guilford.

Matthys, W. (1997). Residential behaviour therapy for children with conduct disorders. *Behavior Modification, 21*, 512–532.

Myers, M. G., Brown, S. A., & Vik, P. W. (1998). Adolescent substance use problems. In E. J. Mash & R. A. Barkley (Eds.), *Treatment of childhood disorders* (2nd ed., pp. 692–729). Guilford Press: New York.

Mitchell, J., Hoberman, H., Peterson, C., Mussell, M., & Pyle, R. (1996). Research on the psychotherapy of Bulimia Nervosa: Half empty of half full. *International Journal of Eating Disorders, 20*, 219–229.

Randall, J., Henggeler, S., Pickrel, S., & Brondino, M. (1999). Psychiatric comorbidity and the 16-month trajectory of substance-abusing and substance-dependent juvenile offenders. *Journal of the American Academy of Child and Adolescent Psychiatry, 38*(9), 1118–1124.

Reinecke, M. A., Dattilio, F. M., and Freeman, A. (Ed.). (2003). *Cognitive therapy with children and adolescents: A casebook for clinical practice* (2nd ed.). New York: Guilford.

Reynolds, W. M. (1998). *Adolescent psychopathology scale*. Odessa, FL: Psychological Assessment Resources.

Scholte, E., & Van Der Ploeg, J. (2000). Exploring factors governing successful residential treatment of youngsters with serious behavioral difficulties: Findings from a longitudinal study in Holland. *Childhood, 2*, 77–93.

Stevens, I. (2004). Cognitive-behavioral interventions for adolescents in residential care in Scotland: An examination of practice and lessons from research. *Child and Family Social Work, 9*, 237–246.

Underwood, L., Barretti, L., Storms, T., & Safonte-Stumolo, N. (2004). A review of clinical characteristics and residential treatments for adolescent delinquents with mental health disorders. *Trauma, Violence, & Abuse, 5*(3), 199–242.

Valliant, P. (1993). Cognitive and behavioral therapy with adolescent males in a residential treatment center. *Journal of Child and Youth Care*, 8 (3), 41-49.

Wilson, G., & Fairburn, C. (1993). Cognitive treatments for eating disorders. *Journal of Consulting and Clinical Psychology, 61*, 575–583.

Witt-Browder, A. (2000). Clients in partial hospital settings. In J. White & A. Freeman (Eds.), *Cognitive-behavioral group therapy for specific problems and populations* (pp. 361–384). Washington, DC: American Psychological Association.

Wright, J., Thase, M., Ludgate, J., & Beck, A. (1993). The cognitive milieu: Structure and proces. In J. Wright, M. Thase, A. Beck, & J. Ludgate (Eds.), *Cognitive therapy with inpatients* (pp. 61–87). New York: Guilford.

Wright, N. (1995). Social skills training for conduct disordered boys in residential treatment: a promising approach. *Residential Treatment for Children and Youth, 12*, 25–32.

Zimmerman, P. (1999). Desperation and hope in the analysis of a "thrown-away" adolescent boy. *Psychoanalytic Psychology, 16*(2), 198–232.

Chapter Ten

CBT Groups in Medical Settings

Jessica L. Stewart & Christina Esposito

Traditionally, mental health professionals have provided services to children and adolescents in schools, outpatient clinics, and inpatient facilities. However, the field of psychology in the 21st century has emphasized a team health approach to prevent and reduce disease and illness by treating the physical and psychological symptoms of the patient. Mental health providers continue to accept new roles and responsibilities, which allow them to contribute to patient care in medical settings. In recent years, it has been predicted that the field of psychology's contribution to the prevention, assessment, treatment, and management of chronic and acute illnesses will play a significant role in the future development of the profession as a whole (Levant, Ragusea, Reed, et al., 2001). Thus, the amount and kinds of services provided to children and adolescents in medical settings are on the rise. Medical settings may include primary care physician offices, healthcare clinics, medical hospitals, rehabilitation facilities, as well as school-based healthcare centers. While each of these environments presents benefits and limitations to the provision of services, each is an available resource for professionals seeking to increase the availability of opportunities to impart clinical care to young people in need.

This chapter will outline the ways in which clinicians may provide group therapy services to children and adolescents within a variety of medical settings. The importance of considering the contribution of psychological factors to health and wellness of children and adolescents will be presented to provide a rationale for the inclusion of psychological intervention in settings traditionally emphasizing physiological health. Similarly, we will discuss the benefits to physical health that strong cognitive, emotional, and behavioral skills provide. Specific psychological difficulties often associated with children's experiences of medical illnesses and conditions will be reviewed, as well as psychological conditions frequently presenting in medical settings in the absence of physical health concerns. We highlight not only the effects of illness and treatment for children facing chronic conditions, but also those identified as at-risk for illnesses (i.e., obese children), those who experience life-threatening situations (e.g., accidents or acute illness episodes), those adversely effected by the illness of a loved one, and children presenting with "traditional" mental health concerns (e.g., depression, anxiety, Attention-Deficit/Hyperactivity Disorder, etc.), as they may also benefit from intervention within medical settings.

In addition, given the unique characteristics of medical settings, we will discuss several important considerations for the incorporation of group therapy, including assessment of potential group members, the application of a cognitive-behavioral conceptualization to concepts of health and wellness, specific goals applicable within these settings, and potential obstacles that may present for the formation and maintenance of groups in medical environments. The ultimate aim of this chapter will be to outline the benefits of, considerations for, and basic structure of the provision of cognitive-behavioral group therapy for children and adolescents within medical settings for the purposes of prevention and intervention.

Of note, included in this text is a chapter on the application of a group cognitive-behavioral therapy (CBT) model of treatment with children and adolescents with chronic illness (CI). That chapter reviews the literature on the prevalence of CI in young people, its impact on psychological functioning, the available literature on empirically supported group interventions, and barriers to effective inclusion of psychological services as part of the treatment regimen. Most importantly, that chapter outlines the conceptualization of needs and provision of treatment for several chronic health conditions in young people that is based on the CBT model. Thus, we will not include that information in this chapter.

The objectives for readers of this chapter relate to obtaining familiarity with the benefits and feasibility of including group CBT within medical settings to provide services to children and adolescents. No specific treatment protocol will be offered, as so much depends on the specific purpose of group and population being serviced, and to consider all of these factors within each of the group formats offered (related to intervention and prevention) would comprise a volume all its own. The cognitive-behavioral conceptualization of health and wellness, as well as specific cognitive and behavioral goals applicable to a treatment program within healthcare settings, are offered as a template for those interested in incorporating group CBT with children and adolescents into the medical health arena—a worthwhile and timely direction for the field of pediatric psychology.

RATIONALE FOR THE INCLUSION OF PSYCHOLOGICAL SERVICES WITHIN MEDICAL TREATMENT

Integrated Approach to Services

One of the most important trends in the current healthcare structure is increased levels of integration. The demand for "one-stop shopping" in healthcare services is growing. An integrated delivery system may include primary care providers, specialists, psychologists, social workers, and home healthcare agencies. The role of the psychologist within this integrated model includes assessment, consultation, treatment planning, referral to outside resources, and direct intervention via individual, group, and family modalities. No matter the service being provided, the mental health professional must collaborate effectively with other members of the team for optimal patient response. A successful collaboration will rely on an integrated, biopsychosocial model of patient care (Haley et al., 1998). In fact, it is likely that most successful collaborations between mental health professionals and primary care services occur when the two programs are located in the same facility or clinic.

There are a number of advantages to physical proximity. First, when psychological services are a component of the primary care system the stigma of an outside referral decreases (Bray & Rogers, 1995). Parents are often more willing to seek aid from a mental health professional with their pediatrician's recommendations, especially within the same familiar clinic. Low income or minority families with numerous barriers to healthcare (e.g., transportation, financial resources) value the convenience of mental health services offered in the same setting as the primary care provider. In the case of the provision of group therapy services, this is especially beneficial when the group includes a parent-involvement component.

Another advantage to providing mental health services within the medical setting is the availability of formal and informal consultation between the primary care providers and mental health specialists. Open avenues of communication will allow for a team approach to care for all of the child's health needs through a comprehensive conceptualization of the presenting problems, ultimately resulting in better care across disciplines. Finally, integration can facilitate the referral process by recognizing mental health professionals as a convenient and efficient referral option (Haley et al., 1998).

Impact of Medical Illness/Conditions on Psychological Function

The recognition that psychological factors play a role in health and in illness has been well documented for decades and progressively a more commonplace assumption. Specific to the needs of children and adolescents facing medical difficulties, psychological complications can result from being at risk for disease, diagnosis and prognosis of an illness, the illness' impact on social and academic functioning, the impact of treatment on functioning, physiological changes (including medication regimens) that result in psychological symptoms, and lifestyle changes. As all aspects of an individual's functioning (e.g., social, emotional, behavioral, and academic) are interrelated, if the illness experience negatively impacts one area of functioning (i.e., social isolation because of embarrassment over physical condition, etc.), it will undoubtedly result in negative repercussions in other areas (i.e., an increase in depressive symptoms and less motivation for academic success). The interrelated nature of functioning is also of concern for those children who may present within a medical setting for mental health services but are not, themselves, necessarily medically ill. Although the multidirectional influence of these factors makes separating them into categories for discussion (e.g., cognitive, emotional, social, behavioral, or academic) difficult, we will briefly consider some specific ways that illness, disease, or the susceptibility for illness negatively affect the functioning of children and adolescents.

Cognitive. Cognitive abilities such as memory, concentration, attention, problem-solving, and inhibition may be negatively impacted by several aspects of physiological functioning. Medication side effects (including pain medications), some prescribed treatments (e.g., in the case of radiation treatment of cancers), and secondary effects of the illness itself (e.g., pain that exacerbates fatigue, dehydration, and malnutrition) may interfere with a child's mental capacities and functioning. As will be discussed later, the disease experience may also result in negative thoughts related to one's competencies and self-efficacy that may interfere with effective cognitive functioning. Increased anxiety about the potential to develop an illness given one's risk factors may also limit capacity for cognitive functions such as attention, concentration, and motivation.

Emotional.   Chronic illness or being at risk for developing a chronic illness may result in subsequent feelings of helplessness or a lack of control over one's circumstances. Especially in the case with children and adolescents, understanding that sometimes terrible illnesses happen to people (either the child or loved ones) without cause, or the risk factors are present to no fault of one's own, may be quite difficult and produce a sense of confusion that fosters anxiety of all that is both unknown and not well understood. This is especially true about the origin of a condition or uncertain prognoses. In addition, medication side effects may include a degree of physiological arousal that mimics anxiety and serves to strengthen that experience for the patient, as well as emotional instability and dysregulation.

Social.   Social difficulties may result from direct experiences associated with an illness (e.g., limitations on being able to participate in social interactions, etc.), as well as from other emotional, cognitive, or behavioral symptoms (e.g., anxiety that limits one's comfort in engaging with others, memory and attention difficulties that may become embarrassing around peers, behavioral acting-out that results in peer rejection). In addition, peers may be uncomfortable around children and adolescents who display physiological differences or difficulties, such as when young people lose their hair as a result of chemotherapy or a young burn-victim is visibly and permanently. Social isolation is not unusual in youth with CI and adversely affects the management of the illness and academic and emotional functioning. As school-age children rely on feedback from peers to develop self-appraisals, CBT in a group format is a beneficial intervention for this population due to the peer interaction component and the availability of validation for feelings of fear, grief, and sadness surrounding their medical condition.

Peer influence also has a direct impact on treatment adherence, especially with older school age children and adolescents. Age appropriate developmental stages, such as trying to "fit in" with peers, hinder children from remaining faithful to treatment schedules. For example, adolescents with cystic fibrosis have reported not following prescribed medication schedules because they did not want to be seen as different from others or risk the loss of a romantic relationship (Christian & D'Auria, 1997). The social comparison facilitated by group participation aids in changing attitudes, beliefs, and opinions and assists in reversing habitual patterns of noncompliance to develop new patterns of behavior. Self-monitoring, goal setting, behavioral contracting, and corrective feedback done in a group setting provides the child with a support network to reinforce changes necessary for treatment compliance (Fielding & Duff, 1999).

Behavioral.   Having to manage one's own illness experience or the impact of the medical condition of a loved one wears on the emotional and cognitive resources of anyone, especially children and adolescents who may not yet have developed more effective coping strategies to handle these kinds of challenges. As a result, behavioral changes (such as acting out, withdrawal and isolation, clinginess, developmental regression, and appetite or sleep disturbances) may be a natural byproduct of an illness experience (personal or shared) given that young people may be prone to lower tolerances for frustration and stress, increased sensitivity to stressful situations or to perceived social rejection, and difficulty managing and expressing the myriad of emotions that accompany these kinds of situational demands (e.g., anger, sadness, guilt, confusion, helplessness, worry).

Academic.   Given these possible cognitive, emotional, social, and behavioral changes, academic performance is bound to be challenged by a reduction in available resources within the child and an increase in external demands associated with the illness situation. Frequent absenteeism would be expected given the necessity of medical appointments, flare-ups in symptoms, bouts of not feeling well-enough to attend school, and so forth.

Benefits of Psychological Skills on Health and Well-Being

Improving the psychological functioning of young people facing medical difficulties may improve both the condition itself and the ramifications it presents in the areas of functioning above. A child who is equipped with effective emotional coping and problem-solving skills is less likely to experience anxiety or resistance and more likely to adhere to unpleasant treatment regimens, for example. The origin of resistance relates to the perception that there exists a greater risk than one can manage (e.g., a child believing that he will be uncomfortable, helpless, and in pain if he cooperates with a difficult treatment procedure will be less likely to do so). Children who adhere to treatment recommendations will likely show a better response to their treatments than their peers who disengage and oppose what they fear or dislike. The possession of effective psychological and interpersonal skills translates to a greater sense of self-efficacy, the perception that one's choices and actions may actually impact one's condition, and a stronger likelihood of the youth making healthier choices and behaviors that will more likely benefit his condition.

Psychological Difficulties That Can Accompany Illnesses in Youth

Youth facing chronic or life-threatening illnesses have the potential to experience a number of psychological difficulties. Specifically, they are susceptible to the development of anxiety related to the unknown aspects of their diagnosis, potentially poor prognosis, their ability to effectively manage the physical changes or treatment regimen associated with the illness, their ability to maintain effective academic and/or social functioning, etc. Depressive symptoms may surface that also relate to the prognosis of the illness, helplessness and a lack of control over the development or direction of the illness, new limitations on functioning (e.g., social, behavioral, academic), loss of independence, loss of availability of social interactions and relationships, and perceiving that they are no longer the same and "damaged" somehow (an additional loss, of a sense of a competent self). Depression may also result as related to feelings of guilt for burdening family members with changes in routine, restrictions on activities, restrictions on time with each other (e.g., for parents not able to spend time with siblings because of one's illness-related needs and vice versa), financial strain, and even the basic worry family members experience about their health status and future. Some severely depressed children and adolescents may experience feelings of hopelessness related to their prognosis and contemplate suicide.

Children may also experience anger and frustration as a result of health-status changes and the demands and limitations that treatment may impose, as well as limitations in their abilities and functioning across settings. Youth may evidence behavioral difficulties as a result of their anger, frustration, depression, or anxiety that can include defiance and opposition to parents, teachers, friends, and medical staff. They may act-out toward peers out of jealousy because "it's not fair." They may act out angrily because they cannot effect changes in their condition. They may defy rules and expectations at home or in school as a means for controlling whatever aspects they can when they have so little control over their condition or because they feel so often under the control of others (e.g., numerous medical professionals and parents).

CONSIDERATIONS FOR THE INCLUSION OF GROUP PSYCHOLOGICAL SERVICES IN MEDICAL SETTINGS

Collaboration between Professionals in Medical Settings

An advantage of providing CBT interventions in the medical setting is the ease of referrals to the mental health team. Primary care physicians and other medical specialists are more likely to make a referral to a mental health provider when it is a colleague working in the same setting. Establishing relationships with the medical staff will initiate referrals for children with psychosocial issues that coexist with a chronic illness, as well as psychological issues alone. This collaborative relationship is also advantageous to motivating the patient into therapy. Parents are more likely to follow the advice of their primary care physician who recommends a mental health professional who they have worked with or referred to in the past, because of the trusting relationship that parents and pediatric patients have with the primary care physician. Ongoing feedback and clear communication to the medical specialist will enhance the collaborative relationship.

Success in providing therapeutic interventions in the medical setting relies on the mental health specialist becoming a team player and working side by side with pediatric professionals. In addition, the mental health professional must effectively communicate important information to the treating physician and medical staff that may impact their treatment of the child (such as observed symptoms, concerns for functioning that may be a result of side effects of medication, etc). Communication between professionals treating the same patients is important for the optimal level of provision of services, so long as confidentiality limitations are discussed with the referring physicians, the patients, and the legal guardians and are upheld (see further discussion below).

Referral Process

The referral process starts when the medical professional suspects that psychosocial problems are present. One tool used by pediatricians is the *Pediatric Symptom Checklist* (Jutte, Burgos, Mendoza, Ford, & Huffman, 2003), which is a 35-item checklist designed to be filled out by parents of 6- to 12-year-old children to assess their impressions of their children's psychosocial function. It can be completed and scored in less than five minutes and is utilized by pediatricians or medical staff to help determine if a referral to a mental health professional is warranted. Mental health professionals working within medical environments are responsible for educating medical professionals about troublesome symptoms and indications of the need for psychological assessment and intervention. This includes the potential for psychological effects of physiological conditions that may negatively affect the medical course of treatment or prognosis.

Assessment of Potential Group Members

Prior to admittance into a CBT group, a multidimensional assessment should be completed by the mental health professional. A strengths-based approach to assessment will identify competencies of the child and family. Assessment should also emphasize the cultural factors in each setting or domain of functioning assessed. A CBT assessment includes the child and parent's cognitive capacity, health beliefs, motivation to change, developmental stage, and level of psychological stress. Clinicians should also assess potential group members for their willingness to engage in the change process within a group format, as some members may not be good candidates for group inclusion if they are not comfortable interacting personally with others, are experiencing denial to a degree that addressing issues is not feasible, or are resistant to participation in therapy in general. Motivational factors and barriers to treatment from the parents' perspective are critical assessment considerations to avoid dropouts. Information from the school staff, when possible, is also instrumental in assessing the child's current level of functioning and suitability for a group format, as well as the parents' capacity to participate in the child's treatment process.

Several measures are available to assess depression, anxiety, and other emotional and behavioral experiences in children and adolescents, such as the *Children's Depression Inventory* (Kovacs, 1985), the *Child Behavior Checklist* (Achenbach & Edelbrock, 1983), the *Child version of the Anxiety Disorders Interview Schedule for DSM-IV* (Silverman & Albano, 1996), the various components of the *Beck Youth Inventories—Second Edition* (BYI; Beck, Beck, & Jolly, 2005), the *Multidimensional Anxiety Scale for Children* (March, Parker, et al., 1997), and the *Behavior Assessment System for Children—Second Edition* (BASC-2, Reynolds & Kamphaus, 2002). Measures of psychological functioning will provide the mental health specialist with information on the level of distress the child is experiencing, and allow for tracking of symptoms throughout the course of treatment. In addition, assessment that is based on empirically supported measures allows for easily understood impressions to be shared with the medical professionals on the team in chart notes. A child who is experiencing severe psychological distress (i.e., significant levels of depression or anxiety) may not be a good candidate for involvement in group treatment until symptoms are stabilized via individual intervention. Any youth who is at risk for becoming suicidal should be treated in individual therapy until clinical judgment deems him or her ready for a group therapy format.

Other assessment tools available target the health status of children who may be in treatment for their own chronic illness. The *Child Health Questionnaire* measures 14 health concepts, and physical and psychosocial well-being of children 5 years of age and older (Kozinetz, Warren, Berseth, Aday, Sachdeva, & Kirkland,1999). This questionnaire can be utilized to assess a child's perceptions of his or her illness, which may surface in group therapy and be targeted for modification if necessary. In addition, information should be obtained from interviewing medical staff, family members, and school personnel (when available and as permitted by guardians). (For additional measures related to the assessment of specifically CI youth, see chapter 25.)

Inclusion/Exclusion Considerations

Numerous dynamics affect group composition. Age, developmental level, and psychological maturity should be taken into consideration. In the ideal situation, the group also reflects a mix of gender and ethnicity (Friedberg & Crosby, 2001). This may not be realistic in medical settings when attempting to form groups with similar psychological needs due to a chronic illness. It may be unlikely to have enough members for group who are experiencing the same physical condition, making a homogenous group impossible. However, it may not be necessary to form homogeneous groups according to the specific disease because treatment goals may overlap across chronic illnesses. For example, children with diabetes and severe asthma may share similar feelings of isolation, exclusion from activities, and anxiety over acute symptoms. It is more important to consider the psychosocial adaptation and commonalities in adjustment to illness than to be concerned with comprising groups with members of the same illness "category." It may be beneficial, in some circumstances, to separate groups of children from adolescents based on severity or terminal nature of their condition/status, as developmental understanding and approach to treatment of issues such as death and dying, for example, would be unique. This is also true when the group is for young people who are not themselves chronically ill, but may be receiving intervention to adjust to the illness of a parent or loved one. When designing groups from a prevention approach to promote wellness, it may be helpful to form more heterogeneous groups for the sake of having diversity of age and experience with the topic to facilitate peer modeling, scaffolding of skills, and social comparison.

Confidentiality

An important issue to consider when working collaboratively within medical settings is that of confidentiality. Essentially, mental health professionals must understand practices surrounding the sharing of information between team members, family members, and patients. While services are to be provided to the children and adolescents, the referral was made by a medical professional monitoring the youth's overall treatment and progress. Therefore, it is important to understand the extent to which information is expected to be recorded in medical charts, the boundaries related to how much detail of patient participation and progress to include when consulting directly with team members, and how much information is shared with parents participating (or not) in the family component of treatment, if applicable. The same confidentiality considerations regarding parental right-to-know about content of group sessions that exist in other settings exist here. Typically, medical team members appreciate knowing how active patients are in the therapy process, disclosure of experiences related to symptoms and side effects, improvement or deterioration of relevant symptoms, and other information helpful for their work in addressing the physiological condition and patient status.

Given the impact of physical health problems and chronic illness on the developmental, emotional, behavioral, social, and academic functioning of children and adolescents, mental health treatment is a natural extension of existing healthcare services aimed to improve the illness-experience, potential for treatment success, and maintenance of optimal functioning. Unfortunately, few models exist in the literature to address the provision of group therapy services for this population of young people. Models that do exist are not descriptive or empirically validated, are not based on a sound theoretical model, and are loosely structured so that effectiveness and accuracy of reproduction is questionable (Plante, Lobato, & Engel, 2001). Our emphasis in this chapter is not to present a specific model of group therapy, but to discuss the general application of CBT within a group modality for work with children and adolescents within medical settings for a variety of purposes and formats. What follows is not an outline of a specific program of intervention for a specific illness presentation, but a presentation of the ways in which mental health professionals may expand their services into medical settings for the benefit of greater numbers of children and adolescents in the capacity of prevention and intervention.

COGNITIVE-BEHAVIORAL GROUP THERAPY IN MEDICAL SETTINGS

A Goodness of Fit

Medical settings are unique environments, in that their purpose is to provide time-limited, cure/treatment-focused interventions in a brief and rapid fashion with follow-up, if any, on an as-needed basis and often at the discretion of patients (and in the case of young people, their guardians). Managed-care limitations have dictated that patient-professional interactions are brief and focused, not comprehensive to address secondary issues. The inclusion of a therapeutic group intervention within these environments must bear in mind these parameters of typical service-delivery and aim to follow, at least to some degree, the same style and trends without compromising the care delivered within the structure of the group. Based on the theoretical underpinnings of the CBT model, it is a natural and logical fit when considering a model of psychological intervention within medical settings.

Behavioral issues contribute to health and disease in many ways and psychoeducation regarding these issues can begin with children and adolescents. The U.S. Department of Health and Human Services (2000) has identified that eight of the top 10 leading health indicators are behavioral issues. These include alcohol, tobacco use, diet, physical activity, suicide, violence, unintentional injuries, and unsafe sex. Utilizing cognitive-behavioral techniques to promote healthy lifestyles and prevent disease in children is an innovative method for taking a more proactive approach to mental health services.

Cognitive-behavioral group therapy in medical settings has demonstrated effective treatment outcomes for adults (Spira, 1997); however, CBT in this modality for children has not been well-researched to date. Even in the absence of problem-specific protocols, the cognitive-behavioral model of assessment and intervention typically incorporated for use with children and adolescents in other settings is well suited for inclusion in medical settings given the solution-focused, time-limited, educational, and skill building components. The structure of individual sessions (e.g., the initial agenda, goals for session, review of between-session work, specific topic, practice exercises, and assignment of homework), for example, facilitates a process through which patients progress that is focused and purpose-driven. Medical interventions similarly consist of data gathering, assessment to formulate and adjust conceptualization, and the prescription of specific strategies or interventions to improve the situation.

In addition, CBT is short-term and focuses on changing specific cognitions and behaviors that, in this case, relate to health, illness, and wellness. As such, practical therapy that works quickly and encourages patient responsibility and action toward change will be more readily accepted by medical staff. Furthermore, CBT strategies and techniques can be explained to pediatric medical specialists in language they can understand and appreciate, allowing for effective collaboration to meet shared treatment goals. In addition, physicians collaborating with mental health professionals can support and encourage the behavioral interventions and cognitive changes within their patients through follow-up and in ongoing care.

Formats for Group Intervention

"Medical settings" refers to inpatient settings (e.g., hospitals, rehabilitation centers, and the like), primary care physician offices, community clinics, and school-based medical clinics. Potential group participants may include those youth currently experiencing medical difficulties, those who may be experiencing adjustment difficulties resulting from the medical situation of a loved one, those with mental health conditions or symptoms, those at-risk for developing either medical or mental health conditions (e.g., those involved in drug or alcohol abuse, sexually promiscuous youth, obese and sedentary youth, children who have an immediate family member with a significant mental illness), and youngsters who have experienced traumatic accidents or injuries that require psychological intervention.

Medical health illnesses/conditions. As discussed above, when a child or adolescent is experiencing a chronic and/or life-threatening illness, the potential exists for the youth to experience psychological difficulties. Group therapy may facilitate the management of emotional, social, cognitive, and behavioral changes that result from that illness or negatively influence its prognosis and the child's wellbeing. Group therapy may be primarily for the sake of providing a supportive environment with similarly ill peers (e.g., to provide modeling and social comparison of functioning), to address a specific symptom presentation (e.g., anxiety related to invasive medical procedures, depression and social isolation that results from physical disfigurement), or to increase behavioral and emotional skills necessary for the management of a difficult treatment regimen (e.g., problem-solving skills, activity scheduling, and contingency contracts in the management of juvenile diabetes). The goals relate to the development of effective skills relevant to coping, self-expression, interpersonal relationships, and problem-solving. Cognitive-behavioral groups afford young people the exposure to similar peers for the benefit of comparing and validating some of their experiences, even if the specific conditions or situations vary. In addition, youth involved in group therapy with peers facing similar circumstances benefit from the modeling of others regarding how one can interpret, react, and cope with their experiences and the challenges that medical illness or disease may present.

Psychological intervention. Some children will be brought to the attention of medical professionals not because of medical symptoms but because of psychological or behavioral ones. Typically, distressed parents first turn to their pediatricians for advice and guidance to address these concerns. Common symptoms observed by parents (or reported by school professionals) that may lead to a medical appointment include depression, anxiety, attention difficulties, oppositional behavior, hyperactivity, aggression, social withdrawal, changes in appetite or sleep, changes in activity level, school refusal/phobia, adjustment difficulties following difficult transitions, grief or bereavement following loss, or severe mood swings. Adolescents may also present with more self-destructive behaviors such as eating disorder symptoms, self-injury, substance abuse, and suicidal ideation. Hopefully, physicians will rule out any medical cause for symptoms and then seek to refer the child or adolescent appropriately to a mental health professional. If that professional is down the hall, the referral is more comfortably made by the physician and more readily accepted and followed-through with by the child's guardian. Group therapy within the primary care physician's office may seek to address any one of these presenting problems and may include a parent education component, as well. For a presentation of the literature addressing efficacy of treatments and specific group protocols for the psychological presentations just listed, readers are directed to the relevant chapters within this text.

Prevention. Group therapy may be offered within medical settings for the provision of prevention services to promote the maintenance of health and optimal physical functioning. Groups designed for this purpose have the opportunity to provide support and information to a population who may not reach out to or be referred to mental health professionals on their own. By marketing "wellness groups" rather than "group therapy" some patients may be more accepting of group participation. Groups for the sake of prevention will be largely educational in nature, but when addressing health and wellness it is important to consider health beliefs of members and their families and their perceptions of what is "healthy," for example. Group therapy addressing the prevention of illness and the promotion of healthier living should explore the belief systems of members regarding the topics, their susceptibility to illness, how people develop illnesses, participation in treatment, ability to impact one's own physical health, and so forth, so as to ensure that the educational material is absorbed and inaccurate beliefs or perceptions about health and wellness can be modified effectively. Examples of health-related prevention-focused group therapy topics include smoking cessation; substance use, abuse, and abstinence; healthy sexuality, such as sexually transmitted diseases, pregnancy, and abstinence; nutrition, exercise, and fitness; healthy body image; eating disorder awareness and prevention; stress management; and date-related violence.

An advantage of conducting wellness groups in medical settings is that topics addressed may be considered less threatening or taboo because they appear to relate to physical health issues that less frequently carry the stigma that mental health topics do. In addition, it is a more conducive atmosphere for involving parents or family in the therapy, as approaches to physical health management typically include familial support. Families also may be more willing to participate within the familiar medical settings as compared to unfamiliar mental health environments. Parents can also be educated by both the mental health professionals and the primary care team on how to help make lifestyle changes to avoid negative health consequences for their family.

Specific populations of children and adolescents could form homogeneous wellness or therapy groups. For example, an adolescent group for overweight teens may focus on diabetic prevention and decreasing pediatric obesity. Jelalian and Saelens (1999) reviewed empirically supported treatments for pediatric obesity for children ages 8- to 12-years old. Behavioral interventions (e.g., behavioral contracting, stimulus control, self-monitoring, response cost, token economy, homework exercises, parent training, and parent weight loss) that focused on modifying eating patterns and increasing physical activity were found superior to education alone. Prevention groups such as this are ideal for medical settings because of the opportunities to interact with the healthcare staff to further reinforce attention to the health risks of children and further support efforts through concerned monitoring of progress.

Grief and bereavement related to a loved one's illness.   Children and youth participating in group therapy services within medical settings may be experiencing grief related to the loss of a loved one (e.g., a parent, sibling, grandparent, or close friend), or related to the smaller scale, daily losses that come with the transitions and sacrifices within families when one member is ill. (For a more detailed review of a CBT protocol for the treatment of grief and bereavement with young people, please see chapter 14 on grief and loss.) Group CBT with these youth aims to provide a supportive peer environment to explore ways in which loss and adjustment difficulties influence emotional, cognitive, behavioral, social, and academic functioning and to facilitate the development of skills for improving each. An emphasis is on promoting a realistic perspective of the loss, its impact on one's entire situation (not just the negative aspects), and one's abilities to effectively manage difficulties and adjust.

Accidents/traumatic experiences.   Some young patients may present within medical settings following accidents or injuries that may result in traumatization, such as car accidents, fires, accidental dismemberment, shootings and other violent crimes, or involvement in natural disasters. Trauma-reactions may also result from invasive medical procedures (such as spinal taps and bone marrow aspirations). Trauma-related symptoms include emotional dysregulation (either a flattening of affect or an increase in arousal), withdrawal, re-experiencing and intrusive thoughts about the event, and the like. Cognitive-behavioral group therapy incorporated within medical settings can address these cognitive, emotional, and behavioral difficulties by aiming to reduce distressing symptoms and return patients to a more effective level of functioning. Readers are directed to chapter 12 of this text for a more thorough review of the literature and treatment considerations of post-traumatic stress.

CBT Conceptualization of Health and Illness

From a cognitive-behavioral framework, illness, health, wellness, and consequences of each are stimuli that activate the belief systems within individuals. Young people facing illness (including mental) or potential health crisis may, for example, experience doubts about their competence to handle the condition or treatment, fears about progression and outcome, worries and guilt for the effects on loved ones, beliefs about their inability to control the situation or aspects of it, fears about the abilities of others to help or care for them, and so forth. If children have existing schema related to these themes, the illness or condition will exacerbate those pre-existing schema, strengthening those thoughts and the resulting emotional reactions of anxiety, anger, depression, helplessness, guilt, hopelessness, and the like. Moreover, especially in the case of children and young people who may not yet have developed beliefs about their competencies related to such life-altering situations, the way in which the illness or situation is viewed will affect the response to it.

For example, the reactions of children and adolescents seen for group intervention within medical settings not for their own medical health reasons but because of the loss or illness of a loved one will depend on many factors including their perception and beliefs about the illness and death and dying. Children seen following a traumatic accident, for example, may be experiencing negative emotional and behavioral symptoms that result from inaccurate beliefs about their safety and vulnerability, the inefficacy of others to protect them, their responsibility for the event, the roles of others in the event, etc. Some conceptualization based on the cognitive-behavioral model related to the development of behavioral, emotional, cognitive, and social difficulties has been presented under previous headings above.

The adjustment to chronic illness or being at-risk for its development requires a process of acceptance and commitment to a treatment regimen or lifestyle changes for the sake of managing or preventing that illness. Not all patients progress through that process, and may respond to diagnosis or prognosis with a perspective that is less than accepting or committed as the result of distorted cognitions. Denial as a cognitive strategy for managing the worries, doubts, and uncertainty of the situation reduces the emotional experiences of fear, anxiety, sadness, and anger, but results in a lack of commitment to the process of illness management (e.g., treatment). Children who utilize this ineffective coping strategy will not have a favorable illness outcome and experience additional difficulties as a result of not effectively dealing with the realistic aspects of their situations. Similarly, if the illness is viewed, for example, as a punishment for past wrongful deeds, youth may experience feelings of shame, guilt, and sadness that lessen the likelihood they will feel motivated to change their situation and may accept the illness but not the possibility for impacting the prognosis and outcome.

CBT assists children and adolescents to accurately perceive their situation by restructuring maladaptive beliefs (related to, for example, one's ability to cope effectively with the changes and challenges of the illness and treatment) and, therefore, negative emotions that would exacerbate unhealthy coping such as avoidance, denial, etc. As CBT aims to increase awareness of automatic thoughts related to one's situation (or possible, future situation), challenge the accuracy of those perceptions, and then alter those that are inaccurate or distorted to facilitate more positive and adaptive behavioral and emotional reactions to the situation, it is fitting to apply this model within the context of situations that require accurate perception, acceptance, and adjustment to very realistic circumstances. Children and adolescents experiencing a chronic illness are susceptible to distorted views of themselves and their situation because of the life-threatening nature of illness itself and the stress that such a condition would produce—facing one's mortality will undoubtedly invoke thoughts and questions about one's readiness and competence to manage what's ahead, especially for young people who may struggle just to understand the magnitude of these concepts. For those with positive beliefs related to one's ability to handle the situation effectively, this situation is less threatening and more easily accepted as realistic.

As the application of CBT within medical settings is not solely for the purposes of treating ill youth, intervention can be applied to facilitating wellness within medical settings, as well. Those who are otherwise healthy may be prone to a lack of awareness of the possibility they may become ill at some point as the result of distorted beliefs about their ability to control with certainty their physiological status. For example, as is especially true developmentally for young people, some individuals' belief systems contain the faulty assumption that "it can't happen to me." Many people believe that "if I eat right, exercise, and take care of myself, I will not get sick." For those who are in denial about the possibility that chronic illness may present for anyone, the diagnosis of a condition would be devastating because it would not fit with the unrealistic expectations for "the way the world works." In addition, those who possess stereotypes about who "gets sick" and who is spared (the "belief in the just world"), will be less likely to take preventative measures that would reduce the likelihood of contracting an illness (such as for those people who believe that only obese people "get" diabetes, or only homosexuals or IV-drug-users contract HIV/AIDS).

A health belief system determines one's health-related behaviors (such as diet, exercise, compliance with treatment regimens, utilization of resources and support). This includes issues related to mental health as well as the ability to manage difficult and stressful situations that present. CBT facilitates the promotion of accurate beliefs and corresponding attitudes that result in consistent behaviors within one's health perspective to promote wellness and healthy choices. In addition, CBT facilitates the acquisition and utilization of skills to manage situations that may present.

COGNITIVE-BEHAVIORAL STRATEGIES AND INTERVENTIONS

The prevention and/or management of physical or psychological illnesses require effective skill development and maintenance in childhood that continues into and throughout adulthood. Children and adolescents participating in group CBT within medical settings ideally will acquire a repertoire of emotional coping, problem-solving, cognitive awareness, and interpersonal skills that will afford them the opportunities to make behavioral and social choices that maintain healthier lifestyles for a better quality of life. Protocols that structure the application of specific cognitive and behavioral strategies for issues that may present in medical settings are outlined in those problem-specific chapters included in this text. Generally speaking, the following goals with examples of accompanying cognitive and behavioral interventions are applicable within medical settings for improving overall health status and well-being: (1) *emotional identification, expression, and coping skills* that include anger management and increased frustration tolerance; (2) *stress management skills* that include relaxation, imagery, and activity scheduling for healthy options for recreational enjoyment; (3) *cognitive awareness and control* that includes the identification of automatic thoughts, thought-stopping techniques, journaling, identifying the evidence, thought challenging, and restructuring of distorted beliefs; (4) *acceptance* that relies on realistic cognitive appraisal; (5) *behavioral change* through self-monitoring, social-comparison, "experiments," reinforcement by others and the self; (6) *problem-solving skills* (cognitive and social); (7) *interpersonal skills* such as communication, empathy, perspective taking; and (8) *self-advocacy and assertiveness skills* through self-talk and self-instruction, empowerment, and assuming responsibility for choices within one's control. The selection of specific interventions will be based on the cognitive-behavioral conceptualization of the issues facing group members, potential limitations within specific settings, and developmental level of participants. For example, behavioral interventions are perhaps the most appropriate methods for changing maladjustment in very young children. Individual problem chapters will outline specific interventions.

POTENTIAL CHALLENGES AND STRATEGIES FOR MANAGEMENT

Comorbidity

It is possible that children and adolescents presenting for treatment within medical settings will be experiencing a combination of psychological difficulties in and of themselves, or as a result of or in combination with medical illness, traumatic event, or the illness of others. It is important to consider the appropriateness of the group make-up for the needs of the individual child and to prioritize which difficulties would require immediate intervention. For example, a young person at risk for diabetes may also carry a diagnosis of a severe mood disorder. The clinician must determine which issue is most pressing (is the youngster effectively medicated so that focus could be on the issues related to the prevention of diabetes, or would her mood instability reduce the likelihood of benefiting from involvement in the prevention group). Given that what is being proposed here is the general inclusion of psychological services within medical settings, the population parameters are not specified and may include a variety of presenting problems—several, potentially, within the same child or adolescent.

Setting Differences

Although the premise of this chapter is to outline the provision of group CBT to children and adolescents within medical settings, there are inherent differences within what is collectively termed "medical settings." As mentioned above, this may include inpatient settings such as pediatric units within a hospital or rehabilitation facility, outpatient community medical clinics, primary care physician offices, and school-based medical clinics. Each setting will be different in terms of procedures for group establishment, referral, structure, and participation, as well as the populations and presenting problems seen. It is more likely that inpatient medical settings will present youth who's primary diagnosis is medical in nature (and likely acutely significant) or psychological in response to the medical illness or death of a loved one, while the children and adolescents who are referred within outpatient and school-based clinics will likely be chronically-ill patients (with less severe, more manageable conditions) or those presenting with primary psychological difficulties. There will also likely be differences between populations seen within outpatient clinics, in terms of demographic variables (e.g., socioeconomic status, race, ethnicity) and specific illness risk-factors seen within, for example, community-based medical clinics as opposed to private physician offices. This should be considered in terms of availability of patient resources (e.g., such as transportation or financial means to continue on an ongoing basis in group), exposure to health-related information, cultural influences on health beliefs, and so forth. Group facilitators should take these variables into account when developing the structure, frequency, and demands of the group (including homework assignments and family involvement).

It is also important to know and reduce the impact of setting-specific limitations as much as possible to facilitate equal opportunities for patient involvement. For example, logistical considerations such as a space for conducting group that is wheelchair or handicap accessible, the ability of inpatients to leave their rooms or availability of staff to monitor those inpatients who may require machine or intravenous monitoring, the length of groups within outpatient settings given insurance limitations, the ease of patients finding the rooms within large facilities, availability of clerical support and materials (e.g., for having handouts available, for assisting with insurance billing, parking), privacy of the group location or displays to ease patient concerns regarding confidentiality,and so forth. In the hustle and bustle of some medical settings, the ability to conduct a 45 to 60 minute group therapy session smoothly and privately may be challenging and this challenge should not be assumed to be easily conquered.

Attrition/Noncompliance

When developing groups, it is important to consider the likelihood that members will be invested in not only the process for themselves but in their role within the dynamic of the group as a whole. Moreover, keeping in mind that the populations being discussed include medically or psychologically involved youth, limitations associated with illness or conditions may also reduce the likelihood members may be able to remain in group for the duration of the sessions. We mentioned the possibility that patient resources may also limit their ability to afford group membership, for example, if there is a fee. Given the impact of psychological functioning on physiological functioning discussed above, the important role mental health professionals play in restructuring distorted health beliefs and facilitating effective skill development, and the ethical assumption that mental health professionals provide at least some pro bono services, we respectfully remind readers that we are talking about the potentially long-term health and wellness of children and families. It is possible that reducing or eliminating the fee involved for the participation of children and adolescents in CBGT and prevention therapy may increase participation numbers and reduce attrition rates. This is a legitimate suggestion for the management of at least economic factors affecting attrition of group members, and one we hope more mental health professionals will consider seriously.

SUMMARY AND FUTURE CONSIDERATIONS

This chapter offered an overview of the various reasons and modalities for providing group intervention within medical settings for children and adolescents. It did not address the provision of CBGT with a particular population, per se, or promote any one program of intervention or prevention (CBT or otherwise); but instead focused on aspects of the medical environment that facilitate the provision of psychological services, as well as the avenues in which CBT can be applied to group therapy with young people to improve overall health and well-being. We presented an overview of the cognitive-behavioral conceptualization of illness, wellness, and symptom manifestation for the purposes of outlining the relevance of this model as it applies within medical settings for use with young people. Considerations for group design, member assessment and selection, strategies and technique selection, and potential obstacles to treatment were also discussed. We believe that, in the absence of an existing "gold standard" for group therapy intervention in medical settings to address all populations and presenting problems, CBT is an effective approach that is flexible enough to address a variety of psychological needs associated with medical and mental health and wellness in several capacities from prevention to intervention.

RECOMMENDED READINGS

Clay, D. L. (2004). *Helping schoolchildren with chronic health conditions: A practical guide*. New York: Guilford.

Erickson, S. J., Gerstle, M., & Feldstein, S. W. (2005). Brief interventions and motivational interviewing with children, adolescents, and their parents in pediatric health care settings: A review. *Archives of Pediatrics & Adolescent Medicine, 159*(12), 1173–1180.

Plante, W. A., Lobato, D., & Engel, R. (2001). Review of group interventions for pediatric chronic conditions. *Journal of Pediatric Psychology, 26*(7), 435–453.

Power, T. J., DuPaul, G. J., Shapiro, E. S., & Kazak, A. E. (2003). *Promoting children's health: Integrating school, family, and community*. New York: Guilford.

Roberts, M. C. (Ed.), *Handbook of pediatric psychology* (3rd ed). New York: Guilford.

REFERENCES

Achenbach, T. M., & Edelbrock, C. (1983). *Manual for the child behavior checklist and revised child behavior profile*. Burlington: University of Vermont, Department of Psychiatry.

Beck, J. S., Beck A. T., & Jolly, J. (2005). *Manual for the Beck youth inventories of emotional and social adjustment*. San Antonio, TX: Harcourt Brace.

Bray, J. H., & Rogers, J. C. (1995). Linking psychologists and family physicians for collaborative practice. *Professional Psychology: Research and Practice, 26*, 132–138.

Christian, B. J., & D'Auria, J. P. (1997). The child's eye: Memories of growing up with cystic fibrosis. *Journal of Pediatric Nursing, 12*, 3–12.

Fielding, D., & Duff, A. (1999). Compliance with treatment protocols: Interventions for children with chronic illness. *Archives of Disease in Children, 80*, 196–200.

Friedberg, R. D., & Crosby, L. E. (2001). *Therapeutic exercise for children: A professional guide*. Sarasota, FL: Professional Resource Press.

Haley, W. E., McDaniel, S. H., Bray, J. H., Frank, R. G., Heldring, M., Bennet Johnson, S., et al. (1998). Psychological practice in primary care settings: Practical tips for clinicians. *Professional Psychology: Research and Practice, 29*(3), 237–244.

Jelalian, E., & Saelens, B. E. (1999). Empirically supported treatments in pediatric psychology: Pediatric obesity. *Journal of Pediatric Psychology, 24*, 223–248.

Jutte, D. P., Burgos, A., Mendoza, F., Ford, C. B., & Huffman, L. C. (2003). Use of the Pediatric Symptom Checklist in a Low-Income, Mexican American Population. *Archives of Pediatrics & Adolescent Medicine, 157*(12), 1169–1176.

Kovacs, M. (1985). The Children's Depression Inventory (CDI). *Psychopharmacology Bulletin, 21*, 995–998.

Kozinetz, C. A., Warren, R. W., Berseth, C. L., Aday, L. A., Sachdeva, R., & Kirkland, R. T. (1999). Health status of children with special health care needs: Measurement issues and instruments. *Clinical Pediatrics, 38*(9):525–533.

Levant, R. F., Ragusea, S. A., Reed, G. M., DiCowden, M., Sullivan, F., Stout, C. E., et al. (2001). Envisioning and accessing new roles for professional psychology. *Professional Psychology: Research and Practice, 32*(1), 79–87.

March, J., Parker, J., Sullivan, K., et al. (1997). The multi-dimensional anxiety scale for children (MASC): Factor structure, reliability, and validity. *Journal of the American Academy of Child and Adolescent Psychiatry, 36*, 554–565.

Plante, W. A., Lobato, D., & Engel, R. (2001). Review of group interventions for pediatric chronic conditions. *Journal of Pediatric Psychology, 26*, 435–453.

Reynolds, C. R., & Kamphaus, R. W. (2002). *The clinician's guide to the behavior assessment system for children (BASC).* New York: Guilford.

Silverman, W. K., & Albano, A. M. (1996). *Anxiety disorders interview schedule for DSM-IV, child and parent versions.* San Antonia, TX: Psychological Corporation.

Spira, J. L. (1997). Understanding and developing psychotherapy groups for medically ill patients. In J. L. Spira (Ed.), *Group therapy for medically ill patients* (pp. 3–51). New York: Guilford.

U.S. Department of Health & Human Services. (2000, November). *Healthy people 2010: Leading health indicators.* Retrieved June 15, 2002, from http://www.health.gov/healthypeople/document/html/uih/uih_bw/uih_4htm.

Part Three

PRESENTING PROBLEMS

Chapter Eleven

Cognitive-Behavior Group Treatment for Anxiety Disorders

Ellen Flannery-Schroeder, Christine B. Sieberg,
& Elizabeth A. Gosch

Anxiety disorders represent one of the most common forms of psychopathology among children and adolescents (e.g., Bernstein & Borchardt, 1991; Kashani, Orvaschel, Rosenberg, & Reid, 1989). Prevalence estimates have been reported to be as high as 21% (Kashani & Orvaschel, 1990) with most averaging around 10%. Anxiety disorders have been shown to remain stable throughout childhood and adolescence in the absence of treatment and have been associated with moderate to severe disruptions in child development and later adjustment (Mattison, 1992). Research suggests that anxious children may experience difficulties in their social and peer relations (e.g., Hartup, 1983; Strauss, Forehand, Smith & Frame, 1986), academic achievement (e.g., Benjamin, Costello, & Warren, 1990; King and Ollendick, 1989), and future emotional health (e.g., Beidel, 1991; Cantwell & Baker, 1989; Feehan, McGee, & Williams, 1993). Several researchers have noted the link between anxiety in childhood and anxiety in adulthood. For example, adults with anxiety disorders report anxiety in childhood (e.g., Öst, 1987; Sheehan, Sheehan, & Minichiello, 1981). In addition, researchers have suggested a link between separation anxiety disorder in childhood and panic and agoraphobia in adulthood (e.g., Berg, Marks, McGuire, & Lipsedge, 1974; Gittelman-Klein & Klein, 1973; Zitrin & Ross, 1988).

In response to increasing recognition of the debilitating nature of childhood anxiety disorders, treatment research has flourished and cognitive-behavioral interventions have shown real promise in helping children with clinical levels of disorder (e.g., Barrett, Dadds, & Rapee, 1996; Cobham, Dadds, & Spence, 1998; Kendall, 1994; Kendall, Flannery-Schroeder, Panichelli-Mindel, Southam-Gerow, Henin, & Warman, 1997). In fact, cognitive-behavioral treatments for anxiety disorders (e.g., Kendall, 1994; Kendall et al., 1997) have been deemed "probably efficacious" as determined by proposed criteria (Chambless & Hollon, 1998).

Kendall (1994) conducted a randomized clinical trial including 47 children with an anxiety disorder randomly assigned to either a cognitive-behavioral treatment or a wait-list control condition. Results indicated that 64% of treated children no longer met criteria for their primary anxiety disorder at post-treatment. A one year follow-up (Kendall, 1994) and a three year follow-up (Kendall & Southam-Gerow, 1996) demonstrated maintenance of treatment gains. A second randomized clinical trial, using a sample of 94 children with an anxiety disorder randomly assigned to a cognitive-behavioral treatment or a wait-list, demonstrated 71% of treated cases to no longer have their primary diagnosis at post-treatment (Kendall et al., 1997). Maintenance of treatment gains was evident at a one-year and seven-year follow-up (Kendall et al., 1997; Kendall, Safford, Flannery-Schroeder, & Webb, 2004).

Cognitive-behavioral treatments have been extended from individual formats to family formats as well. For example, Barrett, et al. (1996), using a modification of Kendall's *Coping Cat* program for use with Australian youth, added a family management component to the cognitive-behavioral treatment with good effects. Seventy-nine children with anxiety disorders were randomly assigned to one of three conditions: cognitive-behavioral treatment (CBT), cognitive-behavioral treatment plus family management (FAM), and a wait-list control. Approximately 70% of treated children, versus 26% of wait-list children, did not meet criteria for an anxiety disorder at post-treatment. One-year and 6-year follow-ups demonstrated maintenance of treatment effects (Barrett et al., 1996; Barrett, Duffy, Dadds, & Rapee, 2001).

More recently, cognitive-behavioral treatments using group formats have begun to receive research attention. Group therapy may confer unique benefits including, but not limited to, improved cost-benefit ratios, social interactions with peers (e.g., positive peer modeling), and opportunities to be exposed to multiple anxiety-provoking situations. Cognitive-behavioral group treatments for anxiety will be the focus of the present chapter.

This chapter will begin with an overview of childhood anxiety disorders, their prevalence, phenomenology, and comorbidity patterns along with the long-term outcomes associated with these disorders. Commonly used assessment techniques and instruments for anxiety are evaluated, followed by a cognitive-behavioral conceptualization of anxiety disorders in childhood and the rationale for group treatment. The remainder of the chapter will provide a detailed description of a cognitive-behavioral group treatment protocol, a review of the extant literature using similar cognitive-behavioral group approaches, and a summary of potential difficulties inherent in the practice of group CBT. Finally, a case study will be presented as an exemplar.

OVERVIEW OF CHILDHOOD ANXIETY DISORDERS

Of all psychiatric disorders in adulthood, anxiety disorders are the most common (Kessler, McGonagle, Zhao, Nelson, Hughes, Eshleman, et al., 1994). This statistic also holds true for children and adolescents (Bernstein & Borchardt, 1991; Fergusson, Horwood & Lynskey, 1993; Kashani & Orvaschel, 1990) for whom prevalence rates have been found to range from 6 to 20% (e.g., Anderson, Williams, McGee, & Silva, 1987; Kashani & Orvaschel, 1990; Last, Strauss, & Francis, 1987; Last, Perrin, Hersen, & Kazdin, 1992; Strauss & Last, 1993). It has been estimated that 13 of every 100 children and adolescents age 9–17 exhibit some form of anxiety (U.S. Department of Health and Human Services, 1999). Gender disparities also exist with girls being diagnosed more frequently than boys. Some of the most frequently occurring childhood anxiety disorders include Generalized Anxiety Disorder, Separation Anxiety Disorder, Social Phobia, and Specific Phobia. Other anxiety disorders that may present in childhood include Obsessive-Compulsive Disorder, Panic Disorder, and Post-Traumatic Stress Disorder.

While many children "worry," most often the worry is transitory and does not cause substantial impairment. If, however, the worry is excessive and uncontrollable, regards several life domains, and persists for six months or more, a diagnosis of Generalized Anxiety Disorder (GAD) may be warranted (American Psychiatric Association, 2000). Health, school, disasters, and personal harm are among the most common domains of worry among children (Weems, Silverman, & La Greca, 2000). Worrying often occurs in the absence of a precipitating event, occurs more days than not, and may be accompanied by physical symptoms such as muscle tension, fatigue, and irritability. Children with GAD are often highly perfectionistic and demonstrate cognitive distortions in which small errors are perceived as utter failures. They also tend to be eager-to-please and rule abiding, making them appear as "little adults" (Kendall, Krain, & Treadwell, 1999; Strauss, 1990). These traits are often perceived as socially desirable, thus complicating identification of the problem.

Many adults with GAD report being anxious for as long as they can remember (Rapee, 1985); however, GAD is more prevalent in children age 12 and older (Strauss, Lease, Last, & Francis, 1988; Tracey, Chorpita, Douban, & Barlow, 1997). Interestingly, GAD is also not gender-specific until adolescence, when more girls than boys, are diagnosed—a trend also found in adults (Kendall, 1994; Bowen, Offord, & Boyle, 1990).

Separation anxiety disorder involves a fear of being separated from a parent, caregiver, or loved one. A child with separation anxiety fears that, upon separation, something bad is likely to happen to the child, the attachment figure, or both. For example, a child may refuse to visit a friend's house because the parent might be in an accident, kidnapped, or killed such that the parent and child will never again be reunited. Often separation anxiety manifests as refusal to attend school, frequent trips to the nurse's office, multiple calls home from school, and/or an inability to sleep alone in one's bed. It is certainly true that some separation concerns are developmentally normative; however, separation anxiety disorder involves significant distress and impairment that is no longer age- or stage-appropriate. As with GAD, physical symptoms such as nausea and headaches may manifest when separation occurs or is anticipated. Repeated nightmares involving themes of separation are also common. Separation anxiety disorder has an onset before age 18 and, not surprisingly, is more prevalent in childhood than adolescence (Silverman & Dick-Niederhauser, 2004).

In social phobia, a child fears social or performance-based situations. The child worries that, in these situations, he or she may do something perceived as stupid or dumb resulting in embarrassment or humiliation. The age of onset is typically early to middle adolescence but may occur as early as age eight (Beidel, Morris, & Turner, 2004). While in the social or performance-based situation, the child may exhibit symptoms that mirror a panic attack, such as sweating, heart racing, or shortness of breath. As a result, a child will often avoid the situation altogether or may endure it with considerable distress. Social phobia may result in missing out on strategic developmental interactions with peers and others. Common manifestations of the disorder include poor friendship development and refusal to talk in class, give presentations, eat in public, or interact with teachers or peers.

While some specific fears and worries (e.g., monsters, bugs, the dark, water, needles) are quite typical in a child's development, excessive or persisting worries that result in significant distress and/or avoidance are suggestive of a specific phobia. Prevalence rates of specific phobias are extremely variable, though they are generally higher in girls than in boys (King, Muris, & Ollendick, 2005). The *DSM-IV* classifies specific phobias into the following categories: Animal Type, Natural Environment Type, Blood-Injection-Injury Type, Situational Type, and Other Type (e.g., choking, contracting an illness, vomiting). Both the animal and natural environment types typically have childhood onsets while the onset of the situational subtype is bimodal with one peak in childhood and another during the mid-twenties (American Psychiatric Association, 2000).

Obsessive-compulsive disorder (OCD) is characterized by recurrent obsessions and/ or compulsions that interfere and cause distress in one's life. Prevalence rates of OCD are estimated to be between 0.5 and 1% of children and adolescents (American Psychiatric Association, 2000). The average age of onset of OCD in children is 10 years, with boys more likely to have an earlier onset than girls (March, Franklin, Leonard, & Foa, 2004). Common obsessions (i.e., recurrent or persistent thoughts, images or impulses) include contamination, harm to self or others, sexual urges, religiosity, aggressive themes, and a need to confess. Common compulsions (i.e., repetitive and purposeful behaviors done in response to the obsession) include checking, washing, touching, counting, praying, hoarding, and straightening (March, Franklin, Leonard, & Foa, 2004; Swedo, Rapoport, Leonard, Lenane, & Cheslow, 1989).

Finally, Panic Disorder, while less common than the afore-mentioned anxiety disorders, is important to note because it can be quite immobilizing. Panic Disorder is characterized by recurrent and unexpected panic attacks. Panic disorder is most commonly diagnosed in adolescent girls though it has been shown to affect both children and adolescents, regardless of gender, in up to 10% of the pediatric psychiatric population (Kearney, Albano, Eisen, Allan & Barlow, 1997; Last & Strauss, 1989).

Anxiety disorders are highly comorbid with other childhood psychiatric disorders. Anxiety disorders frequently co-occur with other anxiety disorders, resulting in comorbidity rate estimates to be upwards of 50% (e.g., Benjamin et al., 1990; Kashani & Orvaschel, 1990). Comorbidity rates for anxiety and depression have been reported to be between 13–73% (Curry, March, & Hervey, 2004); comorbidity rates for anxiety and disruptive behavior disorders (e.g., Attention Deficit Hyperactivity Disorder, Oppositional Defiance Disorder, Conduct Disorder) appear to approximate 30% (e.g., Anderson, et al., 1987; Geller, Biederman, Griffin, Jones, & Lefkowitz, 1996; Last, Perrin, Hersen, & Kazdin, 1992). Additionally, substance abuse has been shown to be co-morbid with PTSD, OCD, Social Phobia, and GAD (Curry et al., 2004).

ASSESSMENT OF ANXIETY

Accuracy in assessment is critical to proper diagnosis, case formulation, treatment planning, and evaluation. Assessment is a practice that is not only useful in the initial stages of treatment (e.g., case conceptualization, treatment planning) but important during and after treatment (e.g., evaluations of treatment progress and outcomes) as well. Given the covert nature of anxious distress, children's self-reports are deemed crucial to an accurate assessment. However, there exists considerable debate about who is able to report most accurately regarding a child's internal distress—parent or child. Some studies have suggested that children may be the best reporters of their own anxious distress (e.g., Edelbrock, Costello, Dulcan, Conover, & Kala, 1986; Jensen, Traylor, Xenakis, & Davis, 1988); others have suggested that parents may be better reporters of their children's anxious distress (e.g., DiBartolo, Albano, Barlow, & Heimberg, 1998; Rapee,

Barrett, Dadds, & Evans, 1994; Schniering, Hudson, & Rapee, 2000). Given the conflicting nature of the literature, a multimethod assessment approach is recommended. The combination of child, parent, teacher, and peer reports regarding the child's behaviors across contexts via a variety of assessment methods (e.g., diagnostic interview, paper-and-pencil reports, behavioral observations) is likely to provide the most comprehensive clinical assessment.

Diagnostic Interviews

A diagnostic interview is often considered the most critical piece of a clinical assessment. Diagnostic interviews may be structured or unstructured, the latter permitting flexibility in questioning in order to gather additional information as necessary. Diagnostic interviewing allows for the collection of rich clinical data derived from the interviewee's verbal reports as well as observations of behavior and interpersonal interactions. However, one of the limitations of such interviews is generally the time necessary to complete them. Structured and semi-structured interviews will vary in length depending on a number of variables (e.g., talkativeness of interviewee, extent of clinical symptomatology, interviewer experience) (Velting, Setzer, & Albano, 2004).

The *Anxiety Disorders Interview Schedule for DSM-IV, Child and Parent Versions* (ADIS-IV; Silverman & Albano, 1996a, 1996b) is a semi-structured interview designed to assess anxiety disorders in children and adolescents. The ADIS-IV is conducted separately with parents and children, and although designed for the diagnosis of anxiety disorders, the inclusion of other disorders (e.g., dysthymia, attention deficit hyperactivity disorder, panic disorder) allows for differential diagnoses and the assessment of comorbid conditions. Clinician severity ratings (CSR; 0–8) are assigned to each diagnosis and permit an assessment of the impairment associated with the disorder. Only those disorders receiving a CSR between 4 and 8 are considered in the clinical range.

Other structured diagnostic interviews have been used to assess anxiety disorders in children and adolescents. These include the *Diagnostic Interview for Children and Adolescents* (DICA-R; Herjanic & Reich, 1997), the *Schedule for Affective Disorders and Schizophrenia for School-aged Children* (K-SADS; Kaufman et al., 1997), and the *National Institute of Mental Health Diagnostic Interview Schedule for Children* (NIMH DISC-IV; Shaffer, Fisher, Lucas, Dulcan, & Schwab-Stone, 2000). The DICA-R, K-SADS, and NIMH DISC-IV are all designed to assess a broad range of childhood disorders, including anxiety. The ADIS-IV is the only interview, however, specifically designed for assessing anxiety disorders. As such, it is often considered the "gold standard" in the assessment of anxiety disorders in children and adolescents (Greco & Morris, 2004). Nonetheless, collective evidence suggests that structured diagnostic interviews provide reasonably accurate data regarding children's anxious distress (Schniering, Hudson, & Rapee, 2000).

Self-Report Measures of Anxiety

Typically, self-report measures provide information ancillary to diagnoses. They are used to garner additional information on children's thoughts, feelings, and behaviors, allow for more discrete responding, and are generally quick and easy to administer. Self-report measures may be global in nature, assessing anxiety as a broad construct, or they may be syndrome specific, assessing specific symptoms of anxiety or anxiety within certain contexts or situations (e.g., social anxiety).

Global measures.   For many years, the *Revised Children's Manifest Anxiety Scale* (RCMAS; Reynolds & Richmond, 1985), *Fear Survey Schedule for Children-Revised* (FSSC-R; Ollendick, 1983), and the *State-Trait Anxiety Inventory for Children* (STAIC; Spielberger, 1973) were the instruments of choice in global assessments of anxiety. These global measures of anxiety are downward extensions of corresponding adult versions. As such, they may have limited utility with children and adolescents (Perrin & Last, 1992). While both the RCMAS, FSSC-R, and the STAIC have not been found to adequately distinguish among anxiety disorders or between anxiety disorders and other disorders (e.g., Hodges, 1990; Hoehn-Saric, Maisami, & Wiegand, 1987; Strauss, Last, Hersen, & Kazdin, 1988), these measures have been found to adequately distinguish children with anxiety disorders from nonclinical controls (Ollendick, 1983; Perrin & Last, 1992; Stark, Kaslow, & Laurent, 1993).

More recent attempts to measure the global construct of anxiety have tried to address some of these limitations. The *Multidimensional Anxiety Scale for Children* (MASC; March, Parker, Sullivan, Stallings, & Connors, 1997) and the *Screen for Anxiety and Related Emotional Disorders* (SCARED; Birmaher, et al., 1997) were specifically designed to serve as sensitive and specific screening tools for anxiety disorders in childhood and adolescence. The MASC is a 39-item, 4-point Likert-type child-report measure with four main factors: physical symptoms; social anxiety; harm avoidance; and separation anxiety. The MASC has demonstrated strong psychometric properties in epidemiological and clinical studies (March et al., 1997), as well as in a school-based sample (March, Sullivan, & Parker, 1999).

The SCARED is a 66-item, 3-point Likert-type child-report measure consisting of nine DSM-IV-linked subscales: panic disorder, generalized anxiety disorder, social phobia, separation anxiety disorder, obsessive-compulsive disorder, specific phobia (animal, blood-injection-injury, and environmental-situational types), and traumatic stress disorder. A parent-report version is also available. Both versions of the SCARED have demonstrated excellent internal reliability and good retest reliability in clinical samples (Birmaher et al., 1997; Birmaher, Brent, Chiappetta, Bridge, Monga, & Baugher, 1999) and in a community sample (Muris et al., 1998).

Syndrome-specific measures.   Numerous inventories assess the specific syndromes associated with anxiety. Symptoms of social phobia are assessed by both the *Social Phobia and Anxiety Inventory for Children* (SPAI-C; Beidel, Turner & Morris, 1995) and the *Social Anxiety Scale for Children* (SASC-R; La Greca, 1998; La Greca, Dandes, Wick, Shaw, & Stone, 1988). Items on the SPAI-C are theory-driven and as such do not directly correspond to the DSM-IV criteria (Greco & Morris, 2004). The SPAI-C is comprised of three subscales: fear of negative evaluation; generalized social avoidance and distress; and social avoidance and distress with new or unfamiliar peers. Items on the SASC-R more directly correspond to DSM criteria. Both measures have demonstrated excellent internal consistency and high retest reliabilities (La Greca, 1998; Beidel et al., 1995). Other syndrome specific measures include the *Penn State Worry Questionnaire for Children* (PSWQ-C; Chorpita, Tracey, Brown, Collica, & Barlow, 1997) and the *Childhood Anxiety Sensitivity Index* (CASI; Silverman, Fleisig, Rabian, & Peterson, 1991), the latter of which measures fear of anxiety-related somatic symptoms.

Parent and Teacher Measures of Child Anxiety

As recommended in the assessment literature, a thorough and comprehensive assessment often incorporates information garnered from multiple informants. In the case of children, the perspectives of parents and teachers are especially useful. One of the most common inventories used by parents and teachers to assess internalized distress, as well as a broad range of other problems, is the *Child Behavior Checklist* (CBCL) and the *Teacher Report Form* (TRF; Achenbach, 1991a, 1991b; Achenbach & Rescorla, 2001). The measures yield a Total Behavior Problem score as well as three factor scores (Internalizing, Externalizing, and Social Competence) and nine narrow-band scales. Three of the narrow-band scales are relevant to anxiety: Anxious/Depressed, Withdrawn, and Somatic Complaints. Despite being oft used for the assessment of anxiety, the anxiety-related subscales of the CBCL and TRF may better represent a broad negative affectivity rather than being specific to anxiety (Chorpita, Albano, & Barlow, 1998; Chorpita & Daleiden, 2002). Few parent-report measures of global or specific anxiety exist—the parent versions of the STAI-C and the SCARED are notable exceptions.

Behavioral Observations

Behavioral observations can be a useful supplement to interview and paper-and-pencil measures. They may be structured or naturalistic and often involve notations of children's verbalizations, body posture, body movements, facial expressions, and the like. Two examples of structured observations are the *Behavioral Avoidance Task* and the *Youth Speech Sample*. The *Behavioral Avoidance Task* (BAT) involves requiring a child to confront a feared object, situation, or event and recording the behavioral features of the child's performance (e.g., self-reported fear levels, proximity to feared stimulus, physiological reactions, latency to respond). While they may provide ancillary information difficult to obtain through interview and self-report formats, BATs may be difficult to implement with particular types of fears, lack standardization, and may not generalize to naturalistic settings.

COGNITIVE-BEHAVIORAL CONCEPTUALIZATION

The cognitive-behavioral model posits three dimensions of anxiety: physiological; cognitive; and behavioral—all of which may be considered adaptive emotional responses. On a physiological level, anxiety may alert a child to impending danger via activation of the autonomic nervous system (ANS). When the ANS is activated, physiological responses such as sweating, tightening of the muscles, headaches, and stomach pains may occur as a child's body prepares for "fight or flight" (Albano & Kendall, 2002). Cognitively, a child may perceive the dangerousness of the situation through estimations of his or her own ability to cope. When a child does not believe that he or she can cope, these beliefs may manifest behaviorally through avoidance of anxiety-provoking situation, tantruming, or crying.

Maladaptive levels of anxiety have several etiological explanations. Barlow (2000), for example, conceptualizes anxiety disorders as stemming from three vulnerabilities, termed the "triple-vulnerability model." The three vulnerabilities include (1) genetic vulnerabilities; (2) general psychological vulnerabilities originating from uncontrollable and unpredictable threat; and (3) more specific psychological vulnerabilities stemming from early learning experiences.

Some evidence from twin and family studies suggest that anxiety disorders may be genetically mediated; other studies indicate that temperament may spur anxiety disorders (Manassis, Hudson, Webb, & Albano, 2004). Numerous twin studies have demonstrated that genetics accounts for approximately 30–40% of the variance in anxious symptomatology and disorder (e.g., Andrews, Stewart, Allen, & Henderson, 1990a; Andrews, Stewart, Morris-Yates, Holt, & Henderson, 1990b; Jardine, Martin, & Henderson, 1984; Kendler, Neale, Kessler, Heath, & Eaves, 1992; Torgersen, 1983; Tyrer, Alexander, Remington, & Riley, 1987). Several studies appear to suggest the inheritance of a general predisposition rather than the heritability of individual disorder(s) (e.g., Andrews et al., 1990b; Torgersen, 1983).

Behavioral inhibition, a temperamental feature characterized by irritability in infancy, fearfulness in toddlerhood, and shyness, wariness, and withdrawal in childhood, has also been associated with an increased vulnerability to anxiety disorder(s) (e.g., Biederman et al., 1993; Kagan, 1989, 1997; Rosenbaum et al., 1993). Kagan and colleagues found that approximately 15% of Caucasian American children exhibited this temperamental trait (Kagan, 1989). Biederman and colleagues found that rates of anxiety disorders were highest among children who had been identified as behaviorally inhibited throughout childhood (Biederman, Rosenbaum, Chaloff, & Kagan, 1995). Prospective studies have demonstrated that children identified as behaviorally inhibited at 21 months were more likely than uninhibited children to develop anxiety disorders over the next 5 to 10 years (Biederman et al., 1993; Hirshfeld et al., 1992).

Traumatic, stressful, and/or uncontrollable life events have been identified as factors that may precipitate anxious distress. Children have been found to demonstrate increases in anxiety, somatic complaints, and avoidance behaviors in the aftermath of traumatic events such as earthquakes, fires, and storms (Dollinger, 1986; Dollinger, O'Donnell, & Staley, 1984; Terr, 1981; Yule & Williams, 1990). Several researchers have suggested that children with an anxiety disorder may experience significantly more stressful life events (e.g., parental separations, starting new school, parental divorce, death of family member) than children without anxiety disorders (Benjamin et al., 1990; Goodyer & Altham, 1991; Rapee & Szollos, 1997), and the occurrence of stressful life events in childhood has been found to be associated with an increased risk of anxiety disorder (e.g., Tiet, et al., 1998).

Specific psychological vulnerabilities have been conceptualized in terms of social learning theory (Bandura, 1977). Children can learn specific anxiety responses through modeling—children's fears may be exacerbated by witnessing anxious symptoms in adults or hearing adults talk excessively about potential harm. Children can also learn anxiety responses through classical conditioning. As an example, if a child trips and falls down on the soccer field and, as a result, fails to score the winning goal, he or she may be harshly criticized or teased by peers. The child may then develop a generalized anxiety response in other social situations. Alternatively, children may avoid anxious situations as a method to cope with their anxiety. The two-factor theory proposed by Mowrer (1960) maintains that children are negatively reinforced by lessened anxiety resulting from increases in their avoidant responses. Parents or other adults in the lives of anxious children may also reinforce this avoidant or dependent behavior. For example, a child who is selectively mute may never be encouraged to speak if a parent is always his or her "voice." Similarly, if a parent allows a socially anxious child to stay home from school each morning that the child cries, the child's anxiety will decrease in the short-term, thus reinforcing the avoidant behavior (e.g., crying in attempts to remain at home) and increasing the likelihood that the child will behave similarly when future social situations are anticipated.

GROUP TREATMENT

Cognitive-behavioral therapy (CBT) has been found to be effective for anxious children (Barrett et al., 1996; Eisen & Silverman, 1993; Kane & Kendall, 1989; Kendall, 1994; Kendall et al., 1997; Mansdorf & Lukens, 1987; Ollendick, Hagopian, & Huntzinger, 1991; see also Kazdin & Weisz, 1998; Ollendick & King, 1998). In fact, CBT has been denoted as having met the criteria for "probably efficacious" treatment for anxiety disorders in youth (see Chambless & Hollon, 1998; Ollendick & King, 1998). Though the efficacy of CBT in children with anxiety disorders has been demonstrated, there is increasing interest in the efficacy of using CBT for childhood anxiety disorders in a group format.

A number of studies have begun to evaluate the efficacy of group approaches to the treatment of anxiety disorders in childhood. Most of these studies use treatment protocols that are comprised of similar elements. One of these protocols is presented here. Flannery-Schroeder & Kendall (1996) developed an 18-session manualized group therapy protocol for the treatment of anxiety disorders in children. The program combines a cognitive-behavioral approach with a single-gender group format. Thus, the resulting therapy integrates elements of a behavioral approach (e.g., exposure, relaxation training, role-plays) with a cognitive one (e.g., cognitive restructuring, problem solving) and occurs in a group setting. The group therapy approach parallels the individually based treatment of anxiety disorders in youth (Kendall, 2000) evaluated by Kane and Kendall (1989), Kendall (1994), and Kendall and colleagues. (1997).

The rationale for the use of a group format involves several factors. First, the use of a group treatment for childhood anxiety disorders is rooted in a theoretical basis. Anxiety disorders often have a dysfunctional social, and often evaluative, component (particularly social phobia and generalized anxiety disorder). Groups provide unique opportunities for social interactions with peers (e.g., practice in initiation and maintenance of relationships, peer modeling, peer reinforcement, and peer feedback), social reward, normalization, and multiple exposures to feared interpersonal contexts, objects, and/or situations (Albano, Marten, Holt, Heimberg, & Barlow, 1995; Flannery-Schroeder & Kendall, 2000; Heimberg, Dodge, Hope, Kennedy, Zollo, & Becker, 1990). Further, group treatments may be more cost- and time-efficient than individual therapy formats, an important consideration for any intervention.

The overall goal of the treatment is to provide children with the skills necessary for them to successfully cope in a variety of anxiety-provoking situations. The group program is also divided into two segments: a skill-building segment and a practice segment. In addition, the therapist meets separately with parents of group members between the fourth and fifth group sessions. Individual sessions between the therapist and group member(s) are arranged for those children who have difficulty keeping up or those who are absent from session(s).

The first nine sessions comprise the cognitive/educational component of the treatment. Throughout the treatment, concepts and skills are presented in a sequential order from easy to more difficult. Cognitive-behavioral strategies are presented as a 4-step plan to cope with anxiety. To facilitate recall of the steps, the following acronym (FEAR) is used:

Feeling Frightened?
Expecting Bad Things To Happen?
Attitudes and Actions That Will Help
Ratings and Rewards

As outlined by the acronym, several important concepts are introduced sequentially to the children during the training segment of the program, beginning with the awareness of bodily reactions to feelings and developing recognition of those reactions that are specific to anxiety. The children are trained to use those physical reactions as cues to the presence of anxiety. Second, the children are encouraged to focus on their self-statements and, third, to make modifications in their "self-talk," as appropriate. This is introduced using a cartoon sequences with blank thought bubbles that the children complete. Emphasis is placed on the need to devise a "plan" for more effective coping in the anxiety-provoking experience. The fourth concept introduced is self-rating and reward, even for partial success. Additionally, Show That I Can (STIC) tasks are assigned to the children as homework in order to reinforce the information presented during the sessions, and "Buddy" assignments are used to increase group cohesion as well as hone group members' social skills. Children use the Coping Cat Notebook and Workbook to facilitate learning (Kendall, 1993).

The second half of the treatment (the practice segment) consists of applying the newly acquired skills in a variety of graduated exposures to anxiety-eliciting situations. These situations are tailored to the individual fears of the children. It is likely that within any group there may be a great deal of variability in the worries and concerns of the children. The therapist must be sensitive to the individual needs of each child as well as work on a more global or group level. The practice segments begin with exposures taking place within the group, then progress to exposures involving the group as a whole, then to exposures involving individual group members. Application of strategies to *in vivo* situations provides success experiences, which are incompatible with previous expectations, and provides evidence (to the child, group, and others) that change is taking place. Finally, the last session involves the making of a videotaped commercial about learning to cope with anxiety. The commercial is developed by the group and promotes cooperation, problem solving, and group cohesion. In addition, the commercial serves to consolidate the information learned throughout the treatment and to reinforce each child's role and participation within the group. Each group member is given a copy of the commercial to take home with them.

In sum, the treatment consists of helping the children to recognize signs of anxious arousal and to use these as cues for the use of the anxiety management strategies practiced in the treatment program. Specifically, the program places the greatest emphasis on the following elements of the treatment program: (1) affective education (e.g., awareness of bodily reactions when anxious); (2) identification and modification of anxious self-talk; (3) relaxation training; (4) problem-solving skills training; (5) contingent reinforcement; and (6) graduated exposure to and practice of newly acquired skills in anxiety-eliciting situations. Noteworthy too are the group-based strategies which are emphasized in order to encourage responsibility, problem-solving, and cohesion among group members: (1) group participation in a sequence of learning tasks and assignments, with form of participation varied to fit with each group member's level of readiness and social skill; (2) therapist structuring of session format to encourage expression of anxious affect within an atmosphere of tolerance and respect for the uniqueness of each member's experience; (3) the setting of goals for the group as well as for the individual members; (4) the use of cohesion-building tasks and games to strengthen the ties among group members; and (5) homework assignments designed to enhance group cohesion ("Buddy" assignments).

Research on the efficacy of cognitive-behavior group therapy (CBGT) is emerging (e.g., Barrett, 1998; Flannery-Schroeder & Kendall, 2000; Manassis et al., 2002; Mendlowitz, Manassis, Bradley, Scapillato, Miezitis, & Shaw, 1999; Muris, Meesters, & van Melick, 2003; Rapee, 2000; Silverman, Kurtines, Ginsburg, Weems, Lumpkin, & Carmichael, 1999; Spence, Donovan, & Brechman-Toussaint, 2000). Barrett (1998) evaluated a cognitive-behavioral group family-based intervention for childhood anxiety disorders. Sixty children were randomly assigned to GCBT, GCBT plus family management (GCBT+FAM), and wait list control (WLC). At posttreatment, both treatments were superior to the WLC, and there was no significant difference between GCBT and GCBT+FAM. At 12-month follow-up, 64.5% of GCBT, and 84.8% if GCBT+FAM no longer met criteria for an anxiety disorder. Results indicated that CBT interventions for childhood anxiety disorders could be effectively administered in a group format. Silverman and colleagues (1999) also reported a randomized clinical trial comparing GCBT with concurrent parent sessions to WLC. Sixty-four percent of children in GCBT no longer met criteria for their principal anxiety diagnosis, compared with 13% of those in WLC. Treatment gains were maintained at 3-, 6-, and 12-month follow-up. Similarly, Mendlowitz et al. (1999) found GCBT with and without concurrent parental involvement to reduce symptoms of anxiety and depression in a sample of children with an anxiety disorder. Spence and colleagues (2000) found similar results using a sample of 50 children diagnosed with social anxiety disorder. Rapee (2000) and Toren and colleagues (Toren et al., 2000), in investigations of the efficacy of group cognitive-behavioral treatment involving families, found the treatments to be associated with significant reductions in children's anxious symptoms versus waiting-list control conditions. Though the evidence for the efficacy of GCBT for childhood anxiety disorders in comparison to wait-list control is promising, studies directly comparing individual to group CBT are needed.

Flannery-Schroeder and Kendall (2000) conducted the first randomized clinical trial evaluating the efficacy of GCBT and individual cognitive-behavioral therapy (ICBT) for 8- to 14- year old children diagnosed with childhood anxiety disorders (i.e., Generalized Anxiety Disorder, Separation Anxiety Disorder, Social Phobia). The research compared the efficacy of the cognitive-behavioral group intervention (GCBT) with that of a cognitive-behavioral individual intervention (ICBT) and a wait-list control condition (WL). The cognitive-behavioral therapy protocol that was used for both GCBT and ICBT conditions consisted of the previously reviewed 18-week manualized intervention (Flannery-Schroeder & Kendall, 1996). Groups were single-gendered and consisted of four children. The three conditions (GCBT, ICBT, WL) were compared on dependent measures including: (1) diagnostic status; (2) child self-reports of anxiety, depression, coping, competence, and social functioning (e.g., loneliness, friendships, social activities); (3) parental-reports of child's adaptive functioning, anxiety, coping, competence, and social functioning; and (4) teacher-reports of adaptive functioning. Analyses of diagnostic status revealed that significantly more treated children (73% individual, 50% group) than wait-list children (8%) did not meet diagnostic criteria for their primary anxiety disorder at post-treatment. Dependent measures of child-reported anxiety and coping and several parent-report measures of anxiety, adaptive functioning and coping demonstrated the superiority of the treatment conditions compared to the wait-list condition. Measures of social functioning failed to discriminate among conditions. Treatment gains were maintained at a 3-month and one-year follow-up (Flannery-Schroeder, Choudhury, & Kendall, 2005).

More recently, Manassis and colleagues (2002) compared the efficacy of GCBT and ICBT with parental involvement for childhood anxiety. Children and parents reported significantly decreased anxiety, and clinicians blind to condition reported significantly improved global functioning regardless of treatment modality. Improvement was maintained at 1-year follow-up with no differences found between modalities.

Given the promise of group cognitive-behavioral formats in group versus no treatment designs and group versus individual format designs, a next step is to compare the efficacy of group CBTs to placebo interventions and/or other active therapies (Ollendick & King, 1998). In line with this recommendation, Muris and colleagues (Muris, et al., 2002) examined the efficacy of a group cognitive-behavioral treatment ($n = 10$) versus a psychological placebo (i.e., emotional disclosure [ED]; $n = 10$) and a no-treatment control group ($n = 10$). Results demonstrated that the group CBT significantly reduced anxiety and depressive symptoms whereas the ED and no-treatment conditions did not.

OVERCOMING POTENTIAL OBSTACLES

The literature on the effectiveness of CBGT interventions is relatively limited, though what has been published is promising. There are, however, potential obstacles that need to be addressed when implementing group cognitive-behavioral interventions with anxious children.

First, one must determine whether it is feasible to conduct group cognitive-behavioral treatment at all. That is, is the flow within the treatment clinic sufficient to form therapy groups? If recruitment of group participants is slow, delays in the formation of groups may result in participant attrition (Himle, Van Etten, & Fischer, 2003).

Second, several decisions regarding group composition must be made. Age of group members is an important consideration. "What is the optimal age for group treatment?" and "Should groups be composed of similar or varied ages?" are questions that need to be addressed when forming treatment groups. The extant literature on the efficacy of group cognitive-behavioral therapies for childhood anxiety disorders have largely used similar age ranges (approximately 7–14 years old; e.g., Barrett, 1998; Flannery-Schroeder & Kendall, 2000; Manassis et al., 2002; Mendlowitz et al., 1999; Rapee, 2000; Spence et al., 2000; Toren et al., 2000); however, some studies have looked exclusively at adolescents (e.g., Ginsburg & Drake, 2002; Masia, Klein, Storch, & Corda, 2001; Thienemann, Martin, Cregger, Thompson, & Dyer-Friedman, 2001). The use of cognitive strategies in group treatment typically determines the lower limits of age as children younger that 6 or 7 have not yet developed the ability to engage in metacognition (i.e., thinking about one's own thinking), a skill necessary to the successful use of cognitive strategies.

The decision to include similar age ranges or disparate ones remains the purview of the therapist. It may be that group mates similar in age have more in common, thus resulting in interventions that are more effective. However, dissimilarly aged group mates may benefit if the older children serve as "coaches" and/or "leaders" for younger members. In the latter case, older children gain leadership skills and a deeper understanding of session material, while younger children may benefit if the older children represent more effective models of coping techniques. However, caution is warranted in the case of dissimilarly aged groups. Attention must be paid to the developmental appropriateness of session content and materials (e.g., therapy workbooks). If 7-year-olds are grouped with 11-year-olds, for example, care must be taken to ensure that the session content is pitched neither too low for the older children nor too high for the younger children. Future research is needed to enable therapists to make empirically formed decisions regarding the ages of group members.

Similarly, gender of group members and size of groups represent issues of concern. Treatment outcome studies have tended to evaluate mixed-gender groups (e.g., Mendlowitz et al., 1999; Rapee, 2000; Silverman et al., 1999; for an exception, see Flannery-Schroeder & Kendall, 2000). However, the potential advantages and disadvantages of mixed-gender groups remain unclear. In the Flannery-Schroeder and Kendall (2000) study, group members in a single-gender (female) group evidenced clear disinhibition in sessions. For example, during one session, all group members (including two socially inhibited girls) began dancing on a tabletop—behaviors very atypical of the girls outside of the therapy room. While merely anecdotal, this clinical example underscores a need for research to evaluate the impact of single- versus mixed-gender groups on treatment outcomes.

Additionally, "What group size is optimal?" and "Does group size interact with gender and age composition?" remain questions unanswered in the literature. Group cognitive-behavioral studies have evaluated groups typically ranging in size from three to six members. Eight group members appear to represent the maximum size considered by researchers due to concerns about anxious children's fears with respect to large groups (Mendlowitz et al., 1999). There may be a clinical rationale for choosing a small versus larger group size. For example, it could be argued that certain anxiety disorders (e.g., social phobia) are better treated in smaller groups. However, the converse could be argued as well. It may be that children with social phobia are better treated in larger groups given the increased social interaction opportunities afforded by such. Again, future research is needed to determine which group sizes are most advantageous for which children.

Maintaining confidentiality within a group of children or adolescents presents special challenges. It is often the case that group mates are referred from the same local area. Thus, there stands a good chance that group mates may be acquainted with one another, share a friend in common, or be likely to cross paths in the near future. It is advisable to discuss the importance of confidentiality and its limits prior to the initiation of the first group session. Group members may develop a deepened appreciation and respect for the maintenance of confidentiality if they (and their parents) complete agreements of confidentiality at the outset of therapy. This will help to ensure that everyone feels free to disclose within group sessions. Given the nature of anxiety, however, it would be expected that some group members would find discussion of their experiences as embarrassing or humiliating when in a group setting. This reluctance would be especially heightened for group members with dissimilar anxious symptomatology in an otherwise homogeneous group.

Another potential difficulty exists in the ability of the therapist to address group member's individual needs. As most cognitive-behavioral group sessions reviewed in this chapter ran approximately 90 minutes, a mere 18 minutes can be devoted to each individual member in a 5-person group. This leaves little time to develop a personalized treatment plan for each group member. Additionally, some cautions against the use of group treatment involve concerns that group members may either learn or trivialize the symptoms exhibited by other group members. Anxious children, in particular, may develop a complicity in insisting that particular anxiety-provoking situations are indeed dangerous despite a therapist's attempts to use cognitive-restructuring techniques or *in vivo* exposures to demonstrate the contrary. Conversely, teasing may occur within a group leading to a variety of untoward outcomes (e.g., lowered self-esteem, discouragement, embarrassment).

CASE EXAMPLE

Myriel, a sandy-haired 10-year-old girl, was referred by the school psychologist to the child anxiety clinic for problems attending school. Myriel stubbornly refused to ready herself for school each morning, and her mother reported significant difficulty in getting her to the car to drive her to school. On occasion, Myriel's mother reported having to "drag her" to the car during which time Myriel was mildly combative. Myriel reported an intense dislike of school, had few friends, was exceedingly shy, and appeared sullen and withdrawn much of the school day. Her mother reported that she routinely avoided social situations and hated to have any amount of attention focused upon her. On a structured clinical interview, Myriel met criteria for Social Phobia (Generalized Type) and Major Depressive Disorder.

Beth, age 8, was referred to the child anxiety clinic by her mother because of Beth's unwillingness to remain alone, even for brief moments. Beth's mother reported that Beth had "meltdowns" whenever she and her mother were to be apart. Over the last school year, Beth made frequent trips to the school nurse complaining of stomachaches, which abated upon reuniting with her mother. Most recently, Beth had surgery to correct a heart defect, and while in the hospital, she refused to allow her mother to leave her side even to use the bathroom. Parents also reported difficulty in Beth's behavioral self-control and inattention as well as an extreme fear of spiders. Beth's mother was currently undergoing treatment for generalized anxiety and her father had been diagnosed with Attention Deficit Hyperactivity Disorder (ADHD). Beth was diagnosed via a structured diagnostic interview with Separation Anxiety Disorder, ADHD, and a Specific Phobia.

Alexis, an 11-year old girl, was referred by her parents out of their concern for her worrying and perfectionistic behaviors. Alexis was worrying about making mistakes in her schoolwork, became excessively nervous upon tests and oral reports, and within the past year, had begun to see her grades drop from As to Bs and Cs due to failure to complete several key homework projects. Alexis appeared to believe that if the homework was unable to be completed perfectly, it was not to be done at all. Alexis had tremendous difficulty in managing her frustration levels in the face of challenging schoolwork and frequently "blew up" after making minor errors. Additionally, Alexis had difficulty sleeping independently at night and required a parent to lie down with her. Her parents reported bedtime to be especially difficult as Alexis's worries would escalate during this time. Her concerns about tomorrow's test would soon turn to worries about her performance in the next grade, progressing rapidly to fear of leaving home for college, having enough money to buy a house when she grew up, and to anxiety about her parents' dying despite their good health. Using a structured diagnostic interview, Alexis received a diagnosis of Generalized Anxiety Disorder.

Myriel, Beth, and Alexis were treated in an 18-week clinic-based group cognitive-behavioral treatment for children with anxiety disorders. The group treatment was based on the *Coping Cat* program developed by Kendall and colleagues and followed the outline presented earlier in this chapter. Development of group cohesion was a primary concern during the initial sessions. To facilitate group unity and rapport among group members, the girls were encouraged to choose a name for their group. "Lion Queens" was selected and a poster emblazoned with the name was colored and hung in the therapy room during sessions. Each session began with an individual review of homework, called Show That I Can (STIC) tasks and Buddy tasks, during which the therapist modeled positive feedback, tolerance, and respect for group members. The STIC tasks allowed session content to be personalized to each child's unique manifestation(s) of anxiety. Buddy tasks were highly structured assignments to contact other group members between sessions in order to build group cohesion and provide social skills practice.

The first session focused on building rapport among the group members, introducing them to the treatment program, and encouraging their participation. To facilitate group interaction, the girls played a get-to-know-you game, decorated their homework journals, and took a group tour of the clinic. Early in treatment, Myriel was quiet during sessions but answered questions when asked by group members or the therapist. Beth was extremely social, extraordinarily talkative, and frequently was out of her seat and sidling herself up next to her group mates. She frequently interrupted group members during the homework review to relay her own experiences but with the ultimate effect of generating much laughter and interpersonal ease among all members.

The next few sessions focused on affective education, particularly, the identification of one's own somatic reactions to anxiety and relaxation training (Step 1: "Feeling Frightened?"). Myriel began to distinguish between her anxious and depressed feelings noting how each made her body feel (e.g., she reported that her body felt "shaky" when nervous but "heavy" when sad). Among other affective education tools, the therapist introduced the "feelings thermometer," a large picture of a thermometer with ratings from 0 to 8 that identify low to high levels of anxiety, in order to help the girls begin to identify how much anxiety they felt in different situations. The thermometer emphasized the distinctions among varying levels of fear and worry and provided a useful language for describing the degree of their emotional distress. Beth began to create a list of anxiety-provoking situations involving separation from her mother in which she used the feelings thermometer to rank order the difficulty levels associated with each (e.g., staying upstairs while her mother is downstairs = 3, mother arriving late to pick up Beth after a session = 6, sleeping over at grandmother's house = 8). Alexis' list of anxiety-provoking situations included a progression of situations in which she made larger and more serious mistakes (e.g., making a mistake on a nongraded class assignment = 4, making a mistake on a graded homework assignment = 6, making a mistake on a test = 7) as well as some situations involving sleeping independently (e.g., parents staying with her at bedtime for 10 minutes = 5, parents staying for 5 minutes = 7).

Later sessions focused on the identification and modification of self-talk, problem-solving skills training, and self-rating and reward. In the session focusing on the modification of anxious self-talk to coping self-talk (Step 2: "Expecting Bad Things to Happen?"), Beth reported thinking that "something bad will happen" to her mother when she and Beth are separated. In particular, Beth worried about the possibility of her mother being involved in an auto accident. The therapist and group mates helped Beth to develop coping thoughts including, "My mother is a woman who knows how to take care of herself," "My mother is a good driver," and "If my mother does get into an accident, it will most likely be just a fender-bender."

In the problem-solving session (Step 3: "Actions and Attitudes That Can Help"), the group focused on learning the steps to solving a problem. As an example, Myriel devised ways to cope when she experienced fear and worries in the mornings before school. She and group mates generated a list of potential solutions with no regard to their potential utility. After all ideas were exhausted, the group evaluated each potential solution. Those deemed unlikely to help were eliminated while those deemed promising were highlighted. In Myriel's case, the group's initial list included solutions such as "concentrate on the things you like about school," "fake sick," "call your buddy," and "meet a friend at the school's front door." Myriel's final plan included meeting up with a friend, taking time for deep breathing and relaxation before school, and focusing on the high points of the day (e.g., art class or journal club).

The final skill taught was self-reward (Step 4: "Ratings and Rewards"). The group members received instruction on how to rate their own attempts to cope on a 0–8 scale with 8 signifying maximum effort. The therapist emphasized the importance of rewarding *effort*, and not merely positive results. The group mates each made "reward menus" in which they listed both material and social incentives for use in rewarding efforts to cope with anxiety. Sample rewards included colorful pens, movie tickets, sports equipment, staying-up-late privileges, time with parent(s), sleepovers, and ice cream outings. Prior to the second half of treatment, the acronym for the four step coping plan (i.e., FEAR) was revealed and the coping plan was reviewed.

Throughout the sessions in the first half of treatment, Alexis was very concerned with staying on task and accomplishing the goals of the session. She frequently reprimanded group mates for off-task behavior and chastised them for infractions of session "rules." While Alexis demonstrated complete mastery of all session content as well as "perfectly" completed homework, Beth demonstrated difficulty in staying on task, remembering session content, and had a propensity to arrive at sessions with lost, incomplete, or forgotten homework. Myriel, initially reticent, slowly warmed to the group and by mid-treatment, was actively engaged in sessions and demonstrated good social interactions with group mates.

Sessions in the second half of treatment consisted of applying the newly acquired skills in a variety of graduated exposures to anxiety-eliciting situations, and group cooperation was very important in this phase of treatment. The anxiety-eliciting situations were tailored to the individual fears of the children as these varied across the group. However, the therapist also strove to address concerns shared by group members by developing group exposures. The practice segments began with imaginal exposures taking place within the group, then progressed to *in vivo* exposures involving the group as a whole, then to in vivo exposures involving individual group members. In the group *in vivo* phase, the group members together accomplished superordinate goals. For example, one group *in vivo* exposure involved a scavenger hunt in a nearby park. Beth, the group member with separation anxiety, was responsible for leading the group to the park with minimal directions, Alexis was to make intentional errors during the group quest (e.g., returning to the therapist with an incorrect item), and Myriel, the third group member with social anxiety, had to report back to the therapist and provide an oral review of the group's activities during the scavenger hunt. Thus, each child's unique anxieties were tapped in a task that could not be accomplished without the cooperation and courageous behaviors of each group member. For some exposures, group members with similar fears were paired to accomplish various tasks. For example, Myriel and Alexis shared social concerns. One *in vivo* exposure required the pair to prepare and administer a survey on the usefulness of mistake making. In this exposure, Myriel received practice in approaching and asking questions of strangers while Alexis designed the survey and ultimately, benefited from the "data" gathered. This data, when summed, demonstrated that most survey participants reported seeing value in making mistakes, acknowledged the universality of mistake making, and exhibited a tolerance for the mistakes of others. In this manner, both girls' fears were targeted through a single task.

Finally, the last phase of exposures involved each member tackling *in vivo* exposures independently. Myriel completed a series of social exposures—she gave speeches, initiated conversations with peers and adults (familiar and unfamiliar), joined an art class, and began riding the school bus to and from school. Beth completed a series of exposures, which increased in the degree of separation required—she remained home alone for short periods of time, independently entered convenience stores to make purchases, and slept over at a cousin's house without her parents. In addition, Beth worked on her fear of spiders by progressing from exposures to pictured spiders to plastic spiders to live, but contained, spiders. Alexis tackled *in vivos* that targeted her perfectionism as well as other concerns (e.g., tardiness, sleeping independently). Group mates offered creative ideas and support during the pre-exposure preparation, observed during the exposures, and offered hearty congratulations upon their successful completion.

SUMMARY

Anxiety disorders in children are prevalent, impairing, and often of long-standing duration. However, we can now add "treatable" to this list. Cognitive-behavioral treatments have shown real promise in the treatment of anxiety disorders in childhood and adolescence. While individual and family formats have received a good deal of research attention to date, the emerging literature on the efficacy of group cognitive-behavioral treatments for childhood anxiety is compelling. There appear to be distinct advantages for the use of group approaches with anxious children and adolescents. Group formats may afford more plentiful opportunities for peer modeling, peer interaction, and peer support and reinforcement of treatment-induced changes. They may help to normalize and destigmatize the experience of anxiety as well as to increase generalization of therapy-learned techniques due to a wider exposure to varying anxiety symptoms and concerns. Furthermore, groups parallel the social milieu for most children, and especially adolescents, in that the importance of peers and social groups are paramount during these years. Last, few can deny the cost and time savings inherent in group treatments.

While the research on group cognitive-behavioral treatments holds great promise, we still remain unclear on exactly how or why and for whom such groups work. Researchers must ascertain those conditions in which group cognitive-behavioral formats are preferred and those in which they are less preferred or inadvisable.

RECOMMENDED READINGS

Barrett, P. M. (1998). Evaluation of cognitive-behavioral group treatments for childhood anxiety disorders. *Journal of Clinical Child Psychology, 27*, 459–468.

Flannery-Schroeder, E. C., & Kendall, P. C. (1996). *Cognitive-behavioral therapy for anxious children: Therapist manual for group treatment.* Ardmore, PA: Workbook Publishing.

Flannery-Schroeder, E. C., Choudhury, M., & Kendall, P. C. (2005). Group and individual cognitive-behavioral treatments for youth with anxiety disorders: 1-year follow-up. *Cognitive Therapy and Research, 29*, 253–259.

Flannery-Schroeder, E. C., & Kendall, P. C. (2000). Group and individual cognitive-behavioral treatments for youth with anxiety disorders: A randomized clinical trial. *Cognitive Therapy and Research, 24*, 251–278.

Manassis, K., Mendlowitz, S. L., Scapillato, D., Avery, D., Fiksenbaum, L., Freire, M., Monga, S., & Owens, M. (2002). Group and individual cognitive-behavioral therapy for childhood anxiety disorders: A randomized trial. *Journal of the American Academy of Child and Adolescent Psychiatry, 41*, 1423–1430.

Mendlowitz, S. L., Manassis, K., Bradley, S., Scapillato, D., Miezitis, S., & Shaw, B. F. (1999). Cognitive-behavioral group treatments in childhood anxiety disorders: The role of parental involvement. *Journal of the American Academy of Child and Adolescent Psychiatry, 38*, 1223–229.

Muris, P., Meesters, C., & Van Melick, M. (2002). Treatment of childhood anxiety disorders: A preliminary comparison between cognitive-behavioral group therapy and a psychological placebo intervention. *Journal of Behavior Therapy and Experimental Psychiatry, 33*, 143–158.

Rapee, R. M. (2000). Group treatment of children with anxiety disorders: Outcome and predictors of treatment response. *Australian Journal of Psychology, 52*, 125–129.

Silverman, W. K., Kurtines, W. M., Ginsburg, G. S., Weems, C. F., Lumpkin, P. W., & Carmichael, D. H. (1999). Treating anxiety disorders in children with group cognitive-behavioral therapy: A randomized clinical trial. *Journal of Consulting and Clinical Psychology, 67*, 995–1003.

REFERENCES

Achenbach, T. M. (1991a). *Manual for the Child Behavior Checklists/4–18 and 1991 Profile.* Burlington: University of Vermont.

Achenbach, T. M. (1991b). *Manual for the Teacher Report Form and 1991 Profile.* Burlington: University of Vermont.

Achenbach, T. M., & Rescorla, L. A. (2001). *Manual for ASEBA School-Aged Forms and Profiles.* Burlington: University of Vermont, Research Center for Children, Youth, and Families.

Albano, A. & Kendall, P. (2002). Cognitive behavioral therapy for children and adolescents with anxiety disorders: Clinical research advances. *International Review of Psychiatry, 14*, 129–134.

Albano, A. M., Marten, P. A., Holt, C. S., Heimberg, R. G., & Barlow, D. H. (1995). Cognitive-behavioral group treatment for social phobia in adolescents: A preliminary study. *Journal of Nervous and Mental Disease, 183*, 649–656.

American Psychiatric Association. (2000). *Diagnostic and statistical manual of mental disorders* (4th ed., text rev.). Washington, D.C.: Author.

Anderson, J. C., Williams, S., McGee, R., & Silva, P.A. (1987). DSM-III disorders in preadolescent children. *Archives of General Psychiatry, 44*, 69–76.

Andrews, G., Stewart, G. W., Allen, R., & Henderson, A. S. (1990a). The genetics of six neurotic disorders: A twin study. *Journal of Affective Disorders, 19*, 23–29.

Andrews, G., Stewart, G. W., Morris-Yates, A., Holt, P., & Henderson, A. S. (1990b). Evidence for a general neurotic syndrome. *British Journal of Psychiatry, 157*, 6–12.

Bandura, A. (1977). *Social learning theory.* Englewood Cliffs, NJ: Prentice-Hall.

Barlow, D. (2000). Unraveling the mysteries of anxiety and its disorders from the perspective of emotion theory. *American Psychologist, 55*(11), 1245–1263.

Barrett, P. M. (1998). Evaluation of cognitive-behavioral group treatments for childhood anxiety disorders. *Journal of Clinical Child Psychology, 27,* 459–468.

Barrett, P., Dadds, M., & Rapee, R. (1996). Family treatment of child anxiety: A controlled trial. *Journal of Consulting and Clinical Psychology, 64,* 333–342.

Barrett, P. M., Duffy, A. L., Dadds, M. R., & Rapee, R. M. (2001). Cognitive-behavioral treatment of anxiety disorders in children: Long-term (6-year) follow-up. *Journal of Consulting and Clinical Psychology, 69,* 135–141.

Beidel, D. C. (1991). Social phobia and overanxious disorder in school-age children. *Journal of the American Academy of Child and Adolescent Psychiatry, 30,* 545–552.

Beidel , D. C. , Morris, T. L., & Turner, M .W. (2004). Social phobia. In T. L. Morris & J. S. March (Eds.), *Anxiety disorders in children and adolescents* (2nd ed., pp. 141–163). New York: Guilford.

Beidel, D. C., Turner, S. M., & Morris, T. L. (1995). A new inventory to assess childhood social anxiety and phobia: The Social Phobia and Anxiety Inventory for Children. *Psychological Assessment, 7,* 73–79.

Benjamin, R. S., Costello, E. J., & Warren, M. (1990). Anxiety disorders in a pediatric sample. *Journal of Anxiety Disorders, 4,* 293–316.

Berg, I., Marks, I., McGuire, R., & Lipsedge, M. (1974). School phobia and agoraphobia. *Psychological Medicine, 4,* 428–434.

Bernstein, G.A. & Borchardt, C.M. (1991). Anxiety disorders of childhood and adolescence: A critical review. *Journal of the American Academy of Child and Adolescent Psychiatry, 30,* 519–32.

Biederman, J., Rosenbaum, J. F., Bolduc-Murphy, E. A., Faraone, S. V., Chaloff, J., Hirshfeld, D. R., & Kagan, J. (1993). A 3-year follow-up of children with and without behavioral inhibition. *Journal of the American Academy of Child and Adolescent Psychiatry, 32,* 814–821.

Biederman, J., Rosenbaum, J. F., Chaloff, J., & Kagan, J. (1995). Behavioral inhibition as a risk factor for anxiety disorders. In J. S. March (Ed.), *Anxiety disorders in children and adolescents* (pp. 61–81). New York: Guilford.

Birmaher, B., Brent, D. A., Chiappetta, L., Bridge, J., Monga, S., & Baugher, M. (1999). Psychometric properties of the Screen for Child Related Emotional Disorders (SCARED): A replication study. *Journal of the American Academy of Child and Adolescent Psychiatry, 38,* 1230–1236.

Birmaher, B., Khetarpal, S., Brent, D., Cully, M., Balach, L., Kaufman, J., & Neer, S. M. (1997). The Screen for Anxiety Related Emotional Disorders (SCARED): Scale construction and psychometric characteristics. *Journal of the American Academy of Child and Adolescent Psychiatry, 36,* 545–553.

Bowen, R., Offord, D., & Boyle, M. (1990). The prevalence of overanxious disorder and separation disorder in the community: Results from the Ontario Mental Health Study. *Journal of the American Academy of Child Psychiatry, 25,* 753–758.

Cantwell, D. P., & Baker, L. (1989). Stability and natural history of DSM-III childhood diagnoses. *Journal of the American Academy of Child and Adolescent Psychiatry, 28,* 691–700.

Chambless, D. L., & Hollon, S. D. (1998). Defining empirically supported therapies. *Journal of Consulting & Clinical Psychology, 66,* 7–18.

Chorpita, B. F., Albano, A. M., & Barlow, D. H. (1998). The structure of negative emotions in a clinical sample of children and adolescents. *Journal of Abnormal Psychology, 107,* 74–85.

Chorpita, B. F., & Daleiden, E. L. (2002). Tripartite dimensions of emotion in a child clinical sample: Measurement strategies and implications for clinical utility. *Journal of Consulting and Clinical Psychology, 70,* 1150–1160.

Chorpita, B. F., Tracey, S. A., Brown, T. A., Collica, T. J., & Barlow, D. H. (1997). Assessment of symptoms of worry in children and adolescents: An adaptation of the Penn State Worry Questionnaire. *Behaviour Research and Therapy, 35,* 569–581.

Cobham, V. E., Dadds, M. R., & Spence, S. H. (1998). The role of parental anxiety in the treatment of childhood anxiety. *Journal of Consulting and Clinical Psychology, 66,* 893–905.

Curry, J. F., March, J. S., & Hervey, A. S. (2004). Comorbidity of childhood and adolescent anxiety disorders: Prevalence and implications. In T. Ollendick & J. S. March (Eds.) *Phobic and anxiety disorders in children and adolescents: A clinician's guide to effective psychosocial and pharmacological interventions* (pp. 116–140). New York: Oxford University Press.

DiBartolo, P. M., Albano, A. M., Barlow, D. H., & Heimberg, R. G. (1998). Cross-informant agreement in the assessment of social phobia in youth. *Journal of Abnormal Child Psychology, 26,* 213–220.

Dollinger, S. J. (1986). The measurement of children's sleep disturbances and somatic complaints following a disaster. *Child Psychiatry and Human Development, 16,* 148–153.

Dollinger, S. J., O'Donnell, J. P., & Staley, A. A. (1984). Lightening -strike disaster: Effects on children's fears and worries. *Journal of Consulting and Clinical Psychology, 52*, 1028–1038.

Edelbrock, C., Costello, A. J., Dulcan, M. K., Conover, N. C., & Kala, R. (1986). Parent–child agreement on child psychiatric symptoms assessed via structured interview. *Journal of Child Psychology and Psychiatry, 27*, 181–190.

Eisen, A. R., & Silverman, W. K. (1993). Should I relax or change my thoughts? A preliminary examination of cognitive therapy, relaxation training, and their combination with overanxious children. *Journal of Cognitive Psychotherapy, 7*, 265–279.

Feehan, M., McGee, R., & Williams, S. M. (1993). Mental health disorders from age 15 to age 18 years. *Journal of the American Academy of Child and Adolescent Psychiatry, 32*, 1118–1126.

Fergusson, D. M., Horwood, L. J., & Lynskey, M. T. (1993). Prevalence and comorbidity of DSM-III--R diagnoses in a birth cohort of 15 year olds. *Journal of the American Academy of Child and Adolescent Psychiatry, 32*(6), 1127–1134.

Flannery-Schroeder, E. C., Choudhury, M., & Kendall, P. C. (2005). Group and individual cognitive-behavioral treatments for youth with anxiety disorders: I-year follow-up. *Cognitive Therapy and Research, 29*, 253–259.

Flannery-Schroeder, E. C., & Kendall, P. C. (1996). *Cognitive-behavioral therapy for anxious children: Therapist manual for group treatment*. Ardmore, PA: Workbook Publishing.

Flannery-Schroeder, E. C., & Kendall, P. C. (2000). Group and individual cognitive-behavioral treatments for youth with anxiety disorders: A randomized clinical trial. *Cognitive Therapy and Research, 24*, 251–278.

Geller, D. A., Biederman, J., Griffin, S., Jones, J., & Lefkowitz, T. R. (1996). Comorbidity of juvenile obsessive-compulsive disorder with disruptive behavior disorders. *Journal of the American Academy of Child and Adolescent Psychiatry, 35*, 1637–1646.

Ginsburg, G. S., & Drake, K. L. (2002). School-based treatment for anxious African-American adolescents: A controlled pilot study. *Journal of the American Academy of Child and Adolescent Psychiatry, 41*, 768–775.

Gittelman-Klein, R., & Klein, D. F. (1973). School phobia: Diagnostic considerations in light of imipramine effects. *Journal of Nervous and Mental Disease, 156*, 199–210.

Goodyer, I. M., & Altham, P. M. (1991). Lifetime exit events and recent social and family adversities in anxious and depressed school-aged children. *Journal of Affective Disorders, 21*, 219–228.

Greco, L. A., & Morris, T. L. (2004). Assessment. In T. L. Morris & J. S. March (Eds.), *Anxiety disorders in children and adolescents* (2nd ed., pp. 98–121). New York: Guilford.

Hartup, W. W. (1983). Peer relations. In P. Mussen (Ed.), *Handbook of child psychology* (pp. 103–96). New York: Wiley.

Heimberg, R. G., Dodge, C. S., Hope, D. A., Kennedy, C. R., Zollo, L. J., & Becker, R. E. (1990). Cognitive behavioral group treatment for social phobia: Comparison with a credible placebo control. *Cognitive Therapy and Research, 14*, 1–23.

Herjanic, B. & Reich, W. (1997). Development of a structured psychiatric interview for children: Agreement between child and parent on individual symptoms. *Journal of Abnormal Child Psychology, 25*, 21–31.

Himle, J.A., Van Etten, M., & Fischer, D.J. (2003). Group cognitive behavioral therapy for obsessive-compulsive disorder: A review. *Brief Treatment and Crisis Intervention, 3*(2), 217–229.

Hirshfeld, D. R., Rosenbaum, J. F., Biederman, J., Bolduc, E. A., Faraone, S. V., Snidman, N., Reznick, J. S., & Kagan, J. (1992). Stable behavioral inhibition and its association with anxiety disorder. *Journal of the American Academy of Child and Adolescent Psychiatry, 31*, 103–111.

Hodges, K. (1990). Depression and anxiety in children: A comparison of self-report questionnaires to clinical interview. *Psychological Assessment, 2*, 376–381.

Hoehn-Saric, E., Maisami, M., & Weigand, D. (1987). Measurement of anxiety in children and adolescents using semi-structured interviews. *Journal of the American Academy of Child and Adolescent Psychiatry, 28*, 541–545.

Jardine, R., Martin, N. G., & Henderson, A. S. (1984). Genetic covariance between neuroticism and the symptoms of anxiety and depression. *Genetics Epidemiology, 1*, 89–107.

Jensen, P. S., Traylor, J., Xenakis, S. N., & Davis, H. (1988). Child psychopathology rating scales and interrater agreement: I. Parents' gender and psychiatric symptoms. *Journal of the American Academy of Child and Adolescent Psychiatry, 27*, 442–450.

Kagan, J. (1989). Temperamental contributions to social behavior. *American Psychologist, 44*(4) 668–674.

Kagan, J. (1997). Temperament and the reactions to unfamiliarity. *Child Development, 68*, 139–143.

Kane, M. T., & Kendall, P. C. (1989). Anxiety disorders in children: A multiple-baseline evaluation of a cognitive-behavioral treatment. *Behavior Therapy, 20*, 499–508.

Kashani, J. H., & Orvaschel, H. (1990). A community study of anxiety in children and adolescents. *American Journal of Psychiatry, 147*, 313–318.

Kashani, J. H., Orvaschel, H., Rosenberg, T. K., & Reid, J. C. (1989). Psychopathology in a community sample of children and adolescents: A developmental perspective. *Journal of the American Academy of Child and Adolescent Psychiatry, 28*, 701–706.

Kaufman, J., Birmaher, B., Brent, D., Rao., U., Flynn, C., Moreci, P., Williamson, D., & Ryan, N. (1997). The Schedule for Affective Disorders and Schizophrenia for School-aged Children—Present and Lifetime Versions (K-SADS-PL): Initial reliability and validity data. *Journal of the American Academy of Child and Adolescent Psychiatry, 36*, 980–988.

Kazdin, A. E., & Weisz, J. (1998). Treating psychological problems of youth: Status of empirically supported treatments. *Journal of Consulting and Clinical Psychology, 66*, 19–36.

Kearney, C. A., Albano, A. M., Eisen, A. R., Allan, W. D., & Barlow, D. H. (1997). The phenomenology of panic disorder in youngsters: An empirical study of a clinical sample. *Journal of Anxiety Disorders, 11*, 49–62.

Kendall, P. C. (1993). *A coping cat workbook*. Ardmore, PA: Workbook Publishing.

Kendall, P. C. (1994). Treating anxiety disorders in youth: results of a randomized clinical trial. *Journal of Consulting and Clinical Psychology, 62*, 100–110.

Kendall, P. C. (2000). *Cognitive-behavioral therapy for anxious children: Therapist manual*. Ardmore, PA: Workbook Publishing.

Kendall, P. C., Flannery-Schroeder, E. C., Panichelli-Mindel, S. P., Southam-Gerow, M. A., Henin, A., & Warman, M. J. (1997). Treating anxiety disorders in youth: a second randomized clinical trial. *Journal of Consulting and Clinical Psychology, 65*, 366–380.

Kendall, P. C., Krain, A., & Treadwell, K. (1999). Generalized anxiety disorders. In R. T. Ammermann, M. Hersen, & C. G. Last (Eds.), *Handbook of prescriptive treatments for children and adolescents* (2nd ed., pp. 155–171). Needham Heights, MA: Allyn & Bacon.

Kendall, P. C., Safford, S., Flannery-Schroeder, E., & Webb, A. (2004). Child anxiety treatment: Outcomes in adolescence and impact on substance use and depression at 7.4 year follow-up. *Journal of Consulting and Clinical Psychology, 72*(2), 276–287.

Kendall, P. C., & Southam-Gerow, M. (1996). Long-term follow-up of a cognitive-behavioral therapy for anxiety-disordered youth. *Journal of Consulting and Clinical Psychology, 64*, 724–730.

Kendler, K. S., Neale, M. C., Kessler, R. C., Heath, A.C. & Eaves, L. J. (1992). Major depression and generalized anxiety disorder: Same genes, (partly) different environments? *Archives of General Psychiatry, 49*, 716–722.

Kessler, R. C., McGonagle, K. A., Zhao, S., Nelson, C. B., Hughes, M., Eshleman, S., Wittchen, H. U., & Kendler, K. (1994). Lifetime and 12 month prevalence of DSM-III-R psychiatric disorders in the United States: Results from the National Comorbidity Survey. *Archives of General Psychiatry, 51*, 8–19.

King, N. J., Muris, P., & Ollendick, T. H. (2005). Fears and phobias in children: Assessment and treatment. *Child and Adolescent Mental Health, 10*(2), 50–56.

King, N. J., & Ollendick, T. H. (1989). Children's anxiety and phobic disorders in school settings: Classification, assessment, and intervention issues. *Review of Educational Research, 59*, 431–470.

La Greca, A. M. (1998). *Social anxiety scales for children and adolescents: Manual and instructions for the SASC, SASC-R, SAS-A*. Miami, FL: University of Miami, Department of Psychology.

La Greca, A. M., Dandes, S. K., Wick, P., Shaw, K., & Stone, W. L. (1988). Development of the Social Anxiety Scale for Children: Reliability and concurrent validity. *Journal of Clinical Child Psychology, 17*, 84–91.

Last, G. C., Perrin, S., Hersen, M., & Kazdin, A. E. (1992). DSM-III-R anxiety disorders in children: Sociodemographic and clinical characteristics. *Journal of the American Academy of Child and Adolescent Psychiatry, 31*, 1070–1071.

Last, C. G., & Strauss, C. C. (1989). Panic disorder in children and adolescents. *Journal of Anxiety Disorders, 3*, 87–95.

Last, C. G., Strauss, C. G., & Francis, G. (1987). Comorbidity among childhood anxiety disorders. *Journal of Nervous and Mental Disease, 175*, 726–730.

Manassis, J., Hudson, J., Webb, A., & Albano, A. (2004). Beyond behavioral inhibition: Etiological factors in childhood anxiety. *Cognitive and Behavioral Practice, 11*, 3–-12.

Manassis, K., Mendlowitz, S. L., Scapillato, D., Avery, D., Fiksenbaum, L., Freire, M., Monga, S., & Owens, M. (2002). Group and individual cognitive-behavioral therapy for childhood anxiety disorders: A randomized trial. *Journal of the American Academy of Child and Adolescent Psychiatry, 41*, 1423–1430.

Mansdorf, I. J., & Lukens, E. (1987). Cognitive-behavioral psychotherapy for separation anxious children exhibiting school phobia. *Journal of the American Academy of Child and Adolescent Psychiatry, 26*, 222–225.

March, J., Franklin, M., Leonard, H., & Foa, E. (2004). Obsessive-Compulsive disorder. In T. Morris & J. March, *Anxiety disorders in children and adolescents* (2nd ed., pp. 212–240). New York: Guilford.

March, J. S., Parker, J. D. A., Sullivan, K., Stallings, P., & Conners, C. K. (1997). The Multidimensional Anxiety Scale for Children (MASC): Factor structure, reliability, and validity. *Journal of the American Academy of Child and Adolescent Psychiatry, 36*, 554–565.

March, J. S., Sullivan, K., & Parker, J. (1999). Test-retest reliability of the Multidimensional Anxiety Scale for Children. *Journal of Anxiety Disorders, 13*, 349–358.

Masia, C. L., Klein, R. G., Storch, E. A., & Corda, B. (2001). School-based behavioral treatment for social anxiety disorder in adolescents: Results of a pilot study. *Journal of the American Academy of Child and Adolescent Psychiatry, 40*, 780–786.

Mattison, R. E. (1992). Anxiety disorders. In S. R. Hooper, G. W. Hynd, & R. E. Mattison (Eds.), *Child psychopathology: Diagnostic criteria and clinical assessment* (pp. 179–202). Hillsdale, NJ: Erlbaum.

Mendlowitz, S. L., Manassis, K., Bradley, S., Scapillato, D., Miezitis, S., & Shaw, B. F. (1999). Cognitive-behavioral group treatments in childhood anxiety disorders: The role of parental involvement. *Journal of the American Academy of Child and Adolescent Psychiatry, 38*, 1223–1229.

Mowrer, O. (1960). *Learning theory and behavior.* New York: Wiley.

Muris, P., Meesters, C., & Van Melick, M. (2002). Treatment of childhood anxiety disorders: A preliminary comparison between cognitive-behavioral group therapy and a psychological placebo intervention. *Journal of Behavior Therapy and Experimental Psychiatry, 33*, 143–158.

Muris, P., Merckelbach, H., Mayer, B., van Brakel, A., Thissen, S., Moulaert, V., & Gadet, B. (1998). The Screen for Child Anxiety Related Emotional Disorders (SCARED) and traditional childhood anxiety measures. *Journal of Behavior Therapy and Experimental Psychiatry, 29*, 327–339.

Ollendick, T. H. (1983). Reliability and validity of the Revised Fear Survey Schedule for Children. *Behaviour Research and Therapy, 21*, 685–692.

Ollendick, T. H., Hagopian, L. P., & Huntzinger, R. M. (1991). Cognitive-behavioral therapy with nighttime fearful children. *Journal of Behavior Therapy and Experimental Psychiatry, 22*, 113–121.

Ollendick, T. H., & King, N. J. (1998). Empirically supported treatments for children with phobic and anxiety disorders: Current status. *Journal of Clinical Child Psychology, 27*, 156–167.

Öst, L. G. (1987). Age of onset of different phobias. *Journal of Abnormal Psychology, 96*, 223–229.

Perrin, S., & Last, C. G. (1992). Do childhood anxiety measures measure anxiety? *Journal of Abnormal Child Psychology, 20*, 567–578.

Rapee, R. (1985). Distinction between panic disorder and generalized anxiety disorder. *Australian and New Zealand Journal of Psychiatry, 19*, 227–232.

Rapee, R. M. (2000). Group treatment of children with anxiety disorders: Outcome and predictors of treatment response. *Australian Journal of Psychology, 52*, 125–129.

Rapee, R. M., Barrett, P. M., Dadds, M. R., & Evans, L. (1994). Reliability of the DSM-III-R childhood anxiety disorders using structured interview: interrater and parent–child agreement. *Journal of the American Academy of Child and Adolescent Psychiatry, 33*, 984–992.

Rapee, R. M., & Szollos, A. (1997, November). *Early life events in anxious children.* Paper presented at the 31st Annual AABT Convention, Miami, FL.

Reynolds, C. R., & Richmond, B. O. (1985). *Revised Children's Manifest Anxiety Scale (RCMAS): Manual.* Los Angeles: Western Psychological Services.

Rosenbaum, J. F., Biederman, J., Bolduc-Murphy, E. A., Faraone, S. V., Chaloff, J., Hirshfeld, D. R., & Kagan, J. (1993). Behavioral inhibition in childhood: A risk factor for anxiety disorders. *Harvard Review of Psychiatry, 1*, 2–16.

Schniering, C. A., Hudson, J. L., & Rapee, R. M. (2000). Issues in the diagnosis and assessment of anxiety disorders in children and adolescents. *Clinical Psychology Review, 20*, 453–478.

Shaffer, D., Fisher, P., Lucas, C., Dulcan, M. K., & Schwab-Stone, M. E. (2000). NIMH Diagnostic Interview Schedule for Children — Version IV (NIMH DISC-IV): Description, differences from previous versions, and reliability of some common diagnoses. *Journal of the American Academy of Child and Adolescent Psychiatry, 38*, 28–38.

Sheehan, D. V., Sheehan, K. E., & Minichiello, W. E. (1981). Age of onset of phobic disorders: A reevaluation. *Comprehensive Psychiatry, 22*, 544–553.

Silverman, W. K., & Albano, A. M. (1996a). *The Anxiety Disorders Interview Schedule for DSM-IV: Child Interview Schedule.* San Antonio, TX: Psychological Corporation.

Silverman, W. K., & Albano, A. M. (1996b). *The Anxiety Disorders Interview Schedule for DSM-IV: Parent Interview Schedule.* San Antonio, TX: Psychological Corporation.

Silverman, W., & Dick-Nierderhauser, A. (2004). Separation anxiety disorder. In T. Morris & J. March, *Anxiety disorders in children and adolescents* (2nd ed., pp. 164–188). New York: Guilford.

Silverman, W. K., & Eisen, A. R. (1992). Age difference in the reliability of parent and child reports of child anxious symptomatology using a structured interview. *Journal of the American Academy of Child and Adolescent Psychiatry, 31*, 117–124.

Silverman, W. K., Fleisig, W., Rabian, B., & Peterson, R. A. (1991). Child Anxiety Sensitivity Index. *Journal of Clinical Child Psychology, 20*, 162–168.

Silverman, W. K., Kurtines, W. M., Ginsburg, G. S., Weems, C. F., Lumpkin, P. W., & Carmichael, D. H. (1999). Treating anxiety disorders in children with group cognitive-behavioral therapy: A randomized clinical trial. *Journal of Consulting and Clinical Psychology, 67*, 995–1003.

Silverman, W. K., & Nelles, W. B. (1988). The Anxiety Disorders Interview Schedule for Children. *Journal of the American Academy of Child and Adolescent Psychiatry, 27*, 772–778.

Silverman, W. K., Saavedra, L. M., & Pina, A. A. (2001). Test-retest reliability of anxiety symptoms and diagnoses with Anxiety Disorders Interview Schedule for DSM-IV: Child and parent versions. *Journal of the American Academy of Child and Adolescent Psychiatry, 40*, 937–944.

Spence, S. H., Donovan, C., & Brechman-Toussaint, M. (2000). The treatment of childhood social phobia: The effectiveness of a social skills training-based, cognitive-behavioural intervention with and without parental involvement. *Journal of Child Psychology and Psychiatry, 41*, 713–726.

Spielberger, C. (1973). *Manual for the State-Trait Anxiety Inventory for Children.* Palo Alto, CA: Consulting Psychologists Press.

Stark, D., Kaslow, N. J., & Laurent, J. (1993). The assessment of depression in children: Are we assessing depression or the broad-band construct of negative affectivity? *Journal of Emotional and Behavioral Disorders, 1*, 149–159.

Strauss, C. C. (1990). Overanxious disorder in childhood. In M. Hersen & C. G. Last (Eds.), *Handbook of child and adult psychopathology: A longitudinal perspective* (pp. 237–246). New York: Pergamon Press.

Strauss, C. C., Forehand, R., Smith, K., & Frame, C. L. (1986). The association between social withdrawal and internalizing problems of children. *Journal of Abnormal Child Psychology, 14*, 525–535.

Strauss, C. C., & Last, C. G. (1993). Social and simple phobias in children. *Journal of Anxiety Disorders, 7*, 141–152.

Strauss, C. C., Last, C. G., Hersen, M., & Kazdin, A.E. (1988). Association between anxiety and depression in children and adolescents with anxiety disorders. *Journal of Abnormal Child Psychology, 16*(1), 57–68.

Strauss, C. C., Lease, C. A., Last, C. G., & Francis, G. (1988). Overanxious disorder: An examination of developmental differences. *Journal of Abnormal Child Psychology, 16*, 433–443.

Swedo, S. E., Rapoport, J. L., Leonard, H., Lenane, M., & Cheslow, D. (1989). Obsessive-compulsive disorder in children and adolescents: Clinical phenomenology of 70 consecutive cases. *Archives of General Psychiatry, 46*(4), 335–341.

Terr, L. C. (1981). Psychic trauma in children: Observations following the Chowchilla school bus kidnapping. *American Journal of Psychiatry, 138*, 14–19.

Thienemann, M., Martin, J., Cregger, B., Thompson, H. B., & Dyer-Friedman, J. (2001). Manual-driven group cognitive-behavioral therapy for adolescents with obsessive-compulsive disorder: A pilot study. *Journal of American Academy of Child and Adolescent Psychiatry, 40*, 1254–1260.

Tiet, Q. Q., Bird, H. R., Davies, M., Hoven, C., Cohen, P., Jensen, P. S., & Goodman, S. (1998). Adverse life events and resilience. *Journal of American Academy of Child and Adolescent Psychiatry, 37*, 119–1200.

Toren, P., Wolmer, L., Rosental, B., Eldar, S., Koren, S., Lask, M., Weizman, R., & Laor, N. (2000). Case series: Brief parent-child group therapy for childhood anxiety disorders using a manual-based cognitive-behavioral technique. *Journal of the American Academy of Child and Adolescent Psychiatry, 39*, 1309–1312.

Torgersen, S. (1983). Genetic factors in anxiety disorders. *Archives of General Psychiatry, 40*, 1085–1089.

Tracey, S. A., Chorpita, B. F., Douban, J., & Barlow, D. H. (1997). Empirical evaluation of DSM-IV generalized anxiety disorder criteria in children and adolescents. *Journal of Clinical Child Psychology, 26*, 404–414.

Tyrer, P., Alexander, J., Remington, M., & Riley, P. (1987). Relationship between neurotic symptoms and neurotic diagnosis: A longitudinal study. *Journals of Affective Disorders, 13*, 13–21.

U.S. Department of Health and Human Services. (1999). *Mental Health: A Report of the Surgeon General.* Rockville, MD: U.S. Department of Health and Human Services.

Velting, O. N., Setzer, N. J., & Albano, A. M. (2004). Update on and advances in assessment and cognitive-behavioral treatment of anxiety disorders in children and adolescents. *Professional Psychology: Research and Practice, 35*, 42–54.

Weems, C. F., Silverman, W. K., & LaGreca, A. M. (2000). What do youth referred for anxiety problems worry about? Worry and its relation to anxiety and anxiety disorders in children and adolescents. *Journal of Abnormal Child Psychology, 28*, 63–72.

Yule, W., & Williams, R. (1990). Post-traumatic stress reactions in children. *Journal of Traumatic Stress, 3*, 279–295.

Zitrin, C. M., & Ross, D. C. (1988). Early separation anxiety and adult agoraphobia. *Journal of Nervous and Mental Disease, 176*, 621–625.

Chapter Twelve

Group Cognitive-Behavior Therapy to Address Post-Traumatic Stress Disorder in Children and Adolescents

Annita B. Jones & Jessica L. Stewart

Although few studies have evaluated the prevalence rates of Post-Traumatic Stress Disorder (PTSD) in children and adolescents, it is currently estimated that between 3 and 15% of girls and 1 to 6% of boys meet full criteria for PTSD (The National Center for Post-Traumatic Stress Disorder, 2001). A review of several studies exploring the prevalence of trauma exposure in school-aged samples indicates that trauma rates may be as high as 40 to 70% (Feeny, Foa, Treadwell, & March, 2004). PTSD in children may be the result of being a victim or witness of a violent crime/act, accident, or natural disaster, or the result of physical or sexual abuse. Though not all children who experience a traumatic event will experience symptoms that warrant the full diagnosis of PTSD, the emotional, cognitive, and behavioral responses to trauma are unique and result in dysfunction on some level and to at least some degree (e.g., the victim's belief system changes related to safety and one's own powerlessness, there are physiological changes following the event and during post-trauma re-adjustment). Intervention on some level can be beneficial to resolve the deleterious effects of trauma on physiological and psychological functioning that manifests in post-traumatic symptoms (PTS).

This chapter will briefly discuss the symptom presentation that comprises a formal diagnosis of PTSD, as well as the various risk factors that contribute to its development. Whether a child or adolescent meets full criteria for PTSD or presents with PTS, the negative impact of traumatic experience on the psychological, social, and behavioral functioning of young people will be discussed to provide a rationale for the involvement of seriously affected youth (meeting full diagnostic criteria or not) in treatment. As the literature on psychological treatment of PTSD in young people is limited and typically subsumes the inclusion of components validated in studies with adult victims, some of the components suggested by experts to be most effective are offered. A full review of the extensive literature on PTSD is beyond the scope and purpose of this chapter. The few studies available that investigate the effectiveness of cognitive-behavioral therapy (CBT) within a group context to address PTSD among youth are summarized. We then offer an intervention protocol based on an empirically validated CBT group model, validated in one of the studies reviewed, for use with children and adolescents experiencing PTS or PTSD. Finally, we discuss potential obstacles in the treatment of PTSD in young people for consideration by practitioners.

POST-TRAUMATIC STRESS DISORDER

Definition

PTSD is a complex syndrome that, according to the *Diagnostic and Statistical Manual of Mental Disorders-IV-Text-Revision* (*DSM-IV-TR*; American Psychiatric Association, 2000), includes the following symptoms for at least one month that cause significant impairment in social, occupational, academic, and other important areas of functioning: (1) exposure to (by personal involvement or witnessing) a situation that caused or threatened to cause death or severe injury to one's self or others and results in a response by the victim of fear and helplessness; (2) a continual re-experiencing of the event through nightmares, flashbacks, or episodes of intense distress to events similar in nature to the original trauma; (3) persistent avoidance of anything related to the event, including thoughts, feelings, or discussions and avoidance of situations similar in nature to the traumatic event, as well as detachment from others and affective numbing; and (4) persistent hyperarousal that can be seen in sleep problems, hypervigilance, irritability, concentration and focus problems, and an exaggerated startle response (APA, 2000). Children are especially vulnerable to the development of PTSD in that they already are typically in a position of helplessness to circumstances around them, often experience fear in response to unknown and confusing situations, and have not yet developed mature coping skills to process new, confusing, or emotionally powerful events.

Risk Factors

The development of PTSD is the result of a number of risk factors related to a traumatic event, including the specific nature of the traumatic event, one's degree of involvement in it, the reaction of others (such as parents or family members) involved in the situation, as well as the results of the trauma (for example, the death of a parent, loss of safety and psychosocial security, or change in living situation following severe natural disaster). Demographic characteristics, such as age, gender, premorbid psychological functioning, parents' level of psychopathology prior to and since the trauma, family functioning, and cognitive style also have been found to contribute to the development of PTSD (Cohen, 1998; Goenjian et al., 1995; Green et al., 1991; Joseph, Brewin, Yule, & Williams., 1993). These and other still-unknown risk factors contribute to the unique presentation of PTSD symptoms for each child and there is evidence that children at differing developmental levels may exhibit different symptom presentations (Cohen, 1998).

Impact of Trauma

The effects of trauma include cognitive (e.g., difficulty with concentration, intrusive memories, images, or thoughts about the event, nightmares), emotional (e.g., emotional lability, increased anxiety, depression, fearfulness, apathy or "numbing"), physiological (e.g., increased arousal, sleep disturbance, appetite disturbance, hypervigilance, sensory sensitivity), and interpersonal (e.g., discomfort in social situations, mistrust for the motives and intentions of others, withdrawal and isolation). Especially in children, these difficulties may manifest in behavioral regression (e.g., clinginess, wetting the bed, frequent crying, sucking the thumb) or behavioral acting out (e.g., angry outbursts, irritability, aggression, risky behaviors). Not all children experiencing these PTS following exposure to traumatic events will develop formal PTSD or require psychological intervention. Some psychological and behavioral changes are to be expected for anyone involved in a traumatic event; however, many young people will return to pre-trauma functioning with few lasting difficulties—especially if the appropriate degree of social support is available.

However, psychological, emotional, and physiological difficulties following exposure to trauma that are left untreated may lead to lasting deficits in cognitive, emotional, behavioral, interpersonal, and academic/vocational functioning. Research has shown that the effects of unresolved traumatic experiences on young people may include involvement in the juvenile justice system (Eth, 2000), altered neurophysiology such as the fight or flight response for future stressors (Pfefferbaum, 1997), an altered sense of conscience and responsibility (Goenjian et al., 1999), a negative attributional style and lower estimates of self-efficacy (Saigh, Mroueh, Zimmerman, & Fairbanks, 1995), lowered academic performance (Saigh, Mroueh, & Bremmer, 1997), and lower enrollment in higher education (Duncan, 2000). Overall, research has identified widespread difficulties for children and adolescents exposed to at least one traumatic event that include behavioral, emotional, interpersonal, academic, and health problems, as well as suicidal behavior (Giaconia et al., 1995). These effects have the potential to be lasting and, if untreated, may result in a longer course of treatment due to the conditioning established at the time of the traumatic incident remaining unchallenged (and possibly reinforced) for such a long period of time.

Treatment

While psychopharmacology can be effective in symptom management (e.g., relief of anxiety, sleep disturbance, depression, inability to modulate affect, etc.) in some young people with PTSD, it has been shown to be most effective in combination with CBT (Smyth, 1999). Mental health intervention has the opportunity to facilitate the healthy processing of traumatic events to lessen symptoms that interfere with functioning. Individual therapy is one way that allows for each person's specific situation, symptoms, and needs to be addressed directly and at a pace that is most effective for the individual. However, for many, especially young people, a group setting allows for exposure to similar peers who have also experienced a trauma and, most likely, similar psychological and physiological reactions to it. This opportunity for "normalizing" of experiences provides children and adolescents with opportunities for social comparison and self-monitoring when acquiring new skills and processing something as difficult as trauma. In addition, the group therapy environment affords members the opportunity to experience competence in assisting peers with their healing process—something especially relevant when addressing PTSD, in that children are struggling with issues of competence given the experience of being victimized and/or powerless. Unfortunately, while therapeutic intervention to address PTSD with adult populations has been adequately investigated, studies pertaining to the psychological treatment of young people are scarce in the literature, though on the rise in numbers.

Although empirical treatment outcome studies for PTSD in children and adolescents are few in number, experts agree that treatment should include direct exploration of and exposure to the trauma (in a safe way), use of specific stress management techniques, identification and restructuring of inaccurate attributions related to the trauma, and (when possible) include parents/guardians in treatment (Cohen, 1998; Cohen, Berliner, & March, 2000; Feeny, et al., 2004). It has specifically been suggested that interventions such as relaxation, desensitization, and other behavioral techniques and cognitive restructuring are helpful in treating PTSD in young people (Deblinger et al., 1990). Of the four controlled studies summarized by Cohen (1998), three lent support for the use of CBT interventions that include these aspects of treatment in effectively reducing the symptoms of PTSD. According to Feeny and colleagues (2004), however, research investigating the most effective treatments is increasing. Findings suggest that not only are cognitive-behavioral interventions most effective for adults, they are also receiving strong support for use in the treatment of children.

Feeny and her colleagues (2004) reviewed the four available studies to date that have specifically investigated the efficacy of cognitive-behavioral group therapy (CBGT) with children and adolescents (one is reviewed in more detail below and serves as the basis for the model suggested for use in this chapter). Of them, three included exposure to trauma narratives and stress inoculation interventions, such as psychoeducation, relaxation, cognitive restructuring, and problem-solving (Goenjian et al., 1997; March, Amaya-Jackson, Murray, & Shulte, 1998; Stein et al., 2003). Although the fourth did not include exposure specifically, children did discuss their experiences and resulting feelings (Chemtob, Nakashima, & Hamada, 2002; Feeny, et al., 2004). Each of these studies resulted in significant decreases in PTSD symptoms. There are methodological limitations to these findings (such as the absence of control groups for comparison in two studies and a nonrandomly assigned group in another), but results are promising both for the use of a group modality to address PTSD and the benefits of a cognitive-behavioral approach. Overall, it is suggested that group therapy to address PTSD with children and adolescents should aim to educate members about what are common responses to trauma, teach coping strategies to manage symptoms and re-experiencing of the trauma, and restructure distorted cognitions.

March and his associates (1998) conducted a validation study of an 18-week CBT based, group therapy protocol to address PTSD with children who have experienced a single-incident trauma. Their protocol included psychoeducation, exposure to trauma narratives, anxiety management techniques (e.g., muscle relaxation, diaphragmatic breathing, training to gauge distress levels), problem solving for anger control, development of positive self-statements, and relapse prevention. The Multi-Modality Trauma Treatment (MMTT) protocol was developed from combining effective components of

CBT treatments for use with adults with PTSD, pediatric anxiety, and disruptive behavior disorders (March et al., 1998). Results were promising, indicating significant improvement in PTSD symptoms, anxiety, depression, and anger, as well as a shift from external to internal locus of control. Their findings remained significant at 6-month follow-up, suggesting that changes in group members were more than temporary. Given its inclusion of sound CBT interventions, especially those continually supported in the literature for use in addressing PTSD (albeit with an adult population), this model is the basis for the protocol presented here, as modified and explained in detail below.

CONSIDERATIONS FOR INCLUSION IN GROUP THERAPY

Assessment

Proper individual assessment by facilitators prior to group inclusion is essential to consider the various risk factors for PTSD and their influence on the individual presentation and needs of each member. Despite the existence of numerous measures to assess symptoms consistent with PTSD in young people, Cohen (1998) believes that none are optimal alone and, instead, suggests that clinical interview is the best assessment tool for determining the presenting issues for each potential group member and the appropriateness of inclusion in group treatment. Cohen (1998) suggests that interviews with children ask questions directly and clearly about the traumatic event and resulting symptoms. Facilitators should also be aware of premorbid psychological difficulties and additional current clinical concerns that may be factors in or the result of PTSD.

When composing a group of children or adolescents for therapeutic intervention it is important to consider the experiences of each group member for similarity, and to be cognizant of the possibility of further traumatizing some group members by exposure to the kinds of situations that other group members may have been involved in (i.e., including rape victims and natural disaster survivors in the same group may be detrimental to both as experiences or resulting symptoms are shared). In addition, developmental considerations must be addressed, such as age level and cognitive ability of each child. How recent the traumatic event was, whether it was a single event or ongoing exposure, how long symptoms have persisted, and whether symptom onset was delayed or immediate are also to be considered when forming a group for therapeutic intervention so as to, again, ensure some degree of relatedness for individual members to the group to facilitate cohesiveness, supportive understanding, and normalizing of reactions between members.

Assessment should be multidimensional and include interviews with parents, family members, teachers, and significant others (March, 1995). While no measure for the assessment of PTSD or monitoring of symptoms has been identified as a "gold standard" (Cohen, 1998), there are a number of measures that exist to assess the nature and extent of behavioral and emotional symptoms related to exposure to traumatic events, including the *Child Post-Traumatic Stress Disorder Reaction Index* (CPTSD-RI; Frederick, 1985; Pynoos et al., 1987), the *Impact of Events Scale for Children* (Horowitz, Wilner, & Alvarez, 1979), the Lifetime Incidence of Traumatic Events (LITE, Greenwald & Rubin, 1999), the *Acute Stress Checklist for Children* (ASC-Kids, Kassam-Adams, Baxt, & Shrivastava, 2003), the *Child and Adolescent Trauma Survey* (March, 1999), the

Clinician-Administered PTSD Scale—Child and Adolescent Version (Nader et al., 1994), the *Children's PTSD Inventory* (Saigh et al., 2000), the *Child PTSD Symptom Scale* (CPSS; Foa, Johnson, Feeny, & Treadwell, 2001), the *Trauma Symptom Checklist for Children* (TSCC, Briere, 1996), the *Trauma Symptom Checklist for Young Children* (TSCYC, for children ages 2–12; Briere et al., 2001), the *Los Angeles Symptom Checklist* (LASC, for use with adolescents; Foy, Wood, King, King, & Resnick, 1997), and the *Child Report of Post-traumatic Symptoms* and *Parent Report of Post-traumatic Symptoms* (CROPS and PROPS, respectively; Greenwald & Rubin, 1999; Greenwald et al., 2002). If dissociative symptoms are present or suspected, assessment can include the *Adolescent Dissociative Experiences Scale* (A-DES, Armstrong, Putnam, Carlson, Libero, & Smith, 1997). As with all of these measures, significantly high scores may warrant further evaluation and a delay in group participation until symptoms can be stabilized enough for engagement in the group process and specific interventions.

In addition, some measures that have been validated for related symptoms in general (such as anxiety or behavioral disturbances) can be used to identify areas of distress for children and adolescents who have been clinically identified as having PTSD or PTS. Examples of some additional measures to assess specific symptoms associated with PTSD that may be useful in conjunction with a thorough clinical interview and in combination in a multimethod assessment include the *State-Trait Anxiety Scale* (Spielberger, 1970), the *Children's Depression Inventory* (Kovacs, 1985), the *Child Behavior Checklist* (Achenbach & Edelbrock, 1983), the *Child Version of the Anxiety Disorders Interview Schedule for DSM-IV* (Silverman & Albano, 1996), the *Multidimensional Anxiety Scale for Children* (March, Parker et al., 1997), and the *Behavior Assessment System for Children, Second Edition* (BASC-2, Reynolds & Kamphaus, 2002). This list is by no means exhaustive, though it offers a general idea of the ways in which children's present symptomatology may be assessed by measures other than trauma-specific. It is important to assess the presence of clinically significant symptoms of PTSD, not solely whether full diagnostic criteria is met, as children who evidence a significant symptom presentation should be included in treatment as well (Cohen, 1998).

Clinical interview and use of formal assessment measures will afford clinicians the ability to begin to conceptualize the presentation of each group member. Assigning a level of symptomatology or a formal diagnosis of PTSD will assist in formulating the make-up of the group. But clinicians must also consider the nature of the presentation in terms of the traumatic history of each group member. Judith Herman (1992), in her landmark book *Trauma and Recovery,* introduced the concept of Type I and Type II traumas. Differentiating between these will have a great impact on which version of the group format presented below will be appropriate for your group setting. Type I traumas are more discrete and often occur following a single event in one's life such as natural disaster, violent crime, an exposure to a drive-by shooting, etc., which is outside the normal experience of the person. Type II trauma refers to a pattern of experiences that occurs over time, by numerous perpetrators, with acute intensity and unpredictability. It is the inconsistency that is most damaging since, remembering classical conditioning, behavior is quickly acquired by continuous reinforcement, longer lasting with intermittent reinforcement, and extinguished by no reinforcement. Inconsistency tends to cause the most lasting belief system, behaviors, and patterns of choices or compliancy.

Group Readiness

As has been discussed in other chapters of this volume, not all children and adolescents with a particular diagnosis or presentation are appropriate candidates for group inclusion. The decision to include each member will depend on developmental considerations, cognitive ability, symptom presentation and severity, specific experiences related to trauma, comorbidity of other diagnoses, personality functioning, social skills, the other members being considered for group, and the availability of resources to ensure follow-through. Perhaps the most important factor when considering youth as appropriate candidates for group inclusion relates to their willingness to engage in the therapeutic process, their readiness for change. Especially given the active nature of the CBT process, members must be willing to attend group, participate (even if in actively listening to the interactions of others until comfortable to volunteer on their own), and follow-through with between-session work (a central component in CBT). Members who are not acknowledging their difficulties or not invested in attending may undermine the group cohesiveness and their ability (and that of others) to benefit from treatment. Especially relevant in the treatment of PTSD is the need to establish a safe and trusting environment for all members. Those who are not committed to this goal or who may lack the appreciation and respect for this importance should not be included in group until individual work can increase their awareness and acceptance of the nature of their difficulties and needs.

Benefits of Group

Adolescence is a major developmental stage for identity construction, social belonging, emotional regulation, and hippocampus growth—all of which are impaired by childhood maltreatment. This "double whammy" makes adolescence an even more complex time of life for those diagnosed with PTSD. Group therapy, although an adjunct to individual therapy, can be an amazing environment for victims of trauma to learn from each other. Such learning can include reframes others have tried in similar situations that, when shared, help "normalize" that horrible things occur to many people and have a similar impact for all. Self-perceptions often expressed in such therapy groups include bad, evil, ugly, flawed, helpless, hopeless, stupid, and so forth, and to hear that others feel similar feelings can be very destigmatizing (Beck, 2005). Most traumatized adolescents feel painfully isolated and "different" than their peers. Helping them feel they belong with others whose appearance and behaviors appear relatively normal and who have experienced similar trauma can be healing and a great source of comfort and relief for those who otherwise believe they are "the only ones" who felt the way they did.

Given the heterogeneous presentation of PTSD symptoms and experiences, treatment requires individual assessment and an individualized approach, even when the modality is a group format. The CBT model requires that facilitators identify individual needs during clinical interview, formulate a conceptualization of the belief system of each member as it relates to the presenting problems, and outline treatment strategies to address the individual schema at work in perpetuating symptoms and dysfunction. This affords facilitators the ability to individualize treatment while applying techniques appropriately within a group format and incorporating the natural benefits inherent in the group environment.

THE APPLICATION OF CBT TO GROUP THERAPY FOR YOUTH WITH PTS AND PTSD

Cognitive-Behavioral Conceptualization of Trauma Response

PTSD manifests many symptoms that are conditioned reactions pairing sensory input, existing belief systems, generalized feelings, and cognitive distortions based on the concomitant trauma logic (e.g., "no one can be trusted," "everyone will hurt me if I don't stay away from them or hurt them first," "nowhere is safe," "safe and vulnerable cannot exist together") (Chu, 2000). Other common cognitive distortions include: (1) "I have to be perfect or I'm horribly incompetent or worthless"; (2) "I must be loved by everyone or I am a failure"; (3) "things should be fair and just or I cannot tolerate it"; (4) "everything should be as I expect or it is wrong and must be changed"; and (5) "the world is a dangerous place and I'm incapable of functioning in it because I cannot be completely safe" (Smyth, 1994). *Black and white thinking* occurs as a natural by-product of the "sense of foreshortened future" that is one of the main symptoms of PTSD according to the *DSM-IV-TR* (APA, 2000). Recognizing the anxiety underlying the continuous reinforcement loop of PTSD is helpful to the clinician in understanding the trauma survivors' perception of chronic helplessness and terror despite evidence to the contrary.

Common distortions in thinking are naturally strengthened by trauma, as the brain reverts to the primitive limbic system (the less rational, more emotional part of the brain) during those times (Lewis, Amini, & Lannon, 2001). Among these distortions are (1) *overgeneralizing* —following trauma the victim resorts to trauma logic that reduces the likelihood of objective thinking and everything becomes about the self as an attempt to create some sense of control when there was none; (2) *awfulizing*—this fits with the "sense of foreshortened future" in which the person sees everything as horrible and believes that it will remain so until death; (3) *overpersonalizing*—the trauma reverts the person to a very primitive brain, leaving the victim with a sense of fight/flight/freeze, nonverbal level of functioning whereby everything is perceived as threatening, there is no other reality but the one that is overwhelmed and out of control; (4) *discrediting or discounting*—due to lowered self-esteem compliments are interpreted as (a) this person doesn't really know the truth, (b) this person wants something, (c) this person is trying to make me feel better (trust is relatively destroyed by trauma); and (5) *shoulding/musting*—as ways of having absolute expectations of the self or others which are more easily managed and judged. Incidentally, when these expectations are not met regarding the self, the logical internalization is guilt and shame, while of others the results are disappointment and shame for failure in not being able to control everything external.

Options for Group Treatment

The assessment of the child or adolescent for severity of symptoms (e.g., Type I or Type II trauma, comorbidity, and ruling out physical and more congenital problems), allows for appropriate placement in terms of inclusion in group treatment. Essentially, those who are assessed to be clearly of a Type I PTSD and those functioning relatively well in all areas despite Type II PTSD status are appropriate for inclusion in outpatient groups. Those experiencing more comorbid PTSD and more intense symptoms are more likely to be seen in settings such as clinics, RTFs, or group-home facilities. The most complex Type II PTSD patients are likely most appropriately treated in a trauma-based hospital facility or other structured setting with skilled staff around the clock. Group therapy can expose members to the stressors of others, thus risking triggering or exacerbating members' own personal traumas. The amount of structure needed to support group members following group depends on how stable they are determined to be at admission to the group and what resources may exist in their natural environments. An additional consideration for determining the appropriate environment for group members engaged in active treatment of PTSD may be to utilize the Subjective Units of Distress Scale (SUDS, Wolpe, 1958). The following guidelines are a blend of several clinicians' outlines relative to their comfort and their experiences in group settings, as well as our own experiences. Members whose SUDS intensity level is more consistently 1 to 4 are considered most appropriate for outpatient treatment. The initial protocol will be appropriate for this population. Those with SUDS from 5 to 7 may need an additional layer of support both before and after the group sessions, perhaps within a group home or partial hospital setting. Those with higher SUDS, 8 to 10, may need to be within an inpatient setting if any group protocol is used to provide the appropriate level of adjunctive support to match their more intensive psychological needs.

Goals for Treatment

The treatment goals for CBGT with children and adolescents with significant PTS or PTSD may vary, but typically include several necessary components for stabilization and skill building. Treatment focus should include goals for: (1) psychoeducation regarding typical post-traumatic symptoms, beliefs, and patterns; (2) reduction in episodes of panic states associated with flashbacks; (3) reduction in the intensity of anger and rage; (4) decrease in negative self-talk that reinforces the symptomatic behaviors and beliefs; (5) increase in relaxation skills; (6) increase in ability to identify and modulate affect; (7) the identification, desensitizing to, and development of tolerance for intensive intrusive stimuli; (8) development of a hierarchy of components of traumatic event(s) that fit the SUDS; (9) identification of current life situations that evoke intrusive material and the development of coping skills to counter them; (10) restructuring of cognitive distortions; (11) learning to identify and utilize available resources for support in maintaining gains and overall safety; and (12) training to prevent relapse.

Cognitive-Behavioral Group Therapy for PTSD

The model used as a basis for what we present here is the Multi-Modality Trauma Treatment (MMTT; March et al., 1998) with some adaptations to suit the particular populations being addressed in this chapter. The group therapy format resulting from work done by March and colleagues consists of 18 prescribed sessions with some individual work interspersed at certain intervals plus one "booster" session.

MMTT aims to promote the "habituation of conditioned anxiety, necessary revision of maladaptive trauma-induced cognitive schemas, skillful coping with disturbing affects and physiological sensations, and reduction of collateral symptoms such as anxiety, anger, depression, grief, and disruptive behaviors" (March et al., 1998, p. 588). The emphasis is on exploring the trauma for the sake of identifying its impact on each member and breaking the association between those events/memories and present negative emotional, physiological, and cognitive experiences. Work in and out of session is to emphasize skill building and cognitive restructuring (even if done more indirectly with younger children through activities that facilitate the challenging and altering of distorted perceptions) to cope effectively with symptoms and ultimately minimize them.

The general session outline in Table 12.1 and the suggested activities listed in Table 12.2 are appropriate for those with Type I Trauma (SUDS 1–4). Those with more complex trauma histories, Type II (SUDS 5–10), will use the amended group format with many of the same activities offered in Table 12.2. The suggested activities are merely examples—others may be substituted at the comfort of the clinicians leading the group, as long as the intended intensity level evoked remains similar. The specific group session will be divided into thirds—welcome, group activity, as well as grounding and plans for departure. The welcome will consist of a statement of the goal for the session and a "checking in" with each member that includes reviewing the previous week and sharing new relevant information. The majority of the group will be spent introducing and practicing the week's group topic. Finally, an activity to "ground" participants, review skills and resources for monitoring symptoms outside of group, and the assignment of between-session work will bring group to a close.

Session 1: Welcome, introductions, overview of the group process, and plans and goals for each session. The format and expectations for group are discussed to begin to establish a safe environment (such as rules about respect, confidentiality, conflict resolution, turn-taking, and attendance). Choose from the list of suggested activities if necessary. Give homework to consider what their goals are for the group experience. *Amended for Type II:* More structure and direction is necessary for this level of intensity (Rinsley, 1994). Following the welcome, introduction and overview of the plans and goals for the group sessions, encourage each member to discuss any previous group experience they might have had and what they would like to be different in this group—ask them for specific goals. Choose from the suggested activities in Figure 12.1 as needed. Instruct the members what their options are for family/staff availability following group and what their homework is. (A critical task for the clinical leaders of these groups within inpatient or partial settings is to communicate with the staff who will be working with the group members after group each session. The staff may need to learn skills to help the group members practice the group lessons, just as family members who are supporting participants.)

Session 2: In this and subsequent groups, review the homework from the week before and discuss any difficulties the members had implementing the assignment. Introduce the concept of PTSD, diagnostic criteria and typical symptoms that are experienced by most people. Ask the members if they experience any of the symptoms and which ones are most troublesome to them. Homework may be to identify some particular time that is difficult for them outside group. *Amended for Type II*: Remembering the additional structure needed for this population, frame the definitions in terms that are more general and less triggering or likely to accidentally evoke contagion. Perhaps, allow them

Table 12.1 General Outline of Session Content for CBGT Addressing PTSD

Session	Content/Focus	Homework
1	Welcome, overview of group, goal-setting	Individual goals for group
2	PTSD overview, personal experiences	Identify personal difficulties
3	Introduce progressive, cue-controlled differential muscle relaxation	Practice relaxation techniques
4	Teach diaphragmatic breathing, identification of triggers	Practice techniques, list of triggers
5	Introduce SUDS and practice assigning ratings	identify and rate a feeling and note whether positive or negative
6	Anger/rage, defining and using SUDS continuum	Identify instance of anger along their continuum
7	Introduce problem-solving, while beginning to identify belief systems	Practice problem-solving and report on results
8	Sharing of homework; responding vs. reacting; management versus control; interpreting feedback; identifying negative self-talk	Worksheet of negative beliefs and possible challenges
9	Repeat session 8, connecting more to the concept of the effect of trauma on the beliefs of survivors	Continue
10-G	Introduce stimulus hierarchy, rehearse relaxation techniques, begin SUDS for use with trauma	Practice intervention to step 4 on SUDS
10-I	Individual session: member reviews trauma & constructs hierarchy with clinician; challenging inaccurate beliefs	Write narrative to the stage they are able to process
11, 12, 13	Review narratives with rehearsal of interventions, clinician/members normalize reactions to trauma, provide corrective information; intro of in-vivo exposure	In-vivo exposure to lower-levels of intrusive material
14, 15	Continue narrative exposure, each member rehearsing intervention skills & receiving cognitively challenging feedback from group while progressing in continuum	Cognitive rehearsal of higher level points on continuum
16	Identify cognitive distortions in members' narratives, construct cognitive distortion-counter cognition pairs	Review distortion/counter pairs
17	Review of progress through sessions, introduce relapse prevention, discuss concerns about end of group	Think about ways in which personal goals have been met
18	Certificate for "Becoming the Boss of PTSD" (March et al., 1998). Sharing of personal growth & accomplishment	

Note: The above protocol can be modified according to the nature of PTSD presentation and the specific setting.

to give their diagnosis and what they believe to be the reason PTSD has been chosen. Homework may be to bring to group an example of symptomatic behavior of which they are either self-aware or were told by family/staff.

Session 3: Introduce progressive, cue-controlled differential muscle relaxation and have the members practice during the session. The homework will be to practice the relaxation once per day. *Amended for Type II*: Same as Type I. Homework may be the same.

Session 4: Teach diaphragmatic breathing as a method of proactively addressing early panic episodes associated with triggering stimuli. Homework is to practice these

Table 12.2   Examples of Techniques for In-Session Work

Welcome and introductions
Open with 3 questions: (1) How do you feel? (2) What are you thinking? (3) What would you like to accomplish in this group?

Teaching the SUDS "'thermometer"
Introduce the concept of scaling or rating along a continuum. (For ease of member familiarity, a diagram of a thermometer may be useful to start.) Explain to the group members that they were to imagine first something they are familiar with, perhaps the weather. Describe weather from 1, the mildest, to 10, the most intense storm they can imagine. Have the members draw their own continuum in any form they like (materials needed are sketch pads, markers or crayons and tape). Post the finished project around the room and discuss the similarities and differences in their continuums.

Techniques for modulating intense intrusive symptoms
1. Imagine a split screen on which the intrusive symptom can be viewed. The intense material is on one side while the other side is the relaxing or safe place for balancing and grounding. Utilize dials, rheostats, switches, and the like, as methods of "turning down" the intensity of affect or any other intrusive symptom. The concept of a picture-in-picture television is often used by one of us (JS) with success, as it allows the child some control in switching back and forth but acknowledges that both the intrusive and the relaxing are present while encouraging a sense of mastery over the intrusion.
2. Draw a secure container such as a vault, box, bubble, etc., and draw or write the intense material inside.
3. Write or draw each step of the trauma event on separate pieces of paper, seal each in a plastic bag or envelope and burn, flush, or rip into shreds and throw away.
4. Make a collage of the trauma event or something symbolic of it using magazines, newspaper clippings, etc.
5. Keep a list of triggers through all channels of information processing (i.e., all senses) and make a list of strategies to use when facing the presence of these triggers.
6. Make two columns on a piece of paper: one titled "Intrusive Thoughts", and one "Challenges." Write the thought or feeling that feels overwhelming on the side labeled Intrusive Thoughts. Write a challenging belief on the opposite side:

Intrusive	Challenge
I am selfish	I need to take care of myself
I am stupid	Something I do well is....
I am bad	Everyone makes mistakes

Self-soothing Activities
1. Fill a box with objects for each sense that is distracting and/or self-soothing. Examples might be a soft stuffed animal, a picture of your dog, a pack of your favorite gum, a handkerchief with your favorite cologne on it, a copy of your favorite song, and so forth.
2. Write about your favorite vacation or activity at school or party.
3. Create a collage about a time that was very relaxing for you.
4. Especially for adolescents and older children: create a relaxing, positive, warm environment with smells of a favorite lotion or candle, wrap in a warm soft blanket, lower lights and sounds, listen to soothing (not stimulating) music, and so forth.

End of Session "Grounding"
Let's take a few minutes and develop a safe place to which we will return at the end of each group. Your safe place can be wherever you want, real or imagined, and needs to have all the smells, tastes, colors, doors, windows, trees, pillows, books, sounds such as music or silence such as a walk in the woods, whatever helps you feel safe and "grounded." Grounded means firmly in this room, at this time, and able to make plans for the remainder of the day. Homework is to practice remaining grounded while noticing and recording any times they feel overwhelmed or "triggered" (explanation of this term may be necessary).

techniques several times per day and to begin identifying and listing triggers. *Amended for Type II:* Teach the breathing with as much rehearsal in group as possible and have them paired with someone in the group to coach them outside the group. They could have as homework practicing the breathing numerous times per day perhaps while watching themselves in the mirror or with their partner from group.

Session 5: Introduce the concept of SUDS, having the group members make their own drawing to represent the incremental continuum (age appropriately, for example, in the form of a thermometer, a racetrack, etc.). Homework is to identify and rate some feeling during the week and note whether they consider it positive or negative. *Amended for Type II*: Perhaps provide ready-made diagrams (such as a thermometer) that may be used more liberally with these groups as they may be more concrete in their thinking. Ask them to rate feelings or thoughts and ask family/staff to offer feedback on whether they agree (a way to help the group member connect with how others view their manifestations of feelings and thoughts and provide a comparison for judging their own assessments.)

Session 6: Discuss anger and rage, asking the group members to give their definitions by either their own feeling states or by observing them in others (often easier than owning these intense feelings when initially discussed). Help them create their own continuum of angry feelings using a similar drawing to the SUDS example. Homework will be to note a particular time and event when they can identify a feeling along the anger continuum they have made. *Amended for Type II*: Rehearse the relaxation and breathing techniques learned at the beginning of the session. Define the feelings of anger and rage, asking the members to give examples they saw on TV or in a movie or heard in a song. Using examples at a distance helps the member practice distancing techniques. Maintain a cognitive discussion about anger and healthy uses and expression for the feeling. Homework will be to observe anger in others, checking with family/staff or another member for validation of the observations.

Session 7: Introduce a logical problem-solving approach that includes identifying the problem, stepping away to develop options, considering consequences and discussing pros and cons of various solutions. Ask the members to identify any belief systems that are evident during the process. Homework will be to use this technique in a situation and report the results. *Amended for Type II*: Ask the group members to identify a small problem they faced in the past week discussing whether the decision they made worked in the way they hoped. Define a logical problem-solving approach as above, asking the members to repeat the information and give examples if necessary to enhance understanding. Ask the group members to think of an example in a story, movie, etc., where someone resolved a problem without losing control of angry feelings. Role play one of the situations they described trying different decisions and discussing the possible outcomes. Discuss which new skills learned thus far could be most helpful in managing anger. Homework will be to try to manage a situation differently than they initially react.

Session 8: Draw on the members' successful group rehearsals and homework reports to provide examples of situations they have responded to rather than reacted. Ask them to each provide a positive statement about the group member in the next seat. Ask each how believable the positive remark was to hear. Challenge any negative self-talk that occurs during the discussion, asking for members to offer alternative interpretations. Use one of the journal activities to facilitate the CBT negative statement-positive reframe. Introduce the concept of control versus management of situations. Lead the discussion to the parts of life over which some control can be had versus those where skills in exercising caution and knowing how to get help can be discriminated. Homework will consist of completing a worksheet of negative beliefs and possible challenges. *Amended for Type II*: Present a similar discussion maintaining as much concreteness as necessary depending on the stability of the interactions and reports from family/staff of behavior in the milieu. Suggest the same homework but with the assistance of family/staff.

Session 9: Repeat session 8 connecting more to the concept of the effect of trauma on the beliefs of survivors. *Amended for Type II*: Repeat as for Session 8.

Session 10: Review the SUDS drawings. Ask the members to create another continuum explaining the concept of stimulus hierarchy. Have the group rehearse the relaxation and breathing techniques learned in earlier sessions. Explain to the group that the continuum will now be used to provide steps toward the event that caused their PTSD. They will then learn how to intervene at each step preventing escalation to the 10 on their continuum. End the group with rehearsal of relaxation and breathing. Homework will be to practice intervening to step four. *Amended for Type II*: The same as above allowing the continuum to go only to 4. Alert family/staff of the group content.

At this point in the process, the clinician meets with each group member individually, in which the youth reviews the traumatic event and constructs the continuum with the clinician. The clinician supports the member in maintaining stability during the review and provides corrective cognitions for the inaccurate belief systems that have resulted from the trauma. Individual needs for additional skills are assessed and reported to the appropriate individual therapists. For those with Type II trauma histories, the same intervention is provided maintaining the strict structure that allows containment of affect and intrusive material. Family/staff should be closely involved with this stage of the group therapy. Homework will be for the members to each write a narrative to the stage they are able to process.

Sessions 11, 12, 13: Explore the narratives of each member, providing rehearsal of interventions, at all levels, during the narrative exposure. Structure the narratives over the three sessions beginning with the members who have demonstrated assimilation of new skills. Members are encouraged to give feedback that normalizes other members' responses to the trauma, as well as offer corrective information to challenge misattributions and distortions. Imaginal exposure is practiced and graded *in-vivo* exposure is introduced. Homework will be *in vivo* exposure to lower levels of intrusive material and appropriate interventions used, whether perceived as successful or not. (When reviewing the homework, the clinician should always find some aspect of the intervention that was successful and provide feedback to the member, generalizing to the entire group when possible.) *Amended for Type II*: Present the same format exercising similar caution maintaining the structure and containment of the stimulus and cognitive, relaxation, breathing techniques for intensity management. Homework should be to process the group discussion with family/staff and rehearse containment skills.

Sessions 14, 15: Continue the narrative exposure from previous sessions allowing each member to rehearse intervention skills and receive cognitively challenging feedback from the group. Encourage each member to approach the highest level of intensity using all learned skills to remain grounded. Homework should be cognitive rehearsal of the remaining difficult points on the continuum. *Amended for Type II*: Same as previous sessions at amended level.

Session 16: Identify the cognitive distortions in each members' narratives and notes and draw attention to how they are complicating the healing process. Ask the members to write the cognitive distortion and the counter cognition (whether they believe it yet or not) and review it for homework. *Amended for Type II:* Same as previous sessions at amended level.

Session 17: Review all the processing in all sessions, introducing the concept of relapse prevention by practicing on a regular basis the skills learned for symptomatic reactions. Encourage expression of any concerns about group sessions coming to an end. For homework, members should think about ways in which they have met or progressed toward meeting personal goals established at the start of group, along with skills they have acquired, for sharing in the final group. *Amended for Type II*: Same as previous sessions with the added discussion of how to deal with the ending of group. Family/staff will need to be particularly supportive following the last sessions.

Session 18: Each member receives a certificate for "Becoming the boss of PTSD" (March et al, 1998). Review again as a group all the progress each has achieved and how they can continue to heal and grow. *Amended for Type II:* Award each the certificate as above with praise for all the positive work toward healing and acknowledging all the achievements each has accomplished.

Variations may be made to this group model as appropriate. For example, repeating this group a second time may be beneficial for those with more severe trauma histories to allow further practice while they continue to receive individual therapy and develop a healthy support system.

CONCLUSION AND RECOMMENDATIONS

Given the scarcity of literature available to guide group treatment of children and adolescents with PTSD and PTS, it is important to rely on the components shown most effective in either individual treatment with young people or in work with adults. Specific techniques and intervention strategies must be modified for use with younger group members and those with more severe presentations; however, a thorough assessment and clinical case conceptualization guided by cognitive-behavioral principles will afford clinicians and those providing treatment to this population a sound base from which to begin. Specific interventions may be adjusted depending on the comfort-level of each clinician, the make-up of the group (including participants' age level), and the setting in which group is conducted. The model presented here is an adaptation of the program developed by March and colleagues (1998), which takes into account experimental findings in the field of trauma treatment. It was also empirically validated to show improvement in PTSD symptoms and presentation, making it a strong model and one that is likely to produce positive effects in the treatment of a population so deserving of successful intervention. A great deal more research is warranted to support this model, as well as identify potential benefits of other treatment approaches for use in expanding the available treatment options for young people struggling with the effects of trauma.

RECOMMENDED READINGS

Beck, J. (2005). *Cognitive therapy for challenging problems: What to do when the basics don't work.* New York: Guilford.

Cohen, J. A. (1998). Practice parameters for the assessment and treatment of children and adolescents with posttraumatic stress disorder. *Journal of the American Academy of Child and Adolescent Psychiatry, 37*(10S), 4S–26S.

Cohen, J. A., Berliner, L., & March, J. S. (2000). Treatment of children and adolescents. In E. Foa, T. Keane, & M. Friedman (Eds), *Effective treatments for PTSD* (pp. 106–138). New York: Guilford.

Feeney, N. C., Foa, E. B., Treadwell, K. R. H., & March, J. (2004). Posttraumatic stress disorder in youth: A critical review of the cognitive and behavioral treatment outcome literature. *Professional Psychology: Research and Practice, 35*(5), 466–476.

Herman, J. L. (1992). *Trauma and recovery*. New York: Basic Books.

March, J., Amaya-Jackson, L., Murry, M., & Schulte, A., (1998). Cognitive-behavioral psychotherapy for children and adolescents with post-traumatic stress disorder following a single-incident stressor. *Journal of the American Academy of Child and Adolescent Psychiatry, 37*(6), 585–593.

REFERENCES

Achenbach, T. M., & Edelbrock, C. (1983). *Manual for the child behavior checklist and revised child behavior profile.* Burlington: University of Vermont, Department of Psychiatry.

American Psychiatric Association (2000). *Diagnostic and Statistical Manual of Mental Disorders, 4th ed.* (*DSM-IV-TR*). Washington, DC: American Psychiatric Association.

Armstrong, J., Putnam, F. W., Carlson, E., Libero, D., & Smith, S. (1997). Development and validation of a measure of adolescent dissociation: The adolescent dissociative experience scale. *Journal of Nervous & Mental Disease, 185,* 491–497.

Beck, J. (2005). Cognitive *Therapy for challenging problems: What to do when the basics don't work.* New York: Guilford.

Briere, J. (1996). *Trauma Symptom Checklist for Children (TSCC) professional manual.* Odessa, FL: Psychological Assessment Resources.

Briere, J. Johnson, K., Bissada, A., Damon, L., Crouch, J., Gil, E., et al. (2001). The Trauma Symptom Checklist for Young Children (TSCYC): reliability and association with abuse exposure in a multi-site study. *Child Abuse & Neglect, 25,* 1001–1014.

Chemtob, C. M., Nakashima, J., & Hamada, R. S. (2002). Psychosocial intervention for post-disaster trauma symptoms in elementary school children. *Archives of Pediatric and Adolescent Medicine, 156,* 211–216.

Chu, J. (2000). *Rebuilding shattered lives: The responsible therapy of complex post traumatic and dissociative disorders.* New York: Wiley.

Cohen, J. A. (1998). Practice parameters for the assessment and treatment of children and adolescents with posttraumatic stress disorder. *Journal of the American Academy of Child and Adolescent Psychiatry, 37*(10S), 4S–26S.

Cohen, J. A., Berliner, L., & March, J. S. (2000). Treatment of children and adolescents. In E. Foa, T. Keane, & M. Friedman (Eds.), *Effective treatments for PTSD* (pp. 106–138). New York: Guilford.

Deblinger, E., McLeer, S. V., & Henry, D. (1990). Cognitive-behavioral treatment for sexually abused children suffering post-traumatic stress: Preliminary findings. *Journal of the American Academy of Child and Adolescent Psychiatry, 29,* 747–752.

Duncan, R. D. (2000). Childhood maltreatment and college drop-out rates: Implications for child abuse researchers. *Journal of Interpersonal Violence, 15*(9), 987–995.

Eth, S. (2000). PTSD in children and adolescents. *Review and Psychiatry, 20*(1), 59–68. Washington, DC: American Psychiatric Association.

Feeney, N. C., Foa, E. B., Treadwell, K. R. H., & March, J. (2004). Posttraumatic stress disorder in youth: A critical review of the cognitive and behavioral treatment outcome literature. *Professional Psychology: Research and Practice, 35*(5), 466–476.

Foa, E. B., Johnson, K., Feeny, N. C., & Treadwell, K. R. T. (2001). The Child PTSD Symptom Scale (CPSS): Preliminary psychometrics of a measure for children with PTSD. *Journal of Clinical and Child Psychology, 30,* 376–384.

Foy, D. W., Wood, J. L., King, D. W., King, L. A., & Resnick, H. S. (1997). Los Angeles Symptom Checklist: Psychometric evidence with an adolescent sample. *Assessment, 4,* 377–384.

Frederick, C. J. (1985). Selected foci in the spectrum of posttraumatic stress disorders. In J. Laube & S. A. Murphy (Eds.), *Perspectives on disaster recovery* (pp 110–131). Norwalk, CT: Appleton-Century-Croft.

Giaconia, R. M., Reinherz, H. Z., Silverman, A. B., Pakiz, B., Frost, A. K., & Cohen, E. (1995). Traumas and post traumatic stress disorder in a community population of older adolescents. *Journal of the American Academy of Child and Adolescent Psychiatry, 34,* 1369–1380.

Goenjian, A. K., Pynoos, R. S., Steinberg, A. M., Najarian, L. M., Asarnow, J. R., Karayan, I., et al. (1995). Psychiatric comorbidity in children after the 1988 earthquake in Armenia. *Journal of the American Academy of Child and Adolescent Psychiatry, 34*(9), 1174–1184.

Goenjian, A. K., Karayan, I., Pynoos, R. S., Minassian, D., Najarian, L. M., Steinberg, A. M., et al. (1997). Outcome of psychotherapy among early adolescents after trauma. *American Journal of Psychiatry, 154*, 536–542.

Goenjian, A. K., Stilwell, B. M., Steinberg, A. M., Fairbanks, L. A., Galvin, M. R., Karayan, I., et al. (1999). Moral development and psychopathological interference in conscience functioning among adolescents after trauma. *Journal of the American Academy of Child and Adolescent Psychiatry, 38*(4), 376–384.

Green, B. L., Korol, M., Grace, M. C., Vary, M. G., Leonard, A. C., Gleser, G. C., et al. (1991). Children and disaster: Age, gender, and parental effects on post traumatic stress disorder symptoms. *Journal of the American Academy of Child and Adolescent Psychiatry, 30*(6), 945–951.

Greenwald, R., & Rubin, A. (1999). Brief assessment of children's post-traumatic symptoms: Development and preliminary validation of parent and child scales. *Research on Social Work Practice, 9*, 61–75.

Greenwald, R., Rubin, A., Jurkovic, G. J., Wiedemann, J., Russell, A. M., O'Connor, M. B., et al. (2002, November). *Psychometrics of the CROPS & PROPS in multiple cultures/translations.* Poster session presented at the annual meeting of the International Society for Traumatic Stress Studies, Baltimore.

Herman, J. L. (1992). *Trauma and recovery.* New York: Basic Books.

Horowitz, M., Wilner, N., & Alvarez, W. (1979). Impact of event scale: A measure of subjective stress. *Psychosomatic Medicine, 41*, 209–218.

Joseph, S. A., Brewin, C. R., Yule, W., & Williams, R. (1993). Causal attributions and post traumatic stress in adolescents. *Journal of Child Psychology and Psychiatry, 34*(2), 247–253.

Kassam-Adams, N., Baxt, C., & Shrivastava, N. (2003, October). *Development of the Acute Stress Checklist for Children (ASC-Kids).* Poster presented at the 19th Annual Meeting of the International Society of Traumatic Stress Studies, Chicago.

Kovacs, M. (1985). The Children's Depression Inventory (CDI). *Psychopharmacology Bulletin, 21*, 995–998.

Lewis, T., Amini, F., & Lannon, R. (2001). *A General Theory of Love.* New York: Vintage Books.

March, J. S. (1995). *Anxiety disorders in children and adolescents.* New York: Guilford.

March, J. (1999). Assessment of pediatric Post-traumatic stress disorder. In P. Saigh & J. Bremmer (Eds.), *Post-traumatic stress disorder* (pp. 199–218). Boston: Allyn & Bacon.

March, J., Amaya-Jackson, L., Murry, M., & Schulte, A., (1998). Cognitive-Behavioral Psychotherapy for Children and Adolescents with Post-traumatic Stress Disorder Following a Single-Incident Stressor. *Journal of the American Academy of Child and Adolescent Psychiatry, 37*(6), 585–593.

March, J., Parker, J., Sullivan, K., et al. (1997). The multi-dimensional anxiety scale for children (MASC): Factor structure, reliability, and validity. *Journal of the American Academy of Child and Adolescent Psychiatry, 36*, 554–565.

Nader, K., Blake, D., Kriegler, J., & Pynoos, R. (1994). *Clinician administered PTSD scale for children (CAPS-C), current and lifetime diagnosis version and instructional manual.* Los Angeles: UCLA Neuropsychiatric Institute and National Center for PTSD. National Center for Post Traumatic Stress Disorder (2001). Department of Veteran Affairs, Washington, DC.

Pfefferbaum, B. (1997). Post traumatic stress disorder in children: A review of the past ten years. *Journal of the American Academy of Child and Adolescent Psychiatry, 36*(11), 1503–1511.

Pynoos, R. S., Frederick, C., Nader, K., et al., (1987). Life threat and post-traumatic stress in school-age children. *Archives of General Psychiatry, 44*, 1057–1063.

Reynolds, C. R., & Kamphaus, R. W. (2002). *The clinician's guide to the behavior assessment system for children (BASC).* New York: Guilford.

Rinsley, D .B. (1994). *Treatment of the Severely Disturbed Adolescent.* Northvale, NJ: Jason Aronson.

Saigh, P. A., Yasik, A. E., Oberfield, R. A., Green, B. L., Halamandaris, P. V., et al. (2000). The children's PTSD inventory: Development and reliability. *Journal of Traumatic Stress. 13*(3), 369–380.

Saigh, P. A., Mroueh, M. N., & Bremmer, J. D. (1997). Scholastic impairments among traumatized adolescents. *Behaviour Research & Therapy, 35*(5), 429–436.

Saigh, P. A., Mroueh, M. N., Zimmerman, B. J., & Fairbanks, J. A. (1995). Self-efficacy expectations among traumatized adolescents. *Behaviour Research & Therapy, 33*(6), 701–704.

Silverman, W. K., & Albano, A. M. (1996). *Anxiety disorders interview schedule for DSM-IV, child and parent versions.* San Antonia, TX: Psychological Corporation.

Stein, B. D., Jaycox, L. H., Kataoka, S. H., Wong, M., Tu, W., et al. (2003). A mental health intervention for school children exposed to violence. *Journal of the American Medical Association, 290*, 603–611.

Smyth, L. (1999). *Overcoming PTSD*. New York: New Harbinger.

Smyth, L. D., & Sheppard Pratt and Enoch Pratt Hospital. (1994). *A manual for the treatment of post-traumatic stress disorder, specific phobias, social phobias generalized anxiety disorder, panic disorder, obsessive-compulsive disorder*. Havre de Grace, MD, RTR Publishing.

Spielberger, C.D. (1970). *Preliminary manual for the state-trait anxiety inventory for children*. Palo Alto, CA: Consulting Psychologist's Press.

Wolpe, J. (1958). *Psychotherapy by reciprocal inhibition*. Stanford, CA: Stanford University Press.

Chapter Thirteen

Helping Children and Adolescents Dealing with Divorce

Barbara A. Schaefer & Marika Ginsburg-Block

Jordan, your mom and I have really been struggling to make things work out together this past year, but we haven't been very successful. We have come to realize that as much as we both love you kids immensely, we can't live together anymore and our marriage is ending. We are getting a divorce...

Messages similar to this one are not unusual in American society today. The United States has one of the highest rates of divorce in the world (4.19 per 1,000 population) when compared to English-speaking countries of Australia, Canada, and the United Kingdom (2.28 to 2.74), as well as select developed countries in South America, Asia, and non-English-speaking Europe (0.42 to 2.69; United Nations, 2000). In 2004, approximately one million American couples were divorced (National Center for Health Statistics, 2005). Divorce rates peak within 3 to 5 years of marriages and 63% of divorcing couples are married less than 10 years; however, couples may split at any point across 5 to 30 years of marriage and beyond, with only 12% of divorces occurring among couples married for 20 or more years (U.S. Department of Health and Human Services [DHHS], 1995). Forty percent of these marriages end with children involved, and more than a million children are directly impacted by their parents' divorce each year (Trzcinski & Genheimer, 2000). Moreover, during the course of childhood from birth to age 18, it is estimated that approximately 60% of children will live in a single-parent household at some point (Furstenberg & Cherlin, 1991).

As divorces and subsequent remarriages occur, shifts in household composition are evident. From 1970 to 2000, American family household composition has changed dramatically, with the percentage of married couples with children under age 18 decreasing from 40.3 to 24.1% (U.S. Census Bureau, 2001). In 1990, 20.8% of American married couple family households (5.3 million) involved at least one step-child under age 18, with roughly half of these households including only step children, and the other half encompassing a blend of both step-children and biological children (U.S. Census Bureau, 1992). Variability associated with parent gender and age is also evident. According to the U.S. Census Bureau (2005), in 2001, about 1 in 5 recently married men lived with children ages 1 to 17 years, whereas for women the ratio was about 1 in 3. In addition, nearly 60% of recently married women lived with their own children under age 18, but less than 20% of men live with their offspring. The majority of divorcing couples over age 45 (78.2% of men and 73.3% of women) had one or more children. In addition, among those people who have remarried, approximately 90% of men and women had at least one child (U.S. Census Bureau, 2005).

For American children, family composition is increasingly complex. In 2000, 69.1% of children under age 18 lived with two parents—of which 88.2% lived with both biological parents, 9.3% lived with one biological and one step-parent, and 2.5% lived with another combination (including adoptive parents)—and 26.6% of children lived with one parent (22.4% with their mother; 4.2% with their father; U.S. Census Bureau, 2000). Notably, all but 2 to 4% of children were the offspring of at least one of the adults in the household in which they lived (U.S. Census Bureau, 2003). Complex influences of culture/ethnicity on living arrangements are also evident, given that variability in marriages, households, and family configurations appears to be associated with particular ethnic groups (Orbuch, Veroff, & Hunter, 1999). Ten years after couples' initial marriages, disruption is lowest among Asian American women (20%) as compared to other ethnic groups (Whites 32%, Hispanics 34%, African Americans 47%; Bramlett & Mosher, 2002). Divorce rates are also associated with partners' educational and income level, and likelihood of divorce after separation also varies based on certain individual and family characteristics (Bramlett & Mosher, 2002).

This chapter will explore the impact of divorce on children and adolescents, the group-based interventions that have been investigated, the outcomes of these interventions, and the implications for mental health professionals.

IMPACT OF DIVORCE

Multiple factors seem to be involved in understanding the impact of divorce on the well-being of youth. Hetherington, Bridges, and Insabella (1998) analyzed five contributing factors related to child adjustment in divorces, including individual risk and vulnerability (e.g., child gender, developmental status, temperament, predivorce adjustment), family composition (e.g., single vs. two-parent home, remarriage, custody status), stress and socioeconomic disadvantage (e.g., income loss, task overload), parental distress (e.g., depression, anxiety, emotional lability, loneliness), and family process (e.g., altered roles, conflict, parent–child relations). Given that evidence for these factors is mixed, the authors argue for a transactional model for use in predicting youth's adjustment after divorce and remarriage that encompasses all five possibilities. While all of these factors may be relevant, changes in family process and economic status have been the most widely studied.

As articulated by Lindblad-Goldberg (1989), "it is not *who* is in the family that matters, but *how* the family is organized and how the individuals interact, adapt, and cope" (p. 118, italics added). The impact of divorce on individual family members ranges from subtle to dramatic. Maccoby and Mnookin (1992) identified four co-parenting patterns after separation, including (1) cooperative, (2) conflicted, (3) disengaged, and (4) mixed. These parenting patterns can impact children's perceptions, reactions, and adjustment to separation and divorce in both obvious and subtle ways. Indeed, children's and teenagers' ability to adapt to the many changes inherent in the separation, divorce, and post-divorce process may be affected by co-parenting style (Maccoby & Mnookin, 1992). Established authoritative parenting styles may shift with divorce and evolve into different, possibly less adaptive styles (more authoritarian or permissive) for the single custodial parent (Avenevoli, Sessa, & Steinberg, 1999). Moreover, parents' and children's roles, level of responsibility at home, and other aspects of family life may also change. For example, it is not uncommon for fathers—who are more often the noncustodial parent—to have a reduced role, or eventually nonexistent contact over time (Furstenberg, Peterson, Nord, & Zill, 1983). A national study (Nord, Brimall, & West, 1997) showed that for children who were in contact with their nonresident fathers, only 31% of nonresident fathers participated in their children's school activities during the school year as compared to 75% of resident fathers in two-parent families.

In addition to the possible impact on family processes, the economic impact of divorce can also affect children, particularly those who live with custodial mothers. Noncash public assistance is received by 15% of households of recently divorced men, but twice as many households of recently divorced women (34%) received such assistance, demonstrating that divorce has a greater economic impact on women and children than on men (U.S. Census Bureau, 2005). According to the U.S. Census Bureau (2000), 16% of Americans were living in poverty in 1997; however, 32% of custodial mothers were living in poverty, in comparison to 11% of custodial fathers. Perhaps reflecting time availability, children in two-parent families benefit from being read to more often than those in divorced, separate, never married or widowed parents, and also are more likely to participate in extra-curricular activities such as clubs, sports, and so forth. (U.S. Census Bureau, 2000). Additional potential risks for children of divorce have been identified by Carlson (1995) as they relate to single-parent homes (e.g., poverty, social bias, dropping out, adjustment, resilience).

Children's Responses to Parental Divorce

> *Jordan's initial disbelief and shock dissipated and revealed deep hurt and anxiety about what this meant for her and her family. While in retrospect, she recognized that her parents had often argued and interacted angrily, she had never realized this would lead to divorce and she felt guilty for causing some of the arguments. Anger toward her parents and siblings also emerged and she avoided them by spending much time at her friends' houses. Her schoolwork declined in the following weeks as she lost interest in her classes.*

Children in Jordan's position commonly experience a broad range of emotions in response to the news of parents' impending divorce, and coping with this news is not easy. Moreover, children's age and developmental status influence their perceptions of divorce, with feelings of abandonment, self-blame, confusion, ambivalence, and anger typically emerging at various ages (see Kurdek, 1986). Possible developmental tasks or stages of children's responses to parental divorce have been theorized by Wallerstein (1983), which include: (1) recognizing the reality of parents' separation, (2) disengaging from parent conflicts, (3) resolving loss, (4) resolving of anger and self-blame, (5) accepting finality of divorce, and (6) achieving realistic, independent expectation regarding own future relationships. Negotiating these tasks is impacted by contributing factors within the situation, within the child, within the residential parent, and within the nonresidential parent—each of which can be influential on children's adjustment (Ellis, 2000).

Divorce has the potential to impact children's short- and long-term adjustment and well-being, and studies reveal differences between children of divorced parents and those whose parents did not divorce (Chase-Lansdale, Cherlin, & Kiernan, 1995; Cherlin, Chase-Lansdale, & McRae, 1998; Emery, 1999; Grych & Fincham, 1999; Stevenson & Black, 1995). Summarizing 92 studies' findings on the effects of divorce on children through college-aged youth (N > 13,000), Amato and Keith's (1991) meta-analysis revealed poorer adjustment among children of divorce than among children with intact marriages. Significant effect sizes were found and indicated that divorce impacts multiple areas of children's functioning including academic achievement, conduct, psychological adjustment, self-concept, and social adjustment, as well as parent–child relations. Notably, these group differences are small, rather than large, so while some children of divorced parents may have difficulties not all children of divorce fare worse than those from intact families. The proportion of children who may need intervention is unknown:

> ...a minority of children do experience adjustment problems and are in need of therapeutic intervention. The type of therapeutic intervention suited for children varies according to the type and severity of the adjustment problems and the length of time they are expressed by the child. The major types of therapeutic interventions include child-oriented interventions and family-oriented interventions. (Amato, 1994 , p. 156)

Regardless of the various factors that may influence children's adjustment to divorce, it is clear that divorce has substantial potential to impact children's adjustment and school functioning. Estimates of between 1 in 4 and 1 in 5 children of divorce may experience substantial distress, adjustment problems, or mental health concerns (Hetherington et al., 1998).

While divorce may result in negative outcomes for many children, our knowledge of likely protective factors lends itself to the development of promising prevention and intervention strategies. For example, correlational research illustrates that continued involvement of noncustodial parents is related to a host of favorable child outcomes, including school-based outcomes (Nord & West, 2001). Children are more likely to earn mostly A grades in school, less likely to repeat a grade in school, and less likely to be suspended or expelled from school when their nonresident fathers are involved in their schooling. When nonresident mothers participate in at least one school-based activity during the year, their children are more likely to earn mostly A grades in school.

Consequently, mental health specialists and school personnel need to be prepared to assist children as their family situation transitions. For school psychologists, Carlson (1995) recommends annual screening of student populations for high-risk family situations (e.g., a change in status experienced within last year or expected within the next year) and completion of family assessments to identify potential referrals. In addition, counselors and psychologists can network with community mental health professionals and can notify social and religious groups about school-based support program offerings so as to better connect with children from families experiencing divorce. Parents and teachers are also important referral sources and need to be alert to signs of difficulty in their children and students. A "healthy" divorce, one that is constructive rather than destructive, is possible (Everett & Everett, 1994), but even these reasonably amicable divorces can impact children and youth substantially. Parents and future step-parents need to be educated about how their behavior and interactions may impact children's adjustment in the home, school, and community settings. Furthermore, school-based mental health professionals should be prepared to offer child-based individual and group intervention services (Carlson, 1995).

EFFECTIVE INTERVENTIONS

The need to identify and apply empirically supported interventions has been identified by various mental health professions in practice guidelines and research (e.g., American Psychological Association, American Psychiatric Association, American Academy of Child and Adolescent Psychiatry; see Kazdin, 2000, Nathan & Gorman, 1998, and the Task Force on Promotion and Dissemination of Psychological Procedures, 1995). Among the types of interventions with substantial empirical support is cognitive-behavior therapy (Hoagwood & Erwin, 1997). Based on that approach, groups for children dealing with separated or divorced parents have been developed both in conjunction with parenting groups and as stand-alone interventions. These groups have been utilized in both school and clinic settings to address children's needs, and various levels of empirical support have been presented. Advantages of school-based groups are that most children attend school regularly, and that peers can provide social support and personal perspective on the experience of divorce (Stolberg & Mahler, 1994). Two prevention programs have been shown to be effective in working with youth experiencing parental divorce and are presented below.

Jordan's teachers and parents both noticed the changes in her attitude and behavior, and requested that she be seen by the school counselor. After two individual sessions, the counselor recommended that Jordan participate in one of the divorce groups that he and the school psychologist co-facilitate during the school year. Jordan and her parents agreed that this might be beneficial.

Child-Focused Programs

The *Divorce Adjustment Project* (DAP; Stolberg & Garrison, 1985; Stolberg & Mahler, 1994) children's support group is a 14-week program, with components encompassing support, skill-building, and problem-solving. Four randomly assigned groups of children experiencing divorce (Transfer, Skills, & Support; Skills & Support, Support only, Divorce controls), and a separately obtained intact family control group were included for comparison purposes. Support sessions encompassed such activities as games, writing newspaper articles, and discussing picture-stimulus materials. Skill-building focused on labeling feelings, self-control exercises, problem solving (whose problem is it, is it controllable or not?), and anger control interventions. Special topics activities and a corresponding Kids Book, designed for home-based drawing and writing activities and additional practice, were utilized. Four parent workshops were also part of the program, and included a Parents Book that provided guidance to parents about divorce-related topics and how to talk with their children about divorce (Stolberg & Mahler, 1994). Positive results were obtained for treatment groups compared to no-treatment controls, as lower levels of pathology and clinical symptoms (both internalizing and externalizing) were evidenced at post-test and a year later at follow up.

The *Children of Divorce Intervention Program* (CODIP; Pedro-Carroll, Alpert-Gillis, & Cowen, 1992) initially drew from the DAP work and expanded to create the most well-researched, school-based intervention to date with positive outcomes documented across various age groups. CODIP was initially designed to provide support and build coping skills for 4th- to 6th-grade suburban children experiencing the effects of divorce (Alpert-Gillis, Pedro-Carroll, & Cowen, 1989). Subsequently, CODIP has expanded to include manual-based programs for kindergarten through 8th-grade children (Pedro-Carroll, 1994; Pedro-Carroll & Alpert-Gillis, 1997a; Pedro-Carroll, Alpert-Gillis, & Sterling, 1997; Pedro-Carroll, Sutton, & Black, 1999). Designed as a school-based children's support group co-facilitated by a male-female team, CODIP activities address various feelings, perceptions, and reactions associated with divorce, as well as incorporating games and activities aimed toward improving self-esteem (Alpert-Gillis, Pedro-Carroll, & Cowen, 1989). The structure of the program is similar for all age groups and tailored based on children's developmental level. For example, age-appropriate books, board games, and activities are used for kindergarten whereas older participants (e.g., 7th-grade students) use more sophisticated reading supplements, activities and assignments.

The CODIP group leaders work with a group of approximately 5 to 10 children for 45 minutes each week over a 12 to 15 week time period (see Pedro-Carroll & Alpert-Gillis, 1997b for a more detailed overview). The program curriculum is designed to address group cohesiveness, explore divorce-related concepts and feelings, build communication competencies, and reinforce children's positive perceptions of themselves and their families (Pedro-Carroll & Alpert-Gillis, 1997b). These objectives are addressed through group work and activities, and leaders are expected to communicate with both parents about how his or her child is reacting to the program, as well as ways to improve relations between parent and child. Communication plays a large role in the program and is emphasized for child-to-child relationships, parent-to-child relationships, and parent-to-parent relationships.

Research on CODIP outcomes by Pedro-Carroll and her colleagues has shown positive results using pre- and post-test control group designs (Alpert-Gillis, Pedro-Carroll, & Cowen, 1989; Pedro-Carroll & Cowen, 1985; Pedro-Carroll, Cowen, Hightower & Guare, 1986). Pedro-Carroll and Alpert-Gillis (1997b) found significant improvements in adjustment for 5- to 6-year-old program participants. Using teacher, parent, child, and group leader ratings on various scales, children demonstrated improvements in tolerating frustration, demonstrating appropriately assertive behaviors, and interacting with classmates (Pedro-Carroll & Alpert-Gillis, 1997b). CODIP participants were less anxious and less disruptive, had a greater understanding of divorce and acknowledged that it was not their fault, and were less worried about what changes had occurred (Pedro-Carroll & Alpert-Gillis, 1997b). Outcome research with 2nd- to 3rd- grade children (Albert-Gillis, Pedro-Carroll, & Cowen, 1989) revealed that participants showed greater levels of adjustment, coping ability, and acceptance of diverse family structures in comparison to a control group. Similarly, 4th- to 6th-grade participants in a 10-week CODIP program were less anxious, had fewer school problems, and reported less self-blame and improved problem-solving abilities (Pedro-Carroll & Cowen, 1985); however, self-competence and self-esteem were unchanged. Given these findings, CODIP has been identified as an effective program (DHHS, 2005).

> *Initially hesitant to speak up in the CODIP group setting, once Jordan felt comfortable and able to trust the group members, she gradually opened up about her feelings and fears regarding her parents' divorce and her new living situation. While still sad and angry at times, Jordan found group feedback and peer support helpful in recognizing that others were dealing with similar issues. Moreover, the group members and program activities helped her to understand that she was not responsible for her parents divorce, and there were things she could do to manage situations and to cope with the changes in her life.*

Parent-Focused Intervention Programs

Given that children's adjustment can be uniquely impacted by parents' interactions during the divorce process, interventions targeting parents and parent–child interactions are also important to consider. While these programs have typically been conducted either via the court, community, or clinical settings, these models could potentially be utilized in the school setting as well. Wolchik, Sandler, Winslow, and Smith-Daniels (2005) presented an overview of parent-focused interventions encompassing both brief informational programs and those comprised of multisession programs. Brief programs included Shifflett and Cummings' (1999) work, Kramer and Washo's (1993) *Children First* program, and Arbuthnot and Gordon's (1996) *Children in the Middle* video-based program. Initial outcome data suggest that self-reported inter-parent conflict may decrease, and parents report they involve their children in inter-parent conflict less frequently.

Children in the Middle (CIM; Arbuthnot & Gordon, 1994b, 2005) has been identified as a model program (DHHS, 2005). The CIM parent program is a one- or two-session (90 to 120 minutes), skills-based program comprised of a 37-minute video (also available in Spanish or open-captioned) that provides scenarios demonstrating appropriate and inappropriate parent interactions and communication skills. Suggestions for addressing children's feelings and reactions are also incorporated, and the program includes two parent guidebooks and a teacher's manual. Some positive outcomes for the parent intervention have been presented (Arbuthnot & Gordon, 1996). The child version of the CIM video (30 minutes; Arbuthnot & Gordon, 1994a) parallels the parent version and focuses on appropriate coping mechanisms. A guidebook for children's issues is also available. However, this child-focused program does not yet appear to have been established or evaluated as a stand-alone program. Indeed, Wolchik and colleagues (2005) noted that while the preliminary data on these brief informational programs for parents may be promising, "the design of the evaluations was weak…and *effects on child outcomes have yet to be demonstrated*, so it is difficult to have confidence in the efficacy of brief informational programs" (p. 67, italics added).

The multisession intervention programs identified by Wolchik and colleagues (2005) include the 12-session Single Parents' Support Group for residential mothers (SPSG; Stolberg & Garrison, 1985), 14-session *Parenting Through Change* program for divorced mothers with boys (PTC; Forgatch & DeGarmo, 1999), and the 11-session *New Beginnings Program* for residential mothers (NBP; Wolchik et al., 1993). As cited in Wolchik et al. (2005), evaluation of the SPSG program did not reveal improvement in parenting skills or child adjustment using a quasi-experimental design (Stolberg & Garrison, 1985). Utilizing a randomized control group design and a 30-month follow-up, PTC findings revealed boys' greater compliance with mothers' directives, and compliance was associated with greater positive parenting practices and less coercive discipline (Martinez & Forgatch, 2001). Two rigorous studies of the NBP have been conducted using randomized assignment to treatment and control groups (Wolchik et al., 1993; Wolchik et al., 2000), and experimental results indicated lower child behavior problems and aggression, better adjustment in the mother, improved mother–child relationships, and more effective discipline skills. Notably, inclusion of a child-focused intervention component did not result in improvements beyond those effects found for the mother-only program (Wolchik et al., 2000). Moreover, 6-year follow-up studies have documented group differences and positive outcomes for program participants and their children (Wolchik et al., 2002), and shown that those youth at greatest risk at the pre-intervention time point benefit the most from the intervention program (Dawson-McClure, Sandler, Wolchik, & Millsap, 2004). Given these outcomes, Wolchik and colleague's (1993) New Beginnings' Children of Divorce Parenting Intervention Program and child focused programs have been identified as effective programs for preventing mental health disorders in school-aged children (Domitrovich & Greenberg, 2000).

Considerations in Practice

Professionals who work with children and adolescents will likely encounter many youth who are dealing with issues related to changing family situations and divorce. These children may feel isolated and alone in their experiences and can benefit from psycho-educational intervention and support in a peer group setting. To intervene successfully, professionals should select and utilize programs with empirical support. Given the empirical evidence for the effectiveness and attention to implementation of CODIP and NBP interventions for children and parents, respectively, these would appear to be the best choices available for conducting programs to assist children and families dealing with divorce. Both utilize cognitive-behavioral strategies to assist participants in exploring their feelings and reactions to divorce-related events and anticipated transitions, as well as to encourage peer support and to focus on developing coping skills and strategies. Depending on the target participants, these programs could be developed and evaluated in a variety of settings, including schools, community or religious centers, or clinics.

The goal of group interventions for children of divorce is to provide a supportive, safe environment within which students' feelings can be validated, misconceptions about divorce can be explored, commonalities of experience across individuals can be identified, and coping skills reinforced. Among the potential obstacles facing group leaders are identification and recruitment of group members, obtaining parental consent for child participation, confidentiality, and documenting effects of participation. As it is not clear which children may be at greatest risk for poor adjustment to divorce, identifying potential group participants most in need of help may be a challenge. Suggestions for recruiting and screening group members in schools have been provided by Corey and Corey (1992) and could be similarly applied in other settings. These include notification about and recruitment for the divorce group by: hallway posters with tear-off contact information, public-address announcements, newspaper articles, contact with school personnel (teachers, counselors, administrators, nurses), homeroom announcements, parent letters or bulletins, peer referrals, and student handbooks. Screening of potential participants is suggested and is perhaps best accomplished by a private session between candidate and group leader to determine whether the candidate is capable of participating and likely to benefit (Corey & Corey, 1992).

Prior to group participation, informed consent needs to be obtained. However, the individual required to consent may vary by state, practice setting, and participants' age (e.g., Pennsylvania now permits youth age 14 or older to independently consent to outpatient treatment; Minor's Consent to Mental Health Treatment Act, 2004). Parents may be hesitant to permit their children's involvement in group interventions out of concern for possible social stigmatization or anticipated custody issues. Parents may need to be educated about the likely needs of their children during the divorce process, and parents and youth should be informed about the benefits and potential risks of participation in the group intervention. Confidentiality of communications occurring within the group setting is also an element to consider, as parents may desire to know what is discussed in the group setting. Clarification of the goals of participation and limitations of confidentiality, as well as clear encouragement of ongoing parent–child communication, should occur with the child and parents prior to beginning the group. Lastly, practitioners should be encouraged to collect data to support the efficacy of their intervention work so that additional evidence for programs can be established.

SUMMARY

More than a million children are impacted by parental divorce each year. Divorce creates a period of upheaval and change for both parents and children that can result in high levels of stress and potential distress among family members. Mental health providers in school and community settings can provide helpful support for family members affected by this process. Cognitive-behavioral groups like the CODIP and NBP have been shown to be beneficial and effective interventions for youth and parents, and practitioners are encouraged to conduct evaluations of their own group work to determine its effectiveness.

ACKNOWLEDGMENT

We thank Aura Novak for her assistance in collecting and reviewing materials for this chapter.

RESOURCES

Children of Divorce Intervention Program (CODIP) is available from: Children's Institute, 274 N. Goodman Street, Suite D103, Rochester, New York 14607, (877) 888-7647 (toll free), http://www.childrensinstitute.net/
New Beginnings Program is available from: Dr. Sharlene Wolchik, Professor, Department of Psychology, Arizona State University, P.O. Box 871104, Tempe, AZ 85287-1104, Phone: (480)-965-3326, Fax: (480) 965-8544, Email: wolchik@asu.edu.

REFERENCES

Alpert-Gillis, L. J., Pedro-Carroll, J. L., & Cowen, E. L. (1989). The Children of Divorce Intervention Program: Development, implementation, and evaluation of a program for young urban children. *Journal of Consulting and Clinical Psychology, 57*, 583–589.

Amato, P. (1994). Life-span adjustment of children to their parents' divorce. *The Future of Children, 4*(1), 143–163.

Amato, P. R., & Keith, B. (1991). Consequences of parental divorce for the well-being of children: A meta-analysis. *Psychological Bulletin,* 110, 26–46.

Arbuthnot, J., & Gordon, D. A. (1994a). *Children in the middle — Children's version* [Videotape]. (Available from the Center for Divorce Education, P.O. Box 15900, Athens, OH, 45701)

Arbuthnot, J., & Gordon, D. A. (1994b). *Children in the middle — Parent's version* [Videotape]. (Available from the Center for Divorce Education, 1005 East State Street, Suite G, Athens, OH, 45701)

Arbuthnot, J., & Gordon, D. A. (1996). Does mandatory divorce education for parents work? A six-month outcome evaluation. *Family and Conciliation Courts Review,* 34, 60–81.

Arbuthnot, J., & Gordon, D. A. (2005). *Children in the middle — Parent's version* (revised & updated) [Videotape]. (Available from the Center for Divorce Education, 1005 East State Street, Suite G, Athens, OH, 45701)

Avenevoli, S., Sessa, F. M., & Steinberg, L. (1999). Family structure, parenting practices, and adolescent adjustment: An ecological examination. In. E. M. Hetherington (Ed.), *Coping with divorce, single parenting, and remarriage: A risk and resiliency perspective* (pp. 65–90). Mahwah, NJ: Erlbaum.

Bramlett, M. D., & Mosher, W. D. (2002). Cohabitation, marriage, divorce, and remarriage in the United States. *Vital Health Statistics, 23*(22). Washington, DC: National Center for Health Statistics.

Carlson, C. (1995). Best practices in working with single-parent and stepfamily systems. In A. Thomas & J. Grimes (Eds.). *Best practices in school psychology — III.* (pp. 1097–1110). Washington, DC: National Association of School Psychologists.

Chase-Lansdale, P. L., Cherlin, A. J., & Kiernan, K. E. (1995). The long-term effects of parental divorce on the mental health of young adults: A developmental perspective. *Child Development,* 66, 1614–1634.

Cherlin, A. J., Chase-Lansdale, P. L., & McRae, C. (1998). Effects of parental divorce on mental health throughout the life course. *American Sociological Review,* 63, 239–249.

Corey, M. S., & Corey, G. (1992). *Groups: Process and practice* (4th ed.). Pacific Grove, CA: Brooks/Cole.

Dawson-McClure, S. R., Sandler, I. N., Wolchik, S. A., & Millsap, R. E. (2004). Risk as a moderator of the effects of prevention programs for children from divorced families: A six-year longitudinal study. *Journal of Abnormal Child Psychology, 32,* 175–190.

Domitrovich, C. E., & Greenberg, M. T. (2000). The study of implementation: Current findings from effective programs that prevent mental disorders in school-aged children. *Journal of Educational and Psychological Consultation, 11,* 193–221.

Ellis, E. M. (2000). *Divorce wars: Interventions with families in conflict.* Washington, DC: American Psychological Association.

Emery, R. E. (1999). *Marriage, divorce, and children's adjustment* (2nd ed.). Thousand Oaks, CA: Sage.

Everett, C., & Everett, S. V. (1994). *Healthy divorce.* San Francisco: Jossey-Bass.

Forgatch, M. S., & DeGarmo, D. S. (1999). Parenting through change: An effective prevention program for single mothers. *Journal of Consulting and Clinical Psychology, 67,* 711–724.

Furstenberg, F. F., & Cherlin, A. J. (1991). *Divided families: What happens to children when parents part.* Cambridge, MA: Harvard University Press.

Furstenberg, F. F., Peterson, J., Nord, C., & Zill, N. (1983). The life course of children of divorce: Marital disruption and parental contact. *American Sociological Review, 48,* 656–668.

Grych, J. H., & Fincham, F. D. (1999). Children of single parents and divorce. In W. K. Silverman & T. H. Ollendick (Eds.). *Developmental issues in the clinical treatment of children* (pp. 321–341). Needham Heights, MA: Allyn & Bacon.

Hetherington, E. M., Bridges, M., & Insabella, G. M. (1998). What matters? What does not? Five perspectives on the association between marital transitions and children's adjustment. *American Psychologist, 53,* 167–184.

Hoagwood, K., & Erwin, H. D. (1997). Effectiveness of school-based mental health services for children: A 10-year research review. *Journal of Child and Family Studies, 6,* 435–451.

Kazdin, A. E. (2000). *Psychotherapy for children and adolescents: Directions for research and practice.* New York: Oxford University Press.

Kramer, L., & Washo, C. A. (1993). Evaluation of a court-mandated prevention program for divorcing parents: The Child First Program. *Family Relations, 42,* 179–186.

Kurdek, L. A. (1986). Children's reasoning about parental divorce. In R. D. Ashmore & D. M. Brodzinsky (Eds.), *Thinking about the family: Views of parents and children* (pp. 233–276). Hillsdale, NJ: Erlbaum.

Lindblad-Goldberg, M. (1989). Successful minority single-parent families. In L. Combrinck-Graham (Ed.), *Children in family contexts: Perspectives on treatment* (pp. 116–134). New York: Guilford.

Maccoby, E. E., & Mnookin, R. H. (1992) *Dividing the child: Social and legal dilemmas of custody.* Cambridge, MA: Harvard University Press.

Martinez, C. R., & Forgatch, M. S. (2001). Preventing problems with boys' noncompliance: Effects of a parent training intervention for divorcing mothers. *Journal of Consulting and Clinical Psychology, 69*, 416–428.

Minor's Consent to Mental Health Treatment Act, Pennsylvania Act 147 of 2004.

Nathan, P. E., & Gorman, J. M. (1998). *A guide to treatments that work.* London: Oxford University Press.

National Center for Health Statistics. (2005). Births, marriages, divorces and deaths: Provisional data for 2004. *National Vital Statistics Reports, 53*(21). Hyattsville, MD: Author.

Nord, C. W. & West, J. (2001). *Fathers' and mothers' involvement in their children's schools by family type and resident status.* (NCES Publication No. 01-032). Washington, DC: U.S. Department of Education, National Center for Education Statistics, Office of Educational Research and Improvement.

Nord, C. W., Brimhall, D., & West, J. (1997). *Fathers' involvement in their children's schools.* (NCES Publication No. 98-091). Washington, DC: U.S. Department of Education, National Center for Education Statistics, Office of Educational Research and Improvement.

Orbuch, T. L., Veroff, J., & Hunter, A. G. (1999). Black couples, White couples: The early years of marriage. In E. M. Hetherington (Ed.), *Coping with divorce, single-parenting, and remarriage: A risk and resiliency perspective* (pp. 23–43). Mahwah, NJ: Erlbaum.

Pedro-Carroll, J. L. (1994). *Children of Divorce Intervention Program Procedures Manual: Support groups with 4th–6th grade children* (2nd ed.). Rochester, NY: Primary Mental Health Project.

Pedro-Carroll, J. L., & Alpert-Gillis, L. (1997a). *Children of Divorce Intervention Program: A procedures manual for conducting support groups—Kindergarten and first grade children* (3rd ed.). Rochester, NY: Children's Institute.

Pedro-Carroll, J. L., & Alpert-Gillis, L. J. (1997b). Preventive interventions for children of divorce: A developmental model for 5 and 6 year old children. *The Journal of Primary Prevention, 18*, 5–23.

Pedro-Carroll, J. L., Alpert-Gillis, L. J., & Cowen, E. L. (1992). An evaluation of the efficacy of a preventive intervention for 4th–6th grade urban children of divorce. *Journal of Primary Prevention, 13*, 115–130.

Pedro-Carroll, J. L., Alpert-Gillis, L., & Sterling, S. (1997). *Children of Divorce Intervention Program: A procedures manual for conducting support groups — Second and third grade children* (3rd ed.). Rochester, NY: Children's Institute.

Pedro-Carroll, J. L., & Cowen, E. L. (1985). The Children of Divorce Intervention Program: An investigation of the efficacy of a school-based prevention program. *Journal of Consulting and Clinical Psychology, 53*, 603–610.

Pedro-Carroll, J. L., Cowen, E. L., Hightower, A. D., & Guare, J. C. (1986). Preventive intervention with latency-aged children of divorce: A replication study. *American Journal of Community Psychology, 14*, 277–289.

Pedro-Carroll, J. L., Sutton, S. E., & Black, A. E. (1999). *Children of Divorce Intervention Program: A procedures manual for conducting support groups with seventh and eighth grade students.* Rochester, NY: Primary Mental Health Project.

Shifflett, K., & Cummings, M. E. (1999). A program for educating parents about the effects of divorce and conflict on children: An initial evaluation. *Family Relations, 48*, 79–89.

Stevenson, M. R., & Black, K. N. (1995). *How divorce affects offspring: A research approach.* Dubuque, IO: Brown & Benchmark.

Stolberg, A. L., & Garrison, K. M. (1985). Evaluating a primary prevention program for children of divorce: The Divorce Adjustment Project. *American Journal of Community Psychology, 13*, 111–124.

Stolberg, A. L., & Mahler, J. (1994). Enhancing treatment gains in a school-based intervention for children of divorce through skill training, parent involvement, and transfer procedures. *Journal of Clinical and Consulting Psychology, 62*, 147–156.

Task Force on Promotion and Dissemination of Psychological Procedures. (1995). Training in and dissemination of empirically validated psychological treatments: Report and recommendations. *The Clinical Psychologist, 48*, 3–23.

Trzcinski, E., & Genheimer, E. (Eds.). (2000). *Children and divorce: A Michigan family impact seminars briefing report.* Michigan State University & Wayne State University. Retrieved October, 10, 2005 from http://icyf-ftpwebsvr.icyf.msu.edu/icyf/briefng2.html.

United Nations (2000). *Demographic yearbook: 2000*. Retrieved on September 16, 2005 from http://unstats. un.org/unsd/demographic/products/dyb/dyb2000/Table25.pdf.

U.S. Census Bureau. (1992). *Marriage, divorce, and remarriage in the 1990's*. (Current Population Reports, P23-180). Washington, DC: Author.

U.S. Census Bureau. (2000). *Population profile of the United States: 2000 — Chapter 6: From birth to seventeen: The living arrangements of children: 2000* (pp. 6.1–6.5; Internet release) Retrieved September 16, 2005 from: http://www.census.gov/population/pop-profile/2000/chap06.pdf

U.S. Census Bureau. (2001). *Living together, living alone: Families and living arrangements, 2000* (Current Population Reports P20-537). Washington, DC: Author.

U.S. Census Bureau. (2003). *Children's living arrangements and characteristics: March 2002*. (Current Population Reports, P20-547). Washington, DC: Author.

U.S. Census Bureau. (2005). *Number, timing, and duration of marriages and divorces: 2001*. (Current Population Reports, P70-97). Washington, DC: Author.

U.S. Department of Health and Human Services. (1995). Advance report of final divorce statistics, 1989 and 1990. *Monthly Vital Statistics Report, 43* (9S). Washington, DC: Author.

U.S. Department of Health and Human Services (2005). *SAMSHA model programs*. Retrieved from http://modelprograms.samhsa.gov/.

Wallerstein, J. S. (1983). Children of divorce: The psychological tasks of the child. *American Journal of Orthopsychiatry, 53*, 230–242.

Wolchik, S. A., West, S. G., Sandler, I. N., Tien, J., Coatsworth, D., Lengua, L., et al. (2000). An experimental evaluation of theory-based mother and mother-child programs for children of divorce. *Journal of Consulting and Clinical Psychology, 68*, 843–856.

Wolchik, S. A., Sandler, I. N., Millsap, R. E., Plummer, B. A., Greene, S. M., Anderson, E. R., et al. (2002). Six-year follow-up of preventive interventions for children of divorce: A randomized controlled trial. *Journal of the American Medical Association, 288*, 1874–1881.

Wolchik, S. A., Sandler, I. N., Winslow, E., & Smith-Daniels, V. (2005). Programs for promoting parenting by residential parents: Moving from efficacy to effectiveness. *Family Court Review, 43*, 65–80.

Wolchik, S. A., West, S. G., Westover, S., Sandler, I. N., Martin, A., Lustig, J., et al. (1993). The children of divorce parenting intervention: Outcome evaluation of an empirically based program. *American Journal of Community Psychology, 21*, 293–331.

Chapter Fourteen

A Cognitive-Behavioral Group Approach to Grief and Loss

Jessica L. Stewart & Laura M. Sharp

Death and the dying process is a very real stressor in the lives of many children and adolescents. Researchers estimate that as many as 90% of high school students have personally experienced the death of someone who they cared about, such as the loss of a family member, friend, or pet (Ewalt & Perkins, 1979; Harrison & Harrington, 2001). By the time a child reaches the age of 18 years, research suggests that he or she will witness thousand of deaths (Kroen, 1996). These deaths may range from the impersonal deaths in books, on cartoons, in news media, and in movies to the personal deaths of pets, family members, and friends. Trying to protect children from death is a futile effort. The most frequent experiences of death are the deaths of parents and grandparents followed by deaths of siblings and friends. Deaths of adolescent friends are most likely to arise from unexpected deaths due to car accidents, homicide, and suicide (Corr, Nabe, & Corr, 1994). In 2002 alone, for example, 2,443,387 people died (National Center for Health Statistics, 2005). Those people were mothers, fathers, grandparents, aunts, uncles, siblings, teachers, pastors, and little league coaches.

In most cases, the death of an individual will affect one child, and in some cases, it may affect several children. Explaining death and dying to a child, as well as the grief process, is not an easy task for many parents, as they often face questions such as "what facts to give to tell the child?" and "what can we do to help him cope?" Further complicating this is the reality that the child's loved one was in all likelihood also their own loved one, thus leaving the parent to not only attempt to aid the child in grieving but also to grieve for his or her own loss.

Because of these and other factors, children often have a difficult time navigating through grief and adults have an equally difficult time aiding in the process. Although there is no single formula for guiding children and adolescents through grief (Kroen, 1996), group therapy, particularly the cognitive-behavioral group therapy (CBGT) as will be discussed in this chapter, may facilitate the grieving process by strengthening emotional expression and coping and the process of acceptance and adaptation that is bereavement. For the sake of differentiating some key terms used throughout this chapter, we offer the following definitions given by Worden (1996). Grief refers to "the child's personal expression, thoughts, and feelings associated with death" (p. 11). The process of mourning is that which children go through on their way to adapting to their loss, which is known as bereavement.

Following the death of a loved one, most people tend to show symptoms of clinical depression for about 2 months, but otherwise the "majority of the population appears to cope effectively with bereavement-related distress and most people do not experience problematic grief" (Center for the Advancement of Health [CFAH], 2003, p. 10]. Sad and withdrawn behavior that lasts longer than two months and interferes with a person's functioning, however, may indicate the onset of clinical depression in addition to normal grieving (Christ, Siegel, & Christ, 2002). The bereavement process has been shown to be associated with clinical depression, anxiety, physiological changes, and social functioning (Hogan, Greenfield, & Schmidt, 2001). As described by Kubler-Ross (1993), grief is a process comprised of distinct stages that mourners pass through, though not necessarily in the same order, with the same degree of intensity, or for the same duration. Denial, anger, bargaining, depression, and acceptance are steps along the bereavement process, and children and adolescents may need help to navigate them effectively, given the cognitive, emotional, and behavioral experiences in each stage. These stages will be discussed in more detail in the cognitive conceptualization section of this chapter.

The presentation of symptoms in children and adolescents related to these stages may vary and not resemble what is assumed based on the manifestation of the same emotional or behavioral reactions in adults. For example, sadness and depression in children may manifest as irritability or a low frustration tolerance. Each individual may progress through stages differently, but no individual is exempt from the grieving process when faced with the death of a loved one. If this process is not sufficiently managed it may interfere with natural emotional maturation and security, in that these children may not be adequately able to cope with future loss, issues of mortality (including their own), or attachment and relationships with loved ones. In addition, for example, young people who have suffered the death of a parent are more likely to display dependant personality traits, introversion, delinquency in adolescence, suicidal ideation, and preoccupation with loss (Masterman & Reams, 1988).

The grief of children and adolescents follows a life-long developmental trajectory. The loss may be felt throughout the individual's lifespan, especially at life milestones such as graduation from high school or college, beginning a job, getting married, becoming a parent, and growing older than the loved one who has died (Worden, 1996; Silverman, 2000). Therefore, working towards "closure" may not be a helpful or realistic goal for group therapy. Accepting the loss, adjusting to the life changes it brings, and becoming more comfortable with the death at this point in the individual's life are more appropriate goals and ones that can be accomplished through CBGT. Hogan and her colleagues suggest the importance of considering the role of personal growth (that includes the positive ways in which the mourner is transformed) associated with the bereavement process, that has been studied and found to be a measurable construct in adolescents (Hogan & DeSantis, 1996a; Hogan et al., 2001; Neimeyer & Hogan, 2001).

Not all children require therapeutic intervention to successfully navigate bereavement and the grief process. In fact, given that most people (children, adolescents, and adults alike) manage the bereavement process effectively, grief counseling may not be indicated or helpful for all mourners and, in fact, may have negative consequences (CFAH, 2003). Formal psychological interventions are likely more beneficial for those experiencing what is known as complicated grief (also referred to in the literature as traumatic or pathological grief), though debate exists within the literature regarding this term as a distinct clinical concept (CFAH, 2003). Moreover, the concept of complicated or traumatic grief is not well-defined in the literature. Grief reactions to this degree may significantly impact both psychological and emotional well-being and physical health beyond what is considered "normal" grief.

GRIEF, LOSS, AND TRAUMA

In discussing treatment aimed at addressing child and adolescent grief and loss related to death, it is important to make a distinction between intervention that emphasizes traditional grief reactions (emotional, psychological, physiological, academic, and social) and that which is compounded by factors other than the loss of the person being mourned. In addition to the loss of a loved one to death, traditional grief responses may be experienced when individuals suffer other kinds of losses (e.g., the loss of one's home and possessions to fire, a child's loss of a sense of normalcy or security during divorce, loss of a sense of belonging and friendship when a family relocates, and the like). For further information on coping with divorce, see chapter 13.

An especially important clinical distinction should be addressed related to the experiences of grief and trauma. There are commonalities between the traditional grief response and the reaction to loss following a traumatic incident. Although the stages and process of grieving are typically consistent across situations of loss, the experience of loss because of a traumatic situation often includes a physiological response. When a child experiences the death of a loved one due to a traumatic situation (i.e., a natural disaster, war, or violent crime), the loss is coupled with fear, danger, and sensory-based memories of a threatening situation that produce intense physiological and emotional responses. These emotional and physiological responses associated with the traumatic loss may continue to occur over time until the situation is processed and resolved. This makes for a different clinical presentation and unique therapeutic considerations from those emphasized in traditional grief treatment presented in this chapter. A review of treatment for post-trauma situations is presented in chapter 12.

ASSESSMENT AND GROUP MEMBER IDENTIFICATION AND CONSIDERATIONS

While many children have support and resources in place to facilitate adequate coping and healing, many may not. Thus, group interventions may be necessary. While children referred to group intervention for grief may have experienced similar situations or losses, it is imperative that assessment for group identification be conducted. This should be done by acquiring information known to those making referrals, such as school counselors or psychologists, primary care physicians, clergy, social workers, parents, teachers, coaches, and such. For children who, for example, have pre-existing emotional difficulties, limited family resources, and lose a parent due to death, teachers may be able to recognize when the loss is reported that this is a child who will likely benefit from additional intervention (group involvement) to receive assistance with the grief process that would normally be assumed to come from family involvement and support.

The individual differences in coping and reaction from child to child may relate to the individual's view of self and world, their age when exposed to the death, the nature of the relationship with the loved one who is dying or has died, that person's role in the family, the circumstances of the death (e.g., sudden, the result of a chronic situation, via violent means), the degree of involvement in the procedure or rituals surrounding the passing and burial, and the support and resources available to them to assist in navigating the grief process (Tedeschi, 1996). In addition, the process of bereavement is influenced by past experiences with death, ideas in general about death, developmental understanding of death (Kroen, 1996; Worden, 1996), and how much the death impacts other aspects of life (i.e., change in socioeconomic status, relocation, additional psychological difficulty if the death was the result of a traumatic situation, the grieving process of those around the child, and so forth).

In addition, the child's gender may be a factor in how their symptoms present (i.e., based on societal norms that influence the expression of sadness in boys and girls and their tendency to seek help and support from others). Similarly, cultural and racial differences in emotional expression and the utilization of social support are factors to consider when assessing a child's emotional or behavioral presentation and needs. Each child may present with a different manifestation of grief reactions (e.g., more angry than sad, more anxious or fearful for the safety of other loved ones, insecurity about one's own mortality, a more overt behavioral coping style). All potential contributing factors to the presentation of any child or adolescent being considered for group involvement must be assessed via clinical interview and history gathering prior to his or her inclusion, and considered within the conceptualization of that individual's needs and the make up of the larger group.

Assessment Considerations

Assessment begins with an assurance that the child's level of distress is significant enough to warrant the application of psychological intervention and the inclusion in group therapy. Each group member should be individually interviewed by the facilitator(s) so that rapport may begin to develop and the process and goals of group can be presented. Issues such as confidentiality, how to express that he or she does not wish to participate at a particular time, and responding to the emotions of others may all need to be explored prior to admission to group. It is also important for the group leader to assess the individual's readiness for the group. Individuals who are experiencing extremely intense grief symptoms or are not able to be empathetic toward the losses of others may benefit from individual counseling sessions before or instead of attending a support group.

In addition to clinical interview, appropriate assessment using standardized measures whenever possible will more accurately identify the issues bringing each child to group. There are few measures developed specifically for assessing the severity of grief reactions in children and adolescents, as most are designed with adults, adult patients, and caregivers in mind. Some that may be helpful depending on the ages of members and circumstances of their grief include: the *Hogan Sibling Inventory of Bereavement* (Hogan, 1988), the *Hogan Inventory of Bereavement* (Hogan & DeSantis, 1996b), and several scales developed by Jimerson and colleagues associated with the

Grief Support Curriculum (Lehmann, Jimerson, & Gaasch, 2001), including the *Jimerson Facilitator Rating of Child's Adjustment* (FRA), *Jimerson Caregiver Rating of Child's Adjustment* (CRA), and *Jimerson Youth Common Grief Reactions Checklist* in caregiver report (JYCGC-CR) and self-report (JYCGRC-SR) forms. As existing grief measures validated for use with the adult population are questionable in terms of validity to measure a concept that is still not well-defined empirically (Hogan, et al., 2001), caution must be taken when incorporating these measures into the assessment of children. Administration and wording of items will likely need to be modified. Information obtained may still be useful in conceptualizing the cognitive, emotional, physiological, social, and behavioral experiences of youth being considered for group, even if scores need to be interpreted cautiously or are invalid. Measures that may provide beneficial information include the *Hogan Grief Reaction Checklist* (HGRC; Hogan, et al., 2001), the *Texas Revised Inventory of Grief* (Faschingbauer, Zisook, & DeVaul, 1987), the *Inventory of Traumatic Grief* (Prigerson, Maciejewski, Reynolds, Bierhals, Newsom, Fasiczka, et al., 1995; Prigerson & Jacobs, 2001; Boelen, Den Bout, DeKeijser, & Hoijtink, 2003), and the *Pathological Grief Questionnaire* (Prigerson, Frank, Kasl, Reynolds, Anderson, Zubenko, et al., 1995).

Though not specifically developed to measure grief reactions, tools assessing symptoms of depression, anxiety, anger, hopelessness, and behavioral disturbance may indicate the emotional and behavioral impact of the loss on the child considered for group, and indicate if additional, more immediate and direct services are warranted for a particular child or adolescent experiencing significant emotional distress and impairment in functioning. Examples of such measures include: the *Children's Depression Inventory* (Kovacs, 1985), the *Child Behavior Checklist* (Achenbach & Edelbrock, 1983), the child version of the *Anxiety Disorders Interview Schedule for DSM-IV* (Silverman & Albano, 1996), the *Revised Children's Manifest Anxiety Scale* (Reynolds & Richmond, 1985), the *Multidimensional Anxiety Scale for Children* (March, Parker, Sullivan, Stallings, & Connors,,1997), the *Behavior Assessment System for Children—Second Edition* (BASC-2, Reynolds & Kamphaus, 2002), and the *Beck Youth Inventories—Second Edition* (BYI-II, Beck, Beck, & Jolly, 2005).

When considering members for group participation, it is important to examine the developmental level of the child (CFAH, 2003), not simply his or her age. While typically groups could be outlined by specific age ranges (i.e., young children, school-aged children, pre-adolescents, and adolescents), children whose developmental level and understanding of death may be below that of peers their chronological age may benefit more from inclusion in a group with developmentally similar children. A basic understanding of death involves five concepts (Brent & Speece, 1993; Corr, 1995)—universality (i.e., all people die), irreversibility (i.e., once truly dead, the physical body can never be brought back to life), nonfunctionality (i.e., the living body ceases to engage in life's activities and functions), causality (i.e., what truly brings about death), and noncorporeal continuation (i.e., existing in some form after the death of the physical body). The cognitive and developmental levels of children and adolescents influence their ability to understand these concepts. Young people typically do not have the benefit of a large repertoire of experiences to provide a context for thinking about and understanding death, and are vulnerable to confusion and maladaptive emotional and behavioral responding, especially young children.

Developmental Aspects of Grief

When discussing death with children (ages 6–10), it is important to be as age-appropriately direct as possible. Children's confusion about death can increase their fears and anxieties surrounding the death (Kroen, 1996). Most children at this stage understand that death is permanent, though some young children may misunderstand death as a temporary state of sleeping or suspension where the person continues to exist and will awaken at some time and return to a full life (Kroen, 1996). Thus, it is important to use direct language (e.g., death, died, etc.) and avoid vague terms such as "passed away" or "went to heaven." We recall one situation in which a parent told a young child that his aunt "went to heaven." Upon visiting his grandmother's house several weeks later, he noticed his aunt's coat hanging on the coat rack, and excitedly ran through the house stating, "Aunt Beth is back from heaven, 'cause she never goes away without her coat." Some common responses that children may have at this age include anger, denial, idealization, guilt, and fear (Kroen, 1996).

Preadolescents (ages 10–12) understand that death is permanent. They can also appreciate concepts such as the significance of rituals, what causes death, and the impact that the death will have on them and their families (Kroen, 1996). Children of this age may deny their feelings about the death or deny that the death will have an impact on their lives. When preadolescents deny their feelings, they may act out in ways that often include anger or violence.

Adolescents (ages 13–18) possess an understanding of death that is comparable to that of adults. Because of their characteristic egocentrism and tendency to perceive themselves with immortality, when faced with death it is often more difficult for them to accept death than it is for adults (Kroen, 1996). Their emotions may vary widely and change quickly. Some may become depressed and withdraw from family and friends, discontinue engaging in the activities they used to enjoy, spend a great deal of time alone, or evidence changes in sleep or eating patterns.

CBGT may be employed to facilitate the resolution of significant difficulties in emotional, psychological, social, or academic functioning that may be related to grief due to a recent loss as well as to unresolved grief that may not be recent. The nature and focus of the group for each presentation will primarily be the same, but it will be important to emphasize for the latter the ways in which this lack of resolution inhibits successful moving-on and functioning, so that their loss and their reaction to it (at the time and its impact presently) will become a priority for the child or adolescent to begin addressing directly. Young people receiving therapeutic intervention shortly after suffering their loss will be already more focused on their grief process given that their loss is more of a current, immediate stressor obviously impacting them in the present.

Family Support

It is important to note that treatment will be most effective when caregiver involvement is also emphasized. Family members are an important part of the bereavement process for children and adolescents and may assist best in that process when they are given information related to natural symptoms and behaviors following loss, ways to help children grieve at different developmental stages, how to best care for themselves, how to speak to children about death, warning signs of more severe responses such as depression, and the importance of maintaining typical routines and limits they set for their children. Maximizing the informed support available to young people will facilitate greater success in group therapy outcome.

COGNITIVE-BEHAVIORAL CONCEPTUALIZATION

The cognitive-behavioral model postulates that one's reactions to a stressful event are largely the result of one's perception of that event, its impact on the individual, and one's ability to cope with it. Although observable grief responses vary greatly, those typically observed in children and adolescents include sadness, anxiety, grief, and anger/acting out (Worden, 1996). Specifically, these emotions, while considered "normal" for a limited duration, when excessive can be viewed from the cognitive-behavioral perspective as the result of misinterpretations of the reality of the loss, one's ability to effectively cope with the loss, and one's perception of the consequences of the loss and its impact on all aspects of life.

Specifically, in Worden's (1996) report of his two-year study conducted to provide a clearer picture of whether or not children experience seriously disturbed emotion and behavior following the death of a parent, he included cognitions identified as relating to these four responses. Sadness tended to relate to the loss of shared activities and experiences with the deceased parents, while anxiety was related to a fear of losing another loved one, as well as fear about their own safety and the changes to their lives. Guilt was related to regret for things not done with the parents, affection not expressed, or apologies not given, while anger and acting out behavior was related to feelings of abandonment toward God for taking the parents away, toward a parent for leaving, and toward the surviving parent (e.g., if he or she started dating (Worden, 1996). Children who were more aggressive were also more fearful for the safety of the surviving parent, less able to speak about the dead parent, and exhibited a lower sense of self-efficacy. These findings support a cognitive-behavioral conceptualization of grief reactions, in that the children observed to experience these distressing emotions also tended to have irrational beliefs or fears that accompanied the emotions, such as those related to losing other loved ones, irrational beliefs about their role in the parent's death, and distorted thoughts about the nature of death in terms of it being a purposeful abandonment or the result of an unfair God.

In terms of the widely accepted phases of grief proposed by Kubler-Ross (1993), the cognitive components dictating the quality of experience at each stage and the progression through the stages is evident in the description of the phases: denial, anger, bargaining, depression, and acceptance. Children who are in the denial stage are likely unable to view the death as permanent, real, or the result of the actual circumstances causing it, and therefore, they are unable to exhibit behavioral and emotional responses consistent with reality, causing greater distress. Examples of cognitive distortions associated with this stage may include, "Grandma's not dead, she's just gone away," or "It's my fault dad died, it wasn't an accident it was because I was so mean to him." The anger experienced is likely the result, as mentioned above, of a lack of acceptance of reality and the maintenance of beliefs such as, "Dad *should* still be alive," "It's not fair (right) that mommy's gone," "Everyone I love dies," or "I don't deserve this pain."

Children and adolescents in the bargaining stage are likely still making faulty assumptions related to the degree that they have any influence over this situation being real—that the loved one's death is somehow within their control (e.g., "I promise to be a good girl if grandpa comes back"). Dysfunctional beliefs related to the depression experienced in the fourth stage of Kubler-Ross's model may relate to beliefs such as, "I can't be okay without mom," or "I'll never feel normal again." Finally, acceptance is marked by more realistic thinking about the loss of the loved one and what that means for the grieving child. This may include thoughts such as, "Even though I will always miss him, I know I will be okay," "We can get through this time together as a family," or "Although I know she won't be there, I know mom will be watching me at graduation next spring."

Facilitating the progression through these stages is the aim of cognitive-behavioral therapeutic intervention—that is, to assist children in identifying their beliefs, thoughts, and feelings related to the loss (even if they are not aware of the distorted nature of them) so that their responses become progressively more realistic in nature and, ultimately, more adaptive and healthier. The tasks associated with the bereavement process, as outlined by Worden (1996), relate, essentially, to acceptance. This includes acceptance of one's emotional experiences (e.g., it is okay to be sad, angry), the reality that the loved one is not coming back (e.g., to move on and adjust to life without the parent is not a betrayal of the parent), and that one can and will move forward. This acceptance can be facilitated by the reality-oriented, present-focused, solution-focused, approach of CBT, in that examining ones' current situation with a realistic perspective, based on facts and not on "what-ifs" or fears, is the nature of cognitive-behavioral intervention. Even if, due to developmental limitations, this process is indirectly accomplished, it is still the group facilitator's aim to identify the distorted thoughts of each member that are resulting in maladaptive grief, and seek to bring these distortions to light for modification in the direction of more realistic interpretation. This can be done through a variety of strategies and specific cognitive and behavioral interventions, appropriately considered given the child's developmental level.

In times of stress, young children may exhibit apparent developmental regression, displaying behaviors or emotional reactions typically seen in earlier stages of development (e.g., angry and aggressive outbursts, withdrawal, wanting to sleep with parents, refusal to do chores or schoolwork, a reoccurrence of bedwetting, disturbances in sleep and appetite, increased crying and clinginess). They may engage in a more magical view of the world, including the perception that their actions (e.g., stating "I hate you" or "I wish you were dead!" to a loved one, disobeying rules) caused the loved one's death. Many children will cognitively understand that the death is not their fault, though they may need support in dispelling these irrational beliefs and feelings of guilt. Adolescents, on the other hand, understand the nature of death; however, they are also typically more egocentric in their perspective and may be susceptible to distortions regarding how unique their experience is, that they are alone in their grief, and that no one can help them to cope or mourn because no one else can understand. Compared to their peers who had not experienced the death of a parent, bereaved adolescents expressed more anxiety and fear over time and believed that their schoolwork and behavior were inferior to their peers (Worden 1996). To avoid thinking about death, an adolescent might engage in risky behaviors (Noppe & Noppe, 1996), or engage in deep thinking and exploration of death. It is this exploration that, if guided through cognitive-behavioral intervention, may lead to the identification of distorted thought processes and the subsequent restructuring of them to be more realistic in nature through specific techniques in group.

COGNITIVE-BEHAVIORAL GROUP THERAPY

The emphasis within CBGT will be on members' identification, expression, and exploration of emotions and behaviors related to their grief so that facilitators may become aware of the beliefs and thoughts that underlie these responses. It is typically easier for members to discuss their feelings openly, as many members have not been familiarized with the thought-feeling-behavior connection and may be less skilled at identifying automatic thoughts and their related underlying schema. Facilitators, based on the emotions expressed by the members, should attempt to communicate the nature of participants' thoughts that may be perpetuating ineffective bereavement to the group so that normalization of rational beliefs may be promoted by consensus and distorted thinking can be addressed by members. The method for communicating these underlying thoughts to the group members will depend on the developmental level of the group (such as through open discussion with older members or within behavioral activities, for example, for younger children). The application of these principles with adolescents may not be as confusing, though with young children it is more difficult to conceptualize. Take, for example, a group of early school-aged children exhibiting significant anxiety, irritability, and angry outbursts following the loss of loved one. They are asked to collectively contribute to a story about the death of a parent. Each child is asked to describe why the son in the story would be crying and yelling at his family members. The facilitator will listen to the explanations given and begin to formulate a conceptualization as to the beliefs and fears that the group members may be experiencing. He or she will then, in the context of the story, encourage open discussion of those reasons with the members to encourage them to explore whether or not the "son's" worries are true and reactions are common. Even though the group members are too young to discuss distorted versus realistic beliefs overtly, they are capable of discussing how people feel and why, if most people would feel similarly, how the death may affect others, and what can be done to help others to cope with the death and the aftermath of the loss.

The CBT model traditionally affords therapists a variety of cognitive and behavioral techniques. The selection and application of these techniques will be guided by the conceptualization, the dynamics of the group, and developmental level of group participants. Regardless of the nature of the techniques selected for use (behavioral or cognitive), the facilitators continually conceptualize the needs of the situation based on the cognitive distortions at work. Addressing those distortions may take a primarily behavioral or cognitive approach, depending on the age of the members (with younger members most likely benefiting from behavioral interventions, and older members a combination of both behavioral and cognitive techniques; Christner, Allen, & Maus, 2004). The empathetic peer environment affords members the opportunity for normalizing of grief responses and modeling of effective coping and other skills.

The importance of CBGT facilitating the progression through the stages of bereavement rests on the ability of facilitators to restructure the dysfunctional or distorted beliefs of the group members through discussion or behavioral activities. Let us now consider a specific outline for conducting CBGT with grieving children, modeled loosely after a group outline presented by Masterman and Reams (1988) that appears to be standard for most bereavement groups in the literature, though none have received empirical support for efficacy. We offer this model based on traditional components of bereavement group as applied through a CBT framework. The length of group and the activities outlined will be dictated by the age of the children and, potentially, by setting limitations. Table 14.1 offers a specific outline of sessions for CBGT work

Session Outline

In many cases, these groups will consist of approximately eight sessions, each lasting about 45 to 60 minutes (depending on age of members). Sessions will begin with a brief review (about 10 minutes) of the week between sessions to reorient members to the group process that includes equal opportunity of sharing of thoughts and feelings, and to encourage dialogue of a nonthreatening nature. This may be done by reviewing the "best thing" and "worst thing" that has happened for each member in the time between this and their last meeting. Next, homework or between session work is reviewed (10 minutes) to facilitate exploration of thoughts and feelings relevant to the group by offering a concrete topic. It is important that this is reviewed each week, as it helps monitor what members are doing between sessions but also helps to facilitate generalization of the skills taught in group to the members' daily situations. The next 20 to 35 minutes is used to explore the main topic for the session (see Table 14.1) in an age-appropriate way. Then, 5 minutes toward the end of the session consists of a physical activity to facilitate the release of emotional energy brought up by the discussion and to assist in transitioning out of group. This may take the form of something more active, such as stretching or a physical game, or something passive like relaxation exercises. Each session ends with giving feedback to and receiving feedback from the participants. It is important for the facilitator to point out things that went well in the group (e.g., "I know this was a tough session, I'm really impressed with how each of you contributed to our discussion.") Also, it is essential to obtain feedback from the group. This occurs on two levels: (1) by asking each member what he or she is taking from this session this week, and (2) by asking each member what he thought about the group (e.g., things that were helpful and things that were not).

Progression of Weekly Sessions

Session 1 aims to orient members to each other and to group rules and structure. Facilitators offer acceptance of members' apprehension or feelings about being in group, and encourage sharing of thoughts and worries about what group will be like. It is important to provide members with information about the topics to be covered in future groups to help relieve anxiety and to facilitate an understanding of bereavement by mentioning what is important enough to be covered. Members are also oriented to CBT, in that the connection between the way we think about things and the way we then feel and act is presented in an age-appropriate manner. For example, it may be explained to younger children that a snow-day may produce happiness or disappointment: happiness because

Table 14.1 Session Content of CBT Group Therapy ("Healing Hearts") for Grief and Loss

Week	Topic	Tasks	Possible Interventions	Possible Homework
1	Orientation to group process and building of trust between members.	Explanation: of group format, use of home-work, the CBT model, topics to be covered.	Introduction to "best" and "worst" of the week; psychoeducation about grief process.	Draw a picture or write a description of the family with the loved one in it.
2	Brief discussion of the deceased and reaction to loss.	To begin the discussion of the loss; initial expression of emotions related to loss.	Presenting the loved one positively to other members; activities to label emotions.	Bring in photo, poem, statement for in-session ritual.
3	Funeral rituals; thoughts and feelings about funerals (did they participate? etc), death, after-death.	To openly discuss (and identify) thoughts about the nature of death and loss; create in-group service to serve as memorial/ritual.	Make a collective list of possible feelings and thoughts (differentiating them) for normalizing and modeling.	Develop way to memorialize person, ways in which person is still in member's life.
4	Changes in the family or members' life as a result of the death.	Examining ways in which the loss has caused other changes; identifying feelings and thoughts about the death and the other losses as separate.	Making a collective list of feelings and emotions associated with loss, as well as a list of changes. Identify shared experiences and normalize responses.	Make a list of things that are different without the loved one; daily ways the loved one is noticeably absent.
5	Denial of death, issues of desired reunion, and anger or suicidal ideation	To promote the sharing of feelings of denial or anger related to unrealistic wishes for the deceased's return; acceptance of the loved one's absence.	The "journey jar," exploration of wishes related to the deceased parent's return.	Drawing or writing of the family in the present, without the loved one.
6	Concerns for future and moving forward	To discuss beliefs and feelings related to future deaths (including child's own), parent's remarriage, continuing of family, betrayal of loved one.	Discussion of family traditions and holidays, and changes to them.	Make a list with family of events and traditions coming up, with new roles and responsibilities
7	Preparation for termination; changes since starting group	Identification of beliefs related to progress made and readiness to cope on own; identification of gains; identification of other available support.	Comparing of feelings at the start of group with now, pictures to represent their changes.	Drawing or writing of the family in the future, without the loved one.
8	Termination; evaluation of the group; closure.	Members share what they liked and didn't like about group; say goodbye to other members; acknowledgement of courage to participate.	Write a collective story about group, members, and their courage to face loss. Compile "coping list" for members in future.	To continue using strategies learned to cope, and accessing support as needed.

the student gets to go sledding with mom instead of going to school, or disappointment if it is the student's birthday and they will now miss their party in class. Also, the "best thing" and "worst thing" exercise mentioned above is introduced and modeled by facilitators. A list of coping strategies is begun in the first session and added to each week for use by members following group termination. The assignment of homework is described and begun.

Session 2 is comprised of members describing the deceased loved one, the circumstances of the death, how long ago it was, and other factual information. This can be done by having the members develop a memory book about the deceased person. While this can be done in session, this can also be a useful and engaging between-session strategy. Facilitators begin to encourage disclosure of the members' emotional reactions since the time of the death to model that emotional reactions of differing degrees are normal. All responses, no matter how limited in detail, are accepted to promote sharing, as members are comfortable. Facilitators may need to initiate the discussion with experiences of their own to model how to express certain facts and emotions.

Session 3 involves the discussion of funeral service and rituals, members' participation in those rituals (either in planning or attendance), their thoughts and feelings about them, and fears or misunderstandings about death, burial, or "what happens next." An in-session ritual is conducted to allow for members to individually express losses and symbolically work toward "goodbye," especially if they did not have the opportunity to participate in family services. As the homework was to bring in something for the in-session memorial exercise, members may post pictures of the deceased in the room, participate in a favorite hobby they enjoyed with the deceased, bring in a favorite food of the deceased, and so forth. Members can share their experiences with various post-death practices as a way to discuss cultural and familial differences and emphasize that there is no one way for mourners to say goodbye. Facilitators can more directly assess members' automatic thoughts about death and what impact that has on each individual. The emphasis is not on answering the question of what happens after death, but to identify and validate the group members' beliefs or concerns for the purpose of working toward acceptance that the loved one is no longer alive.

Session 4 focuses on changes to the family since the death (e.g., changes in living arrangements, in parents or other family members, in routines, in responsibilities, and the like.). The goal is to begin to identify how the loss affects members in multiple ways, in addition to the loss of the person itself. Identifying feelings associated with the changes will allow members to begin to learn to separate what emotions connect to which thoughts (e.g., "So, you are really sad that your dad died, but you are also angry that your mom isn't spending as much time with you because she's working more."). Members may gain a realistic perspective on their feelings of loss by ranking which changes or issues are the hardest to deal with. The session ends by having the members begin problem solving ways that they can address the changes and express their feelings about the changes to others within the family.

Session 5 consists of discussing issues related to denial about the loved one's death or members' wishes for the parent to come back using the homework acknowledging realistic ways their absence affects members. Thoughts and feelings are validated as common through sharing of what it would be like if the loved one were to return or still be present. Talk about what happens after death, anger for not being able to be with and loved one anymore, and suicidal ideation as common reactions are talked about.

In Session 6, worries about the future and moving forward are discussed, including fear of the child's own death, of the death of other loved ones, of the possible changes in the family (e.g., parent's remarriage or the possibility of a stepfamily, moving in with grandparents), and of forgetting the loved one. This issue of betrayal of the deceased (by moving on or accepting the loss) is explored for distorted thoughts, to validate this concern, and to discuss more functional perspectives.

Session 7 prepares members for termination and what that means for the child as another "loss." Members talk openly about why they came to group, what they learned, how they changed, and what group ending means (i.e., loss of support, that they are not "supposed to" hurt anymore). Facilitators can share their own positive and negative feelings to model expression and coping with a pending loss. It is also important to discuss alternative ways in which members may continue to receive support.

In Session 8, members evaluate the group verbally in an open discussion of the good and bad aspects of group. Continued contact and support between members is encouraged. It may be appropriate to have a small ceremony to "celebrate" their courage to talk about their feelings and accept and adjust to losing their loved one.

Overcoming Potential Obstacles

As the grief experience of children and adolescents is as unique as the factors that contribute to it, so may be the needs of the individual members that comprise a group for therapy. While ultimately the goal is to identify and modify members' belief systems and resulting emotional and behavioral responses toward acceptance of the loss, individual member factors may negatively impact the overall direction of the group. For example, members who struggle with pre-existing emotional disturbance prior to the loss (e.g., the presence of depressive episodes, significant anxiety, bipolar disorder, severe Attention-Deficit/Hyperactivity Disorder) may have difficulty focusing on the tasks of group, in that their emotional needs exceed what is related to the grief response.

In addition, similar age does not necessarily indicate similar degree of prior exposure to death, and members may therefore present with a very different worldview of death, making their degree of need for an understanding of something novel, perhaps, very different than for other members. The approach to facilitating an understanding of death and loss for the sake of acceptance may be different for different members. Also, it may be possible that the availability of group members may be limited, and therefore, in order to conduct group therapy the members may be of varying ages and developmental levels. This is not ideal but not necessarily a negative thing, as it may allow for greater modeling and potentially for siblings to attend the same group. If this is the case, treatment would still maintain the same goal of acceptance of the loss and its impact on each member's life, but the strategies and techniques employed may differ from member to member, with some older members benefiting from a leadership role in assisting younger members (so long as this is not to the detriment of the older child, which may be the case, for example, when a male child loses a father this may mimic the expectation for that child to be the "man of the house.").

Though it may be ideal to have a homogeneous group in terms of factors such as members' history of experience with death, developmental age, and nature of the relationship with the deceased, this may be unlikely in a number of institutional or community settings. Group facilitators may therefore have to conceptualize these factors as they contribute to each member's needs in group, and how the lack of homogeneity with regards to these factors may limit cohesiveness. Facilitators should attempt to consider, then, encouraging a broader understanding of loss of a loved one, so that each member recognizes that, though different, each other member's experience allows him or her to be empathetic, understanding, and struggling with similar feelings and thoughts about the loss.

Finally, issues of confidentiality, as relevant in any group, may present as difficult with children who interact outside of the group setting. It is important to impress upon members the importance of protecting the rights and feelings of each member by limiting the discussion of group content to the group environment. While outside relationships between members may be a healthy addition to the benefits of relationships within group, they must maintain the confidentiality of the group process. Confidentiality is also of concern with regards to the extent that parents may desire information about what is said or done in group. This issue can be minimized by requesting the understanding of parents or caregivers at the onset of group therapy that information disclosed within the group is to remain in the group for the emotional safety and comfort level of members, and that general summaries of group discussion and progress will be offered to parents periodically throughout the group process or anytime upon request.

CASE EXAMPLE

The following is an example of a grief therapy group, Healing Hearts, conducted by one of us (LS) with school-aged children, within the school setting, according to the protocol outlined above. The group sessions were limited to approximately 30 minutes, however, due to the constraints of class schedules. Members were individually invited to participate by one of the facilitators, who also explained the nature of the group (to address feelings about the loss of a parent), the kinds of other children who will be in the group (e.g., grades and gender), and what activities will take place (e.g., games, art activities, and talking). Six children, all boys, in 3rd through 5th grade who had a parent die, participated. Four boys lost their fathers, while two boys had lost mothers. Each group session began with a warm up where everyone shared their "best" and "worst" thing that happened since the group was last together. These could range from the small (i.e., "I played soccer on Saturday") to the big (i.e., "My mom and sister had a big fight this morning"), and everything in between. This sharing time was short and discussion of these statements was kept to a minimum. Each group session ended with 5 minutes of deep breathing, relaxation exercises, and guided imagery that were taught to the group. This served to allow the children to transition back into their school day after talking about highly emotionally charged issues. If a student was not emotionally ready to return to academic tasks, the student was given the option of a brief individual intervention to promote grounding and management of residual difficult emotions, or some personal time to sit quietly, put water on his face, and to prepare himself to return to the school day.

Practical aspects of the group were discussed, including the group length, topics to talk about, and homework. The "best" and "worst" group warm-up was explained and done by each group member including the facilitators. During the group, the children were given folders to keep their group materials in. They were asked to decorate them anyway they wished but they needed to have their names on them. Group rules were then developed with input from all members and summarized by the facilitators resulting in no more than eight. Rules included keeping hands and feet to oneself, talking one at a time, and being nice to others. The concept of confidentiality was discussed, presented as "What is said in group by other members, stays in group." The members were encouraged to talk about group with their families, but only information they or the facilitators said and not other members. It was also discussed that members don't have to talk and could "pass" if they were not comfortable sharing. The reason for the group was presented, in terms of educating the members that sometimes people who have a loved one die may need a place to share their feelings, to make sense of what happened, and to learn new skills to help them feel better. We discussed various ways people may feel or behave when they are trying to figure out what to do after someone dies. This psychoeducation also included the idea that sometimes when we have so many feelings at once it may be confusing and we need help figuring them out one at a time, including where they come from. With this age group this was the extent of the introduction to CBT for the moment. We then played a question game to orient the members to the process of the facilitators asking questions and the members taking turns to answer them (e.g., questions included favorite color, any pets, most favorite and least favorite class). Then the children were encouraged to ask each other questions in a similar format, to promote group interaction. Finally, the breathing and relaxation exercises were taught and practiced and members were told that these exercises will help them be able to return to class after discussing difficult things in-group. Specifically, members were taught diaphragmatic breathing and progressive muscle relaxation so they could begin to learn to identify their physiological experiences of tension and relaxation, and begin to learn to have some control over these states.

Over the next 7 weeks we conducted group following the outline in Table 14.1, including our "best" and "worst" activity at the start of session, an activity during session to achieve the desired tasks of the given week, and the relaxation and imagery activity at the end of session. We also assigned homework to facilitate the transfer of what was discussed in group to the members' processing outside of group in between session. Examples of specific activities we included to meet our goals each week are as follows.

In Session 2, members named the person who died and presented a few things about that person that made him or her special, including reviewing the drawings/writings brought in for homework. They also mentioned how the person died, and what they remember feeling or worrying about at the time of the death. Physical reactions were discussed to help limit how much feelings were to be relied on initially, such as changes in sleep, feeling tired, changes in eating, more or less play, etc. "Feelings Bingo" was included to encourage the identification and appropriate labeling of emotions by members.

In Session 3, we talked about what happened after their parents died, in terms of the funeral or ritual services. We also conducted an in-session memorial service to honor their deceased parents with pictures, poems, and statements or letters brought in by the members for homework. The aim was to encourage individual members to share their feelings regarding the service they may or may not have attended and give them the opportunity to say "goodbye" in a supportive setting. This allowed us to also gain access to members' beliefs about what happens after death and alleviate fears related to what their parent has gone through since dying. We focused on validating that it is typical to be scared, worried, or confused by not knowing about "what's next," but did not seek to answer those questions, and instead promote the acceptance and management of those feelings and the loss with symbolically saying goodbye.

In Session 4, we decorated "Memory Boxes," which entailed members sharing memories of their parent and finding ways to "save" those memories of life with the parent in a special box, either via pictures, making their own drawings, including items from particular memories, etc. We also reviewed the homework which was for members to think about ways the deceased person is still present and an influence in their lives. While decorating the boxes, we openly discussed feelings of loss and missing the parent, the things that were important to them that they would place in the boxes, times that they would want to remember with their parents, and ways in which the parent's death has changed other things about the members' lives. Several of the boys began to share feelings of anger toward their fathers for dying and frustration at their mothers who were struggling with single motherhood. This sharing was especially beneficial knowledge for one boy, "Matthew," who during interview for inclusion in group expressed feeling guilty for being angry with his father, and hurt feelings based on his distorted interpretation that his mother's emotional distance was because she blamed him for his father's death or didn't love him. Observing other boys express the same feelings and thoughts provided a sense of relief and validation for Matthew, as he began to share for the first time his own feelings. He also appeared to benefit from learning from the other members that he can still love his mother even if he was angry (as two of the boys expressed this indirectly by, on the one hand, verbalizing how they feel when their mothers keep to themselves and are often sad, but also by including their mothers in the decorations on their memory box). He also evidenced, in his sharing, that he began to realize that maybe it wasn't that his mother didn't love him anymore because the other boys' mothers also were acting different since the death of the father (a shift in his distorted thinking to a healthier perspective). As facilitators, we knew ahead of time from the interviews the distorted nature of some of Matthew's thoughts, and helped to facilitate the discussion that would result in this shared expression for the sake of normalizing what is healthy responding and what might be normal thoughts but skewed in some fashion (that "my mother can only love one person, and since dad is gone she can't and doesn't love me anymore…that's why she ignores me.").

In Session 5, we addressed changes in the family that are affecting group members and were alluded to in session 4 and the assigned homework topic. This was accomplished by using a technique developed by one of us (LS), the "Journey Jar" activity, which consists of members taking slips of paper with incomplete sentences on them out of a jar to promote expression of thoughts and experiences. Incomplete sentences included, "The worst thing about the death has been…," "The thing that surprised me most about the death has been…," "The thing I miss the most is…," "What is different now is…," "My living parent doesn't…," "If my parent were still here…," and "I wish I could tell my parent…" We encouraged the discussion to head in the direction of identifying any unrealistic desires to be reunited with the deceased parents or holding on to unrealistic expectations that the parent will come back or that things will not change.

Session 6 involved a discussion of what things in the future might be like without their parents. This was facilitated by first reviewing the assigned homework, which had members reflect and write about ways the family is different in the present. Specifically, we talked about holiday traditions and what role the deceased parent used to play and how that role may be filled differently now. Members shared thoughts that someday "another dad will be there instead" to cut down the Christmas tree, and so forth. These feelings and thoughts were common to many members, and the fact that they tended to share concerns or thoughts about what is ahead for the family was an obvious source of comfort, as then members began to share what they would like and what they would not about those changes. It was emphasized that although many things would change, this did not mean they were forgetting their parent or "letting go" of him or her, and that it was okay to continue finding ways that their deceased parent could remain with them through all future changes. As Thanksgiving was approaching, the activity shifted to members picking what responsibilities they could now assume to help with maintaining family traditions, and how their deceased parents could be included somehow. Homework was to discuss these ideas with their family members and to list ways in which future events will still be positive and enjoyable.

In Session 7, members were asked to share their homework assignments and what it was like to talk about a future without the deceased parents. Their feelings now were compared with those at the time the group started, and members shared what they got out of attending group, what was good or bad about group, and what ending group meant for them. They were asked to draw pictures of themselves at the start of group and now. Coping skills for the future were talked about, in terms of what they could do if they were angry, sad, or scared again, and the reality that they may feel these negative emotions again sometime when the holidays come, or when more changes happen in their lives. We also discussed that despite group ending, there are additional sources of support available and how to take advantage of those resources. Homework was assigned to draw a picture of their family in the future, without the deceased parents, but with something in the picture they can keep for themselves to include their parents in their lives, even if the family "picture" is different.

During the final session, we had a "party" to discuss what we had talked about over the last 7 weeks, how the members felt differently from the start of group, ways they had learned to manage negative emotions, and how they can continue to use those skills in the future. Members "evaluated" the group by telling us what we should do the same for the next group and what we should add or take out. We also wrote a collaborative story about a group of six students who had the courage to talk about and face tough feelings and loss and how they all began to feel better and stronger, even if they still got sad sometimes.

SUMMARY

The issues discussed above relate to the implementation of CBGT to address grief and loss with children and adolescents, and are meant to provide group facilitators with an understanding of how to effectively merge this well-supported model of treatment with a traditional format of intervention for a difficult emotional process. It requires an understanding of the underlying principles of CBT (as discussed in chapter 1), that will allow facilitators the ability to continually conceptualize the experiences of group members for the sake of promoting changes in beliefs and behaviors related to the loss and related to the nature of grief and bereavement. It is important to consider the appropriateness of including a particular child in therapeutic intervention in the first place, as well as what that child's specific emotional and behavioral problems may be, where he or she is in terms of the stages of grief, and his or her developmental level. Once a group is formed, CBT considers these individual group member factors in seeking to meet the overarching goal of identifying underlying distorted beliefs that perpetuate an ineffective bereavement process. These beliefs are then modified via specific cognitive and behavioral interventions to facilitate healthy progression toward the acceptance of loss. Skill-building, in terms of problem-solving, self-awareness, self-expression, and coping, is also an emphasis of CBGT, and this aim is accomplished through techniques chosen based on conceptualization of the underlying needs of the group members, their grief experience, and their developmental levels.

Although little empirical research exists as to the effectiveness of any one grief and loss curriculum, we belief that the application of an empirically-supported model of intervention, such as CBT, to the group therapy modality with children and adolescents can effectively facilitate the acceptance of loss of a loved one that is bereavement.

SUGGESTED BOOKS FOR CHILDREN

Death of a Friend
Bahr, M. (2000). *If Nathan were here*. Eardman's.
Buchanan Smith, (1992). *A taste of blackberries*. Harper Trophy

Death of a Sibling
Cohn, J. (1994). *Molly's rosebush*. Albert Whitman.
Old, W. C. (1995). *Stacy had a little sister*. Albert Whitman.
Yeomans, E. (2000). *Lost and found: Remembering a sister*. Centering Corporation.

Death of a Parent
Brisson, P. (1999). *Sky memories*. Delacorte.
Clifton, L. (1988). *Everett Anderson's goodbye*. Henry Holt.
Madenski, M. (1991). *Some of the pieces*. Little, Brown.
Napoli, D. J. (2002). *Flamingo dream*. Greenwillow Books.
Powell, S. (1991). *Geranium morning*. First Avenue Editions.
Sgouros, C. (1998). *A pillow for my mom*. Houghton Mifflin.
Spelman, C. (1996). *After Charlotte's mother died*. Albert Whitman.
Vigna, J. (1991). *Saying goodbye to daddy*. Albert Whitman.

Death of Grandparent
Bruchac, J. (1993). *Fox song*. Philomel Books.
de Paola, T. (2000). *Nana upstairs and Nana downstairs*. Puffin Books.
Doray, M. (2001). *One more wednesday*. Greenwillow Books.
Joosse, B. M. (2001). *Ghost wings*. Chronicle Books.
Jukes, M. (1994). *Blackberries in the dark*. Yearling Books.
Luenn, N. (1998). *A gift for Abuelita*. Rising Moon.
Nobisso, J. (2000). *Grandpa loved*. Gingerbread House.
Thurman, C. (1989). *A time for remembering*. Simon & Schuster.

SUGGESTED BOOKS FOR ADOLESCENTS

Brook, N. & Blair, P. D. (2003). *I wasn't ready to say goodbye*. Ingram.
Cromie, R. (1998). *After you lose someone you love*. Free Spirit.
Grollman, E. A. (1993). *Straight talk about death for teenagers: How to cope with losing someone you love*.
    Houghton Mifflin.

Grollman, E. A. & Malikow (1999). *Living when a young friend commits suicide: Or even starts talking about it.* Houghton Mifflin.

Grollman, E. A., & Johnson, J. (2001). *A teenagers book about suicide.* Centering Corporation.

Krementz, J. (1988). *How it feels when a parent dies.* Random House.

Myers, E. (2004). *When will I stop hurting: Teens, Loss, and grief.* Rowman & Littlefield.

Scrivani, M. (1991). *When death walks in.* Centering Corporation.

Traisman, E. S. (1992). *Fire in my heart, ice in my veins.* Centering Corporation.

REFERENCES

Achenbach, T. M., & Edelbrock, C. (1983). *Manual for the child behavior checklist and revised child behavior profile.* Burlington: University of Vermont, Department of Psychiatry.

Beck, J. S., Beck, A. T., & Jolly, J. B. (2005). *Beck youth inventories* (2nd ed.). San Antonia, TX: Harcourt Assessment.

Boelen, P. A., Den Bout, J. V., DeKeijser, J., & Hoijtink, H. (2003). Reliability and validity of the Dutch version of the Inventory of Traumatic Grief (ITG). *Death Studies, 27*(3), 227–248.

Brent, S. B., & Speece, M. W. (1993). "Adult" conceptualization of irreversibility: Implications for the development of the concept of death. *Death Studies, 17*, 203–224.

Center for the Advancement of Health (2003). *Report on bereavement and grief research.* http://owww.cfah.org/pdfs/griefreport.pdf.

Christ, G. H., Siegel, K., & Christ, A. E. (2002). Adolescent grief: "It never really hit me…until it actually happened." *Journal of the American Medical Association, 288,* 1269–1278.

Christner, R. W., Allen, J. S., & Maus, M. R. (2004, Winter). An overview for selecting CBT techniques in the treatment of youth in schools, *Insight, 24*(2), 8–10.

Corr, C. A. (1995). Children's understandings of death. In K. J. Doka (Ed.), *Children mourning, mourning children* (pp. 3–16). Washington DC: Hospice Foundation of America.

Corr, C. A., Nabe, C. M., & Corr. D. M. (1994). *Death and dying, life and living.* Pacific Grove, CA: Brooks/Cole.

Ewalt, P. L., & Perkins, L. (1979). The real experience of death among adolescents: An empirical study. *Social Casework, 60*, 547–551.

Faschingbauer, T. R., Zisook, S., & DeVaul, R. A. (1987). The Texas Revised Inventory of Grief. In S. Zisook, (Ed.). *Biopsychosocial aspects of bereavement* (pp. 109–123). Washington, DC: American Psychiatric Press.

Harrison, L., & Harrington, R. (2001). Adolescents' bereavement experiences: Prevalence, association with depressive symptoms, and use of services. *Journal of Adolescence, 24*, 159–169.

Hogan, N. S. (1988). The effects of time on the adolescent sibling bereavement process. *Pediatric Nursing, 14*(4), 333–335.

Hogan, N. S., & DeSantis, L. D. (1996a). Adolescent sibling bereavement: Toward a new theory. In C. Corr & D. B. Balk (Eds.), *Helping adolescents cope with death and bereavement* (pp. 173–195). Philadelphia: Springer.

Hogan, N. S., & DeSantis, L. D. (1996b). Basic constructs of a theory of adolescent sibling bereavement. In D. Klass, P. R. Silverman, & S. L. Nickman (Eds.), *Continuing bonds: New understandings of grief* (pp. 235–254). Washington, DC: Taylor & Francis.

Hogan, N. S., Greenfield, D. B., & Schmidt, L. A. (2001). Development and validation of the Hogan Grief Reaction Checklist. *Death Studies, 25*, 1–32.

Kovacs, M. (1985). The Children's Depression Inventory (CDI). *Psychopharmacology Bulletin, 21*, 995–998.

Kroen, W. C. (1996). *Helping children cope with the loss of a loved one: A guide for grownups.* Minneapolis, MN: Free Spirit.

Kubler-Ross, E. (1993). *On death and dying.* Collier Books.

Lehmann, L., Jimerson, S. R., & Gaasch, A. (2001). *Grief support group curriculum: Facilitator's handbook.* Philadelphia: Taylor & Francis.

March, J., Parker, J., Sullivan, K., Stallings, P., & Conners, C. K. (1997). The multi-dimensional anxiety scale for children (MASC): Factor structure, reliability, and validity. *Journal of the American Academy of Child and Adolescent Psychiatry, 36*, 554–565.

Masterman, S. H., & Reams, R. (1988). Support groups for bereaved preschool and school-aged children. *American Journal of Orthopsychiatric Association 58*(4), 562–570.

National Center for Health Statistics (2005). Retrieved from http://www.cdc.gov/nchs/fastats/deaths.htm.

Neimeyer, R. A., & Hogan, N. S. (2001). Quantative of qualatative? Measuresment issues in the study of grief. In M. Stroebe, R. O. Hansson, W. Stroebe, & B. H. Schut (Eds.), *Handbook of bereavement research: Consequences, coping, and care* (pp. 89–118). Washington, DC: American Psychological Association Press.

Noppe, L. D., & Noppe, I. C. (1996). Ambiguity in adolescent understandings of death. In C. A. Corr & D. E. Balk (Eds.), *Handbook of adolescent death and bereavement* (pp. 25–41). New York: Springer.

Prigerson, H. G., Frank, E., Kasl, S. V., Reynolds, C. F., Anderson, B., Zubenko, G. S., et al. (1995). Complicated grief and bereavement-related depression as distinct disorders: preliminary empirical validation in elderly bereaved spouses. *American Journal of Psychiatry, 152*, 22–30.

Prigerson, H. G., & Jacobs, S. C. (2001). Traumatic grief as a distinct disorder: A rationale, consensus criteria, and a preliminary empirical test. In M. Stroebe, R. O. Hansson, W. Stroebe, & B.H. Schut (Eds.), *Handbook of bereavement research: Consequences, coping, and care* (pp. 613–645). Washington, DC: American Psychological Association Press.

Prigerson, H. G., Maciejewski, P. K., Reynolds, C. F., III, Bierhals, A. J., Newsom, J. T., Fasiczka, A., Frank, E., Doman, J., Miller, M. (1995). The Inventory of Complicated Grief: a scale to measure certain maladaptive symptoms of loss. *Psychiatry Research, 59*, 65–79.

Reynolds, C. R., & Kamphaus, R. W. (2002). *The clinician's guide to the behavior assessment system for children (BASC)*. New York: Guilford.

Reynolds, C. R., & Richmond, B. O. (1985). *Revised Children's Manifest Anxiety Scale*. Los Angeles, CA: Western Psychological Services.

Silverman, P. R. (2000). *Never too young to know*. New York: Oxford University.

Silverman, W. K., & Albano, A. M. (1996). *Anxiety disorders interview schedule for DSM-IV, child and parent versions*. San Antonia, TX: Psychological Corporation.

Tedeschi, R. G. (1996). Support groups for adolescents. In Corr, C. A. & Balk, D. E. (Eds.), *Handbook of Adolescent Death and Bereavement* (pp. 293–311). New York: Springer.

Worden, J. W. (1996). *Children and grief: When a parent dies*. New York: Guilford.

Chapter Fifteen

Cognitive-Behavioral Group Treatment for Child Sexual Abuse

Mark J. Johnson & Alicia Young

Healthcare and research professionals note that sexual abuse is a significant problem affecting a substantial number of today's children and youth (Sedlack & Broadhurst, 1996). Therapeutic and research efforts are frequently hampered by the fact that there is no universally accepted definition of child sexual abuse (Haugaard, 2000). These definitions vary depending on the context and purpose of the definition (Bonner, Logue, Kaufman, & Niec, 2001). A broad definition provided by Bonner and colleagues (2001) describes sexual abuse as "the involvement of dependent, developmentally immature children and adolescents in sexual activities they do not fully comprehend and to which they are unable to give informed consent" (p. 1002). This definition speaks to the exploitative nature of sexual abuse and Faller (1993) notes that there are three interrelated factors that are useful in determining if a sexual act was abusive. These include:

Power differential—power is derived from a difference between the victim and perpetrator in either status or size.

Knowledge differential—the perpetrator has a more extensive knowledge base regarding the significance and implications of a sexual relationship. This often implies a difference in age, intellect and/or developmental status between victim and perpetrator.

Gratification differential—the goal of the sexual act is not mutual gratification, but instead the perpetrator is seeking to sexually gratify him or herself.

In 2003, Child Protective Services (CPS) investigated 906,000 reports of child maltreatment, of these, 9.9% were victims of child sexual abuse (U.S. Department of Health and Human Services, 2005). Because CPS typically only investigates situations where the abuse is perpetrated by a caretaker, this percentage does not reflect the true prevalence of child sexual abuse. A recent review of the literature found that 16.8% and 7.9% of women and men respectively have experienced sexual abuse as a child (Putnam, 2003). Some reviews of national data indicate that girls are sexually abused three times more often than boys (Sedlack & Broadhurst, 1996), although there are data that suggests the higher percentage of sexual abuse among females may be related to differences in reporting of abuse rather than actual incidence of sexually abusive experiences (Larson, Terman, Gomby, Quinn, & Behrman, 1994).

The average age of victims reporting sexual abuse is from 9 to 11 years (Gomes-Schwartz, Horowitz, & Cardarelli, 1990), but recent statistics indicate that children are consistently vulnerable to sexual abuse from age three and up (Sedlak & Broadhurst, 1996). Sexual abuse occurs in all racial, cultural, and economic groups, but studies have found that children from families with the lowest income are 18 times more likely to be sexually abused (Sedlak & Boradhurst, 1996). This finding may be related to a higher number of families of lower socioeconomic status being involved in social services, thus the abuse was more likely to be reported (Finkelhor & Barron, 1986). Other risk factors that have been associated with sexual abuse include the presence of a stepfather in the home or living with someone other than natural parents, parental substance abuse, parental mental health problems, decreased contact with mother due to working outside of the home, disability or illness, and parents who have a conflictual relationship (Finkelhor & Barron, 1986).

OVERVIEW OF THE PRESENTING PROBLEM

The effect of child sexual abuse varies widely and is influenced by characteristics of the abuse, family dynamics, developmental level of the child, child's perception of the abuse, and emotional support provided to the child following the abuse (Beichtman, Zucker, Hood, DaCosta, Akman, & Cassavia 1992; Bonner et al., 2001; Elliott, & Briere, 1994; Cohen & Manarinno, 1996; Kendall-Tackett, Williams & Finkelhor, 1993; King, Tonge, Mullen, Myerson, Heyne, & Ollendick, 1999). As a group, children do not respond to sexual abuse with one particular symptom or syndrome (Saywitz, Mannarino, Berliner, & Cohen, 2000). Sexually abusive experiences have been linked to behavioral, emotional, cognitive, academic, and even physical effects (Bolton et al., 1989; Bonner et al., 2001; Cohen & Mannarino, 1993; Fergusson, Horwood, & Lynskey, 1996; Kendall-Tackett et al., 1993). Initially, the most common symptoms are sexualized behavior (Friedrich, Grambsch, Damon, Hewitt, Koverola, Lang, & Wolfe, 1992) and symptoms associated with Post Traumatic Stress Disorder (PTSD), such as nightmares and sleep disturbance, fearfulness, and avoidance of abusive stimuli (Conte & Schuerman, 1988; Kendall-Tackett, 1993; McLeer, Deblinger, Henry, & Orvashel, 1992). Sexually abused children present with more psychiatric symptoms than nonabused children (Finkelhor & Browne, 1986; Kendall-Tackett, 1993). Cohen & Mannarino (1993) found that when evaluated within six months after the abuse was reported and investigated, most of the children met criteria for a psychiatric disorder. However, the majority of children in this sample did not exhibit sufficient symptoms to meet criteria for chronic disorders. The most common disorder was Adjustment Disorder (61%); a smaller percentage of children in this study met criteria for other disorders, such as Major Depressive Disorder (12%) and PTSD (6%). Thus, while there is not a child sexual abuse syndrome that clearly separates children who have been sexually abused from nonabused children, sexually abused children are consistently found to struggle with issues of trust and negative attributions related to the abuse.

Some evidence suggests the type of sexually abusive experience may impact the symptoms exhibited by the child. In a retrospective study, Hulme and Agrawal (2004), investigated an adult sample of women who experienced child sexual abuse and grouped them according to their experiences (i.e., familial vs. extrafamilial; contact vs. noncontact; use of threat or force; age difference of 5 or more years). They found that women who experienced sexual abuse that included forceful physical contact from a family member reported more emotional difficulties than women who experienced nonforceful, nonphysical sexual abuse by an extrafamilial member. The study also found that sexually abused women who also experienced other forms of physical and emotional maltreatment were more likely to have experienced sexual abuse that included the use of force and/or threats. This finding is consistent with other research that found that the severity of behavioral and mental health symptoms increased when the abuse was perpetrated by the father or father figure, when threats/force were used, when there were other forms of maltreatment, and/or when the child experienced negative postabuse responses from his or her support system (Faller, 1993; Beichtman et al., 1992; Gomes-Schwartz et al., 1990).

Three models have emerged in an effort to conceptualize the effects of childhood sexual abuse as there is no DSM diagnostic category. The most widely-known theory is the PTSD model (e.g., Friedrich, 1995; King et al., 1999). This model emphasizes the behavioral and cognitive effects associated with a traumatic event and provides a framework for therapeutic practice. However, as discussed above, not all children who are sexually abused present with symptomatology sufficient to diagnose PTSD. The second theory is known as the traumagenic factors model. In this model, Finkelhor and Browne (1986) note that the sequelae to experiences of sexual abuse can be grouped into four general categories. These include traumatic sexualization (aversive feelings, overvaluing the sexual relationship, and/or sexual identity problems), stigmatization (feeling damaged or responsible for the abusive experience), betrayal (feeling as if one cannot trust others), and powerlessness (a feeling of vulnerability and inability to prevent negative things from happening). The third is the information-processing of trauma model that emphasizes psychosocial impacts such as dissociation and hyperarousal (e.g., Friedrich, 1995). A combination of these models lends to a conceptualization that encompasses the wide range of these symptom sequelae and provides a framework for therapeutic intervention (Friedrich, 1995, 1996).

Researchers have also investigated possible gender differences in the effects of childhood sexual abuse. Finkelhor's (1990) review of the literature cites several studies investigating immediate, 6-12 month follow-up, and long-term effects of sexual abuse. These studies suggest that boys and girls respond similarly to sexual abuse (Conte, Berliner, & Shuerman, 1986; Kelley, 1988; Tong, Oates, & McDowell, 1987). According to teacher and parent reports immediately after disclosure and at follow-up, boys are moderately less symptomatic; however boys' self-evaluations indicated similar symptom levels as girls' self-evaluations (e.g., Tong et al., 1987). Some differences in symptom response between girls and boys are noted in the literature (Banyard, Williams, & Siegel, 2004). Based on teacher and parent report, boys are found to exhibit more externalizing behavior problems such as aggression while girls exhibit more internalizing symptomatology such as a depressed mood (Finkelhor, 1990).

Results for long-term effects are similar for both genders in that approximately one third report no symptoms, while the remaining survivors report significant anxiety, depression, dissociation, sexual problems, sleep disruption, low self-esteem, lower levels of religiosity, suicidal ideation, drug use, marital disruption, and anger (Finkelhor 1990, King et al., 1999). Research further indicates that long-term effects are dependent on whether or not children receive treatment. In one particular study (Gomes-Schwartz et al., 1990), the children that initially presented with the highest number of symptoms showed the most significant improvement over time.

Some research findings suggest little difference in symptoms between genders in response to sexual abuse (Banyard, Williams, & Siegel, 2004; Finkelhor, 1990), however, boys and girls do respond differently to treatment (Friedrich, 1995). Friedrich (1995) suggests that generally speaking, boys respond less well to therapies that encourage them to talk and/or those that make them feel vulnerable. Those symptom differences that have been noted indicate that initial treatment may need to focus more on cognitive and behavioral symptoms for boys and cognitive and affective symptoms for girls. Thus, therapy with boys may need to be more directive and abuse specific with a focus on cognitive and behavioral sequelae. This is supported by the work of Cohen, Deblinger, and Mannarino (1995) who have shown that both boys and girls respond well to trauma focused cognitive-behavioral treatment similar to that described in this chapter.

ASSESSMENT AND GROUP IDENTIFICATION

Investigations to determine if sexual abuse has occurred are generally completed by child protection services (CPS) and/or law enforcement personnel. Faller (1993, 1996) has provided a thorough description of this evaluative process and guidelines for professionals are provided by the American Professional Society on the Abuse of Children (1995). The details of the investigative process are beyond the scope of this chapter and the reader is encouraged to review these documents for information on this topic. Assessment, as described in this chapter, takes place after the investigative process by CPS and law enforcement has been completed and focuses on the behavioral and mental health symptoms the child exhibits. This assessment is important for the purpose of determining if the child is appropriate for group intervention and for planning an appropriate course of treatment.

Deblinger and Heflin (1996) highlight the need to gather information from as many sources as possible when assessing children who have been sexually abused. This may include observation, use of psychological assessment instruments, and interviews with the victim, family members (including the perpetrator if it is familial abuse), teachers, other mental health professionals, and social services/law enforcement professionals involved in the investigative process. Deblinger & Heflin (1996) further emphasize that since Trauma Focused Cognitive Behavior Therapy (TF-CBT) attends to cognitions, emotions and behaviors, special attention should be given to obtaining a thorough assessment of these factors.

Depending on the age and developmental level of the child, a number of caregiver and self-report measures may be helpful. The Behavior Assessment System for Children—Second Edition (BASC-2; Reynolds & Kamphaus, 2004) provides a multimethod and multidimensional assessment system that offers information about a wide range of internalizing and externalizing symptoms exhibited by the child. Appropriate for an age range of 2 to 25, the BASC-2 is a very useful instrument for getting a "snapshot" of how the child is perceived to be functioning in a number of different contexts. The BASC-2 also includes multiple assessment options that include parent, teacher and self-report forms as well as a method for direct observation of classroom behavior and a structured interview format to obtain a developmental history of the child.

Several self-report and caregiver report instruments provide important information on the child's cognitions, fears, and concerns following a traumatic event. The Trauma Symptom Checklist for Children (TSC-C; Briere, 1996), is a self-report measure normed for children age 8 to 16. The TSC-C provides information on children's level of symptomatology in six areas: anxiety, depression, anger, posttraumatic stress, dissociation, and sexual concerns. The Trauma Symptom Checklist for Young Children (TSC-YC; Briere, 2005) is a caregiver questionnaire normed for children age 3 to 12 that provides information on the same domains as the TSC-C, but provides a more detailed assessment of PTSD by assessing symptoms related to intrusion, arousal, and avoidance. The Children's Impact of Traumatic Events Scale (CITES-R; Wolfe, Gentile, Michienzi, Sas, & Wolfe, 1991), a caregiver interview measure normed for children age 8 to 16, provides information related to intrusive thoughts and perceptions of blame, guilt, betrayal, stigmatization, and helplessness. Deblinger and Heflin (1996) report that they have found the CITES-R to be particularly helpful in identifying areas of dysfunctional thought, while the TSC-C includes factors that assess when a child is experiencing difficulty with anger and/or dissociation as these areas are not specifically assessed with other instruments.

The Children's Sexual Behavior Inventory (CSBI; Friedrich, 1997) is completed by the parent/caregiver. Since sexualized behavior is a common behavior problem for children who have been sexually abused, this instrument provides a norm-based assessment for this problem. When developing the CSBI, Friedrich (1997) found that elevated scores on the CSBI were highly correlated with experiences of sexual abuse. In many cases, some form of sexualized behavior will need to be addressed during the course of treatment. These instruments are also helpful in assessing progress in treatment when used as a pre- and post-treatment measure.

Two other assessment instruments developed by Spaccarelli (1995) may also be effective in assessing children's responses to sexual abuse. The Checklist of Sexual Abuse and Related Stressors (C-SARS; Spaccarelli, 1995) assesses whether or not 70 stressful events (i.e., threats, bribery, seduction) frequently associated with sexual abuse occurred when the child was abused. The C-SARS has been positively related to parent and therapist reports of behavior problems and stress (Spaccarelli, 1994). The Negative Appraisals of Sexual Abuse Scale (NASAS; Spaccarelli, 1995) is a 56-item self-report measure of perceptions of threat or harm related to sexual victimization. For each item, the child is asked to use a likert-scale to rate the strength of perception. The NASAS has been shown to be effective in assessing PTSD symptoms, depression and anxiety (Bonner et al., 2001). Spaccarelli (1995) warns that given the reading and comprehension level needed to complete the items, the C-SARS and NASAS may not be appropriate for children under the age of 12.

Extra care should be taken when considering a child for inclusion in a therapy group. Children who exhibit difficulties with suicidal ideation, psychotic process, significant sexualized behaviors, and other serious mental health problems may be better served on an individual basis until these difficulties are better controlled.

CBT CONCEPTUALIZATION OF THE PROBLEM

Cognitive-behavioral approaches are based on the understanding that cognitions, behaviors and emotions are interdependent. A cognitive-behavioral conceptualization of child sexual abuse relies heavily on learning theory, and a subset of information-processing theory called emotion-processing. As with other forms of trauma, when a child is sexually abused, his or her maladaptive coping skills, which may have been helpful while the abuse was occurring, generalize and become disruptive in nonabusive situations (Perrin, Smith, & Yule, 2004).

Learning theory offers one explanation of why these maladaptive coping skills generalize and become disruptive. Learning theory posits that the presentation of a stimulus will elicit a response. Stimuli within the environment at the time the unconditioned stimuli was presented may also become conditioned stimuli and elicit the same response. Therefore, a traumatic event can be thought of as an unconditioned stimulus, which elicits an unconditioned response, and those stimuli in the background become conditioned stimuli leading to avoidance responses (Perrin, Smith, & Yule, 2004). Similarly, the re-experiencing symptoms common in PTSD such as flashbacks are comparable to a conditioned fear response. Learning theory further suggests that repeated exposure to a conditioned stimulus (specific place, smells, and the like) in the absence of the unconditioned stimulus (sexual event) should produce a decrease and finally extinguish the conditioned response (avoidance, re-experiencing). This would explain those whose symptoms ameliorate with time. However, for those who do develop PTSD, the avoidance symptoms prevent exposure to the trauma-related conditioned stimuli and block the extinction process. A study by Falls (1998) provides evidence that associations held between conditioned stimuli, unconditioned stimuli and the unconditioned response might not be erased from memory despite extinction. Therefore, an understanding of learning theory indicates that part of an effective treatment for children who have experienced sexual abuse may include exposure to stimuli that were present in the context where the abuse occurred so they can learn that the presence of those stimuli in a safe environment does not mean that the abuse will follow.

Information-processing theory adds to learning theory by taking into account children's appraisal of the event, the meaning assigned to the event, and addresses recent evidence (Falls, 1998) that memory is not extinguished. This specific subset of information-processing theory has been forwarded by Foa and colleagues (Foa & Kozak, 1986; Foa, Steketee, & Olasov-Rothbaum, 1989) and is called emotion processing. This model asserts that traumatic events are consolidated and stored as fear networks in memory. The fear network includes characteristics of the trauma, the child's appraisal of the dangerousness and meaningfulness of the event, as well as his or her response to the trauma. While the child remains in the context in which the abuse is occurring, this fear network is adaptive as it acts to prevent further trauma; however, even after the child is removed from the abusive context, the network may be triggered by trauma-related stimuli. This memory trigger increases the likelihood of hyperarousal, avoidance, and re-experiencing. Depending on the child's appraisal of the situation and assigned meaningfulness of the event, the child's basic assumptions about safety and self-efficacy may change leading to an increase in perceived threat attached to previously neutral stimuli. Foa and colleagues (1989) argue that this conceptualization of sexual abuse indicates that in-vivo and imaginal exposure in treatment can provide corrective feedback necessary to counter the fear network.

Other researchers (Brewin, 2001; Salmon & Bryant, 2002) argue that this model does not account for the affective symptoms exhibited by those experiencing PTSD and suggest a cognitive neuroscience approach. This approach accounts for dissociative and emotional responding by suggesting that encoding of sensory, motor, and physiological memories associated with the traumatic events occur by bypassing the hippocampus. These memories are called "situationally accessible memories" and when trigged by cues result in a re-experiencing of physical sensations and emotions experienced during the trauma. Brewin (2001) argues that effective therapy accesses these situationally accessible memories and elaborates on them verbally so they become stored as "verbally accessible memories" which can then be retrieved consciously and edited. More traditional cognitive-behavioral strategies of confronting and changing maladaptive beliefs can then be employed during treatment (Ehlers & Clark, 2000).

GROUP TREATMENT

In their review of the literature on treatment outcome for children who have experienced sexual abuse, Finkelhor and Berliner (1995) determined that specific psychological intervention to address the sequelae of sexual abuse is beneficial. A meta-analysis completed by Reeker, Ensing, and Elliott (1997) concluded that group interventions for victims of sexual abuse are effective. A number of well-designed studies have compared the use of Cognitive-Behavior Treatment (CBT) with more traditional therapies in treatment of sexual abuse (Cohen, Berliner, & March, 2000). In a review of studies investigating treatment of sexually abused children, Cocoran (2004) found that cognitive-behavioral treatment protocols showed "a clear advantage" (p. 75) in reducing PTSD symptoms associated with child sexual abuse compared to treatment provided to control groups. Most of the studies reviewed by Cocoran (2004) highlighted the benefit of including the nonoffending parent in treatment. A study by King and colleagues (2000) found that when CBT is provided to the child only, treatment had a positive impact on reducing PTSD symptoms when assessed at the end of treatment, but at a 3 month follow-up assessment, children who had parental involvement fared significantly better.

Trauma Focused Cognitive-Behavioral Treatment has been shown to be effective when provided in a group and/or individual format (Saunders, Berliner, & Hanson, 2004). The National Crime Victims Research and Treatment Center (Saunders et al., 2004) has identified TF-CBT as a well-supported and efficacious treatment to address the sequelae of child sexual abuse. Cohen, Deblinger, and Mannarino (2005) have provided a summary of the research that shows evidence of the effectiveness of TF-CBT. The protocol for TF-CBT, as described in Cohen et al. (2005) and Deblinger & Heflin (1996), includes identification of feelings, stress management, cognitive coping, gradual exposure, cognitive processing, and psychoeducation. In the research protocols, these components were provided to children between the ages of 3 to 13, and the nonoffending parent over the course of 12 individual and family sessions. While the research protocol provides a template for a 12-session program, the treatment protocol itself is considered fluid and can be adapted to match the needs and/or pace of the group participants (Deblinger & Heflin, 1996). Deblinger and Heflin (1996) note that this may be necessary when the child presents with multiple diagnoses or when there are complicated family dynamics and/or legal circumstances.

Most of the components included in the treatment protocol will be familiar to professionals who have used CBT treatments. However, gradual exposure, a significant component of this approach, varies somewhat from other cognitive-behavioral approaches. Research has shown that prolonged exposure and systematic desensitization are effective interventions to reduce symptoms of PTSD in adults (Foa, Rothbaum, Riggs, & Murdock, 1991). However, these interventions can be overwhelming to children (Deblinger & Heflin, 1996). Therefore, the TF-CBT protocol combines prolonged exposure and systematic desensitization in a manner that is more effective with children. Termed *gradual exposure* by the authors, issues related to sexual abuse are first explored in an abstract manner. Over the course of several sessions, the child is gradually exposed to more detailed aspects of the anxiety producing elements of his or her own abusive experiences. As the child learns how to handle the anxiety that accompanies the memory of that experience, he or she is less likely to utilize negative coping strategies and is more likely to use the positive coping strategies previously taught in therapy (Deblinger & Heflin, 1996; Cohen et al., 2005). Gradual exposure to the anxiety that accompanies the processing of the abuse can be uncomfortable for children and some therapists may be reluctant to have children experience this discomfort. Given that gradual exposure may be difficult for children to accomplish, particularly in a group therapy format, therapists may find that children will need several supplemental individual therapy sessions to complete the gradual exposure process. Our clinical experience has shown that when most children are able to complete the gradual exposure process sufficiently in supplemental individual sessions, the process has been reinforced when they are able to share an abbreviated and structured version with the group. Cohen and colleagues (2005) note that they are currently conducting a dismantling study to determine if gradual exposure and cognitive reprocessing are necessary components for a positive therapeutic outcome; it is possible that these components may be found to be either unnecessary or essential for a positive outcome.

The following is a template of a 12-module group intervention model that has been adapted from the protocol for TF-CBT as described by Deblinger & Heflin (1996) and Cohen and colleagues (2005). Although the authors note that their treatment protocol can be used with groups of children, written descriptions of the protocol are for individual and family therapy sessions. While the protocol described in this chapter is consistent with the CBT approach described and used in the research by Deblinger & Heflin (1996) and Cohen and associated (2005), adaptations have been made to make the program applicable to a group format. Deblinger and Heflin (1996) note that although the research protocol describes 12 sessions, some children may need up to 40 sessions to complete the therapeutic work. Therefore, in describing the group format, we have used the term "modules" rather than sessions, as particular client groups may need more than the proscribed number of sessions to thoroughly address the therapeutic task.

The following protocol, presented in Table 15.1, assumes that there were some initial sessions with the child and caregivers to complete the assessment process prior to beginning group treatment. As mentioned above, the protocol includes supplemental individual therapy sessions to complete the gradual exposure portion of treatment. Finally, for some modules, we have included additional techniques that we have found helpful in working with groups of children. We have described those techniques as "variations" throughout the protocol. These variations are designed to remain consistent with the CBT protocol, but to provide the reader with additional materials or techniques that have been helpful in introducing or reinforcing a particular concept with children.

OVERCOMING POTENTIAL OBSTACLES

Sexualized behavior (also frequently called inappropriate sexual behavior or sexually abusive behavior) is a common symptom for children who have been sexually abused (Friedrich et al., 1992). Children who exhibit sexualized behavior problems are more likely to have experienced disruptions in placement, exhibit socialization problems, and may be at increased risk for additional incidents of sexual abuse (Silovsky & Bonner, 2003; Silovsky & Niec, 2002). Therefore, any intervention program for sexual abuse needs to be prepared to address sexualized behavior problems as well. Careful consideration should

Table 15.1   Sample Treatment Protocol for Child Sexual Abuse

Module 1–Introduction to Group/Identification of Feelings

Even in a group format, leaders should be able to cover the information in this module in one session.

Children's Group	**Parent or Caregiver Group**
In this module, it will be important to provide opportunity for getting to know other members of the group, practice sharing in a group environment and establish some group rules.	In the parallel parent group, the purpose of the group and issues of confidentiality are discussed. Parents are encouraged to describe the way that the abuse has affected his or her life. Parents are asked to share the thoughts and feelings he or she experienced when he or she found about the abuse and how he or she presently feels. Deblinger and Heflin (1996) highlight several suggestions to facilitate the parent group.
• Modeling how to share personal information in the group: Introductory activities, such as having each member share his or her name, age, grade, and something unique to him/her (favorite flavor of ice cream, favorite topping on pizza, etc.) can be helpful. Group leaders model how to share in a group setting by going first and actively participating in the general sharing.	• Even though they have agreed to participate in therapy, some parents may question the veracity of the child's report of maltreatment. In the initial sessions, confronting those thoughts and feelings may have a negative impact on the therapeutic relationship. Deblinger and Heflin (1996) note that a parent's thoughts and feelings regarding the abuse often changes over the course of treatment.
• General introduction to the group: Group members will have met with group leaders for an assessment prior to the beginning of the group; therefore, each member of the group should know the purpose of the group. However, this needs to be established with all group members present. Group structure, confidentiality, and group rules should be discussed and identified in the initial session.	• The parent may have been too open in sharing his or her feelings regarding the abuse, or do not know how to broach the subject of the abuse with their child. Parents are encouraged to be discrete in how and when they speak about the abuse when around the child. Parents are also informed that future sessions will address how to talk with the child about the abuse.
• Identification of feelings: Group members are encouraged to identify as many feelings as possible. Positive, negative and ambivalent feelings are discussed. Children are presented with scenarios and asked to identify the feeling(s) he or she would have in the situation. Drawings, photographs, role-playing, or books can be helpful in teaching children how to identify feelings that other's express. Children are asked to identify feelings he or she experienced during the abusive experience. Finally, children are asked to express how it felt to participate and share about the abuse in the group.	• Parenting skills are introduced and discussed in this session. Information about reinforcement of appropriate behavior and appropriate consequences for inappropriate behavior are introduced.

Variation: (Children's Group) General identification of feelings can be facilitated by using a children's animated movie. Watch a segment of the film, then pause the film and ask the children to identify the feeling the character is experiencing. Emphasis can be placed on how one can determine how a person feels by attending to facial expression, body position, and volume of voice. The cognitive triad can also be introduced in this way by asking what the character is thinking, feeling and doing.

(Continued)

Table 15.1   Continued

Module 2—Stress Management

The ability to relax and regulate one's reaction to anxiety is an important skill. We have found that stress management techniques, while relatively simple, are best learned through practice and repetition. Therefore, relaxation and stress management techniques discussed in this module can be practiced at the end of future sessions.

Children's Group	Parent or Caregiver Group
Relaxation and stress management techniques are reviewed in this module. Each child is asked to identify what he or she does to relax (i.e., music, drawing, exercise, etc.). Relaxation techniques such as progressive muscle relaxation are taught and practiced in this session. Deblinger and Heflin (1996) indicate that it is important to remind children to not use these relaxation techniques to facilitate sleep as this may preclude the use of these skills in reducing anxiety when doing therapeutic work.	Parents are taught the same relaxation skills that are taught to the children. Parents are encouraged to practice these skills through the week. When possible, the parents are asked to practice relaxation skills with the children throughout the week. Parents are also taught how stress management can be helpful for them (Walker, 2001).

Powers & Spirito (1998a, 1998b) provide an overview of the use of relaxation and biofeedback with children. Koeppen (1974) is one source that provides a relaxation script for use with elementary age children.

Module 3—Cognitive Processing

The cognitive triangle and cognitive distortions are taught in this module. The cognitive triangle/triad is a key concept in cognitive behavior therapies. The reader is encouraged to review Deblinger and Heflin (1996), Weist and Danforth (1998), and Kendall and Hollon (1979) for more information on how to implement cognitive behavior interventions with children. With a wealth of information and multiple teaching methods to use in this module, this module is typically covered in two or three group therapy sessions.

Children's Group	Parent or Caregiver Group
In this module, the cognitive triangle highlighting the interdependent relationship between thoughts, feelings, and behaviors, is introduced to the children. Deblinger and Heflin (1996) and Seligman, Reivich, Jaycox, and Gillham, (1995) provide some excellent examples of how to introduce this topic in therapy.	In the parallel parent group, parents are introduced to the cognitive triangle and ABC model. Parents are encouraged to consider how their child's behavior may be affected by their thoughts and feelings about the abuse and other events in his or her life. Parents are also taught how to recognize and dispute negative thoughts he or she may experience. Use of the Best Friend Role Play or other empty chair techniques is useful in helping the parent practice disputing negative thoughts. Parents are also taught the same "Thinking Errors" and corrective thoughts that are taught to the children (Burton, et al., 1998).

- In one session, the cognitive triangle or the ABC (Adversity, Beliefs, and Consequences) model (Ellis, 1962; Seligman, et al., 1995) is introduced to the children through the use of written scenarios, cartoon drawings, puppet-shows and/or role-play. Scenarios and role-plays are developed that have similar circumstances, but the character processes the situation differently. Subsequently, the character behaves differently.
- In another session, the method of disputing negative thoughts by replacing them with positive thoughts is addressed. Seligman and colleagues (1995), and Deblinger and Heflin (1996) have some excellent examples of how to teach children to dispute negative thoughts. Scenarios, role-plays, and use of puppets are helpful in teaching this concept in a group setting. One example, the Best Friend Role-Play (Deblinger & Heflin, 1996) has the child convince a friend that the negative thoughts he or she is experiencing are not accurate.

Parenting skills continue to be reviewed in the parenting group each week.

- For some children, categorizing the negative thoughts as a type of "Thinking Error" may be helpful as each "thinking error" can have a readily identifiable corrective thought. Burton and colleagues (1998) provide a list of thinking errors that children are able to understand and identify.

Variation:

- A teaching method shown to be highly effective called Active Student Responding (ASR; Heward, 1996) is useful in quickly assessing that the children understand a concept. For example, using flashcards with feeling words or faces to represent a feeling, the children respond in unison by raising the card that matches the feeling the person is experiencing in the scenario, role-play, etc. At a glance, the group leader sees the response, provides feedback, and reinforces the concept while each group member remains actively engaged. Giving each child a small whiteboard with dry-erase markers on which they write or draw their answer can also be an effective way to facilitate Active Student Responding.
- As mentioned above, a children's animated film can be helpful in teaching children the interrelation of thoughts, feelings, and actions. The children watch a short segment of the movie and the children identify the thoughts, feelings and actions of the character.
- Learning the "Thinking Errors" can be facilitated through the use of a memory game. Using 3×5 cards, write all of the thinking errors on cards of one color and the corrective responses on cards of a different color. Laying the cards out face down in a grid, have the children turn the cards over and attempt to match the thinking error with the corrective response. When a match is made, a scenario illustrating the correction of the thinking error is shared with the group.

Module 4—Sexuality Education and Gradual Exposure

In this module, the group focus is on providing appropriate sexuality education and gradual exposure to the anxiety associated with the sexual abuse experience. As mentioned above, the gradual exposure portion of treatment may be difficult for children to complete in a group format. Therefore, supplemental individual/family therapy sessions may be necessary for the child to accomplish this therapeutic task. Although the actual number of individual/family therapy sessions needed to complete the gradual exposure process may vary, the research protocol completed this process in 2–3 therapy sessions. Deblinger and Heflin (1996, p. 74) provide a useful sample hierarchy of the gradual exposure process:

1. General information about child sexual abuse.
2. Nonabusive interactions with the offender.
3. The disclosure and resulting investigation.
4. The first episode of abuse.
5. Additional types of abusive contacts.
6. Other specific episodes of abuse (associated with special events such as holidays, birthdays, beginning or ending of the school year).
7. The most disturbing or embarrassing abusive episodes.

Deblinger and Heflin (1996) provide excellent examples of techniques that are useful in completing the gradual exposure process in individual/family therapy sessions. Examples include reenactment with play materials, creating therapeutic journals/drawings regarding the abuse, visualization, and in-vivo exposure. When the child has completed the gradual exposure in the individual/family sessions, he or she is asked to summarize one incident to share with the group using the following format:

- Who abused him or her,
- Where the abuse occurred,
- When the abuse occurred, and
- What happened (can be a brief description).
- The child is also encouraged to share at least one thought and one feeling he or she experienced as a result of the abuse.

The authors have found that general information regarding sexual abuse and sexuality education can be appropriately provided in the group format. Therefore, while children are being presented with this information in the group format, gradual exposure is completed in the supplemental individual/family therapy sessions. Finally, in a structured manner, the children share information about their experience of abuse with the group. It is important that the group leaders maintain a supportive group environment for the sharing of personal experience.

(Continued)

Table 15.1   Continued

Children's Group	Parent or Caregiver Group
In this module, the process of gradual exposure begins. In the group, children are provided with developmentally appropriate and accurate information about sexual abuse and human sexuality. Portions of books such as It's Perfectly Normal (Harris, 1994), or What's the Big Secret (Brown & Brown, 1997) are used to provide accurate information regarding human sexuality. Books and drawings may also be used to facilitate discussion on sexual abuse. The Very Touching Book (1983), and other books written by individuals who have been sexually abused are helpful in broaching this subject with children. Diagrams included in the book, Treatment Exercises for Child Abuse Victims And Children With Sexual Behavior Problems (Johnson, 1998) are helpful in talking about the effects of sexual abuse. Following the general discussion of human sexuality and sexual abuse, the children are asked to generate ideas about what sexually abused children might think or feel about the abuse. Reviewing the effects of sexual abuse and human sexuality typically takes 2–3 sessions.	During this module, parents participate in the individual/family therapy sessions to complete the gradual exposure exercises. These supplemental sessions include individual therapeutic work with the child to complete the gradual exposure process. The parent also meets individually with the therapist to complete his or her own gradual exposure process. Parents are also presented with suggestions on how to talk with and support his or her child through the gradual exposure process. As the gradual exposure process nears completion, family sessions allow the child to share what they have processed with the parent. The therapist instructs and models how to support and encourage the child through this process (Deblinger & Heflin, 1996).
When the children have completed the gradual exposure process in the supplemental individual/family therapy sessions, the children are asked to share their experience with the group. Using the format of Who, Where, When, and What—each child shares a summary of the experience that he or she has processed in the supplemental individual/family therapy sessions. The child shares at least one thought and feeling he or she experienced related to the abuse. Group members provide support and encouragement to each other and they share how it feels to receive the support of peers in the group.	Group sessions with the parents in this module are used to provide information about healthy sexuality and to allow the parent to share what he or she has learned about him/herself and his or her child through the gradual exposure process. For the sexuality education process, parents are shown the portions of the books that are being used in the children's group. Parents also receive additional information regarding normal sexual development and how to handle problematic sexual behavior in children (Bonner, Walker, & Berliner, 1999; Gordon & Schroeder, 1995; Johnson, 1999; Sandfort & Rademakers, 2000; Silovsky & Bonner, 2003).
The exact number of sessions needed to complete the sharing of sexually abusive experiences depends on the size of the group and the amount of time needed to share experiences. However, group leaders should count on using two sessions to complete this portion of the module. Sharing and hearing this information can be difficult for the group members and group leaders. Therefore, it is important to end each session with an enjoyable activity that defuses the anxiety of the group participants.	

Module 5—Cognitive Processing of Abuse Experiences

In this module, the children and parents learn to dispute the negative and dysfunctional thoughts associated with the abuse experience. The therapist, having made note of negative or dysfunctional thoughts shared during the gradual exposure process, helps the child and parent in disputing those thoughts. Methods learned earlier in therapy are applied to abuse specific thoughts.

Children's Group

A review of how to dispute negative thoughts may be needed using material that is not abuse-focused. Following this review, the children begin to process the abusive experience by learning how to dispute or correct negative thoughts. Deblinger and Heflin (1996) identify the more common areas of maladaptive cognitions that will need to be addressed in this module, and they include:

- Abuse attributions—why did the abuse occur and who is responsible?
- Social reactions—how did others react to learning about the abuse experience?
- Sexuality—what type of inaccurate information about sexuality did the child learn as a result of the abuse experience?

The use of role-play has been shown to be very effective in helping the children process the abuse (Deblinger & Heflin, 1996). In this module, the power of group therapy is particularly evident as group members are able to help peers complete this process and identify multiple ways to dispute negative thoughts.

Parent or Caregiver Group

In this module, the parent group mirrors the children's group. Parents review how to dispute negative thoughts and then they begin to address the negative cognitions he or she may have about the abuse experience. Parents may also benefit from use of role-play in this module.

Module 6—Safety Skills

Children's Group

In this module, children learn appropriate safety skills regarding sexual abuse. Issues such as OK-Touches vs. Not OK-Touches, personal boundaries (Johnson, 1998), sexual behavior rules (Bonner, et. al., 1999; Silovsky & Bonner, 2003), and the importance of telling an adult when abuse occurs. A variety of methods or techniques can be used in this module depending on the age or developmental level of the children in the group (Silovsky & Niec, 2002). For example, to teach personal boundaries, the therapist may want to use hula hoops to illustrate personal space.

Parent or Caregiver Group

The parent group receives similar instruction regarding safety skills for sexual abuse. It is helpful to combine the child and parent groups for a joint session and allow the child to share with the parents what he or she has learned about personal boundaries, sexual behavior rules, and different types of touching.

Module 7—Review

This module serves to review what the child has learned through the therapy process. The child and parent group is combined and the information that has been provided during the course of the group is reviewed. The author has found that this can be accomplished in a fun manner by making a homemade board game using poster board and questions written on 3×5 cards (Corder [2000] has templates for a board game that the therapist can adapt for this purpose). The child and his or her parent participate in answering questions about information provided in the group. One moving piece for the entire group is used so that the group must cooperate and exhibit what they have learned to reach the goal and win the game.

be given as to whether a particular child who exhibits sexualized behavior problems is appropriate for inclusion in the TF-CBT treatment group. In some cases, the clinician may need to work with the child and family to decrease the incidence of sexualized behavior before inclusion in the TF-CBT group. Cognitive-behavioral approaches are shown to be effective in addressing sexualized behavior problems in children and the reader is encouraged to review the literature that describes intervention programs for sexualized behavior problems (Bonner et al., 1999; Burton et al., 1998; Johnson, 1998; Letourneu, Schoenwald, & Sheidow, 2004; Silovsky & Niec, 2002).

Clinical services are provided to children in a variety of settings; including schools, community counseling centers, therapeutic foster care, and residential care. Cohen and colleagues (2005) note that they have provided TF-CBT to children and a nonoffending caregiver in kinship and foster care as part of their research protocol and found the therapy to be effective. However, due to circumstances in the child's life, a consistent parent or caregiver may not be available to participate in treatment. For example, children may be placed in residential care following multiple foster care placements due to persistent behavioral difficulties. This is problematic given that research indicates caregiver involvement is an important treatment component for the sequelae of sexual abuse (Cohen, 2005). Nonetheless, many clinicians practice in settings where caregiver participation is not consistent or possible. Thus, the authors would like to illustrate how TF-CBT can be adapted to these situations by providing a case example of a child in residential care who received TF-CBT treatment without caregiver involvement. However, when a foster home was identified for the child, the foster parents participated in therapy sessions to facilitate the transition into their home.

CASE EXAMPLE

Michael was a 10-year-old Caucasian male receiving treatment in a residential setting. Michael was placed in residential care after he had exhibited significant behavior problems and needed to be removed from his third therapeutic foster care placement. Michael was one of six children who had been removed from his parent's care due to substantiated sexual abuse by Michael's stepfather. History obtained from Children and Youth Services (CYS) indicated that not only was Michael sexually abused by his stepfather when his mother was out of the home, the stepfather also instructed and encouraged Michael and his male siblings to engage in sexual activity with his female siblings. Michael's mother had not been involved in his life in the one and one-half years since he had been removed from her care and CYS had deemed that other relatives were not an appropriate placement option. Therefore, at the time that Michael was placed in residential care, no consistent caregiver could be identified.

The assessment process indicated that Michael was of above-average intelligence, but caregiver and self-report measures indicated that he exhibited clinically significant externalizing behavior problems, including sexual behavior problems. Michael participated in a number of therapeutic activities and groups addressing issues such as social skills and anger management as part of his treatment program in residential care. One of these groups was a TF-CBT group with an emphasis on processing the sexual abuse he endured and reducing sexual behavior problems. Although Michael did not have a caregiver to participate in a parallel treatment group, supplemental individual therapy sessions were provided to complete the gradual exposure process consistent with the description provided above.

Michael had no difficulty completing the therapeutic work pertaining to the cognitive triad and relaxation skills. However, Michael had significant difficulty with the gradual exposure process. He expressed shame (Feiring & Taska, 2005; Feiring, Taska, & Chen,

2002) and negative attributions (Deblinger & Runyon, 2005) related to his abuse and the sexual behavior that occurred between himself and his siblings. Michael was reluctant to process any aspect of the abuse and he became reticent and defiantly opposed therapeutic intervention. After a number of intervention techniques had been unproductive, Michael eventually began the gradual exposure process by participating in a role-play that included him being interviewed as an expert on sexual abuse for a television show by the therapist (Corder, 2000; Deblinger & Heflin, 1996). Using this technique over the course of several sessions, Michael progressed from discussing general information about sexual abuse to sharing his own personal feelings and attributions about his experience of sexual abuse. Michael subsequently shared his thoughts and feelings regarding his abuse with the group and he was relieved to find that his fellow group members were encouraging and supportive. After he processed the abuse, Michael completed cognitive processing of the abuse. Michael became a leader in the group and assisted in the education of his peers in how to combat negative thoughts and feelings about their abuse experience. Michael found that by sharing how he had learned to dispute negative thoughts and feelings, he was able to help his peers through this process and his own therapeutic progress was strengthened.

While in residential care, a foster home was identified for Michael. Michael's foster parents participated in the therapy process for several weeks prior to his being placed into the foster home. Michael shared his experience with the foster parents, including the workbook/journal work that he had done as part of the therapeutic process. The foster parents expressed anxiety about having Michael in their home given Michael's history of sexualized behavior problems. An individualized safety plan including guidelines for providing adequate supervision and structure for Michael was developed. The foster parents learned how to help Michael dispute negative thoughts and feelings. Michael's foster parents used these techniques during the therapy sessions to dispute the negative and inaccurate thoughts associated with the anxiety about having Michael come to live with them. As a result, the foster parents had a specific individualized plan for how to assist Michael and they were able to counteract unwarranted anxiety about Michael being placed in their home.

At a 6-month follow-up appointment with Michael and the foster family, it was reported that Michael was doing well. Parent and self-report measures indicated that he was not exhibiting any externalizing or internalizing symptoms that reached a clinically significant level. He had not engaged in sexualized behavior in the foster home and his foster parents were able to use the techniques learned in therapy to assist Michael in disputing negative thoughts and feelings. Foster parents reported that Michael had continued to use the positive leadership skills that were evident in the therapy group.

SUMMARY

Childhood sexual abuse is a significant problem (Sedlack & Broadhurst, 1996) in that it affects a substantial number of youth every year (U.S. Department of Health and Human Services, 2003). Efforts to address this problem include research (e.g., Beichtman, Zucker, Hood, daCosta, Akman, & Cassavia, 1992; Finkelhor, 1990), the development of assessment tools (Briere, 1996; Friedrich, 1997; Spaccarelli, 1995; Wolfe, Gentile, Michienzi, Sas, & Wolfe, 1991), and intervention strategies (American Professional Society on the

Abuse of Children, 1995; Cohen, Deblinger, & Mannarino, 2005). To date, TF-CBT has been identified as an effective treatment for youth who are victims of childhood sexual abuse (e.g., Cocoran, 2004; Cohen, Berliner, & March, 2000).

Trauma Focused Cognitive Behavior Therapy (TF-CBT) is well supported as an effective treatment (e.g., Cohen, Deblinger, & Mannarino, 2005; Cohen, Deblinger, Mannarino, & Steer, 2004) as it integrates research findings (e.g., Finkelhor & Brown, 1986) and provides a cognitive-behavioral conceptualization of sexual abuse (Perrin, Smith, & Yule, 2004). A TF-CBT treatment approach focuses on the cognitions, emotions, and behaviors youth experience when sexually abused. Research further indicates that TF-CBT intervention strategies are beneficial when provided in individual and group formats (Saunders, Berliner, & Hanson, 2004), however, descriptions of the protocol are for individual and family therapy sessions. Therefore, in this chapter we have adapted the protocol to a group format. Although research indicates that it is important to have parent or caregiver involvement in treatment (King et al., 2000), this may not always be possible due to parental noninvolvement, and placement in residential or foster care settings. Although further study is needed, this chapter suggests that this model can be effectively adapted to a group format in settings/situations where concurrent caregiver involvement is not possible. The findings from ongoing dismantling studies will continue to inform clinicians as to the important components of cognitive-behavioral therapy with children who have experienced sexual abuse.

RECOMMENDED READINGS

Bryant, R. A., & Harvey, A.G. (2000). *Acute stress disorder: A handbook of theory, assessment, and treatment.* Washington, D.C.: American Psychological Association Press.

Bryant, R. A., Sackville, T., Dang, S. T., Moulds, M., & Guthrie, R. (1999). Treating acute stress disorder: An evaluation of cognitive behavior therapy and supportive counseling techniques. *American Journal of Psychiatry, 156*(11), 1780–1786.

Burton, J. E., Rasmussen, L. A., Bradshaw, J., Christopherson, B J., & Huke, S. C. (1998). *Treating children with sexually abusive behavior problems: Guidelines for child and parent intervention.* New York: Haworth.

Cohen, J. A., Deblinger, E., & Mannarino, A. P. (2005). Trauma focused cognitive-behavioral therapy for sexually abused children. In E. D. Hibbs, & P. S. Jensen, (Eds.), *Psychosocial treatments for child and adolescent disorders: Empirically based strategies for clinical practice* (2nd ed., pp. 743–765). Washington DC: American Psychological Association.

Cohen, J.A., Mannarino, A.P., & Deblinger, E. (2006). *Treating trama and traumatic grief in children and adolescents.* New York: Guilford.

Deblinger, E. & Heflin, A.H. (1996). *Treating sexually abused children and their nonoffending parent: A cognitive behavioral approach.* Thousand Oaks, CA: Sage.

Foa, E. B., Keane, T. M., & Friedman, M. J., (2000). *Effective treatments for PTSD: Practice guidelines from the International Society for Traumatic Studies.* New York: Guilford.

Graham, P. (Ed). (2005). *Cognitive behaviour therapy for children and families.* New York: Cambridge University Press.

Myers, J. E. B., Berliner, L., Briere, J., Hendrix, C. T., Reid, T., & Jenny, C. (2002). *The Apsac handbook on child maltreatment.* Thousand Oaks, CA: Sage.

Stauffer, L., & Deblinger, E. (1991). *Let's talk about taking care of you: An educational book about body safety.* Hatfield, PA: Hope for Families.

REFERENCES

American Professional Society on the Abuse of Children. (1995). *Practice guidelines: Psychosocial evaluation of suspected sexual abuse of young children.* Chicago: Author.

Banyard, V. L., Williams, L. M., & Siegel, J. A. (2004). Childhood sexual abuse: A gender perspective on context and consequences. *Child Maltreatment, 9,* 223-238.

Beichtman, J. H., Zucker, K. J., Hood, J. E., daCosta, G. A., Akman, D., & Cassavia, E. (1992). A review of the long-term effects of child sexual abuse. *Child Abuse & Neglect, 16,* 101–118.

Bonner, B., Logue, M. B., Kaufman, K. L., & Niec, L. N. (2001). Child maltreatment. In C. E. Walker & M. C. Roberts (Eds.), *Handbook of clinical child psychology* (3rd ed., pp. 989–1030). New York: Wiley.

Bonner, B. L., Walker, C. E., & Berliner, L. (1999). *Children with sexual behavior problems: Assessment and treatment* (Final Report, Grant No. 90-CA-1469). Washington, DC: Administration of Children, Youth, and Families, Department of Health and Human Services.

Brewin, C. R. (2001) Cognitive and emotional reactions to traumatic events: implications for short-term intervention. *Advances in Mind—Body Medicine, 17,* 163-168.

Briere, J. (1996). *Trauma symptom checklist for children professional manual.* Odessa, FL: Psychological Assessment Resources.

Briere, J. (2005). *Trauma symptom checklist for young children professional manual.* Lutz, FL: Psychological Assessment Resources.

Brown, L. K., & Brown, M. (1997). *What's the big secret: Talking about sex with girls and boys.* Boston: Little, Brown.

Burton, J. E., Rasmussen, L. A., Bradshaw, J., Christopherson, B. J., & Huke, S. C. (1998). *Treating children with sexually abusive behavior problems: Guidelines for child and parent intervention.* New York: Haworth.

Cocoran, J. (2004). Treatment outcome research with the non-offending parents of sexually abused children: A critical review. *Journal of Child Sexual Abuse, 13*(2), 59–84.

Cohen J. A., & Mannarino, A. P. (1993). Sexual abuse. In R. T. Ammerman, C. G. Last, & M. Hersen (Eds.), *Handbook of prescriptive treatments for children and adolescents* (pp. 347–366). Boston: Allyn and Bacon.

Cohen, J., & Mannarino, A. P. (1996). A treatment outcome study for sexually abused preschoolers: Initial findings. *Journal of the American Academy of Child and Adolescent Psychiatry, 35*(1), 42–50.

Cohen, J. A., Berliner, L., & March, J. S. (2000). Treatment of children and adolescents. In E. Foa, T. Keane, & M. Freidman (Eds.), *Effective treatments for PTSD: Practice guidelines from the International Society for Traumatic Stress Studies* (pp. 106–138). New York: Guilford.

Cohen, J. A., Deblinger, E., & Mannarino, A. P. (2005). Trauma focused cognitive-behavioral therapy for sexually abused children. In E. D. Hibbs, & P. S. Jensen, (Eds.), *Psychosocial treatments for child and adolescent disorders: Empirically based strategies for clinical practice* (2nd ed., pp. 743–765. Washington, DC: American Psychological Association.

Cohen, J. A., Deblinger, E., Mannarino, A. P., & Steer, R. A. (2004). A multisite, randomized controlled trial for children with sexual abuse-related PTSD symptoms. *Journal of the American Academy of Child and Adolescent Psychiatry, 43*(4), 393–402.

Conte, J. R., & Schuerman, J. R. (1988). The effects of sexual abuse on children: A multidimensional view. In G. E. Wyatt & G. J. Powell (Eds.), *Lasting effects of child sexual abuse* (pp. 157–170). Newbury Park, CA: Sage.

Corder, B. F. (2000). *Structured psychotherapy groups for sexually abused children and adolescents.* Sarasota, FL: Professional Resource Press.

Deblinger, E., & Heflin, A. H. (1996). *Treating sexually abused children and their nonoffending parent: A cognitive behavioral approach.* Thousand Oaks, CA: Sage.

Deblinger, E., & Runyon, M. K. (2005). Understanding and treating feelings of shame in children who have experienced maltreatment. *Child Maltreatment, 10*(4), 364–376.

Ehlers, A., & Clark, D. M. (2000). A cognitive model of posttraumatic stress disorder. *Behaviour Research and Therapy, 38,* 319–345.

Elliott, D. M., & Briere, J. (1994). Forensic sexual abuse evaluations of older children: Disclosures and symptomatology. *Behavioral Sciences and the Law, 12,* 261–277.

Ellis, A. (1962). *Reason and emotion in psychotherapy.* New York: Lyle Stuart.

Faller, K. (1996). *Evaluating children suspected of having been sexually abused.* Thousand Oaks, CA: Sage.

Faller, K. C. (1993). *Child sexual abuse: Intervention and treatment issues.* Washington, DC: U.S. Department of Health and Human Services.

Falls, W. A. (1998). Extinction: A review of theory and evidence suggesting that memories are not erased with nonreinforcement. In W. O'Donohue (Ed.), *Learning and behavior therapy* (pp. 205–229). Boston: Allyn & Bacon.

Feiring, C., & Taska, L. S. (2005). The persistence of shame following sexual abuse: A longitudinal look at risk and recovery. *Child Maltreatment, 10*(4), 337–349.

Feiring, C., Taska, L., & Chen, K. (2002). Trying to understand why horrible things happen: Attribution, shame, and symptom development following sexual abuse. *Child Maltreatment, 7*(1), 26–41.

Fergusson, D. M., Horwood, L. J., & Lynskey, M. T. (1996). Childhood sexual abuse and psychiatric disorder in young adulthood: II. Psychiatric outcomes of childhood and sexual abuse. *Journal of the American Academy of Child and Adolescent Psychiatry, 35,* 1365–1374.

Finkelhor, D., & Browne, A. (1986). Initial and long term effects: A conceptual Framework. In D. Finkelhor, S. Araji, L. Baron, A. Browne, S. D. Peters, & G. E. Wyatt, (Eds.), *Sourcebook on child sexual abuse* (pp. 143–179), Newbury Park, CA: Sage.

Finkelhor, D. (1984). *Child sexual abuse.* New York: The Free Press.

Finkelhor, D. (1990). Early and long-term effects of child sexual abuse: An update. *Professional psychology: Research and Practice, 21,* 325–330.

Finkelhor, D., & Barron, L. (1996). Risk factors for sexual abuse. *Journal of Interpersonal Violence, 1*(1), 43–71.

Finkelhor, D., & Berliner, L. (1995). Research on the treatment of sexually abused children: A review and recommendations. *Journal of the American Academy of Child and Adolescent Psychiatry, 34,* 1408–1423.

Foa, E. B., & Kozak, M. J. (1986). Emotional processing of fear: Exposure to corrective information. *Psychological Bulletin, 99,* 220–235.

Foa, E. B., Rothbaum, B. O., Riggs, D. S., & Murdock, T. (1991). Treatment of PTSD in rape victims: A comparison between cognitive behavioral procedures and counseling. *Journal of Counseling and Consulting Psychology, 59,* 715–723.

Foa, E. B., Steketee, G., & Olasov-Rothbaum, B. (1989). Behavioural/cognitive conceptualizations of post-traumatic stress disorder. *Behavior Therapy, 20,* 155–176.

Friedrich, W. (1996). An integrated model of psychotherapy with abused children. In J. Briere, L. Berliner, J. A. Bulkley, C. Jenny, & T. Reid (Eds.), *The APSAC handbook on child maltreatment.* Thousand Oaks, CA: Sage.

Friedrich, W. N. (1995). *Psychotherapy with sexually abused boys: An integrated approach.* Thousand Oaks, CA: Sage Publications.

Friedrich, W. . (1997). *Child sexual behavior inventory: Professional manual.* Odessa, FL: Psychological Assessment Associates.

Friedrich, W. N., Grambsch, P., Damon, L., Hewitt, S. K., Koverola, C., Lang, R., & Wolfe, V. (1992). The Child Sexual Behavior Inventory: Normative and clinical comparisons. *Psychological Assessment, 4,* 303–311.

Gomes-Schwartz, B., Horowitz, J. M., & Cardarelli, A.P. (1990). *Child sexual abuse: The initial effects.* Newbury Park, CA: Sage.

Gordon, B. N., & Schroeder, C. S. (1995). *Sexuality: A developmental approach to problems.* New York: Plenum Press.

Harris, R. H. (1994). *It's perfectly normal: Changing bodies, growing up, sex, and sexual health.* Cambridge, MA: Candlewick Press.

Haugaard, J. (2000). The challenge of defining child sexual abuse. *American Psychologist, 55*(9), 1036–1039.

Heward, W. L. (1996). Three low-tech strategies for increasing the frequency of active student response during group instruction. In R. Gardner III, D. M. Sainato, J. O. Cooper, T. E. Heron, W. L. Heward, J. W. Eshleman, & T. A. Grossi (Eds.), *Behavior analysis in education: Focus on measurably superior instruction* (pp. 283–320). Pacific Grove, CA: Brooks/Cole.

Hulme, P. A., & Agrawal, S. (2004). Patterns of childhood sexual abuse characteristics and their relationships to other childhood abuse and adult health. *Journal of Interpersonal Violence, 19*(4), 389–405.

Johnson, T. C. (1998). *Treatment exercises for child abuse victims and children with sexual behavior problems.* South Pasadena, CA: Author.

Johnson, T. C. (1999). *Understanding your child's sexual behavior: What's natural and healthy.* Oakland, CA: New Harbinger Publications.

Kendall, P. C., & Hollon, S. D. (Eds.). (1979). *Cognitive-behavioral interventions: Theory, research and procedures.* New York: Academic Press.

Kendall-Tackett, K. A., Williams, L. M., & Finkelhor, D. (1993) Impact of sexual abuse on children: A review and synthesis of recent empirical studies. *Psychological Bulletin, 113*(1), 164–180.

King, N., Tonge, B., Mullen, P., Myerson, N., Heyne, D., Rollings, S., Martin, R., & Ollendick, T. (2000). Treating sexually abused children with posttraumatic stress symptoms: A randomized clinical trial. *Journal of the American Academy of Child and Adolescent Psychiatry, 39,* 1347–1355.

King, N. J., Tonge, B. J., Mullen, P., Myerson, N., Heyne, D., & Ollendick, T. H. (1999). Cognitive-behavioural treatment of sexually abused children: A review of research. *Behavioural and Cognitive Psychotherapy, 27,* 295-309.

Koeppen, A. S. (1974). Relaxation training for children. *Elementary School Guidance and Counseling, 9,* 14–21.

Larson, C., Terman, D. L., Gomby, D. S., Quinn, L. S., & Behrman R.E. (1994). Sexual abuse of children: Recommendations and Analysis. *The Future of Children, 4*(2), 4-30.

Letourneau, E. J., Schoenwald, S. K., & Sheidow, A. J. (2004). Children and adolescents with sexual behavior problems. *Child Maltreatment, 9*(1), 49–61.

Perrin, S., Smith, P., & Yule, W. (2004). Treatment of PTSD in children and adolescents. In P. M. Barrett & T. H. Ollendick (Eds.), *Handbook of interventions that work with children and adolescents: Prevention and treatment* (pp. 217–242). West Sussex, UK: Wiley.

Powers, S. W., & Spirito, A. (1998a). Biofeedback. In J. Noshpitz, J. Coyle, S. Harrison, & S. Eth (Eds.), *Handbook of child and adolescent psychiatry* (vol 6, pp. 411–417). New York: Wiley.

Powers, S. W., & Spirito, A. (1998b). Relaxation. In J. Noshpitz, J. Coyle, S. Harrison, & S. Eth (Eds.), *Handbook of child and adolescent psychiatry* (vol. 6, pp. 417–422). New York: Wiley.

Putnam, F. (2003). Ten-year research update review: Child sexual abuse. *Child and Adolescent Psychiatry, 2*(3), 269–278.

Reeker, J., Ensing, D., & Elliott, R. (1997). A meta-analytic investigation of group treatment outcomes for sexually abused children. *Child Abuse and Neglect, 21,* 669–680.

Reynolds, C. R., & Kamphaus, R. W. (2004). *Behavior assessment system for children: Second edition manual.* Circle Pines, MN: American Guidance Service.

Salmon K., & Bryant, R. A. (2002). Posttraumatic stress disorder in children: The influence of developmental factors. *Clinical Psychology Review, 22,* 163–188.

Sandfort, G. M., & Rademakers, J. (Eds.). (2000). *Childhood sexuality: Normal sexual behavior and development.* New York: Haworth Press.

Saunders, B. E., Berliner, L., & Hanson, R. F. (Eds.). (2004). *Child physical and sexual abuse: guidelines for treatment* (Revised report: April 26, 2004). Charleston, SC: National Crime Victims Research and Treatment Center.

Saywitz, K. J., Mannarino, A. P., Berliner, L., & Cohen, J. A. (2000). Treatment for sexually abused children and adolescents. *American Psychologist, 55*(9), 1040–1049.

Sedlak, A. J., & Broadhurst, D. D. (1996). *Executive summary of the third national incidence study of child abuse and neglect.* Washington, DC: U.S. Department of Health and Human Services.

Seligman, M., Reivich, K., Jaycox, L., & Gillham, J. (1995). *The optimistic child.* New York: Harper Perennial.

Silovsky, J. F., & Bonner, B. L. (2003). Children with sexual behavior problems. In T. H. Ollendick, & C. S. Schroeder (Eds.), *Encyclopedia of clinical child and pediatric psychology* (pp. 589–591). New York: Kluwer Press.

Silovsky, J. F., & Niec, L. (2002). Characteristics of young children with sexual behavior problems: A pilot study. *Child Maltreatment, 7*(3), 187–197.

Spaccarelli, S. (1994). Stress, appraisal, and coping in child sexual abuse: A theoretical and empirical review. *Psychological Bulletin, 116*(2), 340–362.

Spaccarelli, S. (1995). Measuring abuse stress and negative cognitive appraisals in child sexual abuse: Validity data on two new scales. *Journal of Abnormal Child Psychology, 6,* 703–727.

Tong. L., Oates. K., & McDowell, M. (1987). Personality development following sexual abuse. *Child Abuse and Neglect, II,* 371-383.

U.S. Department of Health and Human Services, Administration on Children, Youth and Families. (2005). *Child Maltreatment 2003.* Washington, DC: U.S. Government Printing Office.

Walker, C. E. (2001). *Learn to relax, 3rd edition: Proven techniques for reducing stress, tension, and anxiety —and promoting peak performance.* New York: Wiley.

Weist, M. D., & Danforth, J. S. (1998). Cognitive-behavioral therapy for children and adolescents. In H. S. Ghuman & R. M. Sarles (Eds.), *Handbook of child and adolescent outpatient, day treatment and community psychiatry* (pp. 235–244). Philadelphia: Brunner/Mazel.

Wolfe, V., Gentile, C., Michienzi, T., Sas, L., & Wolfe, D. A. (1991). The Children's Impact of Traumatic Events Scale: A measure of post-sexual-abuse PTSD symptoms. *Behavioral Assessment, 13,* 359–383.

Chapter Sixteen

Mediating Depression in Youth: A Cognitive-Behavior Group Therapy Approach

Ray W. Christner & McKenzie L. Walker

It is not uncommon to hear an adult describe a child, or maybe more commonly an adolescent, as "moody" or "irritable." While in many cases this may be a simple fluctuation in mood, for other youth this may highlight ongoing and sometimes serious problems. Professionals have historically viewed depression and mood disorders within the context of adulthood. In fact, some believed that children did not have the cognitive capacities to be depressed or that depression was a normal part of growing up. However, more recent reports have suggested that Major Depressive Disorder (MDD) and Dysthymic Disorder (DD) are more common in childhood and adolescence than once was thought (American Academy of Child and Adolescent Psychiatry [AACAP], 1998). Lifetime prevalence rates for 15- to 18-year-olds have been reported to be about 14%, with an additional 11% estimated to have a lifetime history of minor depression (Kessler & Walters, 1998). In adolescents, Depression is often associated with comorbid diagnoses and symptoms, such as an increased risk for substance abuse and a higher risk of suicide (AACAP, 1998). Although the prevalence of Depression before puberty is not well established, some estimates suggest as many as 2% of children may experience depression at a given time. However, many of these children are seen as being disruptive or a behavioral problem rather than depressed (Evans & Andrews, 2005).

CLINICAL COURSE

The clinical course of MDD and DD in youth can be affected by a variety of factors. These factors may occur in isolation or may overlap and result in a cumulative effect. While we often use the global diagnoses of MDD and DD, these contributing factors influence both the clinical course and the manifestation of symptoms so that presentation varies across individuals. The AACAP (1998) has provided a list of some common factors, including demographics, genetic and familial factors, psychopathological factors, educational functioning, psychodynamic factors, cognitive style and temperament, the experience of early adverse events, exposures to negative life events, family relation-ships, and biological factors.

Field, Diego, and Sanders (2001) indicated that parental factors have a strong impact on adolescent depression. Specifically, the decrease in parental relationships, verbal intimacy with parents, and physical affection are all factors found to correlate with depression in adolescents. There is also evidence that an increase in paternal depres-sion correlates with adolescent depression versus rates in non-depressed fathers and their children. Stark and colleagues (1993) noted that there is a greater likelihood that depressed parents will use punitive parenting because of irritation with the child and a lack of energy and emotional functioning necessary to provide appropriate parental support. Research has concluded that families with less support and more conflict and dysfunction increase a child's risk of developing depression (Evans & Andrews, 2005).

Compared to nondepressed peers, adolescents with depression report having nega-tive peer relationships and fewer friends, are viewed as not as popular, and scored lower on measures focusing on well-being and happiness (Field et al., 2001). Social problems in children and adolescents often occur before the onset of depressive symptoms, and subsequently depressive symptoms may then further exacerbate the vicious cycle of so-cial difficulties. This is important, in that the social or interpersonal environment serves an important, though often stressful, context for youth to develop schema and belief systems about themselves and how they fit in with others. Additionally, adolescents with depression have reported higher levels of suicidal ideation than nondepressed peers (Field et al., 2001); a likelihood that clinicians must be prepared to assess and intervene appropriately.

Other behaviors that clinicians must be aware of with regard to children and ado-lescents with depression include spending less time doing homework and having lower grade point averages in school. These, in part, may result from difficulty concentrating, lack of motivation, increase in fatigue, etc. Moreover, it is less likely for depressed youth to spend time exercising or engaging in physical activity. The presence of substance use and abuse in late adolescence for those with a depressive disorder is common (Evans & Andrews, 2005). Those adolescents who are depressed are more likely to use cocaine and marijuana than nondepressed peers (Field et al., 2001).

WHY IS TREATING YOUTH DEPRESSIVE DISORDERS IMPORTANT?

While depressive disorders in youth can be somewhat complex, there is growing evidence that children and adolescents struggling with depression can be treated successfully with certain targeted psychotherapies. One of the most widely studied psychotherapies for depression has been cognitive therapy (Beck, Rush, Shaw, & Emery, 1979), and in recent years, others have discussed the use of cognitive or cognitive-behavioral treatments for depression in youth (Curry & Reinecke, 2003; Friedberg & McClure, 2002; Clarke, Lewinsohn, & Hops, 1990; Lewinsohn, Clarke, Rohde, Hops, & Seeley, 1996). Current research has noted that "about half of Americans will meet the criteria for a DSM-IV disorder sometime in their lifetime, with first onset usually in childhood or adoles-cence" (Kessler, Berglund, Demler, Jin, & Walters, 2005, p. 593). In fact, children and adolescents who are depressed are at an increased risk for experiencing reoccurrences in later adolescence and adulthood (Costello et al., 2002; Lewinsohn, Solomon, Seeley,

& Zeiss, 2000). With this data in mind, as well as the fact that depressive disorders and other mental health condition are linked to difficulties in various areas of life functioning (e.g., school performance, peer problems, family issues), it is incumbent upon mental health professionals to address risk factors and provide early intervention for youth who show signs of mental illness, including depression, to minimize difficulties later in adult functioning. Some have suggested that early intervention of subthreshold depressive features might foster an adaptive cognitive or attributional style among youth, which may reduce susceptibility to depressive episodes later on (Gillham & Reivich, 1999).

DEPRESSIVE DISORDERS IN YOUTH

Identifying children and adolescents with depressive disorders is not an easy task, as comorbid conditions or secondary behaviors (e.g., acting out) often cloud the presentation. Thus, clinicians working with children and adolescents with potential depressive disorders must have a solid understanding of the essential features of these disorders, as well as common co-occurring difficulties. Moreover, while understanding the diagnostic criteria is important, having a solid conceptualization of depression in youth is essential in developing effective treatments.

Major Depressive Disorder

The *Diagnostic and Statistical Manual of Mental Disorders, Fourth Edition, Text Revision* (*DSM-IV-TR*; American Psychiatric Association, 2000) provides guidelines and criteria for the diagnosis of various disorders, including mood disorders. A diagnosis of Major Depressive Disorder requires the client to have at least one major depressive episode lasting for two weeks or longer. The key features of a depressive episode include: (1) a depressed mood (in youth the mood can be irritable); (2) loss of appetite or pleasure in activities; (3) appetite or weight loss or gain of at least 5%; (4) sleep problems in the form of increased or decreased sleep; (5) psychomotor agitation or slowness; (6) lack of energy or fatigue; (7) feelings of worthlessness or excessive guilt; (8) decreased ability to think, concentrate, or make decisions; and (9) perseverative thoughts of death or frequent thoughts or behaviors related to suicide. These symptoms must be present for the majority of the day and occur more days than not over a minimum 2-week period.

Dysthymic Disorder

Dysthymic Disorder, as compared to MDD, is a more chronic presentation of a depressed mood, lasting for more days than not over a 2-year period. This differs slightly with children and adolescents, in that, while the symptoms must be chronic, the interval of symptom presence needs to be for only one year (American Psychiatric Association, 2000). With youth clients, their symptoms may also vary in presentation, as is the case with MDD, as their mood may be more "irritable" rather than "depressed." DD often has an earlier onset than MDD, and it is commonly diagnosed in childhood, adolescence, or early adulthood. The American Psychiatric Association notes that DD tends to be a more chronic illness, and thus, spontaneous recovery is less likely. Evans and Andrews (2005) use the analogy of chronic allergies to illustrate the persistent nature of DD, whereas MDD would be more similar to that of a bad case of the flu.

According to the *DSM-IV-TR* (American Psychiatric Association, 2000) at least two of the following symptoms need to be present in order to diagnose DD: (a) increased or decreased appetite, (b) sleep disturbance, (c) lack of energy or tiring easily, (d) a decreased self-esteem, (e) lack of concentration and decision making difficulties, or (f) hopelessness. There are times with DD that the individual may have a decrease in symptoms for a period of up to two months, though this does not suggest remission.

Differential Diagnosis and Comorbidity

As noted earlier, the diagnosis of depressive disorders (e.g., MDD and DD) in childhood can be difficult. Thus, it is important for professionals to rule out other possible diagnoses before confirming a diagnosis of MDD or DD. While there are many disorders to consider, nonaffective disorders (e.g., disruptive behavioral disorders, anxiety disorders), adjustment disorders with symptoms of depression, bereavement, and general medical conditions are important to evaluate when diagnosing and treating symptoms of depression.

The AACAP (1998) noted that medical disorders can pose a specific obstacle to the process of differential diagnosis, as a variety of chronic illnesses affect patterns of sleeping and eating, as well as the amount of energy an individual will have to expend. Each of these areas is a core criteria in the diagnosis of depression, and thus, must be explored and ruled out by a physician. Moreover, certain medical illnesses can exacerbate any already existing depressive symptoms, while other conditions may bring on a new episode of depression. It is important to understand how the illness is affecting the client to be able to provide the most appropriate interventions for symptom relief. For example, The AACAP (1998) highlighted the importance of noting whether the client is reporting feeling hopeless, worthless, guilty, or are displaying thoughts or actions of suicide. This is important because these feelings are more likely to stem from a depressive disorder rather than a physical illness pointing to the need for a psychotherapeutic intervention. Mental health professionals treating children and adolescents with a depressive disorder should maintain a relationship with the youngsters treating physician, and ongoing consultation is suggested to the benefit of both medical and mental health professionals.

UNDERSTANDING DEPRESSIVE DISORDERS IN YOUTH: A CONCEPTUALIZATION

The manifestation of depressive disorders in children and adolescents often looks different from that within an adult population, as noted above. When working with children and adolescents with depressive disorders, clinicians must obtain a clear case conceptualization to inform treatment. Murphy and Christner (2006) offered a format for consideration when conceptualizing cases involving children and adolescents. Their approach consists of several components including: (1) a problem list, (2) assessment data, (3) developmental consideration, (4) working hypotheses, (5) origin of working hypotheses, (6) antecedents and precipitating factors, (7) maintaining factors, and (8) protective and resiliency factors. However, in addition to this format, clinicians working

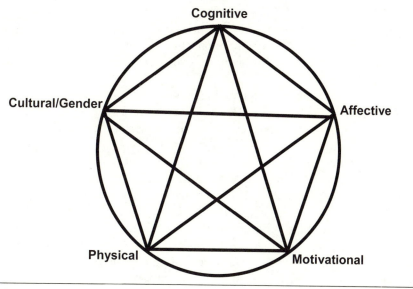

Figure 16.1   Interaction Effect.

with children and adolescents with a depressive disorder must also have a conceptual understanding of depressive symptoms across several domain areas: (1) affective, (2) cognitive, (3) motivational, (4) environmental/interpersonal, (5) physical, and (6) cultural/gender. These aspects are not distinct components of depression, but interact—in terms of one's functioning in each area contributing to that of the other areas—to result in the overall presentation of the client's experience with depression which must be comprehensively conceptualized for the sake of effective treatment (see Figure 16.1).

Affective

Affective components of depressive disorders are commonly recognized by clinicians and include feelings, such as self-loathing, apathy, and sadness. However, when working with youth it is common for other emotions to be displayed, as well. Moore and Carr (2000) suggest that irritability, anxiety, and aggression may be the main features in children with MDD, and sadness and lack of pleasure may be less prominent. Roberts, Lewinsohn, and Seeley (1995) noted that adolescents, however, are more likely to display a depressed mood, sleep problems, poor concentration, appetite disturbances, and lack of interest in pleasurable activities (anhedonia). With some youth clients, it is possible to see a less stable affective presentation, as they exhibit a combination of sadness, anxiety, anger, aggression, irritability, and so forth.

Cognitive

Cognitive components related to depression are two-fold. First are the cognitive deficits that may accompany a depressive disorder or depressive symptoms. These include difficulty concentrating and making decisions, as well as a fixation with morbidity. For children with depressive disorders, it is likely that these deficits are a result of their mood difficulties. However, deficits in regulation skills, such as emotional dysregu-lation, have been consistently linked to depressive disorder, though the evidence is unclear whether these deficits precede the onset of depression (Shaw, Keenan, Vondra, Delliguadri, & Giovannelli, 1997) or occur as a result of depressive symptoms (Garber, Braafladt, & Weiss, 1995).

Cognitive distortions offer another perspective into how cognition influences depres-sive disorders. Most well known in this regard is Beck's cognitive triad (1967), which asserts that negative distortions in perception about the self, the world, and the future result in a depressed mood. Dysfunctional schemas serve as filters that guide what an individual attends to, how he or she perceives it, and what meaning he or she takes from it. The youth's schema paired with situational stimuli (everyday occurrences) produce the child's individual conscious thoughts, also known as automatic thoughts. Thus, a young girl who is depressed may perceive the situation in which her friend is talking to another girl as negative, with automatic thoughts that may include "She doesn't want to be my friend any more," or "Nobody likes me." Although this model generally assumes that depressed youth have more frequent negative thoughts (supported by Zupan, Hammen, & Jaenicke, 1987), other studies have shown that nondepressed youth possess positive self-schema, which are not present in depressed youth (Hammen & Zupan, 1984). This lack of positive self-schema or the existence of negative self-schema or a combination of the two are thought to lead to a negative bias and perception in information processing in youth with depressive disorders.

Motivational

A number of motivational symptoms exist with childhood and adolescent depressive disorders. These include isolation from friends and family, a decrease in academic skills or progress, and an increase in suicidal ideation and actions. Moreover, these children and adolescents are less likely to engage in pleasurable activities. This lack of motivation or energy may make it difficult in treating youth with a depressed mood, and in many cases, may be the entry point for intervention. We should not automatically assume that individuals are motivated to make necessary changes, even though depressive symptoms are often uncomfortable for them. Sometimes, too early in treatment, we "jump" to hav-ing the client take action, only to find them not ready, and subsequently, not following through. Instead, considering the clients' readiness to change and matching interventions to "where the client is" may be more beneficial. Prochaska, DiClemente, and Norcross (1992) originally developed their Stages of Change Model for the treatment of substance abuse. Over the years, their model has been used with a number of problem areas. Free-man and Dolan (2001) offered a revised Stages model, which expanded the work of Prochaska and colleagues. We have found this expanded model to be very useful with youth patients. For further information, see Freeman and Dolan (2001).

Environmental/Interpersonal

Depressed youth often describe experiencing negative psychosocial situations that have "led to" or exacerbated their negative mood. These events can include acute situations, such as a loss of a friendship or poor performance in school, as well as those events that are chronic, such as family conflict, chronic illness, ongoing peer conflicts, etc. While the acute situations may result in a short-term depressive state, chronic events or frequent acute events may lead to more severe mood difficulties. Abramson, Seligman, and Teasdale (1979) noted that experiencing negative, uncontrollable situations is linked to feelings of helplessness and apathy. When these situations are experienced continually, they may lead to the development of negative self-schema (that may include beliefs about one's efficacy and abilities to make changes which impacts treatment motivation, participation, and outcome). Young (1991) suggested that maladaptive or negative schema could be the result of inadequate parenting or ongoing family conflict (e.g., repeated criticisms or rejection). While treatment may not have the capability of removing the environmental or interpersonal problems, by understanding these factors and their influence in the development of depression, clinicians can target the negative thoughts about these events and teach patients problem solving skills to better cope with these issues. In some cases, integrating family-based interventions may be warranted as well.

Physical

Several notable physical manifestations are common in depressive disorders. As noted above, clinicians should seek medical consults when these symptoms are present, as there may be a medical cause. Some of the physical manifestations of depression include changes in sleep patterns, in appetite or eating patterns, as well as complaints of physical illness. These difficulties with sleep may exacerbate feelings of fatigue and sadness and may also contribute to cognitive deficits, such as poor concentration and decision making. While appetite and eating problems may also affect cognitive and affective components, it may also result in increased or decreased weight, which can further bring about social difficulties or negative automatic thoughts. Stark, Christopher, and Dempsey (1993) noted that adolescents with severe depression are more likely to present with weight gain and psychomotor deficits.

Cultural and Gender

Cultural and gender issues are also important when conceptualizing depressive disorders in children and adolescents. Stark, Sander, Yancy, Bronik, and Hoke (2000) noted that girls tend to experience more severe and prolonged episodes of depression. There is also a difference noted in the behaviors of boys in various minority populations, as depression and even anxiety are more commonly displayed through acting out rather than feelings of sadness or fear (Rambaldo et al., 2001). Gibbs (1998) reported an alarming increase in the rate of suicide among African American youth and noted that the identification of suicidal ideas in African American youth may be more difficult, as they express more anger, acting out, and high-risk behaviors. Research on depression in Asian American youngsters has been sparse, though Nagata (1998) indicated that this should not be interpreted as an absence of depression with this population, but rather a possible reflection of the cultural reluctance to pursue mental health services. Ho (1992) has noted that Asian immigrants, however, exhibit an increase in somatic complaints as a result of their internalization of psychological distress.

ASSESSMENT OF DEPRESSION IN YOUTH

The assessment of youth for therapy and diagnosis should be comprehensive and include data from multiple sources (e.g., child, parents, teachers). A number of effective tools exist to assess both the presence and severity of depressive disorders. A full and comprehensive review and descriptions of all available measures and their psychometric properties is beyond the scope of this chapter. However, we will provide a brief review of the assessment tools that we commonly use and that inform our clinical practice. Again, in addition to the measures reviewed below, we recommend that clinicians also consult with the child's or adolescent's physician to rule out any physical causes and to offer medical assessment and treatment, if necessary.

Interviews

Clinical interviews are an essential assessment tool for gathering information about a patient or individual. Many suggest the use of semistructured interviews (Stark et al., 1993; Merrell, 2001). In line with Merrell, we recommend the use of two types of semistructured interviews for depressed patients: (1) interview about psychosocial areas and (2) interview regarding behavioral aspects. With regard to the psychosocial interview, it is imperative to have a working knowledge of the patient's interpersonal functioning, family and peer relationships, school adjustment, history of treatment, and social support system. In addition, questions should specifically address areas of any psychological or social deficits, negative life events, the psychological history of the family, medical history, and social network (AACAP, 2001).

The second type of semistructured interview, which focuses on behavioral aspects, is used to gain information about the child's problem areas. This is beyond merely reviewing symptoms of depression or other disorders, and instead, is used to help identify factors that contribute to the behaviors or mood difficulties (e.g., antecedents and consequences of behaviors). Consistent with work seen in many schools, we advocate for *Functional Behavior Assessments* to be conducted with all youth patients. This offers a means to help manage and control factors within the environment that may be contributing to the patient's mood, and if controlled, affords the opportunity for patients to work on personal factors.

In addition to the semistructured interviews discussed above, we recommend the use of the *Kiddie-Schedule for Affective Disorders and Schizophrenia for School-Age Children* (K-SADS; Orvaschel & Puig-Antich, 1987). The K-SADS can be used with the child and parents, and assesses the potential for individual disorders, as well as the child's level of global impairment. While the K-SADS was originally designed for research and requires a high level of training, skilled interviewers or clinicians can easily adapt its flexible format for clinical use.

With any type of interview, it may be necessary to use a variety of techniques to engage the child. For younger children, clinicians will need knowledge and experience in how to use play interview techniques to augment their semistructured interview.

We have found that using simple adjustments such as using puppets or art activities as part of the interview can enhance engagement of the child. In some cases with notably depressed young children, we have used a cognitive-behavioral adaptation of *Sand Tray* techniques to aid in the interview with success.

Rating Scales

It is important when assessing youth to also utilize self-report measures as well a behavioral rating scales completed by caregivers and teachers. There are a number of broadband and narrow-band scales that are useful. While broadband scales are most useful in initial assessment and to identify or rule out any other comorbid issues, narrow-band instruments can give a more detailed understanding of the child's depression and can also be used for progress monitoring or outcome assessment.

Broadband Measures.   While there are a number of broad-band instruments on the market, two of the most common measures used are the *Achenbach Scales* (Achenbach, 2001) and the *Behavior Assessment System for Children, Second Edition* (BASC-2; Reynolds & Kamphaus, 2004). Both of these offer assessment using parent and teacher versions, as well as self-report inventories that can be completed by the child or adolescent.

The Achenbach Scales consist of the *Child Behavior Checklist* (CBCL), the *Teacher Report Form* (TRF), and the *Youth Report Form* (YRF). Each of these scales assess externalizing and internalizing symptoms of a number of problem areas including aggressive behavior, anxious and depressed symptoms, attention problems, rule-breaking behavior, social problems, somatic complaints, thought problems, and withdrawal. The Achenbach Scales group these problem areas into DSM-oriented scales to assist in diagnosis, including affective problems, anxiety problems, somatic problems, attention deficit/hyperactivity problems, oppositional defiant problems, and conduct problems.

The BASC-2 also offers parent and teacher versions, as well as self-report scales. The BASC-2 assesses both clinical problem areas (e.g., aggression, anxiety, attention problems, atypicality, conduct problems, depression, hyperactivity, learning problems, and withdrawal), as well as adaptive behaviors (e.g., functional communication, leadership, social skills, study skills, adaptability, and resilience). Thus, the use of the BASC-2 can help clarify a youth's diagnostic picture, while also providing information on key assets and strengths that can assist in treatment planning.

Narrowband Measures.   A number of self-report, narrow-band inventories exist for use with children and adolescents. We are specifically focusing on those assessments of mood issues or depression. Beck and his colleagues have developed a number of useful tools to assist in the assessment of depression, including the *Beck Depression Inventory, Second Edition* (BDI-II; Beck, Steer, & Brown, 1996) and the *Beck Youth Inventories, Second Edition* (BYI-II; Beck, Beck, & Jolly, 2005).

The BDI-II consists of 21 items and is intended to assess the severity of depression in adolescents and adults (ages 13 and up). Higher scores on the BDI-II are associated with increased levels of depression (e.g., mild depression = scores of 14 to 19; moderate depression = score of 20 to 28; severe depression = score over 28). In addition to the traditional BDI-II, Beck, Beck, and Jolly (2005) developed the BYI-II. The BYI-II consists of five scales (e.g., self-concept, anxiety, depression, anger, and disruptive behavior), and are used with youth ranging in age from 7 to 18 years. The child responds to 20 items (written at a second grade level) by indicating how true the item is for him or her, using a 4-point scale. Raw scores are converted into T-scores, with scores from 55 to 59 being mildly elevated, 60 to 69 being moderately elevated, and 70 plus being extremely elevated. While all five scales can be given to a child, a unique feature is that each scale can also be given as an individual measure. Thus, when working with depressed youth, clinicians may choose to administer only the BYI-II Depression Scale. We have found the BYI-II to be particularly useful in monitoring progress with children in therapy.

Another useful narrow-band tool is the *Children's Depression Inventory* (CDI; Kovacs, 1992). The CDI is a downward extension of the BDI and can be used with youth patients from 7 to 17 years of age. Similar to the BYI-II, the CDI uses T-scores and a score above 65 is considered clinically significant.

The unique feature of each of the narrow-band measures mentioned is that they can be administered individually or in a group format. This is especially useful when conducting group interventions, as clinicians can use these instruments to assess and monitor outcomes. Recently, we have used the BYI-II periodically throughout a 12-session group (e.g., Session 1, Session 3, Session 6, Session 9, and Session 12) and found it to be useful in monitoring progress and to identify patients who may need further assessment or intervention.

Group Assignment

When assessment data has been collected on youth being considered for group treatment, clinicians must review all information to form a group that can be productive, interactive, and ultimately a positive experience. Clinicians must consider several issues in group member selection. First, the severity of the child's depression is a significant consideration. Given that individuals with differing levels of depression may be dealing with different presenting problems and experiences (e.g., suicidality and hopelessness in more severely depressed youth), we suggest that having group homogeneity regarding the severity of depression should be considered. In addition, having youth who possess similar levels of motivation for change can help facilitate a more productive group. We have included group members who have other comorbid conditions (e.g., generalized anxiety); however, certain comorbid conditions (e.g., drug and alcohol abuse, panic disorder, schizophrenia) require different and sometimes more intensive levels of intervention. Those patients who present as especially severe for group (e.g., suicidal), we often refer for intensive individual work first or, if conducting group work in an intensive treatment program, we request individual psychotherapy to parallel group intervention. Finally, the cognitive functioning level of group members should be considered. Homogeneity across cognitive levels of group members allows facilitators to offer and conduct activities at a level that all participants can grasp and understand.

EVIDENCE-BASED TREATMENT OF DEPRESSION

Evidence of CBT for Depression

Research on the treatment of depression in youth has included studies examining both psychopharmacological and psychotherapeutic interventions. While the treatment of depression often includes a combination of the two, we will focus on psychotherapeutic approaches, specifically those utilizing a cognitive-behavioral model. To date, evidence has shown psychotherapeutic interventions to be efficacious for youth depression (Brent, Holder, Kolko, Birmaher, Baugher, Roth, et al., 1997; Lewinsohn & Clarke, 1999; Stark, Swearer, Kurowski, Sommer, & Bowen, 1996). Much of the research conducted on these interventions has focused on cognitive-behavioral approaches (Weersing, Iyengar, Kolko, Birmaher, & Brent, 2006). The accumulating evidence is promising, suggesting that CBT helps to reduce symptoms of depression for youth patients (Curry & Reinecke, 2003; Weersing et al., 2006). Meta-analyses of CBT outcomes have found moderate to large effect sizes in the reduction of depressive symptoms when compared to wait-list and attention placebo controls (Lewinsohn & Clarke, 1999; Reinecke, Ryan, & DuBois, 1998). Reinecke and colleagues further noted that moderate effect sizes were maintained at follow-up; however, many studies used follow-ups of 3 months or less, and thus, this data should be viewed with caution.

Evidence-Based Cognitive-Behavioral Group Treatment Programs

In addition to CBT in general, CBT group treatments for depression have shown positive outcomes (Stark et al., 1993). The group setting offers opportunities and some benefits beyond what can be provided in individual treatment, such as social learning experiences, skill building practice (e.g., assertiveness), and a forum for modeling behaviors and interpersonal communication with peers. Moreover, when group members help each other, it can instill and increase a members' positive view of the self and serve to reinforce a productive self-schema. Clinicians working with groups help guide group members through a process of identifying thoughts, feelings, behaviors, and symptoms related to a depressed mood and help to build the skill level of participants. Ultimately, as the group progresses there will be little guidance needed from the clinician. (Stark et al., 1993).

While several different evidence-based programs exist for the treatment of depression, two prominent group interventions for youth are the *Adolescent Coping with Depression Course* (Clarke, Lewinsohn, & Hops, 1990) and the *ACTION Program* (Stark & Kendall, 1996). Both of these programs offer a structured program, which focuses on the development of cognitive and behavioral coping skills. Although the limitations of this chapter do not provide the opportunity to review these programs in detail, we provide a brief overview below. Readers are encouraged to consult the individual treatment manuals for both programs for greater detail (see Clarke, Lewinsohn, & Hops, 1990; Stark & Kendall, 1996).

Adolescent Coping with Depression Course (CWD-A). The research examining CWD-A in the treatment of adolescents with depression has, to date, been positive, showing a notable decrease in depressive symptoms as compared to controls (Lewinsohn et al., 1990; Clarke, Rohde, Lewinsohn, Hops, & Seeley, 1999). The entire CWD-A program, including leader manuals and workbooks, can be obtained free of charge by downloading them from the program authors' website at http://www.kpchr.org/public/acwd/acwd.html.

The CWD-A program is a structured group treatment involving a number of patient and therapist resources, including a leader's manual with scripts, a workbook for

Table 16.1   Session Outline of the CWD-A Program
(Clarke, Lewinsohn, & Hops, 1990)

Session Number	Session Topic
Session 1	Depression and Social Learning
Session 2	Self-Observation and Change
Session 3	Reducing Tension
Session 4	Learning How to Change
Session 5	Changing Your Thinking
Session 6	The Power of Positive Thinking
Session 7	Disputing Irrational Thinking
Session 8	Relaxation
Session 9	Communication
Session 10	Communication
Session 11	Negotiation and Problem Solving
Session 12	Negotiation and Problem Solving
Session 13	Negotiation and Problem Solving
Session 14	Negotiation and Problem Solving
Session 15	Life Goals
Session 16	Prevention, Planning, and Ending

group members, and a workbook for parents. CWD-A consists of 16 sessions, and it is consistent with the CBT framework in general, as the program uses direct instruction, modeling, homework, and skill building exercises so that patients learn to better cope with or prevent depression. Table 16.1 offers an outline of the sessions and session topics for the CWD-A program.

The ACTION Program.   The ACTION program (Stark & Kendall, 1996) provides another structured cognitive-behavioral group treatment approach, though it can be used with children as young as 9-years of age through adolescents. The ACTION treatment program includes 30 sessions, about 1 hour each, and teaches skill sets that include relaxation skills, social skills, problem solving skills, and identifying the interaction between cognitions, behaviors, and affect. Child workbooks and therapist treatment manuals are available with this program. The ACTION program has a set sequence of sessions. Table 16.2 offers a brief overview of the session topics.

A MODULAR APPROACH TO COGNITIVE-BEHAVIORAL GROUP TREATMENT WITH DEPRESSION

When reviewing the two treatment programs above, it is evident that both have many aspects in common. For instance, both programs have components addressing relaxation, self-monitoring (or observation), problem-solving instruction, and the modification of maladaptive thoughts, to name a few. Additionally, both of these programs provide psychoeducational aspects about depression, as well as the treatment approach in general. While we are comparing only two programs for depression, other programs for depression and other disorders seem to have similar components. Thus, clinicians looking to offer evidence-based intervention should review programs to ensure they cover these areas, as well as others that are specific to the problem area being addressed.

Table 16.2 Session Outline of the ACTION Program (Stark & Kendall, 1996)

Session Number	Session Topic
Session 1	Introduction; establish appropriate expectations
Session 2	Affective education; establish with-in group incentive system; self-monitoring pleasant emotions
Session 3	Affective education; introduction to active coping orientation; self-monitoring pleasant emotions
Session 4	Affective education; extended coping orientation, pleasant events scheduling; self-monitoring pleasant emotions
Session 5	Affective education; introduction to problem solving; self-monitoring pleasant emotions
Session 6	Affective education; pleasant events scheduling and self-monitoring pleasant emotions; problem-solving game
Session 7	Affective education; pleasant event scheduling; problem-solving game
Session 8	Affective education; application of problem-solving to mood disturbance
Session 9	Application of problem solving to mood disturbance; missing solution activity
Session 10	Introduction to relaxation; exercise and mood
Session 11	Problem solving applied to interpersonal situations; pleasant events scheduling; relaxation as a coping strategy
Session 12	Problem solving applied to interpersonal situations; focus on self-evaluation of solution implementation; relaxation as a coping strategy
Session 13	Spontaneous problem solving; relaxation and problem solving
Session 14	Introduction to cognitive restructuring; identification of depressogenic thoughts
Session 15	Practice catching negative thoughts; cognitive restructuring
Session 16	Improve understanding of cognitive restructuring; practice catching negative thoughts; what's the evidence?; what to do when a negative thought is true
Session 17	Alternative interpretation
Session 18	Alternative interpretation; identifying negative expectations; introduce "what if"?
Session 19	What if?
Session 20	Review of cognitive restructuring; introduction to assertiveness training; generate and rehearse coping statements
Session 21	Positive assertiveness; generation of coping statements
Session 22	Assertiveness training; generation of coping statements
Session 23	Identify personal standards; introduction to self-evaluation training; identification of areas in need of personal improvement
Session 24	Establish goals and subgoals for self-improvement
Session 25	Self-evaluation training/working toward self-improvement
Session 26	Self-evaluation training/working toward self-improvement
Session 27	Self-evaluation training/working toward self-improvement
Session 28	Self-evaluation training/working toward self-improvement
Session 29	Termination issues; programming for generalization
Session 30	Termination issues; programming for generalization

Although the aforementioned programs are presented, for the most part, in a set sequence, many of the sessions are designed to focus on providing training regarding one specific skill or skill set. These skill areas represent modules within the treatment program in which each session builds upon the next to enhance a skill before moving on to the next skill to be taught in the sequence. For instance, the ACTION program described above has several sessions dedicated to problem-solving training—moving from an introduction to problem solving through a game activity, to applying problem solving to mood issues, to problem solving in interpersonal situations. Many clinicians, when considering using manualized protocols or treatment approaches, believe it is inconsistent with the approach to depart from the set order of sessions within the protocol or to use only one session or skill module in isolation from the rest of the manual. This perceived lack of flexibility is a common criticism of manualized approaches to treatment. However, those skilled in using the CBT approach have found ways to be more flexible while maintaining the integrity of treatment approaches. Curry and Reinecke (2003) noted "it is not necessary for modules to be organized in a set sequence, or is it necessary for modular forms of CBT to be group-oriented or highly structured" (p. 100).

Using a flexible, modular approach in treatment is consistent with the CBT case conceptualization model, in which intervention selection is based on the clinician's sound clinical understanding of the child's or adolescent's problem area (Murphy & Christner, 2006). This not only avoids the clinician relying on a trial and error approach, but also circumvents the clinician requiring a patient to learn skills or a skill set which may be unnecessary or which may be one in which he or she is already competent. Thus, a modular approach allows clinicians to use group interventions that are distinct to the group's needs. It is easier to use this approach with individual patients, though through proper assessment and group placement, clinicians can easily determine modules that are directly relevant to the needs of the members of the group.

Research has shown common CBT interventions that seem to characterize successful treatment approaches with children and adolescents (Kaslow & Thompson, 1998; Kazdin & Weisz, 1998), which include: (1) increasing participation in pleasant, mood-enhancing activities; (2) improving social interactions; (3) improving social problem-solving skills; (4) reducing physiological tension; and (5) modifying maladaptive thoughts. Clinicians should use their knowledge of this research to develop the basic modular structure for a group treatment, and then, they may add other modules that may be unique to a given group (e.g., handling being bullied). Curry and Reinecke (2003) refer to this as the "designation of core versus non-core modules" (p. 101).

Individualized Group Treatment Sequence: Within and Between Session Aspects

A modular approach to cognitive-behavioral group intervention allows some structure but also flexibility within a specific session and between sessions. Within a session, there is a standard structure or agenda suggested for clinicians to follow, yet, if needed, there can be modification to the agenda. Table 16.3 offers an outline of a generic agenda used for each session. However, when teaching a new skill to patients in a group, certain aspects may arise that require some modification in the agenda. For instance, one of us (RWC) conducted an adolescent group session which focused on problem-solving training. The group members became very frustrated because they felt they "tried these

Table 16.3   Example of Generic Agenda for Modular Group

Within Session Agenda for One-Hour Group
Assess mood—can use objective (e.g., BYI-II; CDI) or subjective measures (e.g., SUDS)
    (5 minutes)
Set session agenda (5 minutes)
Review previous session and homework (5 minutes)
Discuss any concerns (5 minutes)
Work on specific skill(s) for the module (30 minutes)
Develop and discuss new homework (5 minutes)
Summary and session evaluation (5 minutes)

things" but they were unsuccessful. Rather than adhere to the agenda, it was beneficial to process their experiences and to identify some of the difficulties they had in implementing problem solving in the past. This not only offered reinforcement they that were "being heard," but it also illustrated the skill being taught—that is, there was a problem and we talk through ways to get beyond the barriers. Although this flexibility within session provides opportunities to address issues that arise, clinicians should be cautious, in that some groups may use this to avoid a given task.

Between-session or between-module flexibility, to some extent, was described above. This approach views each session or each module as a component that exists independent of the other sessions or modules. Given this, clinicians can expose a patient to a given skill set without requiring them to have previous training in other skills. This is a benefit not only for groups who start and finish the group process together, but also for groups that may have members entering and leaving at different times. We have found the modular approach particularly useful for implementation with the *rotating group* format described by Stewart, Christner, and Freeman in chapter 1. Some standardized programs, such as CWD-A, are set up to be implemented as a whole program or in these modular components (Clarke et al., 1990). Although there are benefits related to this approach, it also creates some limitations that clinicians should be aware of; mainly, "the loss of a linear sequence of interlaced sessions in which some sessions build upon previously covered materials" (Curry & Reinecke, 2003, p. 101).

Examples of Modules Used with Youth Depression

There are a number of different modules that can be used with youth who are depressed. As noted earlier, research has shown several specific target areas that should be considered in treatment (Kaslow & Thompson, 1998; Kazdin & Weisz, 1998). In Table 16.4, we offer a list of suggested modules for clinicians specifically treating children and adolescents who are depressed. This list is not exhaustive, but reflects some of the components consistent across various programs and research. Selection of modules should be based on the conceptualization of all group members' issues and needs. While it is unlikely that every member of the group will have the "exact" same needs, clinicians should select modules based on the majority need of the group. Many of these modules and activities can be found in treatment manuals, such as CWD-A and the ACTION program, but also can be developed by clinicians based on their knowledge of the literature and evidence-based interventions. Below, we offer examples to outline two of the modules listed.

Table 16.4   Sample of Modules in the Treatment of Youth Depression

Module	Sample of Specific Skills Taught	Sample of Between-Session Work
Introducing the CBT Model	Socializing to the link between the situations, thoughts, feelings, and actions	Writing down an example of the situation, thought, feeling, action connection
Understanding and Monitoring Your Emotions	Labeling emotions Understanding emotional cycles Self-monitoring	Keeping track of how you feel by completing a Mood Diary with mood ratings Completing a Dysfunctional Thought Record
Changing Your Activity	Understanding the benefits of activity Reviewing activity scheduling Selecting pleasant activities Scheduling pleasant activities	Developing a current activity schedule Adding a pleasant activity to your schedule and monitor your mood ⌐ list p. 311
Managing Your Stress	Understanding your signs of stress (e.g., body signals) Reviewing benefits of relaxation Learning relaxation strategies Diaphragmatic breathing Muscle-tension release Imagery	Keeping a Stress Signals Log Practicing the strategy learned Teaching someone else the strategy learned
Changing Your Thoughts	Identifying your thoughts Understanding the link between thoughts, feelings, and behaviors Identifying negative thoughts Naming negative thoughts Challenging negative thoughts Increasing positive counterthoughts	Completing a Dysfunctional Thought Record Completing a Dysfunctional Thought Record with counterthoughts Testing the evidence of your thoughts Practicing catching your negative thoughts and changing them to positive thoughts Coming up with alternative thoughts
Improving Your Social Skills	Starting a Conversation Meeting new people and introducing yourself Improving conversation skills (e.g., joining and leaving) Looking at what others like and dislike Giving and receiving feedback to others Improving listening skills Responding to others	Trying the new skills and journal on how the other person responded Conducting behavioral experiments and tracking the response of others
Enhancing Your Assertiveness	Understanding communication Reviewing what makes good communication Discuss positive and negative characteristics of being assertive Knowing when to be assertive Learning to be assertive	Looking at your own communication style Designing a personal assertiveness plan Using assertiveness imagery about a situation in your life Using and monitoring your assertiveness skills.

Module	Sample of Specific Skills Taught	Sample of Between-Session Work
Improving Your Problem Solving	Defining the problem Brainstorming possible solutions Selecting the best solutions Putting the solution to the test Evaluating the results Applying problem solving in various situations	Completing a problem solving worksheet regarding a problem that happens between sessions Practicing problem solving skills and monitor the outcome Teaching problem solving to someone in your family or at your school
Building Your Self-Efficacy	Creating goals Recognizing the strengths Fighting perfectionism Understanding responsibility Overcoming fears and obstacles	Complete a Strength Finders sheet Develop a list of short-term, mid-term, and long-term goals

Changing your activity. This module is designed to serve three purposes: (1) to have group members monitor their activity, (2) to have group members increase their activity level, and (3) to have group members engage in pleasant activities. Some of the specific activities in this module are listed in Table 16.4. However, below is a specific example of how we use pleasant activity scheduling with a group. In the session prior to introducing this activity, we have group members complete an Activity Schedule of their activities for the past week. For older children and adolescents, we have them complete a record based on half-hour time intervals. For younger children, we often use pictures and have them indicate activities based on morning, afternoon, and evening.

Once we have an idea of what activities they are presently engaging in, we use a Pleasant Activity List to come up with activities they found fun before their depression and activities they believe would be things they would enjoy now and in the near future (see Figure 16.2 for a sample of the Pleasant Activity List.) Using the list, the group discusses activities they enjoy and the reasons they enjoy them. The following illustrates how a therapist can work with the group to identify pleasant activities.

Therapist: Today, we are going to talk about some things we do for fun. I've thought of activities that others enjoy. Take a look at the Pleasant Activity List. You can use the list for some examples or you come up with your own ideas. What kind of things do you do for fun?

Sarah: Nothing. Everything is just boring. I just watch TV and sleep.

Margie: Yeah...not much is fun anymore.

Therapist: It can be difficult to think of fun things when we are depressed because you're right, nothing seems fun anymore. Let's think back to what you have done in the past for fun. What can you think of?

Debi: I loved skateboarding. I have not done it for a while.

Lynn: Walking. I didn't go anywhere, I just liked walking when it's nice outside.

Therapist: Those are great examples. Anyone else?

Monique: Relaxing!

Therapist: What do you mean?

Monique: Just sitting around, listening to music, and letting my head go blank.

Therapist: Great. Some of you talked about energizing activities, but Monique mentioned a more private and relaxing activity. Sara and Margie, what things have you thought of?

Sara: Still nothin'.

Margie: Me too.

Therapist: How about others teenagers you know, do they do things for fun?

Margie: It's like everyone has fun stuff to do. My life is just boring.

Therapist: Name one thing that "everyone" does for fun.

Sara: My friend Beth sings and dances.

Margie: My sister just goes to the mall and talks with friends and shops.

Therapist: Have you tried these things?

Sara: When Beth is over, we goof off.

Therapist: How is it when you "goof off"?

Sara: It makes me laugh.

Therapist: This is a good example, Sara. Sometimes just goofing off, singing and dancing, can be fun.

Sara: I forgot about it. We made each other laugh so hard.

Therapist: Margie, have you tried going to the mall with your sister?

Margie: Yeah.

Therapist: And...how was it?

Margie: It used to be fun. I don't know now.

Therapist: What are some clues you can use to tell you that it might be fun now?

Margie: I guess that it used to be fun before.

Therapist: So, is it possible that if you tried going with her again, it may be somewhat fun?

Margie: I guess anything is possible.

Therapist: Would you be willing to try it as an experiment? Let's see what it's like if you go this week.

After the group members identify pleasant activities, it is important to have them plan one each day in their schedule and to monitor how they felt during and after the activity (using a scale from 0, meaning No Enjoyment at All, to 10, meaning Great Enjoyment). We have also had the group members predict how much they will enjoy an activity before they attempt it to challenge their anticipatory perceptions and expectations, which is especially useful for adolescents who often do not believe they will enjoy the activity at all (Friedberg & McClure, 2002). Again, for older children and adolescents we use a regular schedule, and with younger children we have them develop a picture schedule. This activity is then carried over as the between session work for them to practice until the next session. At the next session, each member talks about what went well and what did not. It is not expected that all activities will be positive.

Changing your thoughts. Identifying and changing negative thinking is a key feature in CBT treatments for individuals, as well as in group settings. Before we can assist children and adolescents in changing their thoughts, we must first facilitate their awareness of what they are thinking. We have found that attempting this too early with group members' own personal situations often results in silence or "I don't know" responses. To address this, our experience has shown that using generic, yet similar, scenarios is

Pleasant Activity List

Energizing Activities	Moving About Activities
Take a walk	See a movie
Go swimming	Watch a sporting event at school
Play a sport (e.g., basketball, tennis, etc.)	Go to the library
Take a bike ride	Go shopping
Go jogging	Walk to a friends
Exercise	Go to the recreation center (e.g., YMCA)
Go fishing	Other: _____
Other: _____	Other: _____
Other: _____	Other: _____
Other: _____	
Socializing Activities	**Calming Activities**
Call a friend	Listen to music
Go to a school dance	Write a letter
Go out with some friends	Journal
Other: _____	Play a computer game
Other: _____	Read a book
Other: _____	Other: _____
	Other: _____
	Other: _____
Pampering Activities	**Other Activities**
Do your hair and makeup	Other: _____
Take a long shower or bath	Other: _____
Eat your favorite food	Other: _____
Buy yourself a present	Other: _____
Read your favorite magazine	Other: _____
Watch your favorite TV show	Other: _____
Other: _____	Other: _____
Other: _____	Other: _____
Other: _____	Other: _____

Figure 16.2   List of Pleasant Activities.

more beneficial to get the group thinking about the thought-feeling-behavior process. We typically begin by providing the group a set of four scenarios to help teach them the skill. An example of a scenario is, "You're supposed to meet a friend at the mall. You're waiting for 15 minutes and she didn't show up. You tried calling her cell phone and she does not answer."

As a group, we discuss each situation and the thoughts, feelings, and behaviors related to the situation. We use a Thought-Feeling-Behavior Connection chart, as illustrated in Figure 1.1 in chapter 1, drawn on a white board to process through the scenarios. The transcript below offers a brief illustration.

> Therapist: So, let's talk about this situation [*writes the situation in the center of the chart*]. If this was you, what would go through your head?
>
> Jasmine: She forgot about me.
>
> Lakita: I wonder if she is okay.
>
> Therapist: What are other thoughts you can come up with?
>
> Rose: I guess I'd worry about her first. Then, I'd get pissed.
>
> Therapist: Rose, those are some ways you may be feeling, but what would be going through your head?
>
> Rose: I hope she's not hurt. But, if she didn't show it would change to...I can't believe she left me solo.
>
> Therapist: Good. [*after about 8 to 10 thoughts*] Let's move on. If we look at what went through your head, how would this make you feel? Rose gave us a few ideas...worried and pissed.
>
> Jasmine: Let down. Sad.
>
> Lakita: Nervous.
>
> Therapist: [*after reviewing the emotions with every thought given*] You each were feeling different things, even though the situation was the same. How come? It's because of the different thoughts, or the different ways of looking at the situation. It's what went through your head. Would this also affect how you behave? What would you do in this situation, based on your thoughts and feelings?
>
> Jasmine: I wouldn't talk to her. If she let me down, I would just avoid her.
>
> Lakita: I'd start calling around to find her.
>
> Rose: Once I got angry, I'd leave a message on her phone. It wouldn't be nice. It's wrong not to show.
>
> Therapist: We now have some ideas of "negative thoughts" and how they affect thoughts, feelings, and then our behaviors. Let's see if we can change to thinking that is more positive, and then see what happens to our feelings and actions.

As you can see from the therapist's last statement, once members are able to identify thoughts, we begin the process of getting them to start thinking about alternative thoughts and testing them out. It is most useful to take each negative thought and have the group brainstorm a number of alternative counterthoughts to it. This allows them to see the range of possible thoughts for every situation and will help to highlight the inaccuracy of *all-or-nothing* thinking.

While these examples are not exhaustive of the activities or modules covered in this approach to treatment, it offers a review of how these sessions may appear. Clinicians new to this approach can rely on group activities provided in a number of group treatment protocols, like those discussed above. Although this approach may be difficult to do at first, as clinicians become skilled in case conceptualization and intervention (or module) selection, it can be both an effective and an efficient approach to treatment.

OVERCOMING OBSTACLES IN GROUP TREATMENT
WITH DEPRESSED YOUTH

Working with youth patients experiencing depressed moods can at times be challenging. Group work with this population may create a compromising atmosphere for some participants, who may feel vulnerable in a setting with a variety of other youth, especially those who have experienced interpersonal relationship problems. Additionally, the features of pessimism and egocentrism in depression brings to question the ability of this population to provide adequate and appropriate feedback to peers regarding their experience of depression and their ability to cope. Given that a child or adolescent with depression is at a greater risk to internalize feedback from other participants in a negative way, this would serve to reinforce their already negative sense of self (Stark et al., 1993). Group leaders must be aware of these issues and observe participants to be sure these do not occur and if they do to address them immediately. We often will process some situations as a group, though with other situations, we will meet individually with a group member (depending on the potential consequences of discussing private or sensitive issues).

Group leaders can use a number of techniques to enhance group compliance and productivity (which may be of issue with patients experiencing problems with motivation and energy, as is the case with depressed youth), as well as to avert potential obstacles and to enhance group success. Self-monitoring one's presentation is important while interacting with the group. Being aware of your body language and wording is very important, youth with depression may have unique perceptions about what is happening in the group (Wright, Beck, & Thase, 2003). Some members may isolate from friends and their peer group or withdraw from the treatment group itself (AACAP, 2001). Thus, maintaining a positive, productive affect will enhance the productivity and compliance of the group. Awareness of even the smallest changes and successes is important to reflect in the therapeutic atmosphere (Young et al., 2001).

Collaboration with the group participants is a very important tool in the therapeutic process. It is important for group members to feel as though they are a part of that therapy process, and they should be working together with one another and with the group leader. When group members are involved and perceive themselves as important contributors to the group process, they are more likely to adhere to therapy (Young et al., 2001; Wright, et al., 2003).

Interventions used in the group setting should be chosen carefully, and they should adhere to the group process and should be consistent with the conceptualization of group members' cases. If a clinician uses interventions too difficult for the group, it will create failure and a reinforcement of the negative self-view. On the other hand, interventions too easy for the group will not be productive and may also reinforce a negative self-view (e.g., "Even the group leader doesn't think I am capable to do more.").

Providing and eliciting feedback on a regular basis will help the group members to stay focused and provide necessary information on the group process. This can also help to intercept and reframe any misperceived interventions or discussions. Feedback also helps the facilitator to understand where the group is in their processing and understanding of interventions being discussed. Summarizing the session content helps to reiterate the "key points" and gives the group leader an assessment of what is being understood.

Moreover, it is important for group leaders to offer a rationale for each technique used, as it increases participation and compliance (Young et al., 2001).

SUMMARY

Depression in childhood and adolescence can be a complex and chronic disorder. Despite the fact that youth depression has only been recently accepted by professionals, there has been considerable growth in our knowledge and understanding about youth depression and interventions. Cognitive-behavioral group interventions have emerged as one of the primary interventions for children and adolescents with depression. A number of structured protocols have been developed and shown to be effective, such as CWD-A and the ACTION program. While these programs serve as excellent sources of intervention, we offer additional thoughts on using a modular approach that utilizes evidence-based intervention to develop a group treatment to meet a specific group's needs. This approach offers a CBT group process that is flexible and integrated, and it represents current views that interventions should be evidence-based, yet tailored to the specific needs of the child (in this case, each child within a group). While modular CBT treatments have not undergone extensive review, clinical practice and some research has shown promise.

REFERENCES

Abramson, L. Y., Seligman, M. E. P., & Teasdale, J. (1978). Learned helplessness in humans: Critique and reformulation. *Journal of Abnormal Psychology, 87,* 49–74.

Achenbach, T. M. (2001). *Manual for the ASEBA school-age forms and profiles.* Burlington: University of Vermont.

American Academy of Child and Adolescent Psychiatry. (1998). Practice parameters for the assessment and treatment of children and adolescents with depressive disorders. *Journal of the American Academy of Child and Adolescent Psychiatry, 37,* 63S–83S.

American Psychiatric Association. (2000). *Diagnostic and statistics manual of mental disorders (4th ed.) Text Revision.* Washington, DC: Author.

Beck, A. T. (1967). *Depression: Clinical, experimental, and theoretical aspects.* New York: Harper & Row.

Beck, A. T., Steer, R. A., & Brown, G. K. (1996). *Beck depression inventory* (2nd ed.). San Antonio, TX: The Psychological Corporation.

Beck, A., Rush, A., Shaw, B., & Emery, G. (1979). *Cognitive therapy for depression.* New York: Guilford.

Beck, J. (1995). *Cognitive therapy: Basics and beyond.* New York: Guilford.

Beck, J. S., Beck A. T., and Jolly, J. (2005). *Manual for the Beck Youth Inventories of Emotional and Social Adjustment* (2nd ed.). San Antonio, TX: The Psychological Corporation.

Brent, D., Holder, D., Kolko, D., Birmaher, B., Baugher, M., Roth, C., et al. (1997). A clinical psychotherapy trial for adolescent depression comparing cognitive, family, and supportive therapy. *Archives of General Psychiatry, 54*(9), 877–885.

Clarke, G. N., Lewinsohn, P. M., & Hops, H. (1990). *Instructor's manual for the adolescent coping with depression course.* Eugene, OR: Castalia Press.

Clarke, G. N., Rohde, P., Lewinsohn, P. M., Hops, H., & Seeley, J. R. (1999). Cognitive-behavioral treatment of adolescent depression: Efficacy of acute group treatment and booster sessions. *Journal of the American Academy of Child and Adolescent Psychiatry, 38,* 272–279.

Costello, E. J., Pine, D. S., Hammen, C., March, J. S., Plotsky, P. M., Weissman, M. M., et al. (2002). Development and natural history of mood disorders. *Biological Psychiatry, 52,* 529–542.

Curry, J. F., & Reinecke, M. A. (2003). Modular therapy with adolescents with major depression. In M. A. Reinecke, F. M. Dattilio, & A. Freeman (Eds.), *Cognitive therapy with children and adolescents: A casebook for clinical practice* (pp. 95–127). New York: Guilford.

Evans, D. L., & Andrews, L. W. (2005). *If your adolescent has depression or bipolar disorder: The teen at risk and you—What you face and what to do about it.* New York: Oxford Press.

Field, T., Diego, M., & Sanders, C. (2001). Adolescent depression and risk factors. *Adolescence, 36,* 491–499.

Freeman, A., & Dolan, M. (2001). Revisiting Prochaska and DiClemente's stages of change theory: An expansion and specification to aid in treatment planning and outcome evaluation. *Cognitive and Behavioral Practice, 8,* 224–234.

Friedberg, R. D., & McClure, J. M. (2002). *Clinical practice of cognitive therapy with children and adolescents: The nuts and bolts.* New York: Guilford.

Garber, J., Braafladt, N., & Weiss, B. (1995). Affect regulation in depressed and nondepressed children and young adolescents. *Development and Psychopathology, 7,* 93–115.

Gibbs, J. T. (1998). African-American adolescents. In J. T. Gibbs, L. N. Huang, & Associates (Eds.), *Children of color: Psychological interventions with culturally diverse youth* (pp. 143–170). San Francisco: Jossey-Bass.

Gillham, J. E., & Reivich, K. J. (1999). Prevention of depressive symptoms in schoolchildren: A research update. *Psychological Science, 10,* 461–462.

Hammen, C., & Zupan, B. A. (1984). Self-schemas, depression, and the processing of personal information in children. *Journal of Experimental Child Psychology, 37,* 598–608.

Ho, M. K. (1992). *Minority children and adolescents in therapy.* Newbury Park, CA: Sage.

Kaslow, N., & Thompson, M. (1998). Applying the criteria for empirically supported treatments to studies of psychosocial interventions for child and adolescent depression. *Journal of Clinical Child Psychology, 27,* 146–155.

Kazdin, A., & Weisz, J. (1998). Identifying and developing empirically supported child and adolescent treatments. *Journal of Consulting and Clinical Psychology, 66,* 19–36.

Kessler, R. C., Berglund, P., Demler, O., Jin, R., & Walters, E. E. (2005). Lifetime prevalence and age of-onset distributions of DSM-IV disorders in the National Comorbidity Survey Replication. *Archives of General Psychiatry, 62,* 593–602.

Kessler, R., & Walters, E. E. (1998). Epidemiology of DSM-III-R major depression and minor depression among adolescents and young adults in the National Comorbidity Survey. *Depression and Anxiety, 7,* 3–15.

Kovacs, M. (1992). *Children's depression inventory.* North Tonawanda, NY: MultiHealth Systems.

Lewinsohn, P. M., & Clarke, G. N. (1999). Psychosocial treatments for adolescent depression. *Clinical Psychology Review, 19,* 329–342.

Lewinsohn, P. M., Clarke, G. N., Hops, H., & Andrews, J. (1990). Cognitive-behavioral group treatment of depression in adolescents. *Behavior Therapy, 21,* 285–401.

Lewinsohn, P. M., Clarke, G. N., Rohde, P., Hops, H., & Seeley, J. R. (1996). A course in coping: a cognitive-behavioral approach to the treatment of adolescent depression. In E. D. Hibbs & P. S. Jensen (Eds.), *Psychosocial treatments for child and adolescent disorders: Empirically based strategies for clinical practice* (pp. 109–135). Washington, DC: American Psychological Association.

Lewinsohn, P. M., Solomon, A., Seeley, J. R., & Zeiss, A. (2000). Clinical implications of "subthreshold" depressive symptoms. *Journal of Abnormal Psychology, 109,* 345–351.

Merrell, K. W. (2001). *Helping students overcome depression and anxiety: A practical guide.* New York: Guilford.

Moore, M., & Carr, A. (2000). Depression and grief. *What works with children and adolescents? A critical review of psychological interventions with children, adolescents, and their families.* London: Brunner-Routledge.

Murphy, V. B., & Christner, R. W. (2006). A cognitive-behavioral case conceptualization approach for working with children and adolescents. In R. B. Mennuti, A. Freeman, & R. W. Christner (Eds.), *Cognitive-behavioral interventions in educational settings: A handbook for practice* (pp. 78–94). New York: Routledge.

Nagata, D. K. (1998). The assessment and treatment of Japanese American children and adolescents. In J. T. Gibbs, L. N. Huang, & Associates (Eds.), *Children of color: Psychological interventions with culturally diverse youth* (pp. 215–239). San Francisco: Jossey-Bass.

Orvaschel, H., & Puig-Antich, J. H. (1987). *Schedule for Affective Disorders and Schizophrenia for School-Age Children* (Epidemiological version, 4th ed.). Pittsburgh: Western Psychiatric Institute and Clinic.

Prochaska, J. O., DiClemente, C.C., & Norcross, J. C. (1992). In search of how people change: Applications to addictive behaviors. *American Psychologist, 47,* 1102–1114.

Rambaldo, L. R., Wilding, L. D., Goldman, M. L., McClure, J. M., & Friedberg, R. D. (2001). School-based interventions for anxious and depressed children. *Innovations in clinical practice: A source book, 19,* 347–358.

Reinecke, M. A., Ryan, N. E., & Dubois, D. L. (1998). Cognitive-behavioral therapy of depression and depressive symptoms during adolescence: A review and meta-analysis. *Journal of the American Academy of Child and Adolescent Psychiatry, 37,* 26–34.

Reynolds, C. R., & Kamphaus, R. W. (2004). *Behavior assessment system for children* (2nd ed.). Circle Pines, MN: American Guidance Service.

Roberts, R. E., Lewinsohn, P. M., & Seeley, J. R. (1995). Symptoms of DSM-III-R major depression in adolescence: Evidence from an epidemiological survey. *Journal of the American Academy of Child and Adolescent Psychiatry, 34,* 1608–1617.

Shaw, D. S., Keenan, K., Vondra, J. I., Delliquadri, E., & Giovannelli, J. (1997). Antecedents of preschool children's internalizing problems: A longitudinal study of low-income families. *Journal of the American Academy of Child and Adolescent Psychiatry, 36,* 1760–1767.

Stark, K. D., & Kendall, P. C. (1996). *Treating depressed children: Therapist manual for "Action."* Ardmore, PA: Workbook Publishing.

Stark, K. D., Christopher, J., & Dempsey, M. (1993). Depression. In R. T. Ammerman, & M. Hersen (Eds.), *Handbook of behavior therapy in the psychiatric setting* (pp. 427–452). New York: Wiley.

Stark, K., Sander, J., Yancy, M., Bronik, M., & Hoke, J. (2000). Treatment of depression in childhood and adolescence. In P. C. Kendall (Ed.), *Child and adolescent therapy: Cognitive-behavioral procedures* (2nd ed., pp. 173–234). New York: Guilford.

Stark, K., Swearer, S., Kurowski, C., Sommer, D., & Bowen, B. (1996). Targeting the child and the family: A holistic approach to treating child and adolescent depressive disorders. In E. Hibbs & P. Jensen (Eds.), *Psychosocial treatments for child and adolescent disorders: Empirically based strategies for clinical practice* (pp. 207–238). Washington, DC: American Psychological Association.

Weersing, V. R., Iyengar, Kolko, D. J., Birmaher, B., & Brent, D. A. (2006). Effectiveness of cognitive-behavioral therapy for adolescent depression: A benchmarking investigation. *Behavior Therapy, 37,* 36–48.

Wright, J. H., Beck, A. T., & Thase, M. E. (2003). Cognitive Therapy. In R. E. Hales, & S. C. Yudofsky, *The American psychiatric publishing textbook of clinical psychiatry* (4th ed., pp. 1245–1284). Arlington, VA: American Psychiatric Publishing.

Young, J. E. (1991). *Cognitive therapy for personality disorders: A schema-focused approach.* Sarasota, FL: Professional Resource Exchange.

Young, J. E., Weinberger, A. D., & Beck, A. T. (2001). Cognitive therapy for depression. In D. Barlow (Ed.), *Clinical handbook of psychological disorders: A step-by-step treatment manual* (3rd ed., pp. 264–308). New York: Guilford.

Zupan, B. A., Hammen, C., & Jaenicke, C. (1987). The effects of current mood and prior depressive history on self-schematic processing in children. *Journal of Experimental Child Psychology, 43,* 149–158.

Chapter Seventeen

Meeting the Treatment Needs of Children with ADHD: Can Cognitive Strategies Make a Contribution?

Lauren Braswell

This volume contains many encouraging reports about the success of cognitive-behavioral (CB) group interventions with children presenting a variety of behavioral and emotional concerns. This chapter is not one of those reports. Perhaps as much as anyone in the field, I would enjoy describing a series of studies that detail how effective CB methods can be with groups of children manifesting symptoms of Attention-Deficit/Hyperactivity Disorder (ADHD). But, in the immortal words of the Rolling Stones, "you can't always get what you want." Or, to restate this in more academically appropriate language, the way can be difficult for clinician-researchers who value the role of evidence in matching children with appropriate treatments. At this juncture, I am clearly older, hopefully wiser, and certainly a more selective fan of the use of cognitive-behavioral methods with ADHD children and their families, in group contexts or otherwise. Although, to finish the Stones refrain, "if you try sometimes, you just might find, you get what you need." And when it comes to the needs of children with ADHD, there are methods to meet some very crucial treatment needs, but cognitive strategies do not play a major role in these methods.

In this chapter, past attempts to apply CB approaches to ADHD will be briefly discussed and current views on effective treatment will be presented. To avoid the complete demoralization of cognitive-behaviorists, the possible value of selective inclusion of certain cognitive elements in the context of accepted treatments will also be considered. These elements include giving greater attention to the role of parents' cognitions in behavioral parent training, refining methods of training self-monitoring/self-evaluation skills to enhance the accuracy of the ADHD child's self-perceptions, and continuing to promote the inclusion of selected approaches to anger management training. To add an even more cautious note to this chapter, concerns about possible iatrogenic effects of treating youth with externalizing difficulties in groups will be considered briefly. Finally, questions for future research of cognitive aspects of treatment will be shared.

A BRIEF HISTORY OF COGNITIVE-BEHAVIORAL INTERVENTIONS AND ADHD

To be sure, the symptoms that characterize children with ADHD—inattention, organizational problem, and impulsive responding—would *seem* to be ideal candidates for CB interventions. If a child is struggling with impulsive behavior, what could be more logical than teaching the child to use verbal self-instructions to encourage more deliberate responding across a variety of problem situations? If a child has difficulty with interpersonal relationships, why not attempt to train interpersonal cognitive problem solving and perspective taking? Twenty years ago, use of these strategies seemed like a reasonable intervention plan. Early work with mildly impaired children was very encouraging (Kendall & Braswell, 1985) as were early efforts with some clinical populations (see review in Braswell & Bloomquist, 1991). But other investigators, such as Abikoff (1991), sounded an early warning that, when applied with children meeting full diagnostic criteria for ADHD, CB methods were not yielding evidence of reliably positive effects. In a school-based intervention for children manifesting disruptive behaviors, many of whom met formal criteria for ADHD, Braswell, August, Bloomquist, Realmuto, Skare, and Crosby (1997) compared the impact of a multicomponent intervention that included parent, teacher, and CB child training groups relative to an informational control condition in which parents and teachers were presented basic information about ADHD and commonly accepted behavior management principles but children received no training. The multicomponent condition included 18 school-based peer training groups in Year 1 and 10 groups in Year 2. Training content included behavioral social skills, interpersonal problem solving, anger management, negative thoughts and feelings management, and conflict resolution skills. Families in either condition could choose to request a free initial screening interview with a child psychiatrist to determine whether additional evaluation and /or consideration of a medication trial would be appropriate. As evaluated at the end of Year 2, multisource assessment was not supportive of the efficacy of the multicomponent condition over the information control condition. Both groups improved, but data from a developmental control suggested these improvements were best attributed to maturation. The results of this study were discouraging, for the findings demanded that I seriously reconsider modes of intervention previously believed to be effective.

The lack of observed effects for children with ADHD is made somewhat more perplexing by the data indicating CB strategies are effective in the treatment of a variety of childhood conditions for which children with ADHD tend to be co-morbid, such as anxiety disorders and problems with conduct and anger management. The reader is referred to other chapters of this book as well as volumes by Kazdin and Weisz (2003) and Kendall (2005) for further information, but the success of CB approaches in treating childhood anxiety disorders and difficulties with conduct problems and anger is particularly striking. It is an open question whether or not the presence of ADHD along with these conditions makes these children less responsive to interventions that have been found effective with samples not co-morbid for ADHD. If the "deficits" that are most central to ADHD—which Barkley (1997) has suggested are core deficits in inhibitory control—precede and, therefore, disrupt the very executive function processes that are addressed in so many CB strategies one would think this might disrupt the success of CB strategies for other disorders. In the absence of clear data on this question, however, no statement made in this chapter should be construed as implying children who present with ADHD in addition to their problems with anxiety or anger could not be candidates for evidence-based treatments for these collateral difficulties. Clearly, continued evaluation of the impact of co-morbidity on treatment efficacy is needed. While the CB interventions targeting children with ADHD have not been particularly successful, fortunately, other types of intervention with this population have yielded results that are more positive.

CURRENT STATUS OF ADHD TREATMENT

Children with ADHD have received a phenomenal level of research attention over the past three decades. The work of many investigators has yielded interesting hypotheses about the nature of the underlying disorder (Barkley, 1997; Nigg, 2001), improvements in assessment (Pelham, Fabiano, & Massetti, 2005) and, of most relevance to the current chapter, a more refined understanding of effective treatment (MTA Cooperative Group, 1999a, 1999b, 2004).

At this juncture, stimulant medication is considered the primary treatment for ADHD. As noted by Martin (2005), response rates to stimulant medications approach at least 70%, responsiveness can be established in a relatively short timeframe, and effect sizes are significant. The results of the landmark MTA study of the treatment of ADHD indicated that carefully managed medication and a combined medication/intensive psychosocial intervention program (which included year-long behavioral parent training, participation in an intensive summer treatment program, and behavioral intervention in the child's school) achieved basically the same degree of improvement on measures of the core symptoms of ADHD relative to the psychosocial treatment condition alone or community care (MTA Cooperative Group, 1999, 2004). The observation that many children in the community care condition were also receiving medication indicates even the right treatment (e.g., psychostimulant medication) will not achieve optimal outcomes unless it is implemented with adequate attention to individual titration and close follow-up. The combined medication and psychosocial treatment condition did result in greater positive change for ADHD children who were also co-morbid for anxiety issues and/or Oppositional Defiant Disorder or Conduct Disorder. In their analysis of the most cost-effective approach to treatment, Jensen and colleagues. (2005) concluded that careful medication management may be the best choice for children with ADHD who are not co-morbid for other disorders. For those who are presenting with co-morbid conditions, the addition of selected psychosocial treatments might be more cost effective due to the greater probability of achieving "normalized" child behavior. Given the high rates of co-morbidity among children with ADHD, this means a relatively large number of children would be served by the addition of psychosocial interventions. In addition, Hinshaw (2005) notes that a significant minority of children with ADHD are not candidates for medication treatment due to failure to respond positively to medications, significant difficulty with medication side effects, and/or philosophical opposition to the use of medication treatments on the part of their parents. Thus, while acknowledging the very positive outcomes achieved with medication treatment, there remains a need for effective nonmedication treatments.

CHOICES OF PSYCHOSOCIAL INTERVENTION

Behavioral Parent Training

Virtually all clinicians and researchers agree on the value of behavioral parent training for the parents and caregivers of children and adolescents with ADHD (Anastopoulos, Shelton, DuPaul, & Guevremont, 1993; Pisterman, McGrath, Firestone, & Goodman, 1989). For more detailed information about parent group interventions the reader is referred to chapter 25 of this volume. At this point, it should be noted that such groups are typically structured to provide parents with information about the disorder as well as help the parents strengthen their skills of positive behavioral management. Common training topics include helping parents learn to use their attention to reinforce appropriate behavior, teaching parents to establish a formal home token reinforcement system, and helping parents learn to implement time-out procedures in a productive manner (Barkley, 1997). Some parent group curricula also begin with teaching parents how to engage in brief periods of more unstructured, child-directed play. From a behaviorist's perspective, spending time in this type of activity enhances the reinforcement value of the parent's attention, and, from a developmentalist's perspective, such activities enhance the quality of the attachment relationship, which may be strained by all the negative interactions created as a result of the child's challenging behavior. Parent group activities typically involve brief didactic presentations, videotaped and *in vivo* modeling of skills to be developed, discussion, and role-play practice. In a subsequent section, this chapter will consider certain cognitive attributes of parents that could impact their experience in parenting groups and/or their response to other interventions.

Social Skills Groups for Children

While virtually all experts on ADHD agree with the value of behavioral parent group training, determining the added value of child-focused interventions such as social skills training groups is more problematic. With a disorder that has such a profound impact on social relationships and social skills (Pelham & Bender, 1982), it seems logical to explore the impact of social skills training. Examining the literature on such training, however, leaves one uncertain about the degree of meaningful change that can be achieved through standard group approaches. A few illustrative studies from this literature will be described.

Pfiffner and McBurnett (1997) conducted an eight-session weekly intervention involving 27 children who met criteria for ADHD. The medication status of these children was varied and not part of the evaluation. The study compared the impact of a child-only group condition, a child group that also involved parents meeting separately in their own group to learn strategies to aid generalization of procedures to home or school, and wait-list control. Group procedures involved skill modules that were believed to be highly relevant to the social skills deficits of children with ADHD, including displaying good sportsmanship, accepting consequences, being appropriately assertive, ignoring provocation, using interpersonal problem solving, and recognizing and dealing with feelings. Training involved brief didactic instruction with symbolic and *in vivo* modeling, role-playing, and behavioral rehearsal. Within each group, games and play activities were incorporated to monitor engagement and provide different contexts for skill practice. A behavioral contingency system was used throughout the group and in the parent generalization condition, parents learned how to apply this system in the home context and as well as how to communicate with teachers about the application of this system in the child's school setting. At posttest and 3 to 4 month follow-up, children in the treatment conditions displayed greater knowledge of social skill information and displayed gains on parent ratings of their social skills. Teacher ratings of school behavior did not indicate improvement, and there were no significant differences between the two treatment groups. This study did not include any peer ratings or observations of social behavior. Thus, the results must be viewed as encouraging but limited.

Using a larger sample of 120 children, all of whom met criteria for either ADHD-Inattentive type or ADHD-Combined type, Antshel and Remer (2003) implemented an 8 week social skills treatment program that targeted behaviors very similar to those addressed in Pfiffner and McBurnett (1997). All children in this study were already being treated with medication. For this study, all parents participated in separately held parent groups during sessions 1, 4, and 8 of the treatment. In these sessions, parents completed assessment measures and received information about behavior management and the treatment their children were receiving. The child training groups were varied in terms of their diagnostic heterogeneity, with some groups composed of children who all manifested the same ADHD subtype, while other groups were mixed in terms of subtype. Assessments occurred at pre-, post-, and 3 month follow-up. Overall, the results obtained did not support the efficacy of SST. In particular, children who were also co-morbid for Oppositional Defiant Disorder did not display improvement. In addition, on some parent ratings, children with ADHD-Inattentive Type who had been in mixed groups were rated as worse on certain dimensions of behavior. This concern will be addressed further in a subsequent section on possible iatrogenic effects of group treatments. Unfortunately, the findings of Antshel and Remer (2003) are consistent with other reports.

In their meta-analysis of social skills training programs for students with various behavior disorders, Kavale, Mathur, Forness, Rutherford, and Quinn (1996) reported that among those participants already receiving medications, there was only an 8% improvement over medication-only group participants. This conclusion is consistent with the more recent work of Abikoff and colleagues (2004) who evaluated the impact of psychostimulant medication combined with an intensive psychosocial intervention in a group for 103 7- to 9-year-old children with ADHD. Of relevance for the current chapter, the psychosocial intervention included social skills training groups that met weekly from October through April of the first year of the study and monthly for the second year. These groups used direct instruction, modeling, videotaped self-feedback, and behavioral rehearsal to train social skills. Groups initially relied on a concrete, externally-determined reward system, but self-evaluation procedures were added by Session 7. With only a few exceptions, the authors reported no advantage in social functioning with the psychosocial intervention group over and above the results achieved with the use of medication. As previously noted, the relative contribution of such social skills training may be different if, in fact, a given child is not a good candidate for medication treatment.

One concern with social skills group training, and, for that matter, most traditional approaches to mental health treatment is that, as it is typically implemented, these approaches require children to take skills learned in one setting and generalize them to another. But children with ADHD seem to do best when interventions are implemented and desired behavior reinforced at the very point of performance of that behavior (Barkley, 2006). In contrast to traditional therapy approaches, the next form of psychosocial treatment to be considered is the very embodiment of the principle of intervening at the point of performance.

Intensive Summer Treatment Program

Over the past 25 years, Pelham and colleagues have developed and continue to refine one of the most successful evidence-based treatments for ADHD (Pelham, Fabiano, Gnagy, Greiner, & Hoza, 2005). As noted by Pelham and colleagues (2005), behavioral interventions have a large evidence base but can be expensive in comparison to treatment with medications and are certainly more difficult to implement well. But, these authors add that behavioral interventions also offer the possibility of teaching skills that directly address the functioning impairments so commonly observed in this population of children. Since 1980, Pelham and colleagues have conducted their 8-week, full day, 5-day per week Summer Treatment Program (STP) targeting 5 to 15 year olds who have been diagnosed with ADHD. Participants spend 3 hours each day in academic activities and the remainder of the day in sports and other recreational activities. These activities include intensive sports skills training in basketball, soccer, baseball, and swimming, for athletic performance appears to be an important factor in peer acceptance and is believed to enhance the child's sense of self-esteem and self-efficacy (Lopez-Williams et al., 2005). Social skills lessons are conducted in brief daily segments, and the intensive behavioral management system that operates throughout the day provides high rates of feedback and shaping in the appropriate use of these skills in all of the child's daily activities. Parents attend behavioral child management training groups and are involved in providing home-based rewards dependent upon the feedback they receive from a daily report card completed by STP staff. After observing the child's response to this intensive behavioral approach, recommendations may be made for the child to also receive a careful evaluation for medication treatment, but in the context of this intervention, medication is viewed as a secondary intervention. Pelham and colleagues. (2005)note that as of 2003 nearly 90 empirical studies had been conducted on various aspects of the STP and the program has been successfully exported to other sites. The overall treatment program has been able to document very large behavioral changes, and the power of individual subcomponents of the intervention has been demonstrated.

Unfortunately, yet understandably, the pragmatics of time and funding limitations mean the STP can only extend for 8 weeks, but as indicated in Pelham and colleagues. (2005), the 360 hours of treatment provided in this 8 weeks equals approximately 7 years of traditional weekly social skills training. Program staff conduct different forms of follow-up during the school year, such as a Saturday treatment program and booster sessions for parents throughout the school year. Unfortunately, the contribution of this aspect of the program has not been systematically evaluated. The developers of this program argue that the chronic nature of ADHD symptomatology demands relatively more intensive psychosocial interventions than are commonly provided in the classic model of weekly individual, family, or group therapy. These authors also note that they do not expect that with a condition as chronic as ADHD that treatment gains would persist without continued intervention. Thus, this intensive approach can be viewed as somewhat analogous to medication treatment, for while the child is actively engaged in the program, it is highly effective, and when it is withdrawn, behavior deteriorates (Chronis et al., 2004).

While the STP is a behaviorally intensive form of intervention in which the program contingencies seem to set the tone for the behavior of those involved, some intervention settings have been vulnerable to possible unintended negative effects that seem to arise from the aggregation of young people with disruptive behavior disorders.

Caveat Regarding Aggregating Children with Disruptive Behavior Disorders

Some would view it as understandable to question the wisdom and sanity of any mental health professional who willingly chooses to meet with a group of children with ADHD. The nature of the core symptoms of this disorder, e.g. inattention, impulsivity, and hyperactivity, offer a foreshadowing of the ways in which such an experience could go wrong or at least become a *de facto* stage for the display of inappropriate behavior rather than a training context that promotes skill building. And, in reality, it is only in the last ten years that treatment outcome researchers have begun to give some long overdue attention to measuring all aspects of outcome, whether positive or negative. Thus, in addition to establishing the effectiveness of selected interventions, group work with children manifesting externalizing disorders such as ADHD, ODD, or Conduct Disorder, is complicated by the possibility that aggregating these youth could lead to iatrogenic effects. While most of the research addressing this question involves work with children meeting criteria for Conduct Disorder or adjudicated delinquents, given the high co-morbidity among the disruptive behavior disorders, it seems wise for those working with ADHD youth to be attentive to this data.

As originally discussed by Dishion, McCord, and Poulin (1999), even interventions that achieve their primary positive goal, such as reducing aggression, could also produce negative outcomes, such as increasing the probability that the youth involved smoke cigarettes, spend time with deviant peers, and/or manifest other forms of deviant behavior. Treatment outcome researchers in the past have not been particularly attentive to assessing for possible iatrogenic or negative contagion effects. The probability that these effects could, however, occur does not really seem so surprising given what is known about how peers can influence the development of deviant behavior. In their review of this literature, Gifford-Smith , Dodge, Dishion, and McCord (2005) note that there is reason to be concerned about possible iatrogenic effects, but it is important to understand that these effects seem to be influenced by several important factors. For example, age of the child seems to matter, with adolescents being more likely to be influenced by their peers than younger children. Interestingly, the level of experience of the group leader may also contribute, with iatrogenic effects most likely with an inexperienced leader. Who else is in the group also seems to play a role, with the work of Feldman (1992) suggesting that groups composed of both deviant and nondeviant peers are less likely to show iatrogenic effects than groups composed of all deviant peers. The role of group composition may, however, be complex. As noted in the earlier discussion of Antshel and Remer (2003), when ADHD-Inattentive types (who would tend to be less behaviorally impulsive) were grouped with ADHD-Combined types, the Inattentive types were rated as showing some behavioral deterioration from pretreatment scores. Dishion and Dodge (2005) hypothesize that the effects of aggregating deviant peers may be most pronounced with groups who are only moderately deviant, such as selected prevention groups, and could be less of a factor among youth who are either clearly not deviant or among those who are already manifesting high rates of deviant behavior.

The take home point for the current reader could be that in the absence of strong evidence for the positive effects of a given program, one may need to think twice before placing a child with ADHD into a group treatment situation. This conclusion might be most appropriate if the child in question is a teenager with only mild disruptive behavior and/or there is uncertainty about the experience level of the group leader.

With this overview of some of the strong points and problematic issues concerning psychosocial treatments for children with ADHD, the reader now has a basis for considering what might be accomplished by the selective addition of cognitive contents or strategies.

COGNITIVE ELEMENTS THAT COULD ENHANCE THE TREATMENT OF CHILDREN WITH ADHD

Attending to the Role of Cognitions in Behavioral Parent Group Training

Researchers have long been curious about the relationship between parent attitudes and parent behavior and how this connection impacts child adjustment (Bugental & Johnston, 2000; Stogdill, 1936). Within the more specific domain of behavioral parenting groups, there has been a trend towards greater attention to the attributions, expectancies, and cognitive problem-solving skills of parents (Griest, Forehand, Rogers, Breiner, Furey, & Williams, 1982; Treacy, Tripp, & Baird, 2005; Webster-Stratton, 1994). Parent beliefs about the causes (intentional vs. unintentional) and controllability of child behavior can affect both the parent's emotional and disciplinary response to the child (Johnston, Patenaude, & Inman, 1992). Smith and O'Leary (1995) observed that the combination of child blaming attributions regarding misbehavior and negative emotional arousal in the parent is particularly likely to result in overreactive, harsh parenting behaviors. While harsh, overreactive responding is certainly not desirable, Harrison and Sofronoff (2002) speculate that other parents may be vulnerable to going to the other extreme and be at risk to develop a sense of "learned helplessness" if they have unrealistic expectations about being able to control child behavior.

In addition to beliefs and expectations regarding child behavioral control, parents may also struggle with unhelpful beliefs or misconceptions about treatment that could interfere with making optimal progress. For example, extreme beliefs about the role of medication—either viewing it as a panacea or a poison—could make it difficult for a parent to make evidence-based choices about the child's treatment plan. Some investigators, such as dosReis, Zito, Safer, Soekem, Mitchell, and Ellwood (2003), have studied parent perceptions of and satisfaction with stimulant medication. Using a group of parents whose children had been on medication an average of 3 years, these investigators found generally positive perceptions of medication effectiveness, but these parents also endorsed a number of beliefs that are at odds with current knowledge. For example, 17% of parents thought medications were not effective with adolescents and adults with

ADHD, 25% thought medication use could impact their child's height, and over 50% believed sugar increased hyperactivity symptoms.

In a fascinating offshoot of the MTA study, Hoza and colleagues (2000) found that even nontreatment-related beliefs may have an association with treatment outcome. These investigators observed that even after controlling for the effects of treatment condition, more negative child outcomes were associated with reported use of dysfunctional discipline by mothers and fathers, low self-esteem in mothers, low parenting efficacy expectations in fathers, and fathers' tendency to explain child noncompliance in terms of inadequate effort and bad mood on the part of the child. Thus, parent attitudes and expectations seem capable of influencing treatment response and/or poor response to treatment can have an understandable but perhaps unhelpful effect on parent attitudes.

In their discussion of methods of enhancing behavioral parent training, Chronis, Chacko, Fabiano, Wymbs, and Pelham (2004) have also called for greater attention to the role of parental cognitions, noting that "parental expectations regarding their involvement in BPT, their child's involvement in BPT, the duration of treatment, the focus of treatment, and the effectiveness of the treatment for their child may affect a parent's attendance and engagement in treatment" (p. 12).

More recently, Treacy, Tripp, and Baird (2005) studied the effectiveness of a 9 week stress management program for parents of children with ADHD. Program content included a focus on problem-solving skills and cognitive restructuring in addition to education about ADHD, parent rights and resources, family communication skills, discipline skills, and parent self-care skills. Relative to a wait list control group, mothers participating in the treatment program reported significant reductions in parenting stress and significant improvements in parenting style, such as decreases in verbosity, overreactivity, and laxness. The only change reported in participating fathers was a decrease in verbosity. Observed changes were maintained at 6 and 12 month follow-up assessments.

In considering how parental beliefs and expectations might be addressed in BPT groups, it is important to acknowledge the difficult nature of the task. On the one hand, the leader wants to provide parents with enough solid information about ADHD that parents are able to move beyond inappropriate blaming of the child or inappropriate self-blame. On the other hand, the leader also wants to help parents nurture the view that parental choices and actions do matter so the parent can feel empowered to face the many challenges that come with raising a child with ADHD. This balancing act may be best accomplished by leaders who allow and encourage questions and reflections on the part of the parents, particularly when new information is being presented. For example, the group leader might pause periodically and literally ask "How does this information impact your views about ADHD?" If a group is too large and/or not yet ready for more open discussion, the leader could provide brief feedback sheets for parents to complete anonymously. These responses could be collected and read out loud to initiate discussion of these concepts. It may also help if the leader provides parents with examples of commonly occurring unhelpful expectations and beliefs, such as those appearing in charts created for use in treatment by Bloomquist (2006). With these examples to consider, the leader could then ask parents to think about the long term impact on the child if the parent continues to endorse a particular unhelpful belief or expectation. For example, if some parents share, anonymously or otherwise, that they tend to think that their child with ADHD is the source of all the family's difficulties, Bloomquist (2006) recommends the therapist ask the group to consider what is helpful or unhelpful about continuing to think this thought each day. Through discussion it would be useful to lead the group to consider how having such thoughts is likely to impact parent behavior towards the child and then consider how this behavior might further influence the actions and emotions of the child.

Self-Regulation Training

Self-monitoring or self-evaluation approaches typically involve helping a child learn to notice the occurrence of or make a rating about some easily defined aspect of his or her behavior. In their recent meta-analysis of self-regulation interventions for children with ADHD, Reid, Trout, and Schartz (2005) examined the impact of self-monitoring, self-monitoring plus reinforcement, self-management (which involves some form of self-monitoring coupled with an additional step of comparing one's self-evaluation to an external standard or criterion, such as the ratings of an adult in the situation) and self-reinforcement (which is similar to self-monitoring plus reinforcement, but in this case the self-reinforcement is self-administered). Reid and colleagues concluded that the majority of effect sizes calculated for these forms of intervention were moderate to large, meaning .6 or greater. Some studies included students who were on medication throughout the self-regulation intervention and even in these cases, strong effect sizes were observed for increasing on-task behavior and decreasing inappropriate/disruptive behavior. These authors noted that adding self-regulation to ongoing medication treatment seemed to result in stabilizing or decreasing the variability of the behaviors observed. While the authors are clear to caution that all of their studies were based on a relatively small number of cases, their data support the inclusion of self-regulation methods in multimodal treatment for children with ADHD.

At this point, the reader may be saying, "fine, but how does this relate to group work with these children?" Fortunately, Hinshaw and colleagues (Hinshaw, 2005; Hinshaw, Henker, & Whalen, 1984a) have already clarified how self-evaluation could be accomplished in a group context through implementation of the "Match Game." This procedure, which is suitable for use in both child groups and small classroom settings, was originally adapted from Turkewitz, O'Leary, and Ironsmith (1975). At the point of introducing this procedure, the group leader or teacher clarifies a specific behavioral criterion for reinforcement, such as *waiting for others to finish speaking* or *keeping one's hands off others*. It may be necessary to spend some time modeling what this criterion behavior looks like and role-playing violations of this criterion. Then at various points during ongoing group activities, the leader has the group pause and displays a "Match Game" sheet that presents the behavioral criterion and includes a rating scale ranging from 1 (not at all good) to 5 (great). The leader then asks the children to reflect on their own behavior over the last interval and rate themselves on how well they have executed the criterion behavior. The leader explains that he or she will also be rating the child and, if the child's rating is within one point of the leader's rating the child earns a bonus point for accurate self-evaluation. Hinshaw (2005) emphasizes the importance of having the group co-leaders role-play the self-evaluation process as part of the teaching of this skill. He recommends that in early role plays the leader should portray a child giving himself an overly generous self-assessment so the co-leader can then model providing corrective feedback about why his or her rating is at odds with the child's self-rating.

After the process has been modeled, the children can then complete their rating sheets while the leaders discuss and complete their ratings. Each child then shares his or her rating and the reasons for this choice and the leader does the same, again, being very careful to give highly detailed feedback on the specific child behaviors that resulted in the assigned rating. Typically, the game would be enacted more frequently during early group/class sessions to allow the children more practice in developing their self-evaluation skills. Then in later sessions, the leader can choose to lengthen the interval between self-evaluations, dependent upon the needs of the group. In an experimental evaluation of a similar self-evaluation process, Hinshaw, Henker, and Whalen (1984a) trained ADHD children to evaluate their behavior and then examined the effects of this self-evaluation procedure versus traditional external reinforcement system. The effects of this manipulation were examined both with and without concurrent use of medication. The results indicated that the most positive behavior was displayed by the group on medication and enacting the self-evaluation procedure. Variations on this self-evaluation task have also been incorporated into some of the social skills groups previously described and the intensive summer treatment program.

In addition to promoting positive behavior, self-evaluation efforts like the "Match Game" are of interest, as repeated use of these procedures might help address the tendency of children with ADHD to have a distorted self-appraisal. The importance of targeting accurate self-appraisal has been highlighted by a growing body of evidence confirming the tendency of children with ADHD to have a positive illusory bias with regard to their self-assessments (Antshel & Remer, 2003; Diener & Milich, 1997; Hoza et al., 2004). As discussed by Hoza and colleagues, this bias may represent a sort of double-edged sword in the psychological life of the child. Some degree of positive distortion may be adaptive in helping these children avoid demoralization in the face of frequently negative feedback from peers and adults. On the other hand, problem recognition and accurate self-awareness are typically necessary first steps towards positive behavior change, so a positive illusory bias could impede efforts towards change and/or lower motivation to change.

It remains a very open question whether repeated experience with formalized self-assessment exercises can counter or prevent the development of a positive illusory bias. The results obtained by Hoza and colleagues occurred *after* the children had participated in extensive treatment, so that would suggest that once established, such a view might be difficult to change. This observation would argue for early intervention with the self-appraisals of children, but development research would caution that young children do not have the ability and/or the interest to focus on themselves as an object of self-evaluation until some time between the ages of 6 and 8 (Harter, 1985). Given the lag in maturity level that is frequently observed in children with ADHD, the age at which self-evaluation can begin with these children may even be slightly older.

But at some point, at least some adolescents with ADHD do transition into greater self-awareness and more accurate self-appraisal. As a very informal aside, I am frequently called on to meet with college students with ADHD as they implement particular academic accommodations to help them be successful in my courses. In examining this rather select group of young people who have been successful enough to make it into college despite their ADHD, it is striking the degree to which they manifest ownership of their issues. This aspect of their presentation is particularly noticeable if one has also had occasion to work with younger adolescents in whom this degree of self-awareness is completely absent. Some of these college students have been asked to share their thoughts or explanations for how they achieved this adaptive self-awareness. While terribly unwise to make too much out of a small number of anecdotal comments, it is interesting how many of these individuals note that they don't really know what words or processes helped them make this transition to greater self-responsibility. They do know, however, that they became motivated to be more engaged in their own treatment and self-help efforts when they began to realize they were not going to achieve some important personal goal, such as making it into a competitive design program or maintaining an important relationship, unless they began to respond more appropriately to their own needs. These responses make me wonder how motivational interviewing techniques that have been popularized in the field of chemical dependency treatment might be used with adolescents who are having difficulty understanding the value of adaptive problem ownership (Hettema, Steele, & Miller, 2005; Rollnick & Miller, 1995).

Anger Management

Finally, cognitive behavioral methods designed to enhance anger management may offer some added value for those children with ADHD who are prone to inappropriate expressions of anger. Targeting anger issues seems like a productive focus given that poor anger management can have such a costly impact on relationships within the home, with peers, and in the school setting. In addition, difficulties with anger may be the aspect of the child's behavior that is most likely to get the child moved into a more restrictive educational setting when otherwise he or she might have been able to function in a regular classroom.

Building on earlier work by Goodwin and Mahoney (1975) who had ADHD children practice remaining self-controlled in the face of verbal taunts, Hinshaw, Henker, and Whalen (1984b) trained small groups of children with ADHD in the use of stress inoculation methods. The children first learned about various physiological cues that serve as early warning signs of anger. Children are then trained in a variety of cognitive and behavioral strategies for coping with anger, including the use of ideas like engaging in distracting thoughts, reminding oneself of the goal of remaining calm, engaging in deep breathing, or other forms of simple relaxation. A number of practice opportunities are then created so the children can try out the use of their selected coping methods, first with easier examples, but eventually with challenging tasks, such as being the victim of taunts by others. In the evaluation of this training, Hinshaw and colleagues (1984b) compared this form of stress inoculation training with a control group that had just been exposed to more general principles of social problem solving and perspective taking. In addition, half of each group received psychostimulants while the other half received placebos. These interventions were evaluated by comparing the children's responding in pre and post treatment provocation situations. The children who had received the stress inoculation training earned significantly higher ratings on a global measure of self-control. This group also displayed more deliberate use of coping strategies. Children who were medicated responded in a less intense manner than children on placebo, but there were no medication-related differences in the content of the children's behavior.

This useful training format has been incorporated into the successful Anger Coping Program and Coping Power Program developed by Lochman and colleagues (Larson & Lochman, 2002; Lochman, Barry, & Pardini, 2003). In the Lochman program applications, the anger coping skills are first practiced with puppets prior to engaging in live action role-plays, which may be a very wise modification for use with highly reactive children with ADHD. In addition, this program emphasizes behavioral rehearsal of problem-solving and anger coping skills through the children's creation of demonstration videotapes. Again, this highly appealing mode of rehearsal is relatively more likely to hold the attention of the elementary school child co-morbid for both ADHD and anger management issues.

THOUGHTS FOR FURTHER EXPLORATION

Given that the first commitment of all serious clinicians and researchers is to the well-being of the client and not to a particular form of treatment, it would seem that the first order of business must be to do a better job promoting those treatments that have demonstrated effectiveness. Parents, teachers, physicians, and all those influencing the decisions made about child treatment need to know that the interventions with the greatest demonstrated effectiveness are carefully managed psychostimulant medication, parent involvement in a behavioral parenting group, and, if available, child involvement in an intensive summer treatment program with related school consultation. The skills of a cognitive-behavioral clinician could be put to good use helping parents explore the beliefs or expectancies that cause them to be reluctant to implement proven treatments for their child. Without parental commitment to being an informed consumer of evidence-based care, the child with ADHD is very unlikely to receive timely or appropriate treatment.

Just as Martin (2005) has challenged the psychiatric community and pharmaceutical industry to come up with truly novel compounds that offer more refined treatment for ADHD rather than just more "me too" drugs, it appears that authors such as Hinshaw (2005) and Strayhorn (2002) have urged those of us interested in psychosocial approaches to move beyond the stagnation of the past 15 years. As much as many clinicians and researchers, not to mention families, would like to discover a form of weekly child-focused group treatment that can make a lasting impact on children with ADHD, our current understanding of the disorder and existing treatment outcome research suggest this traditional form of treatment delivery is not particularly useful. Is it possible that something less intensive than the summer treatment program, but more intensive than weekly sessions could be useful for these children? That is an empirical question. Do we know that cognitive behavioral treatments that have proven effective in treating childhood anxiety, depression, and/or conduct problems can be equally effective with children co-morbid for ADHD? That, too, is an empirical question. And, of particular interest, what interventions can be implemented at the middle and high school level to increase the odds that more students with ADHD will become the kind of effective, engaged self-advocates that are so impressive at the college level? Clearly, many questions remain for investigators and clinicians concerned with developing and refining psychosocial interventions that will better meet the needs of children with ADHD.

REFERENCES

Abikoff, H. (1991). Cognitive training in ADHD children: Less to it than meets the eye. *Journal of Learning Disabilities, 24*, 205–209.

Abikoff, H., Hechtman, L. Klein, R. G., Gallagher, R., Fliess, K., Etcovitch, J., et al. (2004). Social functioning in children with ADHD treated with long-term methylphenidate and Multimodal psychosocial treatment. *Journal of the American Academy of Child and Adolescent Psychiatry, 43*, 820–829.

Anastopoulos, A. D., Shelton, T. L., DuPaul, G. J., & Guevremont, D. C. (1993). Parent training for attention-deficit hyperactivity disorder: Its impact on parent functioning. *Journal of Abnormal Psychology, 21*, 581–596.

Antshel, K. M., & Remer, R. (2003). Social skills training in children with Attention Deficit Hyperactivity Disorder: A randomized-controlled clinical trial. *Journal of Clinical Child and Adolescent Psychology, 32*, 153–165.

Barkley, R. A. (1997). *ADHD and the nature of self-control.* New York: Guilford.

Barkley, R. A. (1997). *Defiant children: A clinician's manual for parent training* (2nd ed.). New York: Guilford.

Barkley, R. A. (2006). *Attention deficit hyperactivity disorder: A handbook for diagnosis and Treatment* (3nd ed.). New York: Guilford.

Bloomquist, M. L. (2006). *Skills training for children with behavior problems: A parent and practitioner guidebook...*(revised ed.). New York: Guilford.

Braswell, L., August, G., Bloomquist, M. L., Realmuto, G., Skare, S., & Crosby, R. (1997). School-based secondary prevention for children with disruptive behavior: Initial outcomes. *Journal of Abnormal Child Psychology, 25,* 197–208.

Braswell, L., & Bloomquist, M. L. (1991). *Cognitive-behavioral therapy with ADHD children: Child, family, and school interventions.* New York: Guilford.

Bugental, D. G., & Johnston, C. (2000). Parental and child cognitions in the context of the family. *Annual Review of Psychology, 51*, 315–344.

Chronis, A., Fabiano, G., Gnagy, E., Onyango, A., Pelham, W., Lopez-Williams, A., et al. (2004). An evaluation of the summer treatment program for children with attention deficit/hyperactivity disorder using a treatment withdrawal design. *Behavior Therapy,35*, 561–85.

Dishion, T. J., & Dodge, K. A., (2005). Peer contagion in interventions for children and adolescents: Moving towards an understanding of the ecology and dynamics of change.*Journal of Abnormal Child Psychology, 33*, 395–400.

Dishion, T. J., McCord, J., & Poulin, F. (1999). When interventions harm: Peer groups and problem behavior. *American Psychologist, 54,* 755–764.

dosReis, S., Zito, J., Safer, D., Soeken, K., Mitchell, J., & Ellwood, L. (2003). Parental perceptions and satisfaction with stimulant medication for attention-deficit hyperactivity disorder. *Journal of Developmental & Behavioral Pediatrics, 24*, 155–161.

Feldman, R. A. (1992). The St. Louis experiment: Effective treatment of antisocial youths in prosocial peer groups. In J. McCord and R. Tremblay (Eds.), *Preventing antisocial behavior: Interventions from birth through adolescence* (p. 233-251). New York: Guilford

Gifford-Smith, M., Dodge, K., Dishion, T. J., McCord, J. (2005). Peer influence in children and adolescents: Crossing the bridge from developmental to intervention science. *Journal of Abnormal Child Psychology, 33*, 255–265.

Goodwin, S. & Mahoney, M. (1975) Modification of aggression through modelling: an experimental probe *Journal of Behaviour Therapy and Experimental Psychiatry, 6,* 200–202.

Griest, D. L., Forehand, R., Rogers, T., Breiner, J., Furey, W., & Williams, C. A. (1982). Effects of parent enhancement therapy on the treatment of outcome and generalization of a parent training program. *Behavior Research and Therapy, 20*, 429–436.

Harrison, C., & Sofronoff, K. (2002). AD/HD and parental psychological distress: Role of demographics, child behavioral characteristics, and parental cognitions. *Journal of the American Academy of Child and Adolescent Psychiatry, 41*, 703–712.

Harter, S. (1985). *The Self-Perception Profile for Children: Revision of the Perceived Competence Scale for Children (Manual).* Denver, CO: University of Denver.

Hettema, J., Steele, J., & Miller, W. R. (2005). Motivational interviewing. *Annual Review of Clinical Psychology, 1*, 91–111.

Hinshaw, S. P. (2005). Attention-deficit/Hyperactivity Disorder. In P. C. Kendall (Ed.), *Child and adolescent therapy: Cognitive-behavioral procedures* (3rd ed, pp. 82–112). New York: Guilford.

Hinshaw, S. P., Henker, B., & Whalen, C. K. (1984a). Cognitive-behavioral and pharmacologic interventions for hyperactive boys: Comparative and combined effects. *Journal of Consulting and Clinical Psychology, 52,* 739-749.

Hinshaw, S. P., Henker, B., & Whalen, C. K. (1984b). Self-control in hyperactive boys in anger-Inducing situations: Effects of cognitive-behavioral training and of methylphenidate. *Journal of Abnormal Child Psychology, 12,* 55–77.

Hoza, B., Owens, J. S., Pelham, W. E., Swanson, J. M., Conners, C. K., Hinshaw, S. P., et al. (2000). Parental cognitions as predictors of child treatment response in attention deficit/hyperactivity disorder. *Journal of Abnormal Child Psychology, 28,* 569–584.

Hoza, B., Gerdes, A., Hinshaw, S. P., Arnold, L. E., Pelham, W. E., Molina, B. S. G., et al. (2004). Self-percep-tions of competence in children with ADHD and comparison children. *Journal of Consulting and Clinical Psychology, 72,* 382–391.

Johnston, C., Patenaude, R., & Inman, G. (1992). Causal attributions for hyperactive and aggressive child behaviors. *Social Cognition, 10,* 255–270.

Jensen, P. S., Garcia, J. A., Glied, S., Crowe, M., Foster, M., Schlander, M., et al. (2005). Cost-effectiveness of ADHD treatments: Findings from the multimodal treatment Study of children with ADHD. *American Journal of Psychiatry, 162,* 1628–1636.

Kavale, K. A., Mathur, S. R., Forness, S. R., Rutherford, R. B., & Quinn, M. M. (1996). Effectiveness of social skills training for students with behavior disorders: A Meta-analysis. In T. Scruggs & M. Mastrupieri (Eds.), *Advances in learning and behavioral disabilities* (vol. 11; 1-26). Greenwich, CT: JAI Press.

Kazdin, A. E., & Weisz, J.R. (Eds.) (2003). *Evidence-based psychotherapies for children and adolescents.* New York, NY: The Guilford Press

Kendall, P. C., & Braswell, L. (1985). *Cognitive-behavioral therapy for impulsive children.* New York: Guil-ford.

Kendall, P. C., & Braswell, L. (1993). *Cognitive-behavioral therapy for impulsive children* (2nd ed.). New York: Guilford.

Kendall, P. C. (2005). *Child and adolescent therapy: Cognitive-behavioral procedures* (3rd ed.). New York: Guilford.

Larson, J. & Lochman, J. E. (2002). *Helping schoolchildren cope with anger: A cognitive-behavioral interven-tion.* New York: Guilford.

Lochman, J. E., Barry, T. D., & Pardini, D. (2003). Anger control training for aggressive youths. In A. E. Kazdin & J. R. Weisz (Eds.), *Evidence-based psychotherapies for children and adolescents* (pp. 263–281). New York: Guilford.

Lopez-Williams, A., Chacko, A., Wymbs, B., Fabiano, G., Seymour, K., Gnagy, E., et al. (2005). Athletic perfor-mance and social behavior as predictors of peer acceptance in children diagnosed with attention-deficit/ hyperactivity disorder. *Journal of Emotional and Behavioral Disorders, 13,* 173–181.

Martin, A. (2005). The hard work of growing up with ADHD. *American Journal of Psychiatry, 162,* 1575–1577.

MTA Cooperative Group. (1999). 14-month randomized clinical trial of treatment strategies for attention deficit hyperactivity disorder. *Archives of General Psychiatry, 56,* 1073–1086.

MTA ooperative Group. (2004). The National Institute of Mental Health MTA follow-up: 24-month outcomes of treatment strategies for attention-deficit hyperactivity disorder. *Pediatrics, 113,* 754–761.

Nigg, J. T. (2001). Is ADHD an inhibitory disorder? *Psychological Bulletin, 127,* 571–598.

Pelham, W. E., & Bender, M. E. (1982). Peer relationships in hyperactive children: Description and treatment. In K. Gadow & I. Bialer (Eds.), *Advances in learning and behavioral disabilities* (vol. 1, pp. 365–436). Greenwich, CT: JAI Press.

Pelham, W. E., Fabiano, G. A., Gnagy, E. M., Greiner, A. R., & Hoza, B. (2005). The role of summer treatment programs in the context of comprehensive treatment for Attention-deficit/Hyperactivity Disorder. In E. D. Hibbs & P. S. Jensen (Eds.), *Psychosocial treatments for child and adolescent disorders: Empirically based Strategies for clinical practice* (2nd ed., pp. 377–409). Washington, DC: American Psychological Association Press.

Pelham, W. E., Fabiano, G. A., & Massetti, G. M. (2005). Evidence-based assessment of Attention-deficit/Hy-peractivity Disorder in children and adolescents. *Journal of Clinical Child Psychology, 34,* 449–476.

Pfiffner, L. J., & McBurnett, K. (1997). Social skills training with parent generalization: Treatment effects for children with Attention Deficit Disorder. *Journal of Consulting and Clinical Psychology, 65,* 749–757.

Pisterman, S., McGrath, P., Firestone, P., & Goodman, J. T. (1989). Outcome of parent-mediated treatment of preschoolers with Attention Deficit Disorder with Hyperactivity. *Journal of Consulting and Clinical Psychology, 57,* 636–643.

Reid, R., Trout, A. L., & Schartz, M. (2005). Self-regulation interventions for children with Attention Deficit/ Hyperactivity Disorder. *Exceptional Children, 76,* 361–377.

Rollnick, S., & Miller, W. R. (1995). What is motivational interviewing? *Behavioral and Cognitive Psychotherapy, 23*, 325–334.

Shelton, T. L., Barkley, R. A., Crosswait, C., Moorehouse, M., Fletcher, K., Barrett, S., et al. (2000). Multimethod psychoeducational intervention for preschool children with disruptive behavior: Two year post-treatment follow-up. *Journal of Abnormal Child Psychology, 28,* 253–266.

Smith, A. M., & O'Leary, S. G. (1995). Attributions Londerville, S., & Main, M. (1981). Security of and arousal as predictors of maternal discipline. attachment, compliance, and maternal training. *Cognitive Therapy and Research, 19,* 345-357.

Strayhorn, J. M. (2002). Self control theory and research. *Amercian Journal of Child and Adolescent Psychiatry, 41,* 7–16.

Stogdill, R. M. (1936). Experiments in the measurement of attitudes toward children: 1899–1935. *Child Development, 7,* 31–36.

Treacy, L., Tripp, G., & Baird, A. (2005). Parent stress management training for Attention-deficit/Hyperactivity Disorder. *Behavior Therapy, 36,* 223–233.

Turkewitz, H., O'Leary, K. D., & Ironsmith, M. (1975). Generalization and maintenance appropriate behavior through self-control. *Journal of Consulting and Clinical Psychology, 43,* 577-583.

Webster-Stratton, C. (1994). Advancing videotape parent training: A comparison study. *Journal of Consulting and Clinical Psychology, 62,* 583–593.

Webster-Stratton, C. (2005). The incredible years: A training series for the prevention and treatment of conduct problem in young children. In E. D. Hibbs & P. S. Jensen (Eds.), *Psychosocial treatments for child and adolescent disorders: Empirically based trategies for clinical practice.* Washington, DC: American Psychological Association Press.

Chapter Eighteen

Cognitive-Behavior Group Therapy for Angry and Aggressive Youth

John E. Lochman, Nicole Powell, Caroline Boxmeyer,
Annie M. Deming, & Laura Young

In this chapter, we will provide an overview of anger and aggression in children and adolescents, noting how childhood aggression can be a central risk marker for later serious antisocial behavior. A cognitive-behavior model describing the development and maintenance of children's aggressive behavior will be presented, and this contextual social-cognitive model serves as a foundation for cognitive-behavioral group interventions for aggressive children. Cognitive-behavioral group interventions have certain advantages relative to individually-delivered intervention, including the opportunity for role-playing and peer modeling of skills, peer reinforcement of positive behavior, and greater cost-efficiency. Relevant evidence-based group interventions will be noted, and a case example from the Coping Power program will be provided to illustrate key intervention goals. Finally, obstacles to group treatment with aggressive children will be discussed, along with potential methods for addressing these obstacles.

ANGER AND AGGRESSION IN CHILDREN AND ADOLESCENTS

Aggression can be defined as behavior that may result in harm to a person or an object (Pettit, 1997). Within our youth population, behavioral patterns involving aggression, acting-out, and other generally disruptive behavior patterns represent the highest referral rates for mental health services. In addition, these behavioral patterns showed an increase from the 1960s through the 1990s (Achenbach & Howell, 1993).

Researchers and clinicians show much interest in childhood aggression for several reasons. Aggression in childhood is a risk factor for negative outcomes in adolescence and adulthood including substance use, delinquency, school dropout, and violence (Lochman, Whidby, & Fitzgerald, 2000). Aggression in youth tends to lead to violent, antisocial behavior in later years (Moffitt & Caspi, 2001). Nearly all antisocial adults showed signs of conduct disorder as children. According to Farrington (1995), approximately half of any sample of antisocial children continues with their antisocial behavior in adolescence. Subsequently, half of the antisocial adolescents continue on to become antisocial adults. These behavior patterns not only harm the aggressive individual, but also have obvious negative implications for other individuals and society at large.

Aggressive behavior is a hallmark sign of the *DSM-IV-TR* diagnoses of oppositional defiant disorder and conduct disorder. However, many children who exhibit aggression might have a subclinical condition or other diagnosable condition that affects their behavior. For example, research indicates that aggression coincides with several disorders, including Attention Deficit Hyperactivity Disorder (ADHD), depression, and anxiety (e.g., Zoccolillo, 1992).

Aggressive children are likely to experience negative reactions from parents, peers, and teachers. These negative reactions then in turn affect behavior and outcomes. For example, the combination of aggressive behavior and peer rejection leads to increased risk of depression and anxiety symptoms. The combination of depression and conduct problems in turn places children at a higher risk for early onset substance use (Miller-Johnson, Coie, Maumary-Gremaud, Lochman, & Terry, 1999).

COGNITIVE-BEHAVIORAL CONCEPTUALIZATION OF INTERVENTION

Aggressive behavior and the development of antisocial behavior can be conceptualized within a cognitive-behavioral framework. One such framework is the contextual social-cognitive model, which was significantly influenced by Novaco's work with aggressive adults and Crick and Dodge's (1994) social information processing model.

According to Patterson, Reid, and Dishion (1992), antisocial behaviors during adolescence are the result of a developmental trajectory influenced by familial and personal factors. The contextual social-cognitive model assumes that factors in a child's social and psychological development and family environment relate to childhood aggression and later delinquency and substance use (Lochman & Wells, 2002a).

Loeber (1990) theorized that poor parenting practices affect childhood aggression. Then, children's aggressive behavior becomes more prevalent, influencing developmental processes that heighten the risk of negative outcomes such as substance abuse and conduct disorder. As children become more oppositional, they experience more negative reactions from parents, peers, and teachers, leading to distortions in social information-processing. As they are experiencing these negative reactions, their bond with their school decreases and their academic progress weakens, causing these children to be more susceptible to deviant peer group influences. By adolescence, this trajectory can result in an increased risk of substance use, delinquency, and school failure. Therefore, the contextual social-cognitive model posits that two types of factors contribute to adolescent antisocial behavior: (1) child level factors, including poor social cognitive skills and lack of social competence, and (2) parent level factors, including inconsistent or harsh discipline and low caregiver involvement with the child.

Child-Level Factors

The contextual social-cognitive model focuses on how a child responds to interpersonal conflicts or frustrations. Two distinct sets of cognitive processes are at work during an interpersonal interaction: (1) the child's perceptions and attributions of the problem, which affect the child's level of anger and involve the first three steps of Crick and Dodge's (1994) model, followed by (2) the child's plan for a response to the situation, which involves the final three steps of Crick and Dodge's model.

During the first three steps, children encode internal and external cues, interpret these cues, and formulate a goal. Research has shown that aggressive children have particular difficulties during the early stages of information processing because of their problems encoding incoming information and in interpreting other's intentions correctly. For example, aggressive children exhibit a hostile attribution bias, in that they view other's intentions as hostile more often than their nonaggressive peers. Aggressive children also tend to generate interpersonal goals such as power and dominance more than their nonaggressive peers.

The final three steps involve accessing possible responses, choosing a response, and enacting that response. Compared to nonagressive peers, aggressive children tend to generate fewer solutions and their solutions are of poorer quality. Their solutions often involve aggression and do not often include verbal assertion. Aggressive youth also exhibit a belief that aggression is an appropriate and effective method to achieve a goal.

The steps in the social-cognitive model are impacted by schemas, another important child level construct (Lochman, White, & Wayland, 1991). An individual's schemas can include generalized expectations about oneself and others, and can form the basis for perceptions of current events. For example, aggressive boys tend to base their perceptions of their own aggressive behavior on prior expectations more than nonaggressive boys do (Lochman & Dodge, 1998).

Parent-Level Factors

Research has shown that children's aggressive behavior is influenced and maintained by parenting practices. Harsh and/or inconsistent discipline, poor parental monitoring, vague commands, low parental involvement, and maternal depression have all been found to contribute to children's aggressive behavior (Downy & Coyne, 1990; Patterson et al., 1992). Parents' social-cognitive processes have also been examined for their contribution to children's aggressive behavior. Additionally, the relation between parenting practices and aggressive behavior can be thought of as bidirectional, in that poor parenting contributes to the onset of aggressive behavior which in turn results in negative reactions from parents and impedes the use of effective parenting practices.

Research indicates that child-level factors and parent-level factors both contribute to childhood aggression and an outcome of adolescent antisocial behavior. Thus, the contextual social-cognitive model posits that prevention and intervention should focus on both types of factors in order for treatment to be successful.

ASSESSMENT AND GROUP IDENTIFICATION

In assessing for appropriate involvement in group treatment, it is imperative to gain a comprehensive understanding of the child's symptoms, strengths, weaknesses, and possible diagnoses. It is also critical to examine the child's social-cognitive skills, as these are a central component of therapy with aggressive children (Lochman & Wells, 2002a). We will first focus on behavioral assessment measures and then proceed to measures of social-cognitive skills.

Behavioral Assessment

The four main assessment methods include norm-referenced tests, interviews, observations, and informal assessment procedures. This discussion will focus on norm-referenced tests and rating scales. However, note that by interpreting each of the four methods individually and then resolving any major discrepancies among them, we can formulate a stronger conceptualization of the issues in order to guide treatment decisions (Sattler, 2001).

The battery of tests and rating scales available for aggression assessment includes a variety of narrow- and broad-band scales. Narrow-band scales assess specifically for the characteristics of aggression, and thus provide specific information on aggressive behavior and the diversity of externalizing symptoms (Collett, Ohan, & Myers, 2003). However, as these scales have typically been used for research purposes, their clinical value is limited by a lack of normative data and psychometric information.

Broad-band scales provide a more comprehensive assessment of general competencies and problem areas (Collett et al., 2003). As these scales often provide normative data and cut-off scores useful for classification and comparison, clinicians rely more heavily on broad-band scales to inform their clinical decisions. However, these scales offer a limited depth of understanding. As they assess numerous areas of functioning, fewer questions can be allotted for each specific area. Additionally, they often confound aspects of externalizing behavior into one subscale, resulting in a blurred picture of aggressive characteristics (Collett et al., 2003).

The broad-band, norm-referenced measures that have proven useful in assessing for aggression are measures of behavioral, social, and emotional competencies across a range of internalizing to externalizing problems. The *Behavior Assessment System for Children — Second Edition* (BASC-2; Reynolds & Kamphaus, 2004), *Revised Behavior Problem Checklist* (RBPC; Quay & Peterson, 1996), and the *Conners' Rating Scales — Revised* (CRS-R; Conners, 1997) provide integrative approaches to assessment across multiple informants. Despite the general, broad-band nature of these measures, both the CRS-R and the RBPC focus primarily on externalizing problems. The *Personality Inventory for Children-Second Edition* (PIC-2; Wirt, Lachar, Seat, & Broen, 2001) and its self-report companion, the *Personality Inventory for Youth* (PIY; Lachar & Gruber, 1995), also include measures of disruptive behavior and delinquency.

Some broad-band, norm-referenced measures such as the *Reynolds Adolescent Adjustment Screening Inventory* (RAASI; Reynolds, 2001), the *Student Behavior Survey* (SBS; Lachar, Wingenfeld, Kline, & Gruber, 2000), and the *Child Behavior Checklist* (CBCL) and its teacher (TRF) and child counterparts (YSR) (Achenbach, 1991a, 1991b, 1991c) are designed for use as screening measures. These measures use a range of informants to assess for verbal and physical aggression, oppositional defiant behavior, and conduct problems.

There are several non-normed, narrow-band rating scales that measure specific conceptualizations and components of aggression. The *Overt Aggression Scale* (OAS;

Yudofsky, 2003) was developed for use in inpatient psychiatric settings and is most appropriate for seriously aggressive individuals who typically score beyond the range of rating scales for aggression. The *Children's Aggression Scale* (CAS; Halperin, 2003) distinguishes between verbal, physical, provoked, and initiated aggression across various settings and individuals and is more relevant for outpatient youth who demonstrate mild to severe acts of aggression. The *Proactive and Reactive Aggression Scale* (PRA; Dodge, 2003) focuses on the proactive or reactive motivations behind aggressive acts. The *Direct and Indirect Aggression Scale* (DIAS; Bjorkqvist, 2003) makes a distinction between direct confrontational forms of aggression and indirect forms of aggression.

Assessment for Inclusion in Group Therapy

Many factors are believed to contribute to the development and maintenance of aggressive behavior. While innate characteristics and contextual factors are outside of the influence of therapeutic intervention, such programs can address social competence and social-cognitive skills. These factors are believed to mediate the negative outcomes of aggressive behavior (Lochman & Wells, 2002a). The social-cognitive model of children's aggression suggests that aggressive children demonstrate cognitive distortions when interpreting incoming social information and evaluating social problems, and they show deficiencies in formulating appropriate responses to these problems (Lochman & Wells, 2002a). Consequently, the assessment of a child's social-cognitive skills and functioning is central to understanding the child's therapeutic needs and likelihood of benefiting from group intervention.

While there are a number of measures used for assessing social-cognitive functioning, most have poor validity and are not adequate for assessing social-cognitive skills (van Manen, Prins, & Emmelkamp, 2001). However, the Selman and Byrne test (1974), the *Means-End Problem Solving Inventory* (MEPS; Platt & Spivack, 1989), the *Taxonomy of Problematic Social Situations for Children* (TOPS; Dodge, McClaskey, & Feldman, 1985), and the *Social Cognitive Skills Test* (SCST; Van Manen et al., 2001) do possess clinical utility. These measures use social problem situations, presented through pictures or stories, to assess a child's social cognitive skills and problem solving abilities. The Selman and Byrne test and the MEPS ask the child to relay how a protagonist would react in a situation requiring social-cognitive problem solving abilities. The SCST uses similar means to assess the child's functioning on eight specific social cognitive skills. The TOPS requires the child's teacher to rate, across several situations, how much the child struggles with each situation and the child's likelihood of responding inappropriately.

The Coping Power program for children with conduct problems is an example of a group intervention for which inclusion is assessment-based (Lochman & Wells, 2004). Lochman and Wells have used a multiple-gating approach to measure children's behavior for elevated levels of aggression appropriate for inclusion in the program. First, teachers rated each of their students on severity of verbal aggression, physical aggression, and disruptiveness. Because cognitive functioning is thought to moderate treatment outcome, the teachers also rated each child's cognitive ability. The 22% most aggressive children were then contacted for inclusion in Gate 2 and Gate 3 of the program screening. For

Gate 2, parents gave consent for the teacher to complete the TRF, and for Gate 3, parents completed the CBCL. Children with T-Scores below 55 to 60 on these measures were excluded from the program (Lochman & Wells, 2004). Thus, this program utilizes behavioral assessments to determine need for intervention, as well as cognitive assessment to establish appropriate inclusion in the program.

COGNITIVE-BEHAVIORAL GROUP INTERVENTIONS

A number of group treatment programs have been developed to address cognitive-behavioral deficits associated with anger and aggression in youth. Empirical research has demonstrated positive effects on behavior and social-cognitive functioning following participation in group interventions for children from preschool age to adolescence. Effective group interventions come in a variety of forms; they may be long-term or short-term, they may target children exclusively or may include components for parents and/or teachers, they may be clinic-based or school-based. This section will review several evidence-based group programs for youth, including the Coping Power program.

An example of an effective cognitive-behavioral program for very young children is Webster-Stratton and Hammond's (1997) Dinosaur School. These authors reported that 4- to 7-year-old children with early-onset conduct problems made improvements in their level of behavioral problems in the home following participation in a group intervention addressing factors such as social skills deficits, conflict resolution, and management of intense emotions. Parent involvement in a concurrently run program enhanced the results; however, improvements were apparent for participants of the child group alone, demonstrating that even very young children can benefit from a group intervention.

Adolescents with conduct problems have also been shown to benefit from participation in cognitive-behavioral group interventions, as demonstrated by Feindler and Ecton's (1986) research. After participating in a group intervention in which skills such as relaxation, problem-solving, and coping statements were taught, adolescents displayed less aggressive and disruptive behavior, and made improvements in measures of their social-cognitive functioning.

For school-age children demonstrating angry, aggressive behaviors or other conduct problems, there are several interventions that have documented beneficial effects. The Montreal Delinquency Prevention Program, an intervention that includes a parenting component and a series of child groups for second and third graders, has been shown to reduce the likelihood of adjustment problems, substance abuse, and delinquent behaviors in the preteen and teenage years (e.g., Tremblay, Kurtz, Masse, Vitaro, & Pihl, 1995).

Anger Coping, an 18-session cognitive-behavioral intervention targeting children in the 4th through 6th grades, has similarly been shown to reduce participants' likelihood of future substance abuse and conduct problems (Lochman, Dunn, & Wagner, 1997). More immediate effects include reduced disruptive behavior, increased on-task behavior, less parent and teacher-rated aggression, and improvements in self-esteem (Lochman et al., 1997). Improvements in self-esteem and lower rates of substance use have been maintained at a 3-year follow-up, though other behavioral improvements have not persisted (Lochman, 1992).

To improve outcome and preventative effects, Anger Coping was revised and expanded, resulting in the Coping Power Program, a multi-component intervention for late elementary- to early middle school-aged children and their parents. In addition to anger management, the 34-session Coping Power child component includes units on goal-setting, emotional awareness, relaxation training, social skills training, problem-solving, and handling peer pressure. Participants are also seen individually on a monthly basis to increase leader-student rapport and to individualize the program as needed. Generalization of treatment effects to the classroom is enhanced through the use of goal sheets which allow teachers to provide daily feedback on students' progress toward behavioral goals.

Coping Power includes a 16-session parenting component designed to run concurrently with the child sessions. Parents are instructed in skills taught in the child component and are encouraged to promote their children's use of these skills at home. The parenting component also addresses parent involvement in academics, management of parents' own stress, behavior management, family communication, and parent–child relationship building.

Support for the Coping Power program has been demonstrated through both efficacy and effectiveness studies. In an initial efficacy study, 183 aggressive boys were randomly assigned to receive the full Coping Power program (child and parent components), the child component only, or no treatment (Lochman & Wells, 2002a). In pre- and post-analyses, both Coping Power groups displayed improvements in measures of social-information processing and locus of control. One year post-intervention, participants displayed lower rates of covert delinquent behavior and parent-reported substance abuse than did the control group (Lochman & Wells, 2004). These results were most pronounced for the full Coping Power program with child and parent components. Coping Power also produced teacher-rated improvements in school behavioral functioning during the follow-up year and these results were primarily attributed to the Coping Power child component.

In the next stage of evaluation, effectiveness studies of Coping Power have been conducted to build on positive efficacy results. In a study involving 245 aggressive children, Lochman and Wells (2002b) reported that Coping Power produced reductions in parents' and teachers' ratings of proactive aggression at the post-intervention assessment. Children who participated in Coping Power and a supplemental classroom intervention also displayed improvements in social competence, problem-solving, and anger-coping skills. At the 1-year follow-up, Coping Power resulted in lower rates of substance use and self-reported delinquency compared to controls (Lochman & Wells, 2003).

Effectiveness studies of the Coping Power program have further documented the intervention's positive effects for a variety of groups including boys and girls (Lochman & Wells, 2002b), aggressive deaf children (Lochman et al., 2001), and a Dutch sample of conduct disordered boys (van de Wiel, Matthys, Cohen-Kettenis, & van Engeland, 2003). In addition, a large scale dissemination study in which school counselors are trained to implement the Coping Power Program in their own schools is currently underway.

OVERCOMING POTENTIAL OBSTACLES

When implementing group interventions with angry and aggressive youth, there are a set of potential obstacles that can interfere with the optimal functioning of the group and which can detract from the effectiveness of the intervention. Four primary issues involve children's reactive behavior in the group, deviancy training and deviant norms, singletons, and the inclusion of highly impulsive ADHD youth. These four issues will be briefly described, and then relevant methods for overcoming these obstacles will be discussed (Lochman & Wells, 1996).

Obstacles

Reactive behavior in groups.   Children who are chosen for a CBT group because of their aggressive behavior with peers can be noncompliant and challenging with adult group leaders and they can readily respond to perceived provocations from other children in the group with flashes of reactive, angry aggression. Reactive aggressive children have difficulty regulating their anger and arousal, causing their "hot" angry cognitions to interfere with their information processing. Children may perceive that other group members are receiving more favorable treatment from group leaders, they may feel that they are being blamed for some problem in the group, or they may feel victimized by a peer's efforts to dominate and control others. Children's emotional reactions to each other in these situations can be highly contagious, and can lead to bursts of aversive, conflictual interpersonal behavior between group members.

Deviancy training and deviant norms.   Group members may reinforce each others' antisocial behavior and antisocial attitudes and create potentially iatrogenic effects (Dishion & Andrews, 1995). The two most prominent explanations for the effect that deviant peer groups have on individuals' behavior are the influence of social norms, and the influence of deviancy training (Lavallee, Bierman, Nix, & Conduct Problems Prevention Research Group, 2005; Patterson, Dishion, & Yoerger, 2000). From a social norm perspective, Wright, Giammarino, & Parad (1986) used the person-group similarity model and found that a high density of aggressive youth in a group may cause the social norms for aggression to shift to a higher level for individuals in the group, making aggressive and antisocial behavior appear to be more socially acceptable.

In addition to being exposed to a number of children with high levels of aggressive behavior in a deviant peer group, the members of the deviant peer group may directly reinforce each other for their antisocial attitudes and behaviors. Delinquent adolescent dyads have been found to provide high rates of positive reinforcement for their partners' deviant talk, while nondeviant dyads provide reinforcement for each others' normative, non-deviant discussions (Patterson et al., 2000). This pattern of reinforcement of rule-breaking talk among deviant dyads directly affects these youths' subsequent substance use and delinquency (Dishion, Eddy, Haas, Li, & Spracklen, 1997). In a key study that demonstrated how deviancy training could be a primary mechanism accounting for the negative effect of aggregating antisocial youth, Patterson and colleagues (2000) found that deviancy training in dyadic interactions partially mediated the effect of boys' involvement with deviant peers in 4th grade and their substance use, police arrests and number of intercourse partners in 8th grade.

Dishion and Andrews (1995) found that deviancy training led young adolescents who were in a group intervention program to have higher rates of tobacco use and more delinquent behaviors at a 1-year follow-up than did control children. These iatrogenic effects remained even at later 3-year follow-ups, especially for youth with more moderate levels of antisocial behavior at baseline (Poulin, Dishion, & Burraston, 2001). The results for social norm explanations for deviant group effects are less clear than deviancy training effects (Lavallee et al., 2005).

These deviant group effects can also be apparent in children's power struggles with group leaders. If a group member is often involved in challenging group leaders, and if that child is relatively well accepted by his or her peers in the group, this can stimulate broad oppositional power struggles between the group and the leaders, and can reduce children's group involvement and motivation for change.

Singletons   The presence of a child who is clearly different from his or her peers in the group on important dimensions may contribute to that individual being ostracized from the group and victimized by peers. Examples of such "singletons" are having one girl in a group of preadolescent boys, having one minority race child in a group, and having a child with low cognitive functioning in a group of children with average intellectual functioning. The singleton child can thus be socially rejected by peers in the group, and can feel distressed and socially incompetent.

Impulsive ADHD children.   Some children can create serious disruptions in group functioning because of their ADHD characteristics, which lead them to impulsively interrupt others and to be in constant physical contact with others because of their uncontrolled hyperactive behaviors. These disruptions can be distinguished from the reactive aggressive behaviors and the deviant group effects described above because they are not intentional disruptions or emotionally charged responses to perceived threats. However, the disruptions caused by ADHD children can seriously disturb the group's ability to work on focused tasks. In addition, an uncontrolled ADHD child can be relatively unable to attend to information presented in the group, and thus will be less likely to remember and incorporate new social cognitive skills.

Ways to Overcome These Obstacles

Intervention structure.   The two primary ways to address problems with children's reactive aggressive behavior and with deviancy training effects are to closely address certain structural issues in the intervention and to provide enhanced behavioral management strategies, as needed. An initial planning issue has to do with the age of the youth in the group. Iatrogenic deviancy training effects seem to be more evident in adolescent-age groups than in preadolescent groups. The inclusion of two group leaders can increase leaders' ability to scan children's behavior continually, and detect subtle signs of peers' reinforcement of deviant behaviors.

Once the group is formed, it is useful to carefully follow aspects of the intervention that involve monitoring and providing consequences for children's behavior. Thus, in our Coping Power groups we place emphasis on having clear Group Rules, starting in the first session, and on providing points for children's adherence to these rules and for their positive participation in group sessions. Other program elements, which alert children to how their behavior can lead to consistent consequences, include the use of weekly goal setting procedures for each group member, having group contingent rewards for the entire group successfully attaining a certain number of points over several months, and working with the parents in the parent group sessions on their ability to provide clearer instructions to the children and to provide consistent consequences for children's positive and negative behaviors. Ongoing contact by the group leaders with the teachers can be critically important in facilitating teachers' abilities to monitor children's social behavior and to provide logical consequences within the school setting.

Group behavioral management strategies. Minor structural changes in the group can be helpful in providing stimulus control to prevent behavioral escalation in the group. Such minor structural changes include changing seating arrangements so that a group leader is between two particularly reactive children. Group leaders' use of nonverbal cues (e.g., eye contact, physical proximity, animated voice tone) can also be an important means for gaining children's optimal attention. Effective group leaders also are able to assist children with making smooth transitions from one group activity to another or from the group back to the class or the waiting room by verbally preparing them several minutes prior to the change of activity, and guiding them through the transition. If some group members are demonstrating high levels of positive involvement in the group, they can also be used to serve as a "buddy" for reactive peers, reminding the peer of group rules.

Major structural changes can also be implemented in the relatively rare occasions when these minor structural changes and usual program structural elements are insufficient to reduce individual children's serious problem behaviors in the group. When a central concern is intense rivalry between two children, leading them to frequently initiate conflict with each other, or when two children are actively involved in deviancy training with each other, the group can be temporarily split into two subgroups. If there are two group leaders, each leader can then work with a subgroup in a more contained way until group members' functioning improves and the subgroups can be reintegrated. In cases with a severely and chronically disruptive individual in the group, the individual can be seen individually rather than in the group for a period of time. If this latter child begins to demonstrate a stronger therapeutic alliance after several individual sessions, then he or she may be carefully reintegrated into the group.

Adjusting the concreteness of group material. In response to having a "singleton" child with lower cognitive functioning in the group, group leaders can adapt intervention content to make it more concrete, and less abstractly metacognitive. The group leaders can spend more time in role-playing and hands-on activities rather in group discussion. In general, it is easier to make the problem-solving training more concrete than the attribution-retraining and perspective-taking sessions in our groups.

Adjustments for ADHD children. When a highly unregulated hyperactive child is in the group, it is useful to consult with the parents and to encourage an evaluation for ADHD and for potential medication management. In group sessions, leaders typically have to provide more frequent and more individually tailored monitoring and feedback for the child's behavior. For example, a group leader can sit next to an ADHD child and use a simple time-sampling chart to indicate when the child has had good on-task behavior in 5 minute blocks during the session.

CASE EXAMPLE FOR COGNITIVE-BEHAVIORAL GROUP INTERVENTION

Coping Power Child Group Session 10: Practice Using Coping Statements for Anger Coping

Mrs. Jones is a licensed clinical social worker who is leading a Coping Power group with five children at the Hope Mental Health Center. She and her co-leader, Ms. Carr, a marriage and family therapy trainee, greet each of the children as they arrive for session ten. The leaders praise the children for being on time and remembering to bring their Coping Power binders.

Mrs. Jones begins the session by asking each child to report on his or her personal behavior goal for the week. Jeremy is a 10-year-old African American boy who was referred to the clinic after being suspended from school for fighting. He proudly states that he met his goal of ignoring teasing from peers four out of five days this week. Mrs. Jones congratulates him and awards him four points. Chris is an 11-year-old Caucasian boy whose disruptive behavior has become more pronounced since his father was incarcerated. Chris sheepishly reports that he forgot to have his teacher sign his sheet indicating whether he met his goal of following directions the first time given in class this week. Ms. Carr asks Chris whether he has any ideas about how he can remember to get his goal sheet signed this coming week. One of the other group members, Becky, who is in Chris' class, offers to serve as a buddy and remind him to bring his goal sheet to the teacher at the same time she does each day. Becky is a 10-year-old multi-ethnic girl who has been diagnosed ADHD. Her parents have declined stimulant medication due to concern that it will stunt her growth. Becky excitedly shares that she met her goal of raising her hand before speaking in class all five days this week. Ms. Carr praises Becky and awards her five points. Mrs. Jones asks Becky what she did to make such a significant improvement in her goal completion from last week. Becky responds that she put a sticker with a picture of a hand on her desk that served as a helpful reminder. Shaquila is an 11-year-old African American girl who has exhibited aggressive behavior and depression symptoms since she was sexually molested by a relative in 1st grade. Shaquila holds up her goal sheet indicating that she met her goal of using an appropriate voice in class two days this week, thus Mrs. Jones awards her two points. The final group member is Miguel, a 10-year-old Hispanic boy who was referred after bringing a knife to school. Miguel states that he met his goal of not being sent to the principal's office five days this week; however, inspection of his goal sheet reveals that he only had it signed one day. Ms. Carr awards him one point and encourages him to remember to have his goal sheet signed so that he can be rewarded for his hard work in the future.

Ms. Carr asks the group members to recall one main point discussed during last week's session. They each give answers indicating that they recall practicing ways to cope with rising levels of anger on their anger thermometers. Becky specifically remembers learning about deep breathing; Miguel about using coping self-statements; and Jeremy about using distraction techniques. Mrs. Jones praises them for remembering these positive coping techniques and awards two points to each group member who completed the homework assignment of recording an anger-arousing event, using their favorite coping technique, and recording the effect on their anger level. She informs the children that they are going to continue to practice using coping self-statements in group today.

In preparation for the group self-control activity, Mrs. Jones asks each child to take out the list they made last week of their three favorite coping statements. Chris is the first to find his list, which includes: (1) "Grow up, don't blow up," (2) "Stay calm, just relax," and (3) "It's not worth fighting." While the other children are searching for their lists, Ms. Carr places a large laminated thermometer on the floor. Once she has the group's attention, Mrs. Jones informs them that they are going to practice using self-control while being provoked by peers, as they have in the three previous sessions. This time, they are going to practice using coping statements while being teased by their peers and will walk up and down the thermometer to show how angry they feel inside. Prior to beginning the activity, Mrs. Jones reminds the children of the rules they must follow during the activity (e.g., no cursing, no racial comments, no physical contact).

Chris is selected to go first and takes his place on the thermometer while the other group members gather around him. "That's the ugliest shirt I've ever seen," Miguel shouts, "where'd you get it, the Ugly Shirt Store?" Jeremy pipes in, "your hair is so red, it looks like it's on fire. Quick, someone call 911!" Chris walks up the thermometer as the teasing makes him angry. "Grow up, don't blow up," he recites loudly, "grow up don't blow up…It's not worth fighting, don't let them bother you…They don't mean it, they're probably just having a bad day." Gradually, Chris starts to walk down the thermometer as the use of coping statements helps calm his anger. Eventually, the teasing dies down as the children run out of ideas and see that the teasing no longer has the desired effect of making Chris angry. Mrs. Jones gives each group member a turn to practice using self-statements to cope with teasing from the group. She pauses the activity and gives Becky a strike when she violates a rule by using a racial slur with Shaquila. Mrs. Jones models appropriate teasing and then resumes the activity. Each group member is given two turns to practice using coping statements, once stating them aloud for the group to hear, and the second time reciting them internally. After each member has had two turns, Ms. Carr leads a discussion of what the children learned from the activity (e.g., "How did you feel when you were teased? What did you say to yourself when you first noticed you were getting angry? Did these thoughts help you cope with your anger? How? What happened to your anger level when you used your coping statements? What happened to the teasing when the group members noticed they weren't getting a reaction from you?").

With 10 minutes remaining, Mrs. Jones begins the session closing activities. She asks each group member to make a positive statement about the member sitting to their right. Miguel compliments Becky on reaching her goal every day this week. Becky apologizes for using a racial slur and compliments Shaquila for not yelling back at her. Shaquila says Jeremy looks nice today. Jeremy tells Chris that he was brave to go first on the self-control activity. Finally, Chris tells Miguel that he was good at remembering his coping statements. Mrs. Jones compliments the group on their good work practicing self control today and informs them that they have each earned their point for following the rules and their point for positive participation. She asks each member to generate a new personal behavior goal for the week while she comes around and tells them their total points and gives them an opportunity to purchase prizes. Shaquila spends 12 of her 20 points to purchase lip gloss. Miguel spends 25 points to purchase a magic trick set to give to his younger brother for Christmas. Jeremy, Chris, and Becky decide to save their points so they can buy larger prizes, respectively: a set of walkie talkies, a Nerf basketball hoop, and a compact disc organizer. Mrs. Jones lets the children use the remaining 5 minutes to play the game of their choosing (Connect Four) and praises them for appropriate turn-taking while they are playing the game. As they leave, she encourages the children to practice using coping statements in situations that make them angry in school or at home this week.

Coping Power Child Group Session 19: Social Problem Solving

After reviewing the children's goals sheets, Mrs. Jones asks them what they recall learning about last week. "I know, I know," Shaquila shouts excitedly, "we talked about the PICC model." "That's right," says Mrs. Jones, "can anyone tell me what the letters P-I-C-C stand for?" "Problem Identification, Choices, and Consequences," shouts Jeremy. "That's right, now who can remember when we can use the PICC model?" asks Mrs. Jones. "When something makes us angry but we don't want to get in a fight," offers Miguel. Ms. Carr praises Miguel for his good answer and reminds the group that the first step is to accurately identify the problem. "Let's play a game," she says, "listen carefully to the following situation and see if you can help figure out what the problem is... Tim has a friend named Bob. He sees Bob walking in front of his house and runs outside and asks him to play. Bob says 'no' and keeps on walking...Can someone tell me what the problem is in this situation?" Becky suggests, "Tim's feelings are hurt because Bob doesn't want to be his friend any more." "That's a good thought Becky, but actually, that would mean that Tim is assuming that Bob doesn't want to be his friend anymore just because he turned down his offer to play. Can someone else think how Tim could describe the problem a little differently?" "He could say that his feelings are hurt because Bob won't play right now and he doesn't know why," says Chris. "Good Chris, that's a more accurate way to describe the problem. "Now, Becky, what do you think Tim's goal is?" "He probably wants to find out why Bob said 'no.'"

"That's right, Becky. Now that we have identified the problem, let's come up with some choices for ways Tim can solve the problem. Let's make a list of as many solutions as possible. Say the first thing that pops into your head. Don't worry about whether the solution is 'right' or 'wrong' or 'good' or 'bad.' Let's see how many we can come up with." Chris says, "Tim could go and find someone else to play with." "Yeah," says Jeremy, "or, Tim could tell Bob 'fine, I didn't really want to play with you anyway.'" "Maybe Tim could ask Bob why he doesn't want to play," says Becky. Shaquila offers, "I think Tim should stop being Bob's friend."

"You all did a nice job coming up with lots of different choices of ways Tim could solve the problem." Now, let's go through and evaluate the consequences of each choice. "What do you think would happen if Tim goes and finds someone else to play with?" Miguel says, "Well, Tim might make a new friend and have someone else to play with, but he might never know why Bob said 'no.' "That's right, Miguel, that is probably a so-so choice because it might help Tim find someone else to play with, but it wouldn't help him meet his goal of finding out why Bob said 'no.' Now, what do you think would happen if Tim tells Bob, 'fine, I didn't really want to play with you anyway' ?" "I think that might make Bob mad and might make him not want to be Tim's friend, when maybe he still wanted to be his friend but just couldn't play right then," says Chris. "That's a good insight, Chris and you are right, that choice is probably a bad one because it won't help Tim meet his goal and might make the problem even worse. Now, what do you think would happen if Tim asks Bob why he doesn't want to play?" Shaquila offers, "Bob might say that he can't play because he has to get home for dinner." "Or Bob might say that he doesn't want to be Tim's friend any more," says Jeremy. "Or, Bob might say 'I don't know' and walk away," says Becky. "You are all right, there are a number of different things that Bob might say and it is hard to know which one he will say. Even though we don't know what Bob will say, this is probably still a good choice because at least Tim will meet his goal of finding out why Bob said 'no.' Now let's look at the last choice. What do you think would happen if Tim decides to stop being Bob's friend and ignores him at school?" "That's not good either," says Miguel "because then they will stop being friends and maybe that's not even what Bob wanted." "Good job Miguel. Now that you have thought about the likely consequences of each choice, which one do you think is best?" "I think choice three is best because at least Tim will find out why Bob doesn't want to play," says Jeremy. "Do you all agree that choice three is best?" asks Mrs. Jones. "YEEEESSS!" scream the group members. "Good job. I agree. It is helpful to use the PICC model to figure out what the problem is, what your goal is, and which choice is most likely to help you meet your goal. Next time, we will talk about how you can use the PICC model to solve problems in your own life and what can make it hard to do so. Good job today, guys!" Mrs. Jones ends the group with positive feedback, the point transactions, and 5 minutes of free play time.

SUMMARY

In this chapter, we have provided a cognitive-behavioral rationale for group-based intervention with aggressive children, and have illustrated its use within our Coping Power program. Cognitive-behavioral group interventions with aggressive children have been delivered in school and clinic settings, and have been provided in conjunction with behavioral management training for parents of the children. Multicomponent cognitive-behavioral group interventions have been found to produce significant reductions in children's aggressive behavior at post-intervention, and research has indicated that these effects have been maintained at follow-up points. A major conclusion from the research findings is that cognitive-behavioral treatment of children's aggressive behavior can alter their developmental trajectory leading to serious antisocial behavior, and serve to prevent delinquency and substance use in the adolescent years. At the same time, there are obstacles that exist for effective cognitive-behavioral group intervention with aggressive children, most notably the possibility of deviancy training within groups for these children. Interventions need to be carefully structured and implemented to reduce these obstacles, and future research is needed to identify optimal therapist behaviors which are essential in handling these obstacles.

RECOMMENDED READINGS

Feindler, E. L. (1991). Cognitive strategies in anger control interventions for children and adolescents. In P. Kendall (Ed.), *Child and adolescent therapy: Cognitive-behavioral procedures* (pp. 66–97). New York: Guilford.

Larson, J., & Lochman, J. E. (2002). *Helping schoolchildren cope with anger: A cognitive-behavioral intervention*. New York: Guilford (paperback edition, 2005, New York: Guilford).

Webster-Stratton, C., & Lindsay, D. W. (1999). Social competence and conduct problems in young children: Issues and assessment. *Journal of Clinical Child Psychology, 28*, 25–43.

REFERENCES

Achenbach, T. M. (1991a). *Manual for the child behavior checklist and 1991 profile.* Burlington, VT: University Associates in Psychiatry.

Achenbach, T. M. (1991b). *Manual for the teacher's report form and 1991 profile.* Burlington, VT: University Associates in Psychiatry.

Achenbach, T. M. (1991c). *Manual for the youth self report and 1991 profile.* Burlington, VT: University Associates in Psychiatry.

Achenbach, T. M., & Howell, C. T. (1993). Are American children's problems getting worse? A 13-year comparison. *Journal of the American Academy of Child and Adolescent Psychiatry, 32*, 1145–1154.

Bjorkqvist, K. (2003). *The direct and indirect aggression scale.* Available from Kaj Bjorkqvist, Professor of Developmental Psychology, PB311, FN65101, Vasa, Finland; kaj.bjorkqvist@abo.fi.

Collett, B. R., Ohan, J. L., & Myers, K. M. (2003). Ten-year review of rating scales. VI: Scales assessing externalizing behaviors. *Journal of the American Academy of Child and Adolescent Psychiatry, 42*, 1143–1170.

Conners, C. K. (1997). *Conners' rating scales-revised: Technical manual.* North Tonawanda, NY: Multi-Health Systems.

Crick, N. R., & Dodge, K. A. (1994). A review and reformulation of social information processing mechanisms in children's social adjustment. *Psychological Bulletin, 115*, 74–101.

Dishion, T. J., & Andrews, D. W. (1995). Preventing escalation in problem behaviors with high risk young adolescents: Immediate and 1 year outcomes. *Journal of Consulting and Clinical Psychology, 63*, 538–548.

Dishion, T. J., Eddy, J. M., Haas, E., Li, F., & Spracklen, K. (1997). Friendships and violent behavior during adolescence. *Social Development, 6*, 207–223.

Dodge, K. A. (2003). *The proactive and reactive aggression scale.* Available from Kenneth Dodge, Duke University, Center for Child and Family Policy, Box 90264, Durham, NC, 27708; dodge@pps.duhu.edu.

Dodge, K. A., McClaskey, C. L., & Feldman, E. (1985). Situational approach to the assessment of social competence in children. *Journal of Consulting and Clinical Psychology, 53*, 344–353.

Downy, G., & Coyne, J. C. (1990). Children of depressed parents: An integrative review. *Psychological Bulletin, 108*, 50–76.

Farrington, D. P. (1995). The challenge of teenage antisocial behavior. In M. Rutter (Ed.), *Psychosocial disturbances in young people* (pp. 83–130). Cambridge: Cambridge University Press.

Feindler, E. L., & Ecton, R. B. (1986). *Adolescent anger control: Cognitive-behavior techniques.* New York: Pergamon Books.

Halperin, J. M. (2003). *The children's aggression scale-teacher version and the children's aggression scale-parent version.* Available from Jeffrey M. Halperin, Department of Psychology, Queens College, 65-3-Kissena Boulevard, Flushing, NY 11367; jeffrey_halperin@qc.edu.

Lachar, D., & Gruber, C. P. (1995). *Personality Inventory for Youth (PIY) manual: Administration and interpretation guide.* Los Angeles: Western Psychological Services.

Lachar, D., Wingenfeld, S. A., Kline, R. B., & Gruber, C. P. (2000). *Student behavior survey.* Los Angeles: Western Psychological Services.

Lavallee, K. L., Bierman, K. L., Nix, R. L., & the Conduct Problems Prevention Research Group (2005). The impact of first-grade "friendship group" experiences on child social outcomes in the Fast Track program. *Journal of Abnormal Child Psychology, 33*, 307–324.

Lochman, J. E. (1992). Cognitive-behavioral interventions with aggressive boys: Three-year follow-up and preventive effects. *Journal of Consulting and Clinical Psychology, 60*, 426–432.

Lochman, J. E., & Dodge, K. A. (1998). Distorted perceptions in dyadic interactions of aggressive and nonaggressive boys: Effects of prior expectations, context, and boys' age. *Development and Psychopathology, 10*, 495–512.

Lochman, J. E., Dunn, S. E., & Wagner, E. E. (1997). Anger. In G. Bear, K. Minke, & A. Thomas (Eds.), *Children's needs II.* Washington, D.C.: National Association of School Psychology.

Lochman, J. E., FitzGerald, D., Gage, S., Kanaly, K., Whidby, J., Barry, T. D., Pardini, D., & McElroy, H. (2001). Effects of a social cognitive intervention for aggressive deaf children: The Coping Power Program. *Journal of the American Deafness and Rehabilitation Association, 35*, 38–61.

Lochman, J. E., & Wells, K. (1996). A social-cognitive intervention with aggressive children: Prevention effects and contextual implementation issues. In R. Dev. Peters & R. J. McMahon (Eds.), *Prevention and early intervention: Childhood disorders, substance use, and delinquency* (111–143). Newbury Park, CA: Sage.

Lochman, J. E., & Wells, K. C. (2002a). Contextual social-cognitive mediators and child outcome: A test of the theoretical model in the Coping Power program. *Development & Psychopathology, 14*, 945–967.

Lochman, J. E., & Wells, K. C. (2002b). The Coping Power program at the middle-school transition: Universal and indicated prevention effects. *Psychology of Addictive Behaviors, 16*, S40–S54.

Lochman, J. E., & Wells, K. C. (2003). Effectiveness of the Coping Power program and of classroom intervention with aggressive children: Outcomes at a 1-year follow-up. *Behavior Therapy, 34*, 493–515.

Lochman, J. E., & Wells, K. C. (2004). The Coping Power program for preadolescent aggressive boys and their parents: Outcome effects at the one-year follow-up. *Journal of Consulting and Clinical Psychology, 72*, 571–578.

Lochman, J. E., Whidby, J. M., & Fitzgerald, D. P. (2000). Cognitive-behavioral assessment and treatment with aggressive children. In P. C. Kendall (Ed.), *Child & adolescent therapy: Cognitive-behavioral procedures* (2nd ed.; pp. 31–87). New York: Guilford.

Lochman, J. E., White, K. J., & Wayland, K. K. (1991). Cognitive behavioral assessment and treatment with aggressive children. In P. C. Kendall (Ed.), *Child and adolescent therapy: Cognitive-behavioral procedures* (pp. 25–65). New York: Guilford.

Loeber, R. (1990). Development and risk factors of juvenile antisocial behavior and delinquency. *Clinical Psychology Review, 10*, 1–42.

Miller-Johnson, S., Coie, J. D., Maumary-Gremaud, A., Lochman, J., & Terry, R. (1999). Relationship between childhood peer rejection and aggression and adolescent delinquency severity and type among African American youth. *Journal of Emotional and Behavioral Disorders, 7*, 137–146.

Moffitt, T. E., & Caspi, A. (2001). Childhood predictors differentiate life-course persistent and adolescence-limited antisocial pathways among males and females. *Development and Psychopathology, 13*, 355–375.

Patterson, G. R., Dishion, T. J., & Yoerger, K. (2000). Adolescent growth in new forms of problem behavior: Macro- and micro-peer dynamics. *Prevention Science, 1*, 3–13.

Patterson, G. R., Reid, J. B., & Dishion, T. J. (1992). *Antisocial boys.* Eugene, OR: Castalia.

Pettit, G. S. (1997). The developmental course of violence and aggression: Mechanisms of family and peer influence. *Psychiatric Clinics of North America, 20*, 283–299.

Platt, J., & Spivack, G. (1989). *The MEPS procedure manual.* Philadelphia: Hahnemann University, Department of Mental Health Sciences.

Poulin, F., Dishion, T. J., & Burraston, B. (2001). 3-year iatrogenic effects associated with aggregating high-risk adolescents in cognitive-behavioral interventions. *Applied Developmental Science, 5*, 214–224.

Quay, H. C., & Peterson, D. R. (1996). *Revised behavior problem checklist, PAR edition.* Odessa, FL: Psychological Assessment Resources.

Reynolds, W. M. (2001). *Reynolds Adolescent Adjustment Screening Inventory: Professional manual.* Odessa, FL: Psychological Assessment Resources.

Reynolds, C. R., & Kamphaus, R. W. (2004). *Behavior Assessment System for Children* (2nd ed.). Circle Pines, MN: American Guidance Service.

Sattler, J.M. (2001). *Assessment of children: Cognitive applications* (4th ed.). La Mesa, CA: Jerome M. Sattler.

Selman, R. L., & Byrne, D. F. (1974). A structural-developmental analysis of levels of role taking in middle childhood. *Child Development, 45*, 803–806.

Tremblay, R. E., Kurtz, L., Masse, L. C., Vitaro, F., & Pihl, R. O. (1995). A bimodal preventive intervention for disruptive kindergarten boys: Its impact through mid-adolescence. *Journal of Consulting and Clinical Psychology, 63*, 560–568.

van de Wiel, N. M. H., Matthys, W., Cohen-Kettenis, P., & van Engeland, H. (2003). Cost effectiveness of the Coping Power program with conduct disorder and oppositional defiant disorder children. *Behavior Therapy, 34*, 421–436.

van Manen, T. G., Prins, P. J. M., & Emmelkamp, P. M. G. (2001). Assessing social cognitive skills in aggressive children from a developmental perspective: The social cognitive skills test. *Clinical Psychology and Psychotherapy, 8*, 341–351.

Webster-Stratton, C., & Hammond, M. (1997). Treating children with early-onset conduct problems: A comparison of child and parent training interventions. *Journal of Consulting and Clinical Psychology, 65*, 93–109.

Wirt, R. D., Lachar, D., Seat, P. D., & Broen, W. E., Jr. (2001). *Personality inventory for children—second edition.* Los Angeles: Western Psychological Services.

Wright, J. C., Giammarino, M., & Parad, H. W. (1986). Social status in small groups: Individual group similarity and the social "misfit." *Journal of Personality and Social Psychology, 50*, 523–536.

Yudofsky, S. C. (2003). *The overt aggression scale.* Available from Stuart C. Yudofsky, Department of Psychiatry and Behavioral Sciences, Baylor College of Medicine, One Baylor Plaza, MS 350, Houston, TX 77030; stuarty@bcm.tmc.edu.

Zoccolillo, M. (1992). Co-occurrence of conduct disorder and its adult outcomes with depressive and anxiety disorders: A review. *Journal of the American Academy of Child and Adolescent Psychiatry, 31*, 547–556.

Chapter Nineteen

Cognitive-Behavioral Groups for Substance-Abusing Adolescents

Emily R. Chernicoff & Shaheen R. Fazelbhoy

For the past 30 years, the National Institute of Drug Abuse (NIDA) has conducted *Monitoring the Future* (MTF), a survey of a nationally representative sample of 8th-, 10th-, and 12th-grade students' use of and attitudes toward alcohol and drugs throughout the United States (2004). The good news is that lifetime and past-month use of cigarettes, alcohol, marijuana, amphetamines, LSD and Ecstasy (MDMA), does appear to have dramatically declined over the past decade. The figures translate into approximately 400,000 fewer youth using substances in 2004 than in 2002. Additional good news is that empirically based prevention and early intervention programs therefore appear to be beginning to have a positive impact.

Despite this heartening evidence, each day, 7,000 children in the United States under the age of 16 continue to sample their first drink. The 2003 data indicate that 54% of 12th-grade students have tried cigarettes, 77% have sampled alcohol, and 46% have experimented with marijuana. In addition, over a quarter of the youth in the United States have smoked marijuana in the past month, and 53% have experimented with other illicit drugs. Alcohol has a negative social and emotional impact as well, as children who began using alcohol by the age of 14 were found to be four times more likely to be involved later in automobile accidents. Another hard, cold fact is that teenage binge drinking has been determined to be a significant predictor of actual suicide attempts (NIAAA, 2004).

Little else is more disturbing than to observe the inevitable interruption of cognitive, behavioral, and emotional growth of the youth who does wind up using drugs or alcohol with any frequency. Poor school attendance, declining academic performance, memory lapses and poor concentration, rebellion against family rules, diminished interest in appearance, changes in friends, altered moods including temper flare-ups, irritability and defensiveness, and general apathy and inertia are documented warning signs that a youth's development is in danger of truncation. (DeWit, Silverman, Goodstadt, & Stoduto, 1995; Dube, Anda, Felitti, Edwards, & Croft, 2002).

Current research examining factors contributing to adolescent substance abuse supports a multiple risk factor model. Stressful life events such as physical, sexual, and emotional abuse, parental discord, bereavement, environmental conditions including economic deprivation, and individual personality factors including temperament, low soothability, low-sociability, and aggression are among the variables most frequently identified as contributing to substance abuse. However, regardless of the combination of stress related risk factors present for any youth, the need for approval and peer substance use were found to supersede all other stress-related risk factors (Swadi, 1999).

Colloquially speaking, it is, in the end, *peer pressure* and *perceived peer pressure*, combined with the ubiquity of substances in our communities that ultimately increase the likelihood that a youth will abuse substances. It is no surprise, then, that cognitive behavioral group therapy (CBGT), which utilizes the very same peer pressure while teaching the adolescent to examine his or her perceptions, has become one of the most commonly applied treatments when prevention has failed to overpower risk factors and professionals are faced with helping the substance-abusing adolescent to "get clean."

OVERVIEW OF THE PROBLEM: DEFINING SUBSTANCE ABUSE

Substance use among children and adolescents remains a major concern for parents, educators, and society at large because of the serious short and long-term negative consequences it has on the physical, social, emotional, and academic development of the youth who use, and the families and communities in which they live.

While some school age youth may use available substances only once or twice in the spirit of experimentation without encountering any negative effects, there do exist drugs that when used only once, may cause death. According to NIDA, even a single session of repeated inhalant abuse can disrupt the heart rhythms and cause death from cardiac arrest or lower oxygen to severe enough levels to cause suffocation.

Complicating the picture is the reality that each of the drugs available to youth contribute to varying distinct physical and emotional problems. Tobacco, alcohol, marijuana or cannabis, amphetamines, cocaine and sedatives, hallucinogens and phencyclidines, inhalants, opioids, steroids, and prescription medications for attention deficit and hyperactivity are not infrequently used together and in varying combinations, ultimately producing a polysubstance abuse or dependency disorder. Given the multiplicity of factors inherent in the chemical properties of each class of drugs, it becomes easy to understand why an adolescent may have difficulty understanding the danger inherent in single and polysubstance use and abuse.

Whether or not a youth is "abusing" a substance is determined by the quantity and frequency of the youth's use of one or more substances and the degree to which substance use negatively impacts his or her physical health, academic performance, self-discipline and social interactions, and the degree to which the youth comes in contact with the juvenile justice system. *The Diagnostic Statistical Manual-IV (DSM-IV-TR*; 2000) makes another specific discrimination between whether a youth is abusing a substance and whether he or she has developed a dependency. *Abuse* is defined as a maladaptive pattern in one or more of four areas: (1) using substances that lead to "clinically significant impairment or distress," as evidenced in failure to do well academically, in repeated school absences, suspensions or expulsions from school, occurring within a 12-month period; (2) recurrent substance abuse in physically dangerous situations such as driving an automobile; (3) recurrent legal problems including arrests for disorderly conduct; and (4) persistent use despite social, emotional, academic or legal problems (p. 110).

One graduates to the more severe diagnosis of *Substance Dependence* when three out of four maladaptive patterns are evidenced over a 12-month period. These maladaptive patterns include (1) *tolerance*, or the marked need for increasing amounts of the substance to achieve a high or experiencing a markedly diminished effect with use of the same amount of the substance; (2) *withdrawal*, manifested by the need to take more or less of the substance to avoid symptoms of withdrawal specific to the drug of choice; (3) more and more of the substance is used in larger amounts over a longer period of time than the user intended; (4) repeated desire or effort to reduce use is unsuccessful; (5) more and more time is devoted to obtaining and using the substance so as to interfere with one's ability to perform academically, interact with one's family and friends, or engage in activities without being high; and (6) the youth continues to use the substance despite that it persistently creates problems in important areas of his or her life.

NIDA's most recent annual *Monitoring the Future* (MTF) statistics estimate that by the 6th grade, between 15 and 20% of students in the study had tried their first cigarette, between 7 and 23% had tried their first alcoholic drink, and between 3 and 6% had tried marijuana by their 12th birthday (2004). The relationship between age of onset of alcohol use and the prevalence of alcohol abuse and dependence in late adolescence and adulthood indicates that more than 40% of the total sample who initiated drinking before age 13 was classified with alcohol dependence at some time in their lives. Rates of alcohol dependence among those who began drinking between 17 and 18 years of age were 24.5 and 16.6%. Age of first use is also associated with a variety of other health problems including early and unwanted pregnancy, depression and suicide, with automobile accidents being four times more likely for those who began drinking by age 14. Suicide, in fact, is the third leading cause of death among teens in the United States, accounting for more deaths than all natural causes combined, and has been strongly linked with binge drinking along with depression, family dysfunction, stress, and impulsivity (NIAAA, 2004).

SUBSTANCE ABUSE AND CO-OCCURRING MENTAL HEATH PROBLEMS

Teenagers who abuse substances have also been found to have frequently coexisting psychiatric disorders that go undiagnosed because they are masked by drug use. A recent NIDA funded study following 182 adolescents who ranged in age from 12 to 18, for 12 months post-treatment for substance abuse found that those who did have co-morbid psychiatric diagnoses who evidenced the externalizing disorders of aggression and delinquent behaviors (including lying, stealing, fighting and destroying property), recovered more slowly than those who did not have underlying psychiatric disorders (Rowe, Liddle, Greenbaum, & Henderson, 2004). However, adolescents who evidenced both externalizing and internalizing disorders (acting out combined with anxiety and depression) obtained the least favorable outcomes, therefore having the highest likelihood of relapse. This outcome was attributed to psychiatric severity, which has similarly been found to be the best predictor of substance abuse treatments in adults. The 12% of the study population that had no co-occurring diagnoses, were initially unresponsive to treatment, but evidenced the best long-term outcomes following treatment, reflecting a recovery rate of 1.5 times that of their peers with co-morbid diagnoses. Youth presenting with exclusively externalizing behaviors (35%) were initially unresponsive to treatment, but did recover, while those presenting with mixed externalizing and internalizing behaviors (48% of the youth in the study) showed a swift response to early treatment but relapsed 1 year later to pre-treatment levels. (The remaining 5% of substance-abusing adolescents diagnosed with internalizing disorders only was too small a group to analyze.)

In the Adverse Childhood Experiences Study (AES), a population-based study of 17,000 middle-class American adolescents undergoing biopsychosocial medical evaluations, Dube, Felitti, Dong, Chapman, Giles, and Ande (2003) concluded that the basic causes of addiction are primarily childhood experience-dependent. These are strongly proportionally related to several specific categories of adverse childhood experiences, including growing up in a household in which one is physically, emotionally or sexually abused, having an alcoholic, mentally ill or imprisoned parent, being exposed to one's mother being abused, or having both parents absent. They further found that the compulsive use of nicotine, alcohol, and injected street drugs increased proportionally in a strong, graded, dose-response manner that closely parallels the intensity of adverse life experiences during childhood. Because adolescents who have experienced these early traumas have very few ways to independently seek relief, they turn to substance abuse, overeating and sexual promiscuity. These coping devices work through their ability to modulate the activity of various neurotransmitters. The authors concluded that addiction overwhelmingly implies prior adverse life experience and that drugs and alcohol are used to conceal shame and mute emotional pain.

Current brain research specific to the use of cocaine and cocaine like substances suggests that substance abuse serves to modulate the activity of neurotransmitters, and that long term changes in neural circuitry are evidenced in brain scans of cocaine users, leading to further compulsive use of the drug. Researchers generalize that youth who abuse substances are forging brain pathways that may interfere with their ability to learn during crucial points in their academic and social development. Even marijuana, long perceived as the mildest of street-drugs, has been found to adversely affect attention span, memory and learning when used heavily (Volkow, 1996).

GROUP COMPOSITION AND PROTOCOL EVALUATION MEASURES

Referrals of substance-abusing youth to group treatment may come from parents, teachers and school counselors, psychiatric inpatient social workers who are responsible for discharge planning, family court or from fellow psychologists. Regardless of the source of referral, clinicians must consider six significant group inclusion factors, including (1) age or developmental stage, (2) sex, (3) the severity of co-morbid psychiatric diagnoses, (4) the youth's stage of readiness for change, (5) drug of choice, and (6) whether or not the group is geared toward "early intervention" for youths who are abusing substances, or toward more formal intervention for youths who have been clearly assessed as being drug dependent and have developed a tolerance and are more likely to go through symptoms of withdrawal.

Ideally, adolescents should be grouped according to their levels of maturity or developmental stage, which can conveniently be divided by whether they are in middle or high school. This allows for more heterogeneity of issues among members. For instance, despite that negative consequences are universal for all members, the high school aged member's loss of phone or driving privileges would hardly be relevant to the twelve year old, who is restricted from his or her use of a video game or television.

Another dilemma particular to running substance abuse groups for adolescents is deciding whether to form a co-ed or a same-sex group. Because girls are better socialized to be able to verbalize their experience, the advantage of a co-ed group is that the girls can model and teach the boys, who may be somewhat alexithymic, and whose entire feeling vocabulary may be limited to anger. However, the disadvantage of on-going flirting, which can drain the group of focus, must be weighed against the previously mentioned advantage. More importantly, because sexual abuse and incest are common precursors to adolescents using substances for the purpose of numbing psychic pain, and because trauma work is included as one unit in this protocol, same-sex groups are more likely to provide the safety necessary for making disclosures possible.

A third consideration relevant to member inclusion is screening for coexisting psychiatric diagnoses. While the literature supports the reality that more often than not co-morbid diagnoses accompany drug abuse, the nature and severity of the disorder has been shown to affect the outcome and relapse rates. Youth with conduct and oppositional disorders tend to be slow to acquire the skills presented in group, yet demonstrate better long-term success, while those who present with significant depression and anxiety tend to respond quickly during treatment, but have a greater relapse rate. It is therefore recommended that those youth who present with depression and anxiety disorders certainly not be ruled out, but rather, that they be included, as long as they are receiving auxiliary treatment specific to those diagnoses and that the referral source indicates that they have been reasonably stabilized and responding to their therapy.

Closely related to co-existing diagnoses is the issue of the youth's readiness to change. Significant about this cohort is that they are most likely to fall within Freeman and Dolan's (2001) "Noncontemplative" first stage of change, in which at first, the notion of getting clean has not even occurred to the youth, which is followed swiftly by resistance to the notion of recovery, or the stage of "Anticomtemplation." While it may seem counterintuitive to include these youth who do not present as overtly motivated to engage in recovery, as previously mentioned, potential members who present with diagnoses of conduct or oppositional disorders have actually empirically proven to be good responders to group substance abuse treatment. The ensuing stages of Precontemplation and Contemplation, or the willingness to accept that there is a need for change, signify the beginning of readiness to engage in clinical work actively.

Finally, the clinician must examine the pros and cons of whether they choose to conduct an early intervention group for youth whose substance use is occasional or only experimental but affecting their lives, a group comprised of youth who have clearly developed an addiction, or a combination of the two. Homogeneity for frequency and degree of use has advantages paralleling those for age and maturity. Combining these cohorts will simultaneously serve to lengthen the anticontemplative stage for those who have only begun to dabble in drugs, thus intensifying their resistance, but also present the reality of the consequences of continuing use. If the choice is made for combining the two, a clinical judgment may be made regarding outliers at either end of the spectrum.

Several tools are available to assess adolescent candidates for appropriateness to treatment. Most popular is the *Substance Abuse Subtle Screening Inventory-Adolescent 2* (SASSI-A2; 2001), which is designed for 12- to 18-year-olds, is a self-administered, double sided, single page inventory of 72 true–false items, 32 of which ask the adolescent to report on a variety of experiences and consequences and frequency of substance use. The beauty of the SASSI-A2 is that it takes only 15 minutes to administer, is easy to use, and has the ability to detect substance abuse problems even when youth predictably attempt to deny or conceal problems (Miller & Lazowski, 2001). However, since the SASSI-A2 has not been available long enough to generate independent psychometric studies, reliability, and validity of this measure is only available from the publisher.

The Personal Experience Screening Questionnaire (PESQ; Winters, 1991) is a 40-item self-report scale examining problem severity, psychosocial risk, and drug use history of each of 12 different substances. The PESQ also contains items that measure defensiveness or exaggerated response style. It has shown to have excellent internal consistency reliability across samples of normal, delinquent, and substance-abusing adolescents, and validity has been demonstrated by significant group differences in PESQ Problem Severity scores between these three types of adolescent samples, as well as differences between groups of adolescents referred or not referred for drug abuse evaluation by school personnel (Winters, 1991).

Hollon and Kendall's Automatic Thoughts Questionnaire (1980) is a 30-item measure of negative automatic thoughts with high internal consistency. It correlates significantly with depression, low self-esteem and hopelessness in children and adolescents (Kazdin, 1990). A version measuring positive thoughts, the ATQ-P, also has high internal consistency and one-month test-retest reliability (Ingram, Kendall, Siegle, Guarino, & McLaughlin, 1995).

Finally, and highly recommended, are the four brief and easy to complete scales available in the public domain at no cost, which have been used in the NIDA Monitoring the Future survey. They include: one 6-item scale measuring physical and psychological reliance on substances, also entitled Monitoring the Future, The Student Survey of Risk and Protective Factors/Favorable Attitudes Toward Antisocial Behavior; a 5-item scale measuring attitudes toward violent behavior; The Social Skills Scale, a 5-item scale measuring the ability to make friends and get along with others; and the Beliefs About Peer Norms, an 8-item scale measuring beliefs about the prevalence and acceptability of drug use among peers.

UNDERSTANDING ADOLESCENT SUBSTANCE ABUSE THROUGH A COGNITIVE BEHAVIORAL LENS

In order to understand what brings a youth to abuse any illegal substance, the cognitive behavioral therapy (CBT) model invites us to first explore which core beliefs provide the scaffolding for the act or behavior of "getting high." These core beliefs are long-standing, embedded, basic assumptions about oneself, one's world, and one's experience of being in the world. They are often derived from our earliest childhood experiences of being members of our families of origin and may be handed down from generation to generation, from parent to child, on a conscious level by literally telling a child who or how they are "supposed" to be (e.g., "You are a one of us, a Smith, and are expected to achieve."). Young Smith learns early on that excellent grades, scoring the highest number of points, or being the yearbook editor "should be" a part of his identity, despite whether or not he has a learning disability, only average intelligence, or little in the way of athletic or creative gifts. This cognitive dissonance between the family script for who one is supposed to be and who one truly is often becomes the armature for engaging in substance abuse. In this case, the internal self-knowledge that one is "different" or "doesn't belong to the clan" may lead to a heightening of the normal need for belonging that the early adolescent experiences as a part of his natural development. Belonging with the kids who identify as "druggies" or the gang who drinks on the weekends easily begins to satisfy the need for belonging that is generated by the dissonance between who he "should be" and who "he feels he is."

Similarly, core beliefs may be transmitted on an unconscious level through the process of parental projection, such as when a parent experiences low self-esteem, denies it within oneself, and projects it onto one's child by being a harsh critic of him or her. The natural consequence of this projection results in the child developing an impaired sense of self-confidence, and the core belief that "I can never get anything right," "I am not good enough," or "I must work harder and always earn approval." It is an easy leap from these cognitions to downward spiraling thoughts such as, "I might as well give up trying," "I might as well get high because nothing matters," or "if I can't be good enough at this or that, I can at least be the coolest and the highest or the go-to gal if any one wants to cop some dope."

Moreover, the source of intergenerationally transmitted core beliefs may be ethnic or cultural, family specific, and even substance-specific attitudes, as seen in the belief "I come from a long line of wooden-legged men, and I should be able to drink without getting drunk like my father and my uncles before me."

The essential adolescent developmental tasks of answering the question "what is me and what is not me," and defining oneself as separate and individuated from one's same-sex parent is often deeply ensconced in a youth's gender schema. Suzie may see her mom, a woman she has adored throughout her childhood, as always socially appropriate and abiding by all the rules. In order for Suzie to begin to experience herself as separate, she may rebel against the "good girl image" she has shared with mom, and in middle school begin to experiment with using drugs to define herself as "not-mom." Thus, core beliefs are also inherent in each consecutive developmental stage, are subject to alteration, and also generate adequate cognitive dissonance to lead a youth to "pick up" a drink or a drug. In this case, the degree to which Suzie feels enmeshed with mom will determine the strength of Suzie's need to define herself as different or "not-mom." If Suzie is afraid she is "too close" or "too like mom," she is more likely to adopt the attitude that she "must" experiment, take risks and "act out" to experience herself as separate and in order to "feel grown up." Whether socially appropriated as a result of one's family scripts, a parent's projection, one's own experience of a disability or limitation, or simply the product of a developmental stage of growth, at different points of development the sense of "who I should be" and "who I am or ought to be according to me or others" may become critical cognitive-behavioral trajectories for a youth regarding whether he or she will experiment with substances, engage in frequent use, or find him or herself in the throes of dependency or addiction.

Once an adolescent internalizes the identity of being a member of a peer group that does use alcohol or drugs, a new schema or template emerges with which the youth now identifies. The newly formed schema of self becomes swiftly embedded and reinforced by frequent socialization with peers while using substances, thus posing one of the chief targets for CBGT. The work of the CBT group is to challenge specifically both the underlying core beliefs that contributed to the need to identify with the substance using peer group, and to dismantle the schema that reinforces the substance use. The CBT group thus functions to attack archaic schemas and faulty thinking and replace them with a new self that is formed not simply by the schema of separation (the dependent "druggie" identity), but rather, true individuation, by teaching the adolescent a process by which he or she may create an authentic self.

A 12-WEEK COGNITIVE BEHAVIORAL/ART THERAPY GROUP (CB/ATG) MODEL FOR ADOLESCENT SUBSTANCE ABUSERS

The following modularized 12-week group is designed to provide members with a time-limited, structured experience that will appeal to youth with various learning styles, provide a psychoeducational format that will support the retention of gains upon the conclusion of the group experience, and pull on each member's strengths. Traditional CBGTs combine didactic and experiential components to accomplish the tasks of teaching, modeling, and practicing the basic elements of incorporating cognitive-behavioral thinking and skills into the youth's repertoire of problem-solving and coping strategies. Ritualization of a weekly agenda provides group members with the safety and predictability necessary to overcome adolescents' initial apprehension and insecurity related to fitting in and "getting it right," as well as help to quell anxieties directly related to the expectation and prospect of not using their substance of choice any more. Ritualizing the agenda also parallels the ritualization of substance abuse that often occurs when kids "get high together," providing a positive substitute experience. Moreover, it becomes a clear structure against which they may begin to rebel early, so that the all-important work of forming a cohesive group may begin more swiftly.

When working with adolescent substance abusers, the additional incorporation of the use of creative arts therapy becomes an especially helpful tool for appealing to the narcissism inherent in this developmental stage. Cognitive Behavioral Art Therapy addresses many of the typical obstacles to treatment. It is not difficult to see the magic created when each member of the group is simultaneously producing their own drawing.

It is as if everyone gets to speak at once, albeit nonverbally. Using drawing also functions to provide members who are less verbally adept to communicate what might otherwise be more difficult using words, proving the old adage that "A picture is worth a thousand words." Moreover, often when youth draw in group, an element of increased interaction and healing humor infuse the experience, allowing for safe inroads into challenging the overly relied upon defenses of denial, rationalization and intellectualization inherent in the adolescent substance abuser's repertoire of coping devices. The sharing of simple media, like paper and markers, becomes a symbolic means of supporting cooperation, resulting in heightened group cohesion. Ensuing sharing and discussion of their art products allows the teenagers an extra measure of safety, in that they may first speak about their drawing rather than themselves. This initial distancing then provides a natural segue to exploring how their drawing speak about the realities of who they are, how they think, and how they behave. The directives for drawings provided in the proposed protocol are specifically designed to illustrate and support the mastery of the skill components of CBT. Clinicians are encouraged to develop their own directives as relevant to themes that arise in any given group.

Setting the Agenda

The first task of the group leader is to establish and model the collaborative setting of the group agendas, which will begin each consecutive group. Simply put, the therapist introduces the group to how they will spend the next 90 minutes. Following a discussion of the rationale for meeting over the next 12 weeks, a primary task of the first meeting is the establishment of a contract in which each member commits to the rules of engagement. The therapist should provide a prepared contract that lists all of the rules and expectations required of membership in the group. Items and issues included are: (a) attendance and timeliness; (b) confidentiality; (c) a discussion regarding respectful communication including acceptable language, put-downs, turn-taking and mutual respect while others are speaking; (d) the function and importance of homework follow-through; (e) bathroom rules; and (f) an indication of what an acceptable response would be if a group member becomes emotionally upset and feels the need to immediately leave the group. Also recommended is that space be left for the inclusion of rules generated by group members during the first discussion, or as a result of experiences in later groups. Each member is expected to sign the contract indicating their commitment to cooperation with their peers. Over the following weeks, each group is begun by inviting members to call out each of the commitments they have made, to reinforce cooperation and members' ownership of the group.

Next, a "temperature-taking" warm-up exercise is introduced. Going around the circle, each member chooses one word to share to describe how he or she is feeling in that moment, along with a corresponding number on an analog scale of 1 to 10. Making one's voice heard and describing "where they are now" serves the gestalt-like function of helping members to feel present and individually acknowledged, while also giving the therapist an indication of the group's mood.

Following these items, which may take between 10 and 15 minutes given the particular tenor of the group on any given day, the actual work begins, with each week building on the former ones, to reinforce mastery of skills. Each, however, introduces both a new skill, and a creative form of expression. Table 19.1 provides a suggested 12-week format that may be adjusted to the needs of the group. Unlike other CBT groups, the use of creative arts requires the therapist to provide group members with equipment and materials for art projects. Suggested: Markers, Craypas, Drawing Paper, Glue, Scissors, old magazines, tape to hang art projects and mural on the wall, a video camera, tapes, and monitor. Note that all role-plays may be videotaped.

OVERCOMING OBSTACLES TO TREATING ADOLESCENT SUBSTANCE ABUSERS IN CB/AT GROUPS

The obvious beauty of the CBT group model is that it provides substance abusing youth with a much needed, highly structured format that is predictable and easily reinforced by group members. Therefore, it provides a high degree of safety for both the group facilitator and the group members. Nonetheless, there are certain challenges inherent

Table 19.1   12-Week Group Treatment Protocol

Week 1: Becoming a Group

- Introduction: Explain and establish rationale for meeting.
  - Simultaneously, have each member design a nametag with markers to wear. This activity serves to redirect anxiety and help members to take in what the therapist is presenting better.
- Present contract, discuss, and get signatures.
- Present Warm Up Exercise, introduce concept of analog scale (therapist models by going first).
- Each member takes a turn at sharing "what has brought them to be a member of this group."
- Each member is asked to state honestly where they see themselves on an analog scale in terms or "readiness" or "investment" in making changes.
- Therapist presents fundamental elements of CBT/ATG.
  - Having a peer support group and safe place.
  - Skill building and developing alternative coping strategies.
  - Explanation of how cognitions work to determine how we act and how we feel.
  - Skill #1: Thought Catching (TC) (therapist provides several examples).
  - Each group member is given opportunity to experience and practice TC.
- Present Logs for each member to use for homework, along with explanation of rationale for homework, explaining the investigative nature of CBT.
- Closure: Repeat Warm-up Exercise as a Warm-down.

Week 2: Stages of Readiness for Change

- Therapist engages group in review of contract elements.
- Adjective/Analog Warm-up.
- Discussion of Homework logs.
  - What was easy, what was hard?
  - Identify members who did not complete task.
  - Using group as coach, have each one use TC to discover the thought that stopped them from doing their homework. Do not be distressed if this is the majority of the group! The work is then simply done in situ, with member coaching.
- Introduce CB/AT Exercise: "Draw a Bridge"
  - Directive: Draw a bridge representing your life. The right end will represent being in recovery. Then draw yourself on the bridge to show where you see yourself today, in relation to wanting to be clean.
  - Lead group in sharing and discussing their hopes, resistances, and fears, listening for beliefs and attitudes related to using vs. recovery. Model alternative thinking.
- Facilitate discussion of Automatic Thinking as introduction to homework.
- Homework: Continue to keep DT log; take 15 minutes this weekend to imagine how life with your family might be different if substance abuse were no longer an issue between you.
- Closure: Warm-down exercise.

Week 3: The Role of Family Relationships in Recovery

- Engage group in review of contract elements.
- Adjective/Analog Warm-up.
- Open group discussion of DT homework logs; troubleshoot problems.
- Introduce Group CB/AT Exercise: "Draw a picture of your family doing something together." If you absolutely can't or don't want to draw people, draw a symbol for each family member. You have 15 minutes to complete it.
  - Facilitate sharing of images enabling each member to begin to describe who is in their family and how they all relate to one another. Look for and discuss similarities and differences to promote group cohesion and feeling of universality.
  - Invite members to share results of their imagery homework, how their using impacts them and their families, including how they feel it may even help to deal with family, and discuss how family life would be different if they were not using substances.
- Introduce the concept of family cognitions and intergenerational transmission of attitudes and beliefs, and have each member identify some of the beliefs they have developed as a result of having grown up in their family.

- Homework: Continue DT logs.
  - Have each member identify one new interactional behavior they will experiment with before the next week, with any family member of their choosing, and report back to the group next week. Role-play as many as time permits
- Closure: Warm-down exercise.

Week 4: The Mind Body Connection

- Engage group in review of contract elements.
- Adjective/Analog Warm-up.
- Open group discussion of DT homework logs; troubleshoot problems.
- Open the floor for members to discuss what occurred when they experimented with a new behavior, using the opportunity to explore what worked, what didn't, or why they did not do homework. Members may bring up any problem encountered during past week they want group's help with.
- Introduce the concept of Brainstorming (no wrong answers).
  - Engage group in brainstorming to generate alternative ways or new interpersonal experiments for each member to choose for homework. Write each one down on the board or newsprint.
  - Role-play some suggested "experiments" using group members to coach one another.
- Resistance and laughter may now be used to segue into presenting a brief psychoeducational explanation of anxiety and the mind/body connection.
  - Engage group in modified progressive muscle relaxation.
- Have the group brainstorm "anxiety-provoking" life situations and list them on the board or newsprint.
- Now, invite the group to choose one encounter from the list with a family member or peer that the majority of the group can most relate to, and walk them through a guided imagery depicting that interpersonal exchange.
  - Engage the group in discussion of their experience of the exposure. Repeat the exercise using a life situation offered by any group member.
  - Discuss the value of preparation, rehearsal, and relaxation in making life changes.
- Homework: Continue keeping your DT log to examine for on-going patterns and areas of attitudinal growth. Try a new experiment or repeat the one from last week using PMR and/or imagery beforehand and report back to the group next time.
- Closure: Warm-down exercise.

Week 5: Dealing with Feelings

- Engage group in review of contract elements. If they have already begun to reinforce one another, this can be done in a swift abbreviated manner.
- Adjective/Analog Warm-up. This also can go faster as group gels.
- Open group discussion of DT homework logs; explore results of interactive homework task. Members may bring up any problem encountered during past week that they want group's help with.
- Facilitator now engages in brief psychoeducational talk about the spectrum of possible feelings inherent in being human, beyond anxiety—inviting the group to call them out—not only anger, but those more difficult to tolerate—hurt, shame, sadness, grief. Discuss how each has a wide range and have the group develop a "Range/Map of Anger" showing gradations (from mildly ticked to enraged) on the board or newsprint.
- Dyadic Exercise: Pick a partner and pick a feeling from a hat (which the therapist has written on small papers) and share a time when you felt that, and how you handled it. Depending on the preference of the group, stay with the same partner or choose a different one and pick another feeling from the hat.
- CBT Art Exercise: Directive: Choose one of the experiences you shared with your partner. On one side of the paper, draw what you felt inside using colors, symbols, or a self-portrait. On the other side, draw what you showed to the world.
  - Have group share products and discuss both the congruencies and incongruities between what we feel and how we behave or what we show the world, and the consequences
  - Begin facilitating group members' understanding of the reciprocal connection between substance use and having and managing feelings. Coach them through an open discussion of what thoughts and feelings trigger the impulse to get high or have a drink.
- Homework: This week keep a log or list of the people, places, things, situations, thoughts, and feelings that trigger your desire to pick up a drug or drink.
- Closure: Warm-down exercise.

(Continued)

Table 19.1   Continued

Week 6: Prelapse, Lapse, and Relapse—"Three Dirty Words"

- Ritual Check In.
- Homework Review: Examine triggers for using. Members may bring up any problem encountered during past week they want group's help with.
- Introduce psychoeducational piece on the realities of relapse as a natural part of the process, the value of planfulness and structure and the notion of internal locus of control, and its importance to remaining clean.
- Task: Distribute blank 3×5 cards. Each member must make an hour-by-hour structured plan for the upcoming weekend, reflecting activities unrelated to getting high. Things as simple as time of awakening, breakfast, and shower should be included along with planned timed with friends and family dinners (e.g., 10 a.m.: get up; 10–10:30 eat breakfast; 10:30–12 do chores, and so forth•   ).
- Use resistance to the task as an opportunity to again practice TC and explore members' beliefs and attitudes toward things such as scheduling and not being spontaneous, doing things without being high with friends, and not being high if/when others are.
  ◦ Troubleshoot problems using CBT fundamentals.
- Introduce CB/AT Exercise: Directive: "On one side of your paper draw yourself tempted to get high. On the other side, draw yourself while or after having said no."
  ◦ Have group explore their responses. Use drawings depicting the inability to resist as an opportunity for group members to discuss cognitions, automatic thoughts re. being judged, loosing friends, etc. and offer suggestions to one another about how to cope with the thoughts, feelings and reactions of others.
- Homework: Follow the plan you've devised on the 3×5 card. Come as close to it as possible and report back to us at next group. Keep your DT logs especially this week.
- Closure: Warm-down exercise.

Week 7: Assertiveness vs. Aggression (Anger Management)

- Ritual Check In
- Homework Review: Troubleshoot. Did you write unrealistic things? What worked or didn't? Why? What do you need to change? What was hardest? Easiest? Discuss your resistances and TC logs.
- Spend 5–10 minutes writing new cards for the following weekend. Members may bring up any problem encountered during past week they want peers' help with.
- Engage group members in open discussion about how group members express their anger—and the difference between being aggressive and assertive. Include inviting members to explore how their family members and friends express their anger—are they aggressive? Assertive? Silent?
  ◦ Each group member writes up a scenario he or she has experienced and has other group members role-play it first aggressively, and then assertively, the coach or director being the member who wrote the scenario.
  ◦ Equipment Needed: Video camera and monitor to record the role-plays which group gets to watch, critique and re-do as needed. Have fun hamming it up to get point across.
- Homework: Try those 3×5 schedules again.
- Closure: Warm-down exercise.

Weeks 8 & 9: Difficult Life Events—We've All Experienced Some…

- Ritual Check In
- Homework Review; trouble shooting. Group suggestions for next time Members may bring up any problem encountered during past week they want group's help with
- Introduce psychoeducational piece on trauma. Have group define, brainstorm, life problems/traumas: parental discord, divorce, losses, family financial problems, parents or siblings who use substances, deaths, girlfriend-boyfriend break-ups, friends moving away, fires, physical, emotional, or sexual abuse, and so forth.
  ◦ Draw one difficult life event of your choosing
  ◦ Open group discussion about art and life events and how they coped and dealt with their feelings, how substance abuse may be connected if at all. This is an open forum for acknowledgement that everybody hurts, that it's okay to talk about it. "Who would you go if this happened to you" is a recommended question to pose.
- Homework: Go for those 3×5 card plans again. This week think about what your resources are. What makes you feel good besides getting high if anything!
- Closure: Warm-down exercise

Week 10: Who and What Are My Resources?

- Ritual 3-part Check In with Homework Review. Members may bring up any problem encountered during past week they want group's help with
- Open discussion about pleasure. What makes you happy/feel good outside of how you used to feel when you were drunk or high? List on newsprint or board. Help members include a variety of things such as a good shower, a funny movie, good music, favorite food, a compliment, a hug, someone being happy to see them, just hanging out with a good friend, a job well done
- CB/ATG Directive: Create two cut and paste collages from magazine images. One a symbolic representation of you before group, and the other of you now.
  - Have each member generate a personal list of people who he or she can consider resources or supports. Family members, school personnel, neighbors, friends, and write next to the name what sort of issues they would talk about with that person. If group members aren't listed, raise that as an observation. Explore how they might remain connected if at all.
  - While group members are working and sharing materials, the therapist presents a psychoeducational explanation of the 12-Step Program model, including sponsorship and distributes brochures provided by local AA/CA/COA Intergroups that group members may review and discuss.
- Homework.
- Closure: Warm-down exercise.

Week 11: About Endings, Losses, and Goodbyes

- Acknowledgement that this is next to last meeting.
- Ritual 3-part Check In with Homework Review; Members may bring up any problem encountered during past week they want group's help with. Engage group in their reactions to previous week's discussion about the 12-step model.
- CBT/AT Directive: "Draw a picture about saying goodbye, an ending, or loss you have experienced in your life."
  - Group engages in discussion about drawings and theme of art as lived, and as related to their substance abuse. Therapist encourages members to incorporate as much CBT understanding of how they have handled endings in the past and how it can now be different given their gains in group.
- Now, repeat Draw a Bridge that was done in 2nd week of group, only taking 5 minutes to draw. Compare and contrast first and last.
- Each member is now directed to write a caution, encouragement and a good wish for each other member in the group that are then shared aloud with one another.
- Therapist provides psychoeducational piece on Relapse as a natural part of recovery.
- Homework: This week, think about the group, what you have gained, how you have grown, what you still need to work on (continuing and future goals; explore how you will identify precursors to relapse).
- Closure: Warm-down exercise.

WEEK 12: Where Do We Go from Here?

- Acknowledgement that this is Closing group.
- Ritual Check In with Homework Review.
- CBT/AT Directive: "Create a Mural" of our experience over the past 12 weeks!" (Therapist provides markers and craypas, as well as large mural paper hung horizontally on the wall so that members have adequate room to work side by side).
  - Follow with discussion of Mural to explore reflected thoughts and feelings; review learning; explore each member's take-away message.
  - Refreshments provided by therapist may be shared during making and processing of mural.
- Each member now takes 5 minutes to write him/herself a letter including goals, hopes, and dreams, congratulating oneself and encouraging future growth. Therapist provides stamped envelopes for members to address.
- Closure: Warm-down exercise.

---

in the work, which are particular to both the stage of adolescence and to the domain of substance abuse.

While they are more often than not themselves "posing" because of their developmentally determined self-consciousness and insecurities, adolescents require absolute authenticity of one another, and in particular, adults. For this reason, the therapist may also be confronted with more than the usual appeals to self-disclose, and may be apt to meet with group members' finger pointing upon his or her most minor infringement. It is essential that therapists conducting substance abuse groups with teenagers be prepared to model a nondefensive stance and a willingness to admit to their own mistakes.

In addition, specific to treating substance-abusing youth is that as budding philosophers they often tend to insist—and truly believe—that they are always right, and they will fiercely defend their positions using the extremely hardened ego defense mechanisms of denial, rationalization, and intellectualization. Moreover, it is here, where CBT is most effective. Teaching the skill of "thought catching," and using one's peers to generate alternative thoughts as well as to reframe cognitions serves to acutely penetrate this triad of defenses, allowing the youth to move from long-wedded beliefs and positions to new ways of thinking about themselves, others, and the world around them.

As mentioned earlier, inclusion of art therapy overcomes several obstacles to treatment. While in most groups it is not always possible for each member to have a turn to work through an issue, when everyone draws, each member has had the opportunity to speak on a simultaneous, nonverbal level. Moreover, because substance abuse is often co-morbid with underlying depression, anxiety, attention, learning disorders, and oppositional defiance, these youth tend to use physical activity as a means to release tension and anxiety. The inclusion of art-making in this CBT model allows for the discharge of excess energy. Members are no longer talking heads, but creative agents, with the act of drawing providing a socially appropriate avenue by which to aggress, albeit against a piece of paper. Finally, the combining of art therapy with CBT helps to overcome what may often be a wide range of cognitive, verbal, and social skills represented in the group.

"War stories," or the detailed accounting by members of their experiences of being high, are also common to these groups. While some accounting of what group members have been through is important to the work, the therapist must keep an eye to when a group member is embarking on one, and assist him or her to use the story in a productive way. For instance, the therapist may interrupt and invite the youth to examine all of the possible consequences that might have happened in that instance, (i.e., physical endangerment or involvement with the legal system), or have the youth stop and consider how much money he or she might have accumulated had they not spent their allowances on their substance of choice. The therapeutic objective in these cases is to deplete the war story of its romantic power, and whenever possible, present reality.

A final word about the weekly assigning of what is traditionally called "homework" in CBT parlance: it is suggested that homework be reframed as a *"Weekly Experiment,"* since nothing is more abhorrent to a teenager than homework!

CASE ILLUSTRATION

Composition

The composition of the following outpatient cognitive-behavioral/art therapy group for substance abusers is representative of the variety of presentations possible in a substance abuse treatment group. It is comprised of 8 members, with 5 boys and 3 girls. Tom, Mary, and Christie exclusively use alcohol, although in varying ways. Tom and Christie are "weekend warriors" who binge drink, but exclusively on the weekends. Mary, who does not binge drink, does however, drink almost every day, while managing to sustain passable grades. Gary, Paul, and Kara smoke marijuana. However, Paul prides himself on not using any other drugs, although he uses daily, smokes throughout the day to maintain a constant "buzz," and admits to often smoking at the bus stop before school. John primarily smokes marijuana to "come down" from his weekend cocaine use, and Gary and Sean admit to using whatever substances are immediately available through their friends. Kara, whose mother is a heroin user and who has been through multiple rehabilitations, smokes only pot, and like Paul, sees no problem with using marijuana, equating it with socially acceptable adult social drinking.

Format and Design Rationale

The group meets for only 6 weeks, but has two sessions per week, on Monday and Friday afternoons, with a renewable contract for a second 6 weeks. The group may then serve multiple purposes by not only providing psychoeducation, CBT skills and practice, but also an all-important safety net before and after the weekend, when youth have the most unstructured time on their hands available for getting high, as well as heightened interaction with family, which is a rich source of conflict for adolescents. Group members come to understand early on that "experiments" (or homework) must be done, and the circumscribed time period allows for in-group practice to remain freshly accessible when members engage in their homework experiments. Since groups 6 through 12 require members to create an hour by hour weekend schedule, the Monday and Friday format provides an opportunity for members to learn to anticipate potential triggers, plan for them, and to process why things went well or didn't immediately afterwards. By having group directly precede and follow weekends, the likelihood that both cognitions and affect are accessible is enhanced, thus minimizing members' tendency to deny, minimize and intellectualize events.

A Note on the Physical Setting

This is critical with a co-ed group. While members sit in the traditional circle, there needs to be adequate space between seats so as not to generate anxiety by physical body contact. The space must also include a table large enough to accommodate all 8 members for art making.

Group II: "Stages of Readiness for Change"

Since it is likely that at least some, if not most, members have not conducted their experiment, the all-important task is to use this as an opportunity to reframe the undone homework. This is a perfect chance to explore how and why it wasn't done and to provide an *in situ* experience of the process of thought catching, using group members to coach and to support those individuals through the task.

Therapist: Ok. Looks like four of you didn't conduct your experiments. Let's take some time to figure out what got in the way and how you stopped yourself from doing it. How about if Christie, Kara, and John help you guys to do this, since they each found a way to do it this weekend. (To Gary, who's been cutting up since group started): Gary, you're the most talkative today, so far? Willing to go first?

Gary: Guess so.

Therapist: So, Gary, tell us about why you didn't do the Thought Catching log.

Gary: Well, if you wanta know the truth, I thought it was just kinda stupid! (Group laughs. Therapist smiles and laughs along with group.)

Therapist: Ok. So you actually thought about it! That's great! And what you thought was "This is stupid?" When did you think about it and what else did you think?

Gary: Actually, it wasn't till last night before I went to bed. I found a piece of paper and pencil and I thought... I thought, "This is stupid!"

Kara: Yeah, I thought that too. But then I tried. Did you?

Gary: Yeah. But nothin' came to me, so I figured, screw it. I'll make it up tomorrow.

Therapist: So, when nothing came to you, were you aware of feeling anything? Think back to that moment with the pencil in you hand.

Gary: I guess I felt stupid.

Therapist: Ok. Glad you're honest with us. So you thought the task was stupid and when you tried to do it, you felt stupid! Then what did you think?

Gary: That I don't even wanta be in this group to begin with! It's bad enough that my parents make me come. I don't have a problem just because I get high sometimes when I hang with my friends. Everyone does! I'm no addict.

The resistance of at least one group member to identifying with having a problem with substances is as inevitable as the sun rising each day, and presents a convenient opening for the group to engage in their first art-making experience. The group is invited to the table where there are markers and paper, and given the Draw a Bridge directive. During the drawing phase, some members may be quiet, while others may chat, discharge anxiety by laughing at their own drawing and even play-fight over hoarding markers. This drawing requires less than ten minutes, and it is helpful to give the group a 3 minute warning so they know when they need to complete their drawing. After collecting the markers, each member shares their drawing, says a few sentences about it, and discusses why they choose to place themselves at any particular point on the bridge.

It is helpful to ask or note several factors aloud, to model how to look at, think about, and talk about their drawings. First, ask, "What is the bridge constructed of?" Is it made of stone, steel or wood? Does it appear sturdy or is it wobbly, and drawn with a wiggly single line? Suggest that the bridge is a symbol of how sturdy their world and footing is in life at the moment. Group members may groan, at this, but are also likely to chime in, examining the similarities and differences between one another's bridges. Next, ask what is beneath the bridge. Is it a small pond? Is it a vast ocean or a river or land? Invite the members to think about whatever is beneath the bridge as the dangers or pitfalls of moving toward recovery, asking them to think and talk aloud about what it's like to be identified as having a substance abuse problem, and what it will be like to be in group. Finally, the placement of the figure may be seen as a significant indicator of each member's stage of readiness to change. The exchange may sound something like this:

Therapist: Now, let's look at where all of you have put yourselves on the bridge. Who wants to go first?

Paul: Well, mine's about an inch over; sorta where Mary put herself. I was gonna not put myself on the bridge at all, but I thought, I'm here, so I'm on the bridge.

Kara: (Laughing, but quite observant) Yeh, but look at how you drew yourself! You look like you're hangin' on for dear life!! Like there are sharks in the water!

Paul: (Laughs) I was thinking of the movie *Jaws* when I was drawing it! Wouldn't wanta fall into the mouth of an Orca!

Kara: Yeah. My mother's an Orca. That's why I'm here!

Therapist: Is there an Orca in your life right now, Paul?

Paul: I guess so. If I get picked up one more time, I could wind up in Juvie Hall. So, I guess my sharks are the police who are all trying to pick me up every weekend!

Christie: Jeez. The police know who you are!?? You need to be here more than me!

Using art is a less direct avenue to identifying one's stage of readiness for change, and therefore far less cerebral and threatening for adolescents. Since "seeing is believing," these drawings serve to cut through denial. It is helpful to keep in mind that any statements made during the art-making and processing segment are opportunities for the therapist to engage members in looking at their automatic thoughts. The group will return to this exercise in the 11th week, after which each member may be given the opportunity to view their original bridge drawings to compare and contrast the two, and note one another's growth.

SUMMARY

Cognitive-behavioral purists may be quick to note that the proposed model for treating substance-abusing youth is infused with more than the usual degree of interactive therapy typical of CBT, and further requires that the clinician take a leap of faith to trust the healing properties of group art psychotherapy to enhance CBT skill building. Moreover, this 12-unit protocol does not span the usual 12 weeks, but rather, is conducted in an expedited fashion, by being held on Fridays and Mondays in order to bracket 6 weekends. It has been our experience that these three added elements function to expedite trust building between members, which swiftly cements group cohesion. They also serve to minimize denial, avoidance, and rationalization by keeping members grounded in reality and reinforcing newly learned cognitive-behavioral skills through immediate repetitions. It has also been our experience that more often than not, because of these factors, as well as the element of fun and humor imparted during art-making, groups have often elected to re-contract, during which the consolidation of skills and learning produces sustained abstinence.

RECOMMENDED READINGS

Kaminer, Y., Burleson, J. A., & Goldberger, R. (2002). Cognitive behavioral coping skills and psychoeducation therapies for adolescent substance abuse. *Journal of Mental Disorders, 190,* 737–745.

Waldron, Holly B., & Kaminer, Y. (2004). On the learning curve: The emerging evidence supporting cognitive-behavioral therapies for adolescent substance abuse. *Addiction,* 99, 93–105.

Wilson, M. (2003). Art therapy in addiction treatment: Creativity and shame reduction. In C. A. Malchiodi, (Ed.), *Handbook of art therapy* (pp. 281–293). New York: Guilford.

REFERENCES

American Psychiatric Association. (2000). *Diagnostic and statistical manual for mental disorder* (4th ed., text revision). Washington, DC: Author.

DeWit, D. J., Silverman, G., Goodstadt, M., & Stoduto, G. (1995). The construction of risk and protective factor indices for adolescent alcohol and other drug use. *The Journal of Drug Issues, 25,* 837–863.

Dube, S. R., Anda, R. F., Felitti, V. J., Edwards, V. J., & Croft, J. B. (2002). Adverse childhood experience and personal alcohol abuse as an adult. *Addictive Behaviors, 27,* 713–725.

Dube, S. R., Felitti, V. J., Dong, M., Chapman, D. P., Giles, W. H., & Ande, R. F. (2003). Childhood abuse, neglect and household dysfunction and the risk of illicit drug use: The adverse childhood experience study. *Pediatrics, 111*(3), 564–572.

Freeman, A., & Dolan, M. (2001). Revisiting Prochaska and DiClemente's Stages of Change Theory: An expansion and specification to aid in treatment planning and outcome evaluation. *Cognitive and Behavioral Practice, 8,* 224–234.

Hollon, S. D., & Kendall, P. C. (1980). Cognitive self statements in depression: Development of an automatic thoughts questionnaire. *Cognitive Therapy and Research, 4,* 383–395.

Ingram, R. E., Kendall, P. C., Siegle, G., Guarino, J., & McLaughlin, S. C. (1995). Psychometric properties of the Positive Automatic Thoughts Questionnaire. *Psychological Assessment, 7,* 495–507.

Kazdin, A. E. (1990). Evaluation of the automatic thoughts questionnaire: Negative cognitive processes and depression among children. *Psychological Assessment, 2,* 73–79.

Miller, F. G., & Lazowski, L. E. (2001). *The adolescent SASSI-A2 Manual: Identifying substance user disorders.* Springville, IN: The SASSI Institute.

National Institute on Drug Abuse (2004). *Preventing drug abuse among children and adolescents: A research-based guide.* Bethesda, MD: National Institutes of Health Publication No. 04–4212(A).

National Institute on Drug Abuse (2006) InfoFacts: High school and youth trends. Available at http://www.nida.nih.gov/Infofacts/Infofaxindex.html.

Rowe, C. L., Liddle, H. L., Greenbaum, P. E., & Henderson, C. E. (2004). Impact of psychiatric comorbidity on treatment of drug abusers. *Journal of Substance Abuse Treatment, 26,* 129–140.

Substance Abuse and Mental Health Services Administration. (2002). SAMHSA Model Programs. Available at http://modelprograms.samhsa.gov.

Swadi, H. (1999). Individual risk factors for adolescent substance use. *Drug and Alcohol Dependence, 55,* 209–224.

Volkow, N. D. (1996). New brain studies yield insights into cocaine binging and addiction. *Journal of Addictive Diseases, 4.* Available at http://www.nida.nih.gov.

Winters, K. C. (1991). *Personal experience screening questionnaire manual.* Los Angeles: Western Psychological Services.

Chapter Twenty

Self-Injurious Behavior

Annita B. Jones

She walked back into the room following her AWOL (residential lingo for runaway). Approaching the counselor, she exposed her forearms which were covered wrist to elbow in scratches. The counselor asked what happened. The ordinarily articulate 14-year-old tearfully replied, "I scratched myself. I don't know why. Please don't tell anybody." "Have you done this before?," asked the counselor. "No, it just occurred to me while I was out walking." During the next hour, the discussion yielded little about what had precipitated the behavior except that the young girl identified that she had not been able to feel real and wanted to see if she could still bleed.

The state residential program for adolescents in 1972 was my first experience with self-injurious behavior in any setting. One valuable lesson learned was to ask adolescents early in treatment if they had ever hurt themselves. Over the next few years, the pattern began to emerge that those who self-injured had similar histories of early childhood maltreatment in some form. Later research has consistently confirmed this observation (Favazza, 1996; Alderman, 1997; Hyman, 1999; Yates, 2004).

INTRODUCTION

Self-injurious behavior (SIB) is not considered a diagnosis in the *Diagnostic and Statistical Manual of Mental Disorders-IV-Text-Revision* (*DSM-IV-TR*; American Psychiatric Association, 2000). Instead, it is a symptom often associated with other diagnoses. While the phenomenon has been identified for many years, it has only recently been described as a treatable symptomatic behavior (Trautmann & Conners, 1994; Favazza, 1987; Simeon & Hollander, 2001). It is estimated that 7% of the population exhibits SIB (Yates, 2004). SIB is typically defined as any behavior causing damage to the self that is used as a paradoxical coping tool. This can take the form of cutting, burning, scratching, eating disorders, substance abuse, evoking violence from others, dangerous/risky activities, neglect of self-care (such as voiding and defecating, wound care, sleep deprivation, and such), unsafe sex, or deliberate sabotage of success (different from the "if I don't try, I can't fail" phenomenon; Jones, 1980). Several of the behaviors included in this definition are appropriate for unique treatment protocols, covered elsewhere in this text. (Readers are directed to the individual chapters on eating disorders and substance abuse for a review of the treatment of these presenting problems.) In addition, this chapter is not intended to address the needs of those children and adolescence who self-injure as a result of severe mental retardation or an autism spectrum disorder. This proposed treatment is relative to behavioral symptoms only, and cannot be incorporated in the treatment of developmentally affected populations.

Throughout this chapter, SIB will primarily relate to behaviors that are self-inflicted and more immediately damaging to the flesh (e.g., cutting, burning, scratching, kicking, or hitting oneself). These behaviors are deliberately harmful to the body and self-defeating to one's perceived identity. Favazza (1987) was one of the first to write exclusively about SIB and the understanding of the person who felt compelled to deliberately use it as a means for coping. Patients with early childhood histories of maltreatment are more likely to self-injure in adolescence (Yates, 2004). Yates offers a thorough review of the literature on the conceptualization and treatment of SIB, concluding that a cognitive-behavioral approach would effectively address this complex developmental phenomenon.

Clinicians who treat those who manifest SIB are often anxious to find consultation...or another referral for the patient. Hospital emergency rooms typically react to self-injuries as if they were suicidal in intent. The countertransferential issues in the treatment of self-injurers are amazingly strong (Simeon & Hollander, 2001). Medical and mental health professionals want to help people heal—watching them self-harm frequently evokes more helplessness than helpers can handle. Unfortunately, the difficult and unique presentation of behaviors and needs makes this population of youth in need of treatment one that is often neglected due to a lack of willingness on the part of mental health professionals, as well as a lack of adequate knowledge and appropriate conceptualization of the nature of SIB.

This chapter will focus on the utilization of group process to facilitate the treatment of SIB according to a cognitive-behavioral framework. The emphasis will be to offer a conceptualization of the behavior so that readers can begin to understand the functions it commonly serves (as reported by those who self-injure) and ways in which to address the emotional, cognitive, and behavioral deficits that precede the behavior. The cognitive-behavioral conceptualization offered throughout this chapter will provide professionals with a theoretical understanding of this self-destructive symptom for the purposes of addressing it within the context of group therapy. There are several considerations for the application of CBT to group therapy with children and adolescents who self-injure that need to be addressed when establishing and conducting group. These will also be presented, as well as an outline to guide session content and progression. Suggestions for monitoring symptoms and cognitive and behavioral interventions to decrease frequency of SIB and increase utilization of healthier, more effective, and less self-destructive means of coping will be offered. Vignettes of sample dialogue are offered to present ways in which facilitators can present relevant topics for discussion and actively explore the process of self-injury (from impulse to aftermath) with the adolescents who engage in it. Potential obstacles and challenges with this unique population will also be highlighted for consideration and, hopefully, anticipation throughout the process of the group.

OVERVIEW OF SIB

Clinical Associations

Self-injury is often a mechanism observed within one or more of several diagnoses, such as Borderline Personality Disorder, in which self-injury is often described by patients as the result of a profound sense of emptiness and loneliness so intense, there is an overwhelming urgency to escape or fill the empty space (Linehan, 1993); Depression, which is frequently marked by self-injury to let others know how badly they feel or numb the "pain" to prevent escalating to a suicidal urgency (Beck, 1995); Post-traumatic Stress Disorder, in which self-injury results when, while reliving traumatic experiences, patients describe the same panicky feelings as at the time of the trauma and the helplessness leads them to take control over the only aspects of their lives they believe they can—their body and when and how they feel inevitable pain (Jones, 1998); Dissociative Disorder (APA, 2000); Oppositional Defiant Disorder, in which self-injury may be the result of loss of control, impulsivity, and acting out in the destruction of property; Conduct Disorder, in that an adrenaline rush may prevent the feeling of pain and poor articulation may lead to demonstrations of self-destructiveness (Woodward & Bernstein, 1994), and so forth. While many who self-injure have early trauma or clinical pathology, Walsh (2006) has identified a subset of self-injurers who appear to be without these variables and perhaps engage in self-injury as the result of societal influence. This is a growing concern for many in the field, as SIB is more often portrayed in the media, movies, and television, and on Internet sites that do not necessarily aim to offer advice for modifying and stopping the behavior but actually attempt to teach young people how to be better self-injurers!

Physiological Association

Since self-injurious behavior is being viewed as a coping tool, albeit lacking in long-term efficacy, it does deserve the respect of a tool that appears to work. We have no medication or other intervention that will match the immediate gratification the patient achieves with self-injury. Physical injury (1) causes massive releases of endorphins, enkephalons, and adrenalin that immediately ease pain (Strong, 1998); (2) can produce dissociation, which temporarily stops all feelings including pain; (3) causes the person to feel part of the body as a way to stop the sense of numbing or dissociation; (4) symbolizes release (e.g., of physiological tension, emotional pressure) through the spilling of blood ("bloodletting"); (5) expresses something externally that is experienced internally; (6) proves to patients, because they bleed, that they are alive when they may be experiencing otherwise; and (7) many other forms of immediate gratification (Trautmann and Conners, 1994). The physiological responses of the body immediately following self-injury serve to reinforce the action—in that self-injurers genuinely receive some form of benefit from the act that reduces their painful emotional experience. This makes extinguishing the behavior and developing more effective coping tools challenging for clinicians working with self-injuring youth. This also reflects the potential for the behavior to be considered an "addiction," given the physiological mechanisms involved in the action-reinforcement association that results in patients reporting they often crave the sensation and experience urges to self-injure.

Individual Presentation

There is no common "face" of the self-injurer. Those who engage in SIB range in age and socioeconomic status, are of varying race and ethnicities, come from a number of cultures, and are of both genders. Perhaps the strongest indication of this assertion is the highly publicized fact that Princess Dianna engaged in SIB. What this means for the group facilitator is that members will be heterogeneous in terms of their reasons, methods, and practices associated with self-injury. While this may challenge cohesiveness within group if members perceive each other to be too different and not able to empathize, what members have in common is that they all rely on a complex mechanism for coping that requires exploration and a greater understanding in order to address it in treatment.

Some self-injurers are extremely sophisticated in their methods and practices. One patient with whom I worked had a formal "cut-down" in her arm (a medical procedure which involves making a cut in the vein so that it is accessible in case of emergency) through which she released blood on a daily basis, even at work. She had a constantly open vein through which she could release blood at any time. The situation became critical when the bandage on the cut-down became loosened resulting in blood spurting all over everyone present. The office staff needed clinical intervention from professionals to deal with the traumatic situation. Another patient, a physician, had learned that he could use a syringe to draw blood out of his vein and then dispose of the blood through health mandated rituals at the hospital where he worked.

COGNITIVE-BEHAVIORAL CONCEPTUALIZATION OF SIB: UNDERSTANDING THE "WHY?"

Just as the population of self-injurers is unique, so are the reasons and means for engaging in the behavior. It is difficult to provide a definitive conceptualization that applies to all self-injurers for all reasons they injure, as so much depends on the origin of the emotional dysregulation (that is a common component of SIB), the function of the behavior, and the additional symptoms and broader diagnostic profile. For example, it has been my observation that depressed patients often use self-injury to deescalate emotional situations before they become suicidal.

Therefore, treatment is to focus primarily on behavioral change and skills building, while using cognitive techniques to gain awareness of distorted or irrational beliefs and assumptions associated with the function of the behavior. A goal of CBT group therapy is to assist members in gaining an awareness of why they engage in SIB—the function the behavior serves. The methods, parts of the body, and the frequency are important variables to chart when working with those who rely on this extreme form of coping, as this information will communicate patterns in the way the behavior itself is carried out. When this information is associated with the timing and circumstances of self-injury, patients can begin to identify its function. Finally, gaining insight regarding the consequence (result or aftermath) of the act allows adolescents the ability to understand the purpose of the behavior fully for the sake of identifying their needs and alternative ways to meet those needs (either in a proactive or reactive way). Physiological factors associated with SIB must also be included in the conceptualization and may help to guide the selection of specific interventions once the function of the behavior is identified.

A tracking form can be used by the clinician, staff or patient to gather data related to the emotion at the time of self-injury (the nature and intensity of it), thoughts experienced, and the need the behavior met at the time to monitor for patterns that emerge. Whenever possible, the patient needs to be the one responsible for documenting this information to encourage accountability, awareness surrounding the reasons for self-injury, and developing more creative individual alternatives for tactics to delay the immediate gratification sought in accomplishing the presenting need. The documentation itself can become a delaying tactic, helping the patient focus on the form and details rather than the urges to act. The relatively comprehensive evaluation found in *Understanding Self-Injury, a Workbook for Adults* (Trautmann & Conners, 1994), is one of the most direct and helpful places for patients to begin to organize their thoughts and beliefs about the SIB and is often the first opportunity that allows them to consider the behavior in cognitive terms. These concepts and considerations can be modified for use with the adolescent population, and incorporated as part of exploration exercises within the group setting so that all members may benefit from the process of identifying and understanding the cognitive-behavioral rationale for the behaviors.

My personal observation has been that patients feel an intense urgency to "*do something*" when internal or external stimulation becomes overwhelming. Unfortunately, the *something* that has become an automatic reaction for those who resort to SIB is harmful to the self. The description heard and observed most often in patients seems most simply to follow the explanation found in Tomkins' Affect Theory (1992). In extremely simplistic terms, the patient first *feels*, either emotionally or physically, then *acts*, and then *thinks*. Viewed through a cognitive-behavioral framework, self-injury is in response to an emotional experience that, itself, is in response to cognition on some level—whether a surface level automatic thought or a schema triggered by an event or flashback, for example. Even in the case of physiological arousal prompting the act, that arousal may be the result of underlying cognitions that have been activated outside of the youth's awareness. Young people are often unaware of their cognitive experiences and may first be able to identify the feeling that led to the urge or need to self-injure. Those who self-injure do so because of a lack of more effective and healthier coping skills to manage intense emotional and physiological experiences.

While the behavior seems repulsive to many, one way to conceptualize it is as an exaggeration of a technique we all use to remedy smaller, extra-stimulating situations. Consider the mosquito bite's resulting itch and our remedy of scratching. The scratching causes mild injury to the skin and nerve endings resulting in temporary numbing. Imagine coping with this sensation both inside and outside of the entire body. This is similar to the experience of being overstimulated for those who self-injure.

A large component of the success of self-injury as purposeful behavior relates to cognitive distortions and an irrational belief system related to one's abilities to cope. Common distorted beliefs include: "SIB is an acceptable way to deal with problems," "Others will know how I feel if I use SIB," "I must act on urges when they occur or I will experience something horrible," all of which are considered negative and counterproductive cognitions (Beck, 1995). Dichotomous thinking is a common distortion observed with adolescent self-injurers, even in terms of physiological arousal (e.g., either aroused or numb). This must be addressed by helping members identify neutrality that will be more functional in appraising situations as realistic events. This is an important goal in working with self-injurers: facilitating the awareness and acceptance of an objective perspective of realistic events as no longer harmful to the person, and promoting, instead, a sense of control over current consequences and outcome.

Given that many patients may present with a number of additional diagnoses, the treatment framework within this chapter will not so much aim to address the underlying diagnostic symptoms (such as PTSD, depression, etc.), but primarily address the behaviors of self-injury as an ultimately ineffective coping mechanism within the context of a broader diagnostic presentation. While members should likely engage in additional group therapy to address other psychological symptoms related to their primary diagnosis, given the harm to the individual inherent within SIB the stabilization of these behaviors should be a priority. As such, often a group of this nature occurs within inpatient settings, but not necessarily. The examples and framework offered can be modified for use in any setting, but considerations should be made for doing so.

ASSESSMENT AND CONSIDERATION OF GROUP MEMBERS

Given the unique nature of this population, there are several equally unique considerations specific to the treatment of self-injurers that must be addressed in the development and process of group CBT with adolescents. Those are reviewed now, in addition to reiterating general inclusion considerations for group treatment with young people, such as those related to age, developmental level, questions of homogeneity versus heterogeneity of group make up, and other issues.

Concurrent Individual Therapy

One requirement for eligibility in a therapy group addressing SIB is ongoing individual therapy. The patient will need to be able to further process what is identified and explored within the group therapy context more significantly, and will need a vast external support network for the general therapeutic process. As mentioned above, many adolescents who engage in self-injury have a history of maltreatment. Therapeutic exploration that seeks to identify thoughts that produce the emotional distress leading to the urge to self-injure will undoubtedly identify difficult and painful memories and thoughts that will make group members vulnerable to triggering of cognitive distortions and exacerbation of emotional experiences.

Acceptance of Need for Behavioral Change

In addition, for group therapy to be effective, adolescents must be able to acknowledge that the SIB is as unhealthy as their difficult emotional experiences, and therefore not an effective tool in the healing process. They must possess the intellectual capabilities to rely, at least to some degree, on cognitive interventions that promote awareness of the thought-feeling-behavior relationship. As, typically, SIB is not seen as frequently in younger children and is more common in adolescents, this standard may not be unrealistic. These youth need to be able to not only recognize this cognitively, but also exhibit a desire and motivation to change their behaviors. This may not be fully achieved until engagement in the group therapy process has begun. The cognitive restructuring involved in moving from perceiving self-injury as a viable coping option to one that is detrimental to their well-being in and of itself is relatively powerful in the healing from SIB. However, be prepared for it to evolve slowly and in stages, as the grief process experienced by group members for the loss of one's "best friend" (a phrase often used by self-injurers) progresses.

Medical Stabilization

Since this pattern of behavior involves the physical body, medical examination and ongoing monitoring is necessary to rule out any underlying physical cause for the behavior, such as a tumor or hormonal imbalance. In addition, a critical element in the appropriateness for inclusion in group therapy relates to medical stabilization. Depending on which form of SIB the patient evidences, medical stabilization is a necessity and a minimum standard for group inclusion. Suppose, for example, an adolescent patient vacillates between cutting forearms, more secretive places such as underneath the breasts, pulling hairs out of the pubic area or underarms, refusing to void or defecate, holding needles in their cheeks, vomiting everything he/she eats, and acting in reckless disregard of the environment, in predictable routine. This patient will need to be in either a very stable supportive home environment or a residential treatment facility since he/she is struggling with cycling SIB that requires close monitoring.

Due to the potential for serious harm inherent in self-injury, it is important to emphasize the stabilization of symptoms that contribute to the likelihood of SIB to facilitate greater successful impact of group therapy. Medication can be important for stabilization. There is no medication that is effective in the treatment of SIB, although some medications can be helpful in symptom management (e.g., to address depression and anxiety symptoms that may contribute to the emotional experiences that result in SIB). Some have reported success with medications that block the pleasure sensation to the brain making SIB less effective as a tool. My personal experience with hundreds of cases has found this true only if the patient truly is motivated to stop the behavior. Otherwise, it seems to add more stress to an already extremely stressful situation (e.g., given the introduction of side-effects, medication regimens, stigma associated with being on medication).

Remembering the potential diagnoses among which SIB can occur, considering certain medications can be critical. In depression, there are a myriad of SSRI's (serotonin reuptake inhibitors), among others that can help with the chemical depression, often comorbid with PTSD (Foa, Keane, & Friedman, 2000). There is no *one* medication shown to be effective in treating PTSD but, again, symptoms may be managed successfully. Medications that have been successfully used include anxiolytics, antidepressants, antipsychotics, sleep aids, and stimulants that can improve attention and focus. Effective symptom management affords group members the ability to concentrate efforts within the context of treatment rather than expend their resources to the management of emotional, physiological, and cognitive distress.

Comorbidity

As discussed above, SIB may accompany a number of diagnoses and it may be the case that potential group members meet criteria for more than one. The more complex patients (those with comorbid diagnoses or multiple incidents of trauma at an early age) are more likely to self-injure relative to the more complicated underlying issues (Favazza, 1996; Yates, 2004). A careful psychological assessment of additional symptomatology is necessary for a better conceptualization of the group member's presenting problems and needs. It is not uncommon for young people engaging in SIB to meet criteria for other problematic psychosocial difficulties, such as depression, anxiety, poor interpersonal relationships, substance abuse, and so forth, and inclusion in other problem-specific treatment groups may be appropriate. In addition, other psychological/congenital diagnoses, such as Pervasive Developmental Disorder, that could be the cause should be ruled out (Shroeder, Oster-Granite, Thompson, 2002), as the appropriate treatment approach would be different.

While clinicians generally avoid diagnosing adolescents with Personality Disorders (Freeman & Rigby, 2003), patterns of Axis II diagnoses are often noted in the presentation of adolescents who self-injure. The consideration of personality disorder traits is as equally important as comorbid Axis I psychological disorders and symptoms, as these traits may be more suggestive of maladaptive interpersonal schema that may undermine involvement in group and affect the adolescent's participation.

Assessment and Interview

Prescreening of prospective patients needs to include the medical results, as mentioned above, consultation with the individual therapist to ensure readiness and support in individual therapy, interview with family members and teachers, a thorough interview with the potential group members that includes a functional behavior analysis, and standardized instruments to assess the degree of symptomatology. Several measures that may be helpful in assessing presenting symptoms and monitoring them throughout the course of treatment include: the *Lifetime Incidence of Traumatic Events* (LITE; Greenwald & Rubin, 1999), the *Acute Stress Checklist for Children* (ASC-Kids; Kassam-Adams, Baxt, & Shrivastava, 2003), the *Child and Adolescent Trauma Survey* (March, 1999), the *Adolescent Dissociative Experiences Scale* (A-DES; Armstrong, Putnam, Carlson, Libero, & Smith, 1997), the *Beck Youth Inventories, Second Edition* (BYI-II; Beck, Beck, & Jolly, 2005), the *Assessment of Self Injurious Coping Behaviors* (Sakheim, 1992), the *Child Behavior Checklist* (Achenbach & Edelbrock, 1983), and the *Behavior Assessment System for Children, Second Edition* (BASC-2; Reynolds & Kamphaus, 2002). If the scores on any of the scales are within the respective clinically significant levels, the potential patients need to be evaluated by a psychologist or psychiatrist who is skilled in working with similar patients with these disorders to determine whether they are stable enough to participate in the group process or if they need additional therapy first to promote physical and emotional stability prior to adjunct therapies such as this group.

CBT GROUP TREATMENT

Regardless of treatment focus, the general group process as discussed by Yalom (1985) needs to be respected for any CBT group. There are several different approaches to take when structuring group therapy for this population. If the patients are in the hospital or intensive residential treatment facility, the group can be open-ended and ongoing with members coming and going as available. If this is an outpatient therapy group, the better course is to have a time-limited group with tightly structured content. Both will be discussed.

Potential group members within inpatient or residential treatment centers may join an ongoing group process at any time that they and the staff feel they are stable enough and ready to benefit from the adjunctive therapy. The group facilitator needs to be aware of classical group dynamics and containment techniques given the possibility for presenting diagnoses of Borderline Personality Traits, Post-Traumatic Stress Disorder, Depression, and other diagnoses that commonly accompany SIB in order to help contain the content of the group interaction and proactively avoid abreactive explosions. Abreactions are a reliving of a previous traumatic event or combination of events that takes the person temporarily to another place and time, resulting in their dissociating from current reality—they are, in effect, caught in another, past reality. Walsh and Rosen (1985) discuss the "contagion" phenomenon, which suggests exposure to another person's traumatic experiences may incidentally traumatize or worsen the already existing symptoms of others. This must be considered within groups that likely include members with PTSD and more severe dissociative disorders, who will need to be able to maintain their containment over traumatic material. A cognitive-behavior al treatment focus is one of the best means by which to maintain focus on current reality (Kluft, 1996). Borderline Personality Disorder patients need to practice managing their affect and impulsivity through cognitive reframe and reprogramming (Linehan, 1993).

The structure for emotional and physical safety needs to be regulated from the initial session, whether sessions will be ongoing or limited in number. Personal experience suggests a ratio of clinician to patient of 1:6. Due to the very intense nature of this group work, facilitators need to continually be aware of all members' respective emotional states and needs to assure safety. To that end, frequent exchanges with the staff (if the group is in residential or inpatient facilities) or individual therapist (regardless of setting) is helpful.

Goals for Treatment

The goals of treatment with this population surprisingly do not include *stopping the behavior*. This approach includes the philosophy that the behavior will cease, slowly and incrementally, as other tools are learned, underlying issues are resolved, and cognitive dissonance is reframed. Ultimately, adolescents in treatment for SIB need to acquire skills to facilitate emotional identification and expression, affective coping, self-regulation, tolerance for discomfort, accurate perception of themselves, others (and their motivations and intentions), and events, and the ability to identify their emotional, physical, and social needs to more effectively meet them prior to experiencing the distress of unmet needs.

This model is eclectic in philosophy, in that it considers biochemical, emotional, behavioral, and cognitive literature. However, the group therapy adjunct presented here will be primarily cognitive-behavioral in its framework and interventions. There are several excellent reasons that cognitive-behavioral therapy (CBT) is an appropriate and fitting treatment approach for use with SIB in young people. CBT allows for a conceptualization that explains these behaviors in terms of a response to cognitive, emotional, and physiological experiences of adolescents. Through the CBT framework, intervention will guide clinicians to view the function of the behavior in terms of distorted beliefs and perceptions more accurately, as well as maladaptive emotional responses and skill deficits (including managing physiological arousal) that result in the reliance on a physiological means of expression and resolution of distress. The vignettes will offer a sampling of dialogue and approaches to engaging in conversation with self-injuring adolescents to ascertain beliefs and perceptions at work within the SIB.

Structure of Group Sessions

At the beginning of each session, facilitators should implement a group "check-in" process that serves to reorient members to the structure and mindset of the group process, including the CBT framework (e.g., terms, the agenda and objectives for session, importance of attending to thoughts and feelings related to the SIB, and the like), and a review of the between-session work. This check-in should also include a discussion of the members' ratings on the Subjective Units of Distress Scale (SUDS) (Wolpe, 1985). This 10-point scale allows the rating of intensity of emotional distress. It is similar to the pain scale used in most medical situations, and for creating a hierarchy of anxiety. Time should be spent in the first two sessions for each member to identify situations that could result in each value on the scale. They should choose a word that describes each increasing level of intensity and draw any figure that adequately represents each level (e.g., a number line, a thermometer, a bar graph, rainbow of colors) with the words that fit in each category. Figure 20.1 provides a sample of a format for members to begin tracking episodes of self-injury outside of group by outlining the emotion experienced

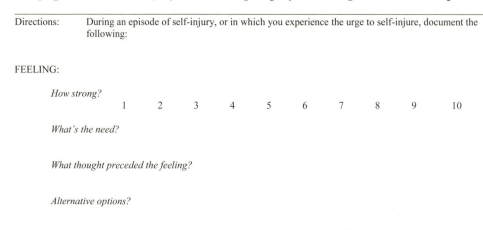

Directions: During an episode of self-injury, or in which you experience the urge to self-injure, document the following:

FEELING:

How strong?

1   2   3   4   5   6   7   8   9   10

What's the need?

What thought preceded the feeling?

Alternative options?

Remember that you may likely have many feelings at once, or feel none at all that you can identify. In that case, record the feeling as NUMB, and still provide the additional information. Provide these pieces of information for each feeling you can identify.

Figure 20.1   Tracking Form for the Functions of SIB.

and its intensity level, the precipitating situation or thought (if able to identify; if not, this can be done within the group when reviewing the homework), the need the injury met, and listing alternative "safe list" options for coping.

Group rules should be reiterated weekly regarding safety, confidentiality, honesty, and sharing versus disclosure. Members should also be reminded about available support resources within and following group. Many of the rules for group should be established within the first session by the group and facilitator collaboratively. However, it is the responsibility of the facilitator to ensure that rules are appropriate for all members and to facilitate an emotionally safe environment in which members may address potentially difficult or painful experiences.

Below is an example of an initial session within an inpatient treatment facility. This initial session may be spaced out over two sessions when the membership is likely to remain stable over the course of several weeks. However, given the limited timeframe of inpatient treatment, the progression of the discussion is presented here in a more rapid fashion than is typical in outpatient services. Given that group therapy to address SIB would be especially beneficial within inpatient settings where self-injurers are more likely to present, the following is offered as an example of a way to move quickly into the process of cognitive-behavior group therapy while maintaining the essential components.

Therapist: We are here to learn more about SIB, to learn why you use it as a coping tool, and ways you can cope instead. Each time we get together we will have a goal for the group—something we hope to accomplish in our short time that will lead each of you to understand the reasons you self-injure, to figure out what need each of you is trying to fill. This is your group, so it is important for everyone to get something out of being here, and to participate in discussions we'll have and assignments to do outside of group between sessions. We will spend a lot of time talking about the way feelings and thoughts go together and cause us to behave in certain ways to deal with the tough thoughts or bad feelings. So to start getting used to that, will each of you please say what you're feeling, thinking, and what you would like to accomplish in this meeting. (*Group facilitator provides unconditional positive regard during this session by not providing corrective feedback but also maintaining clear boundaries.*)

Member 1: I'm feeling nervous, thinking I don't know why I'm here and I would like to know I'm not the only one who struggles with this problem.

Member 2: I'm feeling nothing, thinking I don't want to be here and I don't know what I would like to gain from this.

Member 3: I'm feeling scared, thinking I don't know what to say and I...(*prompt*)... want to understand why I'm hurting myself.

Member 4: I'm feeling angry, thinking I don't need to be here and I don't want anything from this group.

Member 5: What do you want me to say? (*Prompt*) Oh, I'm feeling...I don't know. I'm thinking...I don't know...I don't know what I want to get out of this group meeting.

Member 6: I don't know why I need to be here. I like cutting and burning myself. It stops the feelings. (*Prompt*) I feel stupid, I think this is stupid, and I don't want anything.

T: There seems to be quite a divergent group here today. You're all feeling different things, thinking different things and wanting different things from group. Do you see anything you all have in common?

M4: We all hurt ourselves. We all are very different, though.

T: Yes, indeed, you are! There are similarities in your differences, however. You all have in common that you hurt yourselves. Anyone have an idea why you do that?

M3: It feels good. It makes me feel better.

T: Feel better or feel nothing? (Therapist asks for clarification and prompts the member to think more specifically.)

M3: Maybe...feel nothing. I don't feel it when I'm cutting. Do any of you feel the cuts?

M1: I don't. I just do it when I feel scared or overwhelmed. It makes the feelings go away.

T: How does it do that? Where did you learn to do that?

M5: There's nothing mysterious about it—we just do it. Wanna see my scars?

T: What would your scars say if they could speak?

M5: They would tell you how I feel and make you understand how I feel!

T: Sounds like it's important that others know how you feel. What happens if they understand?

M5: I wouldn't have to tell anyone—they would know just by seeing the cuts or burns.

M1: I feel that way, too. I want people to understand how I feel and the pain is so bad I can't tell anyone—I want to show them.

T: So, others will understand if they "see" your wounds?

M2: Yeah, that's part of it. (*Prompt*) It, like, balances the pain inside with pain outside. I don't feel it when I cut or burn but I can see it. It lets others know how much I hurt. Especially, my mother.

T: What does your mother need to understand?

M2: She never understood how I felt! She always told me to be quiet and not upset anyone with how I felt! She was afraid dad would get mad.

T: And then what would happen?

M2: Nothing.

T: Nothing or you would rather not say?

M2: I'd rather not say.

T: That's more honest. Thank you. Let's review the rules of group.

The facilitator reviews the rules for group, which include honesty (telling the truth but not necessarily everything), confidentiality, that group participation is voluntary and members who are there are willing to work to make important changes, safety (that includes of selves and others, not threatening others even if feeling unsafe), and stabilization of affect (which means letting others know when escalating to implement support services). The group facilitator then presents the purpose of the group, as follows:

T: Some of the purposes of this group are for you to learn how to determine when your impulses to self-injure are triggered, to identify what thoughts go through your head when faced with difficult situations or emotions, to learn to accurately identify different emotions again and different levels of those emotions, and to determine additional coping skills to deal with those thoughts and emotions besides self-injury. We will want to develop a list of ways to self-soothe, reground, and to remember that this is now and the things that happened before are in the past. This is an important concept we will stress in this group and want you to practice outside of group. To begin the list, each of you please tell us one thing that has been helpful when you began to feel overwhelmed.

Allow each member to share one way they have found to regain stability for what will be lower levels on the SUDS. The list of soothing, calming, distracting, delaying, grounding, and orienting tools can be expanded to address each number on the scale, as they are discovered/created through the course of exploration and in vivo situations outside of group. Once members have begun to identify coping techniques for less stressful situations, explain the concept of the SUDS, and the rationale for how and why they will use this scale to identify more difficult emotional situations and, eventually, coping techniques for higher levels. Figure 20.2 illustrates a chart completed by an adolescent girl to outline identified reasons for her self-injury. This documentation may be in any format or medium the adolescent prefers, so long as it allows for an open-ended, ongoing list that is adaptable as the adolescent identifies additional extrastimulating environments and sequences. Ideally, adolescents should aim to identify the feeling and its intensity at the time of self-injury, the need or function that the self-injury serves, identify the thought that preceded it, and identify effective alternative options for coping with the feeling that will serve the same function. It can also be explained that the goal will be for members to be able to identify increases in their arousal levels, apply techniques automatically when distress levels rise, and eventually have higher-level triggers produce only minimal distress. For instance, a therapist might say,

> Now, we are going to focus only on fact-finding so that we may begin to identify triggers. If you, without becoming overwhelmed, think about the very first time you self-injured, what were the circumstances? Pretend you're an observer for the local newspaper. What did you see? How old were you? What happened after you acted? If you told anyone, describe his or her reaction. Let me know if you need to take a break.

The therapist at this point is demonstrating containment of the emotional piece of the overwhelm by offering a "break," also known as a "rest," that facilitates self-regulation—a skill many self-injurers lack. Homework following the first and subsequent sessions will be for members to record episodes of self-injury between sessions using Figure 20.3. When reviewing these forms, collect any repetitions for noting patterns to aid in proactive planning for future situations. In addition, each week members will be assigned between-session work to attempt to incorporate safe list coping strategies during episodes of emotional distress, record these trials, and discuss the outcomes of those trials. Members are continually practicing the identification of thoughts and accurately labeling the corresponding feelings, so that, while it may feel redundant, repetition will facilitate this skill becoming more automatic and patterns in thinking and reacting will be identified. Members will be able to discover the function of their SIB. This awareness naturally leads to an exploration (within group discussions) of alternative ways to meet

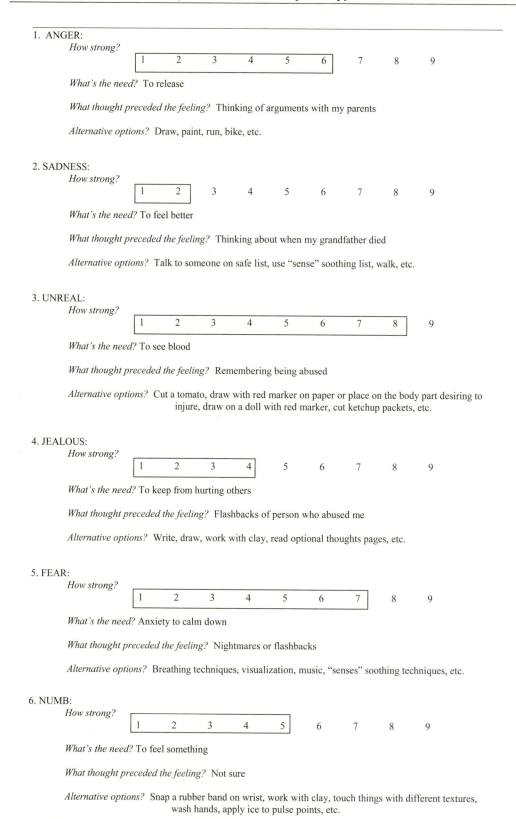

1. ANGER:
    How strong?

    | 1 | 2 | 3 | 4 | 5 | 6 | 7 | 8 | 9 |

    What's the need? To release

    What thought preceded the feeling? Thinking of arguments with my parents

    Alternative options? Draw, paint, run, bike, etc.

2. SADNESS:
    How strong?

    | 1 | 2 | 3 | 4 | 5 | 6 | 7 | 8 | 9 |

    What's the need? To feel better

    What thought preceded the feeling? Thinking about when my grandfather died

    Alternative options? Talk to someone on safe list, use "sense" soothing list, walk, etc.

3. UNREAL:
    How strong?

    | 1 | 2 | 3 | 4 | 5 | 6 | 7 | 8 | 9 |

    What's the need? To see blood

    What thought preceded the feeling? Remembering being abused

    Alternative options? Cut a tomato, draw with red marker on paper or place on the body part desiring to
    injure, draw on a doll with red marker, cut ketchup packets, etc.

4. JEALOUS:
    How strong?

    | 1 | 2 | 3 | 4 | 5 | 6 | 7 | 8 | 9 |

    What's the need? To keep from hurting others

    What thought preceded the feeling? Flashbacks of person who abused me

    Alternative options? Write, draw, work with clay, read optional thoughts pages, etc.

5. FEAR:
    How strong?

    | 1 | 2 | 3 | 4 | 5 | 6 | 7 | 8 | 9 |

    What's the need? Anxiety to calm down

    What thought preceded the feeling? Nightmares or flashbacks

    Alternative options? Breathing techniques, visualization, music, "senses" soothing techniques, etc.

6. NUMB:
    How strong?

    | 1 | 2 | 3 | 4 | 5 | 6 | 7 | 8 | 9 |

    What's the need? To feel something

    What thought preceded the feeling? Not sure

    Alternative options? Snap a rubber band on wrist, work with clay, touch things with different textures,
    wash hands, apply ice to pulse points, etc.

Figure 20.2 Completed Tracking Form for Functions of SIB.

Self-injury Record Form

Client Name: _____ Date: _____ Time: _____

Location: _____ Reporter: _____

Describe situation prior to behavior:

Describe behavior:

Describe aftermath of behavior: (especially notice what was improved!)

What else is noted: (Weather, time of day, day of month, anniversary of loss or trauma, visit w/ parents, therapy session, group session, activity at school, interaction w/ peers, interaction w/ authority figures, drawings or writings found, etc.)

Figure 20.3   Form for Recording Events and Identifying Patterns.

those needs and an exploration of the needs themselves—to ascertain the accuracy of perceptions related to those needs (e.g., whether they are met already in other ways, whether they are truly needs, wants, expectations).

The recommended outline for the first 10-group sessions, held weekly for an hour or an hour and a quarter (depending on the maturity of the group) whether time-limited to 10 or ongoing, follows. Different cognitive and behavioral activities can be used or as the group becomes more trusting and comfortable with the dynamics, the conversation will often carry itself—so long as the therapist monitors pacing, members' needs and distress levels, and facilitates the direction so that members identify and explore under-lying schema and cognitions related to the SIB. The therapist actively prompts members to draw relationships between thinking, feeling, and behaving—in themselves, and in others. If the setting is in a hospital, the turnover will often be frequent so the repetition will be important to help the new members learn the routine. Each time someone new joins, the group will need time to adjust to the change in dynamics. Trust is typically a scarce commodity in patients who self-injure. Each group session will begin with any introductions (if an open-ended group), check-in and SUDS discussion of events during the previous week, as well as a review of safe lists. In addition, weekly session format should resemble the following.

Group Treatment Protocol

Session 1. In addition to the outline provided above, the initial group session should lay the groundwork for members to understand the CBT framework by highlighting the thoughts-feelings-behavior connection. This can be done using the information mem-bers provided during the initial "check in," in that they began to provide feelings and thoughts related to why they self-injure that can begin to formulate the conceptualization for the therapist as to the needs and issues prompting emotional distress and eventual SIB for the members. For example, the anger expressed by one group member because her mother does not understand how she feels suggests that she not only lacks emotional identification and expression skills to tell her mother, but appears to believe that she and her feelings are not worth understanding in her mother's eyes. Perhaps this relates to a deeper level schema about whether or not she is worthy of others' energy and time to be understood, whether others care about how she feels or she is not worthy of caring, etc. The point is, that attending to the beliefs inherent in the statements and feelings of members allows the therapist to begin to feed these observed patterns or connections back to patients for their validation and subsequent awareness. This begins the emphasis throughout group on the thoughts-feelings-behavior connection at the heart of the CBT model. With adolescents, many of these concepts can be discussed directly.

Session 2. The discussion of the SUDS list and a review of the safe lists begun last session are important for the sake of adding new situations and coping techniques identified and utilized during the last week. To review the first homework assignment, members can share instances of lower-level (SUDS level 2–4) emotional difficulty since last session and identify the factors of the situation, their emotions, and their responses. This exercise will be a continuous group activity, as adolescents who engage in SIB struggle with accurate emotional identification and expression. Even discussing diffi-cult situations after the fact allows them to process events and their reactions (feelings, thoughts, and behaviors) while removed from the situation to improve their repertoire of emotional language and expression skills. Homework assignments will subsequently require members to record emotions, thoughts, and responses to stressful events while *in vivo* for practice applying learned skills within the emotionally charged situation. Within session, members will share their experiences and are encouraged to offer feedback to each other regarding possible safe list items they each have found useful.

Session 3. Continue with the SUDS discussion, reviewing safe lists and the use of any tools since last session. If the group has begun to evidence comfort in directly interacting and asking each other for situations for discussion, ask if someone can relate the first experience with self-injury.

Session 4. Following review of SUDS and safe lists, review the between session work to note progress in managing the episodes. Of note: the first time a member is successful in preemptive measures that prevent SIB, avoid any additional celebration other than the usual praise for improvement. The danger in overly celebrating is that the patient will feel an expectation from the group and therapist to maintain abstinence from SIB, which may create too much pressure and prompt an episode.

Encourage another group member to share their first experience with self-injury. In addition, begin to encourage and facilitate member identification of each other's thoughts or feelings that may have led to the SIB. Given that many members report being unable to feel and/or think during times of self-injury, it is beneficial for them to begin to learn to identify the thoughts-feelings-behavior connection involved in the SIB process and may be easier to do initially when viewing someone else's circumstance.

Sessions 5 and 6. Continue with the initial tasks of group, noting progress in managing the feelings and thoughts associated with SIB. Review any new verbal descriptions of the levels of distress. Continue the discussion of the initial instances of SIB for the purposes and how they may connect to present behaviors. Begin to reframe past incidents in cognitive terms, such as: "Knowing what you know now, what would you have done differently in that initial situation of self-injury? What will you do differently in similar situations next time? What did you need that you didn't have then? How can you get that now?" The general goal is to begin to empower the group members to be accountable for their behavior regardless of what has happened or what initiated the SIB—the importance being that they begin to see that what happens now depends on their decisions regarding coping with feelings, urges, and thoughts, and that they must become aware of the connection between these factors and the resulting SIB.

Session 7. (Continue with activities above). Begin to discuss how members can continue developing and rehearsing ways to apply the new awareness of patterns in other environments outside of the group and the facility.

Session 8. Review the charts and safe lists made thus far by each member to identify which items have been the most useful and which have not been helpful, so that members may begin to develop accurate appraisal of effective and ineffective coping strategies, as well as their strengths and needs (e.g., a member no longer engages in SIB in situations that produce anger, but when feeling anxious continues to experience a strong urge and safe list alternatives have not been helpful). In addition, facilitators should assist members in continuing to compare and contrast early versus recent incidents of SIB, looking at the developing patterns for additional ways to intervene earlier in the buildup to acting on self-injurious urges (e.g., given increasing awareness of the function of behaviors, members can develop options for meeting those needs more proactively, rather than experiencing distress that arises from them not being met). Continue discussing termination and how to generalize new skills into the next environment.

Session 9. Continue as above, empowering members to be accountable for their coping responses by emphasizing each member's past week and their attempts to manage situations without SIB, praising even small progress at any point within the pattern (e.g., delaying the behavioral response, being able to lessen the distressing emotion, incorporating safe list activities, identifying thoughts and perceptions of the event, challenging those thoughts for accuracy to diffuse the intense emotion and desire to self-injure). Ask members to make a list of the situations or potential circumstances that worry them most in terms of their ability to effectively cope with distress and apply newly learned skills for review in next weeks' final session.

Session 10. If this is the final session, follow the protocol of previous sessions in terms of reviewing situations since the last group, sharing progress and noting difficulties. Save time to review overall progress since beginning the group and what members need to continue to work on with their individual therapist and/or additional support group involvement. Have members make notes about what they need to continue practicing and how to generalize progress and new skills to the next environments. Review each member's list of special situations of concern and role-play common themes or invite all members to make suggestions for each member's list. Members may write each other inspirational notes for support after group termination, as a means of perpetuating the supportive relationships developed in group for strength later on, or sign a page with a supportive word or name for future affirmation. All members can receive a copy.

If the group is open-ended and continuing on, maintain the protocol, adding exercises to provide psychoeducation and cognitive or behavioral skills related to specific common themes that members may all share (e.g., body dysmorphia, low self-esteem, feeling damaged, feeling crazy) Continue sessions in this manner on an ongoing basis, considering the "graduation" of select members as they progress through treatment and exhibit effective use of healthier coping skills and abstinence from SIB.

The above approach is appropriate for inclusion in all environments. The therapist may be less directive in a more controlled setting, such as inpatient, where there are guaranteed personnel available for potential fallout after group ends. If the group is in an outpatient setting, the structure needs to be more stringent since the patient will be going home to questionable support. Therefore, the containment and skill-building needs outlined above are more of a consideration and need to be more intensely managed in the beginning of the meetings.

Remembering the Thomkins Affect Theory, the importance of connecting to one's cognitive processes is critical in bypassing the feeling and acting parts of the automatic pattern. Anything that can help the patient remember to think instead of act (grounding techniques and objects) may be helpful. The list needs to be ongoing and exhaustive, including something for each sense - sight, sound, smell, touch, taste. For example, the patient may carry a small box in which he/she may keep something soothing to smell, touch, view, taste, and hear.

Some structured activities can be used with this group process. Examples are found in the *Body Image Workbook* (Cash & Pruzinski, 2002) and *The Body Remembers* (Rothschild, 2000). Additional activities that involve skill building for managing affect at the extremes can also be useful. Adolescents who self-injure are relying on one of the few (or the only) skills they have when feeling completely overwhelmed and overstimulated by the many feelings typically surging, especially those from developmentally premature exposure to traumatic experiences (e.g., loss or illness of a parent, childhood maltreatment). There are many skills needed to modulate the intensity of these phenomena and until these skills reach mastery level, the intensity needs to be contained to avoid major overstimulation leading to the use of tools that are already in the patient's self-injury repertoire.

POTENTIAL CHALLENGES

The following vignette is offered to exemplify several potential challenges within group work with adolescent self-injurers: the amount of self-disclosure of details of abuse, sharing "war stories," concurrent self-injury, and the nature of progress in this group.

T: Thank you, S, for sharing the first time you self-injured. When was the last time?

M3: It was last night (voice drops, eye contact stops, fidgeting in the chair).

T: I can see this is an uncomfortable topic for you. Would you like to take a break?

M3: No, I'm ok. Do I have to tell you what I did?

T: In fact, it's better if you don't tell us graphic details (cut or burn, etc.), as that might trigger others. I'm especially interested in how it was different from other times. Please tell us, instead, what you felt before, during and after and, in general what you did differently from the last time you felt compelled to act on something self-injurious.

M3: It was right after a phone conversation with my father (parents divorced; lives with mother; accused father of molesting her—case was unfounded). I didn't want to talk to him but my mother made me. She wanted me to ask him for money. I hate it when she does that!

M4: Yeah, my mom does that, too. Pisses me off!

T: S, you were saying how you felt and you seem to have been angry? What else did you feel?

M3: Scared, I think, when he got mad and yelled at me for asking for the money.

T: What were you afraid would happen?

M3: When he gets mad, he yells and hits. He used to hit me. I felt scared.

[*Break*]

T: S, you were telling us about self-injuring last night. You cut on your left wrist. I notice there are scars of old cuts there. Did some of them need stitches?

M3: Yeah, but this time I cut so I wouldn't need stitches. I didn't want to go to the hospital.

T: Good for you! You made a conscious decision to manage the injury and it was less severe. We'll want to build on that progress!

M3: But I still cut. It's bad.

T: It's unhealthy, but it was less severe than in the past and that's what we want to happen. We will look for any ways the incidents progress toward less harm to your body. Good job! You also identified some of the feelings and we can work on some ways to manage those in the future. It will also be important to talk about what thoughts went through your head that triggered those feelings, like memories or fears about things happening now. You did some of that, and eventually we want to be able to separate the things from the past from the reality of what's now. Sort of like challenging those thoughts and feelings that pop up to see if they are still true or real for what is happening right now. The boundaries with your mom need some work. You'll need to be able to tell her you don't want to be involved with the money issues between her and your dad. It's obvious that situation carries meaning for you that ends up in some pretty negative feelings, and ultimately the urge to self-inure.

M3: That will be hard!

T: Yep! Somebody else will do the easy stuff—you can do the hard work. You already do! We're just going to find some ways that are better for you.

This is an example of a critical step in dealing with those who self-injure. Expect them to self-injure. Some clinicians contract for no self-harm. Experience has taught me that, if inclined, patients will continue to self-injure in more and more discrete methods and not disclose to the therapist—the motive will be to please the therapist instead of work on issues. Staff, therapist, and patients need to document carefully the circumstances of each incident so antecedents and consequences of the behavior can be identified and progress can be pointed out in each follow-up. Even if the progress is that one less stitch was needed, that's forward movement. The patient will feel he/she has failed when they continue to act out. They need time, often protracted time, to allow for the chemical addiction to abate, skills to develop for better emotional management, to desensitize to the feelings they're trying to self-medicate via the SIB, and to replace the SIB with other behaviors and thoughts. This is a deliberate and patient process during which the therapists have to hold the hope.

CONCLUSION

Separations are difficult for adolescents, especially those who self-injure because of childhood maltreatment. Any change is anathema to most humans and added to general developmental stressors of adolescence can trigger acting out behaviors. Group dynamics dictate that there is careful preparation for termination, regardless of whether it occurs after 10 sessions or 50. A specific consideration when working with adolescents who self-injure involves relapse prevention and ensuring that appropriate support services are maintained following group. Making sure the group members know they can contact the therapist with future questions and that a final report will be sent to their individual therapist that includes progress, observations, and suggestions for future growth is important. Expressing your own mixed feelings about ending the time together will help members accept and express their own confusion about the transition. Contacting each member at 3 month intervals for follow-up status is a wonderful way to reinforce that skills continue, and to gather important data about the efficacy of your group.

Best wishes and please remember to care for yourselves when working with patients who manifest symptoms of the level of intensity of this population. It is important to process your own feelings and thoughts following each session with a colleague, especially to monitor countertransference in order to incorporate it into the conceptualization of the group process. Using the same self-soothing skills you encourage the group members to use models healthy behavior for your group...and yourselves.

RECOMMENDED READING

Conners, R. E. (2000). *Self-injury: Psychotherapy with people who engage in self-inflicted violence.* Northvale, NJ: Jason Aronson.

Trautmann, K., & Conners, R. (1994). *Understanding self-injury: A workbook for adults.* Pittsburgh: Pittsburgh Action Against Rape.

Walsh, B. W. (2006). *Treating self-injury: A practical guide.* New York: Guilford.

Yates, T. M. (2004). The developmental psychopathology of self-injurious behavior: Compensatory regulation in posttraumatic adaptation. *Clinical Psychology Review 24*, 35–74.

REFERENCES

Achenbach, T. M., & Edelbrock, C. (1983). *Manual for the child behavior checklist and revised child behavior profile.* Burlington: University of Vermont, Department of Psychiatry.

Alderman, T. (1997). *The scarred soul: Understanding and ending self-inflicted violence.* Oakdale, CA: New Harbinger.

American Psychiatric Association (2000). *Diagnostic and statistical manual of mental disorders, 4th edition* (DSM-IV-TR). Washington, DC: Author.

Armstrong, J., Putnam, F. W., Carlson, E., Libero, D., & Smith, S. (1997). Development and validation of a measure of adolescent dissociation: The Adolescent Dissociative Experience Scale. *Journal of Nervous & Mental Disease, 185*, 491–497.

Beck, J. S. (1995). *Cognitive therapy, basics and beyond.* New York: Guilford.

Beck, J. S., Beck, A. T., & Jolly, J. B. (2005). *Beck Youth Inventories* (2nd ed.). San Antonia, TX: Harcourt Assessment.

Cash, T. F., & Pruzinsky, T. (Eds.). (2002). *Body image: A handbook of theory, research, and clinical practice.* New York: Guilford.

Conners, R. E. (2000). *Self-injury: Psychotherapy with people who engage in self-inflicted violence.* Northvale, NJ: Jason Aronson.

Favazza, A. (1987). *Bodies under siege.* Baltimore, MD: Johns Hopkins University Press.

Favazza, A. (1996). *Bodies under siege* (2nd ed.). Baltimore, MD: Johns Hopkins University Press.

Foa, E. B., Keane, T. M., & Friedman, M. J. (Eds.). (2000). *Effective treatments for PTSD.* New York: Guilford.

Freeman, A., & Rigby, A. (2003). Personality disorders among children and adolescents: Is it an unlikely diagnosis? In M. A. Reinecke, F. M. Dattilio, & A. Freeman (Eds.), *Cognitive therapy with children and adolescents* (2nd ed., pp. 434–464). New York: Guilford.

Greenwald, R., & Rubin, A. (1999). Brief assessment of children's post-traumatic symptoms: Development and preliminary validation of parent and child scales. *Research on Social Work Practice, 9,* 61–75.

Hyman, J. (1999). *Women living with self-injury.* Philadelphia: Temple University Press.

Jones, A. B. (1980). *If I don't try, I can't fail.* [Newsletter]. Decatur, AL: Decatur Mental Health Association.

Jones, A. B. (1998, Spring-Summer). Treatment of self-injurious behavior: Part I: What is SIB? *Healing Magazine.* Orefield, PA: KidsPeace.

Kassam-Adams, N., Baxt, C., & Shrivastava, N. (2003, October). *Development of the acute stress checklist for children (ASC-Kids).* Poster presented at the 19th Annual Meeting of the International Society of Traumatic Stress Studies, Chicago, IL.

Kluft, R. P. (personal communication, circa March 14, 1996).

Linehan, M. M.(1993). *Skills training manual for treating borderline personality disorder.* New York: Guilford.

March, J. (1999). Assessment of pediatric Post-traumatic stress disorder. In P. Saigh & J. Bremner (Eds.), *Post-traumatic stress disorder* (pp. 199–218). Boston: Allyn & Bacon.

Reynolds, C. R., & Kamphaus, R. W. (2002). *The clinician's guide to the behavior assessment system for children (BASC).* New York: Guilford.

Rothschild, B. (2000). *The body remembers: The psychophysiology of trauma and trauma treatment.* New York: W.W. Norton.

Sakheim, D. K. (personal communication, circa June 13, 1992).

Simeon, D., & Hollander, E. (2001) *Self-injurious behaviors: Assessment and treatment.* Washington, DC: American Psychiatric Publishing.

Strong, M. (1998). A *Bright Red Scream: Self-mutilation and the language of pain.* New York: Viking.

Tomkins, S. S. (1992, Rev. ed.). *Affect, imagery and consciousness: Cognition: duplication and transformation of information (affect, imagery, consciousness)* (Rev ed.). New York: Gaunt.

Trautmann, K., & Conners, R. (1994). *Understanding self-injury: A workbook for adults.* Pittsburgh: Pittsburgh Action Against Rape.

Walsh, B. W. (2006). Treating self-injury: A practical guide. New York: Guilford.

Walsh, B. W., & Rosen, P. M. (1985). Self-mutilation and contagion: An empirical test. *American Journal of Psychiatry, 141,* 119–120.

Wolpe, J. (1985). *The practice of behavior therapy* (2nd ed.). New York: Pergamon.

Woodward, B., & Bernstein, C. (1994) *All the president's men* (2nd ed.). Simon and Schuster.

Yalom, I. D. (1985). *The theory and practice of group psychotherapy* (3rd ed.). New York: Basic Books.

Yates, T. M. (2004). The developmental psychopathology of self-injurious behavior: Compensatory regulation in posttraumatic adaptation. *Clinical Psychology Review 24,* 35–74.

Chapter Twenty-One

Guided Social Stories: Group Treatment of Adolescents with Asperger's Disorder in the Schools

Andrew Livanis, Esther R. Solomon, & Daniel H. Ingram

The inclusion of the diagnosis of Asperger's Disorder (AS) in the *DSM-IV* (American Psychiatric Association, 1994) has allowed for more formal investigations of the etiology and prognosis of this disorder. These investigations raised new issues, which will probably dominate research for years to come. One of the issues raised is the need for comprehensive treatment programs for children who meet the diagnostic criteria for this disorder. School personnel, in particular, have had to develop and design treatment procedures for children diagnosed with AS in order to meet their academic, social, and behavioral needs in the schools. Although the bulk of commonly used researched treatment procedures are designed to target the needs of an individual child (Lorimer, Simpson, Myles, & Ganz, 2002; Kuttler, Myles, & Carlson, 1998), there exist very few manualized treatment procedures for the group treatment of AS. A review of current literature shows some promising pilot work by Hetzke (2004) and Barsky (2002); nevertheless, the development and research of group treatment approaches for children diagnosed with AS is at a nascent stage. This chapter will discuss the development and implementation of the *Guided Social Stories* curriculum for adolescents with Autism (AU) and AS. This curriculum has its roots in several research bodies and prior clinical applications.

Research has identified that children with AS and AU have unique neuropsychological profiles that may alternately include difficulties with memory, executive functions, and attention. Therefore, traditional "talk" therapies may not be as effective as is hoped, and may require modifications. Several authors have documented that children with AS and AU tend to show preoccupations with specific topics or areas of interest and will often read excessively on these topics (Wagner, 2002; Bollick, 2001), although there is often very little attempt to incorporate these interests or their manner of data collection (i.e., reading) into social curricula (Moyes, 2002). Therefore, *Guided Social Stories* was designed to work on the interests that children with these profiles exhibited. One clinical method that has been developed for use individually with children diagnosed with AS is the technique of social stories (Gray, 2000). The main character of a social story is the child targeted for support, and the main purpose is to demonstrate the child performing pro-social behaviors successfully.

The use of social stories has been reviewed in several case studies throughout the literature (Lorimer, Simpson, Myles, & Ganz, 2002; Kuttler, Myles, & Carlson, 1998). In these studies, the social story technique was used effectively in an individual situation with children that evidenced a lack of prosocial behaviors and/or a preponderance of oppositional behaviors. However, using this type of individualized intervention is not always easily accomplished in school settings, as it can be time consuming and labor intensive. We hoped to develop in *Guided Social Stories* a more time-efficient method that can be delivered to groups of children who display similar social issues.

Finally, since the students would be asked to use their reading skills during the intervention, reading interventions would be incorporated in order to ensure that the children would benefit as much as possible. Applied behavioral analytic research on the technique of guided notes and active student responses (Heward, 1994) indicates that handouts can be a powerful learning tool, if they include some form of active student participation (i.e., some form of writing). Thus, all these issues must be considered when considering group interventions with AU and AS populations.

OVERVIEW OF PRESENTING PROBLEMS

According to the *DSM-IV-TR*, the diagnostic criteria for AS include (1) severe and sustained impairment in social interaction and (2) the development of restricted, repetitive patterns of behavior, interests and activities (American Psychiatric Association, 2000). The *DSM-IV-TR* further suggests that, in contrast to AU, children with AS display no clinically significant delays or deviance in language acquisition, as well as no delays in cognitive development, which presumes at least average intelligence. This statement has often been misunderstood since children with AS (as well as children with AU who have developed age-appropriate verbal skills through early intervention efforts) generally display difficulties with pragmatic language skills, such as eye contact and listener proximity during discussions. Pragmatic language deficits often cause considerable emotional and social difficulties for children diagnosed with both AU and AS. These difficulties occur due to their appropriate (often better-than-average) semantic and syntactic skills that deceive others into expecting social skills at a level better than other children.

Pragmatic Language Issues and Social Difficulties

One of the symptoms for Asperger's Disorder listed in the *DSM-IV-TR* (American Psychiatric Association, 2000) is the lack of delay in language during early development. However, as the child matures and begins regular exposure to same-age peers (such as in pre-school or in daycare), social difficulties with peers, as well as pragmatic language difficulties, become more and more apparent (American Psychiatric Association, 2000). The difficulties in acquiring the rules necessary to guide language across various social environments are known as pragmatic language difficulties (Landa, 2000). These issues often lead to a variety of social problems commonly seen in children diagnosed with AS.

Landa (2000) reports the use of signals to moderate discussions is an issue. A signal is a verbal or nonverbal cue that is meant to moderate or modify conversations and discussions. For example, we have noticed that eye contact is a problem for children with AS and it impairs their ability to initiate and maintain conversations with others. Indeed, Mundy, Sigman, Ungerer, and Sherman (1986) noted that individuals with AS tend to misunderstand how gaze can be used in a functional fashion during social situations.

Another area that appears to be problematic is the lack of understanding of subtle verbal and nonverbal cues, which signifies to the child's partner their internal wishes or desires (Wing & Attwood, 1987). For example, children with AS often have difficulty identifying when someone has tired of their conversations. This often leads to repeatedly initiating and maintaining topics of interest without regard for the listener's interest in the topic.

Furthermore, difficulties understanding the rules of convention in certain situations can lead to embarrassing or awkward behaviors or displays of intention (Landa, 2000). For example, we have noted many times when a child with AS has announced out loud that he is bored with playing with another individual or has made comments about people's weight or age. Such opinions and observations are expressed by the child in a way that lacks a sense of social nuances and others may subsequently interpret the individual with AS as rude or not sensitive to others' feelings.

In essence, many of the pragmatic language difficulties noted above cause peers or others to misinterpret the child's actions. Those in their social environment may act with indifference or hostility towards the child with AS. The child may not necessarily understand or appreciate the underlying reasons for the environment's actions. Therefore, it has been proposed that direct instruction and practice of prosocial skills should be provided to help the child with AS acclimate to their greater social environment (McCaffe, 2002).

Neuropsychological Findings

Although the interventions for remedying the difficulties that children with AS experience may seem easy to implement, an emerging body of neuropsychological literature on AS may help inform the clinician of which features are necessary to improve treatment success. Many children with AS display issues with attention that interfere with focusing on the task that others in the environment may deem important (Klin, Sparrow, Marans, Carter, & Volkmar, 2000). In treatment, the clinician must be able to control the content of the work so that the child will be able to focus on the appropriate stimuli and learn effectively. Significant executive function issues may cause difficulties with the flexibility of responses, the inhibition of appropriate responses, and the ability to learn from new situations (Hale & Fiorello, 2004). Therefore, the clinician will need to take care to impose intense structure on sessions. The clinician will, moreover, need to explain and define issues, especially in situations when the child is asked to make inferences. Finally, clinicians must consider that the interventions will need to preplan for the generalization of skills. Impairments in behavioral fluency, memory, and word finding may cause difficulties as well (Boucher, 1988). The child with AS is likely to have difficulties fluently recalling verbal or nonverbal behaviors that will result in positive, desired effects. Therefore, repeated practice of skills will need to take place during these sessions to develop automaticity and fluency further.

Prevalence, Course, Comorbidity, and Associated Features of AS

There is a paucity of data available on the prevalence of AS, although there is some limited data available that documents a familial link (Ghaziuddin, Ghaziuddin, & Greden, 2002; American Psychiatric Association, 2000). Furthermore, there is evidence to suggest that AS is a life-long disorder, and thus, prognosis is probably partially dependant upon the individual's environment and its willingness to intervene in appropriate fashions (Ghaziuddin, 2002).

Ghaziuddin, Ghaziuddin, and Greden (2002), in their review of the literature, reported that about 40% of all referrals with a primary diagnosis of AS or AU show evidence of symptoms of other disorders. The authors, in this instance, warn that these reports are not based on community samples, but on small samples or case studies. Major depression was reported as having a high comorbidity with AS and AU. Among the reasons hypothesized for these symptoms are genetic factors, increased awareness of their disability (and subsequent differences when they compare themselves with their peers), and the propensity for social withdrawal (which in turn begins a negative spiral of decreased social reinforcement and avoidance of the environment).

Bejerot, Nylander, and Linstrom (2001) discussed the fact that several traits displayed by individuals with AS or AU are similar to symptoms exhibited by persons with Obsessive Compulsive Disorder (OCD). Indeed, one of the criteria for AS described by the *DSM-IV-TR* is the "restricted repetitive and stereotyped patterns of behavior, interests and activities" (American Psychiatric Association, 2000, p. 84). However, there are differences evident (Ghaziuddin et al., 2002), as individuals with AS often have sensory abnormalities and coordination difficulties, which are not common in individuals with OCD. Furthermore, while the symptoms cause worry and distress in individuals with OCD, individuals with AS or AU find these restricted and stereotyped behaviors to be pleasurable or anxiety reducing (Ghaziuddin et al., 2002).

Symptoms of hyperactivity and impulsivity are also common in AS. At times, parents, staff, and clinicians may feel that an additional diagnosis of ADHD is warranted. *The DSM-IV-TR* stipulates, however, that ADHD should not be diagnosed during the course of a Pervasive Developmental Disorder (American Psychological Association, 2000). Ghaziuddin and colleagues (2002) argue that this is unjustified. Neurological and neuropsychological research has indicated that the etiology of attentional difficulties in AS and ADHD are not always similar (Hale & Fiorello, 2004). Therefore, treatments for hyperactivity should involve intensive functional behavioral analyses before a diagnosis of ADHD is considered.

Individuals with AS often show an interest in developing and maintaining friendships, which is distinguished in *DSM-IV-TR* as a characteristic that differentiates children with AS from children with AU. However, this clear distinction is not always present clinically. One author (AL) has met many children diagnosed with AU or AS who have an interest in participating in social exchanges and who have been frustrated when the environment does not reciprocate their attempts. Qualitative studies such as the one conducted by Carrington, Templeton, and Papinczak (2003) can shed further light on the social world of children with AS from a student perspective. In general, they found that the children with AS interviewed all valued and desired friendship, though concepts such as reciprocity and the sharing of interests and ideas are not well understood by these children. They also found that the adolescents with AS interviewed lacked the insight into what constitutes friendship and they had difficulties using and understanding the language to describe friendship.

ASSESSMENT AND GROUP IDENTIFICATION

In our Guided Social Stories group, the children can be identified for group inclusion through a review of prior school psychological and educational evaluations. The distinction between educational classifications and *DSM-IV-TR* (2000) diagnosis must be considered at this point, as the educational classification of *Autism* corresponds to the diagnosis of Autistic Disorder. Although a diagnosis does not guarantee an educational classification, previous reports of children currently diagnosed with AU tended to include clear background information with recurrent diagnoses of AU across the child's history.

There exists no educational classification, however, that corresponds to the diagnosis of AS. The result of this is that students with a diagnosis of AS are assigned educational classifications which do not reflect the nature or intricacy of the disorder. For example, *Other Health Impaired, Multiple Disabilities,* and *Speech or Language Impaired* are often classifications applied to children diagnosed with AS. Hence, a formal diagnosis of AS may not necessarily be discussed in the students' previous files. Therefore, confirmation of an AS diagnosis may need to occur before the group is formed. This must be considered even in cases where AS was mentioned. Therefore, clinicians need to consider the presenting symptoms rather than simply looking at students' educational classifications.

Clinicians can then identify a group of students who are either currently diagnosed with AU or AS or who have demonstrated behaviors consistent with these disorders. Teacher and parent interviews should be conducted in order to gain a better understanding of the child's clinical history, previous social issues, and academic difficulties. Clinical observations and functional behavioral assessments (FBAs) are also used to collect further information as to current school-wide functioning.

Commercially developed assessment checklists, as well as therapist-designed checklists, can also be used to help identify specific problem behaviors. In this instance, we have used the *Krug Asperger's Disorder Index* (Krug & Arick, 2003), the *Gilliam Asperger's Disorder Scale* (Gilliam, 2001), and the *Asperger Syndrome Diagnostic Scale* (Myles, Bock, & Simpson, 2000). Once an overall diagnostic impression or diagnosis of AS or AU has been established, an assessment checklist targeting various social skills such as eye contact and conversational turn taking should be used. We have created our own checklist for administration to parents and teachers.

Asperger's Disorder or Autistic Disorder?

An issue that should be addressed when discussing assessment is whether the diagnostic construct of AS is different from AU. There have been to date a handful of studies investigating whether individuals with AU and AS differ on various measures. Ozonoff and Griffin (2000), for example, reviewed nine studies investigating the external validity of AS (when compared to AU). Four of the studies found higher overall IQ scores in the AS sample; however, Volkmar and Klin (2000) cautioned that there are no studies comparing cognitive profile differences of students with AU and AS when their overall IQ scores were controlled. Volkmar and Klin also discussed the fact that there are no systematic studies examining treatment efficacy or treatment approach for students with AS or AU.

Other researchers have proposed that the differences between AS and AU are neurologically based (Klin et al., 1995). The working hypothesis is that left hemisphere deficits lead to AU and right hemisphere deficits lead to AS; however, studies utilizing computerized scanning procedures have not consistently demonstrated this dichotomy (Lotspeich et al., 2004; El-Badri & Lewis, 1993; Jones & Kerwin, 1990). These contrasting results have led many clinicians, as well as researchers, to question if AS (Volkmar & Klin, 2000) is simply a "higher" form of AU or High Functioning Autism (HFA).

For the purposes of the Guided Social Stories intervention, we grouped students with diagnoses of AS and AU together, based on the nature of their difficulties rather than diagnosis. Although a diagnosis of AU, AS, or Pervasive Developmental Disorder, Not Otherwise Specified (PDD-NOS) facilitated initial placement into the *Guided Social Stories* program, no differentiation was made on the bases of diagnosis. Instead, treatment followed different courses based on the strengths and needs of the students regardless of specific diagnosis.

COGNITIVE-BEHAVIORAL THERAPEUTIC CONCEPTUALIZATION OF THE PROBLEM

In essence, it appears that both the environment and the child with AS misunderstand one another. The AS child's unique neurological and neuropsychological profile is characterized by variable attention levels, poor memory for behavioral sequences, and a lack of an organizing framework for interpreting both internal and external environments. Two consequences occur: (1) not only does the child with AS misinterpret his or her environment, but (2) his or her actions can cause the environment to characterize the child with AS as "rude," "oppositional," "stubborn," "unfriendly," and "inappropriate." These characterizations often lead the environment to act indifferently or in a hostile manner towards the child with AS. The ironic aspect is that the child with AS then begins to *correctly* interpret the environment as uncaring, hostile, or rejecting.

These never-ending cycles usually begin around the time the need for increased social activity begins for the child (near preschool age). Both the environment and the child often begin a negative spiral in which each interprets the others' actions as negative. The child with AS may begin to react to this difficult situation through active measures (e.g., fighting with others, physical actions) or via passive measures (e.g., withdrawing from the others or escaping activities).

It is important for school staff to understand that that the topography of the behaviors does not infer the function of the behaviors. The function of both of these types of responses can be considered as negatively reinforcing. The child may engage in active behaviors in the hope that these behaviors will change his or her social environment and reduce the hostile cycle in some way. Or, the child may withdraw from the world in the hope that changing his social environment (to an environment with no social stimuli) will reduce the hostile cycle. It should be noted that later these same behaviors might serve other functions as well, though the initial function of the behaviors that school personnel find problematic is that of negative reinforcement.

Another point that should be considered is that the child with AS has decreased self-efficacy in his or her ability to engage in "prosocial" skills. Many children with AS do not believe they can initiate and maintain the behaviors necessary for them to succeed socially. Furthermore, there may have been interventions in the past to teach prosocial signals, but their direct function or purpose was not clearly explained to them. For example, many of the students have exclaimed to us (AL and ES), "What's the big deal about eye contact anyhow?" "How does that help you make friends?" A critical component that needs to be included in an intervention is the inclusion of how this skill relates to the overall goal of initiating and maintaining pleasing social exchanges.

The solution we propose is one that consists of direct instruction and practice of prosocial skills necessary to help the child with AS acclimate to the greater social environment. What is even more important is that we hope to convey to the child the concept that there are less extreme methods to achieve the goal of changing the environment than the behaviors in which the child had been engaging. Essentially, the *Guided Social Stories* curriculum is helpful in teaching alternate behavioral repertoires, their function, and reinforcing the repertoires and their functions through coping-emotive models, as well as *in vitro* and *in vivo* practice.

GROUP TREATMENT USING GUIDED SOCIAL STORIES

Ideally, the clinician will work with the sociobehavioral and pragmatic language issues of AS in their work with children. Initially, we suggest targeting pragmatic language issues, including the lack of use of signals, as well as the lack of awareness of conversational cues, as these skills would need to be taught directly to the students. This conceptualization is not new and has been advocated by many (McAfee, 2002; Myles & Simpson, 2001; Gray, 2000). However, neuropsychological findings and clinical observations would further need to be considered when determining how these skills would be taught to children with AS.

Cognitive Functioning and Reading Development

One criteria for AS in the *DSM-IV-TR* is the lack of intellectual deficits (American Psychiatric Association, 2000). Hans Asperger described these children as "little professors" (Attwood, 1997). Therefore, material used should be age-appropriate, at a level the students should be able to comprehend.

Children with AS often exhibit strengths in reading decoding skills, yet they may exhibit weaknesses in reading comprehension skills (Myles & Simpson, 2001). We have found that although some children with AS may have difficulties with reading comprehension of age-appropriate materials, they often enjoy reading and will seek out reading material that closely approximates their reading comprehension skills. In general, two of the authors (AL and ES) found that children diagnosed with AS will spontaneously read magazines and books when provided a range of themes. A theme children with AS appear to be drawn to is that of the child who is rejected because he or she is somehow different. Another common theme of interest is a mysterious problem that needs to be solved. The characters often solve this mystery with a sense of determination and use of logic (in essence, the main characters need to become little professors and apply the scientific method). For example, the popular Harry Potter series is about an orphan who is disliked by his family but later is found to have a special gift. He then must learn to apply this gift judiciously and systematically in order to solve many mysteries along the way.

Our clinical observations suggest that children with AS enjoy reading passages that contain themes of alienation and mystery, and many children with AS have pointed out the characters' difficulties are similar to their own. They identify readily with characters that experience these issues and enjoy complex story lines.

Attention Issues

As was noted above, children with AS often have difficulties attending to stimuli that others in the environment find important. Therefore, it will be necessary to present highly structured activities in which their interests will be captured and held. Literary characters, such as Harry Potter, offer children with AS a model of a child who struggles in his environment. It appears that children with AS are drawn to models that are similar to themselves. Schunk (1987) indicates that a similarity to a model that one is exposed to is useful in identifying appropriate behaviors, as well as in forming beliefs about those behaviors. Furthermore, the model and the consequences he or she experiences should convey information about the function or importance for the child (Schunk 1987; Zimmerman & Koussa, 1975; Akamatsu & Thelen, 1974). During our interventions, we strived to portray models that present thoughts, feelings, and behaviors that are similar to the AS students with whom we work and whose actions convey functional information about proposed change behaviors (i.e., the models presented often convey information as to why it is important to engage in the behavioral changes).

Another area of importance that needs to be targeted is the child's self-efficacy or his or her belief about his or her capabilities to perform consistently the overt and covert behaviors that will be effective (Bandura, 1997). This belief is affected by the child's successes and failures. The assumption is that children with AS have experienced a great many failures in the social arena; therefore, they have developed low self-efficacy and an internal belief that they cannot engage in particular actions to initiate and maintain social interactions.

Schunk and Hanson (1989) identified coping-emotive models that lead to high rates of self-efficacy for learning. A model that is considered coping-emotive initially portrays distress and experiences difficulties while attempting to display target behaviors. The models then used successive approximations to acquire the targeted behavior and eventually performed the behavior at perfect or near-perfect rates. During this approximation process, the models verbalized positive coping statements, coupled with realistic interpretations of the task (e.g., "I know that this is hard, but I'm starting to understand it, and if I put in some more work, I will understand it even more.").

Therefore, the passages that were presented to the students with AS used other students who also struggle to master various prosocial behaviors. For instance, during stories revolving around appropriate eye contact, the main character identified this as a problem, noted the skill is hard to master, doubts if he can master the skill, and then, progressively shows surprise and satisfaction as he slowly attains the skill. Furthermore, the model questioned school staff members as to why he needed to maintain appropriate eye contact and obtained several functional answers (i.e., the skill is a signal to others that you are ready and willing to initiate and maintain communication).

Executive Functioning and Fluency Issues

One technique that has been used for some time with children identified with AS is social stories (Gray, 2000). A social story is an individualized short story that can be used to help children with AS deal with stressful situations in a constructive way (Sanosti, Powell-Smith, & Kincaid, 2004). Although there have been guidelines as to the types and quantities of sentences that need to be included in each type of social story (Gray, 2000; Gray & Garand, 1993), Sanosti and colleagues (2004) point out that component analyses of social stories have not been conducted, so these guidelines should be taken as suggestions rather than rules. Furthermore, although one recent study has identified a case where the targeted behaviors were maintained even when the social stories were removed (Adams, Gouvousis, VanLue, & Waldron, 2004), poor generalization and maintenance has been noted (Sanosti et al, 2004). Nevertheless, positive results have been demonstrated for increasing life skills such as hand-washing (Hagiwara & Myles, 1999), communication skills (Adams et al., 2004), and appropriate social interactions (Norris & Dattilo, 1999), as well as decreasing disruptive behaviors (Scattone, Wilczynski, Edwards, & Rabian, 2002), and tantrum behaviors (Lorimer, Simpson, Myles, & Ganz, 2002; Kuttler, Myles & Carlson, 1998) in school settings.

In our setting, however, various modifications were made to the social stories design. The first modification was made because groups of children, who had been diagnosed with AS as well as AU, would be targeted. Therefore, the overly individualistic nature of the social stories paradigm might not be beneficial with groups. Instead, social stories were created using coping-emotive models, which incorporated issues, problems, and difficulties that all or most of the children with AS and AU had experienced in the past. Furthermore, the difficulties were framed as "mysteries," where the main character needed to apply the scientific method to solve his or her problems.

Second, the guidelines that were delineated by Gray and Garand (1993) were not used since there were no components analyses that indicated which guidelines (if any) were necessary. Finally, a modification was made based on the applied behavioral analytic literature concerning the concept of active student responses during learning phases (Heward, 1994). Active student responses refer to modifying the learning environment so that the student must maintain an ongoing relationship with the material that he or she is learning. For example, a coordinated set of activities is programmed and introduced into the group session, so as to promote conceptual understanding of material. The student is then provided immediate feedback by staff and by other students through discussion of the materials and their responses. One method of ensuring active student responses described by Heward (1994) is the technique of guided notes, which are teacher-designed handouts with designated areas where the child can write key points. This technique has been used successfully with populations including incarcerated adolescents (Hamilton, Seibert, Gardner, & Talbert-Johnson, 2000), college students with learning disabilities (Lazarus, 1994), and children with mild disabilities (Boyle, 2001). The use of guided notes appears to have improved the rate and amount of learning outcomes in program.

The *Guided Social Stories* curriculum was designed to elicit active student responses during each and every presentation. A story was presented that dealt with a specific skill (e.g., eye contact within a classroom). Within that story, cloze passages were included. The answers for all the cloze passages were found within the story and no inferential reasoning or rewording was necessary. Furthermore, embedded between the cloze passages were additional passages that developed inferential themes and summarized key points (e.g., functional reasons to engage in the skill).

Strategies to Promote Generalization

The stories in the *Guided Social Stories* curriculum were designed to revolve around particular topics, as well as deliver a coordinated set of activities to promote *in vivo* practice. Our desire was to place children in groups and develop a systematized, yet flexible method for delivering these interventions. Our search for viable flexible approaches to delivering these interventions led us to explore the modular cognitive-behavioral therapeutic approach described by Curry and Reinecke (2003). In the modular approach to therapy, sets of skills are arranged in "modules," each of which presents a distinct set of skills. For example, a set of five *Guided Social Stories* and behavioral activities were arranged around the topic of eye contact. This modular approach allows for the selection of modules to match the specific needs of the group, and allows the clinician freedom to create groups based on particular sets of difficulties or problems.

Another advantage noted by Curry and Reinecke (2003) is that the modular approach is useful in addressing comorbidity. As was noted above, children with diagnoses of AS or AU often have comorbid anxiety or depressive disorders. The modular therapeutic approach allows for the development of guided social story modules to target behaviors and cognitive distortions (i.e., systematic misinterpretations of the environment) that are associated with these comorbid disorders.

Within each module, each story deviated slightly from one another in a direct attempt to promote the generalization of skills across settings. For example, in the eye contact module, stories focused on appropriate development of rules for eye contact with peers in one-on-one situations, in groups, and the teacher during class lessons. The appropriate amount of time to spend on eye contact was also discussed as well as when it was appropriate to terminate eye contact.

Group Format

Another difference that distinguishes the *Guided Social Stories* curriculum from traditional social stories is the option of group presentation. Indeed, the group format is an ideal place where students can practice behavioral skills, as well as observe other students practicing these skills. Under focused and structured conditions, other group members can act as models as they struggle together to attain a skill. The sense of group cohesion is intensified as they all discover that the model displays difficulties similar to their own, and they display difficulties similar to one another.

Table 21.1   Organization of a Guided Social Story Session

1. Review of prior out-of-group behavioral experiment

2. Presentation of story

3. Silent reading

4. Discussion of the story and topics

5. Review of responses to the cloze passages

6. Presentation of in-group behavioral experiment

7. Assignment of out-of-group behavioral experiment (i.e., homework)

During a group session, individual group members read the story and then discussed its content. The group leader explored with the group similarities between the story and prior experiences of individual group members (in reality, the stories were designed to be similar to situations described by their teachers or parents). The correct answers were then reviewed (the guided notes), and corrective feedback by the group leader as well as the group members was given in response to errors. Finally, a behavioral activity was designed to help practice the skill. For example, throughout the eye contact module, students were asked to observe and comment about the group leader and a confederate giving eye contact and other group members interacting and giving eye contact.

OVERCOMING POTENTIAL OBSTACLES

Implementing appropriate therapeutic interventions is quite challenging for the clinician. Due to the nature of AS, it is often quite difficult to structure meaningful interactions where children with AS can observe and learn new and difficult social skills. There is always the risk that the targeted child or children will not attend to the points that are presented. Therefore, it is important to have a structure in mind that will facilitate attention to the points that the clinician is interested in targeting.

Moreover, even if the clinician has taken the necessary steps to present an adequate structure, many of the students that we have worked with have experienced difficulty recalling the information they have learned. It is our experience that repetition of material is sometimes necessary, and repeated behavioral practice sessions are likely needed to ensure proper mastery of the material.

The social difficulties that many of the children experience may also cause problems when working with groups of children diagnosed with AS. Due to the history of strained social interactions, children with AS may be primed to view the bulk of their experiences with peers their age as negative and may react with behaviors that are escape or avoidance motivated and have been maintained through negative reinforcement. The group leader should anticipate that the child may "forget" to come for group or arrive late. Furthermore, once in the therapist's office, the child may choose to engage in some other activity that is solitary (e.g., playing a game on the computer or reading) rather than participating in the activities the group leader has planned. At times, we have seen children who have actively participated in groups and have appeared to enjoy themselves only later to complain to their parents that the group was a horrible experience and demand removal from future group activities.

These issues need to be dealt with sensitively and the therapist should always keep in mind the function of these behaviors (i.e., the behaviors have been negatively reinforced in the past, due to long histories of miscommunication between the environment and the child). Initially, it is a good idea to establish a positive and open working relationship with the parents of the children involved and to educate them as to how CBT conceptualizes the difficulties. Then, it is always a good idea to begin the first few sessions with a gradual shaping of social behaviors. For example, an individual child could initially engage in activities such as playing with computers or reading books as long as he or she announces the activity to the other children. Afterward, it would be a good idea to present a game or activity that all the children enjoy and incorporate that into the sessions. Gradually, the children would be presented with the *Guided Social Stories* curriculum during the initial part of the session and then reinforce their cooperation with the *Guided Social Stories* curriculum by having them engage in games or activities that were identified as pleasurable. In this way the children will be reinforced or rewarded for engaging in a social activity. Eventually, the bulk of the session would focus on the *Guided Social Stories* Curriculum.

The language the group leader uses should also be monitored extensively. There is always a risk that when the group leader deviates from the script or "improvises" he or she will use a word or phrase that requires an extensive amount of inferencing on the part of the child. A notable example is the use of metaphors during discourse. The presentation of metaphorical phrases may lead the child to not fully understand the content of the message or, more importantly, misunderstand the message altogether. The clinician would do well to preplan his or her statements in order to minimize the amount of inferencing that would be presented.

CASE EXAMPLE

A case example is provided to detail the effectiveness of one particular module (i.e., eye contact) with four students who participated in group counseling. These four students are presented as they exhibit the effectiveness of the *Guided Social Stories* curriculum across differing reading levels, as well as differing diagnoses. Furthermore, as will be demonstrated, parental involvement affected the outcomes significantly.

Students

The students in this group all attend a suburban middle school and have been classified as children with disabilities. All students received a variety of special educational services and received at least part of their education in self-contained settings. Their parents and teachers were contacted early in the year and asked to complete a therapist-generated questionnaire, which asked them to rate the students on a variety of social skills, including eye contact and conversational turn taking skills. Furthermore, their parents were asked to give their consent for participation in the group intervention, as well as to identify their agreement with the goals and methodology.

Alexander. Alexander is a 13-year-old boy who has a diagnosis of Autism. Alexander's history of communication difficulties was well documented throughout his preschool years (e.g., he did not speak until he was 5 years old and after years of intensive home services). Alexander's reading ability, as measured by standardized assessments, was at least 3 to 4 years above grade level. Before group counseling was initiated, Alexander discussed with the group leader his desire to make friends, though he noted that he did not know how to make friends. The group leader discussed that making friends is a multistep process and that the group was designed to help him develop friendships. Alexander's parents were contacted regarding this group and agreed to the purpose and methodology. They indicated that Alexander engaged in appropriate eye contact at about 30% of the time, and his teachers gave him an average rating of 34%.

Jack. Jack is a 12-year-old boy who was diagnosed with Asperger's Disorder when he was 8 years old. Jack's reading level, as identified by standardized assessments, was at least 2 to 3 years above grade level. Jack recognized that friendships were important and realized he would eventually want to have friends, yet stated he felt that the process was "too difficult" for him to undertake. He and the group leader developed a contract and agreed the group leader would help him develop friendships. Jack's parents were contacted and were in agreement with the proposed group. They indicated that Jack exhibited appropriate eye contact with others 40% of the time, and his teachers gave him an average rating of 38%.

Gus. Gus is a 12-year-old boy who was diagnosed with Asperger's Disorder when he was 7 years old. In addition to his social difficulties, standardized assessment instruments estimated Gus's reading comprehension skills to be significantly below grade level (at least 5 to 6 years below age level). However, his decoding skills were grade appropriate. Despite his reading issues, Gus enjoyed reading comic books and made many attempts to engage in reading. Additionally, his teacher began an intensive reading program, which has shown some short-term benefits. Gus identified that he wanted friends; however, he was unable to figure out how to establish a friendship. Gus's parents were contacted regarding this group, and while they agreed to reluctantly agreed to participation, they did not agree with the purpose and methodology of the group. They indicated that Gus already had mastered the skills the group would target, but noted that this counseling program was better than no counseling program at all. His parents indicated that Gus provided others with appropriate eye contact 85% of the time, while his teachers gave him an average rating of 20%.

Brendan. Brendan is a 14-year-old boy who was diagnosed with Pervasive Developmental Disorder—NOS when he was 4 years old. In addition to his social difficulties, Brendan's reading comprehension skills were estimated by standardized assessments to be significantly below grade level (at least 7 to 8 years below his typically developing peers). His reading decoding skills were found to be age appropriate. As was the case with Gus, Brendan's teacher also began an intensive remedial reading program that demonstrated some positive short-term gains. Brendan's parents were contacted regarding this group and agreed with the methodology as well as the purpose. His parents indicated that Brendan provided others with appropriate eye contact 35% of the time, while his teachers gave him an average rating of 42%.

Group Process

The students were seen for in-group counseling twice a week for the duration of the school year. For the first session, the students were allowed to bring their favorite activity to the therapist's office, such as preferred books or toys. During the second session, the group leader instituted a 3-minute rule in which the students were required to discuss their preferred items (i.e., similar to "show-and-tell"). Structured questions were introduced by the group leader to minimize the anxiety the students may have experienced during this activity. During the third session, the group leader added a popular board game he observed the students playing during lunchtime for half the session, and then, the students were required to discuss their preferred items with the group for the remainder of the session.

It was during the fourth session that the *Guided Social Stories* curriculum was introduced. The first story presented a character named Billy, who supposedly attended the same middle school quite some time ago and who had difficulties with his locker, for which he had to ask his teacher for help. This story was presented during the middle of September when locker issues were common with all the children in the group. This story was intended to introduce the main character and to prepare the students to focus on Billy's similar difficulties experienced by the group members. Indeed, discussions were guided to revolve around their similarities to Billy, such as his locker problem, his reaction to his inability to open the locker, his dislike of the crowds in the hallways, as well as the items he kept in his locker (they happened to be similar to the preferred items that the students brought into the therapeutic environment).

The *Guided Social Stories* curriculum for eye contact was introduced beginning in the fifth session. A list of the topic sequence for stories is presented below in Table 21.2. Accompanying the stories were activities in which the students were asked to observe

Table 21.2   Story Topics Included in the "Eye Contact" Module

Topic	Brief Description
1. Eye contact function	Billy identifies his problem. He wonders if he can ever have good eye contact. He asks adults in his school environment why it is important to have good eye contact. Based on the responses from staff and some thought he identifies the function of eye contact as conveying interest in others, and signaling the desire to start and maintain conversations. Billy is excited because he now understands.
2. Eye contact "empiricism"	Billy sets out to perform an "experiment" and observe reactions to varying degrees of eye contact. When he maintained his baseline eye contact, children gave him little to no attention—some even called him "rude." He voiced that he feels he cannot do this, and seeks help from the school psychologist. The two talk it over, and renewed with confidence he attempts changing the amount of eye contact—this time he stared at the child and never stopped. Other children called him weird. Eventually, through trial and error, he comes up with the "one sentence, one instance of eye contact" rule. Billy is excited because he has, for the first time, maintained good eye contact.
3. Rule modification	Billy's discussions with the speech therapist bring up the fact that eye contact is hard to hold, and somewhat tiring. His therapist points out that it is hard work and not easy, but the benefits outweigh the work that needs to be put in. They also talk about the need to change the rule in the previous story to adjust for eye contact with the teacher while she is giving a group lesson. Billy feels more confident about his eye contact skills, but he acknowledges that it is difficult.
4. Eye contact in others	Billy becomes upset when someone does not engage him in good eye contact. His teacher and he discuss this, and noted that not all children can maintain this skill—there may be other factors interfering. Billy reapproaches the other boy and realizes that he is quite sad about a fight he had with his mother this morning. Billy realizes that your emotional state may influence your eye contact behavior. Billy is finally getting a handle on eye contact.
5. Eye contact rewards	Billy is socially rewarded several times for maintaining good eye contact by his peers and by school staff (borrowing a pen from a peer, teacher pays more attention to his favorite subject). There are instances noted when he does not receive an award, and discussions with his paraprofessional revolve around the idea that eye contact will increase the chances that he will receive social rewards, but does not guarantee it.

the therapist and a confederate attempting to make and maintain appropriate eye contact, observe other peers initiate and hold eye contact, as well as their own attempts to make and hold eye contact while in a large group setting. When students were asked to observe the group leader or a confederate, care was taken to have the adult make a statement doubting his or her ability to adequately engage in appropriate eye contact, and then slowly making statements of increasing confidence, thus further presenting another coping-emotive model.

Homework assignments in which the students were to practice using appropriate eye contact were also assigned. The students were asked to write these assignments in their agendas (where all other academic homework assignments were copied), so that they could remember to practice this skill at home.

Some of the students, as noted above, evidenced poor reading comprehension skills, and it was necessary for the group leader to read the stories aloud to the students. Furthermore, the group leader also provided the answers on a dry erase board for the cloze passages and assisted the students in writing their answers in the appropriate places. A day or two later, the students with reading difficulties were asked if they could recall the essence of the story, and they were able to identify the main points of the story.

The eye contact module lasted 3 weeks, and subsequent modules were rewritten to incorporate reminders to maintain appropriate eye contact. In this way, although the skill was no longer directly taught, it was reviewed throughout the course of the group. Brief descriptions of the topics covered within the module (similar to those presented in Table 21.2) were also sent home to parents so that they could also review the material and reinforce the behaviors they were exhibiting at home.

An analysis of Figure 21.1 and Figure 21.2 indicates increases in eye contact for three of the four students presented. There are some promising findings in these data. This intervention appeared to be effective over time, and in fact, the skill appeared to increase over time. The intervention was used effectively to treat three individuals with similar disorders. Furthermore, at least one of the students who had reading difficulties still managed to evidence positive gains, which implies that grade appropriate reading skills may not be necessary.

Of all the children, Gus did not make any gains according to his parents, and actually regressed according to his teachers. As was noted above, Gus' parents were not in agreement with the purpose and methodology of the group, but reluctantly agreed to

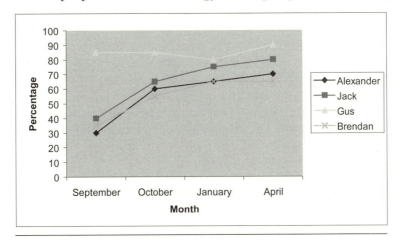

Figure 21.1   Parent Ratings of Percentage of Eye Contact.

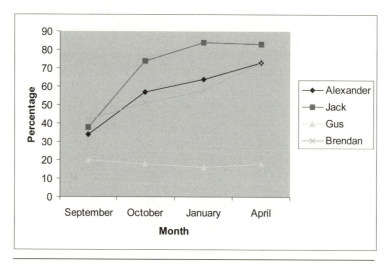

Figure 21.2   Teacher Average Ratings of Eye Contact Over Time.

have him participate. Although the group leader attempted to initiate further dialogue regarding this issue, his parents still did not fully agree to the need for the program.

Other parents not only had agreed with the purpose and methodology of the goals, but also actively sought to cooperate with the treatment to further results. Although specific activities were not assigned for parents in this procedure, the parents of each child remained in frequent contact with the group leader in order to ask what could be done at home to further the treatment. Parents alternately reported discussions of the *Guided Social Stories* curriculum at home, as well as during parent-initiated homework assignments targeting eye contact. These efforts by the parents may explain why increased eye contact appeared to "generalize" at home.

In retrospect, the group leader should have intervened with Gus in a different manner. However, his case highlights the need not only for parental cooperation, but also for their active participation in the treatment of children with AS and AU.

This case example highlighted the use of *Guided Social Stories* to increase eye contact in children with AS and AU. This technique, however, can be used for other skills, as well. Table 21.3 offers other suggested skill topics that could be addressed with this approach.

SUMMARY

AS is characterized by social difficulties, as well as repetitive and stereotyped patterns of behavior. It is challenging for school personnel to develop treatments for this disorder. It is complicated even further since there are few treatment options available. Ideally, school personnel would prefer delivering services within a group setting as it is more cost and time efficient; however, few treatments have been developed that use a group framework.

We hope the framework provided will be useful in practice, where several educational and psychological areas of research have been combined to institute a treatment.

Table 21.3   Examples of Other Guided Social Stories Modules and Examples of Story Topics

Modules	Examples of Story Topics
Vocal tone	How the inflection of various words within a sentence could convey different meanings; how additional information about message content should also be elicited from the other person's body language.
Vocal volume	The identification and implementation of appropriate volumes for the home, school, in large/small groups, and on the phone.
Appropriate listening	How asking questions can be for clarification and to let the other persons know that you are interested in their topics.
Conversational manners	The appropriate use of terms such as "please," "thank you," and "you're welcome," as well as how often these terms should be used.
Initiating conversations	Identification of who should be targeted for a conversation, what topics are appropriate for discussion, which areas are appropriate for discussion, and how all of these areas are relevant on context.
Maintaining conversations	Identification of how long the conversation should be based on the context and the individual, how to tell if the other person is interested in what you are saying, appropriate turn-taking skills.
Identifying negative feelings/moods	Identifying physiological indicators of negative feelings/moods. The focus is not on differentiating feelings, but on identifying bodily sensations (such as heart racing, clenched jaw, shaking legs) to give clues that a negative emotion is occurring.
Coping with negative feelings/moods	Various relaxation strategies are targeted especially those that can be implemented within the classroom setting such as progressive muscle tension and relaxation.

There are four guidelines that were used to develop the stories in the curriculum: (1) the stories should focus on the function of the behavior to be taught; (2) a coping-emotive model should be presented, as the main character should be similar to the children in the group and a systematic method or sequence to solving the problem should be used; (3) active student responses need to be elicited during the stories—in our curriculum we used cloze passages; and (4) structured behavioral practice during the session, as well as homework assignments, are necessary and are built into the structure of the curriculum.

An additional area that should be considered is parental agreement and cooperation. Our experiences have shown that it is often overlooked by school personnel that a collaborative relationship with parents can help in fostering positive results for the children with whom we work. It is important that cooperation, not just agreement, for treatment be sought. We included our own failure as an example to underscore this point. In the future, parental cooperation, in addition to the presentation of the *Guided Social Stories,* should be established.

The *Guided Social Stories* curriculum is presented as an innovative procedure for use with groups of children with AS. These procedures should be further examined by other professionals. Experimental control, even a single case study design, is often difficult to achieve in a school setting. Although experimental control was attempted in this study, adequate control was not used. As noted previously, the field is still in its beginning stages and many ideas will need to be experimentally explored before standardized treatment programs are established.

RECOMMENDED READINGS

Attwood, T. (1997). *Asperger's syndrome: A guide for parents and professionals.* London, UK: Jessica Kingsley.

Gray, C. (2000). *The new social stories book: Illustrated edition.* Arlington TX: Future Horizons.

Klin, A., Volkmar, F. R., & Sparrow, S. (2000). *Asperger syndrome.* New York: Guilford.

McCaffe, J. (2002). *Navigating the social world: A curriculum for individuals with Asperger's syndrome, high functioning autism and related disorders.* Arlington, TX: Future Horizons.

REFERENCES

Adams, L., Gouvousis, A., VanLue, M., & Waldron, C. (2004). Social story intervention: Improving communication skills in a child with an Autism Spectrum Disorder. *Focus on Autism and Other Developmental Disabilities, 19*(2), 87–94.

Akamatsu, T. J., & Thelen, M. H. (1974). A review of the literature on observer characteristics and imitation. *Developmental Psychology, 10,* 38–47.

American Psychiatric Association. (2000). *Diagnostic and statistical manual of mental disorders, text revision* (4th ed.). Washington, DC: Author.

Attwood, T. (1997). *Asperger's syndrome: A guide for parents and professionals.* London, UK: Jessica Kingsley.

Bandura, A. (1997). *Self-efficacy: The exercise of control.* New York: Freeman.

Barsky, S. J. (2002). A comprehensive treatment program for elementary students with Asperger's syndrome. *Dissertation Abstracts International, 63* (1-B).

Bejerot, S., Nylander, L., & Lindstrom E. (2001). Autistic traits in obsessive-compulsive disorder. *Nordic Journal of Psychiatry, 55*(3), 169–176.

Bollick, T. (2001). *Asperger syndrome and adolescence: Helping preteens and teens get ready for the real world.* Gloucester, MA: Fair Winds Press.

Boucher, J. (1988). Word fluency in high functioning autistic children. *Journal of Autism and Developmental Disorders, 18,* 637–646.

Boyle, J. R. (2001). Enhancing the note-taking skills of students with mild disabilities. *Intervention in the School and Clinic, 36*(4), 221–225.

Carrington, S., Templeton, E., & Papinczak, T. (2003). Adolescents with Asperger syndrome and perceptions of friendship. *Focus on Autism and other Developmental Disabilities, 18*(4), 211–218.

Curry, J. F., & Reinecke, M. A. (2003). Modular therapy with adolescents with major depression. In M. A. Reinecke, F. M. Dattilio, & A. Freeman (Eds.), *Cognitive therapy with children and adolescents: A casebook for clinical practice* (pp. 95–127). New York: Guilford.

El-Badri, S. M., & Lewis, M. A. (1993). Left hemisphere and cerebellar damage in Asperger's syndrome. *Irish Journal of Psychological Medicine, 10,* 22–23.

Ghaziuddin, M. (2002). Asperger syndrome: Associated psychiatric and medical conditions. *Focus on Autism and Developmental Disorders, 17*(3), 138–145.

Ghaziuddin, M., Ghaziuddin, N., & Greden, J. (2002). Depression in persons with Autism: Implications for research and clinical care. *Journal of Autism and Developmental Disorders, 32*(4), 299–306.

Gilliam, J. E. (2001). *Gilliam Asperger's disorder scale.* Austin, TX: Pro-Ed Incorporated.

Gray, C. (2000). *The new social stories book: Illustrated edition.* Arlington, TX: Future Horizons.

Gray, C. A., & Garand, J.D. (1993). Social stories: Improving responses of students with autism with accurate social information. *Focus on Autistic Behavior, 8*(1), 1–10

Hagiwara, T., & Myles, B. S. (1999). A multimedia social story intervention: Teaching skills to children with autism. *Focus on Autism and Other Developmental Disabilities, 14,* 82–95.

Hale, B., & Fiorello, C. (2004). *School neuropsychology.* New York: Guilford.

Hamilton, S. L., Seibert, M. A., Gardner, R., & Talbert-Johnson, C. (2000). Using guided notes to improve the academic achievement of incarcerated adolescents with learning and behavior problems. *Remedial and Special Education, 21*(3), 133–142.

Hetzke, J. D. (2004). A sibling-mediated social skills training intervention for children with Asperger's Syndrome: Results from a pilot study. *Dissertation Abstracts International, 65* (3-B).

Heward, W. L. (1994). Three low-tech strategies for increasing the frequency of active participant response during instruction. In R. Gardner, III, D. M. Sainato, J. O. Cooper, T. E. Heron, W. L. Heward, J. Eshelman, & T. A. Grossi (Eds.), *Behavior analysis in education: Focus on measurably superior instruction* (pp. 283–320). Pacific Grove, CAa: Brooks/Cole.

Jones, P. B., & Kerwin, R. W. (1990). Left temporal lobes damage in Asperger's syndrome. *British Journal of Psychiatry, 156,* 570–572.

Klin A., Sparrow, S .S., Marans, W. D., Carter, A., & Volkmar, F. R. (2000). Assessment Issues in children and adolescents with Asperger's Syndrome. In A. Klin, F. R. Volkmar, & S. Sparrow (Eds.), *Asperger syndrome* (pp. 125–155). New York: Guilford.

Klin, A., & Volkmar, F. R. (1996). The pervasive developmental disorders: Nosology and profiles of development. In S. Luthar, J. Burack, D. Cicchetti, & J. Wiesz (Eds.), *Developmental perspectives on risk and psychopathology* (pp. 208–226). New York: Cambridge.

Klin, A., Volkmar, F. R., Sparrow, S. S., Cicchetti, D. V., & Rourke, B. P. (1995). Validity and neuropsychological characterization of Asperger syndrome. *Journal of Child Psychology and Psychiatry, 36,* 1127–1140.

Krug, D. A., & Arick, J.,R. (2003). *Krug Asperger's disorder index.* Austin, TX: Pro-ed Incorporated.

Kuttler, S., Myles, B. S., & Carlson, J. K. (1998). The use of social stories to reduce precursors to tantrum behavior in a student with autism. *Focus on Autism and Other Developmental Disabilities, 13,* 176–182.

Landa, R. (2000). Social Language Use in Asperger Syndrome and High Functioning Autism. In A. Klin, F. R. Volkmar, & S. Sparrow (Eds.), *Asperger syndrome* (pp. 125–155). New York: Guilford.

Lazarus, B. D. (1994). Guided notes, review, and achievement of secondary students with learning disabilities in mainstream content courses. *Education and Treatment of Children, 14*(2), 112–128.

Lorimer, P. A., Simpson, R. L., Myles, B. S., & Ganz, J. B. (2002). The use of social stories as a preventative behavioral intervention in a home setting with a child with autism. *Journal of Positive Behavioral Interventions, 4,* 53–60.

Lotspeich, L., Kwon, H., Schumann, C. M., Fryer, S. L., Goodlin-Jones, B. L., Buonocore, M. H., Lammers, C. R. Amaral, D. G., & Reiss, A. L. (2004). Investigation of neuroanatomical differences between Autism and Asperger syndrome. *Archives of General Psychiatry, 61*(3), 291–298.

McAfee, J. (2002). *Navigating the social world: A curriculum for individuals with Asperger's syndrome, high functioning autism and related disorders.* Arlington, TX: Future Horizons.

Moyes, R. A. (2002). *Incorporating social goals in the classroom: A guide for teachers and parents of children with high functioning autism and Asperger syndrome.* London, UK: Jessica Kingsley.

Mundy, P., Sigman, M., Ungerer, J. A., & Sherman, T. (1986). Defining the social deficits in autism: The contribution of non-verbal communication measures. *Journal of Child Psychology and Psychiatry, 27,* 658–669.

Myles, B. S., Bock, S. J., & Simpson, R. L. (2001) Asperger syndrome diagnostic scale. Los Angeles, CA: Western Psychological Services.

Myles, B. S., & Simpson, R. S. (2001). Understanding the hidden curriculum: An essential social skill for children and youth with Asperger Syndrome. *Intervention in Schools and Clinic, 36*(5), 279–286.

Norris, C., & Dattilio, J. (1999). Evaluating effects of a social story intervention on a young girl with autism. *Focus on Autism and Other Developmental Disabilities, 14,* 180–186.

Ozonoff, S., & Griffith, E.,M. (2000). Neuropsychological function and the external validity of Asperger Syndrome. In A. Klin, F. R. Volkmar, & S. Sparrow (Eds.), *Asperger syndrome* (pp. 25–71). New York: Guilford.

Sanosti, F. J., Powell-Smith, K. A., & Kincaid, D. (2004). A research synthesis of social story interventions for children with autism spectrum disorders. *Focus on Autism and Other Developmental Disabilities, 19*(4), 194–204.

Scattone, D., Wilczynski, S. M., Edwards, R. P., & Rabian, B. (2002). Decreasing disruptive behaviors of children with autism using social stories. *Journal of Autism and Developmental Disorders, 32,* 535–543.

Schunk, D. H. (1987). Peer models and children's behavioral change. *Review of Educational Research, 57,* 149–74.

Schunk, D. A., & Hanson, A. R. (1989). Peer models: Influence on children's self-efficacy and achievement. *Journal of Educational Psychology, 77,* 313–322.

Volkmar, F. R., & Klin, A. (2000). Diagnostic Issues in Asperger Syndrome. In A. Klin, F. R. Volkmar, & S. Sparrow (Eds.), *Asperger syndrome* (pp. 72–96). New York: Guilford.

Wagner, S. (2002). *Inclusive programming for middle school students with autism/Asperger's syndrome.* Arlington, TX: Future Horizons

Wing, L., & Attwood, A. (1987). Syndromes of autism and atypical development. In D. J. Cohen & A. M. Donnellan (Eds.), *Handbook of autism and pervasive developmental disorders* (pp. 3–19). New York: Wiley.

Zimmerman, B. J., & Koussa, R. (1975). Sex factors in children's observational learning of value judgments of toys. *Sex Roles, 1,* 121–132.

Chapter Twenty-Two

Cognitive-Behavior Group Therapy with Children Who Are Ostracized or Socially Isolated

Kimberly Simmerman & Ray W. Christner

Cognitive-Behavior Therapy (CBT) groups with children who are socially isolated or ostracized have rarely been studied for their utility. Evidence suggests that problems such as social anxiety are most effectively treated in group settings (Freeman, Pretzer, Fleming, & Simon, 2004), and social skills training is nearly always completed utilizing other people as models to practice and generalize newly acquired skills (Segrin, 2003). CBT group therapy is an excellent adjunct to other therapeutic interventions, and has been shown to reduce social skill deficits in teenagers with a variety of other psychological disorders (Vickers, 2002). In one study, children with the primary diagnosis of social phobia participated in child-focused CBT groups, and relative to the control group, these children showed significant reductions in both social and general anxiety, which were maintained at a 12-month follow-up (Spence, Donovan, & Brechman-Toussaint, 2000). The researchers' findings also included that fewer children retained the diagnosis of social phobia following treatment, and that there was a trend (though not statistically significant) toward better outcomes if parental involvement was included.

CBT is an evidence-based, straightforward model built on the theory that all individuals operate from preconceived beliefs and assumptions about themselves, others, and the world. These "schemas" are often beyond the understanding and conscious thought of the individual, though they play a major role in shaping how the person interprets and responds to environmental stimuli (Freeman et al., 2004), and in the case of children who are ostracized or isolated, social encounters. Distorted interpretation of social situations can lead to avoidance or rejection by peers. For instance, a child may perceive that other children are actively avoiding him or her when they are actually simply engrossed in an activity.

There are several difficulties associated with childhood social withdrawal, such as poor social problem-solving skills (Harrist, Zaia, Bates, Dodge, & Pettit, 1997; Shure, 2006), aggressive behavior (Baumeister, Twenge, & Nuss, 2002), and later externalizing problems (Kuppersmidt & Cole, 1990). Students who were rejected by their peers are more likely to be suspended from high school, have police contacts, be truant or drop out of school, and are more likely to be retained than their peers (Kuppersmidt & Cole, 1990).

Socially withdrawn children are often not recognized by teachers or parents, especially at younger ages, as their behavior is rarely disruptive. However, the importance of early identification is evident in that socially isolative tendencies are more easily remediated in younger children relative to older children and adults (Adalbjarnardottir, 1995). This supports the notion that early identification and treatment may help socially isolated children learn to interact more effectively and meaningfully, eliminating some of the associated risk factors, and improving their interpersonal relationships and psychological well-being.

This chapter provides an overview of socially isolated and ostracized children, for the sake of highlighting the importance of working with this population of young people to improve skill deficits and overall functioning and well-being. A connection will be drawn between deficits in youth and adult functioning, as well as the possibility that difficulties for these youth will impact following generations. We will discuss the importance of assessing potential group members and considerations for inclusion in group therapy. We also offer a cognitive-behavioral conceptualization of the issues involved within this specific population and their treatment needs. Throughout this chapter, we often refer to these youth within the school setting, in that the educational environment is the largest social component in the lives of children and adolescents. Additionally, given that the school setting provides valuable information about the emotional, social, and behavioral functioning of all youth, and more specifically those who are socially isolated or ostracized, schools are a most likely venue in which to incorporate intervention. We then offer components of effective cognitive-behavioral treatment, with attention to potential obstacles for clinicians to consider to improve efficacy of intervention.

OVERVIEW OF OSTRACIZED OR SOCIALLY ISOLATED CHILDREN

Children who are socially withdrawn have hallmark characteristics that are of clinical interest, in that they tend to engage almost exclusively in passive or active solitary play and may appear shy or avoidant. Social withdrawal is a set of behaviors that tend to be reliably demonstrated and stable over time (Rapport et al., 2001), even from early childhood (Harrist et al., 1997). Several subtypes of social withdrawal have been identified for the purpose of differentiating between children who actively avoid playing with other children, those who want to play but are fearful or anxious, those who simply prefer not to play with others, and those who are rejected by their peers (Harrist et al., 1997). Other researchers have delineated the subtypes differently (e.g., Wasserstein, 1998) based on varying methods of appraisal, but the information relating to the Harrist (1997) subtypes is pertinent to this review. It is important to examine the nature of social withdrawal, as it may be suggestive of possible skill sets and interventions.

The type of withdrawal under which a child may be categorized has a role in determining risk level for later behavioral problems. For example, children who would rather not engage in social activities with other children may tend to have well-developed social skills but prefer not to use them. Similarly, children who are extremely shy and display signs of social anxiety or peer rejection have demonstrated that their social problem solving skills are poor relative to their same-aged peers (Harrist et al, 1997).

These deficits have been closely linked to later aggressive behaviors and aggressive responses to hypothetical social situations, a link that can be seen in very early childhood (Wood et al., 2002).

The most salient correlations over several studies (Wood et al., 2002; Leary et al., 2003; Rapport et al., 2001; Kupersmidt & Cole, 1990; Baumeister et al., 2002) suggest that peer rejection is the form of social withdrawal that is associated most frequently with comorbid aggressive behavior and predicts later aggressive behavior. Children who do not have ample social interactions, whether voluntary or involuntary, are at risk of failing to develop social problem-solving skills and moral judgment (Hart et al., 1998). Rejected children are more likely to behave aggressively than accepted, popular children (Baumeister et al., 2002). This may be because peer rejection adds the components of anxiety and anger. The combination of limited social interactions, anxiety, and anger may be foretelling of later violent behavior.

Kupersmidt and Cole (1990) studied preadolescent peer status as related to later externalizing behavior problems and found that rejected students were more likely to be suspended from high school than nonrejected students. In addition, they were three times more likely to have police contacts than average children, two times more likely to become truant, and disproportionately more likely to drop out of school or to be retained than other children. Even in this study, early childhood aggression, alone or with withdrawal, predicted later externalizing behavior problems more reliably than withdrawal alone (Kupersmidt & Cole, 1990).

Social Anxiety Disorder (SAD) is characterized by intense fear of ridicule and embarrassment in social situations leading to avoidance of feared situations. This disorder is rarely diagnosed in children, although the mean age of onset is age 15 and there may be apparent symptoms of extreme shyness as early as 21 months of age (Kagan, 1989). A single event in a child's life that is perceived as traumatic, such as public rejection, making a major mistake when presenting a speech in front of peers, or being bullied or victimized, may lead to a full expression of a predisposition for SAD (Albano & Barlow, 1996). The notion of predisposition suggests there may be biological or psychological characteristics within the individuals that make them more susceptible to social anxiety.

Calkins and Fox (2002) suggest that self-regulatory processes are important influences in personality development and behavioral adjustment, and that a specific deficit may be an underlying cause of social withdrawal. Claire Kopp (1989) proposed that emotional regulation facilitates healthy adaptation to the environment and allows learning and growth to occur. With exposure to the environment naturally come situations that cause emotional distress and anxiety. The ability to regulate natural emotional responses to environmental conditions helps determine the degree to which healthy coping strategies emerge.

Self-regulation is a child's ability to manage feelings, thoughts, and behaviors across a variety of physical and social contexts in a way that is adaptive and flexible (Volling et al., 2002). Optimal development of affective self-regulation requires repeated exposures to controllable challenges, which teach the child that there is often a delay between initial distress and satisfactory resolution (Perry, 2001). Baumeister and colleagues (2002) explained that an executive deficit in self-regulation might require one to devote more executive energy to stifling emotional responses associated with social withdrawal, thus robbing them of the executive resources required to engage in higher-level reasoning. Emotional stress can interfere with a child's cognitive functioning, and if too much of the child's energy is spent regulating his own behavior and feelings, their learning is interrupted (Gewertz, 2003; Lakes & Hoyt, 2004; Lengua, 2003; Weissberg et al., 2003). Children learn more effectively when they feel attached to their schools, peers, and teachers. Equipping them with social problem solving and self-regulation skills fosters that level of attachment and comfort and will facilitate their learning in general and, specifically, of skills related to interpersonal functioning.

When children who are socially withdrawn do not receive effective interventions to remediate skill deficits, there is a risk that their patterns of behavior may affect later generations. Social withdrawal and its associated behaviors may be passed down from parent to child through a variety of mediating factors. Retrospective studies have explored the connection between child-rearing practices and SAD, and have found that adults with the disorder recall their parents as fostering social avoidance and isolation by limiting social activities, even with close friends and family members (Bruch & Heimberg, 1994; Bruch, Heimberg, Berger, & Collins, 1989). Often, school personnel do not know the family dynamics that may have influenced the development of social withdrawal, so a better understanding of what to look for in children is warranted.

ASSESSMENT AND GROUP MEMBER IDENTIFICATION

Socially withdrawn children are often neglected (Adalbjarnardottir, 1995) when providing interventions, as they are often not disruptive or bothersome to others. The behaviors associated with social isolation or withdrawal are not those that typically attract the attention of adults, and children are often considered "shy." Harrist and colleagues (1997) found that teachers failed to rate children as socially withdrawn despite clinical evidence. This speaks to the importance of educating teachers about social skills and reciprocity, as well as warning signs that a student may require intervention. It is also beneficial to intervene as soon as a student is identified for social skills deficits, as social withdrawal is more stable and persistent in older children and more easily influenced and moderated in younger kids (Adalbjarnardottir, 1995).

In seeking to identify children who would benefit from intervention, it is noteworthy that a recent study found that children who are diagnosed with a learning disability are at greater risk for developing both behavior problems and deficits in social competence (McConaughty & Ritter, 1985). Boys with learning disabilities scored significantly lower than controls for their participation in activities, social contacts with organizations and friends, school performance, and total social competence. Children with learning disabilities are more likely to engage in behaviors, such as interrupting, that disrupt their ability to form meaningful relationships with nondisabled peers (Kam et al., 2004). A correlation between teacher and parent rating scales of behavior and learning disabilities (McConaughty & Ritter, 1985) suggests that children who have difficulty learning academic material in the same way as typically developing children may also struggle with learning the subtleties of social interaction.

To determine whether a child would be a good candidate for group intervention, clinicians should conduct a multidimensional assessment. This assessment should be used to gather data regarding the nature of the child's difficulties, social strengths and weaknesses, other behaviors, readiness for group involvement, and baseline functioning (to be used for progress monitoring). To gather this data, it is essential that clinicians use multiple sources including parents, teachers, and the child themselves. In addition, direct observations are a key aspect to good assessment.

Behavior-Ratings

There are a number of excellent behavior-rating scales available on the market. When selecting instruments, professionals should seek broadband measures, used to look at specific behaviors and competing behaviors, as well as narrow-band measures, designed to assess a specific aspect of emotional or behavioral functioning. This chapter does not permit an exhaustive review of all measures, though we highlight a few we have found useful in our practice.

The *Behavior Rating Inventory of Executive Functions* (BRIEF; Gioia, Isquith, Guy, & Kenworthy, 2000) is a rating scale specifically designed to assess executive function deficits. There are both teacher and parent rating scales, both taking about 10 to 15 minutes to complete. Recently, both a preschool version and self-report version were released to further enhance their utility. Many of the executive deficits assessed using the BRIEF scales have been noted deficient in children who are socially withdrawn. These include the inability to solve problems flexibly (Hart et al., 1998), modulate emotions (Kopp, 1989; & Baumeister et al., 2002), independently generate solutions to problems (Lease, 1995; & Adalbjarnardottir, 1995), or anticipate events, set goals, or develop a plan to complete a task (Hart et al., 1998). Calkins and Fox (2002) also noted that children who are socially withdrawn might also have difficulty monitoring their own behavior for efficacy and ascertaining how their behavior affects others.

Two excellent broadband instruments for assessing children include the *Child Behavior Checklist* (CBCL; Achenbach, 2001) and the *Behavior Assessment System for Children, Second Edition* (BASC-2; Reynolds & Kamphaus, 2004). Both have parent and teacher versions. The CBCL (and the Teacher Report Form, TRF) offer assessment of externalizing and internalizing symptoms including aggressive behavior, anxious and depressed symptoms, attention problems, rule-breaking behavior, social problems, somatic complaints, thought problems, and withdrawal. The BASC-2 provides a measure of various symptoms including aggression, anxiety, attention problems, atypicality, conduct problems, depression, hyperactivity, learning problems, and withdrawal. The BASC-2 also offers adaptive scales that provide useful information for counseling, including functional communication, leadership, social skills, study skills, and adaptability.

There are also several narrow-band scales that are useful to measure social skills and competence, as well as associated distress. Although many of these were generally developed for a different phenomenon than social withdrawal in children, they can provide useful information to the clinician (Kashdan & Herbert, 2001). For example, the *Fear Survey Schedule for Children Revised* (FSSC-R; Ollendick, 1983) identifies anxiety in children and can be applied to previous knowledge about the child to enhance the therapist's understanding. The *Social Phobia and Anxiety Inventory for Children* (SPAI-C; Beidel, Turner, & Morris, 1995) is a self-report scale that is sensitive to children's levels of distress in a variety of natural social settings. Therapists can use this data to differentiate between children with social anxiety and those with other disorders.

The *Beck Youth Inventories of Social and Emotional Adjustment, Second Edition* (BYI-II; Beck, Beck, & Jolly, 2001) have also been very useful. The BYI-II consists of individual scales including the Beck Depression Inventory for Youth (BDI-Y), the Beck Anxiety Inventory for Youth (BAI-Y), the Beck Anger Inventory for Youth (BANI-Y), the Beck Disruptive Behavior Inventory for Youth (BDBI-Y), and Beck Self-Concept Inventory for Youth (BSC-Y). The unique feature of the BYI-II is that clinicians can administer the combination booklet including all of the scales at the initial assessment, and then select specific scales necessary for progress monitoring. Each individual scale only requires 5 to 10 minutes to complete.

Observations

Observing behaviors in natural settings is a valuable tool when assessing children and adolescents for social withdrawal. Observations add a personal component to assessment that serves as a helpful adjunct to interviews, rating scales, and other measures. While traditionally clinicians conduct these observations in a classroom setting, for children who are socially withdrawn or isolated, it is essential to observe in settings that are more interactive, such as on the playground, in the hallway, or at lunch. Mennuti and Christner (2005) noted that schools are a "natural laboratory" for clinicians to observe interpersonal dynamics and to gather data about the problems facing students including antecedents, consequences, and general level of functioning. Freeman, Pretzer, Fleming, and Simon (2004) described another useful way to observe a child's behavior and gather data, which they referred to as an *in vivo* interview. This is when the therapist accompanies the child into a problem situation, while concurrently interviewing the child regarding thoughts, feelings, and so forth.

Interviews

Direct observations and behavior ratings scales are excellent ways of assessing and gathering data on children being considered for group. However, these means of data alone are not sufficient to determine if a child is appropriate for group intervention. The interview should be used for three main purposes: (1) clarifying the other information collected, (2) understanding the specifics of what happens in other settings, and (3) determining the child's readiness for group participation. Clinicians should additionally interview teachers and parents to obtain further clarification. There are a number of questions that can be asked of the child, including how they feel in social situations (e.g., at lunch), what they do with other children outside of school (e.g., being invited to birthday parties), how many friends they have, and how often and what they do with their peers. When working with socially isolated or withdrawn children, it is imperative that therapists ask about and discuss whether the child has been the victim of bullying at school or in the community. Other discussion should be geared to determine if the child is appropriate for group. This may include having them role-play a scenario, discussing their anxiety about group, talking about their goals, and determining their willingness to participate. In addition, we have found that when interviewing the individuals, providing them with the rationale and goals of the group, as well as working with them to develop what they would like to accomplish in group, provides a greater motivation. Also, allow time for the child to ask his or her questions about group or the process, and help him or her find ways to overcome any obstacles regarding group.

CBT CONCEPTUALIZATION OF THE PROBLEM

A CBT model for social withdrawal would include changing coping strategies from avoidant to active, such as thinking and planning solutions, and exploring and restructuring underlying beliefs that govern behavior. This shift in thinking can increase a person's sense of self-efficacy, thus enhancing psychological adjustment (Prins & Ollendick, 2003). Children who are socially isolated or ostracized may interpret the world around them based on distorted views of social interactions, such as the notion that people will remember their inadequacies, judge them for saying the wrong thing, or that any interaction will lead to humiliation. In some cases, some of the children's perceptions may have been accurate, especially in cases where the student has been bullied. Persistent avoidance of social situations, whether voluntary or involuntary, is reinforcing and never allows the individual to habituate to anxiety-provoking encounters (Kendall, Chu, Pimental, & Choudbury, 2000).

Following referral for problems with social interaction, the specific strengths and weaknesses of each child should be assessed and their cases conceptualized based on the CBT model. This process provides a clear picture of the child's problems, which in turn makes his or her behaviors more predictable and understandable (Freeman & Dattilio, 1992). The initial step in creating a case conceptualization is developing a problem list. By gathering information from the patient's developmental history, behaviors, and through a first-hand account, the therapist can form hypotheses about the schemas that govern the individual's behaviors (Freeman & Dattilio, 1992). Given the varied characteristics of socially isolated or ostracized children (Harrist et al., 1997), the treatment protocol and goals would have just as much variety. Once the specific problems are identified for each child, goals and specific strategies can be developed accordingly.

It is important for the therapist to explore the child's schemas and automatic thoughts that govern behaviors, feelings, and interpretations of events. It is important to ask the child to identify as many thoughts about a particular set of circumstances as necessary to better form hypotheses about the underlying schemas. For example, if a child identifies that he feels inept at initiating conversations, ask the child to identify automatic thoughts by asking something like, "What thoughts pop into your head when you want to walk over and say hello to someone?" The child's answers will lend insight into the governing beliefs, such as, "If I say the wrong thing, they'll laugh at me," or "I always have to have something to say or they won't like me." The therapist should share the hypotheses with the child to test for accuracy and to educate the child about the process and theory of CBT. The schemas can help the therapist, collaboratively with the child, to prioritize the problem list and guide which problem should be the primary focus of therapy (Freeman & Dattilio, 1992). If the child's schemas are indicative of severe social anxiety, this may first have to be treated individually to reduce the anxiety level in social situations before attempting group therapy, where the child could then practice and generalize what was developed individually.

Many children who are isolated or ostracized experience anxiety—either as the primary cause of their isolation, which is the case with SAD, or as a result of it, such as in the cases of peer rejection or underdeveloped social skills. Vasey and MacLeod (2001) found that anxious children tend to process information about the world incorrectly. They favor more threatening interpretations of ambiguity relative to their nonanxious peers, and they overestimate the likelihood of danger in the future. Anxious children also demonstrate enhanced memory for threatening information. Lundh and Sperling

(2002) found in their research on post-processing of socially distressing events that people who experience social anxiety process events in negative ways following the event. Such children, who are socially isolated are frequently anxious about interacting and looking foolish or experiencing rejection (Harrist et al., 1997), so they avoid social encounters in their entirety.

There are several aspects of development and the emersion of the ability to connect thoughts, feelings, and behavior that are noteworthy and will help therapists form a comprehensive case conceptualization. The social problem solving skills acquired through typical development involve strengthening executive capacity over time on progressively more complex tasks requiring cognitive flexibility. Adalbjarnardottir (1995) identified four steps individuals use to solve interpersonal problems: (1) definition of the problem, (2) generation of alternative strategies, (3) selection and implementation of a strategy, and (4) evaluation of the outcome. Each of the four steps requires some degree of executive functioning. He examined how well children who were withdrawn performed on these tasks (relative to control subjects) and found that more socially withdrawn children have deficits in many areas of executive functioning, especially perspective-taking ability. The withdrawn children also generate fewer and less complex alternative solutions to each social problem. The children are aware, on some level, of their inability to negotiate social situations effectively, which decreases their sense of self-efficacy (Lease, 1995). They also have lowered outcome expectations and fail to develop strategies to improve their success. The children may have already had negative social experiences due to their inability to understand and integrate the perspective of other participants (Adalbjarnardottir, 1995). This inability is highly correlated with peer rejection.

The generation and internalization of strategies for interacting meaningfully and advantageously in the environment in part depends on effective labeling and communication of feelings and thoughts and developing cognitive schemas related to cause and effect. Both cognitive deficits (Crnic, Hoffman, Gaze, & Edelbrock 2004) and language disorders (Greene & Doyle, 1999) can significantly affect the capacity to understand the benefits of affective self-regulation. Marlowe (2000) posits that "because language is so important in mediating cognition and behavior, children with aberrant language may have much greater difficulty in learning to predict the outcomes of activities and events, and they may fail to mediate their experiences with sufficient specificity" (p. 447). Verbal self-regulation is a critical achievement in regulating internal affective states (Kam et al., 2004; Cole, John-Steiner, Scribner & Souberman, 1978) and self-guided private speech according to Vygotsky (1986), is a sign that children are bringing their behavior under the control of thought. The ability to regulate emotions under psychosocial stress requires focusing attention to details of the situation and the ability to shift attention to less threatening aspects of the environment (Ayduk et al., 2000; Lengua, 2002). Quakley, Reynolds, and Coker (2004) found that children as young as four years old, with simple cues, could distinguish between thoughts, feelings, and behaviors.

Individual CBT can be effective with a variety of disorders, including those associated with decreased capacity for meaningful social interaction. Group treatment can also be introduced as a means of providing a forum to practice and enhance their social skills in a controlled, safe environment. Group treatment also helps reinforce social interaction by providing immediate feedback about what strategies result in successful outcomes. While there is not significant research on group treatment for socially isolated or ostracized youth, we offer a review of the literature that can be extrapolated for these groups.

GROUP TREATMENT

Harrist and colleagues (1997) delineated the different subtypes of social withdrawal, and each of these may require vastly different intervention. Individual characteristics of each child are an important consideration in forming CBT groups because in order for the group to be most effective, the children must be able to benefit from one another. For example, sad or depressed children may self-isolate, but they may not have stable deficits in executive functioning, such as lack of initiation or emotional modulation, once the depression is treated. Their participation in this type of group may be minimal, so other appropriate options such as individual psychotherapy or groups for depression may be more appropriate. Likewise, a child who is actively rejected by his peers may be socially isolated for poor impulse control, socially inappropriate behavior, and difficulty viewing social situations from another child's perspective. This can be irritating to other children, thus resulting in peer rejection (Harrist et al., 1997). Treatment for this type of child could involve cognitive and behavioral techniques to facilitate impulse control, as well as social skills training. Role playing, rehearsal of skills, increase in environmental structure, and providing the child opportunities to engage in small group activities to foster success are all appropriate treatments for such as child. Counselors would be wise to expose withdrawn children to controlled social encounters to allow them to practice their social skills (Adalbjarnardottir, 1995). A group therapy model would be well suited for this purpose.

Many withdrawn children have difficulty monitoring their behaviors for efficacy and they often do not take into account the effect their behaviors have on other children (Calkins & Fox, 2002). This requires that children be taught self-monitoring routines, which they learn through modeling and regular practice. Children may require external cues to self-regulate until it becomes more automatic. Social skills training helps children learn how to listen and look for the social cues from other people and choose an appropriate response that helps them to reach their goal in the social encounter (Segrin, 2003). A program can be modified and tailored to meet the particular needs of each child, and it can have specific goals based on each child's areas of skill deficit.

Ego-resiliency refers to cognitive flexibility or adaptability (Hart et al., 1998). Children who lack flexibility are likely to have unsuccessful social encounters, which may lead either to peer rejection or active avoidance of social situations. This isolation results in decreased opportunities to develop and practice social skills, thus perpetuating the problem. Increasing exposure to social experiences that enhance moral and social judgment may enhance moral reasoning (Hart et al., 1998). This development may in turn lead to heightened curiosity and insight, thus leading to more motivation to learn new social skills.

CBT groups should be carefully formed based on the characteristics of the participants. The cognitive ability and language development of each child should be considered (Freeman et al., 2004), and groups should be generally homogeneous so that all members can learn techniques on the same level of complexity. Children who have poor language skills may need to focus on more behavioral strategies, but children who are more advanced can learn complex cognitive techniques. The nature of each child's isolation is an important factor in that children who actively self-isolate but have adequate social skills require different intervention than children who require social skills training. Children in therapy groups should have similar goals (Freeman et al., 2004) so that they can learn from each other and identify with each other's experiences.

The connection between language and affective self-regulation (Vygotsky, 1930–1935/1978) requires that children be taught the vocabulary of feelings and social problem solving strategies. Marlowe (2000) suggests that children who cannot effectively self-regulate their feelings and behaviors are not in the habit of thinking before they act and must be taught to think routinely and think systematically. Children can be taught language skills as they relate to the systematic instruction of social problem solving skills and strategies as well as developmentally appropriate emotional awareness (Marlowe, 2000). CBT seeks to bring thought and feeling into awareness so that the children understand the connection and feel empowered to influence change over their behaviors.

GROUP TREATMENT COMPONENTS AND ACTIVITIES

Given that children who are socially isolated or rejected may require a different group formats depending on their needs and goals, it is not possible to have a set format for group intervention that will meet the needs of all children. Instead, we suggest that clinicians design groups to the needs of children they are working with, using a three-component process. This process is designed not for specific skills, but instead, is based on having three major components be part of the process: (1) *Group Induction*, (2) *Skills Building and Psychoeducation*, and (3) *Skills Implementation and Processing*. Using this approach, clinicians can have flexibility in choosing specific skills or areas to be addressed, while maintaining a structure to the process that is consistent with the cognitive-behavioral model.

Group Induction Component

The Group Induction component is designed to help set ground rules and limits during the group process, as well as to help group members get to know each other and start building a comfort level. For the most part, this will be accomplished in one session; however, for some groups, there is a value in distributing these skills across two sessions.

Setting limits.   During the first session, the group facilitators should use this time to accomplish several *opening tasks,* used to set a tone for the group. Given that many of these children have not had optimal social experiences, many of them may enter feeling uncomfortable, and thus, setting limits or rules for the group is essential. While the facilitators should have several prepared rules (e.g., keep hands and feet to self, listen when others are talking, use manners when talking), it is important to seek input and collaboration from the members regarding each rule. Collaboration can occur on two levels: (1) have the children explain what the rule means and to give examples, and (2) have the children help develop other rules they feel will make the group a better process. Many times setting the "ground rules" is conducted in a rote and boring way, which does not demonstrate to children that this will be an exciting and worthwhile use of their time. Friedberg and Crosby (2001) suggest having the children cheer each rule they agree with and to boo any rule they disagree with. For fun, we have placed erroneous goals in our initial list to encourage disagreement to be used to facilitate discussion and appropriate negotiation. When setting the ground rules is completed in an open and collaborative manner, the members experience a sense of investment or involvement in the process. It is not enough just to have ground rules, it is imperative that the therapists use the rules to set limits. This is not the case just for the first session, and therapists must monitor and address issues as they arise throughout the group process. When members do not follow the rules, the therapist should address the difficulty and process it with the group. This not only maintains limits, but it also serves as a way to use *in vivo* situations to teach skills and to help facilitators gain access to the automatic thoughts and belief systems of members.

For example, in a group that one of us (RWC) conducted, a child, Harold, was interrupting the other members frequently during a session (Session three). Each time this occurred, Harold was reminded of the rule, and at a point of transition between topics, I processed the situation with Harold and the other group members, as follows:

Dr. C: A few minutes ago, one of the rules was broken. The rule broken was "we listen when others are talking." Let's talk a minute about what it is like for the group when we don't follow the rules.

Harold: Dr. C. I didn't mean it. Jake made me think of somethin'. I wasn't trying to be rude. I won't do it again.

Dr. C.: Harold, I know you didn't mean anything by it, but it is worth talking about. Things like this happen outside of group, and sometimes aren't talked about. Let's use this situation to think about and see how what we do affects others.

Jake: It's okay, Harold. It happens to me always.

Dr. C.: What happens always?

Jake: People cut me off and then I forget what I was sayin'.

Dr. C.: Do others in the group have this happen to them...people interrupting them?

All: Yeah...everyday!

Dr. C.: When people do this, how does it make you feel?

Harold: Like I don't matter.

Jake: Sad.

Dave: It makes me angry.

Ling: I'm like Jake, it makes me sad.

Dr. C.: So, we have some different ways of feeling to the same event. When people interrupt you, what goes through your head or what do you tell yourself?

Dave: I think it's unfair. Why don't people listen?

Harold: My head says, it's happenin' again.

Dr. C.: See when things like this happen, it doesn't make others feel good and they may have negative thoughts. [*Using a thought-feeling-behavior chart presented in Session 2, therapist uses this situation to highlight how thought, feelings, and behaviors work together.*]

We need to work together to make sure that our actions in group don't contribute to other's having these thoughts and feelings. What are suggestions you have so we can be sure we follow the rules?

Dave: I like that we go over the rules each time. That way I don't forget.

Harold: Maybe we could have a signal.

Dr. C.: What do you mean?

Harold: Sometimes, I don't know I'm doin' something. I didn't even think I was butting in on Jake. May be you can give us a sign when we are doing it.

Dr. C.: So, we can keep going over the rules, but we also need a signal to remind you when you are not following them.

All: Yeah.

Dr. C.: Let's come up with some ideas.

Member introduction and group building.   Given that many of the group's members may not be comfortable in group situations initially, it is important to use the first session (if not two) as a way to have the children become comfortable and get to know each other. Again, it is important that this activity be fun and engaging, and the group facilitators should be involved with this, as well as all activities. Facilitators can use many activities for introduction and group building. We prefer using modified versions of *Who Are You?* and *People, Places, and Things*, both described by Vernon (2002) as getting to know you activities.

In *Who Are You?*, group members (including the facilitators) take turns asking each other, "Who are you?" The person being asked responds with something he or she is willing to disclose, and then asks, "Who are you?" In a group format, we modify this a bit, by adding the use of a Koosh ball. We have the children sit in a circle (sometimes on the floor), and give the Koosh ball to one child (usually the one who's first name is alphabetically first). The child then throws to one of the facilitators first, in order for demonstration, and asks, "Who are you?" The facilitator answers and then throws it to another member and asks the question. This continues until all children have at least one or two turns, which should take about 10 to 15 minutes. The following is an example.

Aly: [has the Koosh ball first and throws it to Dr. C] Who are you?

Dr. C.: I'm someone who loves football. Who are you? [throwing the Koosh ball to Samantha]

Samantha: I'm a person who loves music. Who are you? [throwing the Koosh ball to Carly]

Carly: I love collecting Care Bears. Who are you? [throwing the Koosh ball to CeeJay]

CeeJay: I like to play videogames. Who are you? [throwing the Koosh ball to Aly]

Aly: I'm an animal lover...especially dogs and cats. Who are you? [throwing the Koosh ball to Ms. Kim]

Ms. Kim: I love to go for walks outside. Who are you?

For *People, Places, and Things*, you must make a spinner board, by cutting out a circle from poster-board and dividing it into three sections—persons, places, and things. Attach a spinner to the board so it will spin. Each member of the group spins the spinner and describes a person, place, or thing they like, depending on where it lands. An example would be:

Ms. Kim: We want to take some time to get to know each other better. We are going to play a game for a few minutes. I'll begin and spin the spinner. Mine landed on "places," so I'm going to share a favorite place with the group. I love to go to the beach and watch the ocean. Amanda, you're next.

Amanda: [*spins the spinner*] I landed on things.

Ms. Kim: What is one of your favorite things?

Amanda: Bunch. I guess my Gameboy Advanced is the best.

Ms. Kim: Rich, you take a turn.

Rich: [*spins the spinner*] It landed on person. One of my favorite people is Ben Roethlisberger, 'cause I love the Steelers!

The two activities above are designed more for elementary-aged children, but modified versions can be developed for use with adolescents. For instance, we have found that doing an activity around music, movies, or television is useful for teenagers. *I'm the Critic* (Christner, 2005) is an example, which involves teenagers talking about one of their favorite songs or movies and describing what they liked or enjoyed about it and what they did not like or enjoy as much. *You'd Never Guess It* (Christner, 2005) is another example in which adolescents write one thing on paper that no one would guess about them. The papers are put into a bag and the facilitator selects one out of the bag reads it aloud. The group members have to try to guess who wrote the statement, and once the person is identified, they can describe it further to the group.

Each of these tasks is designed as an interactive way to encourage social exchanges, as well as a means of having group members get to know each other. When these activities are presented in a fun and informal manner, most clients, even those who are anxious in social situations, find themselves participating.

Skills Building and Psychoeducation Component

Skills building and psychoeducation can be conducted over a number of sessions, depending on the needs of the group members. Depending on the group and the setting, the number of session during the Skills Building and Psychoeducation Component can vary from three to 15 sessions, or even more in some cases. Each session is designed to teach specific skills to group members that address cognitive skills (e.g., problem solving), social skills, and behavioral response (e.g., self-monitoring). Although the focus is on education and skills building, it does not suggest that the application or generalization of the skills is ignored at this point. Instead, clinicians are encouraged to have the group members learn and practice the skills and refine them during this process.

We have found that many times group members become nervous when they think they need to "now be able to do the skill." We often help group members by telling them a story about *Making Chicken Soup* (Christner, 2006). This story is to help them see that we have a goal in mind (e.g., getting them to feel more comfortable interacting with peers), which is the end product, or the *Chicken Soup*. Our next few sessions are the "cooking process" in which we will add ingredients (e.g., the different skills we are working on), and then conduct *taste tests* (skill practice). Sometimes, the ingredient (or skills) we add will work great and improve the taste, but other times it may not work out as well, and we will need to add more of something or add something different to make improvements in the taste. It is a process of adding ingredients and testing the taste. For young children, you can make this a fun project where they make *Soup Pots* out of paper pockets or bowls, where they add their ingredients or skills learned written on paper slips.

Table 22.1   A Sample of Skills Building and Psychoeducation Topics

Listening skills	Using self-talk
Introducing yourself	Recognizing social cues
Knowing your feelings (labeling emotions)	Monitoring one's self
Joining in	Using self-control
Talking with others (beginning and ending conversation skills)	Taking action to teasing
Making good decisions	Learning to relax
Solving problems (problem solving skills)	Responding to complaints from others
Labeling cognitive errors	Handling embarrassing moments
Cognitive restructuring	Being left out
	Making friends

Table 22.1 offers suggestions of topic areas that can be addressed at each component level. For additional suggestions for group topics, readers are encouraged to reference Erdlen and Rickrode's work in chapter 26 of this handbook. Therapists should use these suggested topics to design a group treatment that is flexible and based on the conceptualizations of each client. There are a number of excellent resources available to obtain activities for each of these skills areas (see Friedberg, Friedberg, & Friedberg, 2001; Friedberg & McClure, 2002; Shure, 2001; Stallard, 2002; Vernon, 2002).

Skills Implementation and Processing Component

The Skills Implementation and Processing component of group intervention with children involves two stages—testing out new skills and processing the outcome. This is best accomplished once the group members have developed a collection of skills. In a traditional sense, this is the time they are engaging in *in vivo* experiences that are at a larger level than just testing one skill at a time.

For instance, one of us (RWC) had a group of 9- and 10-year-old boys who had several social difficulties. Over the course of 10 group sessions, the members learned numerous skills, including things such as watching social cues, knowing when to interject in a conversation, listening to others, asking to participate, monitoring one's self, identifying cognitive distortions, and restructuring negative self-talk. As the students learn individual skills and practiced, parents and teachers reported that many of the children were showing improvement. However, both parents and teachers reported that the skills were not seen in less structured situations, such as the playground. One group member, Jose, continued to be very reluctant to engage in recess activities with peers. During the group, we talked about all the skills he developed and how he could use those to ask if he could play with the other students. We used role-plays, and the other group members used their experiences to portray how some children might react. Jose, then, used his newly acquired skills to address the group members. Jose's "between-session experiment" was to approach a group of students and to ask if he could join in their game. All the members had their own experiments to try for the week. In order to use this as a processing task, we used the *Breaking the Crystal Ball* technique, as described by Friedberg, Friedberg, and Friedberg (2001). This technique offers a way for group members to test and counter their negative predictions regarding an event.

In addition to the skills implementation and processing, groups at this component should discuss maintenance stages and interventions. That is, what do you do when what you have learned doesn't work? It is inevitable, that at some point a group member will face a difficult situation. If he or she has a plan in place to maintain the skills learned, he or she is less likely to revert to old behaviors. We often suggest that as a closing activity in groups, group facilitators work with members to develop a plan of what they can do. *Hitting a Roadblock* (Christner, 2006) is a strategy that can be used, in which these situations are described as similar to driving and coming to an area where the road is closed. The driver has to come up with a plan to get where they want to go, which is similar to the group member who faces a roadblock and needs to problem solve around it. Together, the group members help each other develop their *Map for Success*, which they can use when faced with these situations.

OVERCOMING POTENTIAL OBSTACLES

Segrin (2003) outlines some contraindications and disadvantages to group social skills training, which apply to CBT groups, based on developmental levels of the participants and severity of their individual maladjustment. In order for group treatment of social deficits to be as effective as intended, the participants must have the cognitive ability and attention span to learn the techniques and strategies taught in the group. Some children with profound learning disabilities, for much the same reason as they did not develop interpersonal relationships on their own, may not benefit from more sophisticated training programs (Segrin, 2003). The model for group therapy assumes that not only are the children benefiting from the brief individual time they each receive from the facilitator in the group setting, but they also benefit from each other. The ability to participate actively on some level is a hallmark of group therapy. In settings or groups where the children's cognitive abilities preclude complex tasks, the therapist must focus the sessions on behavioral techniques and relaxation training.

Group members must also be motivated to try something new and learn ways to improve their interpersonal success. Children with low motivation, antisocial personalities who prefer to avoid relationships, or those who choose to self-isolate may not benefit from social skills training or therapy groups (Segrin, 2003). Those problems are better addressed first in individual therapy, at which point it can be determined if the child is ready to integrate into a group. If a child is integrated into a group too soon, not only does the child not benefit, but also the other group members may be hindered.

Group therapy limits the amount of time each child receives direct interaction with the therapist relative to individual therapy. The therapist must possess adequate behavior management skills and the ability to maintain structure if the group is to stay on track (Freeman et al., 2004). A single participant can undermine and disrupt the greater goals of the group. For instance, if a child with social anxiety is unable to tolerate the distress of being in the inherently social group setting, it may affect the other children's interactions. If severe social anxiety incapacitates an individual, this also decreases the likelihood that the child will willingly attend (Freeman et al., 2004). This can be avoided by carefully conceptualizing each child's case and determining if group therapy is the best intervention at that time. In addition, it is encouraged that groups be conducted using coleaders, as this serves for greater structure, as well as for more opportunity to model and demonstrate social interactions.

DISCUSSION

Cognitive behavior therapy has been well-researched and is effective for treating a variety of disorders, but there is limited empirically supported literature on the efficacy of CBT groups in schools. Children who are socially isolated are at-risk for several negative life outcomes including internalizing and externalizing disorders, legal and educational problems, and intergenerational transfer of risk by encouraging isolation in their own children. Schools are where children spend a great deal of time and are closely monitored by teachers, counselors, and other adults in the building, so the sensitivity to the signs of social withdrawal and the potential impact must begin in the classroom and on the playground. School is also the primary forum for social experiences with other children the same age, so it provides the best opportunity to develop and practice social skills within the provision of group CBT.

RECOMMENDED READINGS

Calkins, S. D., & Fox, N. A. (2002). Self-regulatory processes in early personality development: A multilevel approach to the study of childhood social withdrawal and aggression. *Development & Psychopathology, 14*(3), 477–498.

Greenberg, M. T. (1991). *Improving children's understanding of emotions: The effects of the PATHS Curriculum.* Paper presented at the Biennial Meeting of the Society for Research in Child Development (Seattle, WA, April 18–20, 1991).

REFERENCES

Achenbach, T. M. (2001). *Manual for the ASEBA school-age forms and profiles.* Burlington: University of Vermont.

Adalbjarnardottir, S. (1995). How schoolchildren propose to negotiate: The role of social withdrawal, social anxiety, and locus of control. *Child Development, 66,* 1739–1751.

Albano, A. M., & Barlow, D. H. (1996). Breaking the vicious cycle: Cognitive behavioral group therapy for socially anxious youth. In E. D. Hibbs & P. S. Jensen (Eds.), *Psychosocial treatment for child and adolescent disorders: Empirically based strategies for clinical practice* (pp. 43–62). Washington, DC: American Psychological Association.

Ayduk, O., Mendoza-Denton, R., Mischel, W., Downey, G., Peake, P. K., & Rodriquez, M. (2000). Regulating the interpersonal self: Strategic self-regulation for coping with rejection sensitivity. *Journal of Personality and Social Psychology, 79*(5), 776–792.

Baumeister, R. F., Twenge, J. M., & Nuss, C. K. (2002). Effects of social exclusion on cognitive processes: Anticipated aloneness reduces intelligent thought. *Journal of Personality and Social Psychology, 83*(4), 817–827.

Beck, J. S., Beck, A. T., & Jolly, J. B. (2001). *Beck youth inventories of emotional & social impairment.* San Antonio, TX: Psychological Corporation.

Beidel, D. C., Turner, S. M., & Morris, T. L. (1995). A new inventory to assess childhood social anxiety and phobia: The social phobia and anxiety inventory for children. *Psychological Assessment, 7,* 73–79.

Calkins, S. D., & Fox, N. A. (2002). Self-regulatory processes in early personality development: A multilevel approach to the study of childhood social withdrawal and aggression. *Development & Psychopathology, 14*(3), 477–498.

Christner, R. W. (2006, February). *What were you thinking? A cognitive-behavioral approach to changing student behavior.* Workshop presented at Teaching Social Competence: Cognitive Behavior Interventions in School Conference, Immaculata, PA.

Christner, R. W. (2005). *Psychological counseling as a related service: Practical applications for assessment and intervention.* Invited workshop presented for Intermediate Unit No. 1, Coal Center, PA.

Cole, V. John-Steiner, S. Scribner, & E. Souberman (Eds. & Trans.). (1978). *Mind in society: The development of higher mental process. L. S. Vygotsky.* Cambridge, MA: Harvard University Press.

Crnic, K., Hoffman, C., Gaze, C., & Edelbrock, C. (2004). Understanding the emergence of behavior problems in young children with developmental delays. *Infants and Young Children, 17*(3), 223–235.

Freeman, A., & Dattilio, F. M. (1992). *Comprehensive casebook of cognitive therapy.* New York: Plenum.

Freeman, A., Pretzer, J., Fleming, B., & Simon, K. (2004). *Clinical applications of cognitive therapy: Second edition.* New York: Kluwer Academic/Plenum.

Friedberg, R. D., & Crosby, L. E. (2001). *Therapeutic exercises for children: Professional guide.* Sarasota, FL: Professional Resource Exchange, Inc.

Friedberg, R. D., Friedberg, B. A., & Friedberg, R. J. (2001). *Therapeutic exercises for children: Guided self-discovery using cognitive-behavioral techniques.* Sarasota, FL: Professional Resource Exchange.

Friedberg, R. D., & McClure, J. (2002). *Clinical practice of cognitive therapy with children and adolescents: The nuts and bolts.* New York: Guilford.

Gewertz, C. (2003). Hand in hand. *Education Week, 23*(1), 38–41.

Gioia, G. A. Isquith, P. K., Guy, S. C., & Kenworthy, L. (2000). *Behavior rating inventory of executive function.* Lutz, FL: Psychological Assessment Resources.

Greenberg, M. T. (1991). *Improving children's understanding of emotions: The effects of the PATHS Curriculum.* Paper presented at the Biennial Meeting of the Society for Research in Child Development, Seattle, WA, April 18–20, 1991.

Greene, R. W., & Doyle, A .E. (1999). Toward a transactional conceptualization of oppositional defiant disorder: Implications for assessment and treatment. *Clinical Child and Family Psychology Review, 2*(3), 129–148.

Harrist, A. W., Zaia, A. F., Bates, J. E., Dodge, K. A., & Pettit, G. S. (1997). Subtypes of social withdrawal in early childhood: Sociometric status and social-cognitive differences across four years. *Child Development, 68*(2), 278–294.

Hart, D., Keller, M., Edelstein, W., & Hofmann, V. (1998). Childhood personality influences on social-cognitive development: A longitudinal study. *Journal of Personality and Social Psychology, 74*(5), 1278–1289.

Kagan, J. (1989). Temperamental contributions to social behavior. *American Psychologist, 44*, 668–674.

Kam, C., Greenberg, M. T., & Kusche, C. A. (2004). Sustained effects of the PATHS curriculum on the social and psychological adjustment of children in special education. *Journal of Emotional and Behavioral Disorders, 12*(2), 66–78.

Kashdan, T. B., & Herbert, J. D. (2001). Social anxiety disorder in childhood and adolescence: Current status and future directions. *Clinical Child and Family Psychology Review, 4*(1), 37–61.

Kendall, P.C., Chu, B. C., Pimental, S., & Choudbury, M. (2000). Treating anxiety disorders in youth. In P. C. Kendall (Ed.) *Child and adolescent therapy: Cognitive behavioral procedures* (pp. 235–287).

Kubbersmidt, J. B., & Cole, J. D. (1990). Preadolescent peer status, aggression, and school adjustment as predictors of externalizing problems in adolescence. *Child Development, 61*, 1350–1362.

Kopp, C. B. (1989). Regulation of distress and negative emotions: A developmental view. *Developmental Psychology, 25*(3), 343–354.

Lakes, K. D., & Hoyt, W. T. (2004). Promoting self-regulation through school-based martial arts training. *Journal of Applied Developmental Psychology, 25*(3), 283–303.

Leary, M. R., Kowalski, R. M., Smith, L., & Phillips, S. (2003). Teasing, rejection, and violence: Case studies of school shootings. *Aggressive Behavior, 29*, 202–214.

Lease, A. M. (1995). Cognitive and motivational influences on children's social competence and social adjustment. *Dissertation Abstracts International: Section B: The Sciences and Engineering, 56*(3-B), 1703.

Lengua, L. J. (2002). The contribution of emotionality and self-regulation to the understanding of children's responses to multiple risk. *Child Development, 73*(1), 144–161.

Lengua, L. J. (2003). Associations among emotionality, self-regulation, adjustment problems, and positive adjustment in middle childhood. *Applied Developmental Psychology, 24*, 595–618.

Lundh, L., & Sperling, M. (2002). Social anxiety and the post-event processing of socially distressing events. *Cognitive Behavior Therapy, 31*(3), 129–134.

Marlowe, W. B. (2000). An intervention for children with disorders of executive functions. *Developmental Neuropsychology, 18*(3), 445–454.

McConaughty, S. H., & Ritter, D. R. (1985). Social competence and behavioral problems of learning disabled boys aged 6-11. *Journal of Learning Disabilities, 18*(9), 547–553.

McNaught, A. (2004). Stepping out of their shells. *Times Educational Supplement, 4593*, 22–23.

Mennuti, R. B., & Christner, R. W. (2005). School-based cognitive-behavioral therapy (CBT). In A. Freeman (Ed.), *International encyclopedia of cognitive behavior therapy.* New York: Springer/Kluwer.

Olendick, T. H. (1983). Reliability and validity of the revised fear survey schedule for children (FSSC-R). *Behaviour Research and Therapy, 21*, 685–692.

Perry, B. D. (2001). Raising a nonviolent child: Developing self-regulation. *Scholastic Parent & Child, 9*(3), 25–27.

Prins, P. J., & Ollendick, T. H. (2003). Cognitive change and enhanced coping: Missing mediational links in cognitive behavior therapy with anxiety-disordered children. *Clinical Child and Family Psychology Review, 6*(2), 87–105.

Quakley, S., Reynolds, S., & Coker, S. (2004). The effects of cues on young children's abilities to discriminate among thoughts, feelings and behaviors. *Behaviour Research and Therapy, 42,* 343–356.

Rapport, M. D., Denney, C. B., Chung, K., & Hustace, K. (2001). Internalizing behavior problems and scholastic achievement in children: Cognitive and behavioral pathways as mediators of outcome. *Journal of Clinical Child Psychology, 30*(4), 536–551.

Segrin, C. (2003). Social skills training. In W. O'Donohue, J. E. Fisher, & S. C. Hayes (Eds.), *Cognitive behavior therapy: Applying empirically supported techniques in your practice* (pp. 384–390). Hoboken, NJ: Wiley.

Shure, M. (2001). I can problem solve (ICPS): An interpersonal cognitive problem-solving program for children. *Residential Treatment for Children & Youth, 18*(3), 3–14.

Shure, M. (2006, February). *Interpersonal cognitive problem-solving*. General session presented at Teaching Social Competence: Cognitive Behavior Interventions in School Conference, Immaculata, PA.

Spence, S. H., Donovan, C., & Brechman-Toussaint, M. (2000). Treatment of childhood social phobia: The effectiveness of a social skills training-based, cognitive-behavioural intervention, with and without parental involvement. *Journal of Child Psychology and Psychiatry, 41*(6), 713–726.

Stallard, P. (2002). *Think good—feel good: A cognitive behaviour therapy workbook for children and young people*. New York: Wiley.

Vasey, M. W., & McLeod, C. (2001). Information-processing factors in childhood anxiety: A review and developmental perspective. In M. W. Vasey & M. R. Dadds (Eds.). *The developmental psychopathology of anxiety* (pp. 253–277), New York, NY: Oxford University Press.

Vernon, A. (2002). *What works when with children and adolescents: A handbook of individual counseling techniques*. Champaign, IL: Research Press.

Vickers, B. (2002). Cognitive Behaviour therapy for adolescents with psychological disorders: A group treatment programme. *Clinical Child Psychology and Psychiatry, 7*(2), 249–263.

Volling, B. L., McElwain, N. L., Notaro, P. C., & Herrera, C. (2002). Parents' emotional availability and infant emotional competence: Predictors of parent-infant attachment and emerging self-regulation. *Journal of Family Psychology, 16*(4), 447–465.

Vygotsky, L. S. (1986). *Thought and language*. Cambridge, MA: MIT Press.

Wasserstein, S. B. (1998). Empirically-derived subtypes of social withdrawal: Associations with behavioral and cognitive functioning in a naturalistic preschool setting. *Dissertation Abstracts International: Section B: The Sciences and Engineering, 58*(8-B), 4478.

Weissberg, R. P., Resnik, H., Payton, J., & O'Brien, M. U. (2003). Evaluating social and emotional learning programs. *Educational Leadership, March 2003,* 46–50.

Wood, J. J., Cowan, P. A., & Baker, B. L. (2002). Behavior problems and peer rejection in preschool boys and girls. *Journal. of Genetic Psychology, 163*(1), 72–89.

Chapter Twenty-Three

Using Cognitive-Behavior Group Therapy with Chronic Medical Illness

Lamia P. Barakat, Elizabeth R. Gonzalez,
& Beverley Slome Weinberger

Chronic medical illness refers to a range of conditions, both congenital and acquired, that vary in terms of onset, course, incapacitation, treatment demands, and prognosis (Rolland, 1987). Congenital disorders include sickle cell disease and cystic fibrosis, which are inherited and diagnosed shortly after birth, are variable in their course, require preventive intervention, and are life shortening. Many other illnesses develop over the course of childhood. These illnesses may involve intense, invasive, and prolonged treatments with long-term complications resulting from the disease (juvenile diabetes) and the treatment (cancer). Others, such as pediatric headache and recurrent abdominal pain, develop in childhood and have treatments circumscribed for amelioration of pain and its impact on quality of life. In addition, acquired conditions (e.g., obesity and traumatic brain injury) may limit functional ability and interfere with social adaptation.

Chronic medical illness is estimated to affect between 10 to 30% of children in the United States (Newacheck & Taylor, 1992) with many children experiencing more than one condition. The literature suggests that children with chronic medical illness are at risk for problems in physical, academic, and psychosocial functioning depending on demographic and disease characteristics as well as interpersonal and social resistance factors (Wallander, Thompson, & Alriksson-Schmidt, 2003). Although many children with chronic medical conditions show adequate adaptation, adjustment is highly variable (Wallander et al., 2003). A significant number of children will struggle with the influence of physical symptoms and associated treatments on quality of life, social relationships, and psychological functioning (i.e., self-esteem, depression, and anxiety) (Lavigne & Faier-Routman, 1992). Unfortunately, although effective interventions have been identified, a number of barriers and complications have hampered efforts to address the psychosocial risks for these children (Bauman, Drotar, Leventhal, Perrin, & Pless, 1997). Barriers include difficulties recruiting sufficient numbers of children with medical illness, lack of articulation of the theory underlying interventions and an inadequately described program, and problems in coordinating multidisciplinary teams to inform and conduct interventions. These complications also highlight the need to deliver services at points of contact such as schools, community health centers and managed care facilities, and hospitals.

Dubo (1951) provided one of the first published papers on the use of group interventions with children with medical illness. Two recent review papers focused on summarizing the current literature on interventions with children with chronic illness and addressed group interventions (with peers, siblings, parents, or families) and cognitive-behavior therapy (CBT) approaches (Bauman et al., 1997; Plante, Lobato, & Engel, 2001). Over 50 years after Dubo, group interventions comprise more than half of published pediatric intervention studies; however, descriptions of group interventions and empirical evaluation of their effectiveness remain limited (Plante et al., 2001). Many published group interventions do not identify a theoretical approach, use loosely structured play or discussion to provide emotional support, or rely primarily on education to address medical symptoms and psychological adjustment, and there is little empirical evidence of their effectiveness (Plante et al., 2001). In contrast, these review papers concluded that because cognitive-behavioral groups offer a mechanism to model skills, problem-solve with similar others, and meet the developmental goal of peer interaction, they are an effective intervention approach for children with chronic medical illness for whom risk often lies in family and social relationships. Symptom reduction (e.g., pediatric headache, sickle cell disease pain, pediatric overweight), psychosocial adaptation (i.e., psychological adjustment, social functioning, and school adjustment for brain tumor survivors), and self-management (e.g., juvenile diabetes) most frequently serve as the primary targets for group CBT interventions.

OVERVIEW OF PRESENTING PROBLEM

Pediatric overweight, pediatric headache, recurrent abdominal pain, sickle cell disease, juvenile or Type I diabetes, and pediatric brain tumor are the target populations for the group CBT interventions discussed in this chapter. Table 23.1 summarizes information on the onset, course, treatment demands, and outcome of each of these chronic medical conditions based on Rolland's psychosocial typology model (1987) and summarized from Barakat, Kunin-Batson, and Kazak (2001). This typology model describes disease and medical characteristics relevant to psychosocial adaptation. In addition, this chapter builds on the noncategorical approach to chronic medical illness, which suggests that specific illness categories are less important to understanding child psychosocial outcomes than is consideration of stressors common to all illnesses and delineation of illness dimensions for each patient (Gartstein, Short, Vannatta, & Noll, 1999; Rolland, 1987; Stein & Jessop, 1982). Moreover, the noncategorical approach implies that although the group CBT interventions described in this chapter target specific pediatric populations, the interventions may be applied to other medical groups and modified depending on the child's presenting medical symptoms and psychosocial issues (Morison, Bromfield, & Cameron, 2003; Plante et al., 2001).

With documentation that chronic medical illness in children presents a range of stressors that create risk for poor outcomes, variation in psychosocial adaptation is most commonly understood within a risk-and-resistance framework (Wallander et al., 2003; see also Barakat, Lash, Lutz, & Nicolaou, 2005). Objective condition parameters such

Table 23.1 Characteristics of Selected Chronic Medical Illnesses

Illness	Onset	Course	Treatments	Outcome
Pediatric Overweight	Gradual; diagnosed in childhood; hereditary and environmental components	Stable	Appropriate diet; physical activity	Shortened life span; associated health complications; psychological and social problems
Pediatric Headache	Acute; diagnosed in childhood	Relapsing	Medication	Nonfatal; psychological problems noted
Sickle Cell Disease	Acute; most often diagnosed through neonatal screening; hereditary	Relapsing	Prophylactic antibiotic, rest and hydration, pain management, transfusion therapy	Shortened life span; associated health complications; psychological and social problems noted
Recurrent Abdominal Pain	Paroxysmal; diagnosed in childhood	Relapsing	Medication, psychological intervention	Nonfatal; psychological problems noted
Brain Tumor Survivors	Acute; diagnosed in childhood	Stable when in remission and after treatment	Surgery, radiation, chemotherapy, treatments for medical late effects including medication	Potentially fatal; medical late effects of treatment; psychological and social problems noted
Juvenile (Type I) Diabetes	Gradual; diagnosed in childhood or adolescence	Progressive	Blood glucose monitoring, daily insulin injections, modification of diet and exercise	Shortened life span; psychological and social problems noted

as those outlined in the Rolland model (1987), disease severity, and functional status have been shown to impact psychosocial functioning as have demographic variables of gender, age, and family socioeconomic status. Together, demographic and disease-related variables are considered risk factors due to associated higher stress and greater strain on resources. Resistance factors enable resilience and include child and parent cognitive appraisals of self-efficacy and outcome expectations, child and parent adaptive coping, child and parent problem-solving skills, social support, and healthy family functioning; these factors have also been linked to psychosocial adjustment in the empirical literature. Within the risk-and-resistance framework, group CBT interventions aimed at bolstering resistance factors are well suited for children and adolescents with chronic medical conditions.

SYMPTOM REDUCTION

Pediatric Overweight

Pediatric overweight is a rising epidemic in the United States. Based on a body mass index (BMI) above the 85th percentile, approximately 22% of children and adolescents are considered at risk for or are overweight (Jelalian & Saelens, 1999). The consequences of pediatric overweight are severe in that childhood obesity has been associated with adult obesity, current and long-term cardiovascular complications, poor self-esteem and body image, social problems in childhood, adolescence, and adulthood, and adult economic disadvantage (Jelalian & Saelens, 1999). In response, government initiatives have been developed to target pediatric overweight at the local and national levels.

In addition to reduction of weight, the goals of intervention for pediatric over-weight include amelioration of the psychosocial consequences of obesity and attention to children's growth and development (Epstein, Myers, Raynor, & Saelens, 1998). Un-like treatment of obesity for adults, CBT involving both weight reduction and physical activity has been shown to be effective in the short- and long-term in the treatment of pediatric overweight, particularly when conducted prior to adolescence and when behavior therapy and changes in physical activity are included along with education (Epstein et al., 1998; Jelalian & Saelens, 1999). Family involvement in the treatment of pediatric overweight is considered central to the effectiveness of these interventions; however, mustering family support and maintaining weight reduction over time remain significant obstacles.

Assessment and Group Identification

A number of assessment approaches are used to identify overweight children and mea-sure their diet and physical activity. Psychometrically sound measures and commonly used measures are reviewed (Jelalian & Saelens, 1999). As noted, in the context of inter-vention, *percentage overweight* (typically > 20%) and/or *BMI* (at risk for overweight > 85th percentile, overweight > 95th percentile) may be assessed prior to and after, daily, or periodically to identify participants and to measure weight change over time. BMI is associated with body fat and, in children, is computed based on height and weight with consideration given to age and gender (Centers for Disease Control and Prevention, 2005). Continuous assessment and self-monitoring are completed via a *habit book*, in which daily recordings of food intake, calorie intake, and total minutes in activities, both physical and sedentary, are made (Epstein et al., 1995). In terms of standardized self-report measures, the *Eating Behavior Inventory* (O'Neil, Currey, Hirsch, Malcolm, Sexauer, et al., 1979) is often cited and assesses behaviors related to weight loss includ-ing self-monitoring of food intake, eating when hungry or not, and eating habits such as eating when watching TV, speed of eating, and eating snack food.

CBT Conceptualization of the Problem

Traffic-light diet. This dietary program was developed to facilitate understanding of the nutritional value of foods and allow for ease in determining energy intake; it is ad-justed based on age-appropriate, nutritional guidelines (Epstein, Wing, & Valoski, 1985). "Green" foods are go foods; they are low in calories but high in nutrition and may be eaten in unlimited quantities (e.g., vegetables). "Yellow" foods are caution foods; they are moderate to high in calories but are essential for a balanced diet (e.g., dairy foods). "Red" foods are stop foods; they are high in calories and low in nutrition (i.e., junk food and candy). Children learn to limit red foods and obtain appropriate servings of yellow foods. By teaching the traffic-light diet and incorporating self-monitoring of food and calorie intake, children may increase their knowledge of healthy food choices and are provided with immediate feedback regarding the content of their food intake, thereby allowing for reduction in calories and improvement in nutrition.

Physical activity.   Engaging in physical activity is linked to suppression of appetite, increased calorie expenditure, and increased commitment to programs that address obesity (Epstein et al., 1998). Moreover, lifestyle exercise has been supported as most effective (Epstein et al., 1998). Along with increased physical activity, programs now primarily target decreased sedentary activity, which is addressed through a contract for positive contingencies when specific goals are met. Goals are made increasingly difficult, and maintenance is incorporated into the contract.

Stimulus control.   Removal of food of poor nutritional value from the home and marking of remaining foods with red, yellow, and green stickers based on traffic light diet provides stimulus control. In addition, exercise equipment may be visible in the home to serve as cues for physical activity, while cues for sedentary activity may be hidden in cabinets.

Contingency contracting.   The habit book is reviewed nightly, typically by parents who are active participants in the program. Social and concrete reinforcement of children is provided via praise and through an incentive system, using activities and privileges earned for adherence to the program. Reciprocal contracting has been applied with success in which children apply reinforcement to their parents when parents meet their own goals (Epstein et al., 1995). In research studies, contingency management for parents has been incorporated by allowing parents to regain portions of the program fee based on level of attendance at meetings.

Modeling.   Parents are incorporated into programs and follow changes in diet and physical activity in order to serve as a model for their children (Epstein et al., 1998). Children are often encouraged to serve as a model for their parents as well.

Self-monitoring.   Daily completion of the habit book, including recording of food intake and physical activity levels, is a cornerstone of CBT for pediatric overweight. It provides data on adherence to diet and activity and continuous feedback on eating and activity habits, and it forms the basis of administering reinforcement.

Parent problem-solving.   Parent problem-solving follows the tradition of parent training programs and is focused on eating behaviors and physical activity (Epstein et al., 1998).

Group Treatment

As noted, interventions for pediatric overweight are multicomponent treatments and incorporate the family (Epstein et al., 1998; Jelalian & Saelens, 1999); it is not yet clear which components are essential for improved outcomes. However, CBT components beyond those noted, such as cognitive restructuring, have not been supported as important aspects of treatment. The format typically comprises eight weekly or monthly group meetings with follow-up meetings (up to six) in which parents and children learn about diet and exercise programs, goal-setting and behavioral contracting, and delivery of the reinforcement program. The importance of including parents in these programs is well-documented, particularly for preadolescent children. Adolescents may benefit from parent involvement in separate groups; therefore, parents and children most often meet in separate, concurrent groups. Parents focus on gaining mastery in behavior management and problem-solving as well as receiving education on nutrition and physical activity, and setting personal goals. Interventionists maintain phone contact between sessions, and weekly goal-setting/homework is incorporated.

CHRONIC PAIN

Chronic pain may present in the form of headache pain, recurrent abdominal pain, or pain secondary to an illness such as sickle cell disease (SCD). Recurrent pain is a common symptom arising from chronic medical illness and represents a disabling and emotionally distressing problem for many children and their families (Eccleston, Morley, Williams, Yorke, & Mastroyannopoulou, 2002). For example, in one study, one quarter of over 5,000 school-age children in the sample reported experiencing chronic pain (lasting more than 3 months) (Perquin, Hazebroek-Kampscheur, Hunfeld, Bohnene, van Suijlekom-Smit, et al., 2000).

Although pain is primarily managed by pharmacological methods, many children and parents employ nonpharmacologic methods for managing pain to reduce reliance on medication (Barry & von Baeyer, 1997). CBT pain management strategies have the additional benefit of increasing the sense of control children have over their pain, thereby impacting other psychosocial outcomes. This has prompted studies investigating the effectiveness of CBT pain management strategies such as relaxation training, guided imagery, positive coping self-statements, and biofeedback. Group treatment approaches to chronic pain target symptom reduction, with the goal of reducing or eliminating physical symptoms through behavior change (Plante et al., 2001). Eccleston and colleagues (2002) performed a systematic review of published randomized controlled trials of nonpharmacologic interventions to treat chronic pain in children and adolescents; they found only seven studies in which a group-based intervention was used. Consistent with this report, a literature review of empirically supported treatments for disease-related pain in children emphasized that while CBT strategies are promising, the literature base is lacking in well-controlled, manualized studies of adequate sample sizes (Walco, Sterling, Conte, & Engel, 1999).

Assessment and Group Identification

Pain is generally measured via self-report in either prospective or retrospective form (Holden, Deichmann, & Levy, 1999; Walco et al., 1999). A commonly used retrospective measure of pain that allows for child and parent report is the *Pediatric Pain Questionnaire* (PPQ; Varni & Thompson, 1985). This measure asks respondents to rate frequency, intensity, and duration of pain and pain interference with activities and elicits descriptions and location of pain. However, the reliability and validity of retrospective self-reports of pain are limited, as individuals may overestimate pain intensity and duration when reflecting on past pain experiences (van den Brink, Bandell-Hoekstra, & Abu-Saad, 2001).

Prospective measures, such as *paper-and-pencil pain diaries*, may be more valid measures of pain, but there are problems with daily compliance and potential fabrication of data (Palermo, Valenzuela, & Stork, 2003; Stone, Shiffman, Schwartz, Broderick, & Hufford, 2003). When used effectively, paper-and-pencil pain diaries generally require a child to record at least once a day whether pain was experienced, its intensity and duration, any interventions attempted, and the functional consequences of pain (Eccleston et al., 2002). Pain diaries often include a visual analogue scale, which has been shown to be a valid and reliable measure of pain intensity with children (Sanders, Shepherd, Cleghorn, & Woolford, 1994). Children may be required to fill out pain diaries before, during, and after treatment.

In addition, it is useful to assess outcome variables associated with pain, including parent observations of pain and pain behavior, coping responses to pain, and mood. For example, a parent observational measure such as the *Parent Observation Record* (POR) may be used (Sanders, Shepherd, Cleghorn, & Woolford, 1994). This measure requires that parents record the presence or absence of 5 categories of pain behavior in an observation block of 60 minutes throughout the child's day. Regarding coping strategies, Sanders et al. (1994) assessed whether children engaged in active or attention-gaining coping strategies by showing a videotaped vignette and having children rate their likelihood of using each strategy on a Likert-type scale. In the SCD literature, coping strategies are often measured with the *Coping Strategies Questionnaire* (CSQ), which assesses on a Likert-type scale how often children use various pain management strategies (Powers, Mitchell, Graumlich, Byars, & Kalinyak, 2002).

CBT Conceptualization of the Problem

As noted, the goals of group CBT interventions for disease-related pain are to reduce the frequency, intensity, and duration of pain by encouraging children and adolescents to gain mastery over their pain experiences and maintain their daily activities (Chen, Cole, & Kato, 2004). Several factors that maintain pain in children and adolescents, beyond underlying physiological factors, have been identified; these factors are linked to the various components of group CBT interventions for pain.

Self-monitoring. Patients and their families are often unaware or have incomplete understanding of variables surrounding their pain such as "triggers" or potential social reinforcements. Additionally, patients may be poor historians about when they have pain and its frequency and duration. The completion of pain diaries as part of an intervention serves the dual purpose of monitoring any changes in disease activity due to treatment as well as enabling children to self-monitor the frequency, intensity, and duration of their headaches and begin to observe patterns or correlations in their pain activity.

Behavioral coping strategies. Gil and colleagues (Gil, Abrams, Phillips, & Keefe, 1989; Gil, Abrams, Phillips, & Williams, 1992) investigated the role of coping strategies in children and adolescents with SCD and found that coping strategies account for significant portions of the variance in pain, functional outcomes, and psychosocial adjustment. Their research indicated that individuals who use predominantly passive coping experience more severe pain, show greater levels of distress, and use hospital services at a higher rate than individuals who employ active coping. Other researchers have highlighted the role of active coping responses in increasing the child's sense of control over pain versus passive coping responses which may lead to withdrawal, decreased activity, and increased pain (Flor, Birbaumer, & Rudy, 1990; Sanders et al.,

1994; Siegal & Smith, 1989). Behavioral coping strategies, such as relaxation techniques and self-hypnosis, are used. Relaxation techniques may work to decrease overall stress levels, as well as provide children with a means to actively cope with pain. Additionally, these strategies may help provide children with a greater sense of control over their body and disease symptomatology.

Cognitive coping strategies.   Cognitive aspects of coping such as appraisals, beliefs, and expectations play an important role in exacerbating pain (Turk & Meichenbaum, 1994). Interventions have also focused on the role of cognitions in the maintenance of pain. For instance, Kroener-Herwig and Denecke (2002) used an intervention in which children were taught about the significance of dysfunctional and functional cognitions regarding stress and headache. In addition, positive self-talk has been used to enhance coping and counteract problematic stress appraisals, beliefs, and expectations (Sanders et al., 1994).

Social learning processes.   In addition to individual coping strategies in dealing with pain, social learning processes, in particular the response of a person's social environment to pain expression, are increasingly emphasized as important in the maintenance of chronic pain (Sanders, Cleghorn, Shepherd & Patrick, 1996; Sanders et al., 1994). In pediatric chronic illness, the family context of pain may serve to reinforce pain behavior in that caregivers may inadvertently contribute to the maintenance of pain by providing discriminative cues and selective reinforcement for behavioral expressions of pain (Sanders et al., 1994). Moreover, caregiving practices such as attention, nurturance, expression of concern, and emotional reactions of anger and criticism can reinforce pain behavior (Sanders et al., 1994).

Group Treatment

Group CBT interventions for pediatric chronic pain are generally multi-component treatment packages, which does not allow for identification of effective elements of treatment. For example, an intervention applied by Kroener-Herwig and Denecke (2002) for the treatment of pediatric headache in 10 to14 year olds consisted of 8 weekly, 90-minute sessions conducted from a manualized treatment protocol. Treatment components included: psychoeducation about headaches and their underlying pathophysiology, progressive relaxation strategies, ways to cope with stress, cognitive restructuring, positive imagery, self-assertive behavior, and problem-solving. Therapists used two cartoon characters (a young boy "battling" headaches and a "headache dragon") in each session, and children were given homework assignments, which they collected in a folder along with written material on covered topics. In each session, therapists began by reviewing the previous session, introducing the new topic, giving children an opportunity to practice the new skill, providing a playtime intermission involving either physical activity or a creative task, and assigning homework. Similarly, Helm-Hylkema and colleagues (1990) conducted group CBT for the treatment of migraine headache pain with seven children. The intervention consisted of eight therapy sessions, of which four were individual treatment sessions. Group sessions were used to learn relaxation strategies as well as principles of rational emotive therapy to facilitate problem-solving skills around everyday problems.

Family based interventions, such as that administered by Sanders and colleagues. (1994), seek to teach parents ways to help modify pain behavior, as well as support their children's self-management behavior. Additionally, including parents in treatment programs may also help encourage children to practice and utilize their newly learned techniques at home and in school and hospital settings (Barry & von Baeyer, 1997). For example, Sanders and colleagues (1994) used a parent training model in which a comprehensive functional analysis of the child's behavior and family interactions was followed by parent training focused on the social learning components of pain and how to implement behavior modification strategies with children. In an intervention for adolescents with sickle cell disease, parents and other family members are incorporated in the treatment as "support persons" so as to facilitate practice of relaxation, guided imagery, and positive coping self-statement techniques at home, as well as provide parents with a means to decrease disease-related pain (Radcliffe et al., 2004). These interventions may also work to increase self-efficacy related to pain management in that both parents and their children become more empowered to manage pain.

PSYCHOSOCIAL ADAPTATION

Social Skills Training for Children with Brain Tumors

Long-term survival from childhood cancers is increasing, and malignancies that affect the brain are the second most common childhood cancer after leukemia (Carpentieri, Mulhern, Douglas, Hanna, & Fairclough, 1993). However, many survivors experience "medical late effects" or chronic problems related to cancer and its treatment including medical, social, and psychological sequelae (Meadows & Hobbie, 1986). As an example, cardiac, endocrine, and reproductive systems may be altered by particular chemotherapies. For survivors of childhood brain tumors, in addition to cognitive sequelae associated with tumor location, cranial radiation, or intrathecal chemotherapy, decreased social functioning, including low social competence, social withdrawal, and social skills deficits, is reported consistently and rises to a level greater than that reported for children treated for cancers that do not affect the brain and for children with other chronic illnesses (Carpentieri et al., 1993; Mulhern, Carpentieri, Shema, Stone, & Fairclough, 1993). Furthermore, social dysfunction may extend into adulthood (Hays et al., 1992). Therefore, children treated for brain tumors have been identified as being at high risk for difficulties in academic and social functioning, requiring universal assessment and frequent intervention (Barakat, Kunin-Batson, et al., 2003).

A number of reasons have been posited for these pronounced social issues (Die-Trill, Bromberg, LaVally, Portales, SanFeliz, et al., 1996). First, school absence and decreased engagement in activities during active treatment may interfere with the ability to form and maintain friendships with same-age peers (Vannatta, Gartstein, Short, & Noll, 1998). Second, cosmetic manifestations of the illness and enduring functional disability may draw attention to these children in the classroom and result in subsequent dislike or rejection by peers (Mulhern et al., 1993; Vannatta et al., 1998). Third, the neuropsychological consequences of the location of the brain tumor and its associated treatments (particularly cranial radiation and intrathecal chemotherapy) may result in cognitive and affective deficits that impair social skills (Carey, Barakat, Foley, Gyato, & Phillips, 2001). Consequently, there have been efforts to tailor existing social skills training interventions to meet the needs of this medical illness group (Barakat, Hetzke, Foley, Carey, Gyato, & Phillips, 2003).

Assessment and Group Identification

Approaches to identification of children with brain tumors requiring social skills training intervention should include standard measures of social skills, social competence and functioning, and quality of life as well as objective recording of observed social skills, and incorporate child, parent, and teacher perspectives. The *Social Skills Rating System* (Gresham & Elliott, 1990) provides a standard assessment of frequency of positive and negative social behaviors with self, parent, and teacher report formats. Peer nomination or sociometric methods provide insight into children's functioning in their classroom setting as perceived directly by their peers (see Vannatta et al., 1998, for a discussion of peer nomination methods applied to children treated for brain tumors). Quality of life measures in pediatrics often address social functioning. Generic measures of quality of life that apply to children with various chronic medical illnesses include the *Miami Pediatric Quality of Life Questionnaire* (Armstrong, Toledano, Miloslavich, Lackman-Zeman, Levy, et al., 1999) and the *Children's Health Questionnaire* (Landgraf, Abertz, & Ware, 1996). Standard behavior checklists that include scales addressing social competence or social adaptation such as the *Child Behavior Checklist* (Achenbach, 1991) or the *Behavioral Assessment System for Children-Second Edition* (BASC-2; Reynolds & Kamphaus, 2004) may be used.

CBT Conceptualization of the Problem

As with other groups of children who are provided cognitive-behavior, social skills training (e.g., children with learning disorders, children with autism, children with mental retardation, children with attention-deficit hyperactivity disorder), problems in social functioning in children with brain tumors develop and persist due to deficits in nonverbal and verbal social skills as well as social problem-solving abilities and the subsequent lack of acceptance and paucity of social reinforcement by peers (Gresham, 1985). Treatments designed to improve social skills are built on the assumptions that these skills are specific, learned verbal and nonverbal behaviors and include initiations and responses in specific interactions. These behaviors are problematic due to lack of knowledge, lack of acquisition or performance of skills due to another problem, few opportunities for interaction, and/or lack of reinforcement (Elliott & Gresham, 1993). Most commonly, modeling and coaching, reinforcement, direct and self-instruction, and problem-solving are incorporated into cognitive-behavior approaches to social skills training in order to modify perceptions and beliefs about social situations as well as behavioral responses in interactions. Frequently, intervention takes place within peer groups.

For child survivors of brain tumors, gains in social relatedness are often not generalized to the school, activities, and other social settings due in part to misplaced efforts to rebuild prior social networks and activities. This is compounded by peer identification of children with brain tumors as different, limiting opportunities for children to practice and extend their emerging skills (Vannatta et al., 1998). The expectation is that by using behavior and cognitive-behavior strategies, social skills may be formed and generalized to peers and adults in various settings in order to support social competence and functioning (Gresham, 1985).

Group Treatment

Cognitive-behavior, social skills training has been supported as effective in addressing problems in social functioning for select groups of children and under certain conditions (Gresham, 1985), and there is evidence of the effectiveness of social skills training procedures for children treated for brain tumors (Barakat, Hetzke et al., 2003). The group social skills training described here is based on a manualized intervention provided to groups of 6 to 8 school-age children treated for brain tumors; it included a concurrent parent component with children and parents joining together in a final session (Barakat, Hetzke, et al., 2003). Six, biweekly sessions comprised the intervention. This intervention was based in part on an individual social skills intervention for children treated for leukemia (Varni, Katz, Colegrove, & Dolgin, 1993) and integrated key components of established social skills training programs (Elliott & Gresham, 1993; Gresham, 1985).

Education.   Specific social skills, identified as particularly problematic for children with brain tumors, were targeted. These social skills included reading nonverbal cues and nonverbal communication, making conversations, accepting and giving compliments, empathy, and cooperation. Education was provided in multiple sensory formats including verbal instruction, written instructions via posters, and visual instruction through demonstrations. While one set of social skills was targeted at each session, social functioning was shaped over time in that skills from prior sessions were included in the focus of subsequent sessions, application of skills in multiple contexts and situations was emphasized, and the final session targeted skill integration through interaction during a cooperative game and completion party celebration.

Modeling.   Modeling of specific social skills was provided by trained interventionists. Role-plays of social skills used "real life" peer and adult interaction examples and incorporated both "right" and "wrong" models to encourage children to identify appropriate and inappropriate social skills before being encouraged to model the targeted social skills. Topics for role-plays were provided in the manual and taken from problems/issues raised by the participants.

Coaching and positive practice with corrective feedback.   After education and modeling, participants engaged in practice with interventionists and peers followed immediately by corrective feedback from peers and trained interventionists. Feedback was specific in making recommendations for improved interaction based on targeted skills, and at times participants who provided feedback were asked to provide examples or join practice to demonstrate appropriate social skills. In the context of providing corrective feedback, social reinforcement via praise from peers and interventionists was provided. In addition, parents were encouraged to provide social reinforcement when they observed their child engaged in appropriate social skills and to apply corrective feedback when necessary. Furthermore, positive practice in order to promote generalization was incorporated through homework assignments, supported by parents.

Provision of homework assignments targeting specific skills.   Homework assignments were made after each weekly session and were supported through handouts and supply of a homework book. One homework assignment required children to write and perform in a videotaped skit of initiation and maintenance of a conversation with a family member or friend. All homework, including the videotapes, was reviewed at the beginning of each session in a joint meeting of children and parents.

Parent group component.   A parent group was conducted concurrently and focused on reviewing social skills targeted in the intervention, educating parents on the importance of homework for practice, and reinforcing parents' role in generalization by teaching them how to apply corrective feedback, contingent reinforcement, and differential reinforcement. Parents were also encouraged to support homework completion through application of structure and reminders as well as creating opportunities for modeling and practice. Moreover, a significant amount of time was spent discussing observed social skills deficits, addressing current social problems, and group problem-solving of social issues. For example, parents shared ideas on appropriate summer camps for their children, provided suggestions on how to arrange play dates with former or new friends, and shared tips for successful advocacy across settings for their children.

SELF-MANAGEMENT

Type I Diabetes

Type I diabetes is an autoimmune disease that prevents the pancreas from producing sufficient insulin (National Institute of Diabetes and Digestive and Kidney Diseases, 2004). It occurs in about 1 in every 500–600 children, and those affected must receive daily doses of insulin (Wysocki, Greco, & Buckloh, 2003). The long-term complications of diabetes include blindness, kidney disease, and amputation of the leg or foot. Adults with diabetes are also twice as likely to have a heart attack or stroke (National Institute of Diabetes and Digestive and Kidney Diseases, 2004). Diabetes can serve as a model for adherence issues associated with pediatric conditions since treatments are complex, on-going, invasive, and imperative to survival (Delamater, 2000). These treatment regimens can be taxing for children and their families. While many challenges are incurred because of this incurable disease, with appropriate care, people with diabetes can expect typical life expectancies (Mayo Foundation for Medical Education and Research, 2005). However, children and adolescents with diabetes have an increased risk for poor psychosocial adjustment (Wysocki et al., 2003).

CBT interventions, such as stress-management techniques, problem-solving, and conflict resolution, have been found to improve adherence and associated physical and psychosocial outcomes in children with diabetes (Wysocki et al., 2003). Group CBT interventions have been applied to promote adherence in other pediatric populations as well (Baum & Creer, 1986; Greenan-Fowler, Powell, & Varni, 1987), but the focus of this chapter is on juvenile diabetes due to the frequency with which it is studied and the morbidity and mortality associated with nonadherence.

Assessment and Group Identification

Numerous factors must be accounted for when choosing appropriate measures of adherence, especially if the condition being examined requires a multifaceted treatment regimen (La Greca & Bearman, 2003). Adherence to medical regimes has been measured in a variety of forms including drug assays, self-reports, ratings by health professionals, behavioral observations, pill counts, and monitoring devices (La Greca & Bearman,

2003). When evaluating adherence for children with juvenile diabetes, the most successful techniques target a variety of measurement methods and informants (Wysocki et al., 2003), and combinations of objective and subjective measures have been used to assess the effectiveness of intervention programs (Gross, Magalnick, & Richardson, 1985; Satin, La Greca, Zigo, & Skyler, 1989).

For objective, physiologic measures of adherence in Type I diabetes, *total glycosylated hemoglobin level* (HbA1), which analyzes how much glucose a person's red blood cells are exposed to, is commonly used (Delamater et al., 1990; Gross et al., 1985; Satin et al., 1989). Higher HbA1 indicates poorer glycemic functioning. Residual pancreatic ß-cell activity, body mass index, and reflectance meters are other physiologic measures that have been used when measuring adherence in people with diabetes (Delamater et al., 1990; Wysocki, Green, & Huxtable, 1989).

Self-report scales include *A Teenager with Diabetes* (Siegler, La Greca, Citrin, Reeves, & Skyler, 1982) used to gather insight into teenagers' self-perceptions; an adaptation of the *Diabetes-Care Profile* (Davis, Hess, Harrison, & Hiss, 1987) used to gather self-report data on skilled adjustment of insulin dose, diet, and exercise based on blood monitoring; and the *Diabetes Health and Belief Questionnaire*, the *Diabetes Regimen Adherence Questionnaire*, and the *Diabetes Knowledge and Management Skills Assessment Questionnaire,* all used to gather information on the relationship between adherence and health beliefs (Brownlee-Duffeck et al., 1987). Specifically, the Diabetes Health and Belief Questionnaire measures perceived severity of diabetes, perceived severity and susceptibility to complications, and perceived benefits and costs of adherence. The Diabetes Regimen Adherence Questionnaire is a behavioral self-report measure of adherence, and the Diabetes Knowledge and Management Skills Assessment Questionnaire covers diet, insulin injections, insulin reactions, urine testing, foot care, and ketoacidosis and hyperglycemia. Additionally, the *Behavior Modification Test* was developed to assess increases in knowledge and skills taught in a CBT group intervention (Gross et al., 1985), and the *Semantic Differentials* (Osgood, Suci, & Tannenbaum, 1957) is used to measure the difference between parents' and adolescents' perceptions of diabetes.

Based on reports from physicians and parents, *physician ratings of adherence* are used as objective measures (Delamater, 2000), as is the *Behavioral Rating Scale*, a parent-report scale of children's adherence to their medical regimen (Gross et al., 1985).

CBT Conceptualization of the Problem

Health beliefs. As predicted by the health belief model, better adherence and metabolic control have been found to be associated with perceived severity and perceived benefits in a study of adolescents and adults with diabetes (Brownlee-Duffeck et al., 1987). However, within the same sample, greater perceived propensity to complications was not associated with better metabolic control.

Education. Knowledge and skills are necessary for the treatment of all health issues, but they are imperative for proper adherence to multifaceted treatment regimens (Delamater, 2000). However, they are not sufficient. For example, children with high levels of diabetes knowledge have been found to have poor metabolic control (Weist, Finney, Barnard, & Ollendick, 1993). Since knowledge and skills alone are not sufficient to ensure change, group CBT interventions that include parents and involve multiple strategies such as education, self-monitoring, reinforcement, and problem-solving, have been found to be most successful for increasing adherence in pediatric populations (La Greca & Bearman, 2003).

Treatment-related skills and problem-solving. Problem-solving skills include communicating in an assertive yet positive manner (Satin et al., 1989), identifying rewards and self-administering the reward upon completion of the target behavior (Gross et al., 1985), and self-management training in reference to learning about the relationship between behavior and environment (Gross et al., 1985). Targeted treatment-related skills also focus on improving management through improved dietary monitoring and restriction, increased frequency and accuracy of glucose monitoring, and improved skill at adjusting and administering insulin (Anderson, Wolf, Burkhart, Cornell, & Bacon, 1989; Gross et al., 1985; Satin et al., 1989).

Self-management. In reference to diabetes, self-management requires patients to constantly test their blood glucose level and use this information to adjust their eating, exercise, and insulin use (Delamater, 1990). Interventions targeting self-management skills have been somewhat successful in improving metabolic status for youth with diabetes (Anderson et al., 1989; Delamater, 1990; Gross et al., 1985). After being taught specific skills in the group sessions (such as how to accurately record blood glucose data), teens are required to practice as homework and are rewarded for performing the behaviors by parent and or therapist.

Reinforcement. In addition to contingent parental praise, adolescents learn how to reinforce themselves and in some instances, how to reinforce their parents (Gross et al., 1985). Being responsible for selection of rewards and self-delivery has been found to be successful for teens with diabetes. Moreover, teens are taught how to reward their parents with praise when their parents offer assistance with disease management.

Group Treatment

A prototypical CBT group intervention is described by Satin and colleagues (1989). The goals of this intervention were based on enhancing communication within the family concerning diabetes and improving problem-solving skills utilizing role-play and parental simulation. Three to four families met for 6 weekly, 90-minute sessions. The groups included adolescents, one or two of their parents, and a group leader. Each session began with a review of the previous session, allowing time for any remaining questions or comments on the earlier session. Then the topic shifted to the past week, and participants were encouraged to discuss any diabetes-related management issues that may have occurred. An example of such a problem would be getting adolescents to monitor glucose more frequently or how to handle dietary restrictions in the context of social activities. Participants' feelings about the incidents were explored, and all families were encouraged to explore ideas about similar situations they may have experienced at some point. After identifying the problem and expressing feelings that surround it, participants moved to the resolution stage. Everyone contributed to generating possible solutions; this was followed by family role-plays of the problem situations incorporating new approaches. The group leaders served mainly as discussion moderators and did not offer specific advice, instead the focus was on enhancing the family members' communication and problem-solving skills.

During the third session an extra component was implemented; adolescents were instructed to teach their parents how to manage diabetes and the parents reported on their reactions to the experience at the next session. The simulation included a variety of daily tasks such as administration of self-injections, measurement and recording of urinary glucose four times a day, following a meal plan, following and recording an exercise regimen, recording major and minor episodes of hypoglycemia, and having a blood test. After a week, the parents shared their experiences with the group and were encouraged to evaluate their performance.

Another approach to treatment adherence for children with Type I diabetes, Self-Management Training (SMT), is described by Gross and colleagues (1985). For this intervention the parents and children met in separate groups with the rationale being to increase children's comfort in self-disclosure and to sufficiently address the unique, personal and diabetes-related issues of parents and children. There were 8 weekly, 90-minute sessions based on behavior modification training described by Brigham (1982). For the children, sessions included a written lesson presented in a workbook (measurement of behavior, reinforcement, punishment, extinction, shaping, self-management, modifying the behaviors of others, and negotiation and contracting), discussion, modeling, and role-playing exercises. These topics were related to both social issues and practical management issues concerning living with diabetes. Additionally, the children conducted self-management projects related to their medical treatment. Personal self-change strategies and rewards were created and monitored by the participants. To promote generalization, the children were asked to use their skills with their parents. Specifically, they were to praise their parents for offering support to them with their diabetes management.

For the parent component, the same lessons were covered, including role play and modeling exercises. During the sessions, the experimenter would begin with a brief lecture on the day's topic, which was followed by group discussion. Parents would present topics relevant to medical adherence issues and practice their new skills in reference to the examples they generated. While the parents did not receive the behavioral skills text, they were asked to review the weekly lessons with their children and assist in completing the supplementary study guide. Moreover, the parents were also assigned a behavior modification task. The task was to choose a problematic behavior related to the child's diabetes medical regimen and to change their child's target response through reinforcement and/or extinction.

OVERCOMING OBSTACLES TO TREATMENT

Research regarding the different interventions geared towards pediatric chronic illness groups has elucidated many benefits to group CBT interventions. The research is equally informative in highlighting several obstacles that exist to this treatment.

Paucity of Treatment Models

First, an important obstacle to effective group CBT interventions for chronic medical illness is the current dearth of treatment models. While each illness has its respective medical complications and physical impediments, the adversities these families face are often analogous. A generic treatment model, with sufficient flexibility to address disease-specific concerns, could guide therapists treating children with chronic conditions and their families. Moreover, although many published intervention studies with pediatric samples are provided in group formats, these interventions are often not well-delineated nor are they empirically evaluated. Increased descriptions of group CBT interventions that address the utility of the group format explicitly are necessary.

Obtaining Parent Involvement

Second, as evidenced by a number of aforementioned studies (Gross et al., 1985; Satin et al., 1989), parent participation represents a key element in the treatment of chronic medical conditions. Parent participation may contribute to the success of treatment by modeling target behaviors, providing parents with tools of contingency management and reinforcing behavior, and increasing parents' self-efficacy regarding management of their child's medical condition. Obtaining consistent parent involvement in group CBT interventions, however, is often times a difficult task. A potentially useful strategy employs contingency management for parents by incorporating reinforcement administered by the children, the parents themselves, or the researcher.

Participation of Medically Involved Patients

Third, a related concern is the difficulty of soliciting the participation of children who are medically-involved. A chronic medical condition carries with it numerous daily stressors including frequent hospital visits, managing complicated medication regimens, doctors' appointments, and financial constraints. Requiring patients and their families to attend a psychosocial intervention may initially add to their overall stress level, regardless of the proven effectiveness of the offered intervention. Therefore, it is imperative to decrease the burden of participation by providing transportation, reducing the number of sessions, holding sessions on the weekend, conducting sessions through home visits, and/or providing interventions in school settings or during hospital visits.

Identifying Effective Components of Interventions

Finally, it is important to acknowledge that many of the research interventions discussed in this chapter contained multiple components. A randomized controlled trial investigating the effectiveness of a treatment "package" can only vouch for the efficacy of the treatment provided within that package. Unless dismantling studies are done to investigate the efficacy of the separate components of a treatment package, it is impossible to determine accurately which portions of the intervention contributed to the outcome in an intervention. The last obstacle to effective group treatment of chronic medical conditions is therefore our inability at present to identify the effective components of treatments tested in the literature. Therefore, professionals who implement these interventions are cautioned against picking and choosing elements of interventions. At present, the most effective approach may be to provide the entire package.

SUMMARY

Group CBT interventions and associated assessment approaches were described for children with chronic medical conditions. These interventions target children with a range of chronic illnesses and medical presentations, congenital and acquired. Although all the identified conditions are not life-threatening, they share the ability to tax children and their families' resources, limit functional ability, and threaten quality of life and psychosocial adjustment. We focused on the application of group CBT interventions to the treatment of pediatric overweight, amelioration of chronic pain, improvement of social skills, and increase in treatment adherence. Group CBT interventions for children and adolescents with chronic medical illness are promising in their effectiveness; they present challenges associated with the demands of balancing children and families' developmental needs with the demands of illnesses and opportunities to refine the multi-component treatments to better meet the needs of these children.

RECOMMENDED READINGS

Barakat, L. P., Hetzke, J. D., Foley, B., Carey, M. E., Gyato, K., & Phillips, P. C. (2003). Evaluation of a social-skills training group intervention with children treated for brain tumors: A pilot study. *Journal of Pediatric Psychology, 28*, 299–307.

Barakat, L. P., Kunin-Batson, A., & Kazak, A. E. (2003). Child Health Psychology. In A. Nezu, C. Nezu, & P. Geller (Eds.), *Handbook of psychology: Health psychology* (vol. 9, pp. 439–464). New York: Wiley.

Eccleston, C., Morely, S., Williams, A., Yorke, L., & Mastroyannopoulou, K. (2002). Systematic review of randomized controlled trials of psychological therapy for chronic pain in children and adolescents, with a subset meta-analysis of pain relief. *Pain, 99,* 157–165.

Epstein, L. H., Myers, M. D., Raynor, H. A., & Saelens, B. E. (1998). Treatment of pediatric obesity. *Pediatrics, 101*, 554–570.

Gresham, F. M. (1985). Utility of cognitive-behavioral procedures for social skills training with children: A critical review. *Journal of Abnormal Child Psychology, 13*, 411–423.

Jelalian, E., & Saelens, B. E. (1999). Empirically supported treatments in pediatric obesity. *Journal of Pediatric Psychology, 24*, 223–248.

Plante, W. A., Lobato, D., & Engel, R. (2001). Review of group interventions for pediatric chronic conditions. *Journal of Pediatric Psychology, 26*, 435–453.

Wallander, J. L., Thompson, R. J., Jr., & Alriksson-Schmidt, A. (2003). Psychosocial adjustment of children with chronic physical conditions. In M. C. Roberts (Ed.), *Handbook of pediatric psychology* (3rd ed., pp. 141–158). New York: Guilford.

REFERENCES

Achenbach, T. M. (1991). *Manual for the child behavior checklist/4-18.* Burlington: University of Vermont Department of Psychiatry.

Anderson, B. J., Wolf, F. M., Burkhart, M. T., Cornell, R. G., & Bacon, G. E. (1989). Effects of peer-group intervention on metabolic control of adolescents with IDDM randomized outpatient study. *Diabetes Care, 12*(3), 179–183.

Armstrong, F. D., Toledano, S. R., Miloslavich, K., Lackman-Zeman, L., Levy, J. D., Gay, C. L., et al. (1999). The Miami Pediatric Quality of Life Questionnaire: Parent scale. *International Journal of Cancer: Supplement, 12*, 11–17.

Barakat, L. P., Hetzke, J. D., Foley, B., Carey, M. E., Gyato, K., & Phillips, P. C. (2003). Evaluation of a social-skills training group intervention with children treated for brain tumors: A pilot study. *Journal of Pediatric Psychology, 28*, 299–307.

Barakat, L. P., Kunin-Batson, A., & Kazak, A. E. (2003). Child Health Psychology. In A. Nezu, C. Nezu, & P. Geller (Eds.), *Handbook of Psychology: Health Psychology* (vol. 9, pp. 439–464). New York: Wiley.

Barakat, L. P., Lash, L., Lutz, M. J., & Nicolaou, D. C. (2006). Psychosocial adaptation of children and adolescents with sickle cell disease. In R. T. Brown (Ed.), *Pediatric hematology/oncology: A biopsychosocial approach.* New York: Oxford University Press.

Barry, J. B. A., & von Baeyer, C. L. (1997). Brief cognitive-behavioral group treatment for children's headache. *Clinical Journal of Pain, 13*(3), 215–220.

Baum, D., & Creer, T. (1986). Medication compliance in children with asthma. *Journal of Asthma, 23,* 49–59.

Bauman, L. J., Drotar, D. Leventhal, J. M., Perrin, E. C., & Pless, I. B. (1997). A review of psychosocial interventions for children with chronic health conditions. *Pediatrics, 100,* 244–251.

Brigham, T. A. (1982). *Managing everyday problems: A manual of applied psychology for young people.* Pullman: Washington State University.

Brownlee-Duffeck, M., Peterson, L., Simonds, J. F., Goldstein, D., Kilo, C., & Hoette, S. (1987). The role of health beliefs in the regimen adherence and metabolic control of adolescents and adults with diabetes mellitus. *Journal of Consulting and Clinical Psychology, 55*(2), 139–144.

Carey, M. E., Barakat, L. P., Foley, B., Gyato, K., & Phillips, P. C. (2001). Neuropsychological functioning and social functioning of survivors of pediatric brain tumors: Evidence of nonverbal learning disability. *Child Neuropsychology, 7,* 265–272.

Carpentieri, S. C., Mulhern, R. K., Douglas, S., Hanna, S., & Fairclough, D. L. (1993). Behavioral resiliency among children surviving brain tumors: A longitudinal study. *Journal of Clinical Child Psychology, 22*(2), 236–246.

Centers for Disease Control and Prevention Body Mass Index (BMI) for Children and Teens. (2005, September 15). Retrieved September 15, 2005, from http://www.cdc.gov/nccdphp/dnpa/bmi/bmi-for-age.html.

Chen, E., Cole, S. W., & Kato, P. M. (2004). A review of empirically supported psychosocial interventions for pain and adherence outcomes in sickle cell disease. *Journal of Pediatric Psychology, 29*(3), 197–209.

Davis, W. K., Hess, G. E., Harrison, R. V., & Hiss, R. G. (1987). Psychosocial adjustment to and control of diabetes mellitus: Differences by disease type and treatment. *Health Psychology, 6,* 1–14.

Delamater, A. M. (2000). Critical issues in the assessment of regimen adherence in children with diabetes. In D. Drotar (Ed.), *Promoting adherence to medical treatment in chronic childhood illness: Concepts, methods, and interventions* (pp. 173–196). Mahwah, NJ: Erlbaum.

Delamater, A. M., Bubb, J., Davis, S. G., Smith, J. A., Schmidt, L., White, N. H., et al. (1990). Randomized prospective study of self-management training with newly diagnosed diabetic children. *Diabetes Care, 13*(5), 492–498.

Die-Trill, M., Bromberg, J., LaVally, B., Portales, L.A., SanFeliz, A., & Patenaude, A.F. (1996). Development of social skills in boys with brain tumors: A group approach. *Journal of Psychosocial Oncology, 14*(2), 23–41.

Dubo, S. (1951). Opportunities for group therapy in a pediatric service. *International Journal of Group Psychotherapy, 1,* 235–242.

Eccleston, C., Morely, S., Williams, A., Yorke, L., & Mastroyannopoulou, K. (2002). Systematic review of randomized controlled trials of psychological therapy for chronic pain in children and adolescents, with a subset meta-analysis of pain relief. *Pain, 99,* 157–165.

Elliott, S. N., & Gresham, F. M. (1993). Social skills interventions for children. *Behavior Modification, 17*(3), 287–313.

Epstein, L. H., Myers, M. D., Raynor, H. A., & Saelens, B. E. (1998). Treatment of pediatric obesity. *Pediatrics, 101,* 554–570.

Epstein, L. H., Valoski, A. M., Vara, L. S., McCurley, J., Wisniewski, L., Kalarchian, M. A., Klein, K. R., et al. (1995). Effects of decreasing sedentary behavior and increasing activity on weight change in obese children. *Health Psychology, 14,* 109–115.

Epstein, L. H., Wing, R. R., & Valoski, A. M. (1985). Childhood obesity. *Pediatric Clinics of North America, 32,* 363–379.

Flor, H., Birbaumer, N., & Rudy, D. C. (1990). The psychobiology of chronic pain. *Advances in Behaviour Research and Therapy, 12,* 47–84.

Garstein, M., Short, A., Vannatta, K., & Noll, R. (1999). Psychosocial adjustment of children with chronic illness: An evaluation of three models. *Developmental and Behavioral Pediatrics, 20,* 157–163.

Gil, K. M., Abrams, M. Phillips, G., & Keefe, F. (1989). Sickle cell disease pain: Relations of coping strategies to adjustment. *Journal of Consulting and Clinical Psychology, 57*(6), 725–731.

Gil, K. M., Abrams, M. Phillips, G., & Williams, D. A. (1992). Sickle cell disease pain: 2. Predicting health care use and activity level at 9 months follow-up. *Journal of Consulting and Clinical Psychology, 60,* 267–273.

Greenan-Fowler, E., Powell, C., & Varni, J.W. (1987). Behavioral treatment of adherence to therapeutic exercise by children with hemophilia. *Archives of Physical Medicine and Rehabilitation, 68,* 846–849.

Gresham, F. M. (1985). Utility of cognitive-behavioral procedures for social skills training with children: A critical review. *Journal of Abnormal Child Psychology, 13,* 411–423.

Gresham, F. M., & Elliott, S. N. (1990). *The social skills rating system*. Circle Pines, MN: American Guidance Service.

Gross, A. M., Magalnick, L. J., & Richardson, P. (1985). Self-management training with families of insulin-dependant diabetic children: A controlled long-term investigation. *Child and Family Behavioral Therapy, 7*(1), 35–50.

Hays, D. M., Landsverk, J., Sallan, S. E., Hewett, K. D., Patenaude, A. F., Schoonover, D., et al. (1992). Educational, occupational and insurance status of childhood cancer survivors in their fourth and fifth decades of life. *Journal of Clinical Oncology, 10*, 1397–1406.

Helm-Hylkema, H. V. D., Orlebeke, J. F., Enting, L. A., Thussen, J. H. H., & van Ree, J. (1990). Effects of behaviour therapy on migraine and plasma β-endorphin in young migraine patients. *Psychoneuroendocrinology, 15*(1), 39–45.

Holden, E. W., Deichmann, M. M., & Levy, J. D. (1999). Empirically supported treatments in pediatric psychology: Recurrent pediatric headache. *Journal of Pediatric Psychology, 24*(2), 91–109.

Jelalian, E., & Saelens, B.E. (1999). Empirically supported treatments in pediatric obesity. *Journal of Pediatric Psychology, 24*, 223–248.

Kroener-Herwig, B., & Denecke, H. (2002). Cognitive-behavioral therapy of pediatric headache: Are there differences in efficacy between a therapist-administered group training and a self-help format? *Journal of Psychosomatic Research, 53*, 1107–1114.

La Greca, A., & Bearman, K. J. (2003). Adherence to pediatric treatment regimens. In M.C. Roberts (Ed.), *Handbook of Pediatric Psychology* (3rd ed., pp. 141–158). New York: Guilford.

Landgraf, J. M., Abertz, L., & Ware, J. E. (1996). *The CHQ user's manual*, (Second Printing). Boston, MA: HealthAct.

Lavigne, J. V., & Faier-Routman, J. (1992). Psychological adjustment to pediatric physical disorders: A meta-analytic review. *Journal of Pediatric Psychology, 17*, 122–157.

Mayo Foundation for Medical Education and Research (2005). *Type 1 diabetes*. (2005, July 1). Retrieved September 28, 2005, from http://www.mayoclinic.com/invoke.cfm?id=DS00329&dsection=1.

Meadows, A. T., & Hobbie, W. L. (1986). The medical consequences of cure. *Cancer, 58*, 524–528.

Morison, J. E., Bromfield, L. M., & Cameron, H. J. (2003). A therapeutic model for supporting families of children with a chronic illness or disability. *Child and Adolescent Mental Health, 8*, 125–130.

Mulhern, R. K., Carpentieri, S., Shema, S., Stone, P., & Fairclough, D. (1993). Factors associated with social and behavioral problems among children recently diagnosed with brain tumors. *Journal of Pediatric Psychology, 18*, 339–350.

National Institute of Diabetes and Digestive and Kidney Diseases.(2004). *Your guide to diabetes type 1 and type 2*. (NIH Publication No. 05-4016). Washington, DC: U.S. Government Printing Office.

Newacheck, P. W., & Taylor, W. R. (1992). Childhood chronic illness: Prevalence, severity, and impact. *American Journal of Public Health, 82*, 364–371.

O'Neil, P. M., Currey, H. S., Hirsch, A. A., Malcolm, R. J., Sexauer, J. D., Riddle, F. E., et al. (1979). Development and validation of the Eating Behavior Inventory. *Journal of Behavioral Assessment, 1*, 123–132.

Osgood, C., Suci, G., & Tannenbaum, P. (1957). *The measurement of meaning*. Urbana: University of Illinois Press.

Palermo, T. M., Valenzuela, D., & Stork, P. P. (2003). A randomized trial of electronic versus paper pain diaries in children: Impact on compliance, accuracy, and acceptability. *Pain, 107*, 213–219.

Perquin, C. W., Hazebroek-Kampscheur, A. A. J. M., Hunfeld, J. A. M., Bohnene, A. M., van Suijlekom-Smit, L. W. A., Passchier, J. et al. (2000). Pain in children and adolescents: A common experience. *Pain, 87*, 51–58.

Plante, W. A., Lobato, D., & Engel, R. (2001). Review of group interventions for pediatric chronic conditions. *Journal of Pediatric Psychology, 26*, 435–453.

Powers, S. W., Mitchell, M. J., Graumlich, S. E., Byars, K. C., & Kalinyak, K. A. (2002). Longitudinal assessment of pain, coping, and daily functioning in children with sickle cell disease receiving pain management skills training. *Journal of Clinical Psychology in Medical Settings, 9*(2), 109–119.

Radcliffe, J., Barakat, L. P., & Boyd, R. (2004). *A cognitive-behavior pain management intervention for teens with sickle cell disease*. Presented at the Child Health Psychology Conference, Charleston, SC.

Reynolds, C. R., & Kamphaus, R. W. (2004). *Behavior assessment system for children* (2nd ed., BASC-2). Circle Pines, MN: American Guidance Services.

Rolland, J. (1987). Chronic Illness and the life cycle: A conceptual framework. *Family Process, 26*, 203–221.

Sanders, M. R., Cleghorn, G., Shepherd, R. W., & Patrick, M. (1996). Predictors of clinical improvement in children with recurrent abdominal pain. *Behavioural and Cognitive Psychotherapy, 244*(1), 27–38.

Sanders, M. R., Shepherd, R. W., Cleghorn, G., & Woolford, H. (1994). The treatment of recurrent abdominal pain in children: A controlled comparison of cognitive-behavioral family intervention and standard pediatric care. *Journal of Consulting and Clinical Psychology, 62*(2), 306–314.

Satin, W., La Greca, A.M., Zigo, M. A., & Skyler, J. S. (1989). Diabetes in adolescence: Effects of multifamily group intervention and parent simulation of diabetes. *Journal of Pediatric Psychology, 14,* 259–275.

Siegel, L. J., & Smith, K. E. (1989). Children's strategies for coping with pain. *Pediatrician, 16,* 110–118.

Siegler, D. E., La Greca, A. M., Citrin, W. S., Reeves, M. L., & Skyler, J.S. (1982). Psychological effects of intensification of diabetic control. *Diabetes Care, 5*(Suppl. 1), 19–23.

Stein, R. E. K., & Jessop, D. J. (1982). A noncategorical approach to chronic childhood illness. *Public Health Reports, 97,* 354–362.

Stone, A. A., Shiffman, S., Schwartz, J. E., Broderick, J. E., & Hufford, M. R. (2003). Patient compliance with paper and electronic diaries. *Control Clinical Trials, 24,* 182–199.

Turk, D. C., & Meichenbaum, D. (1994). A cognitive-behavioural approach to pain management. In P. D. Wall & R. Melzack (Eds.), *Textbook of pain* (3rd ed., pp. 1337–1348). Churchill Livingstone: Edinburgh.

van den Brink, M., Bandell-Hoekstra, E. N. G., & Abu-Saad, H. H. (2001). The occurrence of recall bias in pediatric headache: A comparison of questionnaire and diary data. *Headache, 41,* 11–20.

Vannatta, K., Gartstein, M. A., Short, A., & Noll, R. B. (1998). A controlled study of peer relationships of children surviving brain tumors: Teacher, peer, and self ratings. *Journal of Pediatric Psychology, 23,* 279–287.

Varni, J. W., & Thompson, K. L. (1985). *The Varni/Thompson Pediatric Pain Questionnaire.* Unpublished manuscript.

Varni, J. W., Katz, E. R., Colegrove, R., Jr., & Dolgin, M. (1993). The impact of social skills training on the adjustment of children with newly diagnosed cancer. *Journal of Pediatric Psychology, 18,* 751–767.

Walco, G. A., Sterling, C. M., Conte, P. M., & Engel, R. G. (1999). Empirically supported treatments in pediatric psychology: Disease-related pain. *Journal of Pediatric Psychology, 24*(2), 155–167.

Wallander, J. L., Thompson, R. J., Jr., & Alriksson-Schmidt, A. (2003). Psychosocial adjustment of children with chronic physical conditions. In M. C. Roberts (Ed.), *Handbook of pediatric psychology* (3rd ed., pp. 141–158). New York: Guilford.

Weist, M., Finney, J., Barnard, M., & Ollendick, T. (1993). Empirical selection of psychosocial treatment targets for children and adolescents with diabetes. *Journal of Pediatric Psychology, 18,* 11–23.

Wysocki, T., Greco, P., & Buckloh, L.M. (2003). Childhood diabetes in psychological context. In M. C. Roberts (Ed.), *Handbook of pediatric psychology* (3rd ed., pp. 141–158). New York: Guilford.

Wysocki, T., Green, L., & Huxtable, K. (1989). Blood glucose monitoring by diabetic adolescents: Compliance and metabolic control. *Health Psychology, 8,* 267–284.

Chapter Twenty-Four

A Relational-Cultural, Cognitive-Behavioral Approach to Treating Female Adolescent Eating Disorders

Andrea Bloomgarden, Rosemary B. Mennuti,
April Conti, & Andrea B. Weller

Eating disorders have become so prevalent that they are now considered one of the most widespread psychiatric problems faced by women and girls (Stice, 2002). In today's society, the pressure to be thin can emanate from a variety of sources including sociocultural factors (e.g., peer influences), family factors (e.g., enmeshment and criticism), negative affect, low self-esteem, and body dissatisfaction (Polivy & Herman, 2002). Body dissatisfaction and dieting are especially pervasive among adolescent girls and young women due to the portrayal of models, movie stars, and diet aids (Costin, 1999). In addition, eating disorders cause many health and psychological hazards to the lives of their victims. If serious enough, they can even cause death (Grave, 2003; Kohn & Golden, 2001).

Eating problems have been found to develop in late childhood and continue throughout late adolescence and into adulthood (Lask & Bryant-Waugh, 2000). Recent studies claim that 5 to 15% of school-aged and high school–aged females experience some symptoms, if not all the criteria for a diagnosable eating disorder (Graber et al., 1994). It has become an epidemic and it is essential that effective treatment be available to support young women in this crisis.

According to Costin (1999), group therapy provides a good opportunity for patients with eating disorders to educate each other from their wide variety of experiences in identification and problem-solving techniques. Group therapy allows patients to feel less secluded in their views and experiences, by sharing and listening to others, thus decreasing a common sense of isolation and facilitating interpersonal learning.

OVERVIEW OF FEMALE ADOLESCENTS
AND EATING DISORDERS

Adolescence presents many changes and stressors for youth. On a physical and psychological level, Attie and Brooks-Gunn (1989) point out that females undergo several developmental challenges including: (1) adjustment to the physical changes of puberty including an increase in body fat; (2) social and emotional changes such as making the transition out of childhood by forming new connections and ties with parents and establishing themselves with peers; and (3) the development of a stable, consolidated identity. According to researchers, the physical changes related to the increase of body fat at pubertal transformation is one of the most significant changes that may contribute to negative eating behaviors, since being thin equates to being good and denotes beauty, competence, and success (Fallon, Katzman, & Wooley, 1994; Mishne, 1986). Thus, self-worth becomes linked with one's level of attractiveness and a body size that meets the standards set in the media. The standards are unrealistic and impossible to achieve for most anyone. It is because of this unrealistic standard set by society that adolescents strive to be thin, no matter how great the cost may be to their own health and bodies (Attie & Brooks-Dunn, 1989).

On a sociocultural level, adolescent girls become shaped by the culturally sanctioned norm to suppress their strengths, identity, and true expression (often referred to as "voice"), in order to preserve relationships. Because girls and women are taught to value relationships more than their own self-expression, they have a heightened sensitivity to cues that suggest damage to a relationship, and in many cases become adept at suppressing their "voice" in order to not lose the relationship. For example, they could agree when they do not agree, feel ashamed of and inhibit strengths so as not to threaten someone else's authority, learn to avoid conflict with others at all costs, even stating they are to blame even when they are not, or trying to convince themselves that they feel differently than they really do. All of these "strategies of disconnection" from themselves are rewarded in that they successfully avoid conflict with parents, peers, and potential dating partners by being agreeable, putting on a smile and in a plethora of ways invalidating their own experience. They become adept at disconnecting from themselves, and grow increasingly more remote from their authentic selves, creating fertile ground for the development of eating disorders, which become the new outlet for expression of disowned feelings.

Individual difference variables hypothesized to be related to developing eating disorders include significant life stressors and affective deficiencies, such as low self-esteem, depressed mood, generalized anxiety, and irritability (Polivy & Herman, 2002). Similarly, personality characteristics such as perfectionist strivings, feelings of ineffectiveness, and self-regulatory deficits are associated with eating disorders. Research conducted by Johnson, Cohen, Kotler, Kasen, and Brook (2002) examined the impact of psychiatric disorders, including anxiety, depressive, disruptive, and personality. Results indicate that females with depressive disorders during early adolescence may be at high risk for the onset of eating problems, including eating disorders, dietary restriction, purging behavior, unusual eating behavior, and recurrent fluctuations in body weight.

Life challenges such as peer influences, media pressures, and personal identification issues including self-esteem, body image, and difficulties with affective expression, may lead adolescent girls to feel "out of control" (Attie & Brooks-Gunn, 1989). While they strive to make good decisions and increase their sense of self, coping patterns, which were adaptive for awhile, become harmful and inevitably contribute to disconnection in relationships, silencing of inner voice, and poor self-esteem (Surrey, 1991; Brown & Gilligan, 1992). According to Steiner-Adair (1991), when adolescents feel that they have lost their ability to verbally express their thoughts, feelings, and opinions, their bodies become the external self that speaks, metaphorically, through behavior. The adolescent's self-worth is evidenced in her attempts to communicate through her illness (Steiner-Adair, 1991). These negative characteristics can potentially pave the path for the development of an eating disorder (Kohn & Golden, 2001; Massey-Stokes, 2000; Mishne, 1986).

Female adolescents may develop eating disorders when faced with numerous challenges and situations, involving physical, cognitive, and social changes that alter many domains of their lives. In order to aid in the recovery of those with eating disorders, it is essential to address cognitions, affect, and behavior while providing education, healthy relationship building, and adaptive coping skills. Group therapy is supported in the literature as an effective form of treatment for adolescents with eating disorders. Special attention to the therapeutic relationship, enhancement of motivation for change, and a cognitive-behavioral conceptualization is suggested. The research on female growth and development that emphasizes the importance of authentic, mutual, and growth fostering relationships supports the use of groups to help girls address their issues in a supportive setting (Daigneault, 2000). Largely, group therapy for adolescent females with eating disorders assists them in feeling less alone in their experiences and validated as they learn about each other, see themselves in each other, and see many common themes or underlying psychological issues they share (Wilson & Vitousek, 1999).

ASSESSMENT

Eating disorders require early identification of symptoms and aggressive intervention in order to prevent many of the severe consequences from occurring. The assessment process is an essential tool to establish diagnoses, develop case conceptualization, implement treatment planning, and track progress on treatment goals throughout the treatment process (Crowther & Sherwood, 1997). The interview, self-report, and behavioral assessments are the three main procedures clinicians use for assessing individuals with eating disorders (Anderson, Lundgren, Shapiro, & Paulosky, 2004). The interview establishes the initial diagnosis, self-report questionnaires guide the clinician to detailed information regarding abnormal eating and psychopathology-related symptoms, and behavioral methods provide a means of self-monitoring (Crowther & Sherwood, 1997; Anderson et al., 2004). Each assessment approach has its strengths and weaknesses. The following discussion will elaborate on the previous information and include specific tools and techniques in order to facilitate the treatment process of eating disorders, namely anorexia nervosa (AN) and bulimia nervosa (BN).

The Interview and Diagnostic Process

Assessment for the presence and severity of an eating disorder requires that the interviewer possess both the knowledge of which questions to ask, and the ability to truly embody a nonjudgmental collaborative stance with the adolescent (Mennuti, Bloomgarden,

& Gabriel, 2005). The interview initially requires open-ended statements and questions for opening a dialogue with the individual about who she is, what her life is like, and how she is feeling about herself. Once the conversation is begun, questions about how she feels about herself in relation to her body and eating can follow more naturally. The details of the eating disorder need to be captured but it is a very personal disclosure, requiring much courage on the part of the adolescent.

It is essential for clinician's to gather a thorough weight history, as well as to evaluate for body image dissatisfaction. It is important to ask questions regarding the individual's feelings and perceptions about body weight and shape, probe the meaning attached to striving for or maintaining ideal weight, and the impact that others' perceptions of weight and shape have had on the individual (Crowther & Sherwood, 1997). Affective disturbance and other psychological issues often coexist with eating disorders; therefore, an assessment of mental health factors is also needed. These include mood disorders, problems with impulsivity, self-harming urges or activities (e.g., cutting oneself), obsessive-compulsive disorder, anxiety disorders, and other addictions (e.g., drug and alcohol). It is essential to clarify the relationship between eating disorders and comorbid disturbances to more effectively treat the individual.

A review of medical issues and overall physical well-being is taken to probe for any signs or symptoms of imminently dangerous medical complications. Questions should include a brief inquiry assessing the presence or absence of each of the following: chest pain or pressure, light-headedness or fainting, dizziness, blood in stool or vomit, any medical conditions that might be affected by the eating problems (e.g., diabetes, appropriate use of insulin), abdominal pain, irregular or scanty menses, sleep apnea, and dental problems (Mennuti, Bloomgarden & Gabriel, 2005).

Diagnostic Measures

Eating Disorder Examination (EDE).   The EDE is a semistructured interview designed to assess psychopathology associated with AN and BN. The 12th edition assesses overeating and methods of extreme weight control, and eating, shape, and weight concern (Anderson et al., 2004). Due to the EDE's well-established psychometric properties (Rizvi, Peterson, Crow, & Agras, 2000; Cooper, Cooper, & Fairburn, 1989) and its ability to assess objective binge episodes, it is the method of choice by many clinicians (Anderson & Maloney, 2001).

Self-Report Questionnaire

Self-report measures serve as screening instruments for the presence of eating and clinical pathology during the assessment process (Anderson et al., 2004). These measures are usually brief and simplistic, relatively inexpensive, and have a cut-off score to indicate a specific level of eating or psychiatric pathology (2004). Self-report questionnaires are useful for augmenting the treatment planning process and for evaluating progress during treatment (Crowther & Sherwood, 1997). However, denial, secrecy, and minimization of the problem create reliability and validity issues (Crowther & Sherwood, 1997). Included below are several psychometrically sound and useful self-report measures.

Eating Attitudes Test (EAT).   The EAT was originally a 40-item self-report questionnaire developed to assess eating attitudes and behaviors. The primary use of the EAT is to identify individuals with various levels and types of eating disturbances (Crowther & Sherwood, 1997). It is an index of the severity of concerns typical among women with eating disorders, particularly in the areas of drive for thinness, fear of weight gain, and restrictive eating (Crowther & Sherwood). The EAT-26 is an abbreviated version to differentiate between severe eating disordered individuals and non-eating disordered individuals (Anderson et al., 2004). Items are written as statements on a Likert scale (i.e., never, rarely, sometimes, often, very often, and always). The EAT-26 is adequately reliable and valid for assessing body image, weight, and dieting (Koslowsky et al., 1992).

Bulimia Test—Revised (BULIT-R).   The primary use of the BULIT-R is to screen for symptoms of BN and to discriminate individuals with BN from individuals with AN and no eating disorders. The BULIT-R consists of 36 items on a 5-point Likert-scale. Examples of questions include, "I feel that food controls my life" and "I eat a lot of food when I'm not even hungry." The BULIT-R results in a value that increases with the severity of the symptomatology. The authors recommend a cutoff score of 104 to identify an individual with BN (Thelen, Farmer, Wonderlich, & Smith, 1991). Research suggests that the BULIT-R has good psychometric properties (Thelen et al., 1991).

Eating Disorder Inventory (EDI-2).   The EDI-2 is a 91-item self-report questionnaire used to measure eating related attitudes and traits. It yields the following eight subscales, including (1) drive for thinness, (2) bulimia, (3) body dissatisfaction, (4) ineffectiveness, (5) perfectionism, (6) interpersonal distrust, (7) interoceptive awareness, and (8) maturity fears (Crowther & Sherwood, 1997). The EDI-2 was adapted from an earlier version (i.e., EDI), which used the 8 subscales, and added: (1) asceticism, (2) impulse regulation, and (3) social insecurity (Anderson et al., 2004). Researchers predict good levels of psychometric validity and reliability with the original version of this measure (Crowther, Lilly, Crawford, & Shepard, 1992). The EDI-2 is one of the most widely used assessment tools for individuals with eating disorders because of its ability to assess many of the core domains of the disturbances (Anderson et al., 2004).

Behavioral Measures

Self-monitoring is a behavioral assessment procedure that monitors an individual's food intake in order to obtain information about eating behavior in the naturalistic environment. Self-monitoring provides the clinician with an assessment of the frequency and timing of meals and snacks and the type of the food consumed, the binging episodes, and other compensatory methods (Crowther & Sherwood, 1997). Self-monitoring becomes a useful tool during CBT to establish regular eating habits (Garner, Vitousek, & Pike, 1997), challenge maladaptive thoughts about food (Garner et al., 1997), increase awareness of internal states and their relationship to food (Crowther & Sherwood, 1997), and to help the clinician guide the patient to realize that "food is just food" (Bowers, 2001, p. 298).

COGNITIVE CONCEPTUALIZATION

Eating disorders, anorexia nervosa (AN), bulimia nervosa (BN) and Eating Disorders Not otherwise Specified (EDNOS), appear to be "multifactoral disorders," as multiple factors influence their onset and contribute to their maintenance (e.g., onset of puberty, parental attachment style, family relationships, peer relationships, media influence, and low self-esteem; Fisher et al., 1995). According to Fairburn and Walsh (2002), an eating disorder can be defined as "a persistent disturbance of eating behavior or behavior intended to control weight, which significantly impairs physical health or psychological functioning. This disturbance should not be secondary to any recognized general medical disorder or any psychiatric disorder" (p. 171).

The perplexing and recalcitrant nature of eating disorders leads theorists from all views (i.e., sociocultural, family, neurobiological, and cognitive-behavioral) to come together and focus on one very important issue—How are eating disorders developed and maintained? Although AN and BN are two distinct disorders, they share many of the same cognitive and behavioral maintenance mechanisms. The only exception is the extreme emphasis individuals with AN place on starvation (Fairburn, Shafran, & Cooper, 1999). The following discussion will address the cognitive conceptualization of eating disorders from a cognitive-behavioral perspective and the dysfunctional thought system that is involved in the development and maintenance the two disorders.

The central features of the cognitive-behavioral model for eating disorders encompass the body self-schema, cognitive biases, negative reinforcement of compensatory behavior by reduction of negative emotion, psychological risk factors that define individuals who are most vulnerable to the development of eating disorders, binge eating, and compensatory behaviors (Williamson, White, York-Crowe, & Stewart, 2004). In addition, many individuals with eating disorders have a long-standing pattern of low self-esteem or negative self-evaluation, which interact with extreme concerns about shape and weight (Wilson, Fairburn, & Agras, 1997). Individuals with AN and BN tend to idealize and evaluate themselves in terms of their appearance because it is more controllable than other areas of their lives. However, strong negative self-evaluation leads individuals with disordered eating to become consistently dissatisfied with appearance, which leads to increasingly lower self-esteem combined with further methods of dietary restraint and compensatory behaviors (Anderson & Maloney, 2001).

The body's self-schema plays an essential role in the development and maintenance of eating disorders. Cognitive theorists have hypothesized that over concern with body weight and shape can result in a self-schema that is activated by external and internal cues. For example, an individual interprets feelings of fullness after a meal as feeling fat (Williamson et al., 2004). Due to the stable nature of a schema, it may resist change; however, it is not immune to change (Garner, Vitousek, & Pike, 1997). Furthermore, cognitive biases, that is, faulty interpretations of self-schema, are activated in individuals with highly developed body self-schema. According to Williamson and colleagues (2004), key stimulus characteristics that readily activate cognitive biases are body/food related information, ambiguous stimuli, and situations that require an individual to reflect on the body.

Negative emotion, such as anxiety, depression, feelings of "fatness," self-hate, and anger, which are often present in individuals with eating disorders, interact with self-schema and cognitive biases to produce a feedback loop (Williamson et al., 2004; Fairburn, Cooper, & Shafran, 2003). Psychological factors, such as obsession with body size, fear of fatness and losing control (i.e., "If I am not in complete control, I may lose all control;" Garner et al., 1997), and perfectionism/obsessionality tend to intensify the state of negative emotion (Williamson et al., 2004). Individuals with eating disorders attempt to escape/reduce negative emotions at any cost, for instance, purging, restricting food intake, and through excessive exercise (Williamson et al., 2004). The regulation of negative affect via compensatory behaviors serves to both negatively reinforce and confirm the need for the behavior (Garner et al., 1997; Williamson et al., 2004). In a study conducted by Waller, Ohanian, Meyer, and Osman (2000) on a group of 50 individuals with BN, the main distinction between purging and non-purging "bulimics" was in the area of perception and self-evaluation. Furthermore, Waller and colleagues found non-purging individuals with BN rated themselves as "more" flawed, lacking in self-control, and relatively unsuccessful in comparison to the purging individuals with BN. The act of vomiting among the purging group helped to reduce awareness and escape the unbearable cognitions, which arise from the core beliefs of shame and defectiveness.

Cognitive theorists argue that eating disorders are developed and maintained by current dysfunctional thinking patterns (Beck, 1995). Furthermore, cognitive-behavioral theorists conceptualize AN and BN in a developmental framework, emphasizing the role of cognitions interceding distressed emotion and abnormal behavior (Bowers, 2001). For example, individuals seek the need for control due to pervasive feelings of ineffectiveness (Fairburn et al., 1999; Vitousek & Manke, 1994). The feelings of ineffectiveness become paralyzing and obsessive for the individual with AN and BN, and they begin to pervade all thinking and activities in which the individual engages (Fairburn et al., 1999). By gaining control of one's eating behavior, the sense of accomplishment, self-worth, and purpose that develop "immediately" are very rewarding (Vitousek & Manke, 1994). The individual also gains control of others in the immediate environment by restricting food (Fairburn et al., 1999). In addition, control over one's weight via starvation, self-induced vomiting, misuse of laxatives and diuretics, and over exercising, is successfully established (Fairburn et al., 2003). The increase in self-worth that results from control over one's life is the reason patients are recalcitrant to treatment. For example, individuals with AN begin to define themselves in terms of anorexia nervosa (Garner et al., 1997) and describe their self-identity as "being anorexic" (Fairburn et al., 1999). The self and dietary restriction become inherently intertwined (Fairburn et al.).

By controlling eating behavior, individuals with eating disorders avoid facing other difficulties in their lives, such as family problems, forming relationships, and sexual pressure (Fairburn et al., 1999). Moreover, an individual with AN and BN is often negatively reinforced for the disorder (i.e., the avoidance of the adult shape and the overwhelming challenges of growing up) and socially reinforced for the disorder (i.e., the initial attention and compliments the weight loss brings the individual as societal standards of beauty become more important; Garner et al., 1997). Furthermore, Vitousek and Manke (1994) suggest that self-schemas of inadequacy, perfectibility, and asceticism, when combined with sociocultural pressures regarding beauty and thinness, create reinforcement for dieting and weight loss, which further maintain the disturbance. However, the emaciated state most patients with AN achieve does not result from the influence of societal standards but from the individual's own maladaptive cognitions and self-reinforcement (Garner et al., 1997).

Low self-esteem tends to play a key role in the development and maintenance of eating disorders. Individuals with AN and BN have more of a global negative view of themselves, which pervades all aspects of their identity and creates a feeling of hopelessness (Fairburn et al., 2003). In a study conducted by Geller, Johnston, and Madsen (1997), participants selected personal attributes, ranked them, and divided a circle into pieces such that the size of each would reflect how much their self-esteem was based upon each attribute. The researchers found higher levels of depression and lower overall self-esteem among samples whose self-evaluation was based more on weight and shape. Furthermore, Geller and colleagues (1998) demonstrated that eating-disordered patients reported greater weight-based self-esteem (mean angle of 144.8 degrees) than psychiatric controls (mean angle of 62.8 degrees) and healthy controls (mean angle 59.5 degrees).

GROUP TREATMENT MODEL: COMBINING RELATIONAL-CULTURAL THEORY WITH COGNITIVE, BEHAVIORAL, AND PSYCHOEDUCATIONAL COMPONENTS

The specific group model conceptualization being proposed here will combine facets of relational-cultural theory of group psychotherapy with cognitive, behavioral, and psychoeducational components of treatment. Adolescents with eating disorders can benefit from the opportunity to learn to experience growth-fostering relationships, which then provide an optimal environment for the clients to utilize the various techniques offered. While cognitive-behavioral therapy and psychoeducation themselves are effective for many, in the context of growth fostering relationships, we propose that clients are likely to benefit even more from the techniques.

The relational-cultural model teaches clients how to participate in "growth-fostering" relationships—that is, experiencing feelings of aliveness, energy, safety, and mutuality from the group experience, the adolescent learns relationship skills that she can enact in the rest of her life. Post-group, she will be more skilled at building relationships that will take her out of isolation, meet her emotional needs, help her to build self-esteem, all of which reduce her need for an eating disorder as a means of coping. Conflict, disagreement, and disconnection are normal aspects of relationships, as learning to experience ruptures and repairs, weathering of different opinions, and respectfully expressing anger provide the adolescent with a new awareness that she can speak her voice openly without either losing the relationship or being criticized for her viewpoint. Typically, she has had demoralizing experiences that have led her to believe that expressing her opinion is useless, giving her reason to turn to her eating disorder as a means of coping with frustration or unexpressed feelings and a source of solace and refuge from unmanageable interpersonal problems. The cognitive, behavioral, and psychoeducational techniques are proven techniques that are helpful, and experiencing them together in the context of growth fostering relationships the adolescent gains a new experience of herself.

Authentic relating is very difficult work, as eating disorders provide the individual a haven in which she can hide and feel safely protected. Learning to experience vulnerability while being emotionally supported is at first a huge risk, often counterintuitive for people who have been emotionally isolated and have built their coping style around silencing themselves. This move from isolation to authentic, connected relating is a lifestyle change that is necessary for a full recovery from an eating disorder.

The purpose of the group is multifaceted. Group members will ideally leave the group in 12 weeks with the following new experience—increased awareness of how food, body image, and emotions are related; reframing of thinking into a more compassionate perspective; decreased judgment of self and others; insight into the function of their eating disorder, leading to an increased ability to progress into healthier self-care behaviors; increased knowledge of alternative coping skills that can be developed and practiced; and an experience of moving into interpersonal connection, increased assertiveness, and using one's inner voice. While these are the standard expectations of what will be achieved by members, each group will be somewhat unique depending on the interpersonal dynamics of the individuals present, as well as how the leader facilitates the process.

The overarching principles guiding the practice of this model of group therapy are derived from the concepts in *Relational Practice Groups*, which is based on the work of Jordon and Dooley (2001). The model provides the foundation for giving group members a new experience in relationship with each other, while weaving in cognitive-behavioral strategies and techniques that will be useful to adolescents struggling with food and body image problems.

Group Structure and Member Selection

The ideal group size is about eight members and two facilitators that co-lead and model the relational process. The session length should be no more than 1.5 hours. All members should be enrolled and start on the same week; new members should not be added after the first week, as this is an important basis for creating emotional safety in the group. It should be expected that every member be there every week, with exceptions rarely occurring. The expectation is that members are making a commitment to themselves and each other, understanding that their behavior impacts others. Facilitators must take responsibility for ensuring that the group starts and ends in a timely fashion, which is also a prerequisite for creating an experience of safety.

Potential group participants should have a pre-group interview with both facilitators. The facilitators need to assess the potential member's readiness for participation in a mutual experience with others, which includes their ability to share time with others, feel that they can benefit from listening as well as talking, and to be able to tolerate the discomfort of conflict with the hopeful experience of learning to resolve it productively. According to Banks (2005), an experience of mutuality is one of "...affecting another person as well as being open to being affected or impacted by the other." (p. 191). Facilitators should select members who seem to be capable and ready for such an experience, as opposed to needing individual therapy where they would have the whole time to focus on themselves.

Other goals of the pre-group interview would be to set individual goals for the participants, as well as help them to conceptualize how the group will function, so that they are prepared for the group experience and able to follow the norms. Information would also be gathered about the participants' eating disorder, so that the facilitators have an awareness of the particular symptoms that the participant is hoping to remediate.

If the facilitators determine that the potential participant is not ready for this type of group, they would recommend other services to the participant that would be a better fit for their needs and goals. Other types of groups, individual therapy, nutritional counseling, and psychiatric assessment are possible other services that would be of use to a person who wants help with eating problems, though who is not a good fit for this particular model of group therapy.

Session Formatting

Jordan and Dooley (2001) describe four parts to the group session format. Each of these is discussed within each session and serves as an agenda for the session. These four components are described below.

Community check-in.   The group commences with each person saying a few words about herself. The facilitators should creatively choose a method that allows for a brief but authentic disclosure of how they are feeling on that day.

Current challenges and competencies.   The leaders invite discussion around a particular topic of relevance, and the group members begin by sharing their current challenges with this particular topic. Current challenges would be difficulties they faced that week or month, challenges they need input about regarding the topic of the day. As each member elaborates about her challenge, she benefits by having her challenge normalized, validated, shared, or understood as she begins to see variations upon a theme, recognizing that similar challenges are faced even if the members appear to be different. Leaders need to guide, support, and be active participants, to ensure that a culture of acceptance of difference and compassion for each other is developed. Participants are encouraged to recognize and name their competencies, too, noticing their resiliency as a way of combating potential feeling of helplessness. Strengths are noted and reinforced, which sets the stage for the next part.

Clarity and choices.   In this part of group, members begin to review and rethink their chosen actions. All actions are considered chosen, even when they feel as though they were automatic or necessary. Whether the group discussion focuses around one individual's particular challenge, and then together, they explore in more detail what her choices were and might have been, or whether the discussion is more general, members benefit from listening to others. Listening to another promotes as much learning as receiving feedback from others. The participants learn to recognize patterns of thought, which typically lead to particular feelings and choices, even if different members' patterns are unique. For example, an individual with anorexia might believe she is worthless, feel overwhelmingly sad, and respond by restricting her eating, whereas an individual who compulsively overeats might have the same thought-feeling pattern though respond by bingeing. Listening to each other poses an opportunity for learning about oneself, supporting each other, decreasing isolation, and feeling the zest of connection. The leader needs to make this process work so that listening participants understand what they can be getting from the listening process—it is an active process that benefits them. Members should not be tuning out, waiting only for their turn to talk. Without proper leadership, members can fail to connect. One person's experience will not automatically inform another's at all times, so listening members' could believe they are not benefiting when listening to irrelevant experiences of others. Moreover, some members who are naturally more extroverted, or who feel an urge for feedback might be unaware of time boundaries and talk more, without awareness of time-sharing. Thus, the leader must be gently in charge, helping them share time effectively, and making explicit the similarities of experience to ensure that members' receive something from the group experience, whether they do more listening or sharing on a given day.

Closing connections.   "What can I take with me from group today?" As in the beginning check-in, a closing check-in invites participants to say a few words about what piece of learning they will take with them that day, encouraging them to be aware of and consolidate their learning. It also helps the group facilitators gauge what is being attained from group.

In sum, CBT is woven throughout, as the leaders are mindful of CBT principles such as recognition of core beliefs, automatic thoughts, and distortions, and points them out at relevant junctures. As the leaders actively participate in creating a culture of compassion for each other, the leaders also weave in relevant comments about how thought patterns create feelings, which lead to actions, and how practicing new ways of thinking will lead to different feelings about self, choice, and ultimately efficacy for choosing healthier actions.

Group Schedule

While the components of this model are described above, it is important for the sessions each week to have a specific content of focus. In Table 24.1, we offer an outline of a 12-week group outline.

Table 24.1   Session Outline for a Relational-Culture, Cognitive-Behavioral Model

Week 1

Introduction to the Relational Model

Introduce ways of relating that promote Jean Baker Miller's "Five Good Things"; explain the norms and expectations of how members will relate to one another to develop meaningful connections that will be mutually healing. The "Five Good Things," according to Jean Baker Miller (1986, p. 3) include (1) Zest, (2) Empowerment, (3) Clarity, (4) Sense of Worth, and (5) Desire for More Relationships.

Week 2

Peer Relationships

Discuss pressures, problems, and areas of difficulty they face in peer relationships. In using the group for support, identify what they need from each other to help them cope better with relationship problems. Ability to give and receive feedback respectfully and nonjudgmentally is a skill that will begin being practiced here but utilized throughout the group program. Recognition of development of an authentic voice, which represents honest self-expression without fear of rejection. Increase awareness of ways they have suppressed their authentic voice in order to maintain relationships.

Week 3

Cognitive-Behavioral Framework of Thoughts, Feelings and Behaviors

Members disclose their typical thought, feeling and behavior patterns around food, body image and self-care, so they can see the common ground, forging a sense of connection even if symptoms are different. Symptoms serve the purpose of coping and have been adaptive to an extent, but taken to an extreme, the symptoms have negative consequences and pose other problems. The cognitive-behavioral framework helps them to recognize automatic thoughts, and helps them practice changing those thoughts.

Week 4

Healthy Relationship with Food

Developing a strategy for normalized eating is crucial to recovery. Choosing small "risks" constitutes a gradual exposure to the problematic pattern. Identify what they "should" be eating, and give themselves permission to do what they know would be healthy for them. Examine current relationships with food, and work toward healthier relationship, including discussion of the necessity of different types of foods (e.g., protein, fat, carbohydrates), so that, ideally, nothing needs to be restricted and they can begin to trust themselves that they can move toward health.

(Continued)

Table 24.1   Continued

Week 5

Distress Tolerance and Behavioral Goals: Part 1

Identify ways that stress is managed, whether it is in the immediate moment or in a chronic way where it aids in the avoidance of feelings. Symptoms of emotional eating, restricting, bingeing and purging have a common purpose—distracting, comforting, avoiding, emotional numbing. New ways of managing stress, both in the moment and in a long-term way, must be developed. Discussion of distress tolerance and introduction of Mindfulness meditation (Linehan, 1993; Kabat-Zinn, 1990) will teach participants new ways to manage difficult moments and learn to face distressing life circumstances more effectively. Change can only happen in conjunction with movement towards healthier eating; the depletion and unhealthy physiological states produced by eating disorder symptoms themselves drive further eating disorder symptoms.

Week 6

Distress Tolerance and Behavioral Goals: Part 2

Assess readiness for change around the eating disorder—each individual develops goals that will move her one-step further along the path of recovery than she was before. For example, while one person might need to plan her meals, another might need to understand how her eating disorder is affecting her life and well-being, physically and emotionally. Each participant considers what risks she is ready to take that will challenge but not overwhelm her. This is important for developing self-efficacy. Instead of standard behavioral goals for the group as a whole, individuals are responsible for figuring out what steps they need to take next. In taking risks, she steps out of eating disorder symptoms whether for a moment or a day, and as she steps out of that dependency she makes room for trying alternative coping. Self-monitoring techniques can be used to help each individual track her goals, her progress, her setbacks. In the context of mutually empowering relationships, participants discuss both their successes and failures in a supportive, nonjudging way. Use of self-monitoring, gradual exposure, and cognitive restructuring can all be used as aids of change, depending on the participant's need or readiness for change.

Week 7

Body Image and Awareness

In an eating disorder, the body is typically a repository of bad feelings and negative energy. The body becomes the medium for experienced displaced negative affect, helplessness, rage, sadness, loss and other undesired emotions. Sometimes the body itself becomes the target, and it is blamed for negative feelings or life's dissatisfactions. The effort to change the body is again misplaced—true empowerment comes not from changing the body per se, but changing one's relationships, life circumstances, thought patterns. Cultural influences on thinking and feeling patterns around body will be explored, with an emphasis on helping participants recognize the effects of the media, family dynamics, prescribed gender roles, or unresolved sexuality issues: any of these could contribute to a negative relationship with one's body. Developing a positive relationship with one's body means learning to recognize it as simply a vehicle through which life is experienced, something to be honored, and something to be taken care of. Experiencing what it feels like to truly notice how one's body feels, without judgment is a new beginning. The longer-term process that will begin to be set in motion is to move from a stance of abuse of the body through eating disorder symptoms to respect and love for the body, through better care of it.

Week 8

Family

Participants will recognize strengths and supports in their family, as well as damaging influences. Examples to be explored: messages learned about self-care, eating, food, and physical appearance; functional role in the family; identification with particular parents' eating patterns; messages about food as giving of nurturance or love; social role of eating in the family and any other facets of family dynamics that might have impacted eating patterns one way or another.

Week 9 to 11

Skills—Assertiveness, Affect Management, Conflict Resolution

Each skill is introduced and its relevance to eating problems expanded upon. Participants identify their distorted beliefs about affect—e.g., its wrong to be angry, weak to need help, dangerous to feel love—that may have developed and keep participants out of fuller relationships. Conflict resolution and assertiveness skills go hand in hand: instead of avoiding conflict, using assertive modes of communication can often be effective in creating change. Drawing from previous discussions about peers and families, specific goals can be set for attempting to make positive changes in relationships that will ultimately help reduce the need for eating disordered behavior. When relationships are satisfying and range of affect is full, the need to be isolated with one's eating disorder atrophies away.

Week 12

Relational Closure and Relapse Prevention

Using a ritual is a good way to ensure that each member says something about what the group as a whole and the individual relationships have meant for her. Honoring endings is an important skill, as experiencing loss while in connection is a way of staying emotionally present and not minimizing the meaning of the ending. Mixtures of affect might be present—happiness for what was gained, loss of what was—as group members will mindfully experience a full range of emotions about what the group has meant and what their lives will be like without it. Example questions that can be asked: "What will you take with you? What do you hope others will take with them? What is the best piece of learning you would like to keep with you? What symbol or image represents what this group has meant for you? What next steps will be important for you? How will you continue to grow your relationships? What areas do you still need to work on? Where will you get support from? In addition to honoring the relationships and verbalizing the gains that have been made in the last 12 weeks, recognizing signs of slipping back into old patterns is equally important to ensure that forward progress will continue to be made even without the group. Expecting setbacks and viewing them not as failures, but opportunities for further growth helps reframe them as a normal occurrence that need not be read as failure. Nonetheless, a commitment to change involves a commitment to attending to setbacks in an active way, whether it means re-engaging in some form of treatment, reaching out for more support, or choosing any response that is assertive and attentive, rather than ignoring and neglectful.

CASE EXAMPLE

The following is an example of how to move group members out of unhealthy joining through symptoms, to sharing in a more personal way about who they are and how the eating disorder is serving as a means of coping. Initially, there may be conversations that constitute symptom sharing, that are not helping each other move towards health. It is the job of the group facilitators to find ways of intervening that move members out of joining in ways that are potentially destructive and guide the conversation towards improved coping or insight.

For example, Jessica, age 13 years old, brings to group her difficulties getting herself to eat dinner with her family. She reports that she sits there, has no desire to eat, feels like everyone is watching her, and her parents are angry with her for not eating. She wants feedback and support from the group. Jenny shares that she too, can't stand eating with her family, and shares ways she has tricked her family into thinking she ate—or in some cases she does eat, but sneaks away from the table to throw up. Rachel explains ways she has learned to hide food in her napkin and slide it off the table into her lap when no one is looking. They laugh and more of the members join in with their examples of similar situations. The norms of relating are moving into an unhealthy dynamic, whereby they bond together over dysfunctional behavior.

The facilitator intervenes: "Jessica, what is needed from the group to help you think differently about this problem?" She hesitates, and then indicates that she doesn't know what she needs. "I just want my parents to leave me alone." The facilitator responds, "But they aren't leaving you alone. Still you have to deal with it—what can we all do to help you with this?" Jessica looks glum and helpless. "I don't know...nothing," she says quietly. "Does anyone else, who can also relate to Jessica's problem, know what you would want from the group to help you with this?"

Rachel answers, "I want to know what to do to make my parents stop getting on my case about eating dinner with me, or get them to stop controlling me. Has anyone in here successfully gotten your parents to understand how you are feeling about your eating problem, and how to deal with you in a way that you feel better about now?" This moves into a discussion about how the members have tried to talk with their parents, in some cases successfully and others not, and they begin to brainstorm creatively about what has worked for some of them. The facilitator goes back and asks Jessica if any of it might work for her to bring the discussion back to the origination point, where the first member asked for help. In this process, the facilitator has now successfully reshaped the focus of the discussion to be more about finding solutions and helping each other with ideas to try, instead of allowing them to digress into details of symptom sharing that served no purpose other than to bond around self-destructive behaviors.

At the end, during the closing, the facilitator asks, "What can each person take from this discussion for yourself that will be useful to you this week? It could be something you would like to try to do differently, some way you are understanding yourself differently, or some new insight you have from hearing this discussion." Group members are given an opportunity to answer the question. Answering this is likely to feel risky—they don't want to say something that sounds stupid. Group members have been encouraged from the beginning, as part of the group norms, to offer positive feedback and support in response to earnest answers—nothing is ever treated as stupid.

"I realized that many of us have trouble eating dinner so I am not feeling so alone now at least." "I realized that I have not really tried to talk to my dad about it. He might be able to understand better than my mother—he's the better listener. I never thought of trying to talk with him about how dinner affects me." "Hiding my food in the napkin just keeps the problem going on and on and then I'm the one stuck with the problem. It might seem like I get away with something in the moment, but here I am, the one who has to go to a group because I have a problem." The group members are now each seeing how the discussion applies to them and each need something different. One member is inspired to try something different—to talk with her father. Another member doesn't know what to do but feels better knowing that others' struggle with it too, another is beginning to see that continuing the behavior is costing her something and while she might enjoy "getting over" on her parents, she is not benefiting in the long run. While they may not all leave with a particular action plan, the leader can gauge that new ideas are being generated, the problems underlying the eating disorder are getting broached, and the conversation has left the group feeling more zestful or energized, more mutual, connected and hopeful as each realizes that they have things to learn from each other.

CHALLENGES

Moving from symptom sharing, which can be a destructive behavior, to being truly connected and in real relationship is a common problem in groups for adolescents. Symptom sharing is even the reason that some people choose not to go to groups—the assumption is that members will learn to develop new symptoms by hearing about others' symptoms. Left unchecked, this can easily happen. Thus, the group leaders need to intervene and redirect the conversation in a timely manner when it begins to happen. It also helps to have it be a stated part of the group norms—that ways of relating need to be mutually supportive and teaching each other new symptoms would be counter to that. Even with that norm in place, however, because talking about symptoms is easier, a habit, a source of bonding, or a way of competing, it normally requires some redirection by group leaders. Consistently, group leaders must enforce the norm, not punitively, but instead seamlessly guide them into more productive and mutually helpful relating. Symptom sharing typically reflects helplessness or failure to see options, so asking members to generate new potential solutions, even if at first group members seem unable to think of anything, is important. The group leaders must have faith in the members and have chosen members who on some level want help and from that place, members will normally come up with new ideas when the leader changes the focus and asks questions that will lead to that kind of thinking.

Facing resistance from the families as group members' newfound assertiveness or empowerment is explored is another common challenge. As in the case described above, one group member decided to try talking with her father about eating dinner as a family and the problems it is raising for her. Perhaps he will welcome her reaching out to him in this way; perhaps not. If she comes back to group next week deflated because she tried it and he said that she needs to stop whining and just eat dinner as a family, then this particular challenge has been demonstrated. The group leader needs to validate that when people recover, they need to behave differently—being aware of what they need, asserting it, and asking for things to be different in their family may yield both positive and negative results. In some cases, family therapy is warranted. The member also needs not to lose hope, or become confused and assume that since it is not working she must give up and remain silent and stuck in her eating disorder. The resistance she faces must not be minimized—if in fact she is facing this, she will need more help from the group to remain courageous, continue to try new ways to communicate, or find additional allies to help her (e.g., a therapist, an other relative, sibling, teacher). Changing themselves can be empowering, but facing the resistance of families can be demoralizing.

Members' own attachment to symptoms and resistance to change may be because the unknown is even more threatening. Movement can be from resistance to change to contemplation about potential change. In the case example, the group member who was invested in hiding her food might not be ready to give that up. Perhaps she feels powerful, expressing her anger at her parents by keeping this secret, feeling like she is "getting over" on them. If she were pressured to give that behavior up prematurely, she might resist. Thus, it is important for leaders to remain mindful of stages of change and that members have their symptoms as the most successful form of coping they have developed to date. As they learn new ideas in group, they might still be hesitant to leave the old ways. While some members are trying out new behaviors, others may be gathering up ideas and insights, and forming mobilization that seems invisible but is gathering momentum to become action at a later point. Thus, as long as group leaders can see that members are creating zestful, useful connections, which lead to insights, better ways of relating, and some new actions for some members, the challenge of resistance to change is likely being managed.

SUMMARY

In closing, eating disorders are prevalent and can be treated in a variety of ways. Given that female adolescents face challenges maintaining their own voice or unique perspective in the context of relationships, the group format potentially provides a corrective experience by offering connection and support from peers as they risk sharing authentically. In addition, in hearing others' stories, they learn more about themselves and may gain insights that would otherwise have been harder to discover, they gain support as they take risks, and build self-confidence with the acceptance they feel from like-minded peers who show concern about their struggle. The group model addressed in this chapter emphasizes the teaching of new ways of relating that can be carried into future relationships. From the group, members learn what it feels like to relate in ways that are truly growth promoting for them and recognize that their recovery must occur in connection, not isolation.

RECOMMENDED READINGS

Fallon, P., Katzman, M. A., & Wooley, S. C. (Eds.). (1994). *Feminist perspectives of eating disorders*. New York: Guilford.

Garner, D. M., & Garfinkel, P. E. (Eds.) (1997). *Handbook of Treatment for Eating Disorders* (pp. 145–177). New York: Guilford.

Miller, J. B., & Stiver, I. P. (1997). *The healing connection: How women form relationships in therapy and in life*. Boston: Beacon Press.

REFERENCES

American Psychiatric Association. (2004). *Diagnostic and statistical manual of mental disorders* (4th ed-text revision). Washington, DC: Author.

Anderson, D. A., Lundgren, J. D., Shapiro, J. R., & Paulosky, C. A. (2004). Assessment of eating disorders: Review and recommendations for clinical use. *Behavior Modification, 28,* 763–782.

Anderson, D. A., & Maloney, K. C. (2001). The efficacy of cognitive-behavioral therapy on the core symptoms of bulimia nervosa. *Clinical Psychology Review, 21,* 971–988.

Attie, I., & Brooks-Gunn, J. (1989). Development of eating problems in adolescent girls: A longitudinal study. *Developmental Psychology, 25*(1), 70–79.

Banks, A. (2005). The Developmental Impact of Trauma. In Comstock, D. (Ed.), *Diversity and Development* (pp. 185–212). Belmont: CA: Brooks/Cole.

Beck, J. (1995). *Cognitive therapy: Basics and beyond*. New York: Guilford.

Bowers, W. A. (2001). Basic principles for applying cognitive-behavioral therapy to anorexia nervosa. *The Psychiatric Clinics of North America, 24*(2), 293–303.

Brown, L. M., & Gilligan, C. (1992). *Meeting at the crossroads: Women's psychology and girls' development*. New York: Ballantine.

Cooper, Z., Cooper, P., & Fairburn, C. (1989). The validity of the eating disorder examination and its subscales. *British Journal of Psychiatry, 154,* 807–812.

Costin, C. (1999). The *eating disorder sourcebook: A comprehensive guide to the causes, treatments, and prevention of eating disorders* (2nd ed.). Los Angeles: Lowell House.

Crowther, J. H., Lilly, R. S., Crawford, P. A., & Shepard, K. L. (1992). The stability of the Eating Disorder Inventory. *International Journal of Eating Disorders, 12,* 97–101.

Crowther, J. H., & Sherwood, N. W. (1997). Assessment. In Garner, D.M., & Garfinkel, P. E. (Eds.), *Handbook of Treatment for Eating Disorders* (pp. 34–49). New York: Guilford.

Daigneault, S. D. (2000) Body talk: A school-based group intervention for working with disordered eating behaviors. *Journal for Specialists in Group Work. 25*(2), 191–213.

Fairburn, C. G., Stice, E., Cooper, Z., Doll, H. A., Norman, P. A., & O'Connor, M. E. (2003). Understanding persistence in bulimia nervosa: A 5-year naturalistic study. *Journal of Consulting and Clinical Psychology, 71*(1), 103–109.

Fairburn, C. G., Shafran, R., & Cooper, Z. (1999). A cognitive behavioural theory of anorexia nervosa. *Behaviour Research and Therapy, 37,* 1–13.

Fairburn, C. G., & Walsh, B. T. (2002). Atypical eating disorders. In C. G. Fairburn & K. D. Brownell (Eds.), *Eating disorders and obesity: A comprehensive handbook* (p. 86). New York: Guilford.

Fallon, P., Katzman, M. A., & Wooley, S. C. (Eds.). (1994). *Feminist perspectives of eating disorders.* New York: Guilford.

Fisher, M., Golden, N. H., Katzman, D. K., Kreipe, R. E., Rees, J., Schebendach, J., et al. (1995). Eating disorders in adolescents: A background paper. *Journal of Adolescent Health, 16,* 420–437.

Garner, D. M., & Blanch, M. T. (2002). Cognitive behavioural treatment of eating disorders. In G. Simos (Ed.), *Cognitive behaviour therapy: A guide for the practising clinician* (pp. 173–200). New York: Taylor & Francis.

Garner, D. M. (1997). Psychoeducational principles in treatment. In Garner, D. M., & Garfinkel, P. E. (Eds.), *Handbook of treatment for eating disorders* (pp. 145–177). New York: Guilford.

Garner, D. M., Vitousek, K. M., & Pike, K. M. (1997). Cognitive-behavioral treatment for anorexia nervosa. In Garner, D. M., & Garfinkel, P. E. (Eds.), *Handbook of treatment for eating disorders* (pp. 94–143). New York: Guilford.

Geller, J., Johnston, C., & Madsen, K. (1997). The role of shape and weight in self-concept: The shape and weight based self-esteem inventory. *Cognitive Therapy and Research, 21,* 5–24.

Geller, J., Johnston, C., Madsen, K., Goldner, E. M., Remick, R. A., & Birmingham, C. L. (1998). Shape and weight-based self-esteem and the eating disorders. *International Journal of Eating Disorders, 24,* 285–298.

Graber, J. A., Brooks-Gunn, J., Paikoff, R. L., & Warren, M. P. (1994). Prediction of eating problems: An 8-year study of adolescent girls. *Developmental Psychology, 30*(6), 823–834.

Grave, R. D. (2003). School-based prevention programs for eating disorders. *Disease Management and Health Outcomes, 11,* 579-592.

Johnson, J. G., Cohen, P., Kotler, L., Kasen, S., & Brook, J. S. (2002). Psychiatric disorders associated with risk for the development of eating disorders during adolescence and early adulthood. *Journal of Consulting and Clinical Psychology, 70*(5), 1119–1128.

Jordan, J., & Dooley, C. (2001). *Relational group practice.* Wellesley, MA: Stone Center Publications.

Kabat-Zinn, J. (1990). *Full catastrophe living.* New York: Delta Publishing.

Kohn, M., & Golden, N. H. (2001). Eating disorders in children and adolescents. *Pediatric Drugs, 3,* 91–99.

Koslowsky, M., Scheinberg, Z., Bleich, A., Mark, M., Apter, A., Danon, Y., & Solomon, Z. (1992). The factor structure and criterion validity of the short form of the eating attitudes test. *Journal of Personality Assessment, 58*(1), 27–35.

Lask, B., & Bryant-Waugh, R. (Eds.). (2000). *Anorexia nervosa and related eating disorders in children and adolescents.* East Sussex, UK: Psychology Press.

Linehan, M. (1993) *Cognitive-behavioral treatment of borderline personality disorder.* New York: Guilford.

Massey-Stokes, M. S. (2000). Prevention of disordered eating among adolescents. *The Clearing House,* 335–340.

Mennuti, R., Bloomgarden, A., & Gabriel, N. (2005). Female adolescents with eating disorders: A cognitive-behavioral approach. In Mennuti, R. B., Freeman, A., & Christner, R. W. (Eds.), *Cognitive-behavioral interventions in educational settings: A handbook for practice* (pp. 464–475). New York: Routledge.

Mishne, J. M. (1986). *Clinical work with adolescents.* New York: Free Press.

Polivy, J., & Herman, C. P. (2002). Causes of eating disorders. *Annual Review of Psychology, 53,* 187–215.

Rizvi, S. L., Peterson, C. B., Crow, J. C., & Agras, W. S. (2000). Test retest reliability of the eating disorder examination. *International Journal of Eating Disorders, 28,* 311–316.

Steiner-Adair, C. (1991). When the body speaks: Girls, eating disorders and psychotherapy. In C. Gilligan, A. G. Rogers & D. L. Tolman (Eds.), *Women, girls and psychotherapy* (pp. 253–266). New York: Harrington Park.

Stice, E. (2002). Risk and maintenance factors for eating pathology: A meta-analytic review. *Psychological Bulletin, 128*(5), 825–849.

Surrey, J. L. (1991). Eating patterns as a reflection of women's development. In J. V. Jordan, A. G. Kaplan, J. B. Miller, I. P. Stiver, & J. L. Surrey (Eds.), *Women's growth in connection: Writings from the Stone Center* (pp. 237–250). New York: Guilford.

Thelen, M., Farmer, J., Wonderlich, S., & Smith, M. (1991). A revision of the bulimia test: The BULIT-R. *Psychological Assessment, 3,* 119–124.

Vitousek, K., & Manke, F. (1994). Personality variables and disorders in anorexia nervosa and bulimia nervosa. *Journal of Abnormal Psychology, 103*(1), 137–147.

Waller, G., Ohanian, V., Meyer, C., & Osman, S. (2000). Cognitive content among bulimic women: The role of core beliefs. *International Journal of Eating Disorders, 28,* 235–241.

Williamson, D., White, M. A., York-Crowe, E., Stewart, T. M. (2004). Cognitive-behavioral theories of eating disorders. *Behavior Modification, 28*(6), 711–738.

Wilson, G. T., & Vitousek, K. M. (1999). Self-monitoring in the assessment of eating disorders. *Psychological Assessment, 11*(4), 480–489.

Wilson, G. T., Fairburn, C. G., & Agras, W. S. (1997). Cognitive-behavioral therapy for bulimia nervosa. In Garner, D. M., & Garfinkel, P. E. (Eds.), *Handbook of treatment for eating disorders* (pp. 67–93). New York: Guilford.

Chapter Twenty-Five

Parent Skill-Building Groups

Carol L. Oster

Parenting education is an important adjunct to the treatment of child and adolescent disorders because parenting style contributes to, moderates, maintains, and affects the emotional, behavioral, and psychological functioning of teens and children. When considering the impact of parent involvement in the treatment of youth, it is important to recognize the unique parent factors contributing to the dynamics of the parent–child relationship, such as the parent's philosophy on parenting, communication style, disciplinary style, level of affection, experiences with their own parents, and beliefs about themselves as parents. Three parenting patterns that are differentiated by relative level of demandingness and warmth—authoritarian, permissive, and authoritative—have been identified and studied in the literature and found to contribute to different patterns of child behavior (Baumrind, 1968). Before outlining the components of a cognitive-behavioral therapy model of group intervention for parents, these parenting styles and the ways in which ineffective parenting is facilitated by the cognitive, emotional, and behavioral functioning of parents will be briefly reviewed for their impact on the functioning of children and adolescents.

Authoritarian parents make high demands for performance and compliance, issue more commands, rely on more coercive methods of child management, and demonstrate low levels of warmth toward their children. Authoritarian methods are highly effective for gaining immediate compliance, but poor at developing long-term pro-social thinking, feeling, and behaving (Stormshak, Bierman, McMahon, Lengua, et al., 2000). They tend to reinforce power motives and aggressive behavior in children, setting up vicious cycles of escalating coercive interactions between parents and children (Patterson, 1982). Permissive parents are warm and supportive, and make relatively few demands for performance or compliance. Lax parenting may represent an abdication of the parental role, sometimes due to parents' own emotional difficulties. Permissive and lax parents rely most on persuasion and emotional appeals, but may resort to coercion and power-assertion when these methods fail. Their style tends to result in lower levels of competence, knowledge, confidence, and self-control in children (Cartwright-Hatton, McNally, White, & Verduyn, 2005).

Authoritative parents combine high demand with warmth, and rely primarily on inductive or educational methods to achieve their goals. They provide value-based rationales for their requests, and recognize and reward behavior that moves in the desired direction. They set clear limits, and respond to misbehavior with ignoring or with natural and logical consequences. Authoritative parenting tends to develop competence, independence, confidence, cooperation, values-based decision-making, and self-control in children (Baumrind, 1968).

Ineffective parenting is related to a variety of environmental stressors, but also is characterized by common errors in cognition, emotion, and behavior, and it is these errors or deficits that parenting education seeks to change. Maladaptive cognitions include inaccurate perception of the child, unrealistic expectations about what children are capable of at different developmental stages, hostile attributions regarding the child's behavior, failure to consider the context of the child's behavior, low belief in the efficacy of parental efforts to modify child behavior, and over-predicting long-term negative consequences of child behavior. These result in reliance on more punitive discipline approaches (Azar & Rohrbeck, 1986; Dix, 1993; Mikeston & Patenaude, 1994; Penderhughes, Dodge, Bates, Pettit, & Zelli, 2000). Parents' beliefs about themselves, children and their behavior, and parenting as a role are derived the same way as other adaptive and maladaptive beliefs: they relate back to early life learning experiences, and are shaped by familial, cultural, religious, social, economic and other influences.

Maladaptive emotional responses are highly correlated with power assertion and child abuse. Parents who experience intense negative affective response to child misbehavior, frustration or anger over perceived lack of control over the child, inability to manage one's own negative affect, and family stress have difficulty controlling their behavioral responses to parenting stress and child misbehavior (Dix, 1991, Kashdan et al., 2004). Parents' emotional dyscontrol can arise from maladaptive beliefs (expectations and attributions) about themselves, their children, and their situation; their own psychological problems; substance abuse; stress; poor modeling of self-control by their own parents, and other factors.

Behavioral excesses or insufficiencies in parenting include excessive use of power and coercion to control a child's behavior; inconsistency in applying child management methods; limited problem-solving ability; limited repertoire of possible responses to children's behavior; use of indirect or unclear commands; allowing insufficient time for the child to respond to commands; giving too many commands; failure to monitor or excessive monitoring of the child's behavior; and failure to reinforce pro-social behavior. Parenting education can effectively intervene in each of these areas, increasing parents' knowledge, building parenting skills, and altering parents' beliefs about the task of parenting and ultimately their parenting behaviors.

ORIGINS OF PARENTING EDUCATION PROGRAMS

Parenting education programs originated with Rudolf Dreikurs (1964) and other Adlerian therapists in the 1950s. The first formal parenting program based on Adlerian theory and methods was *Systematic Training in Effective Parenting* (STEP; Dinkmeyer, McKay, & Dinkmeyer, 1973), which teaches parents to understand the likely goals of children's behavior, apply natural and logical consequences to misbehavior, utilize descriptive praise to encourage pro-social behavior, and develop children's competence. STEP promoted the use of family meetings. Subsequent to Dreikurs' pioneering work, parenting education programs flourished (Forehand & King, 1977; Habisch-Ahlin, 1999; Patterson,

1982; Sanders, Markie-Dadds & Turner, 2003; Webster-Stratton, 1983). The target of change was most often child behavior, with parents acting as intermediary therapists, primarily applying behavioral methods such as time outs and points programs. Parent Effectiveness Training (Gordon, 1970) added communication skills, particularly the use of I-messages and active listening. Active Parenting (Popkin, 1983), another Adlerian-based parenting program, introduced video-based parenting education. Since then, the use of videotaped vignettes to demonstrate problematic and skillful parenting has since become the standard. Videos aid in recall of parenting skills and principles, reduce resistance to change, and encourage and enhance parent participation (Shannon, n.d.; Webster-Stratton, 1996).

Parenting education programs abound today, and include STEP (Dinkmeyer et al., 1973), Parent Effectiveness Training (Gordon, 1970, 2000), Active Parenting Now (Popkin, 2002), Positive Parenting (University of Minnesota, 2004), The Incredible Years (Webster-Stratton, 2006), and Triple-P (Sanders et al., 2003). Studies of the effectiveness of parenting education have yielded common principles and practices regarding group leaders, settings, participants, program goals, program materials, and methods (Matthews & Hudson, 2001; Shannon, n.d.).

GROUP LEADERS

Effective parenting education group leaders have knowledge of child and adolescent physical, cognitive, emotional, and social development; understanding of and sensitivity to individual and group diversity; respect for families and parents; group leadership skills; teaching ability; and the ability to connect with the parents in their groups through the communication of common concerns or characteristics. The leader should espouse a consistent theoretical framework, so that parents receive a coherent philosophy and "toolbox" of strategies and interventions to apply following completion of the training. Formal training in leading parenting education groups is available (and sometimes required) for most published parenting education programs, and sometimes provided free—particularly for those programs provided by university extensions or local and national governments.

Setting

The choice of meeting place should take into account where target parents are likely to be most emotionally and socially comfortable. For some populations, an office or clinic will be suitable, but a church, school, community meeting room, park district, or even a participant's home may be better choices in many situations. Attention to transportation, child care, meeting times, and convenience of the location will increase the likelihood of consistent attendance, particularly for low-income participants. If both parents cannot attend, it is important to find some way to connect with the working parent. Parenting education groups have also met in prisons and hospitals, to reach at-risk parents in those locations. Most parenting education programs are designed for delivery to small groups of four to eight sets of parents, meeting one to two hours a week for six to twelve weeks. Sometimes this is unattractive, impractical, or inappropriate for those for whom the program is intended. Alternative methods include home-study, online, in-home, and community-wide program delivery.

ASSESSMENT OF PARTICIPANTS

Preventive parenting education may be offered to a community at large and open to all comers, but parenting education aimed at secondary or tertiary prevention—intervening when there is an identified problem—may require assessing the parents and/or child prior to including parents in the group. In addition to interviews with parents and children, the most commonly used assessment instruments are the Child Behavior Checklist (Achenbach, 1991), which helps identify internalizing, externalizing, and other problems in children; the Parenting Stress Index (Abidin, 1995), which assesses level of parental satisfaction, efficacy, and stress; and the Conflict Tactics Scale (Straus, Hamby, Finkelhor, Moore, & Runyon, 1998), which determines the level of verbal discussion, verbal aggression, hostile-indirect withdrawal, physical aggression, and spanking parents use to resolve conflict with each other and with children. This instrument is particularly useful for calling attention to the possibility of child abuse. Assessments might seek to clarify:

1. The appropriateness of parental expectations for their children
2. The level of agreement between the parents about expectations
3. The exact nature of the parent–child problem, including how, where, when, how persistently, and with whom the problem occurs
4. Parent and child cognitive, emotional, and behavioral precipitants and reactions to the problem when it occurs
5. The means by which parents discipline their children and the extent of any domestic violence in the family
6. How clearly or inconsistently consequences and rewards are presented
7. The developmental functioning of each child in the family
8. The parents' understanding of community standards for their own and their child's behaviors
9. How normative or nonnormative the child's and parents' behaviors may be
10. Recent changes in the family situation

Parents are helped to assess these areas during parenting education, so prior assessment may only be needed to rule out factors that would preclude participation in the group, such as severe parental psychopathology or inter-partner violence that would be disruptive to the effective functioning of the group.

Groups function best if there is reasonable homogeneity for relevant family, parent, or child characteristics. Almost every program separates groups by developmental age of the child of most concern to the parents, yielding at least three levels: early childhood, school-age, and adolescence. Groups may also form around common diagnostic issues, such as ADHD, developmental or physical disability, internalizing or externalizing disorders, or child abuse and neglect. Some groups are composed entirely of court-referred parents. Common cultural and social values help group participants to bond with each other, reducing isolation and providing needed social support.

GOALS OF PARENTING EDUCATION

Parenting education seeks to improve parents' knowledge, alter the way they think about themselves and their children, build skills and expand behavioral repertoires, clarify or alter values, and foster emotional and behavioral self-regulation. Most parents come to parenting education in order to "fix" a particular child, and indeed, helping children change is a secondary goal, with parents as the primary agents of change. A parallel process emerges in parenting education: the very change processes used to help parents alter their own cognitions, emotions, and behaviors also help them bring about desired or needed changes in themselves, their children and their families. Common goals of parenting education programs are to:

1. Improve parents' knowledge of child development.
2. Increase parents' use of positive, non-coercive methods to develop pro-social behavior in children.
3. Develop alternatives to power-based, coercive, punitive or abusive responses to child misbehavior.
4. Improve parents' emotional and behavioral self-control in response to children.
5. Help parents identify, set, and reinforce reasonable limits for children.
6. Develop parents' problem-solving and conflict resolution skills.
7. Improve communication between parent and child, between parents, and between school and home.
8. Establish or improve parents' social connection and support and reduce parental stress.

MULTI-MODAL APPROACH TO TRAINING

Using a variety of methods and materials increases the likelihood of reaching parents with different learning styles and skills. A multi-modal approach also increases retention, transfer, and generalizability of the program. Best practices (Matthews & Hudson, 2001; Shannon, n.d.) include:

1. Using multiple modalities and activities (videos, written material, lecture, discussion, role-play, interactive learning) to include all learning styles
2. Incorporating cognition, behavior, and emotion in activities and assignments
3. Respecting the cultural values and personal histories of parents and families
4. Using short lectures to introduce new concepts and information
5. Providing clear examples of how children think and act at different ages and stages
6. Having parents anticipate how children would behave in everyday circumstances
7. Directly modeling appropriate parenting practices
8. Using role-play and interactive skill-building to introduce, practice, and reinforce cognitive, behavioral, and emotional change
9. Including regular opportunity for group discussion and comment
10. Building social support and connection between group members
11. Connecting parents to other resources

Videotaped vignettes are available for most formal parenting programs, along with leader guides, parent texts and workbooks, and handouts. Some materials, particularly those developed by universities and governmental agencies, are available free online. Leaders should review materials for consistency with the theoretical approach, reading level required, pertinence to the needs of the group, and focus of the content of a session. Leaders should also provide parents with information about other resources to enhance generalization to siblings, other problems, and future developmental challenges. Before providing parents with lists of online resources, it is important to assure they have access to the internet, and that the online locations of the resources are up to date.

SESSION STRUCTURE

Parenting education sessions include a variety of activities: check-ins, pre-learning activities, videotaped vignettes, didactic presentations, role-plays or other interactive skill-building activities, development and explanation of intersession assignments, and problem-solving. Each session begins with parents checking in with their reflections on the previous session (or on starting the group if it is the first session), efforts to apply what was covered in prior sessions, and questions or concerns. This reviews and reinforces content and skills, and provides an opportunity to correct misinterpretations. It also helps parents to identify progress and problem-solve common difficulties. Brief surveys of knowledge, beliefs, attitudes or behavior, presentations of taped vignettes, problem descriptions, or group discussions of critical incidents prepare the group for the topic of the session. This is followed by didactic presentations that introduce new knowledge or skills, or counter old beliefs and attitudes.

Brief (usually 5 minutes or less) videotaped vignettes are interspersed throughout each session. Videos break down resistance to change by illustrating the universality of parenting dilemmas, and aid in skill development by modeling target behaviors and demonstrating their efficacy. Contemporary parenting videotapes include minority group parents and children, and reduce resistance to what might otherwise be seen as culturally irrelevant or insensitive methods of child rearing. Selection of vignettes can be tailored to the needs of the group. Discussion of each vignette engages parents in reflection and provides opportunity to address concerns about implementing change, particularly where either practical issues or parents' beliefs or values limit willingness to attempt what is being modeled. Modeling of new behaviors by the leader reduces parents' hesitancy about practicing new behaviors in subsequent role-play activities. Discussion following role-play or practice tasks further clarifies new behaviors parents are asked to attempt, and helps adapt tasks for each family, if needed.

Parents are asked to anticipate how they might apply the skill or behavior in their own family in the following week. As with individual cognitive-behavioral therapy, it is best for parents to devise their own plans for applying the lessons each week. If the group is particularly cohesive, they may agree on how they will apply the week's lesson, and make plans for supporting each other in the process. The leaders can provide resources or suggestions for making new skills easier to apply or track. Plans to apply the new knowledge or skill follow Meichenbaum's (1985) routine: Goal, Plan, Do, Check, Attribute, and Reward. Long-term goals (e.g., to increase prosocial behavior, to have a warmer relationship with my child) and weekly goals (e.g., to use descriptive encouragement to reinforce positive behavior; to spend time with my child enjoying an activity together without having to teach, control, or correct him/her) are identified. Parents are helped to make an explicit behavioral plan for implementing the goal: "I will take the time to figure out how to phrase my requests as 'do' rather than 'don't' commands.", "When the problem belongs to my child, I will ask questions to help her think through the problem rather than telling her what to do." Anticipating obstacles and making alternative plans, reminding parents to give themselves time to master a new approach, and granting "permission" to make (nonabusive) mistakes help reduce parents' resistance and anxiety about being able to carry a plan out successfully.

Parents are encouraged to keep track of their attempts to apply the week's lesson in writing, using charts akin to daily thought records or other tools, and to bring those records to each session. This counters mood-congruent recall of failed attempts or children's most recent misbehavior and increases likelihood of follow-through. If methods for recording the events of the week are decided by the parents themselves, they are more likely to "buy into" the task, improving comprehension, and increasing the likelihood that the week's lesson will be remembered and acted upon. Any movement toward change, even a parent's report that, "Well, I thought about it, but I didn't do it," is reinforced and encouraged, to anchor each step toward change in the right direction.

It is critical that parents attribute success to their own effort and behavior. During check-ins at the start of each session, parents are asked to reflect on what they did that made a difference. This increases their sense of efficacy and competence, improves satisfaction with the parenting role, and increases commitment to ongoing change. Parents are encouraged to reinforce themselves and each other for both effort and success in making desired or needed changes. This is also a part of teaching self-care.

SESSION CONTENT

The content and sequence of parenting education "lessons" varies somewhat in response to the characteristics of each group. A good sequence maximizes the likelihood of early success for parents, emphasizes "do" rather than "stop" instructions, and begins with increasing positive child behaviors rather than diminishing problem behaviors. Research suggests that parents' response to this positive focus is more favorable than to an initial focus on reducing children's negative behaviors (DeBord et al., 2002; Shannon, n.d.). The following suggested sequence is presented as a series of lessons. Although most parenting education programs are designed for six to eight weeks, each topic may take more than one group session, and needs to be reinforced after introduction.

Lesson 1. Improve Parents' Knowledge of Child Development

When parents are better aware of appropriate expectations for cognitive, behavioral, and emotional competencies at their child's age and stage of development, they are less likely to respond punitively. They are also more likely to view their child as developing, rather than static, and to view behavior as typical of the age rather than directed at the person of the parent. An early focus on child development emphasizes parents' role as teachers and leads naturally to program emphasis on inductive (educational and nurturing) parenting methods.

Videos, lectures, and handouts on child development, tailored to the ages and other characteristics of the target children are included in the lesson. Group activities include discussion of vignettes and comparison of children to the developmental competencies demonstrated or listed. Learning that 8-year-old girls change "best friends" frequently, reduced Susan's anxiety about her daughter's shifting loyalties, which she had read as signs of poor social skills and judgment. Lydia and Paul had responded to their week-old baby's crying by ignoring her "misbehavior," telling the group, "We thought she was just trying to get attention." When a newborn's normal crying pattern in response to tiredness and hunger was described, they became more responsive to their newborn's needs, narrowly averting their physician's call to Family Services for neglect.

Sharing stories about children's development early in the program helps parents connect with each other, and see that others empathize with the challenges they face. Parents are encouraged to share stories of themselves at the same age and stage of development as their child. Recalling their own childhoods, especially stories of "hijinks," fears, or errors in judgment, helps parents empathize with and understand their children. Marti told the group about her son making a mess of staples while cleaning up his homework area. Later that session, she suddenly remembered that at the same age, she once decided to staple her finger, "just to see what would happen." She realized that her own behavior must have been just as inexplicable to her parents as her son's was to her, and connected with her son's constant experimentation and drive for mastery of his environment, typical of children his age.

Charts of intellectual, emotional, physical, and social development help parents objectify children's behavior and anticipate next stages of development. They usually immediately begin comparing their children to these developmental maps, leading to more objective observations of their children. An early focus on child development helps parents distance themselves from and develop curiosity about children's behavior, reducing reactions based on personalization. It also often moves parents toward a more positive view of their child, inducing positive expectancies and reducing negative attributions. Parents are provided with additional resources for tracking their children's future development.

Lesson 2. Increase Children's Appropriate Behavior

The "product" of successful parenting is usually a confident, competent, cooperative, contributing, and compassionate adult, capable of love, work, and contribution to the larger community. In order to meet these goals, the second focus of parenting education is to increase children's pro-social behavior. Various methods for identifying, teaching, developing, and reinforcing children's adaptive, competent, appropriate behavior are introduced. These include differential reinforcement, descriptive praise, teaching and modeling, making effective requests, and developing warm, supportive relationships with children.

Identify Desired Behaviors. Parents often make vague demands, such as "Think about others for a change!" or "Show some respect!" Video vignettes demonstrate the difficulty children have understanding what parents want when requests or standards are vague. Parents need to practice clearly identifying behaviors children would engage in if they were meeting parental expectations. Sean and Barb wanted their son to "participate in the family." They were able to specify that "participation" meant coming to dinner, asking family members about their day, telling the family about his day, saying good morning and good night, attending his brother's basketball games and telling his brother, "Good game!" These clear behavioral expectations were easier for them to communicate, and were particularly appropriate for their intellectually challenged teenager.

Reinforce Positive Behaviors. All parenting programs introduce parents to basic reinforcement principles, including that the behaviors of their child they attend to are reinforced and thus more likely to recur. Once parents can clearly identify what they want the child to do, it is important to catch the child doing it and respond with reinforcement. Artificial reinforcers, such as point systems and star charts, tend to be discontinued shortly after parenting programs end. Social reinforcers, such as simple recognition of pro-social behavior, descriptive praise, or a hug or handshake, are more likely to be consistently integrated into parenting behavior and maintained following the end of the program. Descriptive praise that attributes some positive underlying characteristic to the child has a strong effect on children's future behavior. Pam's daughter, whose room was often a mess, cleaned and organized her space. Pam commented to her that her room seemed to be so much more spacious, mused aloud that her daughter was a rather organized person, and gave a couple examples of that characteristic. That is, she attributed to her daughter a stable, internal, and global *positive* characteristic that she wanted to encourage.

Teach Desired Skills and Knowledge. Parents sometimes expect behavior that is not within children's repertoires. Duane was appalled when he introduced his teenage son to a baseball scout, and his son mumbled something and walked off to play a video game. Later, he lectured his son about his "rudeness" and criticized his poor social skills. His son began to avoid opportunities to meet scouts. The leader observed that children do not learn through criticism of ignorance, and challenged the group to identify ways for Duane's son to learn appropriate social interactions with adults. They broke down the goal into small, behavioral skills that Duane could teach and model for his son. They then generalized their method to such common expectations as completing homework, cleaning bedrooms, and doing dishes. Teaching a desired behavior requires several parent skills:

1. Breaking the desired behavior into smaller components or steps
2. Giving simple, clear instructions for each step
3. Modeling the target behavior, both as a whole, and in smaller steps
4. Reflecting on the behavior out loud as you model it
5. Explaining the reason for the behavior, to develop value-based, internal motivation
6. Providing the child time to practice and become competent
7. Recognizing and rewarding skill development and progress toward the end goal using descriptive praise and other reinforcers to shape behavior
8. Accurately attributing growth to the child's own efforts, thus attributing realistic positive characteristics to the child
9. Helping the child accurately self-attribute and self-reward

Make Clear, Age-Appropriate Requests.   Cooperative behavior is more likely if parents make clear, direct, age- and stage-appropriate requests. As Susan described a recent argument with her daughter, the group pointed out that she used phrases like, "It might be better if you...," "I would really like you to...," "I think you should...," and other phrases that inadvertently implied that her daughter could choose whether or not to comply. Steve's family therapist observed to the group leader that he tended to try to "jolly" his son into behaving better. She reported Steve tried to stop his son's hitting in the session by tickling him and saying, "Oh come on, Sam. You don't want to be mean, do you?" Sam, age four, jubilantly replied, "Yes I do! I *love* to be mean! It's fun!" Steve made two mistakes: being unclear about his expectations, and unintentionally reward-ing Sam for hitting him by engaging in play. The steps for issuing clear commands and requests include:

1. Issue fewer commands and requests to increase the likelihood of compliance.
2. Time commands when children are more likely to attend and respond, such as dur-ing a break in the action, rather than while they are deeply involved in something else.
3. Direct the child's attention to the issue.
4. Clearly state, in descriptive terms, the expected behavior.
5. Make it clear you expect compliance. State the request as a directive, rather than a question.
6. Allow the child time to comply. Normally compliant children comply with requests one- to two-thirds of the time and begin to comply within about 30 seconds follow-ing the command.
7. Acknowledge and reinforce compliance.

Develop a Warm Relationship.   Children are more compliant when their relation-ships with their parents are warm. Parents are often so exhausted by their attempts to control their children that they do not experience their children as enjoyable. They may report, "I love my child, but I don't *like* my child!" Reintroducing play or other social interactions into the relationship can help to repair the parent–child relationship and regain warmth and affection. Parents who use coercive methods need to be helped to make time for their children where they focus on building the relationship, rather than competing, teaching, correcting, or controlling them. When they do so, they often report they enjoy being with their child for the first time in months or years.

Lesson 3. Decrease Negative Emotional Responding

Parents use more coercive methods when they respond emotionally or impulsively or make hostile attributions about children's misbehavior. Interposing time for reflection between the parent's emotional, defensive impulse and verbal or physical response and helping them to question negative attributions reduce the likelihood of abusive parenting.

Differentiate Immature, Noncompliant and Defiant Behaviors. Relatively little child misbehavior is a direct challenge to parental authority. Some misbehavior results from errors in judgment or self-control that are typical at particular ages and developmental stages. Noncompliance is also not the same as defiance. Children may be noncompliant because they do not hear, attend to, remember, or understand a request. They may not have the physical or emotional ability to comply, may not understand the standards for performance, or may be too distracted, tired or upset to comply. Ignoring, repeating the request at a later time, or teaching needed skills are often more appropriate responses than punishment for non-compliance, depending on the reasons for the behavior. Parents practice differentiating defiance from other forms of misbehavior and determining appropriate responses depending on likely causes.

Challenge General Attribution Errors. A general attribution error results when parents attribute their own misbehavior to situational, time-limited, and environmental or external causes, yet attribute children's misbehavior to global (cross-situational), internal, and enduring characterological traits. The error is evident when parents say such things as, "He's always doing that!", "She's just a brat!" or "He does that on purpose to annoy me," and when they excuse their own loss of control by blaming the child or the situation. Parents must simultaneously hold themselves responsible for controlling their own behavior and increase their awareness of situational contributors to children's behavior.

One way to increase awareness of situational variables is to teach parents to catch themselves using absolute terms, such as *always* and *never*, and to clarify when and under what circumstances the child misbehaves. This task is akin to challenging all-or-none, dichotomous thinking. Allie observed that her son's self-injurious behavior occurred only late at night, after conversations with his girlfriend. This helped her overcome her sense of helplessness, and she set limits on his late-night calls by charging his cell phone in her room. Marti realized that her son was noncompliant when he was deeply involved in some other activity. She learned to time requests better and to secure his attention before making them. Situational analysis helps parents identify where to intervene to change their child's behavior, improves their sense of efficacy, increases empathy, and decreases negative emotional reactions.

Understand the Goals of Children's Behavior. Identifying possible goals of children's behavior is similar to identifying basic mistakes in cognitive therapy. Several parenting education programs refer to four common mistaken goals of children's misbehaviors identified by Dreikurs (1964): power, attention, revenge, and display of inadequacy. When parents view the child's goal solely as mistaken, they tend to respond punitively to the behavior, as if the child has no right to have that goal. It is more often the means to the goal (the observable behavior) that is mistaken, rather than the goal itself. If parents take this perspective and attempt to better understand the "why" of the child's behavior (the goal of it), they can engage in teaching, guiding, and shaping of behavior, so that children meet their understandable (reasonable) goals in more adaptive ways. Table 25.1 reflects these four common goals of misbehavior and provides an understanding of the adaptive need the child is attempting to meet and ways in which parents may be able to more effectively meet those needs. Inviting parents to wonder about the potentially adaptive purposes of their child's behavior interrupts impulsive responding, interposes thought and judgment between impulse and action, and increases empathy for children.

Exert Emotional Self-Control.   Parents are taught behavioral and cognitive methods of self-control. They are encouraged to remove themselves—and allow others to

Table 25.1   Goals and Adaptive Needs of Some Child Misbehavior

Goal	Adaptive Need	Possible Responses
Power	Autonomy, mastery of the environment and self, control over own destiny	Give choices, share decision-making, acknowledge self-control, build mastery, use social exchange theory
Attention	Connection, belonging, recognition, acknowledgement	Attend to child for positive reasons, build relationship, make them a part, acknowledge identity, encourage, provide a secure base
Revenge	Justice, relief from injustice, understanding of the reasons for parents' decisions	Explain rationale and values behind decisions, provide justice, apologize for errors, model and demand respect, give clear commands, use social exchange theory
Inadequacy	Skill building, assistance, stress relief, rest	Build skills, reflect child's resilience, hold to age- and ability-appropriate expectations, allow respite where needed, teach stress management

remove themselves—from conflictual situations until they are able to engage in problem solving with greater behavioral and emotional control. Developing multiple options for temporary respite from child care or management counters a sense of being stuck in conflict. These options include time out for self-care, a retreat to another room, getting someone else to step in for a few minutes, dividing and sharing child care tasks with partners, scheduling regular time off from parenting duties, and use of day care or other care substitutes. Connection with community respite resources is an important adjunct for single parents, parents with several closely spaced children, parents whose children have a disability, and isolated parents. Cognitive self-control methods include practicing coping statements, such as, "I can do this," taking a future perspective, and finding humor in the situation.

Lesson 4. Decrease Child Misbehavior

Parents resort to punishment when they do not have other, well-practiced tools for managing child behavior, when they are distracted or exhausted, and when they are emotionally aroused. Once parents have knowledge of child development, effective methods to elicit desired behaviors, and improved self-control, they can be asked to give up punitive or coercive methods of responding to children's misbehavior.

Counter Myths about Efficacy of Punishment. Parents' punishing behavior is difficult to extinguish because it is usually effective in the short run, reinforcing parents' behavior. The effect is short-lived, because punishment does not develop internal motivation for good behavior. Punishment also decreases parental satisfaction, results in increased parent–child conflict, and is correlated with an increase in overall family violence and child aggressive behavior outside the family. It models power assertion as a means of solving problems. Educating parents about negative effects of punishment, especially physical punishment, counters parents mistaken beliefs about its efficacy and prepares them to try alternatives.

Use "Do" Commands Rather Than "Don't" Commands. One way to decrease the frequency of an unwanted behavior is to reinforce more desirable, incompatible behaviors, referred to as differential reinforcement of other behavior. For example, Steve interrupted his son's hitting behavior in one family therapy session by teaching him to shake hands. Pam helped her daughter decorate her room in an older "teen" style, which encouraged decreased messiness. Using "stop" commands is usually temporarily effective at best, because it does not instruct children what to do instead. "Stop" commands should always be paired with "do instead" instructions.

Reduce the Frequency of Commands. It is easy for parents to notice (and hence, reinforce) misbehavior because misbehavior becomes "figure" against the "ground" of normal or cooperative behavior. Further, some people believe that good parents must correct every instance of misbehavior. As a result, they monitor children too closely, increasing the level of conflict in their relationship with their children. Their children usually complain, "I can't do anything right!" Reducing the frequency of commands and selecting only one or two important behaviors to eliminate or change, provides an opportunity for both parent and child to experience success, gives the child the room to choose better behavior of their own accord, and helps reduce parental stress. Parents must therefore prioritize which behaviors are most important to change, or which behaviors, if changed, will lead to other desirable changes.

Ignore Some Misbehavior. Reducing frequency of commands requires parents to ignore some misbehavior. Much child misbehavior can be ignored without ill effect, and behaviors that have been inadvertently reinforced through negative attention may be extinguished by consistent ignoring. Extinguishing a previously reinforced behavior through ignoring requires consistency, since a variable reinforcement schedule will make a behavior more resistant to extinction. When Marti consistently ignored her son's conflicts, she found that the conflicts themselves decreased and the boy stopped coming to her for resolution. When Mike and Donna subtly ignored their son's pleas for rescue or release from school, increased attention to his resilient behaviors, and directed his attention to other things when he expressed anxiety, his school refusal gradually remitted. Parents need tools and methods for how to ignore misbehavior while remaining relatively unstressed.

Anticipate Development. Parents often catastrophize about the long-term consequences of a child's misbehavior. They fail to credit that children grow out of most misbehaviors, that most misbehaviors are not life-threatening, and that most children grow up to be fine, upstanding citizens. Identifying and challenging catastrophizing beliefs lower parental anxiety and emotional responding. While, of course, some misbehaviors of children must be changed or stopped due to serious safety concerns or because someone's rights are being seriously violated, most child behavior does not fall into these categories.

When Allie's son announced he intended to drop out of school to form a rock band, she and her husband predicted that he would be a failure in life. The group worked through the possible and probable outcomes of their son's announcement, including that the son might change his mind, drop out but later decide he needed to get his GED and college degree, get a job in the trades, and so on. One way to challenge catastrophizing is to exaggerate negative consequences to a humorous extent. The group challenged Allie's catastrophizing cognitions by asking questions, such as, "Will he ever have any job at all? Do you suppose he'll ever move out? Do you think he'll get married and have children?" When Susan's 8-year-old daughter decided to invite only some of her girl-friends to her birthday party, Susan predicted life-long social dysfunction. Challenging her catastrophic prediction, she realized only a few short-term problems might happen, and her daughter would not likely end up a heartless and lonely adult. Pam and Hal reacted to their daughter's poor school performance by fearing she would be a life-long failure, ignoring the fact that their daughter was successful in every other area of life, including at her job.

Use Natural Consequences. Not all behavior can be safely or reasonably ignored. Natural and logical consequences are effective alternatives to punishment. Natural consequences happen as a result of the child's behavior if the parent does not intervene. For example, Pam was convinced to stop calling her daughter out of class every time the daughter had a panic attack and to allow her to suffer the consequences of accumulating detentions for skipping class. As soon as she stopped excusing her daughter from class, her daughter's panic attacks abated, and calls from the school that she had cut class dwindled. When Marti's son complained that his brother would not play with him, rather than inter-rupting what she was doing to supervise their play she calmly responded, "That's what happens when you're mean to him, I guess." Some natural consequences are social: if you are rude or mean, people won't want to be your friend. Some are physical: if you leave your bike out in the rain, it will rust. Some are emotional: if you don't prepare for your presentation, you'll be anxious and embarrassed when the teacher calls on you. Allowing children to experience natural consequences can be very instructive!

Some natural consequences cannot safely be allowed to occur. The baby cannot play with knives, chew on cords, or climb the bookcase. Sometimes, allowing a natural consequence to occur interferes with parents' rights. Letting the child learn that a bike left in the rain will rust may not be a parent's idea of a good investment of money. In such cases, imposing logical consequences is the thing to do.

Use Logical Consequences. Logical consequences are contingencies imposed by pa-rental decision that would not otherwise have occurred. They are clearly connected to the misbehavior; proportional to the misbehavior; time limited—in that there should be an opportunity for the child to demonstrate growth or improvement with a lifting of the consequence; and delivered in a calm, reasonable manner. Parents often impose illogical consequences. For example, they pull children from team sports or after school activities when participation in these activities often teaches the very pro-social skills the parents want children to develop. Parents of children with poor social skills and few friends will sometimes cancel play dates or pull children from social activities just as their children begin to develop enough autonomy and social skill to engage in the usual mischief for their age. Parents are challenged to identify the logical connections between the consequences they usually impose and the behavior that provoked them. Where logical connections cannot easily be identified, they are encouraged to brainstorm alternative, logically connected consequences.

Parents may need to defer action to take time to identify logical consequences for misbehavior, especially if they are emotionally aroused, if they are not able to determine them in advance. Steve and Becky were often so angry with their 4-year-old son that they feared they would hit him, so they locked him in his bedroom when he misbehaved. The next time he misbehaved, they quietly told him they would have to think about what to do, took time to brainstorm possible consequences, and identified and implemented logical consequences that both corrected his behavior and taught him a skill.

Logical consequences may invoke social exchange theory—the observation that social interactions tend to be reciprocated in kind, teaching cooperation and the response cost of treating people poorly. Andrea's 2-year-old slapped and pinched her face whenever Andrea held her. Andrea tried sweet-talking, begging, and slapping the toddler to make her stop, but the child seemed to find it a fun game. The group suggested that the next time, Andrea put the baby on the floor and say, "I don't hold babies who hit me. Maybe you can try again later." Andrea had a hard time holding the line when her daughter sobbed heartbreakingly, but she did follow through. A short time later, she offered the toddler another chance. Repeating the consequence one more time completely extinguished the behavior. This differs from the threat of loss of love used by some parents in that the parent is simply saying what they will and will not do, setting a personal limit. Calmly delivered, without withdrawal of warmth in the relationship, this is a logical consequence rather than a coercive, controlling reaction.

Using natural and logical consequences teaches children to anticipate the likely social and practical outcomes of their behavior, to think ahead, to expect fairness in their dealings with their parents, and to take responsibility for their actions. Eventually, most children are able to identify the natural and logical consequences for their own behaviors. Anticipating consequences helps them control their own behavior.

Use Limited Time-Outs. Effective time-outs help children regain emotional and behavioral self-control in contrast to grounding or sending children to bed without supper, which are punitive or response-cost measures. Guidelines for effective time-outs are:

1. Use time outs to help the child regain self-control rather than as punishment.
2. Identify the task as "calming down," and model removing oneself from emotionally charged situations in order to gain time to think or calm down.
3. Remove the child from whatever is reinforcing the misbehavior.
4. Limit the time out to a short period. For children under 10, the standard is 1 minute per year in age.
5. Start the "timer" when the child is under control. If the child is old enough, end the time out when the child can return to the situation in control of him/herself.
6. Engage the child in reflection on the reason for the time out, and the standards for behavior.
7. Guide the child to engage in the appropriate behavior following the time-out.

Lesson 5. Set Appropriate Limits

Limit-setting establishes the boundaries for appropriate and acceptable behavior. It includes not only the idea of what behavior is considered "out of bounds" or misbehavior, but also what behavior is considered "in bounds" or appropriate. How much informal speech between parent and child is teasing and fun, and when does it become disrespect? How much time should a teenager spend on the computer? When is curfew? When is bedtime? Is a co-ed sleep-over on prom night okay?

Identify Appropriate Limits. Developmentally appropriate limits are within the cognitive, emotional, and behavioral capabilities of the child, and appropriate from a social-developmental perspective. Appropriate limits constantly change as children grow. Changes in society and technology affect what is considered appropriate. Children are not typically allowed to roam the entire day without checking in today, but this was common in the 1950s. When household computers and internet access were first available, standards for children's use of the computer were easy to set, but today even the youngest students are assigned homework that requires computer and internet access. Cell phones are now ubiquitous among high school students, and nearly so among middle school students in some areas. Sometimes, standards change abruptly, rather than gradually, due to local, national, or even international crises. Following highly publicized violent incidents in schools, and particularly in the aftermath of the World Trade Center attacks, many high schools and middle schools began allowing students to carry cell phones in book bags, or stopped enforcing previous "no cell-phone" rules.

Since standards for behavior are shifting targets, parenting education should help parents identify methods for discovering appropriate standards. Parents are encouraged to tap into the collective knowledge and wisdom of school policy, local laws, community consensus, pediatricians, religious and cultural leaders, and other reference groups. They may need help formulating questions to ask pediatricians, encouragement to ask other parents about community standards, reminders to check school handbooks and toy and movie labels, and education about how to access information online. Role-playing is particularly important in helping some parents feel more comfortable calling or talking with someone they don't know—both to communicate their expectations, and to verify community, school, and other standards.

Parents should also consider family, cultural, religious, and neighborhood values in establishing limits. Maladaptive family value systems, often generationally transmitted, must be identified and challenged. Family values often consist of unspoken beliefs about relative power between genders and generations, the value of the individual versus the group, and so on. They may be revealed in commonly used phrases or statements within the family. "If we all pitch in, we'll be done in 20 minutes."; "When I say jump, you say, 'How high?'"; "A man's home is his castle."; "Children should be seen and not heard." Family values create often unspoken expectations for behavior, and can be the source of conflict, particularly as children enter adolescence and young adulthood. Parents need to identify their unspoken values, make them explicit, question their adaptive value, and communicate them effectively. Appropriate limits also recognize the rights of others, including parents and other children. Some parents may need help asserting their own rights as well as those of others, and can be helped to state what they will and will not do.

Communicate Limits Effectively. To be most effective, limits should be communicated ahead of time when possible, presented respectfully, stated positively as "do" versus "don't" directives, and be given in clear, behavioral terms. Limits that embed value-based or practical rationales are more likely to be internalized and remembered. Effective limits take into account the child's ability to comply, and teach necessary skills. For example, to be home on time, a child must know how to read a clock or watch. Timely reminders about limits increase likelihood of compliance. As children develop, rules and limits should be applicable to everyone in the home. Family rules, "house rules," and societal standards are more likely to be viewed by adolescents, in particular, as reasonable, and are therefore more likely to elicit compliance. Stating consequences for breaking a rule or limit in advance and logically connecting consequences to the infraction increase compliance and decrease conflict when rules are broken.

Lesson 6. Teach Problem-Solving and Communication Skills

Problem-solving and communication skills decrease parents' stress and provide another alternative to power assertion as a child-management method. These skills apply not only to parent–child conflicts and problems, but also to marital conflict that often accompanies parent–child difficulties. A prerequisite to effective problem-solving and conflict resolution is that the parent is under emotional and behavioral control, able to respond logically rather than emotionally. Activities that help parents anticipate problems and plan ways to prevent or cope with them increase parents' efficacy and reduce emotional responding.

Use Problem Solving Individually and in Family Meetings. The first task in problem resolution is to clearly identify the problem. The group engages in activities designed to help parents define problems in unambiguous, behavioral terms. Important aspects of problem definition include identifying whose problem it is and who is responsible for fixing the problem. For example, one function of a sibling subsystem is to teach negotiation skills and other social skills. When parents consistently insert themselves into their children's squabbles, children do not learn those skills. At some point in development, incomplete homework becomes the child's problem and responsibility. Too much noise for a parent's comfort is the parent's problem, and the parent can take steps to solve that problem. The usual problem-solving steps are taught: identifying both problem and goal, brainstorming solutions, cost/benefit analysis, prioritizing of options, planning multiple solutions, carrying out the most likely solution, evaluating results, adjusting the plan if necessary, identifying what worked, and celebrating success. Most parenting education groups teach the value, goal, structure and process of family meetings, both as a formal venue for family problem-solving and to plan positive family events.

Attention to communication skills helps parents refine problem solving and limit setting and promote pro-social behavior. Clear communication requires using unambiguous terms, which often can be very difficult for people. Topics covered in this area include:

1. Using I messages
2. Active listening
3. Requesting behavior change before a problem gets out of control
4. Stating personal limits and what one will and will not do, rather than telling the child what to do

5. Sticking to one topic
6. Presenting a unified front
7. Terminating heated discussions and returning to the topic later

Lesson 7. Improve Parental Self-Efficacy and Stress Management

As the parenting education program progresses and child behavior improves, goals for change become moving targets, and parents may minimize gains and maximize remaining problems. Reviewing logs, journals, workbooks, or homework assignments completed during parent training helps them regain perspective and is the first step in relapse prevention and program termination.

To develop or regain a sense of efficacy and take responsibility for continued change, parents must associate change with their own efforts. They must identify what they have done differently, and the impact of those changes on their children, children's behavior, and their own experiences of parenting. Accurate, unexaggerated attributions help them form realistic expectations for the future.

Using a stress inoculation approach (Meichenbaum, 1985), parents are helped to anticipate future developmental stages and the normal cognitive, emotional, behavioral, and social capabilities, limitations, tasks, and challenges that they and their children will face in each stage. For parents of children with special issues, anticipating the development and course of those issues over time, children's likely response to treatment, and long-term planning are part of the relapse prevention plan. Parents are encouraged to anticipate challenges to the changes they have made, identify early signs that the family is getting off track, and plan steps to take in response. These include reviewing materials from the parenting education class, recommitting to new behaviors and cognitions that work but were discontinued, reconnecting with social support and reducing isolation, obtaining respite to regain perspective, and returning for additional training or other therapy. The group takes inventory of the new tools, knowledge, and resources they have as a result of participating in the parenting program, and make explicit plans to keep these actively available at home.

CONCLUSION

When parents come for parenting education, they usually have a particular "problem child" in mind, and are most likely to apply new skills and attitudes to their interactions with that child and to the particular behaviors they identify as problematic. Without specific attention to generalization, they may not apply what they have learned to siblings or to other behaviors, making relapse more likely (Arnold, Levine, & Patterson, 1975; Humphreys, Forehand, McMahon, & Roberts, 1978; Wells, Forehand, & Griest, 1980). Therefore, it is important to train broadly, rather than specifically, throughout the program. Parent–child or parent–parent problems brought up by group members during training should be treated as specific instances of general issues, and general principles, rather than specific solutions, should be addressed. The group should always be challenged to think beyond specifics.

Parenting education has been shown to be effective across cultures, ability levels, socioeconomic statuses, and other parent and family characteristics, providing that the particular practical, educational, and cultural needs of those groups are taken into consideration.

REFERENCES

Abidin, R. R. (1995). *Parenting stress index, 3rd ed.* Odessa, FL: Psychological Assessment Resources.

Achenbach, T. M. (1991). *Manual for the child behavior checklist.* Burlington: University of Vermont Press.

Arnold, J. E., Levine, A. G., & Patterson, G. R. (1975). Changes in sibling behavior following family intervention. *Journal of Consulting and Clinical Psychology, 43,* 683–688.

Azar, S. T., & Rohrbeck, C.A. (1986). Child abuse and unrealistic expectations: Further validation of the Parent Opinion Questionnaire. *Journal of Consulting and Clinical Psychology, 54*(6), 867–868.

Baumrind, D. (1968). Authoritarian vs. authoritative parental control. *Adolescence, 3*(11), 255–272.

Cartwright-Hatton, S., McNally, D., White, C., & Verduyn, C. (2005). Parenting skills training: An effective intervention for internalizing symptoms in younger children? *Journal of Child and Adolescent Psychiatric Nursing, 18*(2), 45–52.

DeBord, K., Bower, D., Goddard, H. W., Kirby, J., Kobbe, A. M., Myers-Walls, J. A., Mulroy, M., & Ozretich, R.A. (2002). *National extension parenting educators' framework.* Washington, DC: U.S. Dept. of Agriculture.

Dinkmeyer, D., McKay, G. D., & Dinkmeyer, D. (1973). *Systematic training for effective parenting.* Lebanon, IN: Pearson.

Dix, T. (1991). The affective organization of parenting: Adaptive and maladaptive processes. *Psychological Bulletin, 120,* 3–25.

Dix, T. (1993). Attributing dispositions to children: An interactional analysis of attribution in socialization. *Personality and Social Psychology Bulletin, 19,* 633–643.

Dreikurs, R. (1964). *Children: The challenge.* New York: Hawthorne.

Forehand, R. L., & King, H. E. (1977). Noncompliant children: Effects of parent training on behavior and attitude change. *Behavior Modification, 1,* 93–108.

Gordon, T. (1970). *Parent effectiveness training.* New York: David McKay.

Gordon, T. (2000). *Parent effectiveness training: The proven program for raising responsible children.* New York: Crown.

Habisch-Ahlin, T. (1999). *Positive discipline: A guide for parents.* Minneapolis, MN: University of Minesota/ Regents of the University of Minnesota. Available at http://www.extension.umn.edu/distribution/familydevelopment/DE7461.html.

Humphreys, L., Forehand, R., McMahon, R., & Roberts, M. (1978). Parent behavioral training to modify child noncompliance: Effects on untreated siblings. *Journal of Behavior Therapy and Experimental Psychiatry, 9,* 235–238.

Mikeston, C., & Patenaude, R. (1994). Parent attributions for inattentive-overactive and oppositional-defiant child behaviors. *Cognitive Therapy and Research, 18*(3), 261–269.

Kashdan, T. B., Jacob, R. G., Pelham, W. E., Lang, A. R., Hoza, B., Blumenthal, J. D., & Gnagy, E. M. (2004). Depression and anxiety in parents of children with ADHD and varying levels of oppositional defiant behaviors: Modeling relationships with family functioning. *Journal of Clinical Child and Adolescent Psychology, 33*(1), 169–181.

Matthews, J. M., & Hudson, A. M. (2001). Guidelines for evaluating parent training programs. *Family Relations, 50*(1), 77–86.

Meichenbaum, D. (1985). *Stress inoculation training.* New York: Pergamon.

Patterson, G. R. (1982). *Coercive family process.* Eugene, OR: Castalia.

Penderhughes, E. E., Dodge, K. A., Bates, J. E., Pettit, G. S., & Zelli, A. (2000). Discipline responses: Influences of parents' socioeconomic status, ethnicity, beliefs about parenting, stress, and cognitive-emotional processes. *Journal of Family Psychology, 14*(3), 380–400.

Popkin, M. (1983). *Active parenting discussion program.* Kennesaw, GA: Active Parenting Publishing.

Popkin, M. (2002). *Active parenting now.* Kennesaw, GA: Active Parenting Publishers.

Sanders, M. R., Markie-Dadds, C. & Turner, K. M. T. (2003). *Theoretical, scientific, and clinical foundations of thetTriple p-positive parenting program: A population approach to the promotion of parenting competence. Parenting research and practice monograph no. 1.* Brisbane, Australia: Families International Publishing.

Shannon, L. C. (n.d.). Best practices in parent education groups seeking to prevent child abuse. National Parenting Education Network. Accessed Dec. 8, 2005,t http://www.ces.ncsu.edu/depts/fcs/npen/BestPra.pdf.

Stormshak, E. A., Bierman, K. L., McMahon, R. J., Lengua, L. J., & Conduct Problems Prevention Research Group (2000). Parenting practices and child disruptive behavior problems in early elementary school. *Journal of Clinical Child Psychology, 29*(1), 17–29.

Straus, M. A., Hamby, S. L., Finkelhor, D., Moore, D. W, & Runyan, D. (1998). *Conflict tactics scale.* Durham, NH: Family Research Laboratory.

Webster-Stratton, C. (1983). Conduct disorders: Intervention approaches. *Nurse Practitioner 8*(5), 23–34.

Webster-Stratton, C. (1996). Videotape modeling intervention programs for families of young children with oppositional-defiant disorder or conduct disorder. In Hibbs, E. D. & Jensen, P. S. (Eds.), *Psychosocial treatment research of child and adolescent disorders: Empirically based strategies for clinical practice* (pp. 435–474). Washington, DC: American Psychological Association.

Webster-Stratton, C. (2006). *The incredible years: A troubleshooting guide for parents of children aged 2–8.* Seattle, WA: Umbrella Press.

Wells, K. C., Forehand, R., & Griest, D. L. (1980). Generality of treatment effects from treated to untreated behaviors resulting from a parent training program. *Journal of Clinical Child Psychology, 9*, 217–219.

Chapter Twenty-Six

Social Skills Groups with Youth: A Cognitive-Behavioral Perspective

Richard J. Erdlen, Jr. & Marcy R. Rickrode

The prevailing *zeitgeist* in 21st-century American education is about meeting academic standards. Too little emphasized, however, is the skill set needed by children and youth to get along with adults and peers in school. Academic skill development will always be the preeminent mission of school, yet we know that employers especially value the prospective employee who works well with a team, is an effective problem-solver, and brings a basic sociability to the work place. These assets are also critical components of one's mental health and quality of life.

The following chapter provides an overview of social competence, its development, and relation to social skills. We discuss the work of several major contributors to the study of social competence and skills while highlighting assessment goals and procedures. The problem of social skill deficits is conceptualized from a cognitive-behavioral perspective and the role of distorted thinking is explained. Specific cognitive and behavioral strategies for working with this population are reviewed and a case example using these techniques is presented. Due to the difficulties surrounding generalization and maintenance of treatment effects, we pay special attention to thoughts about overcoming these obstacles. In addition, we provide several key readings useful for those working with this population, as well those who are interested in further study in this area.

OVERVIEW

What is Social Competence?

Bierman and Welsh (2000) offer a unique conceptualization of social competence. They contend that social competence is the result of a child's ability to integrate behavioral, cognitive, and affective skills successfully in a variety of social contexts and under a variety of social demands. This viewpoint takes into consideration affective and cognitive factors rather than placing most of the focus on specific behavioral responses. Social skills can be viewed as one of several factors that contribute to social competence.

Using this as our basis for understanding social competence, one may question the nature of the relationship between social competence and social skills. A hierarchical model proposed by Merrell (2003) suggests that social competence is a superordinate construct inclusive of those specific verbal and nonverbal behaviors we call social skills. These skills contribute to and facilitate the development of social competence. An additional construct that indirectly affects the development of social competence is that of peer relations. Merrell posits that the quality of one's peer relationships determines the quality of one's social skills and vise versa. These two constructs (peer relations and social skills) have a bidirectional relationship where each influences the other. The all-encompassing and overarching construct that includes social competence as one of its components is adaptive behavior.

Types of Social Skill Deficits

Social skill dysfunction is typically classified in terms of acquisition, performance, or fluency deficits. *Acquisition deficits* involve a complete lack of skill, that is to say the individual has not learned the appropriate behaviors necessary for competence in a given social situation. *Performance deficits,* on the other hand, assume that the basic knowledge of how to perform a given social skill is present; however, the ability or decision to perform this skill in a given context is flawed. *Fluency deficits* refer to a lack of consistent and automatic performance of the behavioral set due to a lack of practice or competent models (Gresham, 2002b). The intervention then is dependent upon the identified deficit. It would be senseless to attempt to teach skills of assertion to an individual who simply is choosing to refrain from exercising these skills. In the same vein, trying to increase performance of a given skill when the basic "how-to" knowledge is unknown would be ineffective.

Dimensions of Social Skills

There are a variety of classification systems available regarding the major categories of social skills; however, we prefer those identified by Caldarella and Merrell (1997) based on their review of 20 years of research. In their meta-analysis, Caldarella and Merrell identified five behavioral dimensions of social skills: (a) peer relations, (b) self-management, (c) academic, (d) compliance, and (e) assertion. These domains were identified by reviewing research on social skills in order to determine the most common factors included in these studies. The researchers then ranked these domains and subskills according to the frequency of their appearance in the reviewed studies. For example, 52.38% of the studies reviewed included factors associated with the peer relations dimension, while 33.33% of the studies were related to the assertion dimension. This taxonomy is valuable for assessment and intervention purposes in that it provides a basis for identifying an individual's social strengths and weaknesses and is a foundation for treatment design.

Development of Social Competence

A logical question to ask for those attempting to intervene with socially challenged youth is, "How does social competence develop?" or, stated another way, "What factors influence whether or not a child will develop into a socially competent adult?" The factors influencing the development of social competence are quite complex and include child, caregiver, and family factors. A study by Smart and Sanson (2001) found certain aspects of a child's temperament, including reactivity (e.g., irritability or negativity), attention regulation (i.e., ability to maintain attention for task completion), and emotion regulation (i.e., the ability to control emotions) to impact later social competence. Furthermore, the fit between these child characteristics and parent expectations also was found to be significant. In their analysis, children with high reactivity and poor parent–child fit generally had the lowest levels of later social skills. Secure attachment and low family stress also were found to be important for social development. In a study by Schmidt, Demulder, and Denham (2002) less securely attached preschoolers were not only rated as less socially competent in kindergarten, but were also more aggressive. Furthermore, Aronen and Kurkela's (1998) work identified several family factors including the quality of family relationships, family health, and socioeconomic status that strongly predicted later social competence in 14- and 15-year-old youth.

Associated Features

Deficits in social skills are core or common features of a variety of developmental disabilities, neurological disorders, and mental diagnoses. The American Association on Mental Retardation (AAMR; 2002) includes "significant limitations...in adaptive behavior" as part of the criteria for establishing the presence of mental retardation. Social skills represent one aspect of adaptive functioning (Sparrow, Cicchetti, & Balla, 2005). Those with autism also exhibit difficulties in their social interactions with others. They may lack basic social skills such as establishing and maintaining eye contact or may have difficulty initiating and sustaining conversations with others. Although having poor social skills is not part of the diagnostic criteria of Attention-Deficit/Hyperactivity Disorder (AD/HD), individuals with this condition often experience trouble with peer relationships due, in part, to higher levels of physical aggression than their peers (Maedgen & Carlson, 2000; see Nixon, 2001 for a review of the literature). Probably the most obvious group that comes to mind when discussing youth who have social difficulties are those diagnosed with Oppositional Defiant Disorder (ODD) or Conduct Disorder (CD). The essential feature of ODD is negative behavior toward authority figures while conduct disorder involves violation of the rights of others or societal norms (American Psychiatric Association, 2000). Both of these disorders involve some sort of social dysfunction.

Impact of Poor Social Competence

The rationale for improving the social skills of youth is easily understood from a review of the long-term implications of poor social competence. Outcomes for those with poor competence, skills, or peer relations include low academic achievement (Wentzel, 1993), drug and alcohol abuse (Greene, Biederman, Faraone, Wilens, Mick, & Blier, 1999), delinquent and aggressive behavior (Matlack & McGreevy, 1994; Rabiner, Coie, Miller-Johnson, Boykin, & Lochman, 2005), school drop-out, and mental health difficulties (Parker & Asher, 1987). It is clear why so much interest and research continues in this area. In order for youth to avoid these abysmal outcomes, it is important to work to improve their skills and relations with others.

SOCIAL SKILLS ASSESSMENT

Youth are often presented for treatment involuntarily by their parents, teachers, counselors, or members of the community. They are in a sense "nominated" by those impacted by or concerned for their level of functioning. In such cases, clinicians are charged with the task of assessing the severity of the youth's difficulties in addition to the need for and focus of treatment. To assist in the selection of specific tools used, it may be helpful to identify and consider one's objectives. Gresham (2002a) identified 12 major goals in social skills assessment and grouped them into four problem-solving stages. Comprising the *Problem Identification Phase* are goals including the identification of social strengths and weakness, the nature of the deficits, and the competing behaviors. Within the *Problem Analysis* phase, possible reasons for or functions of the observed weaknesses are documented by way of functional assessment. This includes careful analysis of the antecedent and consequent factors that may be influencing the youth's skills. In addition, the clinician should assess the social validity or importance of the identified social skills. After these steps are completed, the clinician can identify behaviors to target during intervention. Interventions are then designed by using the data collected in previous steps as a guide (*Plan Implementation*). The *Treatment Evaluation* phase consists of selecting tools to assess progress, evaluate the effects of interventions, and determine how well the youngster is generalizing and maintaining newly learned skills. To assist the clinician in accomplishing these goals, a variety of tools and procedures are briefly described in hopes of making this process most efficient and productive.

Direct Observation

Direct observation of social strengths and weaknesses is often the best method to employ in social skills assessment due to how sensitive observational data is to treatment effects (Gresham, 2002b). In fact, Elliott and Gresham (1987) suggested that observation in one's natural setting is, "the most ecologically valid method of assessing children's social skills" (p. 97). Observing youth at lunch, in the hallway, during collaborative learning activities, or within the community can provide valuable opportunities to witness strengths and weaknesses as well as the environmental conditions present. Merrell (2001; 2003) mentions four essential components of direct observation: (1) using trained observers; (2) establishing operational definitions of behaviors that can be observed with little subjective judgment; (3) using a recording method at the time the behavior occurs (e.g., event, interval, time-sampling, duration, and/or latency recording); and (4) selecting comparison peers. Consideration of these guidelines prior to conducting the observation will facilitate accuracy and time efficiency.

Rating Scales

In addition to direct observation methods, clinicians can obtain valuable information regarding a youth's competencies and deficiencies from parents, teachers, and other caregivers. One way of acquiring quantifiable representations of informant perceptions is by using behavior-rating scales. Several rating scales have been designed for assessing behaviors most often associated with social competence. Gresham and Elliott (1990) developed the *Social Skills Rating System* (SSRS) which contains parent, teacher, and self-report forms for those at the preschool (age 3 to 5 years), elementary (grades K to 6), and secondary level (grades 7 to 12). At the secondary level, the parent form includes a Social Skills and Problem Behaviors scale, while the teacher form adds a third component (Academic Competence). All SSRS forms contain the following three subscales: Cooperation, Assertion, and Self-Control. The parent version adds a fourth subscale (Responsibility), as does the self-report form (Empathy). The SSRS uses a 3-point scale to determine how often each behavior occurs as well as the rater's perception regarding the importance of the skill to the young person's development. A unique feature of the SSRS is the addition of the Assessment Intervention Record. This form provides a way to record the multi-informant ratings and facilitates integrations of this information to identify social behavior strengths and weaknesses as well as interfering problem behaviors.

Another frequently used measure to assess social skills is the *Walker-McConnell Scale of Social Competence and School Adjustment* (WMS; Walker & McConnell, 1995). Unlike the SSRS, the WMS is limited to use in schools as it is designed to elicit perceptions of a student's behavior from school professionals only. There is an elementary and adolescent version used with students in kindergarten through 6 and 7 through 12, respectively. The adolescent version includes four subscales (Self Control, Peer Relations, School Adjustment, and Empathy), as well as a total scale score. Both Adolescent and Elementary versions use a scale that ranges from 1 (never occurs) to 5 (frequently occurs).

The *School Social Behavior Scales, Second Edition* (SSBS) developed by Merrell (2002) is used in conjunction with the *Home and Community Social Behavior Scales* (HCSBS; Merrell & Caldarella, 2002) forming the *Social Behavior Scales*. The SSBS-2 contains two main scales: (1) Social Competence and (2) Antisocial Behavior. The instrument is used by school personnel to rate the social competence and antisocial behavior of youth aged 5 to 18 years. The items on the Social Competence scale are divided into three subscales: Peer Relations, Self-Management/Compliance, and Academic Behavior. The three subscales comprising the Antisocial Behavior scale are labeled Hostile/Irritable, Antisocial-Aggressive, and Defiant/Disruptive. As other instruments reviewed, the SSBS-2 uses a 5-point scale (1 = never, 5 = frequently) to rate youth behavior.

In order to broaden the scope of assessment, Merrell and Caldarella (2002) developed the *Home and Community Social Behavior Scales* (HCSBS), which contain many of the same items as the SSBS-2, though they are rephrased to include behaviors performed in nonschool settings. The two main scales are identical in name to the SSBS-2 Social

Competence and Antisocial Behavior. The Social Competence scale yields two subscales termed Peer Relations and Self-Management/Compliance while the Antisocial Behavior scale includes the Defiant/Disruptive and Antisocial-Aggressive subscales. Like the SSBS-2, the HCSBS uses a 5-point scale where 1 indicates that the behavior never occurs and 5 indicates that it frequently occurs. Together, the SSBS-2 and HCSBS allow the clinician to obtain information regarding the youth's behavior across settings.

Demaray and colleagues (1995) compared the SSRS, WMS, and original version of the SSBS. They concluded that the SSRS was the most comprehensive instrument due to its unique intervention component, broader applicability, multisource approach, and strong reliability and validity. Since this review, Merrell has developed the HCSBS, which can be used in conjunction with the SSBS, addressing the problem presented by Demaray and colleagues regarding its narrow school-only focus.

Interviews

Although direct observations and ratings scales are generally believed to be the most valid and direct measures of social skills, clinicians may need to supplement or complement their assessment by using additional tools. Interviewing is often a useful method for clarifying data collected on the more direct assessments (i.e., direct observations and rating scales) and understanding the environment in which the behavior occurs. Additionally, interviewing may provide an opportunity for the clinician to utilize role-playing as a method of observing the youth's demonstration of important social skills. Spence (2003) suggests that interviewing can be useful for obtaining information from parents and teachers as well. She provides a list of several questions that often provide valuable data and involve inquiries regarding the number of friends an individual has, the type and frequency of contact, the typical duration of the youth's friendships, as well as whether or not the young person is popular or rejected by other children. Additionally, questions may be asked regarding the comfort level of the young person in group social settings (e.g., parties), typical activities during less structured school time (e.g., lunch and recess), the nature of the youth's relationships with adults including parents and teachers, extracurricular or community activities that the individual participates in, as well as specific social settings that trigger anxiety, conflict, or some other discomfort.

Sociometric Techniques

Sociometric techniques are additional tools used in the assessment of social skills and most commonly include peer nomination and peer rating methods. Terry (2000) identifies four main methods for collecting sociometric information. *Peer nomination* involves directing peers within the young person's environment (e.g., classroom) to elect individuals that they like or dislike. The *rank-order* procedure simply involves ordering all peers in a given environment according to the individual's own preferences of, for example, friendship. *Peer rating* methods require classmates to rate one another on a likert scale regarding the extent to which the individual is likeable or meets some other criterion. Finally, *paired comparisons* require individuals to identify the preferred peer in all possible pairs available in a given group. Merrell (2001) suggests that although they are often effective in identifying students that are unaccepted by their peers, sociometric techniques do not actually measure social skills but instead may be assessing peer acceptance or social reputation. Furthermore, these techniques do not provide information regarding why a student is liked or disliked. A third complication is that using such techniques requires permission from parents and administrations, not to mention a group of peers for those being treated in clinical settings. Therefore, although they produce valuable information, sociometric techniques can be difficult to carry out and do not specifically address the nature of the young person's social skills. If they are used, it is important to pair the results with other sources of data to ensure accurate assessment.

CBT CONCEPTUALIZATION OF THE PROBLEM

Rational Beliefs

Social skill deficits may arise from harsh environmental conditions, ineffective parenting, and the lack of adequate role models. These *external* factors generally are not remediable within the context of group therapy. What can be modified, however, are the students' *internal* set of beliefs and schema thought to underlie one's emotional life and behavioral output. A child with a belief system characterized by "musts," for example, may assert, "You *must* treat me fairly (and you're a jerk if you don't)." It is easy to imagine that someone with this entrenched belief would be upset when peers and adults do not conform to his or her expectations. Cognitive-behavior therapy targets irrational beliefs and seeks to dispute ideas that impede one's ability to get along with others. Minimizing irrational beliefs and supplanting them with adaptive, rational alternatives can increase the likelihood of social integration. These concepts related to cognitive-behavior therapy are addressed in chapter 1 of this volume, and thus, will not be discussed further here. However, it is important that clinicians conducting work in social skills development keep these principles in mind, as they may enhance basic social skills instruction.

Social Learning Theory

Another theoretical perspective in understanding social competence and social skills is social learning theory. Social learning, as proposed by its chief theorist, Albert Bandura (cited in Rychlak, 1981), is an attempt to explain how children develop a complex skill set in the social milieu. Bandura's model was based on the interplay of a child's characteristics, a child's specific behaviors, and the environment in a process he termed *reciprocal determinism*. Within this process, children learn new behaviors by observing the behaviors of significant others, like parents, older siblings, or popular peers, and noting which behaviors produce positive outcomes. In other words, the children need not receive direct reinforcement to acquire the new behaviors or their component parts. Seeing that esteemed others receive a payoff is enough to induce the child to imitate the behavior and incorporate it into his or her own behavioral repertoire. Social learning theory "depicts the child as an active participant in learning, with the child's cognition as a central mediator and organizer" (Tharinger & Lambert, 1999, p.148).

From this perspective, children are getting social skill exposure in nearly every social context. This is encouraging for school-based interventionists. When effective models and reinforcement schedules are in place, one would expect the addition of new behaviors, the reorganization of behaviors learned at an earlier age and greater proficiency or fluency in producing effective social skills. Unfortunately, the schools cannot control all of the models to which children are exposed. In addition to negative role models in various media, parents may demonstrate behaviors that seem to work for them in a short-term capacity (e.g., aggressive blustering with store clerks), but which are truly counterproductive for their children. Group facilitation provides a venue where skills that are more effective can be demonstrated, observed, practiced, modified, and rewarded to increase the likelihood of its occurrence *in vivo*.

The actual teaching of a set of social skills, especially for youngsters with identified learning or language deficits, borrows heavily from behavioral principles. Gresham (1997; 2002a) derived a set of guiding principles for the instruction of social skills (see Table 26.1).

Students who are not performing social skills fluently may be lacking awareness of social expectations or lacking the motivation to execute those skills. In the former case, teaching the skill to the naïve student helps to correct the "can't do" issue. The more difficult challenge is to create conditions to elicit social skill performance in the student who "won't do." We are reminded of the student with an emotional disturbance who asked the facilitator why he was teaching social skills. "We know how to do it," the student offered, "we just choose not to" (J.T. Burton, personal communication, December 20, 2005). In our practice, motivation is enhanced by having both genders represented in groups for older students. For younger students, group contingencies can be effective in strengthening social skill performance.

Social Problem Solving

Social problem solving (SPS) approaches date back to the seminal work of Spivack and Shure (1974) with young children. Social problem solving is based on the notion that there are cognitive deficiencies related to social skill deficits. If students can be taught a

Table 26.1   Ten Principles for Social Skills Enhancement

1. Social skills are learned.
2. Social skill difficulties can be acquisition deficits, performance deficits, or fluency deficits.
3. Social skills are contextual and relativistic.
4. Social skills are best taught in naturalistic settings.
5. Social skills are governed by the Principle of Social Reciprocity.
6. Social skills should be taught by the same procedures used to teach academic subjects.
7. There is a direct, positive relationship between the amount and quality of social skill training and the amount of change in social behavior.
8. Social skill training strategies must be accompanied by reductive techniques for the reduction or elimination of interfering problem behaviors.
9. Social skills training must be supplemented by behavioral rehearsal opportunities, performance feedback, and contingency systems in naturalistic settings to promote their occurrence, fluency, and mastery.
10. For social skill to be integrated into a behavioral repertoire, they must be more efficient and reliable in producing desired outcomes as competing behaviors.

way of thinking about interpersonal problems, presumably they can direct that approach to each problem they encounter in naturalistic settings.

Kendall (2006) succinctly indicated the reason for focusing on problem-solving skills—namely, because they occur. Further, he opined that one's success in life depends on the dual ability to recognize a problem and do something about it.

> The youngster and therapist interact in a collaborative problem-solving man-
> ner. In-session activities are practice; life outside a session is the game, and
> coaches provide practice opportunities for the very skills needed in the real
> arena. (Kendall, 2006, p.10)

D'Zurilla and Goldfried (1971) presented an early template for teaching five components of problem solving. Their sequence has been emulated, modified, and rephrased to fit mnemonic terminology. Stark and his colleagues at the University of Texas (2006) reference Kendall's variation of the D'Zurilla and Goldfried paradigm: "the 5 Ps":

*P*roblem—child defines the problem
*P*urpose—child sets the goal of problem solving
*P*lans—child brainstorms possible solutions (obvious or unconventional)
*P*redict and pick—child imagines likely consequences and selects a viable alterna-
    tive
*P*at on the back—child self-monitors progress and rewards effort

Spivack and Shure (1974) built upon the D'Zurilla and Goldfried model of *impersonal* problem solving and directed their attention to the cognitive skills needed to solve *interpersonal* problems effectively. The two cognitive skills they associated with adequate behavioral adjustment included the ability to think of alternative solutions and the ability to think of alternative consequences to solutions. By use of social vignettes, Spivack and Shure developed empirical means of assessing these skills. Finally, they constructed a training program to enhance these skills in children as young as pre-school age. As with each of the problem-solving approaches, the purpose is to address cognitive deficiencies (not distortions) by teaching children *how* to think, not *what* to think. In their review of the extant literature, Sheridan and Walker (1999) identified six steps for a comprehensive SPS model: (1) students learn that they can solve the social problems they encounter, (2) students learn to recognize the existence of a social problem, (3) students learn to brainstorm possible solutions to a problem, (4) students learn to select a strategy and develop a plan, (5) students learn to carry out the plan, and (6) students learn to evaluate their effectiveness.

GROUP TREATMENT

Modeling

In concert with the theoretical conceptualization of social skill development, treatment of social skill deficiencies may incorporate behavioral strategies, cognitive strategies, or some combination of the two. From a social learning (i.e., behavioral) perspective, intervention procedures rely on modeling prosocial behaviors. Sheridan and Walker (1999) provide a clear explanation of how modeling proceeds in social skill instruction. Presuming initial assessment of one's social skill repertoire, a target is selected that matches the identified needs of the student. During skill instruction, the students are provided with a step-by-step explanation of the skill or sequence of skills in question. Next, the skill is modeled either by a peer, teacher, ancillary staff, or via film or videotape. Rather than rely solely on live models, electronic media such as videotape or audiotape can be used to demonstrate the performance of target skills. When a live demonstration is provided, training is enhanced to the extent that the skill is performed in a relevant setting, such as the classroom or playground. With symbolic modeling, the peer model should be one the student can identify with and who receives a reward for positive social behaviors. The third step requires skill performance, typically in role-play procedures. The modeling may proceed in incremental steps from visually imagining the performance of the skill, to verbalizing an effective response to the situation, to finally responding motorically by enacting the response (Sheridan and Walker, 1999).

In practice, we ask students and teachers to contribute to the identification of social skills that need to be addressed. This enhances student ownership and, hence, motivation to try out alternative approaches to their, heretofore, ineffective approaches. When young children with disabilities are instructed in the steps to introducing oneself to a peer, for example, the procedure includes a verbal description (sometimes elicited from participants), modeling by the clinician-leader, and role-play by each group member. Each role-play receives feedback from group members before the next demonstration. Since the performance of new skills requires not only the skill acquisition but also an understanding of when to use it and the incentive to do so, direct reinforcement of behaviors and cognitive restructuring activities are helpful adjuncts to a social learning paradigm.

Coaching

Sheridan and Walker (1999) described two other cognitive-behavioral procedures. The first involves *coaching* students with direct verbal instructions. The coach teaches each step in a social skill sequence, then the coach and students practice the steps (rehearsal), and finally the coach provides feedback to the students. Thus, group participants receive guided practice with the skill set. Sheridan and Walker summarize several empirical studies showing general success with coaching procedures.

In practice, we direct rehearsal of social skills with group participants as one would coach a foul-shooting technique or how to blend a cake mix. With younger children, it may take repeated trials to understand and incorporate the elements of an analogy that will gain the outcome the student desires. To increase the likelihood of internalizing the skill and storing the steps in long-term memory, we ask the participants to become coaches as well. That is, they observe the role play of other participants and suggest refinements for the next try. Students must be attentive to relevant aspects of the skill sequence in order to provide acceptable corrective feedback. Peers also provide feedback to the target student as to whether their role-play would be effective in the "real world."

What sounds good in a group context may not pass the muster on the school playground (J. T. Burton, personal communication, December 20, 2005).

Social Problem Solving

A second cognitive-behavioral procedure is social problem solving. The interpersonal problem-solving approach of Shure (1994) has been refined and is now commercially available as the *I Can Problem Solve* curriculum. The program is suitable for children in Kindergarten through sixth grade, and it was designed with "high-risk" children in mind, according to Elias and Tobias (1996). In the pre-problem-solving phase, children learn to identify feelings and take the perspective of others in a conflict situation. Once in the problem-solving phase children learn to identify the problem, generate solutions, anticipate the consequence of each potential solution, select the best alternative, try it out, and determine its effectiveness.

The SPS model put forth by Elias and Tobias (1996) can be adopted in the classroom or facilitated in a social skills group. To help students understand the core concepts of social problem solving, the authors developed a mnemonic: FIG TESPN. The problem-solving steps associated with the mnemonic are as follows:

Feelings	...cue me to solve a problem.
I	...have a problem.
Goals	...give me a guide.
Think	...of things to do.
Envision	...outcomes.
Select	...my best solution.
Plan	... the procedures, anticipate pitfalls, practice, and pursue it.
Notice	...what happened next and now what?

The authors planned for and encourage teachers to utilize the problem-solving paradigm regularly in the classroom and especially at those "teachable moments" when conflicts arise. For the group facilitator, Elias and Tobias recommend the use of video activities to stimulate critical thinking and to give the problem-solving steps a concrete referent. The effectiveness of their approach is attributed to (1) the focusing and calming effect television and video have on even impaired students; (2) the thinking and problem-solving engendered by open dialogues after the program; and (3) the benefit one derives from rehearsal, guided practice, and role-play that serve to increase the likelihood of generalization outside the group setting.

Common to both the classroom and skills group is a strategy called, "Probe." Probe is a series of nine prompts that lead the student through the FIG TESPN steps. The initial questions relate to evoking a description of the troubling event. Next, the facilitator guides the student through a discussion of current feelings and helps with establishing goals or outcomes. From that point, it is a matter of identifying first attempts at solution, brainstorming alternative solutions, and anticipating results. Then the student is in a position to develop a plan and rehearse or role-play its enactment. Finally, the student will be asked to commit to trying the plan and evaluating its effectiveness.

Cognitive Social Skills Training

A rational-emotive approach to social skills training varies according to the age of the participants. Younger students (5- to 7-year olds) may focus on identifying and labeling feelings and begin linking mistaken thinking with unpleasant feelings. At older ages (8- to 12-year olds), children are exposed to the challenging of beliefs and the disputation of irrational beliefs. By age 13 and beyond, adolescents may be exposed to full disputation of irrational beliefs. Of course, the principle aim is the training of specific social skills. However, the intent also is to develop mediating self-statements; enable participants to regulate their own feelings and manage their own behavior; and to develop the practice of self-reinforcement.

It is interesting to note that the rational-emotive paradigm presented by Bernard and Joyce (1984) utilizes several of the strategies common to models described earlier. There is an element of instruction, presenting a model for observational learning, skill rehearsal, feedback from the facilitator or group members, and practice. For shy and withdrawn children, a typical 12-session program would be conceptualized in three stages: (1) cognitive preparation, (2) cognitive restructuring, and (3) social skill shaping and strengthening. The preparation stage includes a couple of sessions during which participants learn the relationship between one's beliefs and subsequent feelings and behavior. In the middle stage, about four sessions would be devoted to cognitive restructuring. At this point the participants are asked to apply rational-emotive principles to themselves and begin examining their self-statements. The final stage (six sessions) is focused on social skill acquisition and performance. Underlying beliefs and self-statements are examined and rational alternatives reinforced. Then, the beliefs and statements are matched to skills that a withdrawn child would need to become more fully integrated in the learning environment. For example, the self-statement, "I don't have anything interesting to say," would be replaced via modeling and rehearsal with a statement such as, "I like horses and others here probably do too. In fact, they would be interested to hear about my riding lessons."

TREATMENT PROTOCOL

When working with young students with learning and behavioral issues, it is common to find that they do not integrate well with their peers. We have seen that, in the end, these deficits in socializing may be more detrimental to their educational and career options than their academic deficits. The protocol highlighted in Table 26.2 consists of a 10-week group constructed from the treatment models described in the previous section. Topics were culled from the Prepare curriculum (Goldstein, 1999) and the issues commonly relevant to these children. Often these children are on the social periphery and make frequent errors in interpreting social cues and deciding on effective responses. The methodology incorporates the strategies derived from social learning theory, which appear often in the social skills literature. The use of social problem solving strategies and rational-emotive principles is an attempt to strengthen the learning process by enhancing motivation to perform the skills. It is also anticipated that these latter cognitive strategies will make it easier to transfer acquired skills to other environments.

Table 26.2   Ten Week Social Skills Protocol

Week 1	**Feelings**
Objective:	To learn feeling words
	To associate feeling words with their outward expression in others
Activities:	Create a feeling chart. Ask students to write (or have cofacilitator write) the feeling words students generate onto paper strips and tack them onto the wall chart.
	Ask students to pantomime feelings of their choice and ask others to identify the charade.
Week 2	**Thinking and Behavior**
Objective:	To learn words associated with thinking
	To sort different types of behavior
Activities:	Create cartoons with empty thought bubbles. Ask students to supply thoughts, visualizations, and beliefs to match the character's situation.
	Create a T-chart to sort behaviors dichotomously: visible vs. invisible helpful vs. hurtful impersonal vs. personal. Supply behaviors observed in class and ask students to assign them to a column.
Week 3	**A-B-Cs**
Objective:	To learn the connection between thoughts/beliefs and feelings
Activities:	Construct a graphic representation of Actions Beliefs and Consequences. Provide example of how different beliefs about the same event can lead to pleasant or unpleasant feelings.
	Construct a HTFB chart to help students visualize and sort Happenings-Thoughts-Feelings-Behaviors (adapted from Bernard and Joyce, 1984).
Week 4	**FIG TESPN**
Objective:	To learn the mnemonic for solving problems
Activities:	1. Provide a graphic display for explaining each step in the problem-solving process.
	2. Review video available from Tobias (cited in Elias & Tobias, 1996), *FIG TESPN Goes to Middle School.*
Week 5	**Joining a Group**
Objective:	To learn how to join in when a group has formed
Activities:	Identify feelings that might arise when you approach a group. Cartoon situations may help elicit feelings.
	Use the ABC chart or HTFB chart to link feelings with self-statements or beliefs.
	Return to original cartoon. Ask participants to provide a self-statement that would lead to joining in.
	Role-play activity in the playground, the cafeteria and the neighborhood.
Week 6	**Responding to Teasing**
Objective:	To learn ways of responding to teasing that lead to positive outcomes
Activities:	Review the link between thoughts and feelings using the HTFB chart.
	Remind students that once their feelings are settled down (possibly using a feelings "thermometer" to track changes), they are in a better position for problem solving
	Use FIG TESPN steps to problem solve.
	Role play potential responses to teasing.
	Elicit peer feedback.
	Follow-up next time to track in vivo performance.

(Continued)

Table 26.2   Continued

Week 7   Being a Good Sport

Objective: To understand how others might feel after a competitive game
              To become fluent in the expected verbalizations after a game

Activities: Use cartoon figures of players after a game. Ask participants to suggest thought bubbles
              for winners and non-winners.
              Practice overt self-statements in response to good sportsmanship and poor sportsman-
              ship.
              Use FIG TESPN to identify feelings and note a problem.
              Spend time helping students shift from a short-term goal, i.e., avoiding an argument, to a
              long-term goal, .i.e., developing a reputation as someone fun to play with.
              Generate and evaluate solutions.
              Watch video of how others deal with poor sports and how someone might respond after
              a loss.

Week 8   Dealing with Being Left Out

Objective: To develop coping self-statements for times when you are left out of a group or game.

Activities: Solicit personal stories of when someone was left out of a group.
              Use the feeling chart to brainstorm feeling states.
              Facilitator uses overt self-statements to recognize feelings and fill out the HTBF chart.
              Participants role-play self-statements to new scenarios of exclusion.
              Participants use round-robin to brainstorm solutions.
              Create two small groups to work independently on likely outcomes to each solution.
              Participants role-play a recent event in which a member was excluded from an activity in
              school.

Week 9   Dealing with an Accusation

Objective: To generate solutions to a conflict situation

Activities: Use bibliotherapy technique regarding a false accusation. Consult librarian for materials
              and open group with the story.
              At the point of problem identification, stop story and consult ABCs to review how beliefs
              impact emotion. Offer alternative beliefs to the false accusation.
              After a group brainstorm, ask participants to combine ideas to develop a more effective
              response.
              Use the problem resolution phase of the story to find out how the protagonist resolved
              the problem. Ask participants to grade the protagonist on how well he/she used cogni-
              tive strategies.

Week 10   Apologizing

Objective: To consider alternative outcomes to various solutions

Activities: Refer to a personal episode among classmates in which one party was wronged.
              Use a sitcom or video to display alternative ways of making an apology.
              Review the goals for the person who is at fault. What outcome is desired?
              Review the components of an effective apology.
              Role-play apologies from peer coaches. Solicit feedback from the group.
              Ask the person at fault to role-play an apology and solicit feedback.

CASE EXAMPLE

A group of elementary school students with a range of neuropsychological impairments
was determined to have significant social skill deficits. This was determined via the
Social Skill Rating System (SSRS) completed by special education teachers annually for
each student. Further assessment utilized paper and pencil tests to determine an under-

standing of the concepts underlying social skill performance. The school psychologist included informal observation of students in social contexts and observation of directed role-plays within the social skills group.

The students were second and third graders ranging in age from 7- to 9-years old. Nearly all the students were male, and attention deficits and learning disabilities were common comorbid conditions. In general, the group functioned in the average to low average range of intelligence and showed no discernible signs of emotional disturbance. Given the age range, group sessions were adjusted to contain less information and the information was presented at a slower pace with more frequent repetition. The length of each session was adjusted to accommodate student attention span.

Early Session

Use real-life issues to generate motivation and sustain attention.

Therapist: Who has an issue today?

Chris: I do, Dr. Rich.

Therapist: Tell us about it, Chris.

Chris: Joel's been bothering me on the bus.

Therapist: What happened?

(*Chris tells a short story about teasing among classmates on the way to school.*)

Therapist: Who could give me one sentence about Chris' problem? [Problem Identification]

Kate: It makes Chris mad when Joel teases him.

Therapist: Thanks Kate, you're right that this is a teasing issue. Let's look at our ABCs to see if it's really Joel that makes Chris mad.

(*Using graphic organizer, therapist reviews RET principles with the group.*)

TH: What is the Action? Mandy?

Mandy: Teasing.

TH: Right. What is the Consequence? Reggie?

Reggie: He's upset, he's mad.

TH: Right. What is the Belief that comes before feeling mad? Chris?

Chris: I thought Joel was being mean to me.

TH: People usually don't like it when people are mean to them, just like they don't like the taste of sour milk. But what do you believe about Joel's teasing you?

Chris: It means he doesn't like me.

TH: I'm not sure about that. But if you're right, what's so terrible if Joel doesn't like you?

Chris: It means there's something wrong with me. [Cognitive distortion]

TH: Hmmm. Does anybody else think there is something wrong with Chris just because Joel was teasing him? Steve? [Rational disputation]

Steve: Joel was teasing him about his hair sticking up from static. That doesn't mean anything about the person.

TH: In fact, it happens to most people. Maybe Joel doesn't know much about science or maybe he makes friends based on how their hair looks. Would you get mad at somebody like that? Mandy?

Mandy: No, I feel sorry for people who judge people by silly things like that.

TH: So, Chris, not everybody has the same belief you do about the teasing. What is another belief you might have that will lead to you feeling less upset?

Chris: I guess if I believed Joel didn't know much about science or much about me, I could ignore his teasing.

TH: That makes sense to me.

Later Session 1

TH: Last week we talked about a teasing incident on the bus. [Review of the ABCs for dealing with emotional upset]

TH: We decided if Chris would remind himself about the ABCs of becoming upset, he could choose to ignore Joel more easily. He may still find it unpleasant, like a shirt that makes you itchy, but he wouldn't feel mad. What else could Chris do in that situation? Reggie? [Generating alternatives]

Reggie: He could tell the bus driver.

Mandy: He could tell Joel to knock it off.

Steve: He could call him the a—word. That would show him. (*students laugh*)

TH: Let's take a look at that last idea. What would likely happen next? [Anticipating outcomes]

Mandy: Then Joel would get really mad.

Joel: Yeah, I'd knock his lights out.

Chris: Then I'd knock his lights out.

TH: Do we agree that this is not solving the problem?

Steve: Yeah, it just made it worse.

TH: What about Reggie's idea of telling the bus driver?

Chris: Bus drivers don't do anything.

Joel: Only babies tattle to the bus driver.

TH: OK. That might be an idea that sounds good, but doesn't solve the problem. How about Mandy's idea to tell Joel to knock it off?

Reggie: Wouldn't that start a fight again?

Mandy: Not if you did it nicely.

TH: How can we say it so it doesn't sound like mean, fightin' words, but lets Joel know we mean it? Let's all think about that this week. Come up with a way to tell someone we really mean something without sounding bossy or like we're ready to fight. If you need to write it down to remember it, please do so. [Homework]

Later Session 2

TH: Last time we talked about how remembering the ABCs can help you keep from getting upset in school. Then we talked about how Chris could solve the problem of getting teased on the bus. A few ideas didn't seem like they would work too well. For homework I asked you to come up with a way for Chris to tell Joel to "knock off the teasing." To work, Chris has to say it in a way that makes Joel believe him, but doesn't make Joel think Chris is starting a fight. What did you come up with? Steve? [Goal-setting]

Steve: I'll show you. (*Stands up and faces Joel*). Joel you can't keep doing that and I mean it. [Role-play]

TH: Thanks Steve. What did you think of that? Joel?

Joel: He didn't look at me. He was looking over my head.

TH: OK. It works better when you look him in the eye. Anyone else?

Chris: His voice sounded angry.

TH: OK. If you sound angry, the other person might think you're going to start a fight.

Mandy: Can I try?

TH: Sure Mandy. What are you going to do differently so we can watch for it?

Mandy: I'll look him in the eye, use a serious voice, and ask him to stop. (*Stands up and faces Joel*) Joel, please stop teasing me. You make me mad when you do that.

TH: Thanks Mandy, what did the group think of how Mandy did it?

All: She was great!

TH: I think so too. If I had one suggestion, it would be to remember the ABCs. Who makes her mad...?

Joel: I know. It's the "Bs" that make her mad, not teasing.

TH: Good Joel! You show Chris how you would do it.

Joel: (*Stands up and faces Chris. He makes eye contact and uses a serious voice.*) Chris, please stop teasing me. It's no fun and makes me want to play with somebody else.

TH: Good job, Joel. Do you think that would work if Chris said to you?

Joel: I guess it would. I can see why Chris wouldn't want me making fun of his hair.

TH: Next week we're going to talk about times when an apology will make a situation better. For next time, think about times when you wanted an apology or gave an apology. [Homework]

OBSTACLES TO TREATMENT EFFECTIVENESS AND RECOMMENDATIONS

The primary obstacles to running a social skills group relate to treatment effectiveness, which includes long-term and generalizable changes in social functioning. The literature is filled with meta-analyses that show moderate to weak effect sizes of social skills training and/or poor generalization and maintenance of improvements (see Gresham, Sugai, & Horner, 2001 for a review). As a result, an emphasis must be placed upon increasing the likelihood that the interventions applied will result in observable improvement in the youth's skills. Based upon the outcome data regarding the effectiveness of social skills interventions, the following methods are recommended for consideration when designing treatment programs: (a) use of socially valid treatment goals, (b) ensuring the fit between the type of deficit and the intervention chosen, (c) inclusion of socially competent peers, (d) an extension of training into naturalistic settings, and (e) restructuring of the social environment.

Utilizing assessment procedures already reviewed should result in the identification of one or more behaviors to target for intervention. However, it is important to ensure that these target behaviors and skills identified for training are socially valid. Social validity of treatment goals refers to the importance and relevance of these goals to the youth, parents, teachers, and others in the social environment (Hansen, Nangle, & Meyer, 1998). What the therapist considers to be an important skill for the youth to acquire may not match what the youth himself or others view as being important for successful adjustment. As a result, the youth may be resistant to treatment or those in his environment may be dissatisfied with the results. Therefore, it is critical to obtain feedback from the young person himself as well as parents, teachers, and others regarding the goals of treatment, and make adjustments accordingly.

A second critical component of effective social skills training involves matching the particular deficit with an appropriate intervention. Gresham, Sugai, and Horner (2001) attribute the small effect sizes found in the literature in part to the failure to link specific skill deficits with specific intervention strategies. As mentioned earlier, the reason a young person fails to perform a particular social skill (e.g., asking for help) could be attributed to one of two completely different reasons. The youth may not have knowledge regarding the specific steps involved in asking for help (an acquisition deficit) or she may find that being disruptive is a more effective and reliable method for obtaining reinforcement (a performance deficit). In the latter case, it would be inappropriate to utilize modeling, coaching, or behavioral rehearsal if the young person already has these skills in her behavioral repertoire. Therefore, clinicians must be vigilant in assessing the fit or match between the identified problem and the intervention strategies used for remediation.

Leading a social skills group can be particularly challenging for practitioners due to the nature of the problem at hand. As illustrated above, competent models are critical to teaching and reinforcing a given skill. Trying to accomplish this in a group format where many of the members of that group lack good social skills is particularly challenging. One way to overcome this problem is to include typical or particularly socially competent peers in the group. If the group is problem-oriented, this will be more difficult to do. However, including a heterogeneous mix of youth with various social challenges may balance the issues present within the group and permit modeling of various skills by youth who may be more competent in one area than another. Alternatively, the therapist may wish to solicit the assistance of a co-leader. If additional staff is available, collaboration may be possible where two individuals work together in facilitating the social skills group. Krieg, Simpson, Stanley, and Snider (2002) suggest clearly identifying the primary and secondary leader at the onset in order to avoid a power struggle between the two. The value of a secondary leader includes having a competent model readily available to role-play and demonstrate the use of a particular skill. Should a co-leader be unavailable, the practitioner may utilize video models to highlight proper performance of a given skill.

A major drawback of social skills groups is the fact that the youth is removed from the social context in which their social deficit occurs. As a result, the opportunities to practice these skills are often contrived within the context of the group. The important triggers and maintaining factors of the naturalistic setting may not be present within this contrived model, which will likely impact generalization. To overcome this obstacle, it is necessary to include a contextual approach to teaching social skills. Gresham (1997) recommends including incidental teaching in social skills training, especially for those whose primary difficulties involve performance deficits. Incidental teaching involves taking advantage of naturally occurring events in order to teach or enhance the performance of a given skill within the context of the youth's social environment (Gresham, Sugai, & Horner, 2001). By including skills training in the context in which the deficit occurs, the likelihood for generalization is increased.

A final method to consider in treatment design involves restructuring of the social environment so that generalization and maintenance of treatment effects are achieved. First, it is necessary to identify behaviors that may compete with the performance of newly learned skills. Often these behaviors are more efficient and reliable for obtaining reinforcement than the socially skilled behaviors are (Gresham, 1997). In the example above, it was much easier and more efficient to become disruptive rather than wait patiently with one's hand raised prior to receiving help. In such situations, it is important to reduce the power of these negative, maladaptive behaviors and increase the power of the socially skilled behaviors so that newly learned behaviors generalize to all environments. Second, it is critical to include parents, teachers, and peers in treatment due to the crucial roles they play in the provision of consequences and facilitation of generalization. While it is difficult to control peer consequences, parents and teachers can modify their own responses to both maladaptive and skilled behaviors. Adults should provide positive consequences of skilled behavior and work to reduce the effectiveness of maladaptive behavior. Furthermore, these individuals should be made aware of the skills the young person is learning so that prompting and reinforcement of these skills occurs in the natural environment.

SUMMARY

The socially competent youngster is one who moves toward adulthood with favorable odds for mental health, employability, and enhanced quality of life. By contrast, those who remain deficient in social skill acquisition, performance, and fluency are at greater risk for remaining on the perimeter of society. The resulting cost in human suffering, mental health services, and criminal justice involvement entreats educators to do better.

Fortunately, there are lines of empirical investigation spanning decades that have identified important skill sets underpinning social competency. From this research has emerged comprehensive curricula and manualized treatment programs with evidence of efficacy. Kendall (2006) summarized the benefits of manualized treatments for childhood mental health issues. Surely, they provide structure and organization to the intervention. Additionally, manualized treatments offer explicit goals, a recommended sequence of steps toward those goals, and a pace that has empirical support. Examples of structured approaches to treatment were reviewed here.

Ollendick, King, and Chorpita (2006) summarized the arguments against manualized treatments. Some view manuals as promoting a "cookbook" or "cookie-cutter" approach to treatment. Standardized treatment was viewed as delimiting rather than a source of guidance. We acknowledge the controversy and await more empirical data on the subject. Meanwhile, our approach to the facilitation of social skills groups in schools incorporates three separate strands of intervention within a cognitive-behavioral framework, including rational-emotive, social problem solving, and modeling (social learning theory). In clinical experience, this multistrand model holds promise for resolving both skill acquisition and performance issues. Using validated behavioral principles in combination with strategies to correct one's cognitive distortions and deficits may lead to better generalization and transfer. Further research on effectiveness of this eclectic approach is needed.

We close with Kendall's (2006, p. 22) view of our purpose as cognitive-behavioral interventionists.

> By demonstrating, teaching, and honing problem-solving skills, the cognitive-behavioral therapist's efforts coincide with changes to adjustment. The goal is a better-prepared individual-prepared for the inevitable difficulties of life with a set of skills that can facilitate problem resolution.

RECOMMENDED READINGS

Elias, M. J. (1996). *Social problem solving: Interventions in the schools.* New York: Guilford..

Goldstein, A. P. (1999). *The prepare curriculum: Teaching prosocial competencies* (Rev. ed.). Champaign, IL: Research Press.

Gresham, F. M. (2002a). Best practices in social skills training. In A. Thomas & J. Grimes (Eds.), *Best practices in school psychology IV* (pp. 1029–1040). Bethesda, MD: National Association of School Psychologists.

Merrell, K.W. (2003). Assessment of social skills and peer relations. In K.W. Merrell (Ed.), *Behavioral, social, & emotional assessment of children and adolescents* (pp. 311–339). Mahwah, NJ: Erlbaum.

REFERENCES

American Association on Mental Retardation. (2002). *The AAMR definition of mental retardation.* Retrieved December 12, 2005, from http://www.aamr.org/Policies/faq_mental_retardation.shtml

American Psychiatric Association (2000). *Diagnostic and statistical manual of mental disorders* (4th ed., text rev.). Washington, DC: Author.

Aronen, E. T., & Kurkela, S. A. (1998). The predictors of competence in an adolescent sample: A 15-year follow-up study. *Nordic Journal of Psychiatry, 52,* 203–212.

Bernard, M.E., & Joyce, M.R. (1984) *Rational-emotive therapy with children and adolescents: Theory, treatment strategies, preventative methods.* New York: Wiley.

Bierman, K. L., & Welsh, J. A. (2000). Assessing social dysfunction: The contributions of laboratory and performance-based measures. *Journal of Clinical Child Psychology, 29,* 526–539.

Caldarella, P., & Merrell, K. W. (1997). Common dimensions of social skills of children and adolescents: A taxonomy of positive behaviors. *School Psychology Review, 26,* 264–278.

Demaray, M. K., Ruffalo, S. L., Carlson, J., Busse, R. T., Olson, A. E., McManus, S. M., et al. (1995). Social skills assessment: A comparative evaluation of six published rating scales. *School Psychology Review, 24,* 648–671.

D'Zurilla, T. J., & Goldfried, M. R. (1971). Problem solving and behavior modification. *Journal of Abnormal Psychology, 78,* 107–126.

Elias, M. J., & Tobias, S. E. (1996). *Social problem solving: Interventions in the schools.* New York: Guilford.

Elliott, S. N., & Gresham, F. M. (1987). Children's social skills: Assessment and classification practices. *Journal of Counseling and Development, 66,* 96–99.

Goldstein, A.P. (1999). *The PREPARE curriculum: Teaching prosocial competencies* (rev. ed.). Champaign, IL: Research Press.

Greene, R. W., Biederman, J., Faraone, S. V., Wilens, T. E., Mick, E., & Blier, H. K. (1999). Further validation of social impairment as a predictor of substance use disorders: Findings from a sample of siblings of boys with and without ADHD. *Journal of Clinical Child Psychology, 28,* 349–354.

Gresham, F. M. (1997). Social competence and students with behavior disorders: Where we've been, where we are, and where we should go. *Education and Treatment of Children, 20,* 233–250.

Gresham, F. M. (2002a). Best practices in social skills training. In A. Thomas & J. Grimes (Eds.), *Best practices in school psychology IV* (pp. 1029–1040). Bethesda, MD: National Association of School Psychologists.

Gresham, F. M. (2002b). Teaching social skills to high-risk children and youth: Preventive and remedial strategies. In M. R. Shinn, H. M. Walker, & G. Stoner (Eds.), *Interventions for academic and behavior problems II: Preventive and remedial approaches* (pp. 403–432). Bethesda, MD: National Association of School Psychologists.

Gresham, F. M., & Elliott, S. N. (1990). *The Social Skills Rating System.* Circle Pines, MN: American Guidance.

Gresham, F. M., Sugai, G., Horner, R. H. (2001). Interpreting outcomes of social skills training for students with high-incidence disabilities. *Exceptional Children, 67*, 331–344.

Hansen, D. J., Nangle, D. W., & Meyer, K. A. (1998). Enhancing the effectiveness of social skills interventions with adolescents. *Education and Treatment of Children, 21*, 489–514.

Kendall, P. C. (2006). Guiding theory for therapy with children and adolescents. In P. C. Kendall (Ed.), *Child and adolescent therapy: Cognitive-behavioral procedures* (3rd ed., pp. 3–30). New York: Guilford.

Krieg, F. J., Simpson, C., Stanley, R. E., & Snider, D. A. (2002). Best practices in making school groups work. In A. Thomas & J. Grimes (Eds.), *Best practices in school psychology IV* (pp. 1195–1216). Bethesda, MD: National Association of School Psychologists.

Maedgen, J. W., & Carlson, C. L. (2000). Social functioning and emotional regulation in the attention deficit hyperactivity disorder subtypes. *Journal of Clinical Child Psychology, 29*, 30–42.

Matlack, M. E., & McGreevy, M. (1994). Family correlates of social skill deficits in incarcerated and nonincarcerated adolescents. *Adolescence, 29*, 117–133.

Merrell, K. W. (2001). Assessment of children's social skills: Recent developments, best practices, and new directions. *Exceptionality, 9*, 3–18.

Merrell, K. W. (2002). *School Social Behavior Scales, Second Edition.* Eugene, OR: Assessment-Intervention Resources.

Merrell, K. W. (2003). Assessment of social skills and peer relations. In K.W. Merrell, *Behavioral, social, & emotional assessment of children and adolescents* (pp. 311–339). Mahwah, NJ: Erlbaum.

Merrell, K. W., & Caldarella, P. (2002). *Home and community social behavior scales.* Eugene, OR: Assessment-Intervention Resources

Nixon, E. (2001). The social competence of children with attention deficit hyperactivity disorder: A review of the literature. *Child & Adolescent Mental Health, 6*, 172–180.

Ollendick, T. H., King, N. J., & Chorpita, B. F. (2006). Empirically supported treatments for children and adolescents. In P. C. Kendall (Ed.), *Child and adolescent therapy: Cognitive-behavioral procedures* (3rd ed., pp. 492–520).

Parker, J. G., & Asher, S. R. (1987). Peer relations and later personal adjustment: Are low-accepted children at risk? *Psychological Bulletin, 102*, 357–389.

Rabiner, D. L., Coie, J. D., Miller-Johnson, S., Boykin, A. M., & Lochman, J. E. (2005). Predicting the persistence of aggressive offending of African American males from adolescence into young adulthood: The importance of peer relations, aggressive behavior, and ADHD symptoms. *Journal of Emotional and Behavioral Disorders, 13*, 131–140.

Rychlak, J. F. (1981). *Introduction to personality and psychotherapy: A theory-construction approach* (2nd ed.). Boston: Houghton Mifflin.

Schmidt, M. E., Demulder, E. K., & Denham, S. A. (2002). Kindergarten social-emotional competence: Developmental predictors and psychosocial implications. *Early Child Development and Care, 172*, 451–462.

Sheridan, S. M., & Walker, D. (1999). Social skills in context: Considerations for assessment, intervention, and generalization. In C. R. Reynolds & T. B. Gutkin (Eds.), *The handbook of school psychology* (3rd ed., pp. 686–708). New York: Wiley.

Shure, M. (1994). *I can problem solve (ICPS): An interpersonal cognitive problem-solving program for children.* Champaign, IL: Research Press.

Smart, D., & Sanson, A. (2001). Children's social competence: The role of temperament and behaviour, and their "fit" with parents' expectations. *Family Matters, 59,* 10–16.

Sparrow, S. S., Cicchetti, D. V., & Balla, D.A. (2005). Vineland adaptive behavior scales (2nd ed.). Circle Pines, MN: AGS Publishing.

Spence, S. H. (2003). Social skills training with children and young people: Theory, evidence, and practice. *Child and Adolescent Mental Health, 8*, 84–96.

Spivack, G., & Shure, M. B. (1974). *Social adjustment of young children: A cognitive approach to solving real-life problems.* San Francisco: Jossey-Bass.

Terry, R (2000). Recent advances in measurement theory and the use of sociometric techniques. *New Directions for Child & Adolescent Development, 88*, 27–53.

Tharinger, D. J., & Lambert, N. M. (1999). The application of developmental psychology to school psychology practice: Informing assessment, intervention, and prevention efforts. In C. R. Reynolds & T. B. Gutkin (Eds.), *The handbook of school psychology* (3rd ed., pp. 137–166). New York: Wiley.

Walker, H. M., & McConnell, S. R. (1995). *Walker-McConnell Scale of Social Competence and School Adjustment (adolescent version)*. Belmont, CA: Wadsworth/Thomson Learning.

Wentzel, K. R. (1993). Does being good make the grade? Social behavior and academic competence in middle school. *Journal of Educational Psychology, 85*, 357–364.

Part Four

CONCLUSIONS AND FUTURE DIRECTIONS

Chapter Twenty-Seven

Future Directions in CBT Group Treatments

Jessica L. Stewart & Ray W. Christner

Our goal in compiling this handbook was to offer a comprehensive resource outlining the application of the cognitive-behavior therapy (CBT) model to the group modality in working with children and adolescents. We believe, based on our experiences and given support in the literature, that group interventions are an efficient and effective method of service delivery for a wide variety of presenting problems and populations. While cognitive-behavior group therapy (CBGT) has become a common mode of treatment in many inpatient and substance abuse treatment settings, in other settings its use and support is only emerging (e.g., medical settings, school settings, and such). Authors in this handbook have offered a review of using CBGT in a variety of settings, while discussing the potential obstacles that clinician's may face in each environment. Interestingly, while we might expect great differences between settings, much of the appeal for using CBGT in certain environments (e.g., ability to see more patients, social components), as well as the inherent obstacles (e.g., space, patients moving in and out of the system), are fairly common across settings. Therefore, once clinicians have the basic skills and an understanding of implementing CBGT, their ability to do so across settings is more a process of learning idiosyncratic aspects of each environment rather than a specific change to the CBGT model itself.

In addition to its utility in a variety of settings, CBGT has demonstrated efficacy with a number of common presenting problems seen in youth patients. Throughout this handbook, authors offered practical suggestions for a sampling of presenting problems, including depression, anxiety, divorce, grief, sexual abuse, substance abuse, and other issues. We also sought to include CBGT treatment suggestions for targeted issues that are not commonly thought of when discussing CBGT with children and adolescents, including Asperger's Disorder, self-injury, and rejected or ostracized youth.

Unfortunately, despite our effort to put forth a fully comprehensive volume, the growth of cognitive-behavioral interventions (both individual and group) makes the development of a completely comprehensive manual a daunting and likely impossible task. Thus, many other potential avenues for group intervention or treatment with youth are beyond the breadth of this volume, primarily because of the lack of available research or practice guidelines. As chapters within this text are not exhaustive, we offer in this chapter suggestions for potential venues for expanding the application of CBGT.

THE NEED FOR ONGOING RESEARCH

While many of the previous chapters referenced empirical studies and a strong evidence-base, many chapters provided a caveat regarding the limited availability of research support for any group therapy models to address specific problem areas with children. This trend highlights the fact that group treatment of children and adolescents has, as compared to adult populations, not been as widely studied. Our assertion is that the group modality is a fitting, suitable, and beneficial avenue by which child and adolescent clinicians may provide valuable cognitive-behavioral treatment services to the youth population. We believe that, although not all problem areas are well researched to date, with the use of effective progress monitoring child and adolescent group therapy is a viable option. Using existing literature and pairing it with continual assessment of treatment progress, clinicians will be able to address a wide variety of presenting problems across numerous traditional (and unchartered) settings. In addition to continued efficacy studies validating treatment protocols, clinicians in the field need to conduct ongoing case studies and publish outcomes of their group work with certain populations. While some presenting problems are more easily researched using large-scale studies (e.g., anxiety, depression, anger), others (e.g., self-injury, social isolated youth) require research on the part of individual clinicians. With the combination of case and large-scale studies, there is a great opportunity to promote and advance the use of CBGT with children and adolescents.

ADDITIONAL VENUES FOR INCORPORATING SERVICES

Community Settings

Although we included a thorough review of the provision of CBGT within outpatient settings, the literature does not expand the definition of "outpatient settings" to the breadth that we believe professionals should consider. Essentially, we offer that CBGT treatment services could be included in settings that either do not typically offer mental health services or do so primarily from the perspective of support. We challenge readers to consider the availability of settings, such as the YMCA or YWCA, local churches, homeless shelters, and other venues for the provision of group-based mental health services. These settings may help to alleviate the difficulties related to transportation, financial restrictions, availability of space, availability of potential group members, etc. that may otherwise limit the opportunities to conduct worthwhile treatment interventions. Professionals should strongly consider building effective relationships with community members to strengthen the connection for group members and their families between acquiring skills within group and maintaining them within their lives in their communities.

Homeless Youth

Similarly, providing group CBT within community-based clinics other than those specifically for mental health services may allow clinicians to target a specific population more increasingly receiving mention in the literature and media—homeless youth. Young people without homes, insurance, and financial resources will not be members of group therapy services in any other setting than community-based, free services. Typically, however, this population struggles with a variety of (and often severe) environmental stressors and psychological symptoms that require effective treatment, such as depression and other mood disorders, anxiety, PTSD, substance-abuse, prostitution, pregnancy, sexual abuse, HIV/AIDS, personality disorders, and schizophrenia (Kennedy, 1991; Maxwell, 1992; Whitbeck, Hoyt, & Bao, 2000; Whitbeck, Johnson, Hoyt, & Cauce, 2004). Granted, the environmental, interpersonal, and financial limitations of this population of young people may limit their ability to engage faithfully in an ongoing therapeutic relationship. However, the time-limited, solution-focused, skill-building emphasis of CBT suggests that a group modality may be a reasonable and fitting venue in which to offer services that these youth would otherwise not receive but that could make a difference in their functioning and their situations based on decision-making, coping, and problem-solving skills they could acquire in treatment. Research should further investigate the feasibility of offering group CBT to homeless youth in community settings, and the nature of the outcomes of these interventions.

Youth with Schizophrenia

While a diagnosis of a schizophrenic disorder is less frequent in children and adolescents, related symptoms may present in and of themselves or as associated with other disorders in youth (e.g., mood disorders, anxiety disorders, personality disorders, substance abuse). CBT is increasingly being utilized and empirically validated as an efficacious approach to address symptoms and improve skills and functioning of this population of mental health patients (Dickerson & Lehman, 2006; Gaudiano, 2006; Turkington, Kingdon, & Weiden, 2006). Future research should consider this model and the group modality in the treatment of children and adolescents, as well. Group CBT for use with schizophrenic-related symptoms would aim to improve reality testing through cognitive interventions and behavioral experiments, build problem-solving and interpersonal skills, and provide skills for coping with difficult emotions and modifying maladaptive behaviors. These groups would not be limited to inpatient settings and would be a viable component of outpatient treatment, as well, to increase availability of social support and similar peers.

Gay, Lesbian, Bisexual, Transgendered, and/or Questioning Youth

Another population of young people that we felt strongly about devoting more attention to in an individual chapter is that of gay, lesbian, bisexual, transgendered, and questioning (GLBTQ) youth. Unfortunately, again, there is limited research regarding the efficacy of CBT specific to treatment of this population, let alone in the group modality. Literature is increasingly beginning to identify the unique needs of this population who are reportedly, as compared to their heterosexual peers, especially at risk for psychological difficulties including depression and suicide, homelessness, social isolation, anger and violence (Bagley & Tremblay, 2000; Kruks, 1991; Remafedi, French, Story, Resnick, &

Blum, 1998; Russell & Joyner, 2001). Group CBT with this population would allow for an individualized conceptualization of the schema of group members and the GLBTQ population as a whole given their unique experiences. CBT would likely be a fitting model for work with a group more prone to cognitive distortions related to self-efficacy, interpersonal acceptance and rejection and self-worth, given the typical experiences of being other-than-heterosexual in this society. Goals for treatment with this population would likely be to restructure distorted beliefs and negative attributions about one's self-worth and efficacy that may result in difficult emotions, such as anger, depression, shame, guilt, frustration, and confusion. In addition, skill building related to communication, assertiveness, and emotional coping skills would be important.

Next-Generation Immigrants

Young people whose parents immigrate to a new country often have difficulties relating either to the culture their parents emphasize or to the majority culture in which they function on a daily basis. Often times, the difficulty lies in navigating the differences between the environment the parents and family stress and desire to maintain and the environment in which these children must socialize, learn, think, feel, and behave. The literature suggests that difficulties present when young people attempt to acculturate and adopt the rules, expectations, and customs of the majority culture (Oppedal, Roysamb, & Heyerdahl, 2006; Pumariega, Rothe, & Pumariega, 2005). This difficulty may result in conflicts within the home environment, as well as interpersonally for the youth within their peer group. In addition, children and adolescents may experience internal conflicts related to beliefs about identity, guilt, betrayal of their parent's culture or ways, and isolation when perceiving they do not fit into either culture. These potentially distorted perceptions may be detrimental emotionally and/or behaviorally, as young people may begin to experience depression, anxiety, confusion, frustration, anger, guilt, and shame related to these beliefs and behaviors that may lead to further isolation and social and behavioral difficulties (at home or in the larger community).

CONCLUSION

The number of possible topics to address in cognitive-behavioral group therapy with children and adolescents is essentially endless. Many difficulties faced by youth, regardless of the context or specific situation, relate to topics included in this volume and can be addressed by the treatment programs offered. It is our hope that the information included in this text will be useful for the topics specifically addressed, but also as readers consider additional issues facing young people that may be effectively and positively impacted by the provision of group intervention.

REFERENCES

Bagley, C., & Tremblay, P. (2000). Elevated rates of suicidal behavior in gay, lesbian, and bisexual youth. *Crisis: Journal of Crisis Intervention & Suicide, 21*(3), 111–117.

Dickerson, F. B., & Lehman, A. F. (2006). Evidence-based psychotherapy for schizophrenia. *Journal of Nervous and Mental Disorders, 194*(1), 3–9.

Gaudiano, B. A. (2006). Is symptomatic improvement in clinical trials of cognitive-behavioral therapy for psychosis clinically significant? *Journal of Psychiatric Practice, 12*(1), 11–23

Kennedy, M. R. (1991). Homeless and runaway youth mental health issues: No access to the system. *Journal of Adolescent Health, 12*, 576–579.

Kruks, G. (1991). Gay and lesbian homeless/street youth: Special issues and concerns. *Journal of Adolescent Health, 12*(7), 515–518.

Maxwell, B. M. (1992). Hostility, depression, and self-esteem among troubled and homeless adolescents in crisis. *Journal of Youth & Adolescence, 21*(2), 139–150.

Oppedal, B., Roysamb, E., & Heyerdahl, S. (2006). Ethnic group, acculturation, and psychiatric problems in young immigrants. *Journal of Child Psychology and Psychiatry, and Allied Disciplines, 46*(6), 646–660.

Pumariega, A. J., Rothe, E., & Pumariega, J. B. (2005). Mental health of immigrants and refugees. *Community Mental Health Journal, 41*(5), 581–597.

Remafedi G., French S., Story M., Resnick, M.D., & Blum, R. (1998). The relationship between suicide risk and sexual orientation: results of a population-based study. *American Journal of Public Health, 88*, 57–60.

Russell, S. T., & Joyner, K. (2001). Adolescent sexual orientation and suicide risk: evidence from a national study. *American Journal of Public Health, 91*(8), 1276–1281.

Turkington, D., Kingdon, D., & Weiden, P. J. (2006). Cognitive behavior therapy for schizophrenia. *American Journal of Psychiatry, 163*(3), 365–373.

Whitbeck, L. B., Hoyt, D. R., & Bao, W. (2000). Depressive symptoms and co-occurring depressive symptoms, substance abuse, and conduct problems among runaway and homeless adolescents. *Child Development, 71*(3), 721–732.

Whitbeck, L. B., Johnson, K. D., Hoyt, D. R., & Cauce, A. M. (2004). Mental disorder and comorbidity among runaway and homeless adolescents. *Journal of Adolescent Health, 35*(2), 132–140.

Index

Page numbers in italics refer to figures or tables.